GEORGE GROTE

PLATO
AND THE
OTHER COMPANIONS OF SOKRATES

VOLUME III

Elibron Classics
www.elibron.com

PLATO,

AND THE

OTHER COMPANIONS OF SOKRATES.

By GEORGE GROTE, F.R.S.,

AUTHOR OF THE 'HISTORY OF GREECE:'

D.C.L. OXON., AND LL.D. CAMBRIDGE:

VICE-CHANCELLOR OF THE UNIVERSITY OF LONDON:

MEMBER OF THE INSTITUTE OF FRANCE, AND HON. MEMBER OF THE IMPERIAL AND
ROYAL ACADEMIES OF ST. PETERSBURG, KHARKOFF, KÖNIGSBERG, MUNICH,
AMSTERDAM, BRUSSELS, AND TURIN:

HON. MEMBER OF THE HISTORICAL SOCIETIES OF MASSACHUSETTS, AND OF
PHILADELPHIA, U.S. OF AMERICA.

Κάλλιστα γὰρ δὴ τοῦτο καὶ λέγεται καὶ λελέξεται, ὅτι τὸ μὲν ὠφέλιμον
καλόν, τὸ δὲ βλαβερὸν αἰσχρόν.   PLATO, *Republ.* v. 457 B.

Τὸ μὲν οὖν περιττὸν ἔχουσι πάντες οἱ τοῦ Σωκράτους λόγοι, καὶ τὸ κομψὸν
καὶ τὸ καινοτόμον, καὶ τὸ ζητητικόν· καλῶς δὲ πάντα ἴσως χαλεπόν.
                                        ARISTOTEL. *Polit.* ii. 6, 1265 a 10.

IN THREE VOLUMES.

VOL. III.

LONDON:

JOHN MURRAY, ALBEMARLE STREET.

1865.

LONDON: PRINTED BY W. CLOWES AND SONS, STAMFORD STREET,
AND CHARING CROSS.

CONTENTS OF VOLUME III.

————◆————

CHAPTER XXXI.

MENEXENUS.

CHAPTER XXXII.

KLEITOPHON.

CHAPTER XXXII.—*continued.*

CHAPTER XXXIII.

PLATONIC REPUBLIC—ABSTRACT.

CHAPTER XXXIII.—*continued.*

CHAPTER XXXIII.—*continued.*

CHAPTER XXXIII.—*continued.*

CHAPTER XXXIII.—*continued.*

CHAPTER XXXIII.—*continued.*

CHAPTER XXXIV.

REPUBLIC—REMARKS ON ITS MAIN THESIS.

CHAPTER XXXIV.—*continued.*

CHAPTER XXXV.

REPUBLIC—REMARKS ON THE PLATONIC COMMONWEALTH.

CHAPTER XXXV.—*continued.*

CHAPTER XXXV.—*continued.*

CHAPTER XXXV.—*continued.*

CHAPTER XXXVI.

TIMÆUS AND KRITIAS.

CHAPTER XXXVI.—*continued.*

CHAPTER XXXVII.

LEGES AND EPINOMIS.

CHAPTER XXXVII.—*continued.*

CHAPTER XXXVII.—*continued.*

CHAPTER XXXVII.—*continued.*

CHAPTER XXXVII.—continued.

CHAPTER XXXVII.—*continued.*

CHAPTER XXXVII.—*continued.*

CHAPTER XXXVIII.

OTHER COMPANIONS OF SOKRATES.

CHAPTER XXXVIII.—*continued.*

CHAPTER XXXVIII.—*continued.*

CHAPTER XXXIX.

XENOPHON.

CHAPTER XXXIX.—*continued.*

PLATO.

CHAPTER XXXI.

MENEXENUS.

In this dialogue the only personages are, Sokrates as an elderly man, and Menexenus, a young Athenian of Persons and situation of the dialogue. noble family, whom we have already seen as the intimate friend of Lysis, in the dialogue known under the name of Lysis.

Sokr.—What have you been doing at the Senate-house, Menexenus? You probably think that your course Funeral harangue at Athens— Choice of a public orator —Sokrates declares the task of the public orator to be easy— Comic exaggeration of the effects of the harangue. of education and philosophy is finished, and that you are qualified for high political functions. Young as you are, you aim at exercising command over us elders, as your family have always done before you.[a] *Menex.*—I shall do so, if you advise and allow me, Sokrates: but not otherwise. Now, however, I came to learn who was the person chosen by the Senate to deliver the customary oration at the approaching public funeral of the citizens who have fallen in battle. The Senate, however, have adjourned the election until to-morrow: but I think either Archinus or Dion will be chosen. *Sokr.*—To die in battle is a fine thing in many ways.[b] He who dies thus may be poor, but he receives a splendid funeral: he may be of little worth, yet he is still praised in prepared speeches by able orators, who decorate his name with brilliant encomiums, whether deserved or not, fascinating all the hearers: extolling us all—not merely the slain warrior, but the city collectively, our ancestors, and us the living—so admirably that I stand bewitched when I hear them, and fancy myself

---

[a] Plat. Menex. p. 234 B-C.   [b] Plat. Menex. p. 235 A-B.

a greater, nobler, and finer man than I was before. I am usually accompanied by some strangers, who admire as much as I do, and who conceive a lofty estimation both of me and of the city. The voice of the orator resounds in my ear, and the feeling of pride dwells in my mind, for more than three days; during which interval I fancy myself almost in the islands of the blest. I hardly come to myself, or recollect where I am, until the fourth or fifth day. Such is the force of these orators.

Menex.—You are always deriding the orators, Sokrates.[c]

Sokrates professes to have learnt a funeral harangue from Aspasia, and to be competent to recite it himself. Menexenus entreats him to do so.

However, on this occasion I think the orator chosen will have little chance of success: he will have no time for preparation, and will be obliged to speak *impromptu.* *Sokr.*—Never fear: each of these orators has harangues ready prepared. Besides, there is no difficulty here in speaking *impromptu.* If indeed the purpose were to praise the Athenians in Peloponnesus, or the Peloponnesians at Athens, an excellent orator would be required to persuade or to give satisfaction. But when he exhibits before the very hearers whom he praises, there is no great difficulty in appearing to be a good speaker.[d]
Menex.—Indeed! What! do you think you would be competent to deliver the harangue yourself, if the Senate were to elect you? *Sokr.*—Certainly: and it is no wonder that I should be competent to speak, because I have learnt rhetoric from Aspasia (an excellent mistress, who has taught many eminent speakers, and among them Perikles, the most illustrious of all), and the harp from Konnus. But any one else, even less well-trained than me—instructed in music by Lamprus, and in rhetoric by Antiphon—would still be fully competent to succeed in praising Athenians among Athenians.
Menex.—What would you have to say, if the duty were imposed upon you?[e] *Sokr.*—Probably little or nothing of my own. But it was only yesterday that I heard Aspasia going through a funeral harangue for this very occasion: partly suggestions of the present moment, partly recollections of

---

[c] Plat. Menex. p. 235 C. 'Αεὶ σὺ προσπαίζεις, ὦ Σώκρατες, τοὺς ῥήτορας.
[d] Plat. Menex. p. 235 D. Aristotle refers twice to this dictum

as being a true remark made by Σωκράτης ἐν τῷ 'Επιταφίῳ, Rhetoric, i. 9, 1367, b. 8, iii. 14, 1415, b. 30.
[e] Plat. Menex. p. 236 A.

past matters which had occurred to her when she composed the funeral harangue delivered by Perikles. *Menex.*—Could you recollect what Aspasia said ? *Sokr.*—I should be much to blame if I could not. I learnt it from herself, and was near being beaten because I partly forgot it. *Menex.*—Why do you not proceed with it then ? *Sokr.*—I fear that my instructress would be displeased, if I were to publish her discourse. *Menex.*—Do not fear that, but proceed to speak. You will confer the greatest pleasure upon me, whether what you say comes from Aspasia or from any one else. Only proceed. *Sokr.*—But perhaps you will laugh me to scorn, if I, an elderly man, continue still such work of pastime.[f] *Menex.*—Not at all : I beseech you to speak. *Sokr.*—Well, I cannot refuse you. Indeed, I could hardly refuse, if you requested me to strip naked and dance—since we are here alone.[g]

Sokrates then proceeds to recite a funeral harangue of some length, which continues almost to the end.[h] When he concludes—repeating his declaration that the harangue comes from Aspasia—Menexenus observes, By Zeus, Sokrates, Aspasia is truly enviable, if she, a woman, is competent to compose such discourses as that. *(Harangue recited by Sokrates.)*

Sokr.—If you do not believe me, come along with me, and you will hear it from her own lips. *Menex.*—I have often been in company with Aspasia, and I know what sort of person she is. *Sokr.*—Well then, don't you admire her ? and are not you grateful to her for the harangue ? *Menex.*—I am truly grateful for the harangue, to her, or to him, whoever it was that prompted you : and most of all, I am grateful to you for having recited it. *Sokr.*—Very good. Take care then that you do not betray me. I may perhaps be able, on future occasions, to recite to you many other fine political harangues from her. *Menex.*—Be assured that I will not betray you. Only let me hear them. *Sokr.*—I certainly will. *(Compliments of Menexenus after Sokrates has finished both to the harangue itself and to Aspasia.)*

The interval between these two fragments of dialogue is filled up by the recitation of Sokrates : a long funeral harangue in honour of deceased warriors, whom the city

---

[f] Plat. Menex. p. 236 C. ᾽Αλλ᾽ ῎ισως μου καταγελάσει, ἂν σοι δόξω πρεσβύτης ὢν ἔτι παίζειν.

[g] Plat. Menex. pp. 234 C, 236 C.
[h] Plat. Menex. pp. 236 C, 249 C.

directs to be thus commemorated. The period is supposed
Supposed pe-
riod—shortly
after the
peace of
Antalkidas. to be not long after the peace concluded by Antalkidas in 387 B.C. That peace was imposed upon
Sparta, Athens, and the other Grecian cities, by the
imperative rescript of the Persian king: the condition of it
being an enforcement of universal autonomy, or free separate
government to each city, small as well as great.[i]

It had been long the received practice among the Athenians
Custom of
Athens about
funeral ha-
rangues.
Many such
harangues
existed at
Athens, com-
posed by
distinguished
orators or
logographers
—Established
type of the
harangue. to honour their fallen warriors from time to time by
this sort of public funeral, celebrated with every demonstration of mournful respect: and to appoint
one of the ablest and most dignified citizens as
public orator on the occasion.[k] The discourse delivered by Perikles, as appointed orator, at the end
of the first year of the Peloponnesian war, has been
immortalised by Thucydides, and stands as one of the
most impressive remnants of Hellenic antiquity. Since the
occasion recurred pretty often, and since the orator chosen was
always a man already conspicuous,[l] we may be sure that there
existed in the time of Plato many funeral harangues which are
now lost: indeed he himself says in this dialogue, that distinguished politicians prepared such harangues beforehand, in
case the choice of the citizens should fall upon them. And
we may farther be sure, amidst the active cultivation of rhetoric at Athens—that the rhetorical teachers as well as their
pupils, and the logographers or paid composers of speeches,
were practised in this variety of oratorical compositions not
less than in others. We have one of them among the remaining discourses of the logographer Lysias; who could not
actually have delivered it himself (since he was not even a
citizen)—nor could ever probably have been called upon to
prepare one for delivery (since the citizens chosen were
always eminent speakers and politicians themselves, not
requiring the aid of a logographer)—but who composed it as
a rhetorical exercise to extend his own celebrity. In like
manner we find one among the discourses of Demosthenes,

---

[i] See respecting the character of the
peace of Antalkidas, and the manner
in which its conditions were executed,
my History of Greece, chap. 76.

[k] Thucyd. ii. 34.
[l] Thucyd. ii. 34. ὃς ἂν γνώμῃ τε
δοκῇ μὴ ἀξύνετος εἶναι, καὶ ἀξιώματι
προήκῃ.

though of very doubtful authenticity. The funeral discourse
had thus come to acquire an established type. Rhetorical
teachers had collected and generalised, out of the published
harangues before them, certain *loci communes*, religious, patriotic, social, historical or pseudo-historical, &c., suitable to be
employed by any new orator.[m] All such *loci* were of course
framed upon the actual sentiments prevalent among the
majority of Athenians; furnishing eloquent expression for
sympathies and antipathies deeply lodged in every one's
bosom.

The funeral discourse which we read in the Menexenus is
framed upon this classical model. It dwells, with
emphasis and elegance, upon the patriotic common-
places which formed the theme of rhetors generally.
Plato begins by extolling the indigenous character
of the Athenian population; not immigrants from
abroad (like the Peloponnesians), but born from the very soil
of Attica:[n] which, at a time when other parts of the earth
produced nothing but strange animals and plants, gave birth
to an admirable breed of men, as well as to wheat and barley
for their nourishment, and to the olive for assisting their
bodily exercises.[o] Attica was from the beginning favoured by
the Gods; and the acropolis had been an object of competition between Athênê and Poseidon.[p] She was the common
and equal mother of all the citizens, who, from such community of birth and purity of Hellenic origin, had derived the
attributes which they had ever since manifested—attachment
to equal laws among themselves, Panhellenic patriotism, and
hatred of barbarians.[q] The free and equal political constitution of Athens—called an aristocracy, or presidency of the

*Plato in this harangue conforms to the establish-
ed type—Topics on which he insists.*

[m] Aristotel. Rhetoric, i. 5, 1360,
b. 31, i. 9, 1367. Dionys. Hal. Ars
Rhetoric. c. 6, pp. 260-267.
    "Nec enim artibus inventis factum
est, ut argumenta inveniremus: sed
dicta sunt omnia, antequam præci-
perentur: mox ea scriptores observata
et collecta ediderunt" (Quintilian,
Inst. Or. v. 10).
[n] Plat. Menex. pp. 237-245 C. οὐ
γάρ Πέλοπες οὐδὲ Κάδμοι οὐδὲ Αἴγυπτοί
τε καὶ Δαναοὶ οὐδὲ ἄλλοι πολλοί, φύσει
μὲν βάρβαροι ὄντες, νόμῳ δὲ Ἕλληνες,

συνοικοῦσιν ἡμῖν, ἀλλ' αὐτοὶ Ἕλληνες,
οὐ μιξοβάρβαροι οἰκοῦμεν, &c.
[o] Plat. Menex. pp. 237 D, 238 A.
[p] Plat. Menex. p. 237 C.
[q] Plat. Menex. pp. 238 D-239 A-
245 C-D. ἡ ἰσογονία ἡμᾶς ἡ κατὰ
φύσιν ἰσονομίαν ἀναγκάζει ζητεῖν κατὰ
νόμον, καὶ μηδενὶ ἄλλῳ ὑπείκειν ἀλλήλοις ἡ ἀρετῆς δόξῃ καὶ φρονήσεως.
245 D. ὅθεν καθαρὸν τὸ μῖσος ἐντέτηκε
τῇ πόλει τῆς ἀλλοτρίας φύσεως (i. e. of
the βάρβαροι).

best men, under the choice and approval of the multitude—
as it was and as it always had been, is here extolled by Plato,
as a result of the common origin.

Alluding briefly to the victories over Eumolpus and the
Amazons, the orator passes on to the battles of Marathon,
Salamis, and Platæa, which he celebrates with the warmth of
an Hellenic patriot.[r] He eulogizes the generous behaviour
of Athens towards the Greeks, during the interval between
the Persian and the Peloponnesian wars, contrasting it with
the unworthy requital which she received from Sparta and
others. He then glances at the events of the Peloponnesian
wars, though colouring them in a manner so fanciful and delusive, that any one familiar with Thucydides can scarcely
recognise their identity—especially in regard to the Athenian
expedition against Syracuse.[s] He protests against the faithlessness of Sparta, towards the close of the Peloponnesian
war, in allying herself with the common anti-Hellenic
enemy—the Great King—against Athens: and he ascribes
mainly to this unholy alliance the conquest of Athens at the
end of the war.[t] The moderation of political parties in Athens,
when the Thirty were put down and the democracy restored,
receives its due meed of praise: but the peculiar merit
claimed for Athens, in reference to the public events between
403 B.C. and 387 B.C., is—That she stood alone among Greeks
in refusing to fraternise with the Persian King, or to betray to
him the Asiatic Greeks. Athens had always been prompted
by generous feeling, even in spite of political interests, to
compassionate and befriend the weak.[u] The orator dwells
with satisfaction on the years preceding the peace concluded
by Antalkidas; during which years Athens had recovered
her walls and her ships—had put down the Spartan superi-

---

[r] Plat. Menex. pp. 240-241.
[s] Plat. Menex. pp. 242-243.
[t] Plat. Menex. pp. 243-244.
[u] Plat. Menex. pp. 244-245. εἴ τις
βούλοιτο τῆς πόλεως κατηγορῆσαι δικαίως, τοῦτ' ἂν μόνον λέγων ὀρθῶς
κατηγοροίη, ὡς ἀεὶ λίαν φιλοικτίρμων
ἔστι, καὶ τοῦ ἥττονος θεραπίς. Isokrates also, in the Oratio Panegyrica
(Or. iv.), dwells upon this point, as
well as on the pronounced hatred

towards βάρβαροι, as standing features
in the Athenian character (sect. 59-
184). The points touched upon in
reference to Athens by Isokrates are
in the main the same as those brought
out by Plato in the Menexenus, only
that Isokrates makes them subservient
to a special purpose, that of bringing
about an expedition against Persia
under the joint headship of Sparta and
Athens.

ority at sea—and had rescued even the Great King from
Spartan force.[v] He laments the disasters of Athenian soldiers
at Corinth, through difficulties of the ground—and at Lech-
æum, through treachery.   These are the latest political events
to which he alludes.[x]

Having thus touched upon the political history of Athens,
he turns to the surviving relatives—fathers, mothers, Consolation
and exhorta-
children, &c.—of the fallen warriors : addressing to tion to sur-
viving rela-
them words of mingled consolation and exhortation. tives.
He adopts the fiction of supposing these exhortations to have
been suggested to him by the warriors themselves, immediately before entering upon their last battle.[y] This is the
most eloquent and impressive portion of the harangue.   The
orator concludes by a few words from himself, inculcating on
the elders the duty of resignation, and on the youth that of
forward and devoted patriotism.[z]

That this oration was much admired, not merely during
the lifetime of Plato but also long after his death, Admiration
we know from the testimony of Cicero ; who informs felt for this
harangue,
us that it was publicly recited every year on the both at the
time and
day when the annual funereal rites were celebrated, afterwards.
in honour of those citizens collectively who had been slain in
the service of their country.[a]   The rhetor Dionysius[b] recognises the fact of such warm admiration, and concurs generally
therein, yet not without reserves. He points out what he
considers defects of thought and expression — ostentatious
contrasts and balancing of antithetical clauses, after the
manner of Gorgias. Yet we may easily believe that the
harangue found much favour, and greatly extended the reputation of its author. It would please many readers who
took little interest in the Sokratic dialectics.

When Plato first established himself at Athens as a lec-

---

[v] Plat. Menex. p. 245.
[x] Plat. Menex. pp. 245 E, 246 A.
[y] Plat. Menex. pp. 247-248.
[z] Plat. Menex. p. 249 A-C.
[a] Cicero, Orator. c. 44, 151. "At
non Thucydides, no ille quidem haud
paullo major scriptor Plato : nec solum
in his sermonibus, qui διάλογοι di-
cuntur, ubi etiam de industriâ id
faciendum fuit—sed in populari oratione, quâ mos est Athenis laudari eos,
qui sint in præliis interfecti : quæ sic
probata est, ut eam quotannis, ut scis,
illo die recitari necesse sit."
See Plato, Menex. p. 249 B about
these yearly funereal rites, and Lysias,
Epitaph. s. 80.
[b] Dionys. Hal. De Adm. Vi Dic. in
Demosth. p. 1027, compared with Ars
Rhetoric. c. 6, pp. 260-267.

turer (about 386 B.C., shortly after the peace made by Antal-

Probable motives of Plato in composing it, shortly after he established himself at Athens as a teacher—His competition with Lysias —Desire for celebrity both as rhetor and as dialectician.

kidas), he was probably known only by Sokratic dialogues, properly so called : which Dionysius specifies both as his earliest works and as his proper department, wherein he stood unrivalled.[c] In these, his opposition to the Rhetors and Sophists was proclaimed : and if, as is probable, the Gorgias had been published before that time, he had already declared war, openly as well as bitterly, against the whole art of Rhetoric. But it would be a double triumph for his genius, if, after standing forward as the representative of Dialectic, and in that character heaping scornful derision on the rival art of Rhetoric, as being nothing better than a mere knack of juggling and flattery[d]—he were able to show that this did not proceed from want of rhetorical competence, but that he could rival or surpass the Rhetors in their own department. Herein lies the purpose of the Menexenus. I agree with Schleiermacher, Stallbaum, and some other critics,[e] in thinking that it was probably composed not long after the peace of Antalkidas, in competition with the harangue of Lysias now remaining on the same subject. Though the name of Lysias is not mentioned in the Menexenus, yet

[c] Dionys. Hal. De Platon. p. 762. τραφεὶς μὲν ἐν τοῖς Σωκρατικοῖς διαλόγοις ἰσχνοτάτοις οὖσι καὶ ἀκριβεστάτοις, οὐ μείνας δ' ἐν αὐταῖς, ἀλλὰ τῆς Γοργίου καὶ Θουκυδίδου κατασκευῆς ἐρασθείς. Compare p. 761, the passage immediately preceding, and De Adm. Vi Dicendi in Demosthene, pp. 1025-1031.

To many critics Plato appeared successful in the figurative and metaphorical style—δεινὸς περὶ τὸ τροπικόν. But Dionysius thinks him very inferior to Demosthenes even on this point, though it was not the strongest point of Demosthenes, whose main purpose was ὁ ἀληθινὸς ἀγών (Dionys. ibid. p. 1057).

[d] Isokrates, in his last composition (Panathen. Or. xii.), written in very old age, shows how keenly he felt the aspersions of jealous rivals—Sophists less successful than himself — who publicly complained that he despised the lessons of the poets, and thought no teaching worth having except his own—ἀποδεξαμένων δὲ τῶν περιεστώ-

των τὴν διατριβὴν αὐτῶν, ἕνα τὸν τολμηρότερον ἐπιχειρῆσαι ἐμὲ διαβάλλειν, λέγονθ' ὡς ἐγὼ πάντων καταφρονῶ τῶν τοιούτων, καὶ τάς τε φιλοσοφίας τὰς τῶν ἄλλων καὶ τὰς παιδείας ἁπάσας ἀναιρῶ, καὶ φημὶ πάντας ληρεῖν πλὴν τοὺς μετεσχηκότας τῆς ἐμῆς διατριβῆς (sect. 22). That which Isokrates complains of these teachers for saying in their talk with each other, the rhetorical teachers would vehemently complain of in Plato, when he expressed forcibly his contempt for rhetoric in the Gorgias and the Phædrus. One way of expressing their resentment would be to affirm that Plato could not compose a regular rhetorical discourse ; which affirmation Plato would best contradict by composing one in the received manner.

[e] See the Einleitung of Schleiermacher to his translation of the Menexenus; also Stallbaum, Proleg. ad Menex. p. 10, and Westermann, Gesch. der Beredtsamkeit, sect. 66, p. 134.

the rivalry between him and Plato is clearly proclaimed in the Platonic Phædrus : and the two funeral harangues go so completely over the same ground, that intentional competition on the part of the latest, is the most natural of all hypotheses.

Here then we have Plato exchanging philosophy for "the knack of flattery"—to use the phrase of the Gorgias. Stallbaum is so unwilling to admit this as possible, that he represents the Platonic harangue as a mere caricature, intended to make the rhetorical process ridiculous. I dissent from this supposition; as I have already dissented from the like supposition of the same critic, in regard to the etymologies of the Kratylus. That Plato might in one dialogue scornfully denounce Rhetoric—and in another, compose an elaborate discourse upon the received rhetorical type—is noway inconsistent with the general theory which I frame to myself, about the intellectual character and distinct occasional manifestations of Plato.[f] The funeral harangue in the Menexenus proves that, whatever he thought about Rhetoric generally, he was anxious to establish his title as a competent rhetorical composer: it proves farther that he was equal to Lysias in the epideiktic department, though inferior to Perikles. It affords a valuable illustration of that general doctrine which the Platonic Sokrates lays down in the Gorgias—That no man can succeed as a rhetor, unless he is in full harmony of spirit and cast of mind with his auditors; or unless he dwells upon and enforces sympathies, antipathies, and convictions, already established in their minds.[g] A first-rate orator like Perikles, touching the chords of cherished national sentiment, might hope, by such a discourse as that which we

Marginal note: Menexenus compared with the view of rhetoric presented in the Gorgias—Necessity for an orator to conform to established sentiments.

---

[f] Compare also the majestic picture which Plato presents of the ancient character and exploits of the early Athenians, in the mythe commenced in the Timæus (pp. 23-24), prosecuted in the Kritias (pp. 113-114 seqq.), but left by the author incomplete.

[g] Plato, Gorgias, p. 510; see above, ch. xxii. p. 134.

This appears to me the real truth, subject to very rare exceptions. But I do not think it true to say, as the Platonic Sokrates is made to declare in the Menexenus, that it is an easy matter to obtain admiration when you praise Athens among Athenians — though Aristotle commends the observation. Assuredly Perikles did not think so (Thucyd. ii. 35). You have a popular theme, but unless you have oratorical talent to do justice to it, you are likely to disappoint and offend, especially among auditors like the Athenians, accustomed to good speaking. Compare Plat. Kritias, p. 107 E.

read in Thucydides, "adjecisse aliquid receptæ religioni."[h]
No public orator ever appointed by the Senate to pronounce
the funeral harangue, could have expatiated more warmly
than Plato has here done, upon the excellence of the Athenian constitution, and upon the admirable spirit which had
animated Athenian politics, both foreign and domestic. Plato
falls far short, indeed, of the weight and grandeur, the impressive distinctness of specification, the large sympathies,
intellectual as well as popular—with which these topics are
handled by Perikles in Thucydides : but his eulogy is quite
as highflown and unreserved.

In understanding fully the Menexenus, however, we have
Colloquial portion of the Menexenus is probably intended as ridicule and sneer at Rhetoric—The harangue itself is serious, and intended as an evidence of Plato's ability. to take account, not merely of the harangue which
forms the bulk of it, but also of the conversation
whereby it is commenced and concluded. Plato,
speaking always through the mouth of Sokrates, has
to invent some fiction excusing the employment of
his master in the unprecedented capacity of public
orator. What Stallbaum says (in my judgment,
erroneously) about the harangue—appears to me
perfectly true about the conversation before and after it. The
introductory observations, interchanged between Sokrates and
Menexenus, certainly tend to caricature (as Aristophanes[i]
does in the Acharneis and the Equites) the strong effects produced by this panegyrical oratory on the feelings of hearers :
and to depreciate the task of the orator as nothing better than
an easy and amusing pastime. To praise Athens among
Athenian auditors (we are told) is a matter in which few
speakers can fail to succeed, however poor their abilities
Moreover, the great funeral harangue of Perikles is represented as having been composed for him by Aspasia[k]—a

<hr/>

[h] To employ the striking expression
of Quintilian (xii. 10) respecting the
great statue of Zeus at Olympia by
Pheidias.

[i] Aristoph. Acharn. 615, Equit. 640-
887.

The comic exaggeration of Sokrates,
in the colloquial portion of the Menexenus (235, B.C.) goes as far as that of
Aristophanes.

[k] By the language of Plato here,
he seems plainly to bring his own

harangue into competition not merely
with that of Lysias but also with that
of Perikles. But we must not suppose, for that reason, that he necessarily
has in view the Periklean harangue
which we now read in Thucydides, ii.
35-43 : which is the real speech, reported and drest up by Thucydides in
his own language and manner. Probably the Periklean harangue was
preserved separately and in other
reports, so that Plato may have known

female, though remarkable among her sex—who is extolled as
holding the highest place among rhetorical teachers, and is
introduced here, as Aristophanes introduces her in the
Acharneis, when he is putting a construction of discreditable
ridicule on the origin of the Peloponnesian war.   To make a
good funeral harangue (Sokrates says)[1] requires little or no
preliminary preparation : besides, the Rhetors have harangues
ready prepared at home.   All this *persiflage*, in harmony with
the polemics of the Gorgias, derides and degrades the Rhetors
collectively.   But when Plato takes the field against them as
a competitor, in his own rhetorical discourse, he drops the
ironical vein, and takes pains to deliver one really good and
excellent in its kind.   His triumph is thus doubled.   He tells
the Rhetors that their business is a trifling and despicable
one : at the same time showing them that, despicable as it is,
he can surpass them in it, as he professes to surpass Lysias in
the Phædrus.[m]

Such I conceive to be the scope of the dialogue, looked at
from Plato's point of view.   In order to find a person ₐAnachron-
suitable in point of age to be described as the teacher ism of the
of Sokrates, he is forced to go back to the past gene- Menexenus
ration—that of Perikles and Aspasia.   But though less on this
he avoids anachronism on this point, he cannot avoid the
anachronism of making Sokrates allude to events long posterior to his own death.   This anachronism is real, though it
has been magnified by some critics into a graver defect than

---

it without knowing the history of
Thucydides. When I see the extreme
liberty which Plato takes throughout
his harangue in regard to the history
of the past, I can hardly believe that
he ever read Thucydides ; if he ever
read the history, he certainly dis-
regarded it altogether, and threw himself ἐπὶ τὸ προσαγωγότερον τῇ ἀκροάσει
ἢ ἀληθέστερον : like the λογόγραφοι
of whom Thucydides speaks, i. 21.
Lysias among them, though in a less
degree than Plato. Æschines Sokraticus had composed among his
dialogues one entitled 'Ασπασία. See
Xenophon, Œconom. i. 14 ; Cicero de
Inventione, i. 31 ; Plutarch, Perikles,
c. 24-32 ; also Bergk, De Reliquiis
Comœd. Attic. Antiquæ, p. 237.

[1] Aristoph. Acharn. 501.
[m] The remarks of Dionysius of Halikarnassus (in the Epistle to Cn. Pom-
pey about Plato, pp. 754-758) are well
deserving of attention ; especially as
he had before him many writers now
lost, either contemporary with Plato
or of the succeeding generation. He
notices not only Plato's asperity in
ridiculing most of his distinguished
contemporaries, but also his marked
feeling of rivalry against Lysias.
ἦν γὰρ, ἦν μὲν τῇ Πλάτωνος φύσει
πολλὰς ἀρετὰς ἐχούσῃ τὸ φιλότιμον,
&c.
See this subject well handled in an
instructive Dissertation by M. Lebeau
(Stuttgart, 1863, Lysias' Epitaphios
als ächt erwiesen, pp. 42-46 seq.).

it is in truth. Plato was resolved not to speak in his own person, but through that of Sokrates. But he is not always careful to keep within the limits which consistent adherence to such a plan imposes.[n]

[n] Groen van Prinsterer (Prosopographia Platonica, p. 211 seq.) adverts to the carelessness of Plato about exact chronology.

Most of the Platonic critics recognise the Menexenus as a genuine Platonic dialogue. Ast, however, includes it among the numerous dialogues which he disallows as spurious ; and Suckow, Steinhart, and Ueberweg, are also inclined to disallow it. See Ueberweg, Die Aechtheit der Platonischen Schriften, pp. 143-148. These critics make light of the allusion of Aristotle in the Rhetoric — Σωκράτης ἐν τῷ Ἐπιταφίῳ—which appears to me, I confess, of more weight than all the grounds of suspicion adduced by them to prove the dialogue spurious. The presumption in favour of the catalogue of Thrasyllus counts with them, here as elsewhere, for nothing.

CHAPTER XXXII.

KLEITOPHON.

THE Kleitophon is an unfinished fragment, beginning with a short introductory conversation between Sokrates and Kleitophon, and finishing with a discourse of some length, a sort of remonstrance or appeal, addressed by Kleitophon to Sokrates; who makes no reply.

Persons and circumstances of Kleitophon.

Some one was lately telling me (says Sokrates) that Kleitophon, in conversation with Lysias, depreciated the conversation of Sokrates, and extolled prodigiously that of Thrasymachus.

Whoever told you so (replies Kleitophon), did not report accurately what I said. On some points, indeed, I did not praise you; but on other points I did praise you. Since, however, you are evidently displeased with me, though you affect indifference—and since we are here alone—I should be glad to repeat the same observations to yourself, in order that you may not believe me to think meanly of you. These incorrect reports seem to have made you displeased with me, more than is reasonable. I am anxious to speak to you with full freedom, if you will allow it.[a]

Conversation of Sokrates with Kleitophon alone: he alludes to observations of an unfavourable character recently made by Kleitophon, who asks permission to explain.

It would be a shame indeed (rejoins Sokrates), if, when you were anxious to do me good, I could not endure to receive it. When I have learnt which are my worst and which are my best points, I shall evidently be in a condition to cultivate and pursue the latter, and resolutely to avoid the former.

Hear me then (says Kleitophon).

As your frequent companion, Sokrates, I have often listened to you with profound admiration. I thought you superior

Explanation given. Kleitophon expresses gratitude and admiration for the benefit which he has derived from long companionship with Sokrates.
to all other speakers when you proclaimed your usual strain of reproof, like the God from a dramatic machine, against mankind.[b] You asked them, "Whither are you drifting, my friends? You do not seem aware that you are doing wrong when you place all your affections on the gain of money, and neglect to teach your sons and heirs the right use of money. You do not provide for them teachers of justice, if justice be teachable; nor trainers of it, if it be acquirable by training and habit; nor indeed have you studied the acquisition of it, even for yourselves. Since the fact is obvious that, while you, as well as your sons, have learnt what passes for a finished education in virtue (letters, music, gymnastic), you nevertheless yield to the corruptions of gain—how comes it that you do not despise your actual education, and look out for teachers to correct such disorder? It is this disorder, not the want of accomplishment in the use of the lyre, which occasions such terrible discord, and such calamitous war, between brother and brother—between city and city.[c] You affirm that men do wrong wilfully, not from ignorance or want of training; yet nevertheless you are bold enough to say, that wrong-doing is dishonourable and offensive to the Gods. How can any one, then, choose such an evil willingly? You tell us it is because he is overcome by pleasures: well then, that again comes to unwillingness—if victory be the thing which every man wishes: so that, whichever way you turn it, reason shows you that wrong-doing is taken up unwillingly, and that greater precautions ought to be taken upon the subject, both by individuals and by cities."[d]

Such, Sokrates (continues Kleitophon), is the language The observations made by Sokrates have been most salutary and stimu- which I often hear from you; and which I always hear with the strongest and most respectful admiration. You follow it up by observing, that those who

[b] Plato, Kleitoph. p. 407 A. ἐγὼ γάρ, ὦ Σώκρατες, σοὶ συγγιγνόμενος πολλάκις ἐξεπληττόμην ἀκούων, καί μοι ἐδόκεις παρὰ τοὺς ἄλλους ἀνθρώπους κάλλιστα λέγειν, ὁπότε ἐπιτιμῶν τοῖς ἀνθρώποις, ὥσπερ ἐπὶ μηχανῆς τραγικῆς θεός, ὕμνεις λέγων, Ποῖ φέρεσθε, ἄνθρωποι, &c.

[c] Plato, Kleitophon, p. 407 B-C.
[d] Plato, Kleitoph. p. 407 C-D. ὥστε ἐκ παντὸς τρόπου τό γε ἀδικεῖν ἀκούσιον ὁ λόγος αἱρεῖ, καὶ δεῖν ἐπιμέλειαν τῆς νῦν πλείω ποιεῖσθαι πάντ' ἄνδρα ἰδίᾳ θ' ἅμα καὶ δημοσίᾳ ξυμπάσας τὰς πόλεις.

train their bodies and neglect their minds, commit the mistake of busying themselves about the subordinate and neglecting the superior. You farther remark, that if a man does not know how to use any object rightly, he had better abstain from using it altogether: if he does not know how to use his eyes, his ears, or his body—it will be better for him neither to see, nor to hear, nor to use his body at all : the like with any instrument or article of property—for whoever cannot use his own lyre well, cannot use his neighbour's lyre better. Out of these premises you bring out forcibly the conclusion—That if a man does not know how to use his mind rightly, it is better for him to make no use of it:—better for him not to live, than to live under his own direction. If he must live, he had better live as a slave than a freeman, surrendering the guidance of his understanding to some one else who knows the art of piloting men: which art you, Sokrates, denominate often the political art, sometimes the judicial art or justice.[e]

These discourses of yours, alike numerous and admirable—showing that virtue is teachable, and that a man should attend to himself before he attends to other objects—I never have contradicted, and never shall contradict. I account them most profitable and stimulating, calculated to wake men as it were out of sleep. I expected anxiously what was to come afterwards. I began by copying your style and asking, not yourself, but those among your companions whom you esteemed the most[f]—How are we now to understand this stimulus imparted by Sokrates towards virtue? Is this to be all? Cannot we make advance towards virtue and get full possession of it? Are we to pass our whole lives in stimulating those who have not yet been stimulated, in order that they in their turn may stimulate others? Is it not rather incumbent upon us, now that we have agreed thus far, to entreat both from Sokrates and from each other, an answer

---

[e] Plato, Kleitophon, p. 408 A. ἦν δὴ σὺ πολιτικὴν, ὦ Σώκρατες, ἐπονομάζεις πολλάκις, τὴν αὐτὴν δὴ ταύτην δικαστικήν τε καὶ δικαιοσύνην ὡς ἔστι λέγων.

[f] Plato, Kleitoph. p. 408 D. τούτων γὰρ τούς τι μάλιστα εἶναι δοξαζομένους ὑπὸ σοῦ πρώτους ἐπανηρώτων, πυνθανόμενος τίς ὁ μετὰ ταῦτ' εἴη λόγος, καὶ κατὰ σὲ τρόπον τινὰ ὑποτείνων αὐτοῖς, &c.

to the ulterior question, What next? How are we to set to work in regard to the learning of justice?[g] If any trainer, seeing us careless of our bodily condition, should exhort us strenuously to take care of it, and convince us that we ought to do so—we should next ask him, which were the arts prescribing how we should proceed? He would reply—The gymnastic and medical arts. How will Sokrates or his friends answer the corresponding question in their case?

The ablest of your companions answered me (continues Kleitophon), that the art to which you were wont to allude was no other than Justice itself. I told him in reply—Do not give me the mere name, but tell me what Justice is.[h] In the medical art there are two distinct results contemplated and achieved: one, that of keeping up the succession of competent physicians—another that of conferring or preserving health: this last, *Health*, is not the art itself, but the work accomplished by the art. Just so, the builder's art, has for its object the *house*, which is its work—and the keeping up the continuity of builders, which is its teaching. Tell me in the same manner respecting the art called Justice. Its teaching province is plain enough—to maintain the succession of just men: but what is its working province? what is the work which the just man does for us?

To this question your friend replied (explaining Justice)— It is The Advantageous. Another man near him said, The Proper: a third said, The Profitable: a fourth, The Gainful.[i] I pursued the enquiry by observing, that these were general names equally applicable in other arts, and to something different in each. Every art aims at what is proper, advantageous, profitable, gainful, in

Marginal notes:
Questions addressed by Kleitophon with this view, both to the companions of Sokrates and to Sokrates himself.

Replies made by the friends of Sokrates unsatisfactory.

g Plato, Kleitophon, p. 408 E. ἢ δεῖ τὸν Σωκράτην καὶ ἀλλήλους ἡμᾶς τὸ μετὰ τοῦτ' ἐπανερωτᾶν, ὁμολογήσαντας τοῦτ' αὐτὸ ἀνθρώποις πρακτέον εἶναι. Τί τοὐντεῦθεν; πῶς ἄρχεσθαι δεῖν φαμὲν δικαιοσύνης περὶ μαθήσεως;

h Plato, Kleitoph. p. 409 A. εἰπόντος δ' ἐμοῦ, Μή μοι τὸ ὄνομα μόνον εἴπῃς, ἀλλὰ ὧδε—'Ιατρική πού τις λέγεται τέχνη, &c.

i Plato, Kleitoph. p. 409 B. τὸ δ'

ἕτερον, ὃ δύναται ποιεῖν ἡμῖν ἔργον ὁ δίκαιος, τί τοῦτό φαμεν; εἶπε. Οὗτος μὲν, ὡς οἶμαι, τὸ σύμφερον ἀπεκρίνατο· ἄλλος δὲ, τὸ δέον· ἕτερος δὲ, τὸ ὠφέλιμον· ὁ δὲ, τὸ λυσιτελοῦν. ἐπανῆειν δὴ ἐγὼ λέγων ὅτι Κἀκεῖ τάγε ὀνόματα ταῦτ' ἔστιν ἐν ἑκάστῃ τῶν τεχνῶν, ὀρθῶς πράττειν, λυσιτελοῦντα, ὠφέλιμα, τἄλλα τὰ τοιαῦτα· ἀλλὰ πρὸς ὅ, τι ταῦτα πάντα τείνει, ἐρεῖ τὸ ἴδιον ἑκάστῃ τέχνη, &c.

its own separate department : but each can farther describe to you what that department is. Thus the art of the carpenter is, to perform well, properly, advantageously, profitably, &c., in the construction of wooden implements, &c. That is the special work of the carpenter's art: now tell me, what is the special work, corresponding thereunto, of the art called Justice?

At length one of your most accomplished companions, Sokrates, answered me — That the special work peculiar to Justice was, to bring about friendship in the community.[k] Being farther interrogated, he said—That friendship was always a good, never an evil: That the so-called friendships between children, and between animals, mischievous rather than otherwise, were not real friendships, and ought not to bear the name: That the only genuine friendship was, sameness of reason and intelligence :—not sameness of opinion, which was often hurtful—but knowledge and reason agreeing, in different persons.[l]

None of them could explain what the special work of justice or virtue was

At this stage of our conversation the hearers themselves felt perplexed, and interfered to remonstrate with him; observing, that the debate had come round to the same point again. They declared that the medical art also was harmony of reason and intelligence : that the like was true besides of every other art: that each of them could define the special end to which it tended: but that as to that art, or that harmony of reason and intelligence, which had been called Justice, no one could see to what purpose it tended, nor what was its special work.[m]

After all this debate (continues Kleitophon) I addressed the same question to yourself, Sokrates—What is Justice? You answered—To do good to friends, hurt to enemies. But presently it appeared, that the just man would never, on any occasion, do hurt

Kleitophon at length asked the question from Sokrates himself But Sokrates did not answer clearly

---

[k] Plato, Kleitoph. p. 409 C Τελευ-
τῶν ἀπεκρίνατό τις, ὦ Σώκρατές, μοι
τῶν σῶν ἑταίρων ὃς δὴ κομψότατα
ἔδοξεν εἰπεῖν, ὅτι τοῦτ' εἴη τὸ τῆς
δικαιοσύνης ἴδιον ἔργον, ὃ τῶν ἄλλων
οὐδεμιᾶς, φιλίαν ἐν ταῖς πόλεσι ποιεῖν.
[l] Plato, Kleitophon, p. 409 E.
[m] Plato, Kleitophon, p 410 A. καὶ

ἔλεγον (i. e. the hearers said) ὅτι καὶ ἡ
ἰατρικὴ ὁμόνοιά τίς ἐστι, καὶ ἅπασαι αἱ
τέχναι καὶ περὶ ὅτου εἰσίν, ἔχουσι
λέγειν τὴν δὲ ὑπὸ σοῦ λεγομένην
δικαιοσύνην ἢ ὁμόνοιαν, ὅποι τείνουσά
ἐστι, διαπέφευγε, καὶ ἄδηλον αὐτῆς
ὅ, τι πότ' ἐστι τὸ ἔργον

to any one:—that he would act towards every one with a view to good. It is not once, nor twice, but often and often, that I have endured these perplexities, and have importuned you to clear them up.[n] At last I am wearied out, and have come to the conviction that you are doubtless a consummate proficient in the art of stimulating men to seek virtue; but that as to the ulterior question, how they are to find it—you either do not know, or you will not tell. In regard to any art (such as steersmanship or others), there may be persons who can extol and recommend the art to esteem, but cannot direct the hearers how to acquire it: and in like manner a man might remark about you, that you do not know any better what Justice is, because you are a proficient in commending it. For my part, such is not my opinion. I think that you know, but have declined to tell me. I am resolved, in my present embarrassment, to go to Thrasymachus, or any one else that I can find to help me; unless you will consent to give me something more than these merely stimulating discourses.[o] Consider me as one upon whom your stimulus has already told. If the question were about gymnastic, as soon as I had become fully stimulated to attend to my bodily condition, you would have given me, as a sequel to your stimulating discourse, some positive direction, what my body was by nature, and what treatment it required. Deal in like manner with the case before us: reckon Kleitophon as one fully agreeing with you, that it is contemptible to spend so much energy upon other objects, and to neglect our minds, with a view to which all other objects are treasured up. Put me down as having already given my adhesion to all these views of yours.

Proceed, Sokrates—I supplicate you—to deal with me as I
Kleitophon
is on the
point of leav-
ing Sokrates
and going to
Thrasyma-
chus. But
have described; in order that I may never more have occasion, when I talk with Lysias, to blame you on some points while praising you on others. I will repeat, that to one who has not yet received

[n] Plato, Kleitophon, p. 410 A. Ταῦτα δὲ οὐχ ἅπαξ οὐδὲ δὶς ἀλλὰ πολὺν δὴ ὑπομείνας χρόνον καὶ λιπαρῶν ἀπείρηκα, &c.

[o] Plato, Kleitophon, p. 410 C. διὰ

ταῦτα δὴ καὶ πρὸς Θρασύμαχον, οἶμαι, πορεύσομαι, καὶ ἄλλοσε ὅποι δύναμαι, ἀπορῶν—ἐπεὶ εἴ γ᾽ ἐθέλοις σὺ τούτων μὲν ἤδη παύσασθαι πρὸς ἐμὲ τῶν λόγων τῶν προτρεπτικῶν, &c.

the necessary stimulus, your conversation is of inestimable value: but to one who has already been stimulated, it is rather a hindrance than a help, to his realising the full acquisition of virtue, and thus becoming happy.[p]

before leaving he addresses one last entreaty, that Sokrates will speak out clearly and explicitly.

The fragment called Kleitophon (of which I have given an abstract comparatively long); is in several ways remarkable. The Thrasyllean catalogue places it first in the eighth Tetralogy; the three other members of the same Tetralogy being, Republic, Timæus, Kritias.[q] Though it is both short, and abrupt in its close, we know that it was so likewise in antiquity: the ancient Platonic commentators observing, that Sokrates disdained to make any reply to the appeal of Kleitophon.[r] There were therefore in this Tetralogy two fragments, unfinished works from the beginning—Kleitophon and Kritias.

Remarks on the Kleitophon. Why Thrasyllus placed it in the eighth Tetralogy immediately before the Republic, and along with Kritias, the other fragment.

We may explain why Thrasyllus placed the Kleitophon in immediate antecedence to the Republic: because 1. It complains bitterly of the want of a good explanation of Justice, which Sokrates in the latter books of the Republic professes

---

[p] Plato, Kleitophon, p. 410 E. μὴ μὲν γὰρ προτετραμμένῳ σὲ ἀνθρώπῳ, ὦ Σώκρατες, ἄξιον εἶναι τοῦ παντὸς φήσω, προτετραμμένῳ δὲ, σχεδὸν καὶ ἐμπόδιον τοῦ πρὸς τέλος ἀρετῆς ἐλθόντα εὐδαίμονα γενέσθαι.

[q] Diog. L. iii. 59. The Kleitophon also was one of the dialogues selected by some students of Plato as proper to be studied first of all, Diog. L. iii. 61.

[r] M. Boeckh observes (ad Platonis Minoem, p. 11):—" Nec minus falsum est, quod *spurium* Clitophontem plerique omnes mutilatum putant: quem ex auctoris manibus truncum excidisse inde intelligitur, quod ne vetusti quidem Platonici philosophi, quibus antiquissima exemplaria ad manum erant, habuerunt integriorem. Proclus in Timæ. i. p. 7. Πτολεμαῖος δὲ ὁ Πλατωνικὸς Κλειτοφῶντα αὐτὸν οἴεται εἶναι. τοῦτον γὰρ ἐν τῷ ὁμωνύμῳ διαλόγῳ μηδ' ἀποκρίσεως ἠξιῶσθαι παρὰ Σωκράτους. Plané ut in Critiâ, quem ab ipso Platone non absolutum docet Plutarchus in Solone."

M. Boeckh here characterises the Kleitophon as *spurious*, in which opinion I do not concur.

Yxem, in his Dissertation, Uber Platon's Kleitophon, Berlin, 1846, has vindicated the genuineness of this dialogue, though many of his arguments are such as I cannot subscribe to.

He shows farther, that the first idea of distrusting the genuineness of the Kleitophon arose from the fact that the dialogue was printed in the Aldine edition of 1513, along with the spurious dialogues; although in that very Aldine edition the editors expressly announce that this was a mistake, and that the dialogue ought to have been printed as first of the eighth tetralogy. See Yxem, pp. 32-33. Subsequent editors followed the Aldine in printing the dialogue among the spurious, though still declaring that they did not consider it spurious.

to furnish. 2. It brings before us Kleitophon, who announces an inclination to consult Thrasymachus: now both these personages appear in the first book of the Republic, in which too Thrasymachus is introduced as disputing in a brutal and insulting way, and as humiliated by Sokrates: so that the Republic might be considered both as an answer to the challenge of the Kleitophon, and as a reproof to Kleitophon himself for having threatened to quit Sokrates and go to Thrasymachus.

Like so many other pieces in the Thrasyllean catalogue, the Kleitophon has been declared to be spurious by Schleiermacher and other critics of the present century. I see no ground for this opinion, and I believe the dialogue to be genuine. If it be asked, how can we imagine Plato to have composed a polemic argument, both powerful and unanswered, against Sokrates,—I reply, that this is not so surprising as the Parmenidês: in which Plato has introduced the veteran so named as the successful assailant not only of Sokrates, but of the Platonic theory of Ideas defended by Sokrates.

Kleitophon is genuine, and perfectly in harmony with a just theory of Plato.

I have already declared, that the character of Plato is, in my judgment, essentially many-sided. It comprehends the whole process of searching for truth, and testing all that is propounded as such: it does not shrink from broaching and developing speculative views not merely various and distinct, but sometimes even opposite.

Yet though the Kleitophon is Plato's work, it is a sketch or fragment never worked out. In its present condition, it can hardly have been published (any more than the Kritias) either by his direction or during his life. I conceive it to have remained among his papers, to have been made known by his school after his death, and to have passed from thence among the other Platonic manuscripts into the Alexandrian library at its first foundation. Possibly it may have been originally intended as a preparation for the solution of that problem, which Sokrates afterwards undertakes in the Republic: for it is a challenge to Sokrates to explain what he means by Justice. It may have been intended as such, but never prosecuted:—the prepara-

It could not have been published until after Plato's death.

tion for that solution being provided in another way, such as we now read in the first and second books of the Republic. That the great works of Plato—Republic, Protagoras, Symposion, &c.—could not have been completed without preliminary sketches and tentatives—we may regard as certain. That some of these sketches, though never worked up, and never published by Plato himself, should have been good enough to be preserved by him and published by those who succeeded him—is at the very least highly probable. One such is the Kleitophon.

When I read the Kleitophon, I am not at all surprised that Plato never brought it to a conclusion, nor ever provided Sokrates with an answer to the respectful, yet emphatic, requisition of Kleitophon. The case against Sokrates has been made so strong, that I doubt whether Plato himself could have answered it to his own satisfaction. It resembles the objections which he advances in the Parmenidês against the theory of Ideas: objections which he has nowhere answered, and which I do not believe that he could answer. The characteristic attribute of which Kleitophon complains in Sokrates is, that of a one-sided and incomplete efficiency—($\phi\acute{\upsilon}\sigma\iota\varsigma$ $\mu o\nu\acute{o}\kappa\omega\lambda o\varsigma$)—"You are perpetually stirring us up and instigating us: you do this most admirably: but when we have become full of fervour, you do not teach us how we are to act, nor point out the goal towards which we are to move."[s] Now this is precisely the description which Sokrates gives of his own efficiency, in the Platonic Apology addressed to the Dikasts. He lays especial stress on the mission imposed upon him by the Gods, to apply his Elenchus in testing and convicting the false persuasion of knowledge universally prevalent:—to make sure by repeated cross-examination, whether the citizens pursued money and worldly advancement more energetically than virtue:—and to worry the Athenians with perpetual stimulus, like the gadfly exciting a high-bred but lethargic horse. Sokrates describes this not only as the

Margin note: Reasons why the Kleitophon was never finished. It points out the defects of Sokrates, just as he himself confesses them in the Apology.

---

* I have in an earlier chapter (ch. vi. p. 277) cited the passage—"Philosophiam multis locis inchoasti: ad impellendum satis, ad edocendum parum." This is the language addressed by Cicero to Varro, and coinciding substantially with that of Kleitophon here.

mission of his life, but as a signal benefit and privilege conferred upon Athens by the Gods.[t] But here his services end. He declares explicitly that he shares in the universal ignorance, and that he is no wiser than any one else, except in being aware of his own ignorance. He disclaims all power of teaching:[u] and he deprecates the supposition,—that he himself knew what he convicted others of not knowing,—as a mistake which had brought upon him alike unmerited reputation and great unpopularity.[x] We find thus that the description given by Sokrates of himself in the Apology, and the reproach addressed to Sokrates by Kleitophon, fully coincide. "My mission from the Gods" (says Sokrates), "is to dispel the false persuasion of knowledge, to cross-examine men into a painful conviction of their own ignorance, and to create in them a lively impulse towards knowledge and virtue: but I am no wiser than they: I can teach them nothing, nor can I direct them what to do."—That is exactly what I complain of (remarks Kleitophon): I have gone through your course,—have been electrified by your Elenchus,—and am full of the impulse which you so admirably communicate. In this condition, what I require is, to find out how, or in which direction I am to employ that impulse. If you cannot tell me, I must ask Thrasymachus or some one else.

Moreover, it is not merely in the declarations of Sokrates himself before the Athenian Dikasts, but also in the Platonic Sokrates as exhibited by Plato in very many of his dialogues, that the same efficiency, and the same deficiency, stand conspicuous. The hearer is convicted of ignorance, on some familiar subject which he believed himself to know: the protreptic stimulus is powerful, stinging his mind into uneasiness which he cannot appease except by finding some tenable result: but the didactic supplement is not forthcoming. Sokrates ends by creating a painful feeling of perplexity in the hearers, but he himself

The same defects also confessed in many of the Platonic and Xenophontic dialogues.

---

[t] Plat. Apol. So. pp. 28 E, 29 D-E, 36 A-E. προσκείμενον τῇ πόλει ὑπὸ τοῦ θεοῦ ὥσπερ ἵππῳ μεγάλῳ μὲν καὶ γενναίῳ, ὑπὸ μεγέθους δὲ νωθεστέρῳ καὶ δεομένῳ ἐγείρεσθαι ὑπὸ μύωπός τινος· οἷον δή μοι δοκεῖ ὁ θεὸς ἐμὲ τῇ πόλει προστεθεικέναι τοιοῦτόν τινα, ὃς ὑμᾶς ἐγείρων καὶ πείθων καὶ ὀνειδίζων ἕνα ἕκαστον οὐδὲν παύομαι, τὴν ἡμέραν ὅλην πανταχοῦ προσκαθίζων, pp. 36 D, 41 E.

[u] Plat. Apol. So. pp. 21 D-22 D, 33 A. ἐγὼ δὲ διδάσκαλος οὐδενὸς πώποτε ἐγενόμην.

[x] Plat. Apol. So. pp. 23 A, 28 A.

shares the feeling along with them. It is this which the
youth Protarchus deprecates, at the beginning of the Platonic Philêbus;[y] and with which Hippias taunts Sokrates, in
one of the Xenophontic conversations[z]—insomuch that Sokrates replies to the taunt by giving a definition of the Just
(τὸ δίκαιον), upon which Hippias comments. But if the observations ascribed by Xenophon to Hippias are a report of
what that Sophist really said, we only see how inferior he
was to Sokrates in the art of cross-questioning: for the definition given by Sokrates would have been found altogether
untenable, if there had been any second Sokrates to apply
the Elenchus to it.[a] Lastly, Xenophon expressly tells us,
that there were others also, who, both in speech and writing,
imputed to Sokrates the same deficiency on the affirmative
side.[b]

The Platonic Kleitophon corresponds, in a great degree, to
these complaints of Protarchus and others, as well
as to the taunt of Hippias. The case is put, however, with much greater force and emphasis: as
looked at, not by an opponent and outsider, like
Hippias—nor by a mere novice, unarmed though
eager, like Protarchus—but by a companion of
long-standing, who has gone through the full course
of negative gymnastic, is grateful for the benefit
derived, and feels that it is time to pass from the
lesser mysteries to the greater. He is sick of perpetual
negation and stimulus: he demands doctrines and explanations, which will hold good against the negative Elenchus of
Sokrates himself. But this is exactly what Sokrates cannot
give. His mission from the Delphian God finishes with

Forcible, yet respectful, manner in which these defects are set forth in the Kleitophon. Impossible to answer them in such a way as to hold out against the negative Elenchus of a Sokratic pupil.

---

[y] Plato, Philêbus, p. 20 A.
[z] Xenoph. Memor. iv. 4, 9-11.
[a] We need only compare the observations made by Hippias in that dialogue, with the objections raised by Sokrates himself in his conversation with
Euthydêmus, Xen. Mem. iv. 4, 2, and
the dialogue of the youthful Alkibiades
(evidently borrowed from Sokrates)
with Perikles, ib. i. 2, 40-47.
[b] Xenoph. Memor. i. 4, 1. εἰ δέ
τινες Σωκράτην νομίζουσιν, ὡς ἔνιοι
γράφουσί τε καὶ λέγουσι περὶ αὐτοῦ

τεκμαιρόμενοι, προτρέψασθαι μὲν ἀνθρώπους ἐπ' ἀρετὴν κράτιστον γεγονέναι, προαγαγεῖν δ' ἐπ' αὐτὴν οὐχ
ἱκανόν—σκεψάμενοι μὴ μόνον, &c.

See also Cicero, De Oratore, i. 47,
204, in which Sokrates is represented
as saying that *concitatio* (προτροπή)
was all that people required: they did
not need guidance: they would find
out the way for themselves: and
Yxem, Ueber Platon's Kleitophon,
pp. 5-12.

the negative : inspiration fails him when he deals with the affirmative. He is like the gad-fly (his own simile) in stimulating the horse—and also in furnishing no direction how the stimulus is to be expended. His affirmative dicta,—as given in the Xenophontic Memorabilia, are for the most part plain, homebred, good sense,—in which all the philosophical questions are slurred over, and the undefined words, Justice, Temperance, Holiness, Courage, Law, &c., are assumed to have a settled meaning agreed to by every one—while as given by Plato, in the Republic and elsewhere, they are more speculative, highflown, and poetical,[c] but not the less exposed to certain demolition, if the batteries of the Sokratic Elenchus were brought to bear upon them. The challenge of Kleitophon is thus unanswerable. It brings out in the most forcible, yet respectful, manner the contrast between the two attributes of the Sokratic mind: in the negative, irresistible force and originality: in the affirmative, confessed barrenness alternating with honest, acute, practical sense, but not philosophy. Instead of this, Plato gives us transcendental hypotheses, and a religious and poetical ideal ; impressive indeed to the feelings, but equally inadmissible to a mind trained in the use of the Sokratic tests.

We may thus see sufficient reason why Plato, after having drawn up the Kleitophon as preparatory basis for a dialogue, became unwilling to work it out, and left it as an unfinished sketch. He had, probably without intending it, made out too strong a case against Sokrates and against himself. If he continued it, he would have been obliged to put some sufficient reason into the mouth of Sokrates, why Kleitophon should abandon his intention of frequenting some other teacher : and this was a hard task. He would have been obliged to lay before Kleitophon, a pupil thoroughly inoculated with his own negative *œstrus*, affirmative solutions proof against such subtle cross-examination : and this, we may fairly

The Kleitophon represents a point of view which many objectors must have insisted on against Sokrates and Plato.

---

[c] The explanation of Justice given by Plato in the Republic deserves to be described much in the same words as Sokrates employs (Repub. i. p. 332 B) in characterising the definition of Justice furnished by (or ascribed to) the poet Simonides :—

ἠνίξατο, ὡς ἔοικεν, ὁ Σιμωνίδης ποιητικῶς τὸ δίκαιον ὃ εἴη.

assume, was not merely a hard task, but impossible. Hence it is that we possess the Kleitophon only as a fragment.

Yet I think it a very ingenious and instructive fragment: setting forth powerfully, in respect to the negative philosophy of Sokrates and Plato, a point of view which must have been held by many intelligent contemporaries. Among all the objections urged against Sokrates and Plato, probably none was more frequent than this protest against the continued negative procedure. This same point of view—that Sokrates puzzled every one, but taught no one any thing—is reproduced by Thrasymachus against Sokrates in the first book of the Republic:[d] in which first book there are various other marks of analogy with the Kleitophon.[e] It might seem as if Plato had in the first instance projected a dialogue in which Sokrates was to discuss the subject of justice, and had drawn up the Kleitophon as the sketch of a sort of forcing process to be applied to Sokrates: then, finding that he placed Sokrates under too severe pressure, had abandoned the project, and taken up the same subject anew, in the manner which we now read in the Republic. The task which he assigns to Sokrates, in this last-mentioned dialogue, is far easier. Instead of the appeal made to Sokrates by Kleitophon, with truly Sokratic point—we have an assault made upon him by Thrasymachus, alike angry, impudent, and feeble; which just elicits the peculiar aptitude of Sokrates for humbling the boastful affirmer. Again in the second book, Glaukon and Adeimantus are introduced as stating the difficulties which they feel in respect to the theory of Justice; but in a manner totally different from Kleitophon, and without any reference to previous Sokratic requirements. Each of them delivers an eloquent and forcible pleading, in the manner of an Aristotelian or Ciceronian dialogue; and to this Sokrates makes

The Kleitophon was originally intended as a first book of the Republic, but was found too hard to answer. Reasons why the existing first book was substituted.

---

[d] Plat. Republ. pp. 336 D, 337 A, 338 A.

[e] For example, That it is not the province of the just man to hurt any one, either friend or foe, Repub. p. 335 D.

Thrasymachus derides any such definitions of τὸ δίκαιον as the following,—τὸ δέον—τὸ ὠφέλιμον—τὸ λυσιτελοῦν—τὸ ξύμφερον—τὸ κερδάλεον, Repub. i. p. 336 C.

These are exactly the unsatisfactory definitions which Kleitophon describes himself (p. 409 C) as having received from the partisans of Sokrates.

his reply. In that reply, Sokrates explains what he means by Justice: and though his exposition is given in the form of short questions, each followed by an answer of acquiescence, yet no real or serious objections are made to him throughout the whole. The case must have been very different if Plato had continued the dialogue Kleitophon; so as to make Sokrates explain the theory of Justice, in the face of all the objections raised by a Sokratic cross-examiner.[f]

[f] Schleiermacher (Einleitung, v. pp. 453-455) considers the Kleitophon not to be the work of Plato. But this only shows that he, like many other critics, attaches scarcely the smallest importance to the presumption arising from the Canon of Thrasyllus. For the grounds by which he justifies his disallowance of the dialogue are to the last degree trivial.

I note with surprise one of his assertions :—"How" (he asks) " or from what motive can Plato have introduced an attack upon Sokrates, which is thoroughly repelled, both seriously and ironically, in almost all the Platonic dialogues? "

As I read Plato, on the contrary : the truth is, That it is repelled in none, confirmed in many, and thoroughly ratified by Sokrates himself in the Platonic Apology.

Schleiermacher thinks that the Kleitophon is an attack upon Sokrates and the Sokratic men, Plato included, made by some opponent out of the best rhetorical schools. He calls it " a parody and caricature " of the Sokratic manner. To me it seems no caricature at all. It is a very fair application of the Sokratic or Platonic manner. Nor is it conceived by any means in the spirit of an enemy, but in that of an established companion, respectful and grateful, yet dissatisfied at finding that he makes no progress.

CHAPTER XXXIII.

PLATONIC REPUBLIC—ABSTRACT.

THE Republic is the longest of all the Platonic dialogues, except the dialogue De Legibus. It consists of ten books, each of them as long as any one of the dialogues which we have passed in review. Partly from its length—partly from its lofty pretensions as the great constructive work of Plato— I shall give little more than an abstract of it in the present chapter, and shall reserve remark and comment for the succeeding.

The professed subject is—What is Justice? Is the just man happy in or by reason of his justice, whatever consequences may befall him? Is the unjust man unhappy by reason of his injustice? But the ground actually travelled over by Sokrates, from whose mouth the exposition proceeds, is far more extensive than could have been anticipated from this announced problem. An immense variety of topics, belonging to man and society, is adverted to more or less fully. A theory of psychology or phrenology generally, is laid down and advocated: likewise a theory of the Intellect, distributed into its two branches: 1. Science, with the Platonic Forms or Ideas as Realities corresponding to it; 2. Opinion, with the fluctuating semi-realities or pseudo-realities, which form its object. A sovereign rule, exercised by philosophy, is asserted as indispensable to human happiness. The fundamental conditions of a good society, as Plato conceived it, are set forth at considerable length, and contrasted with the social corruptions of various existing forms of government. The outline of a perfect education, intellectual and emotional, is drawn up and prescribed for the ruling class: with many accompanying remarks on the objectionable tendencies of the popular and consecrated poems. The post-existence, as well as the

Declared theme of the Republic—Expansion and multiplication of the topics connected with it.

pre-existence of the soul, is affirmed in the concluding books. As the result of the whole, Plato emphatically proclaims his conviction, that the just man is happy in and through his justice, quite apart from all consideration of consequences—yet that the consequences also will be such as to add to his happiness, both during life as well as after death: and the unjust man unhappy in and through his injustice.[a]

The dramatic introduction of the dialogue, (which is described as held during the summer, immediately after the festival of the Bendideia in Peiræus), with the picture of the aged Kephalus and his views upon old age, is among the richest and most spirited in the Platonic works: but the discussion does not properly begin until Kephalus retires, leaving it to be carried on by Sokrates with Polemarchus, Glaukon, Adeimantus, and Thrasymachus.

Personages of the dialogue.

"Old age has its advantages to reasonable men" (says Kephalus). "If I have lost the pleasures of youth, I have at the same time lost the violent desires which then overmastered me. I now enjoy tranquillity and peace. Without doubt, this is in part owing to my wealth. But the best that wealth does for me is, that it enables me to make compensation for deceptions and injustice, practised on other men in my younger days—and to fulfil all vows made to the Gods. An old man who is too poor to render such atonement for past falsehood and injustice, becomes uneasy in his mind as death approaches; he begins to fear that the stories about Hades, which he has heard and ridiculed in his youth, may perhaps prove true." [b]

Views of Kephalus about old age.

"Is that your explanation of Justice" (asks Sokrates): "that it consists in telling truth, and rendering to every one what you have had from him?" The old man Kephalus here withdraws; Polemarchus and the others prosecute the discussion. "The poet Simonides" (says Polemarchus) "gives an explanation like to that which you have stated—when he affirms, That just dealing consists in rendering to every man what is owing to him."

Definition of Justice by Simonides— It consists in rendering to every man what is owing to him.

---

[a] Plat. Repub. i. pp. 328 A, 350 D, 354 A.
[b] Plato, Republ. i. pp. 330-331.

Compare the language of Cato, more rhetorical and exaggerated than that of Kephalus, in Cicero De Senect. c. 13-14.

" I do not know what Simonides means," replies Sokrates. " He cannot mean that it is always right to tell the truth, or always right to give back a deposit. If my friend, having deposited arms with me, afterwards goes mad, and in that state demands them back, it would not be right in me either to restore the arms, or to tell the truth, to a man in that condition. Therefore to say that justice consists in speaking truth and in giving back what we have received, cannot be a good definition." [c]

Polemarchus here gives a peculiar meaning to the phrase of Simonides: a man owes good to his friends—evil to his enemies: and he ought to pay back both. Upon this Sokrates comments.[d]

[c] Plato, Republ. i. p. 331 C-D.

The historical Sokrates argues in the same manner ⸢in the Memorabilia of Xenophon. See his conversation with Euthydemus, iv. 2; and Cicero, De Offic. iii. 25, 94-95).

[d] Sokrates here remarks that the precepts—Speak truth; Restore what has been confided to you—ought not to be considered as universally binding. Sometimes justice, or those higher grounds upon which the rules of justice are founded, prescribe that we should disobey the precepts. Sokrates takes this for granted, as a matter which no one will dispute; and it is evident that what Plato had here in his mind was, the obvious consideration that to tell the truth or restore a weapon deposited, to one who had gone mad, would do no good to any one and might do immense mischief: thus showing that general utility is both the foundation and the limiting principle of all precepts respecting just and unjust. That this is present to the mind of Plato appears evident from his assuming the position as a matter of course; it is moreover Sokratic, as we see by the Memorabilia of Xenophon.

But Plato, in another passage of the Republic, clothes this Sokratic doctrine in a language and hypothesis of his own. He sets up Forms or Ideas, *per se*. The Just,—The Unjust,—The Honourable,—The Base, &c. He distinguishes each of these from the many separate manifestations in which it is specialised. The Form, though one reality in itself, appears manifold when embodied and disguised in these diversified accompaniments. It remains One and Unchanged, the object of Science and universal infallible truth; but each of its separate manifestations is peculiar to itself, appears differently to different minds, and admits of no˙ higher certainty than fallible opinion. Though the Form of Justice always remains the same, yet its subordinate embodiments ever fluctuate; there is no given act nor assemblage of acts which is always just. Every just act (see Republic, v. pp. 476˙ A-479 A) is liable under certain circumstances to become unjust; or to be invaded and overclouded by the Form of Injustice. The genuine philosopher will detect the Form of Justice wherever it is to be found, in the midst of accompaniments however discrepant and confused, over all which he will ascend to the region of universal truth and reality. The unphilosophical mind cannot accomplish this ascent, nor detect the pure Form, nor even recognise its real existence: but sees nothing beyond the multiplicity of diverse particular cases in which it is or appears to be embodied. Respecting these particular cases there is no constant or universal truth, no full science. They cannot be thrown into classes to which the superior Form constantly and unconditionally adheres. They are midway between reality and non-reality: they are mat-

S.—Simonides meant to say (you tell me) that Justice consists in rendering benefits to your friends, evil to your enemies: that is, in rendering to each what is proper and suitable. But we must ask him farther— Proper and suitable—how? in what cases? to whom? The medical art is that which renders what is proper and suitable, of nourishment and medicaments for the health of the body: the art of cookery is that which renders what is proper and suitable, of savoury ingredients for the satisfaction of the palate. In like manner, the cases must be specified in which justice renders what is proper and suitable—to whom, how, or what?[e]

P.—Justice consists in doing good to friends, evil to enemies. *S.*—Who is it that is most efficient in benefiting his friends and injuring his enemies, as to health or disease? *P.*—It is the physician. *S.*—Who, in reference to the dangers in navigation by sea? *P.*—The steersman. *S.*—In what matters is it that the just man shows his special efficiency, to benefit friends and hurt enemies?[f] *P.*—In war: as a combatant for the one and against the other. *S.*—To men who are not sick, the physician is of no use—nor the steersman, to men on dry land: Do you mean in like manner, that the just man is useless to those who are not at war? *P.*—No: I do not mean that. Justice is useful in peace also. *S.*—So also is husbandry, for raising food—shoemaking, for providing shoes. Tell me for what want or acquisition justice is useful during peace? *P.*—It is useful for the common dealings and joint

Explanation by Polemarchus—Farther interrogations by Sokrates—Justice renders what is proper and suitable: but how? in what cases, proper? Under what circumstances is Justice useful?

ters of opinion more or less reasonable, but not of certain science or unconditional affirmation. Among mankind generally, who see nothing of true and absolute Form, the received rules and dogmas respecting the Just, the Beautiful, &c., are of this intermediate and ambiguous kind: they can neither be affirmed universally, nor denied universally; they are partly true, partly false, determinable only by opinion in each separate case.[1]

[1] Plato, Republic, v. p. 479. οὔτ' εἶναι οὔτε μὴ εἶναι οὐδὲν αὐτῶν δυνατὸν παγίως νοῆσαι, οὔτ' ἀμφότερα οὔτε οὐδέτερον. Τὰ τῶν πολλῶν πολλὰ νόμιμα, καλοῦ τε περὶ καὶ τῶν ἄλλων,

Of the distinction here drawn in general terms by Plato, between the pure unchangeable Form, and the subordinate classes of particulars in which that Form is or appears to be embodied, the reasoning above cited respecting truth-telling and giving back a deposit is an example.

[e] Plato, Republic, i. p. 332 C. ἢ οὖν δὴ τίσι τί ἀποδιδοῦσα τέχνη δικαιοσύνη ἂν καλοῖτο;

[f] Plato, Republic, i. p. 332 E. ὁ δίκαιος ἐν τίνι πράξει καὶ πρὸς τί ἔργον δυνατώτατος φίλους ὠφελεῖν καὶ ἐχθροὺς βλάπτειν;

μεταξύ που κυλινδεῖται τοῦ τε μὴ ὄντος καὶ τοῦ ὄντος εἰλικρινῶς.

transactions between man and man.   *S.*—When we are engaged in playing at draughts, the good player is our useful co-
operator : when in laying bricks and stones, the skilful mason :
much more than the just man.   Can you specify in what particular transactions the just man has any superior usefulness as
a co-operator ?   *P.*—In affairs of money I think.   *S.*—Surely
not in the employment of money.   When you want to buy a
horse, you must take for your assistant, not the just man, but
one who knows horses : so also, if you are purchasing a ship.
What are those modes of jointly employing money, in which
the just man is more useful than others ?   *P.*—He is useful
when you wish to have your money safely kept.   *S.*—That
is, when your money is not to be employed, but to lie idle :
so that when your money is useless, then is the time when
justice is useful for it.   *P.*—So it seems.   *S.*—In regard to
other things also, a sickle, a shield, a lyre—when you want to
use them, the pruner, the hoplite, the musician, must be
invoked as co-operators : justice is useful only when you are
to keep them unused.   In a word, justice is useless for the
use of any thing, and useful merely for things not in use.
Upon this showing, it is at least a matter of no great worth.[g]

But let us pursue the investigation (continues Sokrates).
In boxing or in battle, is not he who is best in striking, best also in defending himself ?   In regard to
disease, is not he who can best guard himself against
it, the most formidable for imparting it to others ?
Is not the general who watches best over his own
camp, also the most effective in surprising and over-
reaching the enemy ?   In a word, whenever a man is effective
as a guard of any thing, is he not also effective as a thief of
it ?   *P.*—Such seems the course of the discussion.   *S.*—Well
then, the just man turns out to be a sort of thief, like the
Homeric Autolykus.   According to the explanation of Simonides, justice is a mode of thieving, for the profit of friends
and damage of enemies.[h]   *P.*—It cannot be so.   I am in

The just man, being good for keeping property guarded, must also be good for steal-ing property—Analogies cited.

---

[g] Plato, Republic, i. pp. 332-333.
Οὐκ ἂν οὖν πάνυ γέ τι σπουδαῖον εἴη ἡ
δικαιοσύνη, εἰ πρὸς τὰ ἄχρηστα χρήσι-
μον ὂν τυγχάνει;

[h] Plat. Rep. i. p. 334 B.   ἔοικεν οὖν
ἡ δικαιοσύνη—κλεπτική τις εἶναι, ἐπ'
ὠφελείᾳ μέντοι τῶν φίλων, καὶ ἐπὶ
βλαβῇ τῶν ἐχθρῶν.

utter confusion.   Yet I think still that justice is profitable to friends, and hurtful to enemies.

S.—Whom do you call friends: those whom a man believes to be good,—or those who really are good, whether he believes them to be so or not: and the like, in reference to enemies?   *P.*—I mean those whom he believes to be good.   It is natural that he should love *them*, and that he should hate those whom he believes to be evil.   *S.*—But is not a man often mistaken in this belief?   *P.*—Yes; often.   *S.*—In so far as a man is mistaken, the good men are his enemies, and the evil men his friends.   Justice, therefore, on your showing, consists in doing good to the evil men, and evil to the good men.   *P.*—So it appears.   *S.*—Now good men are just, and do no wrong to any one.   It is therefore just, on your explanation, to hurt those who do no wrong.   *P.*—Impossible! that is a monstrous doctrine.   *S.*—You mean, then, that it is just to hurt unjust men, and to benefit just men?   *P.*—Yes; that is something better.   *S.*—It will often happen, therefore, when a man misjudges about others, that justice will consist in hurting his friends, since they are in his estimation the evil men: and in benefiting his enemies, since they are in his estimation the good men.   Now this is the direct contrary of what Simonides defined to be justice.[i]

"We have misconceived the meaning of Simonides" (replies Polemarchus).   "He must have meant that justice consists in benefiting your friend, assuming him to be a good man: and in hurting your enemy, assuming him to be an evil man."   Sokrates proceeds to impugn the definition in this new sense. He shows that justice does not admit of our hurting any man, either evil or good.   By hurting the evil man, we only make him more evil than he was before.   To do this belongs not to justice, but to injustice.[k]   The definition of justice—That it consists in rendering benefit to friends and hurt to enemies—is not suitable to a wise man like Simonides, but to some rich potentate

Side notes:

Justice consists in doing good to friends, evil to enemies— But how, if a man mistakes who his friends are, and makes friends of bad men?

Justice consists in doing good to your friend, if really a good man : hurt to your enemy, with the like proviso. Sokrates affirms that the just man will do no hurt to any one. Definition of Simonides rejected.

---

[i] Plato, Republic, i. p. 334 D.   [k] Plato, Republic, i. pp. 335-336.

like Periander or Xerxes, who thinks his own power irresistible.[1]

At this turn of the dialogue, when the definition given
by Simonides has just been refuted, Thrasymachus   Thrasyma-
breaks in, and takes up the conversation with So-   chus takes up
                                                     the dialogue
krates. He is depicted as angry, self-confident to —Repulsive
                                                     portrait
excess, and coarse in his manners even to the length drawn of
                                                     him.
of insult. The portrait given of him is memorable for its
dramatic vivacity, and is calculated to present in an odious
point of view the doctrines which he advances, like the personal deformities which Homer heaps upon Thersites in the
Iliad.[m] But how far it is a copy of the real man, we have no
evidence to inform us.

In the contrast between Sokrates and Thrasymachus, Plato
gives valuable hints as to the conditions of in-   Violence of
structive colloquy. " What nonsense is all this ! " Thrasyma-
                                                     chus—Sub-
(exclaims Thrasymachus). " Do not content your-   dued manner
                                                     of Sokrates—
self with asking questions, Sokrates, which you know Conditions of
                                                     useful collo-
is much easier than answering: but tell us yourself quy.
what Justice is : give us a plain answer : do not tell us that it
is what is right—or profitable—or for our interest—or gainful—or advantageous : for I will not listen to any trash like
this." " Be not so harsh with us, Thrasymachus " (replies
Sokrates, in a subdued tone). " If we have taken the wrong
course of enquiry, it is against our own will. You ought to
feel pity for us rather than anger." " I thought " (rejoined
Thrasymachus, with a scornful laugh) " that you would have
recourse to your usual pretence of ignorance, and would decline answering." *S.*—How can I possibly answer, when you
prescribe beforehand what I am to say or not to say ? If you
ask men—How much is twelve ? and at the same time say—
Don't tell me that it is twice six, or three times four, or four
times three—how can any man answer your question ? *T.*—
As if the two cases were similar ! *S.*—Why not similar ?
But even though they be not similar, yet if the respondent

[1] Here is a characteristic specimen
of searching cross-examination in the
Platonic or Sokratic style : citing
multiplied analogies, and requiring
the generalities of a definition to be

clothed with particulars, that its sufficiency may be proved in each of many
successive as well as different cases.
[m] Homer, Iliad B. 216.

thinks them so, how can he help answering according as
the matter appears to him, whether we forbid him or not?
T.—Is that what *you* intend to do? Are you going to give
me one of those answers which I forbade? *S.*—Very likely
I may, if on consideration it appears to me the proper answer.[n] *T.*—What will you say if I show you another answer
better than all of them? What penalty will you then impose
upon yourself? *S.*—What penalty?—why, that which properly falls upon the ignorant. It is their proper fate to learn
from men wiser than themselves: that is the penalty which I
am prepared for.[o]

After a few more words, in the same offensive and insolent
tone ascribed to him from the beginning, Thrasymachus produces his definition of Justice:—"Justice is
that which is advantageous to the more powerful."
Some comments from Sokrates bring out a fuller explanation, whereby the definition stands amended:—
"Justice is that which is advantageous to the constituted authority, or to that which holds power, in
each different community: monarchy, oligarchy, or
democracy, as the case may be. Each of these authorities makes laws and ordinances for its own interest: declares what is just and unjust: and punishes all citizens who
infringe its commands. Justice consists in obeying these commands. In this sense, justice is everywhere that which is
for the interest or advantage of the more powerful."[p] "I too
believe" (says Sokrates) "that justice is something advantageous, in a certain sense. But whether you are right in
adding these words—' to the more powerful '—is a point for

Marginal: Definition given by Thrasyma-chus—Justice is that which is advantageous to the more powerful. Comments by Sokrates. What if the powerful man mistakes his own advantage?

[n] Plato, Republic, i. p. 337 C.
Εἰ δ' οὖν καὶ μὴ ἔστιν ὅμοιον,
φαίνεται δὲ τῷ ἐρωτηθέντι
τοιοῦτον, ἧττόν τι οἴει αὐτὸν
ἀποκρινεῖσθαι τὸ φαινόμενον
ἑαυτῷ, ἐάν τε ἡμεῖς ἀπαγορεύωμεν,
ἐάν τε μή; Ἄλλο τι οὖν, ἔφη, καὶ σὺ
οὕτω ποιήσεις; ὧν ἐγὼ ἀπεῖπον, τούτων
τι ἀποκρινεῖ; Οὐκ ἂν θαυμάσαιμι, ἦν
δ' ἐγώ, εἴ μοι σκεψαμένῳ οὕτω
δόξειεν.
This passage deserves notice, inasmuch as Plato here affirms, in very
plain language, the Protagorean doc-

trine, which we have seen him trying
to refute in the Theætētus and
Kratylus,—"Homo Mensura,—Every
man is a measure to himself. That
is true or false to every man which
appears to him so."
Most of Plato's dialogues indeed
imply this truth; for no man makes
more constant appeal to the internal
assent or dissent of the individual
interlocutor. But it is seldom that he
declares it in such express terms.
[o] Plato, Republic, i. p. 337 D.
[p] Plato, Republic, i. pp. 338-339.

investigation.q Assuming that the authorities in each state make ordinances for their own advantage, you will admit that they sometimes mistake, and enact ordinances tending to their own disadvantage. In so far as they do this, justice is not that which is advantageous, but that which is disadvantageous, to the more powerful.r Your definition therefore will not hold."

Thrasymachus might have replied to this objection by saying, that he meant what the superior power conceived to be for its own advantage, and enacted accordingly, whether such conception was correct or erroneous. This interpretation, though indicated by a remark put into the mouth of Kleitophon, is not farther pursued.s But in the reply really ascribed to Thrasymachus, he is made to retract what he had just before admitted—that the superior authority sometimes commits mistakes. In so far as a superior or a ruler makes mistakes (Thrasymachus says), he is not a superior. We say indeed, speaking loosely, that the ruler falls into error, just as we say that the physician or the steersman fall into error. The physician does not err *quâ* physician, nor the steersman *quâ* steersman. No craftsman errs *quâ* craftsman. If he errs, it is not from his craft, but from want of knowledge: that is, from want of craft.t What the ruler, as such, declares to be best for himself, and therefore enacts, is always really best for himself: this is justice for the persons under his rule.

To this subtle distinction, Sokrates replies by saying (in substance), " If you take the craftsman in this strict meaning, as representing the abstraction Craft, it is not true that his proceedings are directed towards his own interest or advantage. What he studies is, the advantage of his subjects or clients, not his own. The physician, as such, has it in

Marginal notes:

Correction by Thrasymachus—If the Ruler mistakes, he is *pro tanto* no Ruler—The Ruler, *quâ* Ruler—*quâ* Craftsman—is infallible.

Reply by Sokrates—The Ruler, *quâ* infallible Craftsman, studies the interest of those whom he governs, and not his own interest.

q Plato, Republic, i. p. 339 B.

ἐπειδὴ δὲ ξυμφέρον γέ τι εἶναι καὶ ἐγὼ ὁμολογῶ τὸ δίκαιον, σὺ δὲ προστίθης καὶ αὐτὸ φὴς εἶναι τὸ τοῦ κρείττονος, ἐγὼ δὲ ἀγνοῶ, σκεπτέον δή.

r Plato, Republic, i. p. 339 E.

s Plato, Republic, i. p. 340 B.

t Plato, Republic, i. p. 340 E. ἐπιλιπούσης γὰρ ἐπιστήμης ὁ ἁμαρτάνων ἁμαρτάνει, ἐν ᾧ οὐκ ἔστι δημιουργός· ὥστε δημιουργὸς ἢ σοφὸς ἢ ἄρχων οὐδεὶς ἁμαρτάνει, τότε ὅταν ἄρχων ᾖ.

view to cure his patients: the steersman, to bring his pas-
sengers safely to harbour : the ruler, so far forth as craftsman, makes laws for the benefit of his subjects, and not
for his own. If obedience to these laws constitutes justice, therefore, it is not true that justice consists in what
is advantageous to the superior or governing power. It
would rather consist in what is advantageous to the
governed."[u]

Thrasymachus is now represented as renouncing the ab-

Thrasyma-
chus denies
this—Justice
is the good
of another.
The just
many are
worse off
than the un-
just One, and
are forced to
submit to his
superior
strength.
straction above noted,[x] and reverting to the actualities of life. "Such talk is childish!" (he exclaims, with the coarseness imputed to him in this
dialogue). "Shepherds and herdsmen tend and fatten
their flocks and herds, not for the benefit of the
sheep and oxen, but for the profit of themselves
and the proprietors. So too the genuine ruler in a
city : he regards his subjects as so many sheep,
looking only to the amount of profit which he can draw from
them.[y] Justice is, in real truth, the good of another: it is
the profit of him who is more powerful and rules—the loss of
those who are weaker and must obey. It is the unjust man
who rules over the multitude of just and well-meaning men.
They serve him as being the stronger : they build up his
happiness at the cost of their own. Everywhere, both in
private dealing and in public function, the just man is worse
off than the unjust. I mean by the unjust, one who has the
power to commit wrongful seizure on a large scale. You may
see this if you look at the greatest injustice of all—the case
of the despot, who makes himself happy while the juster men
over whom he rules are miserable. One who is detected in
the commission of petty crimes is punished, and gets a bad
name : but if a man has force enough to commit crime on
the grand scale, to enslave the persons of the citizens, and
to appropriate their goods, instead of being called by a bad
name, he is envied and regarded as happy, not only by the
citizens themselves, but by all who hear him named. Those

u Plato, Republic, i. p. 342.
x Plato, Republic, i. p. 345 B-C.
y Plato, Republic, p. 343 B.

A similar comparison is put into the
mouth of Sokrates himself by Plato in
the Theætêtus, p. 174 D.

who blame injustice, do so from the fear of suffering it, not from the fear of doing it.   Thus then injustice, in its successful efficiency, is strong, free, and overruling, as compared with justice.   Injustice is profitable to a man's self: justice (as I said before) is what is profitable to some other man stronger than he." [z]

Thrasymachus is described as laying down this position in very peremptory language, and as anxious to depart immediately after it, if he had not been detained by the other persons present.   His position forms the pivot of the subsequent conversation.   The two opinions included in it—(That justice consists in obedience yielded by the weak to the orders of the strong for the advantage of the strong—That injustice, if successful, is profitable and confers happiness: justice the contrary)—are disputed, both of them, by Sokrates as well as by Glaukon. [a]

Position laid for the subsequent debate and exposition.

Sokrates is represented as confuting and humiliating Thrasymachus by various arguments, of which the two first at least are more subtle than cogent. [b]   He next proceeds to argue that injustice, far from being a source of strength, is a source of weakness—That any community of men, among whom injustice prevails, must be in continual dispute ; and therefore incapable of combined action against others—That a camp of mercenary soldiers or robbers, who plunder every one else, must at least observe justice among themselves—That if they have force, this is because they are unjust only by halves: that if they were thoroughly unjust, they would also be thoroughly impotent—That the like is true also of an individual separately taken, who, so far as he is unjust, is in a perpetual state of hatred and conflict with himself, as well as with just men and with the Gods: and would thus be divested of all power to accomplish any purpose. [c]

Arguments of Sokrates— Injustice is a source of weakness— Every multitude must observe justice among themselves, in order to avoid perpetual quarrels. The same about any single individual: if he is unjust, he will be at war with himself, and perpetually weak.

Having thus shown that justice is stronger than injustice, Sokrates next offers an argument to prove that it is happier

---

[z] Plato, Republic, i. pp. 343-344.
[a] Plato, Republic, i. pp. 345 A-348 A.
[b] Plato, Republic, i. pp. 346-350.
[c] Plato, Republic, i. pp. 351-352 D.

or confers more happiness than injustice. The conclusion of this argument is—That the just man is happy, and the unjust miserable.[d] Thrasymachus is confuted, and retires humiliated from the debate. Yet Sokrates himself is represented as dissatisfied with the result. "At the close of our debate" (he says) "I find that I know nothing about the matter. For as I do not know what justice is, I can hardly expect to know whether it is a virtue or not; nor whether the man who possesses it is happy or not happy."[e]

Here Glaukon enters the lists, intimating that he too is dissatisfied with the proof given by Sokrates, that justice is every way better than injustice: though he adopts the conclusion, and desires much to hear it fully demonstrated. "You know" (he says), "Sokrates, that there are three varieties of Good:— 1. Good *per se*, and for its own sake (apart from any regard to ulterior consequences): such as enjoyment and the innocuous pleasures. 2. Good both in itself, and by reason of its ulterior consequences: such as full health, perfect vision, intelligence, &c. 3. Good, not in itself, but altogether by reason of its consequences: such as gymnastic training, medical treatment, professional business, &c. Now in which of these branches do you rank Justice?" *S.*—I rank it in the noblest—that is, in the second branch: which is good both in itself, and by reason of its consequences. *G.*—Most persons put it in the third branch: as being in itself difficult and laborious, but deserving to be cultivated in consequence of the reward and good name which attaches to the man who is reputed just.[f] *S.*—I know that this is the view taken by Thrasymachus and many others: but it is not mine. *G.*—Neither is it mine.

Marginal notes:

Farther argument of Sokrates—The just man is happy, the unjust man miserable—Thrasymachus is confuted and silenced. Sokrates complains that he does not yet know what Justice is.

Glaukon intimates that he is not satisfied with the proof, though he agrees in the opinion expressed by Sokrates. Tripartite distribution of Good—To which of the three heads does Justice belong?

---

[d] Plato, Republic, i. pp. 353-354 A.

[e] Plato, Republic, i. fin. p. 354 C. ὥστε μοι γέγονεν ἐκ τοῦ διαλόγου μηδὲν εἰδέναι· ὁπότε γὰρ τὸ δίκαιον μὴ οἶδα ὃ ἔστι, σχολῇ εἴσομαι εἴτε ἀρετή τις οὖσα τυγχάνει εἴτε καὶ οὔ, καὶ πότερον ὁ ἔχων αὐτὸ οὐκ εὐδαίμων ἐστιν ἢ εὐδαίμων.

[f] Plato, Republic, ii. p. 357.

Yet still I think that you have not made out your case against Thrasymachus, and that he has given up the game too readily. I will therefore re-state his argument, not at all adopting his opinion as my own, but simply in order to provoke a full refutation of it from you, such as I have never yet heard from any one. First, I shall show what his partisans say as to the nature and origin of justice. Next, I shall show that all who practise justice, practise it unwillingly; not as good *per se*, but as a necessity. Lastly, I shall prove that such conduct on their part is reasonable. If these points can be made out, it will follow that the life of the unjust man is much better than that of the just.[g]

Glaukon undertakes to set forth the case against Sokrates, though professing not to agree with it.

The case, as set forth first by Glaukon, next by Adeimantus, making themselves advocates of Thrasymachus—is as follows. "To do injustice; is by nature good: to suffer injustice, is by nature evil: but the last is greater as an evil, than the first as a good: so that when men have tasted of both, they find it advantageous to agree with each other, that none shall either do or suffer injustice. These agreements are embodied in laws; and what is prescribed by the law is called lawful and just. Here you have the generation and essence of justice, which is intermediate between what is best and what is worst: that is, between the power of committing injustice with impunity, and the liability to suffer injustice without protection or redress. Men acquiesce in such compromise, not as in itself good, but because they are too weak to commit injustice safely. For if any man were strong enough to do so, and had the dispositions of a man, he would not make such a compromise with any one: it would be madness in him to do so.[h]

Pleading of Glaukon. Justice is in the nature of a compromise for all—a medium between what is best and what is worst.

"That men are just, only because they are too weak to be unjust, will appear if we imagine any of them, either the just or the unjust, armed with full power and impunity, such as would be conferred by the ring of Gyges, which rendered the wearer invisible at pleasure. If the just man could become

<hr />

[g] Plato, Republic, ii. p. 358.   [h] Plato, Republic, ii. pp. 358-359.

thus privileged, he would act in the same manner as the unjust: his temper would never be adamantine enough to resist the temptations which naturally prompt every man to unlimited satisfaction of his desires. Such temptations are now counteracted by the force of law and opinion; but if these sanctions were nullified, every man, just or unjust, would seize every thing that he desired, without regard to others. When he is just, he is so not willingly, but by compulsion. He chooses that course not as being the best for him absolutely, but as the best which his circumstances will permit.

"To determine which of the two is happiest, the just man or the unjust, let us assume each to be perfect in his part, and then compare them. The unjust man must be assumed to have at his command all means of force and fraud, so as to procure for himself the maximum of success; *i. e.* the reputation of being a just man, along with all the profitable enormities of injustice. Against him we will set the just man, perfect in his own simplicity and righteousness; a man who cares only for being just in reality, and not for seeming to be so. We shall suppose him, though really just, to be accounted by every one else thoroughly unjust. It is only thus that we can test the true value of his justice: for if he be esteemed just by others, he will be honoured and recompensed, so that we cannot be sure that his justice is not dictated by regard to these adventitious consequences. He must be assumed as just through life, yet accounted by every one else unjust, and treated accordingly: while the unjust man, with whom we compare him, is considered and esteemed by others as if he were perfectly just. Which of the two will have the happiest life? Unquestionably the unjust man. He will have all the advantages derived from his unscrupulous use of means, together with all that extrinsic favour and support which proceeds from good estimation on the part of others: he will acquire superior wealth, which will enable him both to purchase partisans, and to offer costly sacrifices ensuring to him the patronage of the Gods. The just man,

Comparison of the happiness of the just man derived from his justice alone, when others are unjust to him, with that of the unjust man under parallel circumstances.

on the contrary, will not only be destitute of all these advantages, but will be exposed to a life of extreme suffering and torture.   He will learn by painful experience that his happiness depends, not upon being really just, but upon being accounted just by others."[i]

Here Glaukon concludes. Adeimantus now steps in as second counsel on the same side, to the following effect:[k] *Pleading of Adeimantus on the same side. He cites advice given by fathers to their sons, recommending just behaviour by reason of its consequences.* "Much yet remains to be added to the argument. To make it clearer, we must advert to the topics insisted on by those who oppose Glaukon—those who panegyrise justice and denounce injustice. A father, who exhorts his sons to be just, says nothing about the intrinsic advantages of justice *per se:* he dwells upon the beneficial consequences which will accrue to them from being just.   Through such reputation they will obtain from men favours, honours, commands, prosperous alliances, from the Gods, recompenses yet more varied and abundant.   If on the contrary they commit injustice, they will be disgraced and ill-treated among men, severely punished by the Gods.   Such are the arguments whereby a father recommends justice, and dissuades injustice : he talks about opinions and after consequences only, he says nothing about justice or injustice in themselves.   Such are the allegations even of those who wish to praise and enforce justice.   But there are others, and many among them, who hold an opposite language, proclaiming unreservedly that temperance and justice are difficult to practise—injustice and intemperance easy and agreeable, though law and opinion brand them as disgraceful.   These men affirm that the unjust life is for the most part more profitable than the just.   They are full of panegyrics towards the wealthy and powerful, however unprincipled; despising the poor and weak, whom nevertheless they admit to be better men.[l]   They even say that the Gods themselves entail misery upon many good men, and confer prosperity on the wicked.   Then there come the prophets and jugglers, who profess to instruct rich men, out of many books composed by Orpheus and Musæus, how they

---

[i] Plato, Republic, ii. pp. 361-362.   [k] Plato, Republic, ii. pp. 362-367.
[l] Plat. Rep. ii. p. 364 A-B.

may by appropriate presents and sacrifices atone for all their crimes, and die happy.[m]

"When we find that the case is thus stated respecting justice, both by its panegyrists and by its enemies—that the former extol it only from the reputation which it procures, and that the latter promise to the unjust man, if clever and energetic, a higher recompense than any such reputation can obtain for him—what effect can we expect to be produced on the minds of young men of ability, station, and ambition? What course of life are they likely to choose? Surely they will thus reason: A just life is admitted to be burdensome, and it will serve no purpose, unless I acquire, besides, the reputation of justice in the esteem of others. Now the unjust man, who can establish such reputation, enjoys the perfection of existence. My happiness turns not upon the reality, but upon the seeming: upon my reputation with others.[n] Such reputation then it must be my aim to acquire. I must combine the real profit of injustice with the outside show and reputation of justice. Such combination is difficult: but all considerable enterprises are difficult: I must confederate with partisans to carry my point by force or fraud. If I succeed I attain the greatest prize to which man can aspire. I may be told that the Gods will punish me, but the same poets, who declare the existence of the Gods, assure me also that they are placable by prayer and sacrifice: and the poets are as good authority on the one point as on the other.[o] Such" (continues Adeimantus) "will be the natural reasoning of a powerful, energetic, aspiring, man. How can we expect that such a man should prefer justice, when the rewards of injustice on its largest scale are within his reach?[p] Unless he be averse to injustice, from some divine peculiarity of disposition, or unless he has been taught to abstain from it by the acquisition of knowledge, he will treat the current encomiums on justice as ridiculous. No man is just by his own impulse. Weak men or old men censure injustice, because they have not force enough to commit it with success: which is proved by the fact that any one of

---

[m] Plat. Rep. p. 364 C-E.
[n] Plat. Rep. ii. p. 365 B-D.
[o] Plat. Rep. ii. pp. 365 E, 366 A.
[p] Plat. Rep. ii. p. 366 B-D.

them who acquires power, immediately becomes unjust as
far as his power reaches.

"The case as I set it forth" (pursues Adeimantus) "admits
of no answer on the ground commonly taken by
those who extol justice and blame injustice, from the
earliest poets down to the present day.[q] What they
praise is not justice *per se*, but the reputation which·
the just man obtains, and the consequences flowing from it.
What they blame is not injustice *per se*, but its results. They
never commend, nor even mention, justice as it exists in and
moulds the internal mind and character of the just man; even
though he be unknown, misconceived and detested, by Gods
as well as by men. Nor do they ever talk of the internal
and intrinsic effects of injustice upon the mind of the unjust
man, but merely of his ulterior prospects. They never attempt
to show that injustice itself, in the mind of the unjust man, is
the gravest intrinsic evil; and justice in the mind of the just
man the highest intrinsic good: apart from consequences on
either side. If you had all held this language from the
beginning, and had impressed upon us such persuasion from
our childhood, there would have been no necessity for our
keeping watch upon each other to prevent injustice. Every
man would have been the best watch upon himself, through
fear lest by becoming unjust he might take into his own
bosom the gravest evil.[r]

"Here therefore is a deficiency in the argument on behalf of
justice, which I call upon you,[s] Sokrates, who have
employed all your life in these meditations, to supply.
You have declared justice to be good indeed for its

Marginal notes: Nobody recommends Justice *per se*, but only by reason of its consequences.

Adeimantus calls upon Sokrates to recommend and enforce Justice on its

---

[q] Plat. Rep. ii. p. 366 D-E. πάντων
ὑμῶν, ὅσοι ἐπαινέται φατὲ δικαιοσύνης
εἶναι, ἀπὸ τῶν ἐξ ἀρχῆς ἡρώων ἀρξά-
μενοι, ὅσων λόγοι λελειμμένοι μέχρι
τῶν νῦν ἀνθρώπων, οὐδεὶς πώποτε ἔψεξεν
ἀδικίαν οὐδ᾽ ἐπήνεσε δικαιοσύνην ἄλλως
ἢ δόξας τε καὶ τιμὰς καὶ δωρεὰς τὰς ἀπ᾽
αὐτῶν γιγνομένας· αὐτὸ δ᾽ ἑκάτερον τῇ
αὐτοῦ δυνάμει ἐν τῇ τοῦ ἔχοντος ψυχῇ
ἐνὸν καὶ λάνθανον θεοὺς τε καὶ ἀνθρώπους, οὐδεὶς πώποτε οὔτ᾽ ἐν ποιήσει
οὔτ᾽ ἐν ἰδίοις λόγοις ἐπεξῆλθεν ἱκανῶς
τῷ λόγῳ, &c. Compare p. 362 E.
Whoever reads this will see that
Plato does not intend (as most of his

commentators assert) that the arguments which Sokrates combats in the
Republic were the invention of Protagoras, Prodikus, and other Sophists of
the Platonic century.

[r] Plato, Republic, ii. p. 367 A. εἰ
γὰρ οὕτως ἐλέγετο ἐξ ἀρχῆς ὑπὸ πάντων
ὑμῶν, καὶ ἐκ νέων ἡμᾶς ἐπείθετε, οὐκ
ἂν ἀλλήλους ἐφυλάττομεν μὴ ἀδικεῖν,
ἀλλ᾽ αὐτὸς αὑτοῦ ἦν ἕκαστος ἄριστος
φύλαξ, δεδιὼς μὴ ἀδικῶν τῷ μεγίστῳ
κακῷ ξύνοικος ᾖ.

[s] Plat. Rep. ii. p. 367 E. διότι
πάντα τὸν βίον οὐδὲν ἄλλο σκοπῶν
διελήλυθας ἢ τοῦτο (you, Sokrates).

own grounds, consequences, but still more of a good from its own
and to ex-
plain how intrinsic nature. Explain how it is good, and how
Justice in
itself benefits injustice is evil, in its own intrinsic nature: what
the mind of
the just man. effect each produces on the mind, so as to deserve
such an appellation. Omit all notice of consequences accruing to the just or unjust man, from the opinion, favourable or
otherwise, entertained towards him by others. You must
even go farther: you must suppose that both of them are misconceived, and that the just man is disgraced and punished as
if he were unjust, the unjust man honoured and rewarded
as if he were just. This is the only way of testing the real
intrinsic value of justice and injustice, considered in their
effects upon the mind. If you expatiate on the consequences
—if you regard justice as in itself indifferent, but valuable
on account of the profitable reputation which it procures, and
injustice as in itself profitable but dangerous to the unjust
man from the hostile sentiment and damage which it brings
upon him—the real drift of your exhortation will be, to make
us aspire to be unjust in reality, but to aim at maintaining a
reputation of justice along with it. In that line of argument,
you will concede substantially the opinion of Thrasymachus—
That justice is another man's good, the advantage of the more
powerful: and injustice the good or profit of the agent, but
detrimental to the weaker."[t]

With the invocation here addressed to Sokrates, Adei-
Relation of mantus concludes his discourse. Like Glaukon, he
Glaukon and
Adeimantus disclaims participation in the sentiments which the
to Thrasy-
machus. speech embodies. Both of them professing to be
dissatisfied with the previous refutation of Thrasymachus by
Sokrates, call for a deeper exposition of the subject. Both of
them then enunciate a doctrine, resembling partially, though
not entirely, that of Thrasymachus—but without his offensive
manner, and with superior force of argument. They propose
it as a difficult problem, which none but Sokrates can adequately solve. He accepts the challenge, though with apparent
diffidence: and we now enter upon his solution, which occupies
the remaining eight books and a half of the Republic. All
these last books are in fact expository, though in the broken

[t] Plat. Rep. ii. p. 367 C-D.

form of dialogue.   The other speakers advance scarce any opinions for Sokrates to confute, but simply intervene with expressions of assent, or doubt, or demand for farther information.

I here repeat the precise state of the question, which is very apt to be lost amidst the mæanderings of a Platonic dialogue. Statement of the question as it stands after the speeches of Glaukon and Adeimantus. What Sokrates under-. takes to prove.

First, What is Justice?   Sokrates had declared at the close of the first book, that he did not know what Justice was; and that therefore he could not possibly decide, whether it was a virtue or not:— nor whether the possessor of it was happy or not.

Secondly, To which of the three classes of good things does Justice belong?   To the second class—*i. e.* things good *per se*, and good also in their consequences?   Or to the third class— *i. e.* things not good *per se*, but good only in their consequences?   Sokrates replies (in the beginning of the second book) that it belongs to the second class.

Evidently, these two questions cannot stand together.   In answering the second, Sokrates presupposes a certain determination of the first; inconsistent with that unqualified ignorance, of which he had just made profession.   Sokrates now professes to know, not merely that Justice is a good, but to what class of good things it belongs.   The first question has thus been tacitly dropped without express solution, and has given place to the second.   Yet Sokrates, in providing his answer to the second, includes implicitly an answer to the first, so far as to assume that Justice is a good thing, and proceeds to show in what way it is good.

Some say that Justice is good (*i. e.* that it ensures, or at least contributes to, the happiness of the agent), but not *per se:* only in its ulterior consequences.   Taken *per se*, it imposes privation, loss, self-denial; diminishing instead of augmenting the agent's happiness.   But taken along with its results, this preliminary advance is more than adequately repaid; since without it the agent would not obtain from others that reciprocity of justice, forbearance, and good treatment without which his life would be intolerable.

If this last opinion be granted, Glaukon argues that Justice

would indeed be good for weak and middling agents, but not
for men of power and energy, who had a good chance of
extorting the benefit without paying the antecedent price.
And Thrasymachus, carrying this view still farther, assumes
that there are in every society men of power who despotise
over the rest; and maintains that Justice consists, for the
society generally, in obeying the orders of these despots. It
is all gain to the strong, all loss to the weak. These latter
profit by it in no other way than by saving themselves from
farther punishment or ill usage on his part.

Sokrates undertakes to maintain the opposite—That Justice
is a good *per se*, ensuring the happiness of the agent
by its direct and intrinsic effects on the mind:—
whatever its ulterior consequences may be. He
maintains indeed that these ulterior consequences
are also good: but that they do not constitute the
paramount benefit, or the main recommendation of justice:
that the good of Justice *per se* is much greater. In this point
of view, Justice is not less valuable and necessary to the
strong than to the weak. He proceeds to show, what Justice
is, and how it is beneficial *per se* to the agent, apart from consequences: also, what Injustice is, and how it is injurious to
the agent *per se*, apart from consequences.[u]

*Position to
be proved by
Sokrates—
Justice
makes the
just man
happy per se,
whatever be
its results.*

He begins by affirming the analogy between an entire city
or community, and each individual man or agent.
There is justice (he says) in the entire city—and
justice in each individual man. In the city, the
characteristics of Justice are stamped in larger
letters or magnified, so as to be more easily legible.
We will therefore first read them in the city, and then apply
the lesson to explain what appears in smaller type in the
individual man.[x] We will trace the steps by which a city is
generated, in order that we may see how justice and injustice
spring up in it.

*Argument of
Sokrates to
show what
Justice is—
Assumed
analogy be-
tween the
city and the
individual.*

It is in this way that Plato first conducts us to the formation of a political community. A parallel is assumed between
the entire city and each individual man: the city is a man on
a great scale—the man is a city on a small scale. Justice

---

[u] Plato, Republic, ii.   [x] Plato, Republic, ii. pp. 368-369.

belongs both to one and to the other. The city is described and analysed, not merely as a problem for its own sake, but in order that the relation between its constituent parts may throw light on the analogous constituent parts, which are assumed to exist in each individual man.[y]

The fundamental principle (Sokrates affirms) to which cities or communities owe their origin, is, existence of wants and necessities in all men. No single man is sufficient for himself: every one is in want of many things, and is therefore compelled to seek communion or partnership with neighbours and auxiliaries. Reciprocal dealings begin: each man gives to others, and receives from others, under the persuasion that it is better for him to do so.[z]

Fundamental principle, to which communities of mankind owe their origin—Reciprocity of want and service between individuals—No individual can suffice to himself.

Common needs, helplessness of individuals apart, reciprocity of service when they are brought together—are the generating causes of this nascent association. The simplest association, comprising the mere necessaries of life, will consist only of four or five men: the husbandman, builder, weaver, shoemaker, &c. It is soon found advantageous to all, that each of these should confine himself to his own proper business: that the husbandman should not attempt to build his own house or make his own shoes, but should produce corn enough for all, and exchange his surplus for that of the rest in their respective departments. Each man has his own distinct aptitudes and dispositions; so that he executes both more work and better work, by employing himself exclusively in the avocation for which he is suited. The division of labour thus becomes established, as reciprocally advantageous to all. This principle soon extends itself: new wants arise: the number of different employments is multiplied. Smiths, carpenters, and other artisans, find a place: also shepherds and herdsmen, to provide oxen for the farmer, wool and hides for the weaver and the shoemaker. Presently a farther subdivision of labour is introduced for carrying on exchange and distribution: markets are established: money is coined: foreign merchants will import and export commodities:

---

[y] Plato, Republic, ii. p. 369 A. τὴν τοῦ μείζονος ὁμοιότητα ἐν τῇ τοῦ ἐλάτ- τονος ἰδέᾳ ζητοῦντες.

[z] Plato, Republic, ii. p. 369.

dealers, men of weak body, and fit for sedentary work, will
establish themselves to purchase wholesale the produce brought
by the husbandman, and to sell it again by retail in quantities
suitable for distribution.   Lastly, the complement of the city
will be made up by a section of labouring men who do jobs for
hire: men of great bodily strength, though not adding much
to the intelligence of the community.[a]

Such is the full equipment of the sound and healthy city,
confined to what is simple and necessary.   Those

Moderate equipment of a sound and healthy city —Few wants.

who compose it will have sufficient provision of
wheat and barley, for loaves and cakes—of wine to
drink—of clothing and shoes—of houses for shelter, and of
myrtle and yew twigs for beds.   They will enjoy their cheerful
social festivals, with wine, garlands, and hymns to the Gods.
They will take care not to beget children in numbers greater
than their means, knowing that the consequence thereof must
be poverty or war.[b]   They will have, as condiment, salt and
cheese, olives, figs, and chesnuts, peas, beans, and onions.
They will pass their lives in peace, and will die in a healthy
old age, bequeathing a similar lot to their children.   Justice
and injustice, which we are seeking for, will be founded on a
certain mode of mutual want and dealing with each other.[c]

You feed your citizens, Sokrates (observes Glaukon) as if
you were feeding pigs.   You must at least supply them with
as many sweets and condiments as are common at Athens:
and with beds and tables besides.

I understand you (replies Sokrates): you are not satisfied
with a city of genuine simplicity: you want a city

Enlargement of the city— Multiplied wants and services. First origin of war and strife with neighbours— It arises out of these multiplied wants.

luxurious and inflated. Well then—we will suppose
it enlarged until it comprehends all the varieties of
elegant and costly enjoyment: gold, silver, and
ivory: musicians and painters in their various
branches: physicians: and all the crowd of attendants required for a society thus enlarged.   Such
extension of consumption will carry with it a numerous popu-

---

[a] Plato, Republic. ii. p. 371.
It is remarkable that in this first
outline of the city Plato recognises
only free labour, not slave labour.

[b] Plato, Republic, ii. p. 372 B. οὐχ

ὑπὲρ τὴν οὐσίαν ποιούμενοι τοὺς παῖδας,
εὐλαβούμενοι πενίαν ἢ πόλεμον.

[c] Plato, Republ. ii. p. 372 A.   ἐν
αὐτῶν τούτων χρείᾳ τινὶ τῇ πρὸς ἀλλήλους.

lation, who cannot be maintained from the lands belonging to
the city. We shall be obliged to make war upon our neighbours, and seize some of their lands. They too will do the
same by us, if they have acquired luxurious habits. Here we
see the first genesis of war, with all its consequent evils:
springing from the acquisition of wealth, beyond the limit of
necessity.[d] Having war upon our hands, we need soldiers,
and a considerable camp of them. Now war is essentially a
separate craft and function, requiring to be carried on by
persons devoted to it, who have nothing else to do. We laid
down from the beginning, that every citizen ought to confine
himself exclusively to that business for which he was naturally
fit; and that no one could be allowed to engage in two distinct occupations. This rule is above all things essential for
the business of war. The soldier must perform the duties of
a soldier, and undertake no others.[e]

The functions of these soldiers are more important than
those of any one else. Upon them the security of
the whole community depends. They are the
Guardians of the City: or rather, those few seniors
among them, who are selected from superior merit
and experience, and from a more perfect education,
to exercise command, are the proper Guardians;
while the remaining soldiers are their Auxiliaries.[f]
These Guardians, or Guardians and their Auxiliaries,
must be first chosen with the greatest care, to ensure
that they have appropriate natural dispositions: next their
training and education must be continued as well as systematic. Appropriate natural dispositions are difficult to
find: for we require the coincidence of qualities which are
rarely found together. The Auxiliaries must be mild and
gentle towards their fellow-citizens, passionate and fierce
towards enemies. They must be like generous dogs, full of
kindness towards those whom they know, angrily disposed
towards those whom they do not know.[g]

Assuming children of these dispositions to be found, we
must provide for them the best training and education.

[d] Plato, Republic, ii. p. 373.
[e] Plato, Republ. ii. p. 374.
[f] Plato, Republic, ii. p. 414 B.
[g] Plato, Republic, ii. p. 376.

The training must be twofold: musical, addressed to the

mind: gymnastical, addressed to the body—pursuant to the distribution dating from ancient times.[h] Music includes all training by means of words or sounds: speech and song, recital and repetition, reading and writing, &c.

The earliest training of every child begins from the stories

or fables which he hears recounted: most of which are false, though some among them are true. We must train the child partly by means of falsehood, partly by means of truth: and we must begin first with the falsehood. The tenor of these fictions, which the child first hears, has a powerful effect in determining his future temper and character. But such fictions as are now currently repeated, will tend to corrupt his mind, and to form in him sentiments and opinions adverse to those which we wish him to entertain in after life. We must not allow the invention and circulation of stories at the pleasure of the authors: we must establish a censorship over all authors; licensing only such of their productions as we approve, and excluding all the rest, together with most of those now in circulation.[i] The fables told by Homer, Hesiod, and other poets, respecting the Gods and Heroes, are in very many cases pernicious, and ought to be suppressed. They are not true: and even were they true, ought not to be mentioned before children. Stories about battles between the Gods and the Giants, or quarrels among the Gods themselves, are mischievous, whether intended as allegories or not: for young hearers cannot discriminate the allegorical from the literal.[k]

I am no poet (continues the Platonic Sokrates), nor can I

pretend to compose legends myself: but I shall lay down a type of theological orthodoxy, to which all the divine legends in our city must conform. Every

---

[h] Plato, Republic, ii. p. 376 E.

Τίς οὖν ἡ παιδεία; ἢ χαλεπὸν εὑρεῖν βελτίω τῆς ὑπὸ τοῦ πολλοῦ χρόνου εὑρημένης; ἔστι δέ που ἡ μὲν ἐπὶ σώμασι γυμναστική, ἡ δ᾽ ἐπὶ ψυχῇ μουσική.

This appeal of Plato to antiquity and established custom deserves notice.

[i] Plato, Republ. ii. p. 377. ὧν δὲ νῦν λέγουσι τοὺς πολλοὺς ἐκβλητέον.

Compare the animadversions in Sextus Empiricus about the mischievous doctrines to be found in the poets, advers. Mathematicos, i. s. 276-293.

[k] Plato, Republ. ii. p. 378.

poet must proclaim that the Gods are good, and therefore cannot be the cause of any thing except good. No poet can be allowed to describe the Gods (according to what we now read in Homer and elsewhere) as dispensing both good and evil to mankind. The Gods must be announced as causes of all the good which exists, but other causes must be found for all the evil: the Gods therefore are causes of comparatively few things, since bad things are far more abundant among us than good.[1] No poetical tale can be tolerated which represents the Gods as assuming the forms of different persons, and going about to deceive men into false beliefs.[m] Falsehood is odious both to Gods and to men : though there are some cases in which it is necessary as a precaution against harm, towards enemies, or even towards friends during seasons of folly or derangement.[n] But none of these exceptional circumstances can apply to the Gods.

legends to it. The Gods are causes of nothing but good: therefore they are causes of few things. Great preponderance of actual evil.

It is indispensable to inspire these youthful minds with courage, and to make them fear death as little as possible. But the terrific descriptions, given by the poets, of Hades and the underworld, are above all things likely to aggravate the fear of death. Such descriptions must therefore be interdicted, as neither true nor useful. Even if poetically striking, they are all the more pernicious to be listened to by youths whom we wish to train up as spirited freemen, fearing enslavement more than death.[o] We must also prohibit the representations of intense grief and distress, imputed by Homer to Heroes or Gods, to Achilles, Priam, or Zeus, for the death of friends and relatives. A perfectly reasonable man will account death no great evil, either for himself or for his friend : he will be, in a peculiar degree, sufficient to himself for his own happiness, and will

The Guardians must not fear death. No terrible descriptions of Hades must be presented to them : no intense sorrow, nor violent nor sensual passion, must be recounted either of Gods or Heroes.

---

[1] Plato, Republ. ii. p. 379 C.
Οὐδ' ἄρα ὁ θεὸς, ἐπειδὴ ἀγαθὸς, πάντων ἂν εἴη αἴτιος, ὡς οἱ πολλοὶ λέγουσιν, ἀλλ' ὀλίγων μὲν τοῖς ἀνθρώποις αἴτιος, πολλῶν δὲ ἀναίτιος· πολὺ γὰρ ἐλάττω τὰγαθὰ τῶν κακῶν ἡμῖν. Καὶ τῶν μὲν ἀγαθῶν οὐδένα ἄλλον αἰτιατέον, τῶν δὲ κακῶν ἄλλ' ἄττα δεῖ ζητεῖν τὰ αἴτια ἀλλ' οὐ τὸν θεόν.

[m] Plato, Republic, ii. pp. 380-381.
Dacier blames Plato for this as an error, saying, that God may appear, and has appeared to men, under the form of an Angel or of some man whom he has created after his own image (Traduction de Platon, Tom. i. p. 172).

[n] Plato, Republic, ii. p. 382 C.

[o] Plato, Republic, iii. pp. 386-387.

E 2

therefore endure with comparative equanimity the loss of friends, relatives, or fortune.[p] We must teach youth to be ashamed of indulging in immoderate grief or in violent laughter.[q] We must teach them also veracity and temperance, striking out all those passages in Homer which represent the Gods or Heroes as incontinent, sensual, furiously vindictive, reckless of obligation, or money-loving.[r] The poets must either not recount such proceedings at all, or must not ascribe them to Gods and Heroes.

We have thus prescribed the model to which all poets must accommodate their narratives respecting Gods and Heroes. We ought now to set out a similar model for their narratives respecting men. But this is impossible, until our present investigation is brought to a close: because one of the worst misrepresentations which the poets give of human affairs, is, when they say that there are many men unjust, yet happy—just, yet still miserable:—that successful injustice is profitable, and that justice is a benefit to other persons, but a loss to the agent. We affirm that this is a misrepresentation, but we cannot assume it as such at present, since the present enquiry is intended to prove that it is so.[s]

Type for all narratives respecting men.

From the substance of these stories we pass to the style and manner. The poet will recount either in his own person, by simple narrative: or he will assume the characters and speak in the names of others, thus making his composition imitative. He will imitate every diversity of character, good and bad, wise and foolish. This however cannot be tolerated in our city. We can permit no imitation except that of the reasonable and virtuous man. Every man in our city exercises one simple function: we have no double-faced or many-faced citizens. We shall respectfully dismiss the poet who captivates us by variety of characters, and shall be satisfied with the dry recital of simple stories useful in their tendency, expressing the feeling of the reasonable man and no other.[t]

Style of narratives. The poet must not practise variety of imitation: he must not speak in the name of bad characters.

[p] Plato, Republic, iii. p. 387.
[q] Plato, Republic, iii. p. 388.
[r] Plato, Republic, iii. pp. 390-391.

[s] Plato, Republic, iii. p. 392.
[t] Plato, Republic, iii. pp. 396-398.

We must farther regulate the style of the Odes and Songs, consistent with what has been already laid down. Having prescribed what the sense of the words must be, we must now give directions about melody and rhythm. We shall permit nothing but simple music, calculated less to please the ear, than to inspire grave, dignified, and resolute sentiment. We shall not allow either the wailing Lydian, or the soft and convivial Ionic mood: but only the Phrygian and Dorian moods. Nor shall we tolerate either the fife, or complicated stringed instruments: nothing except the lyre and harp, with the panspipe for rural abodes.[u] The rhythm or measure must also be simple, suitable to the movements of a calm and moderate man. Both good rhythm, graceful and elegant speaking, and excellence of sense, flow from good and virtuous dispositions, tending to inspire the same dispositions in others:[x] just as bad rhythm, ungraceful and indecorous demeanour, defective proportion, &c. are companions of bad speech and bad dispositions. Contrasts of this kind pervade not only speech and song, but also every branch of visible art: painting, architecture, weaving, embroidery, pottery, and even the natural bodies of animals and plants. In all of them we distinguish grace and beauty, the accompaniments of a good and sober disposition—from ungracefulness and deformity, visible signs of the contrary disposition. Now our youthful Guardians, if they are ever to become qualified for their functions, must be trained to recognise and copy such grace and beauty.[y] For this purpose our poets, painters, architects, and artisans, must be prohibited from embodying in their works any ungraceful or unseemly type. None will be tolerated as artists, except such as can detect and embody the type of the beautiful. Our youth will thus insensibly contract exclusive familiarity, both through the eye and through the ear, with beauty in its various manifestations: so that their minds will be brought into harmonious preparation for the subsequent influence of beautiful discourse.[z]

This indeed (continues Sokrates) is the principal benefit

Marginal note: Rhythm and Melody regulated. None but simple and grave music allowed: only the Dorian and Phrygian moods, with the lyre and harp.

---

[u] Plato, Repub. iii. pp. 398-399.
[x] Plato, Republ. iii. p. 400.

[y] Plato, Republic, iii. pp. 400-401.
[z] Plato, Republic, iii. p. 401 C-D.

arising from musical tuition, that the internal mind of a youth becomes imbued with rhythm and harmony. Hence he learns to commend and be delighted with the beautiful, and to hate and blame what is ugly; before he is able to render any reason for his sentiments: so that when mature age arrives, his sentiments are found in unison with what reason enjoins, and already predisposed to welcome it.[a] He becomes qualified to recognise the Forms of Temperance, Courage, Liberality, Magnanimity, and their embodiments in particular persons. To a man brought up in such sentiments, no spectacle can be so lovely as that of youths combining beauty of mental disposition with beauty of exterior form. He may indeed tolerate some defects in the body, but none in the mind.[b] His love, being genuine and growing out of musical and regulated contemplations, will attach itself to what is tempered and beautiful; not to the intense pleasures of sense, which are inconsistent with all temperance. Such will be the attachments subsisting in our city, and such is the final purpose of musical training—To generate love of the Beautiful.[c]

Effect of musical training of the mind—makes youth love the Beautiful and hate the Ugly.

We next proceed to gymnastic training, which must be simple, for the body—just as our musical training was simple for the mind. We cannot admit luxuries and refinements either in the one or in the other. Our gymnastics must impart health and strength to the body, as our music imparts sobriety to the mind.[d] We shall require few courts of justice and few physicians. Where many of either are needed, this is a proof that ill-regulated minds and diseased bodies abound. It would be a disgrace to our Guardians if they could not agree on what is right and proper among themselves, without appealing to the decision of others. Physicians too are only needed for wounds or other temporary and special diseases. We cannot admit those refinements of the medical art, and that elaborate nomenclature and classification of diseases, which the clever sons of Æsculapius have in-

Training of the body—simple and sober. No refined medical art allowed. Wounds or temporary ailments treated; but sickly frames cannot be kept alive.

[a] Plato, Republic, iii. p. 402 A.
[b] Plato, Republic, iii. p. 402 D-E.
[c] Plato, Republic, iii. p. 403 C. δεῖ

δέ που τελευτᾷν τὰ μουσικὰ εἰς τὰ τοῦ καλοῦ ἐρωτικά.
[d] Plato, Republic, iii. p. 404.

vented, in times more recent than Æsculapius himself.[e] He knew, but despised, such artifices; which, having been devised chiefly by Herodikus, serve only to keep alive sickly and suffering men—who are disqualified for all active duty through the necessity of perpetual attention to health,—and whose lives are worthless both to themselves and to the city. In our city, every man has his distinct and special function, which he is required to discharge. If he be disqualified by some temporary ailment, the medical art will be well employed in relieving and restoring him to activity : but he has no leisure to pass his life as a patient under cure, and if he be permanently unfit to fill his place in the established cycle of duties, his life ought not to be prolonged by art, since it is useless to himself and useless to the city also.[f] Our medical treatment for evils of the body, and our judicial treatment for evils of the mind, must be governed by analogous principles. Where body and mind are sound at bottom, we must do our best to heal temporary derangements : but if a man has a body radically unsound, he must be suffered to die— and if he has a mind unsound and incurable, he must be put to death by ourselves.[g]

Gymnastic training does some good in strengthening the body, but it is still more serviceable in imparting force and courage to the mind. As regards the mind, gymnastic and music form the indispensable supplement one to the other. Gymnastic by itself makes a man's nature too savage and violent : he acquires no relish for knowledge, comes to hate discourse, and disdains verbal persuasion.[h] On the other hand, music by itself makes him soft, cowardly, and sensitive, unfit for danger or hardship. The judicious combination of the two is the only way to form a well balanced mind and character.[i]

Value of Gymnastic in imparting courage to the mind— Gymnastic and Music necessary to correct each other.

[e] Plato, Republic, iii. p. 405. φύσας τε καὶ κατάρρους νοσήμασιν ὀνόματα ἀναγκάζειν τίθεσθαι τοὺς κομψοὺς Ἀσκληπιάδας, οὐκ αἰσχρὸν δοκεῖ; Καὶ μάλ', ἔφη, ὡς ἀληθῶς καινὰ ταῦτα καὶ ἄτοπα νοσημάτων ὀνόματα. Οἶα, ὡς οἶμαι, οὐκ ἦν ἐπ' Ἀσκληπιοῦ. P. 406 C.

[f] Plato, Republic, iii. p. 406 C. οὐδενὶ σχολὴ διὰ βίου κάμνειν ἰατρευομένῳ. P. 406 D. οὐ σχολὴ κάμνειν οὐδὲ λυσιτελεῖ οὕτω ζῆν, νοσήματι τὸν νοῦν

προσέχοντα, τῆς δὲ προκειμένης ἐργασίας ἀμελοῦντα. P. 407 D-E. ἀλλὰ τὸν μὴ δυνάμενον ἐν τῇ καθεστηκυίᾳ περιόδῳ ζῆν, μὴ οἴεσθαι δεῖν θεραπεύειν, ὡς οὔτε αὑτῷ οὔτε πόλει λυσιτελῇ. P. 408 A.

[g] Plato, Republic, iii. pp. 409-410.

[h] Plato, Republic, iii. p. 411 D. Μισόλογος δὴ ὁ τοιοῦτος γίγνεται καὶ ἄμουσος, καὶ πειθοῖ μὲν διὰ λόγων οὐδὲν ἔτι χρῆται, &c.

[i] Plato, Republic, iii. pp. 410-411.

Such must be the training, from childhood upwards, of

Out of the Guardians a few of the very best must be chosen as Elders or Rulers— highly edu- cated and severely tested.

these Guardians and Auxiliaries of our city. We must now select from among these men themselves, a few to be Governors or chief Guardians; the rest serving as auxiliaries. The oldest and best of them must be chosen for this purpose, those who possess in the greatest perfection the qualities requisite for Guardians. They must be intelligent, capable, and solicitous for the welfare of the city. Now a man is solicitous for the welfare of that which he loves. He loves those whose interests he believes to be the same as his own; those whose well-being he believes to coincide with his own well-being[k]— the contrary, with the contrary. The Guardians chosen for Chiefs must be those who are most thoroughly penetrated with such sympathy; who have preserved most tenaciously throughout all their lives the resolution to do every thing which they think best for the city, and nothing which they do not think to be best for it. They must be watched and tested in temptations pleasurable as well as painful, to see whether they depart from this resolution. The elders who have best stood such trial, must be named Governors.[1] These few will be the chief Guardians or Rulers: the remaining Guardians will be their auxiliaries or soldiers, acting under their orders.

Here then our city will take its start; the body of Guardians

Fundamental creed re- quired to be planted in the minds of all the citi- zens, respect- ing their breed and relationship.

marching in arms under the orders of their Chiefs, and encamping in a convenient acropolis, from whence they may best be able to keep order in the interior and to repel foreign attack.[m] But it is in- dispensable that both they and the remaining citizens should be made to believe a certain tale,—which yet is altogether fictitious and of our own invention. They must be told that they are all earthborn, sprung from the very soil which they inhabit: all therefore brethren, from

---

[k] Plato, Republic, iii. p. 412. Οὔκουν φρονίμους τε εἰς τοῦτο δεῖ ὑπάρχειν καὶ δυνατοὺς καὶ ἔτι κηδεμόνας τῆς πόλεως; Ἔστι ταῦτα. Κήδοιτο δ' ἂν τις μάλιστα τούτου ὃ τύγχανοι φιλῶν; Ἀνάγκη. Καὶ μὴν τοῦτο γ' ἂν μάλιστα φιλοῖ, ᾧ ξυμφέρειν ἡγοῖτο τὰ αὐτὰ καὶ ἑαυτῷ, καὶ ὅταν μάλιστα ἐκείνου μὲν εὖ πράτ- τοντος οἴηται ξυμβαίνειν καὶ ἑαυτῷ εὖ πράττειν, μὴ δὲ, τοὐναντίον.

[1] Plato, Republic, iii. pp. 413-414. Refer to De Leg. about resisting pleasure as well as pain.

[m] Plato, Republic, iii. p. 415 D.

the same mother Earth : the auxiliaries or soldiers, born with their arms and equipments. But there was this difference (we shall tell them) between the different brethren. Those fit for Chiefs or Rulers, were born with a certain mixture of gold in their constitution : those fit for soldiers or Guardians simply, with a like mixture of silver : the remainder, with brass or iron. In most individual cases, each of these classes will beget an offspring like themselves. But exceptions will some-times happen, in which the golden man will have a child of silver, or brass,—or the brazen or iron man, a child of nobler metal than his own. Now it is of the last importance that the Rulers should keep watch to preserve the purity of these breeds. If any one of their own children should turn out to be of brass or iron, they must place him out among the husbandmen or artisans : if any of the brazen or iron men should chance to produce a child of gold, they must receive him among themselves, since he belongs to them by his natural constitution. Upon the maintenance of these distinct breeds, each in its appropriate function, depends the entire fate of the city : for an oracle has declared that it will perish, if ever iron or brazen men shall become its Guardians.[n]

It is indispensable (continues Sokrates) that this fiction should be circulated and accredited, as the funda-mental, consecrated, unquestioned, creed of the whole city, from which the feeling of harmony and brotherhood among the citizens springs. But how can we implant such unanimous and unshaken belief, in a story altogether untrue? Similar fables have often obtained implicit credence in past times : but no such case has happened of late, and I ques-tion whether it could happen now.[o] The postulate seems extravagant : do *you* see by what means it could be realised? —I see no means (replies Glaukon) by which the fiction could be first passed off and accredited, among these men them-selves : but if it were once firmly implanted, in any one

How is such a fiction to be accredited in the first instance? Difficulty ex-treme, of first beginning ; but if once accredited, it will easily transmit it-self by tradi-tion.

---

[n] Plato, Republic, iii. pp. 414-415.

[o] Plato, Republic, iii. p. 414. Τίς ἂν οὖν μηχανὴ γένοιτο τῶν ψευδῶν τῶν ἐν δέοντι γιγνομένων, ὧν νῦν δὴ ἐλέγο-μεν, γενναῖόν τι εἶναι ψευδομένους πεῖ-σαι μάλιστα μὲν αὐτοὺς τοὺς ἄρχοντας,

εἰ δὲ μή, τὴν ἄλλην πόλιν; Μηδὲν καινὸν, ἀλλὰ Φοινικικόν τι, πρότερον μὲν ἤδη πολλαχοῦ γεγονός, ὥς φασιν οἱ ποιηταὶ καὶ πεπείκασιν, ἐφ' ἡμῶν δὲ οὐ γεγονὸς οὐδ' οἶδα εἰ γενόμενον ἄν, πεῖ-σαι δὲ συχνῆς πειθοῦς.

generation, I do not doubt that their children and descendants would inherit and perpetuate it.[p] We must be satisfied with thus much (replies Sokrates) : assuming the thing to be done, and leaving the process of implanting it to spontaneous and oracular inspiration.[q] I now proceed with the description of the city.

The Rulers and their auxiliaries the body of Guardians must

Guardians to reside in barracks and mess together; to have no private property or home; to be maintained by contribution from the people.

be lodged in residences, sufficient for shelter and comfort, yet suitable for military men, and not for tradesmen. Every arrangement must be made for rendering them faithful guardians of the remaining citizens. It would be awful indeed, if they were to employ their superior strength in oppressing instead of protecting the flock entrusted to them. To ensure their gentleness and fidelity, the most essential guarantee is to be found in the good musical and gymnastic training which they will have received. But this alone will not suffice. All the conditions of their lives must be so determined, that they shall have the least possible motive for committing injustice towards the other citizens. None of them must have any separate property of his own, unless in special case of proved necessity : nor any house or store-cupboard from which others are excluded. They must receive, from the contributions of the remaining citizens, sufficient subsistence for the health and comfort of military men, but nothing beyond. They must live together in their camp or barrack, and dine together at a public mess-table. They must not be allowed either to possess gold and silver, or to drink in cups of those metals, or to wear them as appendages to clothing, or even to have them under the same roof. They must be told, that these metals, though not forbidden to the other citizens, are forbidden to them, because they have permanently inherent in their mental constitution the divine gold and silver, which would be corrupted by intermixture with human.[r]

If these precautions be maintained, the Guardians may be

---

[p] Plato, Republic, iii. p. 415 D. Τοῦτον οὖν τὸν μῦθον ὅπως ἂν πεισθεῖεν, ἔχεις τινὰ μηχανήν ; Οὐδαμῶς, ἔφη, ὅπως ἂν αὐτοὶ οὗτοι· ὅπως μέντ᾽ ἂν οἱ τούτων υἱεῖς καὶ οἱ ἔπειτα, οἱ τ᾽ ἄλλοι ἄνθρωποι οἱ ὕστερον.

[q] Plato, Republic, iii. p. 415 D. Καὶ τοῦτο μὲν δὴ ἕξει ὅπη ἂν αὐτὸ ἡ φήμη ἀγάγῃ.

[r] Plato, Republic, iii. pp. 416-417.

secure themselves, and may uphold in security the entire city. But if the precautions be relinquished—if the Guardians or Soldiers acquire separate property in lands, houses, and money—they will then become householders and husbandmen instead of Guardians or Soldiers: hostile masters, instead of allies and protectors to their fellow-citizens. They will hate their fellow-citizens, and be hated by them in return: they will conspire against them, and will be themselves conspired against. In this manner they will pass their lives, dreading their enemies within far more than their enemies without. They, and the whole city along with them, will be perpetually on the brink of destruction.[s]

If the Guardians fail in these precautions, and acquire private interests, the city will be ruined.

But surely (remarks Adeimantus), according to this picture, your Guardians or Soldiers, though masters of all the city, will be worse off than any of the other citizens. They will be deprived of those means of happiness which the others are allowed to enjoy. Perhaps they will (replies Sokrates): yet I should not be surprised if they were to be the happiest of all. Be that as it may, however, my purpose is, not to make *them* especially happy, but to make the whole city happy. The Guardians can enjoy only such happiness as consists with the due performance of their functions as Guardians. Every man in our city must perform his appropriate function, and must be content with such happiness as his disposition will admit, subject to this condition.[t] In regard to all the citizens without exception, it must be the duty of the Guardians to keep out both riches and poverty, both of which spoil the character of every one. No one must be rich, and no one must be poor.[u] In case of war, the constant discipline of our soldiers will be of more avail than money, in making them efficient combatants against other cities.[x] Moreover, other cities are divided against themselves: each is many cities, and not one: poor and rich are at variance with each other, and various fractions of each of these classes against other fractions. Our city alone, constituted as I propose, will be

Complete unity of the city, every man performing his own special function.

[s] Plato, Republic, iii. p. 417.
[t] Plato, Republic, iv. pp. 420-421.
[u] Plato, Republic, iv. p. 421.
[x] Plato, Republic, iv. p. 422.

really and truly One. It will thus be the greatest of all cities, even though it have only one thousand fighting men. It may be permitted to increase, so long as it will preserve its complete unity, but no farther.[y] Farthermore, each of our citizens is one and not many: confined to that special function for which he is qualified by his nature.

It will devolve upon our Guardians to keep up this form of communion unimpaired; and they will have no difficulty in doing so, as long as they maintain their own education and training unimpaired. No change must be allowed either in the musical or gymnastic training: especially not in the former, where changes are apt to creep in, with pernicious effect.[z] Upon this education depends the character and competence of the Guardians. They will provide legislation in detail, which will be good, if their general character is good—bad, on the contrary supposition. If their character and the constitution of the city be defective at the bottom, it is useless for us to prescribe regulations of detail, as we would do for sick men. The laws in detail cannot be good, while the general constitution of the city is bad. Those teachers are mistaken who exhort us to correct the former, but to leave the latter untouched.[a]

The maintenance of the city depends upon that of the habits, character, and education of the Guardians.

In regard to religious legislation—the raising of temples, arrangement of sacrifices, &c.—we must consult Apollo at Delphi, and obey what he directs. We know nothing ourselves about these matters, nor is there any other authority equally trustworthy.[b]

Religious legislation— Consult the Delphian Apollo.

Our city is now constituted and peopled (continues Sokrates). We must examine it, and see where we can find Justice and Injustice—reverting to our original problem, which was, to know what each of them was, and which of the two conferred happiness. Now assuming our city to be rightly constituted, it will be perfectly good: that is, it will be wise, courageous, temperate, and just. These four constituents cover the whole: accordingly, if we can discover and set out

The city is now constituted as a good city— that is, wise, courageous, temperate, just. Where is its Justice?

[y] Plato, Republic, iv. p. 423.
[z] Plato, Republic, iv. p. 424.
[a] Plato, Republic, iv. pp. 425-426.

[b] Plato, Republic, iv. p. 427 B. τὰ γὰρ δὴ τοιαῦτα οὔτ' ἐπιστάμεθα ἡμεῖς, &c.

Wisdom, Courage, and Temperance—that which remains afterwards will be Justice.[c]

First, we can easily see where Wisdom resides.   The city includes in itself a great variety of cognitions, corresponding to all the different functions in which its citizens are employed.   But it is not called *wise*, from its knowledge of husbandry, or of brazier's and carpenter's craft : since these are specialties which cover only a small fraction of its total proceedings.   It is called *wise*, or well-advised, from that variety of intelligence or cognition which directs it as a whole, in its entire affairs : that is, the intelligence possessed by the chief Guardians or Rulers.   Now the number of persons possessing this variety of intelligence is smaller than the number of those who possess any other variety.   The wisdom of the entire city resides in this very small presiding fraction, and in them alone.[d]

First, where is the wisdom of the city? It resides in the few elder Rulers.

Next, we can also discern without difficulty in what fraction of the city Courage resides.   The city is called courageous from the valour of those Guardians or Soldiers upon whom its defence rests.   These men will have learnt, in the course of their training, what are really legitimate objects of fear, and what are not legitimate objects of fear.   To such convictions they will resolutely adhere, through the force of mind implanted by their training, in defiance of all disturbing impulses.   It is these right convictions, respecting the legitimate objects of fear, which I (says Sokrates) call true political courage, when they are designedly inculcated and worked in by regular educational authority : when they spring up without any rational foundation, as in animals or slaves, I do not call them Courage.   The Courage of the entire city thus resides in its Guardians or Soldiers.[e]

Where is the Courage? In the body of Guardians or Soldiers.

Thirdly, wherein resides the Temperance of the city ? Temperance implies a due relation, proportion, or accord, between different elements.   The temperate man is called, superior to himself: but this expression, on first hearing, seems unmeaning, since the man must also be inferior to himself.   But the ex-

Where is the Temperance? It resides in all and each, Rulers, Guardians, and People. Superiors rule and Inferiors obey.

c Plato, Republic, iv. pp. 427-428.   d Plato, Republic, iv. pp. 428-429.
e Plato, Republic, iv. pp. 429-430.

pression acquires a definite meaning, when we recognise it as implying that there are in the same man's mind better and worse elements: and that when the better rules over the worse, he is called superior to himself, or temperate —when the worse rules over the better, he is called inferior to himself, or intemperate. Our city will be temperate, because the better part of it, though smaller in number, rules over the worse and inferior part, numerically greater. The pleasures, pains, and desires of our few Rulers, which are moderate and reasonable, are preponderant: controuling those of the Many, which are miscellaneous, irregular, and violent. And this command is exercised with the perfect consent and good-will of the subordinates. The Many are not less willing to obey than the Few to command. There is perfect unanimity between them as to the point—Who ought to command, and who ought to obey? It is this unanimity which constitutes the temperance of the city: which thus resides, not in any one section of the city, like Courage and Wisdom, but in all sections alike: each recognising and discharging its legitimate function.[f]

There remains only Justice for us to discover. Wherein

Where is the Justice? In all and each of them also. It consists in each performing his own special function, and not meddling with the function of the others.

does the Justice of the city reside? Not far off. Its justice consists in that which we pointed out at first as the fundamental characteristic of the city, when we required each citizen to discharge one function, and one alone—that for which he was best fitted by nature. That each citizen shall do his own work, and not meddle with others in their work—that each shall enjoy his own property, as well as do his own work—this is true Justice.[g] It is the fundamental condition without which neither temperance, nor courage, nor wisdom could exist; and it fills up the good remaining after we have allowed for the effects of the preceding three.[h] All the four are alike indispensable to make up the entire

---

[f] Plato, Republic, iv. pp. 431-432.

[g] Plato, Republic, iv pp. 432-433.

Καὶ μὴν ὅτι γε τὸ τὰ αὑτοῦ πράττειν καὶ μὴ πολυπραγμονεῖν δικαιοσύνη ἐστιν, καὶ τοῦτο ἄλλων τε πολλῶν ἀκηκόαμεν, καὶ αὐτοὶ πολλάκις εἰρήκαμεν.

P. 433 E. ἡ τοῦ οἰκείου τε καὶ ἑαυτοῦ ἕξις καὶ πρᾶξις δικαιοσύνη ἂν ὁμο-

λογοῖτο.

[h] Plato, Republic, iv. p. 433 C. δο-κεῖ μοι τὸ ὑπόλοιπον ἐν τῇ πόλει ὧν ἐσκέμμεθα, σωφροσύνης καὶ ἀνδρίας καὶ φρονήσεως, τοῦτο εἶναι ὃ πᾶσιν ἐκείνοις τὴν δύναμιν παρέσχεν ὥστε ἐγγενέσθαι, καὶ ἐγγενομένοις γε σωτηρίαν παρέχειν, ἕως περ ἂν ἐνῇ.

Good of the city: Justice, or each person (man, woman, free-man, slave, craftsman, guardian) doing his or her own work— Temperance, or unanimity as to command and obedience between Chiefs, Guardians, and the remaining citizens— Courage, or the adherence of the Guardians to right reason, respecting what is terrible and not terrible—Wisdom, or the tutelary superintendence of the Chiefs, who protect each person in the enjoyment of his own property.[i]

As justice consists in each person doing his own work, and not meddling with that of another—so injustice occurs, when a person undertakes the work of an-other instead of his own, or in addition to his own. The mischief is not great, when such inter-ference takes place only in the subordinate func-tions: when, for example, the carpenter pretends to do the work of the shoemaker, or *vice versâ;* or when either of them undertake both. But the mischief be-comes grave and deplorable, when a man from the subordinate functions meddles with the higher—when a craftsman, avail-ing himself of some collateral support, wealth or party or strength, thrusts himself into the functions of a soldier or auxiliary—or when the Guardian, by similar artifice, usurps the functions of a Chief—or when any one person combines these several functions all at once in himself. Herein con-sists the true injustice, ruinous to the city: when the line of demarcation is confounded between these three classes—men of business, Guardians, Chiefs. That each of these classes should do its own work, is Justice: that either of them should meddle with the work of the rest, and especially that the sub-ordinate should meddle with the business of the superior, is Injustice, with ruin following in its train.[k] It is from these opposite characteristics that the titles Just or Unjust will be rightfully bestowed upon our city.

We must now apply, as we undertook to do, the analogy of the city to the individual. The just man, so far forth

Injustice arises when any one part of the city interferes with the functions of the other part, or undertakes double func-tions.

---

[i] Plato, Republic, iv. p. 433 D.

[k] Plato, Republic, iv. p. 434 B-C.

ἡ τριῶν ἄρα ὄντων γενῶν πολυπραγ-μοσύνη καὶ μεταβολὴ εἰς ἄλληλα, μεγίστη τε βλαβὴ τῇ πόλει καὶ ὀρθό-τατ’ ἂν προσαγορεύοιτο μάλιστα κα-

κουργία—Κακουργίαν δὲ τὴν μεγίστην τῆς ἑαυτοῦ πόλεως, οὐκ ἀδικίαν φήσεις εἶναι;

χρηματιστικοῦ, ἐπικουρικοῦ, φυλακι-κοῦ, γένους οἰκειοπραγία, δικαιοσύνη τ’ ἂν εἴη, καὶ τὴν πόλιν δικαίαν παρέχοι.

as justice is concerned, cannot differ from the just city.

Analogy of the city to the individual—Each man is tripartite, having in his mind Reason, Energy, Appetite. These three elements are distinct, and often conflicting. He must therefore have in his own individual mind three distinct parts, elements, or classes, corresponding to the three classes above distinguished in the city. But is it the fact that there are in each man three such mental constituents—three different classes, sorts, or varieties, of mind ?

To settle this point as it ought to be settled, would require a stricter investigation than our present dialogue will permit : but we may contribute something towards it.[1] It is manifest that there exist different individuals in whom reason, energy (courage or passion), and appetite, are separately and unequally developed : thus in the Thracians there is a predominance of energy or courage—in the Phœnicians, of appetite—in the Athenians, of intellect or reason. The question is, whether we employ one and the same mind for all the three—reason, energy, and appetite ; or whether we do not employ a different mind, or portion of mind, when we exercise reason—another, when we are under the influence of energy—and a third, when we follow appetite.[m]

To determine this question, we must consider that the same thing cannot at the same time do or suffer opposites, in the same respect and with reference to the same thing. The same thing or person cannot at the same time, and in the same respect, both stand still and move. This may be laid down as an universal truth : but since some may not admit it to be so, we will at any rate assume it as an hypothesis.[n] Now in reference to the mind, we experience at the same time various movements or affections contrary to each other : assent and dissent—desire and aversion—the attracting any thing to ourselves, and the repelling it from ourselves : each of these is different from and contrary to the other. As a specimen of desires, we will take thirst. When a man is in this condition, his mind desires nothing else but to drink ; and

[1] Plato, Republic, iv. p. 435 C.

Schleiermacher (in the Introduction to his translation of the Republic, p. 71) considers that this passage of the Republic is intended to note as a desideratum the exposition in the Timæus ; wherein the constituent elements of mind or soul are more fully laid down, and its connection with the fundamental elements of the Kosmos.

[m] Plato, Republic, iv. p. 436 A.

[n] Plato, Republic, iv. p. 437 A.

strains entirely towards that object.   If there be any thing
which drags back his mind when in this condition, it must be
something different from that which pulls him forward and
attracts him to drink.   That which attracts him, and that
which repels him, cannot be the same : just as when the
archer at the same time pulls his bow towards him and
pushes it away from him, it is one of his hands that pulls
and another that pushes.[o]   Now it often happens that a man
athirst refuses to drink : there is something within him that
prompts him to drink, and something still more powerful that
forbids him.   These two cannot be the same : one of them is
different from the other : that which prompts is appetite, that
which forbids is reason.   The rational element of the mind is
in like manner something different or distinguishable from all
the appetites, which tend towards repletion and pleasure.

Here then we have two distinct species, forms, or kinds,
existing in the mind.[p]   Besides these two, however,
there is a third, distinct from both : Energy, Passion,
Courage, which neither belongs to Appetite nor to
Reason.   Each of these three acts apart from, and
sometimes in contrariety to, each of the others.[q]
There are thus three distinct elements or varieties of mind in the individual—Reason, Energy,
Appetite : corresponding to the three constituent
portions of the city—The Chiefs or Rulers—The Guardians
or Soldiers—The Craftsmen, or the remaining Community.[r]
The Wisdom of the city resides in its Elders : that of the
individual in his Reason.   The Courage of the city resides
in its Guardians or Soldiers : that of the individual in his
Energy.   But in the city as well as in the individual, it is
the right and privilege; of the rational element to exercise
command, because it alone looks to the welfare and advantage of the whole compound :[s] it is the duty of the two

Reason, Energy, Appetite, in the individual—analogous to Rulers, Guardians, Craftsmen in the city. Reason is to rule Appetite. Energy assists Reason in ruling it.

---

[o] Plato, Republic, iv. p. 439 A-B.

[p] Plato, Republic, iv. p. 439 E.
Ταῦτα μὲν τοίνυν δύο ἡμῖν ὡρίσθω εἴδη ἐν ψυχῇ ἐνόντα, &c.

[q] Plato, Republic, iv. pp. 440-441.

[r] Plato, Republic, iv. p. 441 C. τὰ αὐτὰ μὲν ἐν πόλει, τὰ αὐτὰ δ᾽ ἐν ἑνὸς ἑκάστου τῇ ψυχῇ γένη ἐνεῖναι, καὶ ἴσα

τὸν ἀριθμόν. P. 443 C. τὰ ἐν τῇ ψυχῇ γένη, &c.

[s] Plato, Republic, iv. pp. 441 E, 442 B. τῷ μὲν λογιστικῷ ἄρχειν προσήκει, σοφῷ ὄντι καὶ ἔχοντι τὴν ὑπὲρ ἁπάσης τῆς ψυχῆς προμηθείαν— Σοφὸν δέ γε (ἕνα ἕκαστον καλοῦμεν) ἐκείνῳ τῷ σμικρῷ μέρει, τῷ ὃ ἦρχέ τ᾽

other elements—the energetic and the appetitive—to obey.
It is moreover the special function of the Guardians in the
city to second the Chiefs in enforcing obedience upon the
Craftsmen: so also in the individual, it is the special function
of Energy or Courage to second Reason in controuling
Appetite.

These special functions of the separate parts being laid

A man is just
when these
different
parts of his
mind exercise
their appro-
priate func-
tions without
hindrance.
down, Justice as well as Temperance will appear
analogous in the individual and in the city. Both
Justice and Temperance reside in all the parts
equally: not in one of them exclusively, as Wisdom
and Courage reside. Justice and Temperance belong to the subordinate as well as to the dominant parts.
Justice exists when each of the parts performs its own function, without encroaching on the function of the others : Temperance exists when all the parts are of one opinion as to the
title of the higher or rational element to exercise command.[t]

A man as well as a city is just, when each of his three sorts
or varieties of mind confines itself to its own legitimate function : when Reason reigns over and controuls the other two,
and when Energy seconds Reason in controuling Appetite.
Such a man will not commit fraud, theft, treachery, perjury,
or any like proceedings.[u] On the contrary, injustice exists
when the parts are in conflict with each other : when either of
them encroaches on the function of the other : or when those
parts which ought to be subordinate rise in insurrection against
that which ought to be superior.

Justice is in the mind what health is in the body, when the

Justice and
Injustice in
the mind—
what health
and disease
are in the
body.
parts are so arranged as to controul and be controuled
pursuant to the dictates of nature. Injustice is in
the mind what disease is in the body, when the parts
are so arranged as to controul and be controuled contrary to the dictates of nature. Virtue is thus the health,
beauty, good condition of the mind : Vice is the disease, ugli-
ness, weakness, of the mind.[x]

Having thus ascertained the nature of justice and injustice,

ἐν αὐτῷ καὶ ταῦτα παρήγγελλεν, ἔχον
αὖ κἀκεῖνο ἐπιστήμην ἐν αὐτῷ τὴν τοῦ
ξυμφέροντος ἑκάστῳ τε καὶ ὅλῳ τῷ
κοινῷ σφῶν αὐτῶν τριῶν ὄντων.

[t] Plato, Republic, iv. pp. 442 C,
443 B.
[u] Plato, Republic, iv. pp. 442-443.
[x] Plato, Republic, iv. p. 444.

we are now in a condition (continues Sokrates) to reply to the question proposed for investigation—Is it profitable to a man to be just and to do justice *per se*, even though he be not known as just either by Gods or men, and may thus be debarred from the consequences which would ensue if he were known? Or is it profitable to him to be unjust, if he can contrive to escape detection and punishment? We are enabled to answer the first question in the affirmative, and the second question in the negative. As health is the greatest good, and sickness the greatest evil, of body: so Justice is the greatest good, and injustice the greatest evil, of mind. No measure of luxury, wealth, or power, could render life tolerable, if we lost our bodily health: no amount of prosperity could make life tolerable, without mental health or justice. As bodily health is good *per se*, and sickness evil *per se*, even apart from its consequences: so justice also is good in itself, and injustice evil in itself, apart from its consequences.[y]

Original question now resumed—Does Justice make a man happy, and Injustice make him miserable, apart from all consequences? Answer—Yes.

Sokrates now assumes the special question of the dialogue to be answered, and the picture of the just or perfect city, as well as of the just or perfect individual, to be completed. He is next proceeding to set forth the contrasts to this picture—that is, the varieties of injustice, or the various modes of depravation and corruption—when he is arrested by Polemarchus and Adeimantus: who call upon him to explain more at large the position of the body of Guardians or Soldiers in the city, in regard to women, children, and the family.[z]

Glaukon requires farther explanation about the condition of the Guardians, in regard to sexual and family ties.

In reply, Sokrates announces his intention to make such provision as will exclude separate family ties, as well as separate property, among these Guardians. The Guardians will consist both of men and women. The women will receive the same training, both musical and gymnastical, as the men.[a] They will take part both in the bodily exercises of the palæstra, in the military drill, and in the combats

Men and women will live together and perform the duties of Guardians alike—They will receive the same gymnastic and musical training.

[y] Plato, Republic, iv. p. 445.   [z] Plato, Republic, v. p. 449.

[a] Plato, Republic, v. p. 452.

of war.   Those who deride these naked exercises as preposterous for the female sex, should be reminded (Sokrates
says) that not long ago it was considered unseemly among the
Greeks (as it still is among many of the *barbari*) for men to
expose their naked bodies in the palæstra: but such repugnance has been overpowered by the marked usefulness of the
practice: the Kretans first setting the example, next the
Lacedæmonians; lastly all other Greeks doing the same.[b]
We maintain the principle which we laid down in the beginning, that one person should perform only one duty—that
for which he is best qualified.   But there is no one function,
or class of functions, for which women as such are peculiarly
qualified, or peculiarly disqualified.   Between women generally, and men generally, in reference to the discharge of
duties, there is no other difference, except that men are
superior to women in every thing:[c] the best women will
be on a level only with the second-best men, but they will be
superior to all men lower than the second-best.   But among
women, as among men, there are great individual differences:
one woman is fit for one duty, another for another: and in
our city, each must be employed for the duty suitable to her
individual disposition.   Those who are best qualified by nature
for the office of Guardians, must be allotted to that office:
they must discharge it along with the men, and must be
trained for it by the same education as the men, musical and
gymnastical.

If an objector accuses us of proposing arrangements contrary to nature, we not only deny the force of the
objection, but we retort the charge.   We affirm that
the arrangements now existing in society, which restrict all women to a limited number of domestic
and family functions, are contrary to nature—and
that ours are founded upon the genuine and real
dictates of nature.[d]   The only difference admissible
between men and women, in the joint discharge of
the functions of Guardians, is, that the easier portion of such
functions must in general be assigned to women, and the

Nature does not prescribe any distribution of functions between men and women. Women are inferior to men in every thing. The best women are equal to second-best men.

---

[b] Plato, Republic, v. p. 452 D.

[c] Plato, Republic, v. p. 455 C-D.

[d] Plato, Republic, v. p. 456 C. κατὰ

φύσιν ἐτίθεμεν τὸν νόμον· ἀλλὰ τὰ νῦν
παρὰ ταῦτα γιγνόμενα παρὰ φύσιν μᾶλλον, ὡς ἔοικε, γίγνεται.

more difficult to men, in consequence of the inferiority of the feminine nature.[e]

These intermingled male and female Guardians, in the discharge of their joint functions, will live together all in common barracks and at common mess-tables. There must be no separate houses or separate family-relations between them. All are wives or husbands of all: no youth must know his own father, no mature man must know his own son: all the mature men and women are fathers or mothers of all the younger: all of the same age are brothers and sisters.[f] We do not intend, however, that the copulation between them shall take place in a promiscuous and arbitrary manner : we shall establish laws to regulate the intermarriages and breeding.[g] We must copy the example of those who regulate the copulation of horses, dogs, and other animals : we must bring together those who will give existence to the best offspring.[h] We must couple, as often as we can, the men who are best, with the women who are best, both in mind and body; and the men who are least good, with the women who are least good. We must bring up the offspring of the former couples— we must refuse to bring up the offspring of the latter.[i] And such results must be accomplished by underhand arrangements of the Elder Chiefs; so as to be unknown to every one else, in order to prevent discontent and quarrel among the body of the Guardians. These Elders will celebrate periodical festivals, in which they will bring together the fitting brides and bridegrooms, under solemn hymns and sacrifices. They must regulate the number of marriages in such manner as to keep the total list of Guardians as much as possible without increase as well as without diminution.[k] The Elders must make an artful use of the lot, so that these couplings shall appear to every one else the effect of chance.

Marginal note: Community of life and relations between the male and female Guardians. Temporary marriages arranged by contrivance of the Elders. No separate families.

[e] Plato, Republic, v. p. 457 B.
[f] Plato, Republic, v. pp. 457-458.
[g] Plato, Republic, v. p. 458 E.
[h] Plato, Republic, v. p. 459 A.
[i] Plato, Republic, v. p. 459 E. δεῖ μὲν ἐκ τῶν ὡμολογημένων τοὺς ἀρίστους ταῖς ἀρίσταις συγγίγνεσθαι ὡς πλειστάκις, τοὺς δὲ φαυλοτάτους ταῖς φαυλοτά-

ταις τοὐνάντιον, καὶ τῶν μὲν τὰ ἔκγονα τρέφειν, τῶν δὲ μὴ, εἰ μέλλει τὸ ποίμνιον ὡς ἀκρότατον εἶναι· καὶ ταῦτα πάντα γιγνόμενα λανθάνειν πλὴν αὐτοὺς τοὺς ἄρχοντας, εἰ αὖ ἡ ἀγέλη τῶν φυλάκων ὅ, τι μάλιστα ἀστασίαστος ἔσται.
[k] Plato, Republic, v. p. 460 A.

Distinguished warriors must be rewarded with a larger licence of copulation with different women, which will produce the farther advantage of having as many children as possible born from their procreation.[1] All the children as soon as born must be consigned to the Chiefs or Elders, male and female, who will conceal in some convenient manner those who are born either from the worst couples or with any bodily imperfection; while they place the offspring of the best couples in special outbuildings under the charge of nurses. Those mothers who are full of milk will be brought here to give suck, but every precaution will be taken that none of them shall know her own child : wet-nurses will also be provided in addition, to ensure a full supply : but all the care of the children will devolve on the public nurses, not on the mothers.[m]

The age for such intermarriages, destined to be procreative *Regulations about age, for procreation— Children brought up under public authority.* for the benefit of the city, must be from thirty to fifty-five, for men — from twenty to forty, for women. No man or woman, above or below these limits of age, will be allowed to meddle with the function of intermarriage and procreation for the public ; which function must always be conducted under superintendance of the authorities, with proper sacrifice and prayers to the Gods. Nor will any man, even within the licensed age, be allowed to approach any woman except by assignment from the authorities. If any infringement of this law should occur, the offspring arising from it will be pronounced spurious and outcast.[n] But when the above limits of age are passed, both men and women may have intercourse with whomsoever they please, except fathers with daughters or sons with mothers : under condition, however, that no offspring shall be born from such intercourse, or that if any offspring be born, it shall be exposed.[o]

How is the father to know his own daughter (it is asked), or the son his own mother ? They cannot know (replies Sokrates) : but each couple will consider every child born in the seventh month or tenth month after their marriage, as their child, and will address him or her by the appellation of

[1] Plato, Republic, v. p. 460 B.   [n] Plato, Republic, v. p. 461 A-B.
[m] Plato, Republic, v. p. 460 C-D.   [o] Plato, Republ. v. p. 461 C.

son or daughter. The fathers and mothers will be fathers and mothers of all the children born at that time : the sons and daughters will be in filial relation to all the couples brought together at the given antecedent period.[p]

The main purpose of such regulations, in respect to family as in respect to property, is to establish the fullest communion between all the Guardians, male and female—and to eliminate as much as possible the feeling of separate interest in any fraction of them. The greatest evil to any city is, that which pulls it to pieces and makes it many instead of one : the greatest good to it is that which binds it together and makes it one. Now what is most efficacious in binding it together, is, community of the causes of pleasure and pain : when each individual feels pleasure from the same causes and on the same occasions as all the rest, and pain in like manner. On the other hand, when the causes of pleasure and pain are distinct, this tends to dissolution ; and becomes fatal if the opposition is marked, so that some individuals are much delighted, and others much distressed, under the same circumstances. That city is the best arranged, wherein all the citizens pronounce the words, *Mine* and *Not Mine*, with reference to the same things : when they coalesce into an unity like the organism of a single individual. To him a blow in the finger is a blow to the whole man : so also in the city, pleasure or pain to any one citizen ought to communicate itself by sympathy as pleasure and pain to all.[q]

Perfect communion of sentiment and interest among the Guardians— Causes of pleasure and pain the same to all, like parts of the same organism.

Now the Guardians under our regulations will present as much as possible this community of *Mine* and *Not Mine*, as well as of pleasures and pains—and this exclusion of the separate individual *Mine* and *Not Mine*, as well as of separate pleasures and pains. No individual among them will have either separate property or separate family relationship : each will have both one and the other in common with the rest.[r] No one will have property of his own to be increased, nor a family of his own to be benefited, apart from the rest : all will be as

Harmony— absence of conflicting interest— assured scale of equal comfort—consequent happiness—among the Guardians.

[p] Plato, Republic, v. p. 461 D.   [q] Plato, Republic, v. p. 462.

[r] Plato, Republic, v. p. 464.

much as possible common recipients of pleasure and pain.[s]
All the ordinary causes of dispute and litigation will thus be
excluded. If two Guardians of the same age happen to
quarrel, they must fight it out: this will discharge their
wrath and prevent worse consequences—while at the same
time it will encourage attention to gymnastic excellence.[t]
But no younger Guardian will raise his hand against an
older Guardian, whom he is taught to reverence as his father,
and whom every one else would protect if attacked. If the
Guardians maintain harmony among themselves, they will
easily ensure it among the remaining inhabitants. Assured
of sufficient but modest comforts, the Guardians will be relieved from all struggles for the maintenance of a family,
from the arts of trade, and from subservience to the rich.[u]
They will escape all these troubles, and will live a life happier
than the envied Olympic victor : for they will gain the victory
in an enterprise more illustrious than he undertakes, and they
will receive from their fellow-citizens fuller maintenance and
higher privilege than what is awarded to him, as well as
honours after death.[x] Their lives are not to be put in comparison with those of the farmer or the shoemaker. They
must not indeed aspire to any happiness incompatible with
their condition and duty as Guardians. But that condition
will itself involve the highest happiness. And if any silly
ambition prompts them to depart from it, they will assuredly
change for the worse.[y]

Such is the communion of sexes which must be kept up for
the duties of Guardians, and for the exigencies of
military defence. As in other races of animals,
males and females must go out to fight, and each
will inspire the other with bravery. The children
must be taken out on horseback to see the encounters from a distance, so that they may be kept clear of
danger, yet may nevertheless be gradually accustomed to

In case of war both sexes will go together to battle—Rewards to distinguished warriors.

[s] Plato, Republic, v. p. 464 D. πάντας εἰς τὸ δυνατὸν ὁμοπαθεῖς λύπης τε καὶ ἡδονῆς εἶναι.
[t] Plato, Republic, v. p. 464 E.
[u] Plato, Republ. v. p. 465 C. τῶν κακῶν ἂν ἀπηλλαγμένοι ἂν εἶεν, κολακείας τε πλουσίων, ἀπορίας τε καὶ ἀλγηδόνας, &c.
[x] Plato, Republic, v. p. 465 D. Πάντων τε δὴ τούτων ἀπαλλάξονται, ζήσουσί τε τοῦ μακαριστοῦ βίου, ὃν οἱ Ὀλυμπιονῖκαι ζῶσι, μακαριώτερον.
[y] Plato, Republic, v. p. 466 A-C.

the sight of it.[z] If any one runs away from the field, he must be degraded from the rank of Guardian to that of husbandman or craftsman. If any man suffers himself to be taken prisoner, he is no loss: the enemy may do what they choose with him. When any one distinguishes himself in battle, he shall be received on his return by garlands and by an affectionate welcome from the youth.[a] Should he be slain in battle, he shall be recognised as having become a Dæmon or Demigod (according to the Hesiodic doctrine), and his sepulchre shall be honoured by appropriate solemnities.[b]

In carrying on war, our Guardians will observe a marked difference in their manner of treating Hellenic enemies and barbaric enemies. They will never enslave any Hellenic city, nor hold any Hellenic person in slavery. They will never even strip the body of an Hellenic enemy, except so far as to take his arms. They will never pile up in their temples the arms, nor burn the houses and lands, of Hellenic enemies. They will always keep in mind the members of the Hellenic race as naturally kindred with each other, and bound to aid each other in mutual defence, against Barbaric aliens who are the natural enemies of all of them.[c] They will not think themselves authorised to carry on war as Hellens now do against each other, except when their enemies are Barbaric.

War against Hellenic enemies to be carried on mildly— Hellens are all by nature kinsmen.

Enough of this, Sokrates, replies Glaukon. I admit that your city will have all the excellences and advantages of which you boast. But you have yet to show me that it is practicable, and how.[d]

The task which you impose (says Sokrates) is one of great difficulty: even if you grant me, what must be granted, that every reality must fall short of its ideal type.[e] One condition, and one only, is essential to render it practicable: a condition which you may ridicule as preposterous, but which, though not probable, is certainly supposable. Either philosophers must acquire the ruling power, or else the present

Question— How is the scheme practicable? It is difficult, yet practicable on one condition— That philosophy and political power should come into the same hands.

---

[z] Plato, Republic, v. pp. 466-467.
[a] Plato, Republic, v. p. 468 B.
[b] Plato, Republic, v. p. 469 B.

[c] Plato, Republic, v. pp. 470-471.
[d] Plato, Republic, v. pp. 471-472.
[e] Plato, Republic, v. pp. 472-473.

rulers of mankind must themselves become genuine philosophers. In one or other of these two ways philosophy and political power must come into the same hands. Unless such condition be fulfilled, our city can never be made a reality, nor can there ever be any respite of suffering to the human race.[f]

The supremacy which you claim for philosophers, (replies Glaukon) will be listened to with repugnance and scorn. But at least you must show who the philosophers are, on whose behalf you invoke such supremacy. You must show that it belongs to them by nature both to pursue philosophy, and to rule in the various cities: and that by nature also, other men ought to obey them as well as to abstain from philosophy.[g]

The first requisite for a philosopher (replies Sokrates) is,

Characteristic marks of the philosopher—He contemplates and knows Entia or unchangeable Forms, as distinguished from fluctuating particulars or Fientia.

that he shall love and pursue eagerly every sort of knowledge or wisdom, without shrinking from labour for such purpose. But it is not sufficient that he should be eager about hearing tragedies or learning the minor arts. Other men, accomplished and curious, are fond of hearing beautiful sounds and discourses, or of seeing beautiful forms and colours.

But the philosopher alone can see or distinguish truth.[h] It is only he who can distinguish the genuine Form or Idea, in which truth consists, from the particular embodiments in which it occurs. These Forms or Ideas exist, eternal and unchangeable. Since Pulchrum is the opposite of Turpe, they must be two, and each of them must be One: the same about Just and Unjust, Good and Evil; each of these is a distinct Form or Idea, existing as One and Unchangeable by itself, but exhibiting itself in appearance as manifold, diverse, and frequently changing, through communion with different objects and events, and through communion of each Form with others.[i] Now the accomplished, but

---

[f] Plato, Republic, v. p. 473 D.
[g] Plato, Republic, v. p. 474 A-B.
[h] Plato, Republic, v. pp. 474-475. τοὺς τῆς ἀληθείας φιλοθεάμονας. P. 475 E.
[i] Plato, Republic, v. p. 476 A. Ἐπειδὴ ἐνάντιον καλὸν αἰσχρῷ, δύο αὐτω εἶναι. Οὐκοῦν ἐπειδὴ δύο, καὶ ἓν ἑκάτερον; Καὶ περὶ δικαίου καὶ ἀδίκου, καὶ ἀγαθοῦ καὶ κακοῦ καὶ πάντων τῶν εἰδῶν πέρι, ὁ αὐτὸς λόγος; αὐτὸ μὲν ἓν ἕκαστον εἶναι, τῇ δὲ τῶν πράξεων καὶ σωμάτων καὶ ἀλλήλων κοινωνίᾳ πανταχοῦ φανταζόμενα πολλὰ φαίνεσθαι ἕκαστον;

unphilosophical, man cannot see or recognise this Form in itself. He can see only the different particular cases and complications in which it appears embodied.[k] None but the philosopher can contemplate each Form by itself, and discriminate it from the various particulars in conjunction with which it appears. Such philosophers are few in number, but they are the only persons who can be said truly to live. Ordinary and even accomplished men—who recognise beautiful things, but cannot recognise Beauty in itself, nor even follow an instructor who points it out to them—pass their lives in a sort of dream or reverie : for the dreamer, whether asleep or awake, is one who believes what is similar to another thing to be not merely similar, but to be the actual thing itself.[l] The philosopher alone, who embraces in his mind the one and unchangeable Form or Idea, along with, yet distinguished from, its particular embodiments, possesses knowledge or science. The unphilosophical man, whose mind embraces nothing higher than variable particulars, does not know—but only opines, or has opinions.[m]

This latter, the unphilosophical man, will not admit what we say. Accordingly, we must prove it to him. You cannot know without knowing Something : that is, Some Ens; for Non-Ens cannot be known. That which is completely and absolutely Ens, is completely and absolutely cognizable : that which is Non-Ens and nowhere, is in every way uncognizable. If then there be anything which is at once Ens and Non-Ens, it will lie midway between these two : it will be something neither absolutely and completely cognizable, nor absolutely and completely uncognizable : it belongs to something between ignorance and science. Now science or knowledge is one thing, its object is, complete Ens. Opinion is another thing, its object also is different. Knowing and Opining belong, like Sight and Hearing, to the class of Entia called Powers or Faculties, which we and others possess, and by means of which—that is, by means of one or other of

Ens alone can be known— Non-Ens is unknowable. That which is midway between Ens and Non-Ens (particulars) is matter only of opinion. Ordinary men attain nothing beyond opinion.

k Plato, Republic, v. p. 476 B.
l Plato, Republic, v. p. 476 B.
m Plato, Republic, v. p. 476 C. Οὐ-

κοῦν τούτου .μὲν τὴν διάνοιαν ὡς γιγνώ-
σκοντος γνώμην ἂν ὀρθῶς φαῖμεν
εἶναι, τοῦ δὲ δόξαν, ὡς δοξάζοντος.

them—we accomplish everything that we do accomplish. Now no one of these powers or faculties has either colour or figure, whereby it may be recognised or distinguished from others. Each is known and distinguished, not by what it is in itself, but by what it accomplishes, and by the object to which it has special relation. That which has the same object and accomplishes the same result, I call the same power or faculty: that which has a different object, and accomplishes a different result, I call a different power or faculty. Now Knowing, Cognition, Science, is one of our faculties or powers, and the strongest of all: Opining is another, and a different one. A marked distinction between the two is, that Knowing or Cognition is infallible—Opining is fallible. Since Cognition is one power or faculty, and Opining another—the object of one must be different from the object of the other. But the object of Cognition is, the Complete Ens: the object of Opining must therefore be, not the Complete Ens, but something different from it. What then is the object of Opining? It is not Complete Ens, but it is still Something. It is not Non-Ens, or Nothing; for Non-Ens or Nothing is not thinkable or opinable: you cannot think or opine, and yet think or opine nothing. Whoever opines or thinks, must opine or think something. Ens is the object of Cognition, Non-Ens is the object of non-Cognition or Ignorance: Opination or Opinion is midway between Cognition and Ignorance, darker than the former, but clearer than the latter. The object of opination is therefore something midway between Ens and Non-Ens.

But what is this Something, midway between Ens and Non-Ens, and partaking of both—which is the object of Opination? To make out this, we must revert to the case of the unphilosophical man. We have described him as not believing in the existence of the Form or Idea of Beauty, or Justice *per se;* not enduring to hear it spoken of as a real Ens and Unum; not knowing anything except of the many diverse particulars, beautiful and just. We must remind him that every one of these particular beautiful things will appear repulsive also: every one of these just and holy particulars,

Particulars fluctuate: they are sometimes just or beautiful, sometimes unjust or ugly. Forms or Entia alone remain constant.

will appear unjust and unholy also. He cannot refuse to admit that each of them will appear under certain circumstances beautiful and ugly, just and unjust, holy and unholy. In like manner, every particular double will appear also a half: every light thing will appear heavy: every little thing great. Of each among these many particulars, if you can truly predicate any one quality about it, you may with equal truth predicate the opposite quality also. Each of them both is, and is not, the substratum of all these different and opposite qualities. You cannot pronounce them to be either one or the other, with fixity and permanence: they are at once both and neither.

Here then we find the appropriate object of Opination: that which is neither Ens nor Non-Ens, but something between both. Particulars are the object of Opination, as distinguished from universal Entities, Forms, or Ideas, which are the object of Cognition. The many, who disbelieve or ignore the existence of these Forms, and whose minds dwell exclusively among particulars—cannot know, but only opine. Their usages and creeds, as to beautiful, just, honourable, float between positive Ens and Non-Ens. It is these intermediate fluctuations which are caught up by their opining faculty, intermediate as it is between Cognition and Ignorance. It is these also, the objects of Opination, which they love and delight in: they neither recognise nor love the objects of Cognition or Knowledge. They are lovers of opinion and its objects, not lovers of Knowledge. The philosopher alone recognises and loves Knowledge and the objects of Knowledge. His mind dwells, not amidst the fluctuating, diverse, and numerous particulars, but in contemplation of the One, Universal, permanent, unchangeable, Form or Idea.

The Many cannot discern or admit the reality of Forms— Their minds are always fluctuating among particulars.

Here is the characteristic difference (continues Sokrates) which you required me to point out, between the philosopher and the unphilosophical man, however accomplished. The philosopher sees, knows, and contemplates, the One, Real, unchangeable, Form or Idea: the unphilosophical man knows nothing of this Form *per se*, and sees only its multifarious

The philosopher will be ardent for all varieties of knowledge—His excellent moral attributes—He will be trained to capacity for active life.

manifestations, each perpetually variable and different from all the rest. The philosopher, having present to his mind this type—and approximating to it, as far as may be, the real institutions and practices—will be the person most competent to rule our city : especially as his education will give him farthermore—besides such familiarity with the Form or Type—as large a measure of experience, and as much virtue, as can fall to the lot of the unphilosophical man.[n] The nature and disposition of the true philosopher, if improved by education, will include all the virtue and competence of the practical man. The philosopher is bent on learning everything which can make him familiar with Universal Forms and Essences in their pure state, not floating amidst the confusion of generated and destroyed realities : and with Forms and Essences little as well as great, mean as well as sublime.[o] Devoted to knowledge and truth—hating falsehood—he has little room in his mind for the ordinary desires : he is temperate, indifferent to money, free from all meanness or shabbiness. A man like him, whose contemplations stretch over all time and all essence, thinks human life a small affair, and has no fear of death. He will be just, mild in his demeanour, quick in apprehension, retentive in memory, elegant in his tastes and movements. All these excellences will be united in the philosophers to whom we confide the rule of our city.[p]

It is impossible, Sokrates (remarks Adeimantus), to answer in the negative to your questions. Nevertheless we, who hear and answer, are not convinced of the truth of your conclusion. Unskilled as we are in the interrogatory process, we feel ourselves led astray little by little at each successive question ; until at length, through the accumulated effect of such small deviations, we are driven up into a corner without the power of moving, like a bad player at draughts, defeated by one superior to himself.[q] Here in this

Adeimantus does not dispute the conclusion, but remarks that it is at variance with actual facts —Existing philosophers are either worthless pretenders, or when they are good, useless.

---

[n] Plato, Republic, vi. p. 484.

[o] Plato, Republic, vi. p. 485 A.

[p] Plato, Republic, vi. pp. 485-486.

[q] Plato, Republic, vi. p. 487 B. Πρὸς μὲν ταῦτά σοι οὐδεὶς ἂν οἷός τ' εἴη ἀντειπεῖν· ἀλλὰ γὰρ τοιόνδε τι πάσχουσιν οἱ ἀκούοντες ἑκάστοτε ἃ νῦν λέγεις· ἡγοῦνται δι' ἀπειρίαν τοῦ ἐρωτᾶν τε καὶ ἀποκρίνεσθαι ὑπὸ τοῦ λόγου σμικρὸν παραγόμενοι, ἀθροισθέντων τῶν σμικρῶν ἐπὶ τελευτῆς τῶν λόγων, μέγα τὸ σφάλμα καὶ ἐναντίον τοῖς πρώτοις ἀναφαίνεσθαι, &c.

This is an interesting remark on the

particular case your conclusion has been reached by steps to which we cannot refuse assent. Yet if we look at the facts, we see something quite the reverse as to the actual position of philosophers. Those who study philosophy, not simply as a branch of juvenile education but as a continued occupation throughout life, are in most cases strange creatures, not to say thoroughly unprincipled: while the few of them who are most reasonable, derive nothing from this pursuit which you so much extol, except that they become useless in their respective cities.[r]

Yes (replies Sokrates), your picture is a correct one. The position of true and reasonable philosophers, in their respective cities, is difficult and uncomfortable. Conceive a ship on her voyage, under the management of a steersman distinguished for force of body as well as for skill in his craft, but not clever in dealing with, or acting upon other men. Conceive the seamen all quarrelling with each other to get possession of the rudder; each man thinking himself qualified to steer, though he has never learnt it—nor had any master in it—nor even believes it to be teachable, but is ready to massacre all who affirm that it is teachable.[s] Imagine, besides, these seamen importuning the qualified steersman to commit the rudder to them, each being ready to expel or kill any others whom he may prefer to them: and at last proceeding to stupify with wine or drugs the qualified steersman, and then to navigate the vessel themselves according to their own views; feasting plentifully on the stores. These men know nothing of what constitutes true and able steersmanship. They extol, as a perfect steersman, that leader who is most efficacious, either by persuasion or force, in seizing the rudder for them to manage: they despise as useless any one who does not possess this talent. They never reflect that the genuine steersman has enough to do in surmounting the dangers of his own especial art, and in watching the stars and the winds:

Sokrates admits the fact to be so—His simile of the able steersman on shipboard, among a disobedient crew.

effect produced upon many hearers by the Sokratic and Platonic dialogues,—puzzling, silencing, and ultimately stimulating the mind, but not satisfying or convincing,—rather raising suspicions as to the trustworthiness of the process, which suspicions have to be turned over and scrutinised by subsequent meditation.

[r] Plato, Republic, vi. p. 487 D.
[s] Plato, Republic, vi. p. 488.

and that if he is to acquire technical skill and practice adequate to such a purpose, he cannot at the same time possess skill and practice in keeping his hold of the rudder whether the crew are pleased with him or not. Such being the condition of the ship and the crew, you see plainly that they will despise and set aside the true steersman as an useless proser and star-gazer.[t]

Now the crew of this ship represent the citizens and leaders of our actual cities : the steersman represents the true philosopher. He is and must be, useless in the ship : but his uselessness is the fault of the crew and not his own. It is not for the true steersman to entreat permission from the seamen, that they will allow him to command ; nor for the wise man to solicit employment at the doors of the rich. It is for the sick man, whether he be poor or rich, to ask for the aid of the physician ; and for every one who needs to be commanded, to invoke the authority of the person qualified to command. No man really qualified will submit to ask command as a favour.[u]

The uselessness of the true philosopher is the fault of the citizens, who will not invoke his guidance.

Thus, Adeimantus (continues Sokrates), I have dealt with the first part of your remark, that the true philosopher is an useless man in cities as now constituted : I have shown you this is not his fault—that it could not be otherwise,—and that a man even of the highest aptitude cannot enjoy reputation among those whose turn of mind is altogether at variance with his own.[x]

I shall now deal with your second observation—That while even the best philosophers are useless, the majority of those who cultivate philosophy are worthless men, who bring upon her merited discredit. I admit that this also is correct; but I shall prove that philosophy is not to be blamed for it.[y]

You will remember the great combination of excellent dispositions, intellectual as well as moral, which I laid down as

[t] Plato, Republic, vi. p. 488 D-E.

[u] Plato, Republic, vi. p. 489 B. τῆς μέντοι ἀχρηστίας τοὺς μὴ χρωμένους κέλευε αἰτιᾶσθαι, ἀλλὰ μὴ τοὺς ἐπιεικεῖς. Οὐ γὰρ ἔχει φύσιν κυβερνήτην ναυτῶν δεῖσθαι ἄρχεσθαι ὑφ᾽ αὑτοῦ, &c.

[x] Plato, Republic, vi. p. 489 D. ἔκ

τε τοίνυν τούτων καὶ ἐν τούτοις οὐ ῥᾴδιον εὐδοκιμεῖν τὸ βέλτιστον ἐπιτήδευμα ὑπὸ τῶν τἀνάντια ἐπιτηδευόντων.

[y] Plato, Republic, vi. p. 489 E. ὅτι οὐδὲ τούτου φιλοσοφία αἰτία, πειραθῶμεν δεῖξαι.

indispensable to form the fundamental character of the true philosopher. Such a combination is always rare. Even under the best circumstances, philosophers must be very few. But these few stand exposed, in our existing cities, to such powerful causes of corruption, that they are prevented from reaching maturity, except by some happy accident. First, each one of those very qualities, which, when combined, constitute the true philosopher,—serves as a cause of corruption, if it exists by itself and apart from the rest. Next, what are called good things, or external advantages, act in the same manner— such as beauty, strength, wealth, powerful connections, &c. Again, the stronger a man's natural aptitudes and the greater his external advantages,—the better will he become under favourable circumstances, the worse will he become, if circumstances are unfavourable. Heinous iniquity always springs from a powerful nature perverted by bad training : not from a feeble nature, which will produce no great effects either for good or evil. Thus the eminent predispositions,—which, if properly improved, would raise a man to the highest rank in virtue,—will, if planted in an unfavourable soil, produce a master-mind in deeds of iniquity, unless counteracted by some providential interposition.

The great qualities required to form a philosopher, become sources of perversion, under a misguiding public opinion.

The multitude treat these latter as men corrupted by the Sophists. But this is a mistake. Neither Sophists nor other private individuals produce mischief worth mentioning. It is the multitude themselves, utterers of these complaints, who are the most active Sophists and teachers: it is they who educate and mould every individual, man and woman, young and old, into such a character as they please.[z] When they are assembled in the public assembly or the dikastery, in the theatre or the camp—when they praise some things and blame others, with vociferation and vehemence echoed from the rocks around—how irresistible will

Mistake of supposing that such perversion arises from the Sophists. Irresistible effect of the public opinion generally, in tempting or forcing a dissenter into orthodoxy.

---

[z] Plato, Republic, vi. p. 492 A. ἢ καὶ σὺ ἡγεῖ, ὥσπερ οἱ πολλοὶ, διαφθειρομένους τινὰς εἶναι ὑπὸ σοφιστῶν νέους, διαφθείροντας δέ τινας σοφιστὰς ἰδιωτικοὺς, ὅ, τι καὶ ἄξιον λόγου—ἀλλ᾽ οὐκ αὐτοὺς τοὺς ταῦτα λέγοντας μεγίστους μὲν εἶναι σοφιστὰς; παιδεύειν δὲ τελεώτατα καὶ ἀπεργάζεσθαι οἵους βούλονται εἶναι καὶ νέους καὶ πρεσβυτέρους καὶ ἄνδρας καὶ γυναῖκας;

be the impression produced upon the mind of a youth who
hears them! No private training which he may have previously received can hold out against it. All will be washed
away by this impetuous current of multitudinous praise or
blame, which carries him along with it. He will declare
honourable or base the same things as they declare to be so:
he will adopt the character, and follow the pursuits, which
they enjoin. Moreover if he resists such persuasive influence,
these multitudinous teachers and Sophists have stronger
pressure in store for him.[a] They punish the disobedient with
disgrace, fine, and even death. What other Sophist, or what
private exhortation, can contend successfully against teachers
such as these? Surely none. The attempt to do so is insane.
There neither is, nor has been, nor will be, any individual
human disposition educated to virtue in opposition to the
training of the multitude:[b] I say *human*, as distinguished
from *divine*, of which I make exception: for in the existing
state of society, any individual who is preserved from these
ascendant influences to acquire philosophical excellence, owes
his preservation to the divine favour.

Moreover, though the multitude complain of these professional teachers as rivals, and decry them as Sophists—yet we must recollect that such teachers
inculcate only the opinions received among the multitude themselves, and extol these same opinions as
wisdom.[c] The teachers know nothing of what is
really honourable and base,—good and evil,—just and unjust.
They distribute all these names only with reference to the
opinions of the multitude:—pronouncing those things which
please the multitude to be good, and those which displease
to be evil,—without furnishing any other rational account.
They call things necessary by the name of just and honour-

The Sophists and other private teachers accept the prevalent orthodoxy, and conform their teaching to it.

[a] Plato, Republic, vi. p. 492 C. καὶ
φήσειν τὰ αὐτὰ τούτοις καλὰ καὶ αἰσχρὰ
εἶναι καὶ ἐπιτηδεύσειν ἅπερ ἂν οὗτοι,
καὶ ἔσεσθαι τοιοῦτον—Καὶ μὴν οὔπω
τὴν μεγίστην ἀνάγκην εἰρήκαμεν. Ποίαν;
Ἣν ἔργῳ προστιθέασι λόγῳ μὴ πεί-
θοντες, οὗτοι οἱ παιδευταί τε καὶ σοφισταί. Ἦ οὐκ οἶσθα ὅτι τὸν μὴ πειθό-
μενον ἀτιμίαις τε καὶ χρήμασι καὶ θανά-
τοις κολάζουσιν; Καὶ μάλα, ἔφη,

σφόδρα.
[b] Plato, Republic, vi. p. 492 D.
[c] Plato, Republic, vi. p. 493 A.
ἕκαστον τῶν μισθαρνούντων ἰδιωτῶν,
οὓς δὴ οὗτοι σοφιστὰς καλοῦσι καὶ ἀντι-
τέχνους ἡγοῦνται, μὴ ἄλλα παιδεύειν ἢ
τὰ τῶν πολλῶν δόγματα, ἃ δοξάζουσιν
ὅταν ἀθροισθῶσι, καὶ σοφίαν ταύτην
καλεῖν.

able; not knowing the material difference between what is good and what is necessary, nor being able to point out that difference to others. Thus preposterous are the teachers, who count it wisdom to suit the taste and feelings of the multitude, whether in painting or in music or in social affairs. For whoever lives among them, publicly exhibiting either poetry or other performances private or official, thus making the multitude his masters beyond the strict limits of necessity—the consequence is infallible, that he must adapt his works to that which they praise. But whether the works which he executes are really good and honourable, he will be unable to render any tolerable account.[d]

It is therefore the multitude, or the general voice of society—not the Sophists or private teachers, mere echoes of that general voice—which works upon and moulds individuals. Now the multitude cannot tolerate or believe in the existence of those Universals or Forms which the philosopher contemplates. They know only the many particulars, not the One Universal. Incapable of becoming philosophers themselves, they look upon the philosopher with hatred; and this sentiment is adopted by all those so-called philosophers who seek to please them.[e] Under these circumstances, what chance is there that those eminent predispositions, which we pointed out as the foundation of the future philosopher, can ever be matured to their proper result? A youth of such promise, especially if his body be on a par with his mind, will be at once foremost among all his fellows. His relatives and fellow-citizens, eager to make use of him for their own purposes, and anxious to appropriate to themselves his growing force, will besiege him betimes with solicitations and flatteries.[f] Under these influences, if we assume him to be rich, well born, and in a powerful city, he will naturally become intoxicated with unlimited hopes and ambition; fancying himself competent to manage the affairs of all governments, and giving himself the empty airs of a lofty potentate.[g]

The people generally hate philosophy—A youth who aspires to it will be hated by the people, and persecuted even by his own relatives.

[d] Plato, Republic, vi. p. 493 C-D.
[e] Plato, Republic, vi. p. 494 A.
φιλόσοφον μὲν ἄρα πλῆθος ἀδύνατον εἶναι—Καὶ τοὺς φιλοσοφοῦντας ἄρα ἀνάγκη ψέγεσθαι ὑπ᾽ αὐτῶν—καὶ ὑπὸ τούτων τῶν ἰδιωτῶν, ὅσοι προσομιλοῦντες ὄχλῳ ἀρέσκειν αὐτῷ ἐπιθυμοῦσι.
[f] Plato, Republic, vi. p. 494 B.
[g] Plato, Republic, vi. p. 494 C. πληρωθήσεσθαι ἀμηχάνου ἐλπίδος, ἡγοῦ-

If there be any one to give him a quiet hint that he has not
yet acquired intelligence, nor *can* acquire it without labour—
he will turn a deaf ear. But suppose that such advice should
by chance prevail, in one out of many cases, so that the youth
alters his tendencies and devotes himself to philosophy—what
will be the conduct of those who see, that they will thereby
be deprived of his usefulness and party-service towards their
own views? They will leave no means untried to prevent
him from following the advice, and even to ruin the adviser,
by private conspiracy and judicial prosecution.[h] It is impossible that the young man can really turn to philosophy, against
obstructions thus powerful. You see that those very excellences and advantages, which form the initial point of the growing philosopher, become means and temptations for corrupting
him. The best natures, rare as they always are, become thus not
only ruined, but turned into instruments of evil. For the same
men (as I have already said) who, under favourable training,
would have done the greatest good, become perpetrators of
the greatest evil, if they are badly placed. Small men will
do nothing important, either in the one way or the other.[i]

It is thus that the path of philosophy is deserted by those
who ought to have trodden it, and who pervert their
exalted powers to unworthy objects. That path—
being left vacant, yet still full of imposing titles
and pretensions, and carrying a show of superior
dignity as compared with the vulgar professions—
becomes invaded by interlopers of inferior worth and ability,
who quit their own small craft, and set up as philosophers.[k]
Such men, poorly endowed by nature, and debased by habits
of trade, exhibit themselves, in their self-assumed exaltation
as philosophers, like a slave recently manumitted, who has

The really great minds are thus driven away from the path of philosophy —which is left to empty pretenders.

μενον καὶ τὰ τῶν Ἑλλήνων καὶ τὰ τῶν
βαρβάρων ἱκανὸν εἶναι πράττειν.
   [h] Plato, Republic, vi. p. 494 D.
ἐὰν δ᾽ οὖν, διὰ τὸ εὖ πεφυκέναι καὶ τὸ
ξυγγενὲς τῶν λόγων, εἰς αἰσθάνηταί τέ
πῃ καὶ κάμπτηται καὶ ἕλκηται πρὸς
φιλοσοφίαν, τί οἰόμεθα δράσειν ἐκείνους
τοὺς ἡγουμένους ἀπολλύναι αὐτοῦ τὴν
χρείαν καὶ ἑταιρείαν; οὐ πᾶν μὲν ἔργον,
πᾶν δὲ ἔπος, λέγοντάς τε καὶ πράττοντας
καὶ περὶ αὐτὸν, ὅπως ἂν μὴ πεισθῇ, καὶ
περὶ τὸν πείθοντα, ὅπως ἂν μὴ οἷός τ᾽

ᾖ, καὶ ἰδίᾳ ἐπιβουλεύοντας καὶ δημοσίᾳ
εἰς ἀγῶνας καθίσταντας;
   [i] Plato, Republic, vi. p. 495 A-B.
   [k] Plato, Republic, vi. p. 495 D.
καθορῶντες γὰρ αὖ ἄλλοι ἀνθρωπίσκοι
κενὴν τὴν χώραν ταύτην γιγνομένην,
καλῶν δὲ ὀνομάτων καὶ προσχημάτων
μεστήν, ὥσπερ οἱ ἐκ τῶν εἰργμῶν εἰς
τὰ ἱερὰ ἀποδιδράσκοντες, ἄσμενοι καὶ
οὗτοι ἐκ τῶν τεχνῶν ἐκπηδῶσιν εἰς τὴν
φιλοσοφίαν.

put on new clothes and married his master's daughter.[1] Having intruded themselves into a career for which they are unfit, they cannot produce any grand or genuine philosophical thoughts, or any thing better than mere neat sophisms, pleasing to the ear.[m] Through them arises the discredit which is now attached to philosophers.

Amidst such general degradation of philosophy, some few and rare cases are left, in which the pre-eminent natures qualified for philosophy remain by some favourable accident uncorrupted. One of these is Theagês, who would have been long ago drawn away from philosophy to active politics, had he not been disqualified by bad health. The restraining Dæmon, peculiar to myself (says Sokrates) is another case.[n] Such an exceptional man, having once tasted the sweetness and happiness of philosophy, embraces it as an exclusive profession. He sees that the mass of society are wrongheaded—that scarce any one takes wholesome views on social matters—that he can find no partisans to aid him in upholding justice[o]—that while he will not take part in injustice, he is too weak to contend singlehanded against the violence of all, and would only become a victim to it without doing any good either to the city or to his friends—like a man who has fallen among wild beasts. On these grounds he stands aloof in his own separate pursuit, like one sheltering himself under a wall against a hurricane of wind and dust. Witnessing the injustice committed by all around, he is content if he can keep himself clear and pure from it during his life here, so as to die with satisfaction and good hopes.

He will perform no small achievement (remarks Adeimantus) if he keeps clear to the end.[p]

True (replies Sokrates)—yet nevertheless he can perform

Marginal note: Rare cases in which a highly qualified philosopher remains—Being at variance with public opinion, he can achieve nothing, and is lucky if he can obtain safety by silence.

---

[1] Plato, Republic, vi. p. 495 E.
[m] Plato, Republic, vi. p. 496 A.
[n] Plato, Republic, vi. p. 496 D.
[o] Plato, Republic, vi. p. 496 D.
καὶ τούτων δὴ τῶν ὀλίγων οἱ γενόμενοι καὶ γευσάμενοι ὡς ἡδὺ καὶ μακάριον τὸ κτῆμα, καὶ τῶν πολλῶν αὖ ἱκανῶς ἰδόντες τὴν μανίαν, καὶ ὅτι οὐδεὶς οὐδὲν ὑγιὲς ὡς ἔπος εἰπεῖν, περὶ τὰ τῶν πόλεων πράττει, οὐδ' ἔστι ξύμμαχος μεθ' ὅτου τις ἰὼν ἐπὶ τὴν τῶν δικαίων

βοήθειαν· σώζοιτ' ἄν, ἀλλ' ὥσπερ εἰς θηρία ἄνθρωπος ἐμπεσὼν, οὔτε ξυναδικεῖν ἐθέλων οὔτε ἱκανὸς ὢν εἰς πᾶσιν ἀγρίοις ἀντέχειν, πρίν τι τὴν πόλιν ἢ φίλους ὀνῆσαι προαπολόμενος ἀνωφελὴς αὑτῷ τε καὶ τοῖς ἄλλοις ἂν γένοιτο—ταῦτα πάντα λογισμῷ λαβὼν ἡσυχίαν ἔχων καὶ τὰ αὑτοῦ πράττων—ὁρῶν τοὺς ἄλλους πιμπλαμένους ἀνομίας, ἀγαπᾷ εἴ πη αὑτὸς καθαρὸς ἀδικίας, &c.

[p] Plato, Republic, vi. p. 497 A.

no great achievement, unless he meets with a community
The philo-
sopher must
have a com-
munity suit-
able to him,
and worthy
of him. suited to him.   Amidst such a community he will
himself rise to greatness, and will preserve the public
happiness as well as his own.   But there exists no
such community anywhere, at the present moment.
Not one of those now existing is worthy of a philosophical
disposition : q which accordingly becomes perverted, and de-
generates into a different type adapted to its actual abode,
like exotic seed transported to a foreign soil.   But this philosophical disposition were planted in a worthy community,
so as to be able to assert its own superior excellence, it would
then prove itself truly divine, leaving other dispositions and
pursuits behind as merely human.

You mean by a worthy community (observes Adeimantus),
It must be
such a com-
munity as
Sokrates
has been de-
scribing—
But means
must be
taken to keep
up a perpe-
tual succes-
sion of philo-
sophers as
Rulers. such an one as that of which you have been drawing the outline ?—I do (replies Sokrates) : with this
addition, already hinted but not explained, that
there must always be maintained in it a perpetual
supervising authority representing the scheme and
purpose of the primitive lawgiver.   This authority
must consist of philosophers : and the question now
arises—difficult but indispensable—how such philosophers are to be trained up and made efficient for the good
of the city.

The plan now pursued for imparting philosophy is bad.
Proper man-
ner of teach-
ing philoso-
phy—Not to
begin at a
very early
age. Some do not learn it at all: and even to those who
learn it best, the most difficult part (that which re-
lates to debate and discourse) is taught when they
are youths just emerging from boyhood, in the intervals of practical business and money-getting.r   After that
period, in their mature age, they abandon it altogether ;
they will scarcely so much as go to hear an occasional lecture
on the subject, without any effort of their own : accordingly
it has all died out within them, when they become mature in
years.   This manner of teaching philosophy ought to be re-

q Plato, Republic, vi. p. 497 B-C.

r Plato, Republic, vi. p. 498 A.
Νῦν μὲν οἱ καὶ ἁπτόμενοι μειράκια ὄντα
ἄρτι ἐκ παιδῶν τὸ μεταξὺ οἰκονομίας
καὶ χρηματισμοῦ πλησιάσαντες αὐτοῦ
τῷ χαλεπωτάτῳ ἀπαλλάττονται, οἱ φιλο-

σοφώτατοι ποιούμενοι — λέγω δὲ τὸ
χαλεπώτατον τὸ περὶ τοὺς λόγους—ἐν
δὲ τῷ ἔπειτα, ἐὰν καὶ ἄλλων τοῦτο
πραττόντων παρακαλούμενοι ἐθέλωσιν
ἀκροαταὶ γίγνεσθαι, μεγάλα ἡγοῦνται,
πάρεργον οἰόμενοι αὐτὸ δεῖν πράττειν.

versed.   In childhood and youth, instruction of an easy character and suitable to that age ought to be imparted; while
the greatest care is taken to improve and strengthen the body
during its period of growth, as a minister and instrument to
philosophy.   As age proceeds, and the mind advances to perfection, the mental exercises ought to become more difficult
and absorbing.   Lastly, when the age of bodily effort passes
away, philosophy ought to become the main and principal
pursuit.[s]

Most people will hear all this (continues Sokrates) with
mingled incredulity and repugnance.   We cannot
wonder that they do so: for they have had no experience of one or a few virtuously trained men ruling
in a city suitably prepared.[t]   Such combination of
philosophical rulers within a community adapted to
them, we must assume to be realised.[u]   Though difficult, it is noway impracticable: and even the multitude will
become reconciled to it, if you explain to them mildly what
sort of persons we mean by philosophers.   We do not mean
such persons as the multitude now call by that name; interlopers in the pursuit, violent in dispute and quarrel with
each other, and perpetually talking personal scandal.[x]   The
multitude cannot hate a philosophical temper such as we depict, when they once come to know it—a man who, indifferent to all party disputes, dwells in contemplation of the
Universal Forms, and tries to mould himself and others into
harmony with them.[y]   Such a philosopher will not pretend to
make regulations, either for a city or for an individual, until
he has purified it thoroughly.   He will then make regulations
framed upon the type of the eternal Forms—Justice, Temperance, Beauty—adapting them as well as he can to human
exigencies.[z]   The multitude, when they know what is really
meant, will become perfectly reconciled to it.   One single
prince, if he rises so as to become a philosopher, and has a
consenting community, will suffice to introduce the system
which we have been describing.   So fortunate an accident can

If the multi-tude could once see a real, perfect, philosopher, they could not fail to love him: but this never happens.

[s] Plato, Republic, vi. p. 498 C.
[t] Plato, Republic, vi. p. 498 E.
[u] Plato, Republic, vi. p. 499 B-C.

[x] Plato, Republic, vi. pp. 499-500.
[y] Plato, Republic, vi. p. 500 C-D.
[z] Plato, Republic, vi. p. 501.

undoubtedly occur but seldom: yet it is not impossible, and one day or other it will really occur.[a]

I must now (continues Sokrates) explain more in detail the studies and training through which these preservers and Rulers of our city, the complete philosophers, must be created. The most perfect among the Guardians, after having been tested by years of exercises and temptations of various kinds, will occupy that distinguished place. Very few will be found uniting those distinct and almost incompatible excellences which qualify them for the post. They must give proof of self-command against pleasures as well as pains, and of competence to deal with the highest studies.[b] But what are the highest studies? What is the supreme object of knowledge? It is the Idea of Good—the Form of Good: to the acquisition of which our philosophers must be trained to ascend, however laborious and difficult the process may be.[c] Neither justice nor any thing else can be useful or profitable, unless we superadd to them a knowledge of the Idea of Good: without this, it would profit us nothing to possess all other knowledge.[d]

Course of training in the Platonic city, for imparting philosophy to the Rulers. They must be taught to ascend to the Idea of Good. But what is Good?

Now as to the question, What Good is? there are great and long-standing disputes. Every mind pursues Good, and does every thing for the sake of it—yet without either knowledge or firm assurance what Good is, and consequently with perpetual failure in deriving benefit from other acquisitions.[e] Most people say that Pleasure is the Good: an ingenious few identify Intelligence with the Good. But neither of these explanations is satisfactory. For when a man says that Intelligence is the Good, our next question to him must be, What sort of Intelligence do you mean?—Intelligence of what? To this he must reply, Intelligence of the Good:

Ancient disputes upon this point, though every one yearns after Good. Some say Intelligence; some say Pleasure. Neither is satisfactory.

[a] Plato, Republic, vi. p. 502.
[b] Plato, Republic, vi. p. 503.
[c] Plato, Republic, vi. p. 504.
[d] Plato, Republic, vi. p. 505. ὅτι γε ἡ τοῦ ἀγαθοῦ ἰδέα μέγιστον μάθημα πολλάκις ἀκήκοας, ᾗ καὶ δίκαια καὶ τἄλλα προσχρησάμενα χρήσιμα καὶ ὠφέλιμα γίγνεται, &c.

[e] Plato, Republic, vi. p. 505 E. ὃ δὴ διώκει μὲν ἅπασα ψυχὴ καὶ τούτου ἕνεκα πάντα πράττει, ἀπομαντευομένη τί εἶναι, ἀποροῦσα δὲ καὶ οὐκ ἔχουσα λαβεῖν ἱκανῶς τί ποτ᾽ ἔστιν, οὐδὲ πίστει χρήσασθαι μονίμῳ, οἵᾳ καὶ περὶ τἄλλα, διὰ τοῦτο δὲ ἀποτυγχάνει καὶ τῶν ἄλλων εἴ τι ὄφελος ἦν, &c.

which is absurd, since it presumes us to know already what
the Good is—the very point which he is pretending to elucidate. Again, he who contends that Pleasure is the Good, is
forced in discussion to admit that there are such things as
bad pleasures : in other words, that pleasure is sometimes
good, sometimes bad.[f] From these doubts and disputes about
the real nature of Good, we shall require our philosophical
Guardians to have emancipated themselves, and to have
attained a clear vision. They will be unfit for their post if
they do not well know what the Good is, and in what manner
just or honourable things come to be good.[g] Our city will
have received its final consummation, when it is placed under
the superintendence of one who knows what the Good is.

But tell me, Sokrates (asks Adeimantus), what do *you* conceive the Good to be—Intelligence, or Pleasure, or
any other thing different from these ? I do not profess to know (replies Sokrates), and cannot tell you.
We must decline the problem, What Good itself is ?
as more arduous than our present impetus will enable us to reach.[h] Nevertheless I will partially
supply the deficiency by describing to you the offspring of
Good, very like its parent. You will recollect that we have
distinguished the Many from the One : the many just particulars, beautiful particulars, from the One Universal Idea or
Form, Just *per se*, Beautiful *per se*. The many particulars
are seen, but not conceived : the one Idea is conceived, but
not seen.[i] We see the many particulars through the auxiliary agency of light, which emanates from the Sun, the God
of the visible world. Our organ and sense of vision are not
the Sun itself, but they are akin to the Sun in a greater degree
than any of our other senses. They imbibe their peculiar
faculty from the influence of the Sun.[k] The Sun furnishes to

*Adeimantus
asks what
Sokrates
says. So-
krates says
that he can-
not answer :
but he com-
pares it by a
metaphor to
the Sun.*

---

[f] Plato, Republic, vi. p. 505 C.

[g] Plato, Republic, vi. p. 506 A.
δίκαιά τε καὶ καλὰ ἀγνοούμενα ὅπῃ ποτὲ
ἀγαθά ἐστιν, οὐ πολλοῦ τινος ἄξιον
φύλακα κεκτῆσθαι ἂν ἑαυτῶν τὸν τοῦτο
ἀγνοοῦντα.

[h] Plato, Republic, vi. p. 506 B-E.
Αὐτὸ μὲν τί ποτ' ἐστὶ τἀγαθὸν ἐάσωμεν
τὰ νῦν εἶναι· πλέον γάρ μοι φαίνεται ἢ
κατὰ τὴν παροῦσαν ὁρμὴν ἐφικέσθαι τοῦ

γε δοκοῦντος ἐμοὶ τὰ νῦν· ὅς δὲ ἔκγονός
τε τοῦ ἀγαθοῦ φαίνεται καὶ ὁμοιότατος
ἐκείνῳ, λέγειν ἐθέλω.

[i] Plato, Republic, vi. p. 507 B. Καὶ
τὰ μὲν (πολλὰ; δὴ ὁρᾶσθαί φαμεν, νοεῖσθαι δὲ οὔ· τὰς δ' αὖ ἰδέας νοεῖσθαι μὲν,
ὁρᾶσθαι δὲ οὔ.

[k] Plato, Republic, vi. p. 508 A. ἡ
ὄψις — ἡλιοειδέστατον τῶν περὶ τὰς
αἰσθήσεις ὀργάνων.

objects the power of being seen, and to our eyes the power of seeing: we can see no colour unless we turn to objects enlightened by its rays. Moreover it is the Sun which also brings about the generation, the growth, and the nourishment, of these objects, though it is itself out of the limits of generation: it generates and keeps them in existence, besides rendering them visible.[1] Now the Sun is the offspring and representative of the Idea of Good: what the Sun is in the sensible and visible world, the Idea of Good is in the intelligible or conceivable world.[m] As the Sun not only brings into being the objects of sense, but imparts to them the power of being seen—so the Idea of Good brings into being the objects of conception or cognition, imparts to them the power of being known, and to the mind the power of knowing them.[n] It is from the Idea of Good that all knowledge, all truth, and all real essence spring. Yet the Idea of Good is itself extra-essential; out of or beyond the limits of essence, and superior in beauty and dignity both to knowledge and to truth; which are not Good itself, but akin to Good, as vision is akin to the Sun.[o]

Here then we have two distinct regions or genera: one, the

The Idea of Good rules the ideal or intelligible world, as the Sun rules the sensible or visible world. conceivable or intelligible, ruled by the Idea of Good—the other, the visible, ruled by the Sun, which is the offspring of Good. Now let us subdivide each of these regions or genera into two portions. The two portions of the visible will be—first, real objects, such as animals, plants, works of art, &c.—second, the images or representations of these, such as shadows, reflexions in water or in mirrors, &c. The first of these two

---

[1] Plato, Republic, vi. p. 509 B. Τὸν ἥλιον τοῖς ὁρωμένοις οὐ μόνον τὴν τοῦ ὁρᾶσθαι δύναμιν παρέχειν φήσεις, ἀλλὰ καὶ τὴν γένεσιν καὶ αὔξην καὶ τροφήν, οὐ γένεσιν αὐτὸν ὄντα.

[m] Plato, Republic, vi. p. 508 C. Τοῦτον (τὸν ἥλιον) τὸν τοῦ ἀγαθοῦ ἔκγονον, ὃν τἀγαθὸν ἐγέννησεν ἀνάλογον ἑαυτῷ, ὅ, τι περ αὐτὸ ἐν τῷ νοητῷ τόπῳ πρός τε τὸν νοῦν καὶ τὰ νοούμενα, τοῦτο τοῦτον ἐν τῷ ὁρατῷ πρός τε ὄψιν καὶ τὰ ὁρώμενα.

[n] Plato, Republic, vi. p. 508 E. Τοῦτο τοίνυν τὸ τὴν ἀλήθειαν παρέχον τοῖς γιγνωσκομένοις καὶ τῷ γιγνώσκοντι

τὴν δύναμιν ἀποδιδὸν, τὴν τοῦ ἀγαθοῦ ἰδέαν φάθι εἶναι, αἰτίαν δ' ἐπιστήμης οὖσαν καὶ ἀληθείας ὡς γιγνωσκομένης, &c.

[o] Plato, Republic, vi. p. 509 B. Καὶ τοῖς γιγνωσκομένοις τοίνυν μὴ μόνον τὸ γιγνώσκεσθαι φαναι ὑπὸ τοῦ ἀγαθοῦ παρεῖναι, ἀλλὰ καὶ τὸ εἶναί τε καὶ τὴν οὐσίαν ὑπ' ἐκείνου αὐτοῖς προσεῖναι, οὐκ οὐσίας ὄντος τοῦ ἀγαθοῦ, ἀλλ' ἔτι ἐπέκεινα τῆς οὐσίας πρεσβείᾳ καὶ δυνάμει ὑπερέχοντος. Καὶ ὁ Γλαύκων μάλα γελοίως, Ἄπολλον, ἔφη, δαιμονίας ὑπερβολῆς! Σὺ γὰρ, ἦν δ' ἐγὼ, αἴτιος, ἀναγκάζων τὰ ἐμοὶ δοκοῦντα περὶ αὐτοῦ λέγειν.—also p. 509 A.

subdivisions will be greatly superior in clearness to the second: it will be distinguished from the second as truth is distinguished from not-truth.[p] Matter of knowledge is in the same relation to matter of opinion, as an original to its copy. Next, the conceivable or intelligible region must be subdivided into two portions, similarly related one to the other: the first of these portions will be analogous to the real objects of vision, the second to the images or representations of these objects: the first will thus be the Forms, Ideas, or Realities of Conception or Intellect—the second will be particular images or embodiments thereof.[q]

Now in regard to these two portions of the conceivable or intelligible region, two different procedures of the mind are employed: the pure Dialectic, and the Geometrical, procedure.   The Geometer or the Arithmetician begins with certain visible images, lines, figures, or numbered objects, of sense: he takes his departure from certain hypotheses or assumptions, such as given numbers, odd and even— given figures and angles, of three different sorts.[r]   He assumes these as data without rendering account of them, or allowing them to be called in question, as if they were self-evident to every one.   From these premises he deduces his conclusions, carrying them down by uncontradicted steps to the solution of the problem which he is examining.[s]   But though he has before his eyes the visible parallelogram inscribed on the sand, with its visible diagonal, and though all his propositions are affirmed respecting these—yet what he has really in his mind is something quite different—the Parallelogram *per se*, or the Form of a Parallelogram—the Form of a Diagonal, &c.   The

To the intelligible world there are applicable two distinct modes of procedure—the Geometrical —the Dialectic. Geometrical procedure assumes diagrams.

<hr/>

[p] Plato, Republic, vi. pp. 509-510. διῃρῆσθαι ἀληθείᾳ τε καὶ μὴ, ὡς τὸ δοξαστὸν πρὸς τὸ γνωστὸν, οὕτω τὸ ὁμοιωθὲν πρὸς τὸ ᾧ ὡμοιώθη.

[q] Plato, Republic, vi. p. 510 B.

[r] Plato, Republic, vi. p. 510 B. ᾗ τὸ μὲν αὐτοῦ (τμῆμα) τοῖς τότε τμηθεῖσιν ὡς εἰκόσι χρωμένη (this is farther illustrated by p. 511 A—εἰκόσι χρωμένην αὐτοῖς τοῖς ὑπὸ τῶν κάτω ἀπεικασθεῖσι) ψυχὴ ζητεῖν ἀναγκάζεται ἐξ ὑποθέσεων, οὐκ ἐπ' ἀρχὴν πορευομένη ἀλλ' ἐπὶ τελευτὴν, &c.

[s] Plato, Republic, vi. p. 510 C. οἱ περὶ τὰς γεωμετρίας τε καὶ λογισμοὺς καὶ τὰ τοιαῦτα πραγματευόμενοι, ὑποθέμενοι τό τε περιττὸν καὶ τὸ ἄρτιον καὶ τὰ σχήματα καὶ γωνιῶν τριττὰ εἴδη καὶ ἄλλα τούτων ἀδελφὰ καθ' ἑκάστην μέθοδον, ταῦτα μὲν ὡς εἰδότες, ποιησάμενοι ὑποθέσεις αὐτὰ, οὐδένα λόγον οὔτε αὑτοῖς οὔτε τοῖς ἄλλοις ἔτι ἀξιοῦσι περὶ αὐτῶν διδόναι, ὡς παντὶ φανερῶν· ἐκ τούτων δ' ἀρχόμενοι τὰ λοιπὰ ἤδη διεξιόντες τελευτῶσιν ὁμολογουμένως ἐπὶ τοῦτο, οὗ ἂν ἐπὶ σκέψιν ὁρμήσωσιν.

visible figure before him is used only as an image or representative of this self-existent Form; which last he can contemplate only in conception, though all his propositions are intended to apply to it.[t] He is unable to take his departure directly from this Form, as from a first principle: he is forced to assume the visible figure as his point of departure, and cannot ascend above it: he treats it as something privileged and self-evident.[u]

From the geometrical procedure thus described, we must

Dialectic procedure assumes nothing and departs from the highest Form, and steps gradually down to the lowest, without meddling with any thing except Forms.

now distinguish the other section—the pure Dialectic. Here the Intellect ascends to the absolute Form, and grasps it directly. Particular assumptions or hypotheses are indeed employed, but only as intervening stepping-stones, by which the Intellect is to ascend to the Form: they are afterwards to be discarded: they are not used here for first principles of reasoning, as they are by the Geometer.[x]
The Dialectician uses for his first principle the highest absolute Form; he descends from this to the next highest, and so lower and lower through the orderly gradation of Forms, until he comes to the end or lowest: never employing throughout the whole descent any hypothesis or assumption, nor any illustrative aid from sense. He contemplates and reasons upon the pure intelligible essence, directly and immediately: whereas the Geometer can only contemplate it indirectly and mediately, through the intervening aid of particular assumptions.[y]

[t] Plato, Republic, vi. p. 510 D-E. τοῖς δρωμένοις εἴδεσι προσχρῶνται, καὶ τοὺς λόγους περὶ αὐτῶν ποιοῦνται, οὐ περὶ τούτων διανοούμενοι, ἀλλ᾽ ἐκείνων περὶ οἷς ταῦτα ἔοικε, τοῦ τετραγώνου αὐτοῦ ἕνεκα τοὺς λόγους ποιούμενοι καὶ διαμέτρου αὐτῆς, ἀλλ᾽ οὐ ταύτης ἣν γράφουσι, καὶ τἄλλα οὕτως· αὐτὰ μὲν ταῦτα ἃ πλάττουσί τε καὶ γράφουσιν, ὧν καὶ σκιαὶ καὶ ἐν ὕδασιν εἰκόνες εἰσὶν, τούτοις μὲν ὡς εἰκόσιν αὖ χρώμενοι, ζητοῦντες δὲ αὐτὰ ἐκεῖνα ἰδεῖν, ἃ οὐκ ἂν ἄλλως ἴδοι τις ἢ τῇ διανοίᾳ.

[u] Plato, Republic, vi. p. 511 A. οὐκ ἐπ᾽ ἀρχὴν ἰοῦσαν, ὡς οὐ δυναμένην τῶν ὑποθέσεων ἀνωτέρω ἐκβαίνειν, εἰκόσι δὲ χρωμένην αὐτοῖς τοῖς ὑπὸ τῶν κάτω ἀπεικασθεῖσιν, καὶ ἐκείνοις πρὸς ἐκεῖνα ὡς ἐναργέσι δεδοξασμένοις τε καὶ τετι-

μημένοις.

[x] Plato, Republic, vi. p. 511 B. τὸ ἕτερον τμῆμα τοῦ νοητοῦ, οὗ αὐτὸς ὁ λόγος ἅπτεται τῇ τοῦ διαλέγεσθαι δυνάμει. τὰς ὑποθέσεις ποιούμενος οὐκ ἀρχὰς ἀλλὰ τῷ ὄντι ὑποθέσεις, οἷον ἐπιβάσεις τε καὶ ὁρμάς, ἵνα μέχρι τοῦ ἀνυποθέτου, ἐπὶ τὴν τοῦ παντὸς ἀρχὴν ἰὼν, ἁψάμενος αὐτῆς, πάλιν αὖ ἐχόμενος τῶν ἐκείνης ἐχομένων, οὕτως ἐπὶ τελευτὴν καταβαίνῃ αἰσθητῷ παντάπασιν οὐδενὶ προσχρώμενος, ἀλλ᾽ εἴδεσιν αὐτοῖς δι᾽ αὐτῶν εἰς αὐτὰ καὶ τελευτᾷ εἰς εἴδη.

[y] Plato, Republic, vi. p. 511 C. σαφέστερον εἶναι τὸ ὑπὸ τῆς τοῦ διαλέγεσθαι ἐπιστήμης τοῦ ὄντος τε καὶ νοητοῦ θεωρούμενον ἢ τὸ ὑπὸ τῶν τεχνῶν καλουμένων, αἷς αἱ ὑποθέσεις ἀρχαὶ, &c.

The distinction here indicated—between the two different sections of the Intelligible Region, and the two different sections of the Region of Sense—we shall mark (continues Sokrates) by appropriate terms. The Dialectician alone has Noûs or Intellect, direct or the highest cognition: he alone grasps and comprehends directly the pure intelligible essence or absolute Form . The Geometer does not ascend to this direct contemplation or intuition of the Form : he knows it only through the medium of particular assumptions, by indirect Cognition or Dianoia; which is a lower faculty than Noûs or Intellect, yet nevertheless higher than Opinion.

Two distinct grades of Cognition—Direct or Superior—Noûs—Indirect or Inferior—Dianoia.

As we assign two distinct grades of Cognition to the Intelligible Region, so we also assign two distinct grades of Opinion to the Region of Sense, and its two sections. To the first of these two sections, or to real objects of sense, we assign the highest grade of Opinion, viz.: Faith or Belief. To the second of the two, or to the images of real objects of sense, we assign the lower grade, viz.: Conjecture.

Two distinct grades of Opinion also in the Sensible World—Faith or Belief—Conjecture.

Here then are the four grades. Two grades of Cognition— 1. Noûs, or Direct Cognition. 2. Dianoia, or Indirect Cognition : both of them belonging to the Intelligible Region, and both of them higher than Opinion. Next follow the two grades of Opinion. 3. The higher grade, Faith or Belief. 4. The lower grade, Conjecture. Both the two last belong to the sensible world; the first to real objects, the last to images of those objects.[z]

Sokrates now proceeds to illustrate the contrast between the philosopher and the unphilosophical or ordinary man, by the memorable simile of the cave and its shadows. Mankind live in a cave, with its aperture directed towards the light of the sun; but they are so chained, that their backs are constantly turned towards this aperture, so that they cannot see the sun and sunlight. What they do see is by means of a fire which is always burning behind them. Between them and this fire there is a wall; along the wall are posted

Distinction between the philosopher and the unphilosophical public, illustrated by the simile of the Cave, and the captives imprisoned therein.

[z] Plato, Republic, p 511 D-E.

men who carry backwards and forwards representations or
images of all sorts of objects; so that the shadows of these
objects by the firelight are projected from behind these
chained men upon the ground in front of them, and pass to
and fro before their vision. All the experience which such
chained men acquire, consists in what they observe of the
appearance and disappearance, the transition, sequences, and
co-existences, of these shadows, which they mistake for truth
and realities, having no acquaintance with any other phenomena.[a] If now we suppose any one of them to be liberated
from his chains, turned round, and brought up to the light of
the sun and to real objects—his eyesight would be at first
altogether dazzled, confounded, and distressed. Distinguishing as yet nothing clearly, he would believe that the shadows
which he had seen in his former state were true and distinct
objects, and that the new mode of vision to which he had been
suddenly introduced was illusory and unprofitable. He would
require a long time to accustom him to daylight: at first his
eyes would bear nothing but shadows—next images in the
water—then the stars at night—lastly, the full brightness of
the Sun. He would learn that it was the Sun which not only
gave light, but was the cause of varying seasons, growth, and
all the productions of the visible world. And when his mind
had been thus opened, he would consider himself much to be
envied for the change, looking back with pity on his companions still in the cave.[b] He would think them all miserably
ignorant, as being conversant not with realities, but only with
the shadows which passed before their eyes. He would have
no esteem even for the chosen few in the cave, who were
honoured by their fellows as having best observed the co-
existences and sequences among these shadows, so as to predict
most exactly how the shadows would appear in future.[c] Moreover if, after having become fully accustomed to daylight and
the contemplation of realities, he were to descend again into

---

[a] Plato, Republic, vii. pp. 514-515.
[b] Plato, Republic, vii. pp. 515-516.
[c] Plato, Republic, vii. p. 516 C.
Τιμαί τε καὶ ἔπαινοι εἴ τινες αὐτοῖς ἦσαν
τότε παρ' ἀλλήλων καὶ γέρα τῷ ὀξύτατα
καθορῶντι τὰ παριόντα, καὶ μνημονεύ-

οντι μάλιστα ὅσα τε πρότερα αὐτῶν
εἰώθει καὶ ἅμα πορεύεσθαι, καὶ ἐκ τούτων
δὴ δυνατώτατα ἀπομαντευομένῳ τὸ μέλ-
λον ἥξειν, δοκεῖς ἂν αὐτὸν ἐπιθυμητικῶς
αὐτῶν ἔχειν καὶ ζηλοῦν τοὺς παρ' ἐκείνων τιμωμένους τε καὶ ἐνδυναστεύοντας;

the cave, his eyesight would be dim and confused in that comparative darkness; so that he would not well recognise the
shadows, and would get into disputes about them with his
companions.   They on their side would deride him as having
spoilt his sight as well as his judgment, and would point him
out as an example to deter others from emerging out of the
cave into daylight.[d]   Far from wishing to emerge themselves,
they would kill, if they could, any one who tried to unchain
them and assist them in escaping.[e]

By this simile (continues Sokrates) I intend to illustrate,
as far as I can, yet without speaking confidently,[f] Daylight of
the relations of the sensible world to the intelligible contrasted
world: the world of transitory shadows, dimly seen light and
and admitting only opinion, contrasted with that of the Cave.
unchangeable realities steadily contemplated and known, illuminated by the Idea of Good, which is itself visible in the
background, being the cause both of truth in speculation and
of rectitude in action.[g]   No wonder that the few who can
ascend into the intelligible region, amidst the clear contemplations of Truth and Justice *per se*, are averse to meddle
again with the miseries of human affairs, and to contend with
the opinions formed by ordinary men respecting the shadows
of Justice, the reality of which these ordinary men have never
seen.   There are two causes of temporary confused vision: one,
when a man moves out of darkness into light—the other
when he moves out of light into darkness.   It is from the
latter cause that the philosopher suffers when he redescends
into the obscure cave.[h]

The great purpose of education is to turn a man round from
his natural position at the bottom of this dark cave, Purpose of a
philosophical
where he sees nothing but shadows: to fix his eyes training, to
turn a man
in the other direction, and to induce him to ascend round from

---

[d] Plato, Republic, vii. p. 517 A.
ἆρ᾽ οὐ γέλωτ᾽ ἂν παράσχοι καὶ λέγοιτο
ἂν περὶ αὐτοῦ ὡς ἀναβὰς ἄνω διεφθαρ-
μένος ἥκει τὰ ὄμματα, καὶ ὅτι οὐκ ἄξιον
οὐδὲ πειρᾶσθαι ἄνω ἰέναι;

[e] Plato, Republic, vii. p. 517 A.
καὶ τὸν ἐπιχειροῦντα λύειν τε καὶ ἀνά-
γειν, εἴ πως ἐν ταῖς χερσὶ δύναιντο
λαβεῖν καὶ ἀποκτεῖναι, ἀποκτιννύναι ἂν ;

[f] Plato, Republic, vii. p. 517. τῆς

γε ἐμῆς ἐλπίδος, ἐπείπερ ταύτης ἐπιθυ-
μεῖς ἀκούειν· θεὸς δέ που οἶδεν
εἰ ἀληθὴς οὖσα τυγχάνει.

This tone of uncertainty in Plato
deserves notice. It forms a striking
contrast with the dogmatism of many
among his commentators.

[g] Plato, Republic, vii. p. 517 C.
[h] Plato, Republic, vii. pp. 517-518.

facing the bad light of the Cave to face the day-light of phi-losophy, and to see the eternal Forms. into clear daylight.   Education does not, as some suppose, either pour knowledge into an empty mind, or impart visual power to blind persons.   Men have good eyes, but these eyes are turned in the wrong direction.   The clever among them see sharply enough what is before them ; but they have nothing before them except shadows, and the sharper their vision the more mischief they do.[i]   What is required is, to turn them round and draw them up so as to face the real objects of daylight.   Their natural eyesight would then suffice to enable them to see these objects well.[k]   The task of our education must be, to turn round the men of superior natural aptitude, and to draw them up into the daylight of realities.   Next, when they shall have become sufficiently initiated in truth and philoso-phy, we must not allow them to bury themselves permanently in such studies—as they will themselves be but too eager to do. We must compel them to come down again into the cave and exercise ascendancy among their companions, for whose benefit their superior mental condition will thus become available.[l]

Coming as they do from the better light, they will, after Those who have emerged from the Cave into full daylight amidst eter-nal Forms, must be forced to come down again and undertake active duties —Their re-luctance to do this. a little temporary perplexity, be able to see the dim shadows better than those who have never looked at anything else.   Having contemplated the true and real Forms of the Just, Beautiful, Good— they will better appreciate the images of these Forms which come and go, pass by and repass in the cave.[m] They will indeed be very reluctant to undertake the duties or exercise the powers of government: their genuine delight is in philosophy ; and if left to them-selves, they would cultivate nothing else.   But such reluc-tance is in itself one proof that they are the fittest persons to govern.   If government be placed in the hands of men eager to possess it, there will be others eager to dispossess them, so that competition and factions will arise.   Those who come forward to govern, having no good of their own, and seeking to

---

[i] Plato, Republic, p. 519 A-B.

[k] Plato, Republic, p. 519 B.   ὧν εἰ ἀπαλλαγὲν περιεστρέφετο εἰς τἀληθῆ, καὶ ἐκεῖνα ἂν τὸ αὐτὸ τοῦτο τῶν αὐτῶν

ἀνθρώπων ὀξύτατα ἑώρα, ὥσπερ καὶ ἐφ' ἃ νῦν τέτραπται.

[l] Plato, Republic, vii. pp. 519-520.

[m] Plato, Republic, vii. p. 520 C.

extract their own good from the exercise of power, are both unworthy of trust, and sure to be resisted by opponents of the like disposition. The philosopher alone has his own good in himself. He enjoys a life better than that of a ruler; which life he is compelled to forego when he accepts power and becomes a ruler.[n]

The main purpose of education, I have said (continues Sokrates) is, to turn round the faces of the superior men, and to invite them upwards from darkness to light—from the region of perishable shadows to that of imperishable realities.[o] Now what cognitions, calculated to aid such a purpose, can we find to teach?[p] Gymnastic, music, the vulgar arts, are all useful to teach, but they do not tend to that which we are here seeking. Arithmetic does so to a certain extent, if properly taught—which at present it is not.[q] It furnishes a stimulus to awaken the dormant intellectual and reflective capacity. Among the variety of sensible phenomena, there are some in which the senses yield a clear and satisfactory judgment, leaving no demand in the mind for any thing beyond: there are others in which the senses land us in apparent equivocation, puzzle, and contradiction—so that the mind is stung by this apparent perplexity, and instigated to find a solution by some intellectual effort.[r] Thus, if we see or feel the fingers of our hand, they always appear to the sense, fingers: in whatever order or manner they may be looked at, there is no contradiction or discrepancy in the judgment of sense. But if we see or feel them as great or small, thick or thin, hard or soft, &c., they then appear differently according as they are seen or felt in different order or under different circumstances. The same object which now appears great, will at another time appear small: it will seem to the sense hard or soft, light or heavy, according as it is seen under different comparisons and relations.[s] Here then, sense is involved in an apparent contradiction, declaring the same object to be

Marginal note: Studies serving as introduction to philosophy—Arithmetic, its awakening power—shock to the mind by felt contradiction.

[n] Plato, Republic, vii. pp. 520-521.
[o] Plato, Republic, vii. p. 521 C. ψυχῆς περιαγωγὴ, ἐκ νυκτερινῆς τινὸς ἡμέρας εἰς ἀληθινὴν τοῦ ὄντος ἰούσης ἐπάνοδον, ἣν δὴ φιλοσοφίαν ἀληθῆ φήσομεν εἶναι.

[p] Plato, Republic, vii. p. 521 C. Τί ἂν οὖν εἴη μάθημα ψυχῆς ὁλκὸν ἀπὸ τοῦ γιγνομένου ἐπὶ τὸ ὄν;
[q] Plato, Republic, vii. pp. 522-523 A.
[r] Plato, Republic, vii. p. 523 C.
[s] Plato, Republic, pp. 523-524.

both hard and soft, great and small, light and heavy, &c. The mind, painfully confounded by such a contradiction, is obliged to invoke intellectual reflection to clear it up. Great and small are presented by the sense as inhering in the same object. Are they one thing, or two separate things? Intellectual reflection informs us that they are two: enabling us to conceive separately two things, which to our sense appeared confounded together. Intellectual (or abstract) conception is thus developed in our mind, as distinguished from sense, and as a refuge from the confusion and difficulties of sense, which furnish the stimulus whereby it is awakened.[t]

Now arithmetic, besides its practical usefulness for arrange-

Perplexity arising from the One and Many, stimulates the mind to an intellectual effort for clearing it up.

ments of war, includes difficulties and furnishes a stimulus of this nature. We see the same thing both as One and as infinite in multitude: as definite and indefinite in number.[u] We can emerge from these difficulties only by intellectual and abstract reflection. It is for this purpose, and not for purposes of traffic, that our intended philosophers must learn Arithmetic. Their minds must be raised from the confusion of the sensible world to the clear daylight of the intelligible.[x] In teaching Arithmetic, the master sets before his pupils numbers in the concrete, that is, embodied in visible and tangible objects—so many balls or pebbles.[y] Each of these balls he enumerates as One, though they be unequal in magnitude, and whatever be the magnitude of each. If you remark that the balls are unequal—and that each of them is Many as well as One, being divisible into as many parts as you please—he will laugh at the objection as irrelevant. He will tell you that the units to which his numeration refers are each *Unum per se*, indivisible and without parts; and all equal among themselves without the least shade of difference. He will add that such units cannot be exhibited to the senses, but can only be conceived by the intellect; that the balls before you are not such units in reality, but serve to suggest

---

[t] Plato, Republic, vii. p. 524 B-C.

[u] Plato, Republic, vii. p. 525 A. ἅμα γὰρ ταὐτὸν ὡς ἕν τε ὁρῶμεν καὶ ὡς ἄπειρα τὸ πλῆθος.

[x] Plato, Republic, vii. p. 525 B.

διὰ τὸ τῆς οὐσίας ἁπτέον εἶναι γενέσεως ἐξαναδύντι, &c.

[y] Plato, Republic, vii. p. 525 C. ὁρατὰ ἢ ἁπτὰ σώματα ἔχοντας ἀριθμοὺς, &c.

and facilitate the effort of abstract conception.[z] In this manner arithmetical teaching conducts us to numbers in the abstract—to the real, intelligible, indivisible unit—the *Unum per se.*

Geometrical teaching conducts the mind to the same order of contemplations; leading it away from variable particulars to unchangeable universal Essence. Some persons extol Geometry chiefly on the ground of its usefulness in applications to practice. But this is a mistake: its real value is in conducing to knowledge, and to elevated contemplations of the mind. It does, however, like Arithmetic, yield useful results in practice: and both of them are farther valuable as auxiliaries to other studies.[a]

Geometry conducts the mind towards Universal Ens.

After Geometry—the measurement of lines and superficial areas — the proper immediate sequel is Stereometry, the measurement of solids. But this latter is nowhere properly honoured and cultivated; though from its intrinsic excellence, it forces its way partially even against public neglect and discouragement.[b] Most persons omit it, and treat Astronomy as if it were the immediate sequel to Geometry: which is a mistake, for Astronomy relates to solid bodies in a state of rotatory movement, and ought to be preceded by the treatment of solid bodies generally.[c] Assuming Stereometry, therefore, as if it existed, we proceed to Astronomy.

Astronomy —how useful —not useful as now taught— must be studied by ideal figures, not by observation.

Certainly (remarks Glaukon) Astronomy, besides its usefulness in regard to the calendar and the seasons, must be admitted by every one to carry the mind upwards, to the contemplation of things not below but on high. I do not admit this at all (replies Sokrates), as Astronomy is now cultivated: at least in my sense of the words, *looking upwards, and looking downwards.* If a man lies on his back, contemplating the ornaments of the ceiling, he may carry his eyes upward, but not his mind.[d] To look upwards, as I understand it, is to

---

[z] Plato, Republic, vii. p. 526 A. εἴ τις ἔροιτο αὐτούς, Ὦ θαυμάσιοι, περὶ ποίων ἀριθμῶν διαλέγεσθε, ἐν οἷς τὸ ἓν οἷον ὑμεῖς ἀξιοῦτέ ἐστιν, ἴσον τε ἕκαστον πᾶν παντὶ καὶ οὐδὲ σμικρὸν διάφερον, μόριόν τε ἔχον ἐν ἑαυτῷ οὐδέν; τί ἂν οἴει αὐτοὺς ἀποκρίνασθαι; Τοῦτο ἔγωγε, ὅτι περὶ τούτων λέγουσιν ὧν διανοηθῆναι μόνον ἐγχωρεῖ, ἄλλως δ' οὐδαμῶς μεταχειρίζεσθαι δυνατόν.

[a] Plato, Republic, vii. pp. 526-527.
[b] Plato, Republic, vii. p. 528 A-C.
[c] Plato, Republic, vii. p. 528 B. ἐν περιφορᾷ ὃν ἤδη στερεὸν λαβόντες, πρὶν αὐτὸ καθ' αὑτὸ λαβεῖν. P. 528 E.
[d] Plato, Republic, vii. p. 529 B.

carry the mind away from the contemplation of sensible things, whereof no science is attainable—to the contemplation of intelligible things, entities invisible and unchangeable, which alone are the objects of science. Observation of the stars, such as astronomers now teach, does not fulfil any such condition. The heavenly bodies are the most beautiful of all visible bodies and the most regular of all visible movements, approximating most nearly, though still with a long interval of inferiority, to the ideal figures and movements of genuine and self-existent Forms—quickness, slowness, number, figure, &c., as they are in themselves, not visible to the eye, but conceivable only by reason and intellect.[e] The movements of the heavenly bodies are exemplifications, approaching nearest to the perfection of these ideal movements, but still falling greatly short of them. They are like visible circles or triangles drawn by some very exact artist ; which, however beautiful as works of art, are far from answering to the conditions of the idea and its definition, and from exhibiting exact equality and proportion.[f] So about the movements of the sun and stars : they are comparatively regular, but they are yet bodily and visible, never attaining the perfect sameness and unchangeableness of the intelligible world and its forms. We cannot learn truth by observation of phenomena constantly fluctuating and varying. We must study astronomy, as we do geometry, not by observation, but by mathematical theorems and hypotheses : which is a far more arduous task than astronomy as taught at present. Only in this way can it be made available to improve and strengthen the intellectual organ of the mind.[g]

In like manner (continues Sokrates), Acoustics or Harmonics must be studied, not by the ear, listening to and comparing various sounds, but by the contemplative intellect, applying arithmetical relations and theories.[h]

After going through all these different studies, the student will have his mind elevated so as to perceive

Acoustics, in like manner—The student will be thus conducted to the highest of all studies—Dialectic; and to the region of pure intelligible Forms.

---

e Plato, Republic, vii. p. 529 D.
f Plato, Republic, vii. pp. 529-530.
g Plato, Republic, vii. p. 530 B.
Προβλήμασιν ἄρα χρώμενοι ὥσπερ γεω-

μετρίαν, οὕτω καὶ ἀστρονομίαν μέτιμεν·
τὰ δ᾽ ἐν τῷ οὐρανῷ ἐάσομεν, &c.
h Plato, Republic, vii. p. 531.

the affinity of method[1] and principle which pervades them all. In this state he will be prepared for entering on Dialectic, which is the final consummation of his intellectual career. He will then have ascended from the cave into daylight. He will have learnt to see real objects, and ultimately the Sun itself, instead of the dim and transitory shadows below. He will become qualified to grasp the pure Intelligible Form with his pure Intellect alone, without either aid or disturbance from sense. He will acquire that dialectical discursive power which deals exclusively with these Intelligible Forms, carrying on ratiocination by means of them only, with no reference to sensible objects. He will attain at length the last goal of the Dialectician—the contemplation of Bonum *per se* (the highest perfection and elevation of the Intelligible) [k] with Intellect *per se* in its full purity : the best part of his mind will have been raised to the contemplation and knowledge of the best and purest entity.[l]

I know not whether I ought to admit your doctrine, Sokrates (observes Glaukon). There are difficulties both in admitting and denying it. However, let us assume it for the present. Your next step must be to tell us what is the characteristic function of this Dialectic power—what are its different varieties and ways of proceeding ? I would willingly do so (replies Sokrates), but you would not be able to follow me.[m] I would lay before you not merely an image of the truth, but the very truth itself ; as it appears to me at least, whether I am correct or not—for I ought not to be sure of my own correctness.

But I am sure that the dialectic power is something of the nature which I have described. It is the only force which can make plain the full truth to students who have gone through the preliminary studies that we have described. It is the only study which investigates rationally real forms and essences[n]—what

---

[1] Plato, Republic, vii. p. 531 D.

[k] Plato, Republic, vii. p. 532 A. οὕτω καὶ ὅταν τις τῷ διαλέγεσθαι ἐπιχειρῇ, ἄνευ πασῶν τῶν αἰσθήσεων διὰ τοῦ λόγου ἐπ' αὐτὸ ὃ ἔστιν ἕκαστον ὁρμᾷ, καὶ μὴ ἀποστῇ πρὶν ἂν αὐτὸ ὃ

ἔστιν ἀγαθὸν αὐτῇ τῇ νοήσει λάβῃ, ἐπ' αὐτῷ γίγνεται τῷ τοῦ νοητοῦ τέλει, &c.

[l] Plato, Republic, vii. p. 532 D.

[m] Plato, Republic, vii. p. 533 A.

[n] Plato, Republic, vii. p. 533 B. ὡς αὐτοῦ γε ἑκάστου πέρι, ὃ ἔστιν

pure Forms, and espe- cially to that of the highest Form—*Good.* each thing is, truly in itself. Other branches of study are directed either towards the opinions and preferences of men—or towards generation and combination of particular results—or towards upholding of combinations already produced or naturally springing up: while even as to geometry and the other kindred studies, we have seen that as to real essence, they have nothing better than dreams [o]—and that they cannot see it as it is, so long as they take for their principle or point of departure certain assumptions or hypotheses of which they can render no account. The principle being thus unknown, and the conclusion as well as the intermediate items being spun together out of that unknown, how can such a convention deserve the name of Science? [p] Pursuant to custom, indeed, we call these by the name of Sciences. But they deserve no higher title than that of Intellectual Cognitions, lower than Science, yet higher than mere Opinion. It is the Dialectician alone who discards all assumptions, ascending at once to real essence as his principle and point of departure: [q] defining, and discriminating by appropriate words, each variety of real essence—rendering account of it to others—and carrying it safely through the cross-examining process of question and answer. [r] Whoever cannot discriminate in this way the Idea or Form of Good from every thing else, will have no proper cognition of Good itself, but only, at best, opinions respecting the various shadows of Good. Dialectic—the capacity of discriminating real Forms and maintaining them in cross-examining dialogue—is thus the coping-stone, completion, or consummation, of all the other sciences. [s]

The Synoptic view peculiar to the Dialec-tician.

Scale and duration of various

The preliminary sciences must be imparted to our Guardians during the earlier years of life, together with such bodily and mental training as may test their energy and perseverance of character. [t] After the age of twenty, those who have distinguished themselves in

---

ἕκαστον, οὐκ ἄλλη τις ἐπιχειρεῖ μέθοδος ὁδῷ περὶ παντὸς λαμβάνειν, &c.

[o] Plato, Republic, vii. p. 533 C. ὡς ὀνειρώττουσι μὲν περὶ τὸ ὂν, ὕπαρ δὲ ἀδύνατον αὐτὰς ἰδεῖν, ἕως ἂν ὑποθέσεσι χρώμεναι ταύτας ἀκινήτους ἐῶσιν, &c.

[p] Plato, Republic, vii. p. 533 D.

[q] Plato, Republic, vii. p. 533 E.

[r] Plato, Republic, vii. p. 534 B. ἢ καὶ διαλεκτικὸν καλεῖς τὸν λόγον ἑκάστου λαμβάνοντα τῆς οὐσίας;

[s] Plato, Republic, vii. p. 534 C-E. ὥσπερ θριγκὸς τοῖς μαθήμασιν ἡ διαλεκτικὴ ἡμῖν ἐπάνω κεῖσθαι, &c.

[t] Plato, Republic, vii. pp. 535-536 D.

the juvenile studies and gymnastics, must be placed studies for the Guardians, from youth upwards. in a select class of honour above the rest, and must be initiated in a synoptic view of the affinity pervading all the separate cognitions which have been imparted to them. They must also be introduced to the view of Real Essence and its nature. This is the test of aptitude for Dialectics : it is the synoptic view only, which constitutes the Dialectician.[u]

In these new studies they will continue until thirty years of age : after which a farther selection must be made, of those who have most distinguished themselves. The men selected will be enrolled in a class of yet higher honour, and will be tested by dialectic cross-examination : so that we may discover who among them are competent to apprehend true, pure, and real, Essence, renouncing all visual and sensible perceptions.[x] It is important that such Dialectic exercises should be deferred until this advanced age—and not imparted, as they are among us at present, to immature youths : who abuse the license of interrogation, find all their homegrown opinions uncertain, and end by losing all positive convictions.[y] Our students will remain under such dialectic tuition for five years, until they are thirty-five years of age : after which they must be brought again down into the cave, and constrained to acquire practical experience by undertaking military and administrative functions. In such employments they will spend fifteen years; during which they will undergo still farther scrutiny, to ascertain whether they can act up to their previous training, in spite of all provocations and temptations.[z] Those who well sustain all these trials will become, at fifty years of age, the finished Elders or Chiefs of the Republic. They will pass their remaining years partly in philosophical contemplations, partly in application of philosophy to the regulation of the city. It is these Elders whose mental eye will have been so trained as to contemplate the Real Essence of Good, and to copy it as an archetype in all their ordinances and administration. They will be the Moderators of the city : but they

---

[u] Plato, Republic, vii. pp. 536-537 C.
καὶ μεγίστη πεῖρα διαλεκτικῆς φύσεως καὶ μή· ὁ μὲν γὰρ συνοπτικὸς διαλεκτικὸς, ὁ δὲ μὴ, οὔ.

[x] Plato, Republic, p. 537 D.
[y] Plato, Republic, vii. pp. 538-539.
[z] Plato, Republic, vii. p. 539 D-E.

will perform this function as a matter of duty and necessity—
not being at all ambitious of it as a matter of honour.[a]

What has here been said about the male guardians and
philosophers must be understood to apply equally to
the female. We recognise no difference in this respect between the two sexes. Those females who have
gone through the same education and have shown
themselves capable of enduring the same trials as
males, will participate, after fifty years of age, in the like philosophical contemplations, and in superintendance of the city.[b]

All these studies, and this education, are common to females as well as males.

I have thus shown (Sokrates pursues) how the fundamental
postulate for our city may be brought about.—That
philosophers, a single man or a few, shall become
possessed of supreme rule; being sufficiently exalted
in character to despise the vulgar gratifications of
ambition, and to carry out systematically the dictates of rectitude and justice. The postulate is indeed hard
to be realised—yet not impossible.[c] Such philosophical rulers,
as a means for first introducing their system into a new city,
will send all the inhabitants above ten years old away into
the country, reserving only the children, whom they will train
up in their own peculiar manners and principles. In this way
the city, according to our scheme, will be first formed: when
formed, it will itself be happy, and will confer inestimable
benefit on the nation to which it belongs.[d]

First forma- tion of the Platonic city —how brought about: diffi- cult, but not impossible.

Plato thus assumes his city, and the individual man forming a parallel to his city, to be perfectly well constituted.
Reason, the higher element, exercises steady controul: the
lower elements, Energy and Appetite, both acquiesce con-
tentedly in her right to controul, and obey her orders—the
former constantly and forwardly—the latter sometimes
requiring constraint by the strength of the former.

But even under the best possible administration, the city,
though it will last long, will not last for ever.
Eternal continuance belongs only to Ens; every
thing generated must one day or other be destroyed.[e]
The fatal period will at length arrive, when the

The city thus formed will last long, but not for ever. After a cer- tain time, it will begin to

[a] Plato, Republic, vii. pp. 539-540.
[b] Plato, Republic, vii. p. 540 C.
[c] Plato, Republic, vii. p. 540 E.
[d] Plato, Republic, vii. p. 541 A.
[e] Plato, Republic, viii. p. 546 A.
γενομένῳ παντὶ φθορά ἐστιν, &c.

breed of Guardians will degenerate. A series of ^{degenerate.} changes for the worse will then commence, whereby the Platonic city will pass successively into timocracy, oligarchy, democracy, despotism. The first change will be, that the love of individual wealth and landed property will get possession of the Guardians: who, having in themselves the force of the city, will divide the territory among themselves, and reduce the other citizens to dependance and slavery.[f] They will at the same time retain a part of their former mental training. They will continue their warlike habits and drill: they will be ashamed of their wealth, and will enjoy it only in secret: they will repudiate money-getting occupations as disgraceful. They will devote themselves to the contests of war and political ambition—the rational soul becoming subordinate to the energetic and courageous.[g] The system which thus obtains footing will be analogous to the Spartan and Kretan, which have many admirers.[h] The change in individual character will correspond to this change in the city. Reason partially losing its ascendancy, while energy and appetite both gain ground—an intermediate character is formed in which energy or courage predominates. We have the haughty, domineering, contentious, man.[i]

Out of this timocracy, or timarchy, the city will next pass into an oligarchy, or government of wealth. The rich will here govern, to the exclusion of the poor. Reason, in the timocracy, was under the dominion of energy or courage: in the oligarchy, it will be under the dominion of appetite. The love of wealth will become predominant, instead of the love of force and aggrandisement. Now the love of wealth is distinctly opposed to the love of virtue: virtue and wealth are like weights in opposite scales.[k] The oligarchical city will lose all its unity, and will consist of a few rich with a multitude of dis-

Marginal notes: 1. Timocracy and the timocratical individual. 2. Oligarchy, and the oligarchical individual.

---

[f] Plato, Republic, viii. p. 547.

[g] Plato, Republic, viii. pp. 547-548 D. διαφανέστατον δ' ἐν αὐτῇ ἐστιν ἕν τι μόνον ὑπὸ τοῦ θυμοειδοῦς κρατοῦν-τος—φιλονείκιαι καὶ φιλοτίμιαι.

[h] Plato, Republic, viii. p. 544 C.

[i] Plato, Republic, viii. pp. 549-550.

[k] Plato, Republic, viii. pp. 550 D-E-

551 A. προϊόντες εἰς τὸ πρόσθεν τοῦ χρηματίζεσθαι, ὅσῳ ἂν τοῦτο τιμιώτερον ἡγῶνται, τοσούτῳ ἀρετὴν ἀτιμοτέραν. ἢ οὐχ οὕτω πλούτου ἀρετὴ διέστηκεν, ὥσπερ ἐν πλάστιγγι ζυγοῦ κειμένου ἑκατέρου, ἀεὶ τοὐναντίον ῥέποντε; also p. 555 D.

contented poor ready to rise against them.[1]   The character
of the individual citizen will undergo a modification similar
to that of the collective city.   He will be under the rule of
appetite : his reason will be only invoked as the servant
of appetite, to teach him how he may best enrich himself.[m]
He will be frugal,—will abstain from all unnecessary expenditure, even for generous and liberal purposes—and will keep
up a fair show of honesty, from the fear of losing what he has
already got.[n]

The oligarchical city will presently be transformed into a

3. Demo-
cracy, and
the democra-
tical indivi-
dual.
democracy, mainly through the abuse and exaggeration of its own ruling impulse—the love of wealth.
The rulers, anxious to enrich themselves, rather
encourage than check the extravagance of young spendthrifts,
to whom they lend money at high interest, or whose property
they buy on advantageous terms.   In this manner there
arises a class of energetic men, with ruined fortunes and
habits of indulgence.   Such are the adventurers who put
themselves at the head of the discontented poor, and overthrow the oligarchy.[o]   The ruling few being expelled or put
down, a democracy is established with equal franchise, and
generally with officers chosen by lot.[p]

The characteristic of the democracy is equal freedom
and open speech to all, with liberty to each man to shape
his own life as he chooses.   Hence there arises a great
diversity of individual taste and character.   Uniformity of
pursuit or conduct is scarcely enforced : there is little restraint
upon any one.   A man offers himself for office whenever he
chooses and not unless he chooses.   He is at war or at peace,
not by obedience to any public authority, but according to
his own individual preference.   If he be even condemned by
a court of justice, he remains in the city careless of the
sentence, which is never enforced against him.   This democracy is an equal, agreeable, diversified, society, with little or
no government : equal in regard to all—to the good, bad, and
indifferent.[q]

So too the democratical individual.   The son of one among

---

[1] Plato, Republic, viii. p. 552.
[m] Plato, Republic, viii. p. 553.
[n] Plato, Republic, viii. p. 554.

[o] Plato, Republic, viii. pp. 555-556.
[p] Plato, Republic, viii. p. 557 A.
[q] Plato, Republic, viii. pp. 557-558.

these frugal and money-getting oligarchs, departing from the habits and disregarding the advice of his father, contracts a taste for expensive and varied indulgences.   He loses sight of the distinction between what is necessary, and what is not necessary, in respect to desires and pleasures.   If he be of a quiet temperament, not quite out of the reach of advice, he keeps clear of ruinous excess in any one direction; but he gives himself up to a great diversity of successive occupations and amusements, passing from one to the other without discrimination of good from bad, necessary from unnecessary.[r]   His life and character thus becomes an agreeable, unconstrained, changeful, comprehensive, miscellany, like the society to which he belongs.[s]

Democracy, like oligarchy, becomes ultimately subverted by an abuse of its own characteristic principle.   Freedom is gradually pushed into extravagance and excess, while all other considerations are neglected.   No obedience is practised: no authority is recognised.   The son feels himself equal to his father, the disciple to his teacher, the metic to the citizen, the wife to her husband, the slave to his master.   Nay, even horses, asses, and dogs, go free about, so that they run against you in the road, if you do not make way for them.[t]   The laws are not obeyed: every man is his own master.

4. "Passage from demo-cracy to des-potism. Cha-racter of the despotic city.

The subversion of such a democracy arises from the men who rise to be popular leaders in it: violent, ambitious, extravagant, men, who gain the favour of the people by distributing among them confiscations from the property of the rich.   The rich, resisting these injustices, become enemies to the constitution: the people, in order to put them down, range themselves under the banners of the most energetic popular leader, who takes advantage of such a position to render himself a despot.[u]   He begins his rule by some acceptable measures, such as abolition of debts, and assignment of

---

[r] Plato, Republic, viii. pp. 560-561 B.   εἰς ἴσον δή τι καταστήσας τὰς ἡδονὰς διάγει, τῇ παραπιπτούσῃ ἀεὶ ὥσπερ λαχούσῃ τὴν ἑαυτοῦ ἀρχὴν παραδιδοὺς, ἕως ἂν πληρωθῇ, καὶ αὖθις ἄλλῃ, οὐδεμίαν ἀτιμάζων, ἀλλ' ἐξ ἴσου τρέφων.

[s] Plato, Republic, viii. p. 561 D-E.

παντοδαπόν τε καὶ πλείστων ἠθῶν μεστὸν, καὶ τὸν καλόν τε καὶ ποίκιλον, ὥσπερ ἐκείνην τὴν πόλιν, τοῦτον τὸν ἄνδρα εἶναι.

[t] Plato, Republic, viii. pp. 562-563 C.

[u] Plato, Republic, viii. pp. 565-566.

lands to the poorer citizens, until he has expelled or destroyed the parties opposed to him. He seeks pretences for foreign war, in order that the people may stand in need of a leader, and may be kept poor by the contributions necessary to sustain war. But presently he finds, or suspects, dissatisfaction among the more liberal spirits. He kills or banishes them as enemies: and to ensure the continuance of his rule, he is under the necessity of dispatching in like manner every citizen prominent either for magnanimity, intelligence, or wealth.[x] Becoming thus odious to all the better citizens, he is obliged to seek support by enlisting a guard of mercenary foreigners and manumitted slaves. He cannot pay his guards, without plundering the temples, extorting perpetual contributions from the people, and grinding them down by severe oppression and suffering.[y] Such is the government of the despot, which Euripides and other poets employ their genius in extolling.[z]

We have now to describe the despotic individual, the pa-
Despotic individual corresponding to that city. rallel of the despotised city. As the democratic individual arises from the son of an oligarchical citizen departing from the frugality of his father and contracting habits of costly indulgence : so the son of this democrat will contract desires still more immoderate and extravagant than his father, and will thus be put into training for the despotic character. He becomes intoxicated by insane appetites, which serve as seconds and auxiliaries to one despotic passion or mania, swaying his own soul.[a] To gratify such desires, he spends all his possessions, and then begins to borrow money wherever he can. That resource being exhausted, he procures additional funds by fraud or extortion ; he cheats and ruins his father and mother; he resorts to plunder and violence. If such men are only a small minority, amidst citizens of better character, they live by committing crimes on the smaller scale. But if they are more numerous, they set up as despot the most unprincipled and energetic of their number, and become his agents for the enslavement

---

[x] Plato, Republic, viii. p 567.
[y] Plato, Republic, viii. pp. 568-569.
[z] Plato, Republic, viii. p. 568 B.
[a] Plato, Republic, ix. pp. 572-573 D.

Ἔρως τύραννος ἔνδον οἰκῶν διακυβερνᾷ τὰ τῆς ψυχῆς ἅπαντα (pp. 574-575) τυραννευθεὶς ὑπὸ Ἔρωτος—Ἔρως μόναρχος, &c.

of their fellow-citizens.[b] The despotic man passes his life always in the company of masters, or instruments, or flatterers : he knows neither freedom nor true friendship—nothing but the relation of master and slave. The despot is the worst and most unjust of mankind : the longer he continues despot, the worse he becomes.[c]

We have thus gone through the four successive depravations which our perfect city will undergo—timocracy, oligarchy, democracy, despotism. Step by step we have passed from the best to the worst—from one extreme to the other. As is the city, so is the individual citizen—good or bad : the despotic city is like the despotic individual,—and so about the rest. Now it remains to decide whether in each case happiness and misery is proportioned to good and evil : whether the best is the happiest, the worst the most miserable,—and so proportionally about the intermediate.[d] On this point there is much difference of opinion.[e]

The city has thus passed, by four stages, from best to worst. Question— How are Happiness and Misery apportioned among them?

If we look at the condition of the despotised city, it plainly exhibits the extreme of misery ; while our model city presents the extreme of happiness. Every one in the despotised city is miserable, according to universal admission, except the despot himself with his immediate favourites and guards. To be sure, in the eyes of superficial observers, the despot with these few favourites will appear perfectly happy and enviable. But if we penetrate beyond this false exterior show, and follow him into his interior, we shall find him too not less miserable than those over whom he tyrannises.[f]

Misery of the despotised city.

What is true of the despotised city, is true also of the despotising individual.[g] The best parts of his mind are under subjection to the worst : the rational mind is trampled down by the appetitive mind, with its insane and unsatisfied cravings. He is full of perpetual perturbation, anxiety, and fear; grief when he fails, repentance

Supreme Misery of the despotising individual.

---

[b] Plato, Republic, ix. pp. 574-575.
[c] Plato, Republic, ix. pp. 575-576.
[d] Plato, Republic, ix. p. 576 D.
[e] Plato, Republic, ix. p. 576 C. τοῖς δὲ πολλοῖς πολλὰ καὶ δοκεῖ.
[f] Plato, Republic, ix. p. 577 A.

[g] Plato, Republic, ix. p. 577 C. τὴν ὁμοιότητα ἀναμιμνησκόμενος τῆς τε πόλεως καὶ τοῦ ἀνδρὸς—εἰ οὖν ὅμοιος ἀνηρ τῇ πόλει, οὐ καὶ ἐν ἐκείνῳ ἀνάγκη τὴν αὐτὴν τάξιν ἐνεῖναι; &c. P. 579 E.

even after he has succeeded. Speaking of his mind as a
whole, he never does what he really wishes: for the rational
element, which alone can ensure satisfaction to the whole
mind, and guide to the attainment of his real wishes, is
enslaved by furious momentary impulses.[h] The man of
despotical mind is thus miserable; and most of all miserable,
the more completely he succeeds in subjugating his fellow-
citizens and becoming a despot in reality. Knowing himself
to be hated by every one, he lives in constant fear of enemies
within as well as enemies without, against whom he can
obtain support only by courting the vilest of men as partisans.[i] Though greedy of all sorts of enjoyment, he cannot
venture to leave his city or visit any of the frequented public
festivals. He lives indoors like a woman, envying those who
can go abroad and enjoy these spectacles.[k] He is in reality
the poorest and most destitute of men, having the most vehement desires, which he can never satisfy.[l] Such is the despot
who, not being master even of himself, becomes master of
others: in reality, the most wretched of men, though he
may appear happy to superficial judges who look only at
external show.[m]

Thus then (concludes Sokrates) we may affirm with confidence, having reference to the five distinct cities
above described—(1. The Model-City, regal or aris-
tocratical. 2. Timocracy. 3. Oligarchy. 4. Democracy. 5. Despotism)—that the first of these is
happy, and the last miserable: the three intermediate cities being more or less happy in the
order which they occupy from the first to the last.

Each of these cities has its parallel in an individual citizen. The individual citizen corresponding
to the first is happy—he who corresponds to the last
is miserable: and so proportionally for the individual corresponding to the three intermediate cities.
He is happy or miserable, in and through himself,

Conclusion—The Model city and the individual corresponding to it, are the happiest of all—That which is farthest removed from it, is the most miserable of all.

The Just Man is happy in and through his Justice, however he may be treated by others. The Unjust Man, miserable.

[h] Plato, Republic, ix. pp. 577-578. μεστὴ ἔσται.
Καὶ ἡ τυραννουμένη ἄρα ψυχὴ ἥκιστα
ποιήσει ἃ ἂν βουληθῇ, ὡς περὶ ὅλης
εἰπεῖν ψυχῆς· ὑπὸ δὲ οἴστρου ἀεὶ ἑλκο-
μένη βίᾳ ταραχῆς καὶ μεταμελείας

[i] Plato, Republic, ix. pp. 578-579.
[k] Plato, Republic, ix. p. 579 C.
[l] Plato, Republic, ix. p. 579 E.
[m] Plato, Republic, ix. pp. 579-580.

or essentially; whether he be known to Gods and men or not—whatever may be the sentiment entertained of him by others.[n]

There are two other lines of argument (continues Sokrates) establishing the same conclusion.

1. We have seen that both the collective city and the individual mind are distributed into three portions: Reason, Energy, Appetite. Each of these portions has its own peculiar pleasures and pains, desires and aversions, beginnings or principles of action: Love of Knowledge: Love of Honour: Love of Gain. If you question men in whom these three varieties of temper respectively preponderate, each of them will extol the pleasures of his own department above those belonging to the other two. The lover of wealth will declare the pleasures of acquisition and appetite to be far greater than those of honour or of knowledge: each of the other two will say the same for himself, and for the pleasures of his own department. Here then the question is opened, Which of the three is in the right? Which of the three varieties of pleasure and modes of life is the more honourable or base, the better or worse, the more pleasurable or painful?[o] By what criterion, or by whose judgment, is this question to be decided? It must be decided by experience, intelligence, and rational discourse.[p] Now it is certain that the lover of knowledge, or the philosopher, has greater experience of all the three varieties of pleasure than is possessed by either of the other two men. He must in his younger days have tasted and tried the pleasures of both: but the other two have never tasted his.[q] Moreover, each of the three acquires more or less of honour, if he succeeds in his own pursuit: accordingly the pleasures belonging to the love of honour are shared, and may be appreciated, by the philosopher; while the lover of honour, as such, has no sense for the pleasures of philosophy. In the range of personal experience, therefore, the philosopher surpasses the other two: he surpasses them no less in exercised

Marginal note: Other arguments proving the same conclusion. Pleasures of Intelligence are the best of all pleasures.

[n] Plato, Republic. ix. p. 580 D. ἐάν τε λανθάνωσιν ἐάν τε μὴ, πάντας ἀνθρώπους τε καὶ θεούς.

[o] Plato, Republic, ix. p. 581.

[p] Plato, Republic, ix. p. 582 A. ἐμπειρίᾳ τε καὶ φρονήσει καὶ λόγῳ.

[q] Plato, Republic, ix. p. 582 B.

intelligence, and in rational discourse, which is his own principal instrument.[r] If wealth and profit furnished the proper means of judgment, the money-lover would have been the best judge of the three : if honour and victory furnished the proper means, we should consult the lover of honour : but experience, intelligence, and rational discourse, have been shown to be the means—and therefore it is plain that the philosopher is a better authority than either of the other two. His verdict must be considered as final. He will assuredly tell us, that the pleasures belonging to the love of knowledge are the greatest : those belonging to the love of honour and power, the next : those belonging to the love of money and to appetite, the least.[s]

2. The second argument, establishing the same conclusion,

They are the only pleasures completely true and pure. Comparison of pleasure and pain with neutrality. Prevalent illusions.

is as follows :—No pleasures, except those belonging to philosophy or the love of wisdom, are completely true and pure. All the other pleasures are mere shadowy outlines, looking like pleasure at a distance, but not really pleasures when you contemplate them closely.[t] Pleasure and pain are two conditions opposite to each other. Between them both is another state, neither one nor the other, called neutrality or indifference. Now a man who has been sick and is convalescent, will tell you that nothing is more pleasurable than being in health, but that he did not know what the pleasure of it was, until he became sick. So too men in pain affirm that nothing is more pleasurable than relief from pain. When a man is grieving, it is exemption or indifference, not enjoyment, which he extols as the greatest pleasure. Again, when a man has been in a state of enjoyment, and the enjoyment ceases, this cessation is painful. We thus see that the intermediate state—cessation, neutrality, indifference—will be sometimes pain, sometimes pleasure, according to circumstances. Now that which is neither pleasure nor pain cannot possibly be both.[u]

[r] Plato, Republic, ix. p. 582 C-D. λόγοι δὲ τούτου μάλιστα ὄργανον.

[s] Plato, Republic, ix. pp. 582-583.

[t] Plato, Republic, ix. p. 583 B. οὐδὲ παναληθής ἐστιν ἡ τῶν ἄλλων ἡδονὴ πλὴν τοῦ φρονίμου, οὐδὲ καθαρά, ἀλλ' ἐσκιαγραφημένη τις, ὡς ἐγὼ δοκῶ

μοι τῶν σοφῶν τινος ἀκηκοέναι.

[u] Plato, Republic, ix. pp. 583-584. Ὁ μεταξὺ ἄρα νῦν δὴ ἀμφοτέρων ἔφαμεν εἶναι, τὴν ἡσυχίαν, τοῦτό ποτε ἀμφότερα ἔσται, λύπη τε καὶ ἡδονή— Ἦ καὶ δυνατὸν τὸ μηδέτερα ὂν ἀμφότερα γίγνεσθαι; Οὔ μοι δοκεῖ. Καὶ μὴν τό

Pleasure is a positive movement or mutation of the mind : so also is pain. Neutrality or indifference is a negative condition, intermediate between the two: no movement, but absence of movement: non-pain, non-pleasure. But non-pain is not really pleasure : non-pleasure is not really pain. When therefore neutrality or non-pain, succeeding immediately after pain, appears to be a pleasure—this is a mere appearance or illusion, not a reality. When neutrality or non-pleasure, succeeding immediately after pleasure, appears to be pain—this also is a mere appearance or illusion, not a reality. There is nothing sound or trustworthy in such appearances. Pleasure is not cessation of pain, but something essentially different : pain is not cessation of pleasure, but something essentially different.

Take, for example, the pleasures of smell, which are true and genuine pleasures, of great intensity : they spring up instantaneously without presupposing any anterior pain—they depart without leaving any subsequent pain.[x] These are true and pure pleasures, radically different from cessation of pain : so also true and pure pains are different from cessation of pleasure. Most of the so-called pleasures, especially the more intense, which reach the mind through the body, are in reality not pleasures at all, but only cessations or reliefs from pain. The same may be said about the pleasures and pains of anticipation belonging to these so-called bodily pleasures.[y] They may be represented by the following simile :—There is in nature a real Absolute Up and uppermost point—a real Absolute Down and lowest point—and a centre between them.[z] A man borne from the lowest point to the centre will think himself moving upwards, and will be moving upwards relatively. If his course be stopped in the centre, he will think

Most men know nothing of true and pure pleasure. Simile of the Kosmos—Absolute height and depth.

γε ἡδὺ ἐν ψυχῇ γιγνόμενον καὶ τὸ λυπηρὸν, κίνησίς τις ἀμφοτέρω ἔστον; ἢ οὔ; Ναί. Τὸ δὲ μήτε ἡδὺ μήτε λυπηρὸν οὐχὶ ἡσυχία μέντοι καὶ ἐν μέσῳ τούτων ἐφάνη ἄρτι; Ἐφάνη γάρ. Πῶς οὖν ὀρθῶς ἔστι τὸ μὴ ἀλγεῖν ἡδὺ ἡγεῖσθαι, ἢ τὸ μὴ χαίρειν ἀνιαρόν; Οὐδαμῶς. Οὐκ ἔστιν ἄρα τοῦτο, ἀλλὰ φαίνεται, παρὰ τὸ ἀλγεινὸν ἡδὺ καὶ παρὰ τὸ ἡδὺ ἀλγεινὸν τότε ἡ ἡσυχία, καὶ οὐδὲν ὑγιὲς τούτων τῶν φαντασμάτων πρὸς ἡδονῆς ἀλήθειαν, ἀλλὰ γοητεία τις.

[x] Plato, Republic, ix. p. 584 B.
[y] Plato, Republic, ix. p. 584 C.
[z] Plato, Republic, ix. p. 584 C. Νομίζεις τι εἶναι ἐν τῇ φύσει τὸ μὲν ἄνω, τὸ δὲ κάτω, τὸ δὲ μέσον; Ἔγωγε.

himself at the absolute summit—on looking to the point from which he came, and ignorant as he is of any thing higher. If he be forced to return from the centre to the point from whence he came, he will think himself moving downwards, and will be really moving downwards, absolutely as well as relatively. Such misapprehension arises from his not knowing the portion of the Kosmos above the centre— the true and absolute Up or summit. Now the case of pleasure and pain is analogous to this. Pain is the absolute lowest—Pleasure the absolute highest—non-pleasure, non-pain, the centre intermediate between them. But most men know nothing of the region above the centre, or the absolute highest—the region of true and pure pleasure : they know only the centre and what is below it, or the region of pain. When they fall from the centre to the point of pain, they conceive the situation truly, and they really are pained : but when they rise from the lowest point to the centre, they misconceive the change, and imagine themselves to be in a process of replenishment and acquisition of pleasure. They mistake the painless condition for pleasure, not knowing what true pleasure is : just as a man who has seen only black and not white, will fancy if dun be shown to him, that he is looking on white.[a]

Hunger and thirst are states of emptiness in the body : ignorance and folly are states of emptiness in the mind. A hungry man in eating or drinking obtains replenishment : an ignorant man becoming instructed obtains replenishment also. Now replenishment derived from that which exists more fully and perfectly, is truer and more real than replenishment from that which exists less fully and perfectly.[b]

Nourishment of the mind partakes more of real essence than nourishment of the body —Replenishment of the mind imparts fuller pleasure than replenishment of the body.

[a] Plato, Republic, pp. 584-585.

Οὐκοῦν ταῦτα πάσχοι ἂν πάντα διὰ τὸ μὴ ἔμπειρος εἶναι τοῦ ἀληθῶς ἄνω τε ὄντος καὶ ἐν μέσῳ καὶ κάτω ;—ὅταν μὲν ἐπὶ τὸ λυπηρὸν φέρωνται, ἀληθῆ τε οἴονται καὶ τῷ ὄντι λυποῦνται, ὅταν δὲ ἀπὸ λύπης ἐπὶ τὸ μεταξύ, σφόδρα μὲν οἴονται πρὸς πληρώσει τε καὶ ἡδονῇ γίγνεσθαι, ὥσπερ δὲ πρὸς μέλαν φαιὸν ἀποσκοποῦντες ἀπειρίᾳ λευκοῦ. καὶ πρὸς τὸ ἄλυπον οὕτω λύπην ἀφορῶντες ἀπει-

ρίᾳ ἡδονῆς ἀπατῶνται ;

[b] Plato, Republic, ix. p. 585 B. Πλήρωσις δὲ ἀληθεστέρα τοῦ ἧττον ἢ τοῦ μᾶλλον ὄντος ; Δῆλον ὅτι τοῦ μᾶλλον. Πότερα οὖν ἡγεῖ τὰ γένη μᾶλλον καθαρᾶς οὐσίας μετέχειν, τὰ οἷον σίτου καὶ ποτοῦ καὶ ὄψου καὶ ξυμπάσης τροφῆς, ἢ τὸ δόξης τε ἀληθοῦς εἶδος καὶ ἐπιστήμης καὶ νοῦ καὶ ξυλλήβδην ξυμπάσης ἀρετῆς ;

Let us then compare the food which serves for replenishment of the body, with that which serves for replenishment of the mind. Which of the two is most existent? Which of the two partakes most of pure essence? Meat and drink—or true opinions, knowledge, intelligence, and virtue? Which of the two exists most perfectly? That which embraces the true, eternal, and unchangeable—and which is itself of similar nature? Or that which embraces the mortal, the transient, and the ever variable—being itself of kindred nature? Assuredly the former. It is clear that what is necessary for the sustenance of the body partakes less of truth and real essence, than what is necessary for the sustenance of the mind. The mind is replenished with nourishment more real and essential: the body with nourishment less so: the mind itself is also more real and essential than the body. The mind therefore is more, and more thoroughly, replenished than the body. Accordingly, if pleasure consists in being replenished with what suits its peculiar nature, the mind will enjoy more pleasure and truer pleasure than the body.[c] Those who are destitute of intelligence and virtue, passing their lives in sensual pursuits, have never tasted any pure or lasting pleasure, nor ever carried their looks upwards to the higher region in which alone it resides. Their pleasures, though seeming intense, and raising vehement desires in their uninstructed minds, are yet only phantoms deriving a semblance of pleasure from contrast with pains:[d] they are like the phantom of Helen, for which (as Stesichorus says) the Greeks and Trojans fought so many battles, knowing nothing about the true Helen, who was never in Troy.

The pleasures belonging to the Love of Honour (Energy or Passion) are no better than those belonging to the Love of Money (Appetite). In so far as the desires belonging to both these departments of mind are under the controul of the third or best department (Love of Wisdom, or Reason), the nearest approach to true pleasure, which it is in the nature of either of them to bestow, will be realised. But in so far as either

Comparative worthlessness of the pleasures of Appetite and Ambition, when measured against those of Intelligence.

---

[c] Plato, Republic, ix. p. 585 E.   [d] Plato, Republic, ix. p. 586.

of them throws off the controul of Reason, it will neither obtain its own truest pleasures, nor allow the other departments of mind to obtain theirs.[e]   The desires connected with love, and with despotic power, stand out more than the others, as recusant to Reason, Law, and Regulation.   The kingly and moderate desires are most obedient to this authority.   The lover and the despot, therefore, will enjoy the least pleasure : the kingly-minded man will enjoy the most.   Of the three sorts of pleasure, one true and legitimate, two bastard, the despot goes most away from the legitimate, and to the farthest limit of the bastard.   His condition is the most miserable, that of the kingly-minded man is the happiest : between the two come the oligarchical and the democratical man.   The difference between the two extremes is as 1 : 729.[f]

I have thus refuted (continues Sokrates) the case of those

The Just Man will be happy from his justice— He will look only to the good order of his own mind —He will stand aloof from public affairs, in cities as now constituted. who contend—That the unjust man is a gainer by his injustice, provided he could carry it on successfully, and with the reputation of being just.   I have shown that injustice is the greatest possible mischief, intrinsically and in itself, apart from consequences and apart from public reputation: inasmuch as it enslaves the better part of the mind to the worse. Justice, on the other hand, is the greatest possible good, intrinsically and in itself, apart from consequences and reputation, because it keeps the worse parts of the mind under due controul and subordination to the better.[g]   Vice and infirmity of every kind is pernicious, because it puts the best parts of the mind under subjection to the worst.[h]   No success in the acquisition of wealth, aggrandisement, or any other undue object, can compensate a man for the internal disorder which he introduces into his own mind by becoming unjust. A well-ordered mind, just and temperate, with the better part governing the worse, is the first of all objects : greater even than a healthy, strong, and beautiful body.[i]   To put his mind into this condition, and to acquire all the knowledge thereunto conducing, will be the purpose of a wise man's life.

[e] Plato, Republic, ix. pp. 586-587.
[f] Plato, Republic, ix. p. 587.
[g] Plato, Republic, ix. pp. 588-589.
[h] Plato, Republic, ix. p. 590.
[i] Plato, Republic, ix. p. 591 B.

Even in the management of his body, he will look not so much to the health and strength of his body, as to the harmony and fit regulation of his mind. In the acquisition of money, he will keep the same end in view: he will not be tempted by the admiration and envy of people around him to seek great wealth, which will disturb the mental polity within him:[k] he will, on the other hand, avoid depressing poverty, which might produce the same effect. He will take as little part as possible in public life, and will aspire to no political honours, in cities as at present constituted—nor in any other than the model-city which we have described.[l]

The tenth and last book of the Republic commences with an argument of considerable length, repeating and confirming by farther reasons the sentence of expulsion which Plato had already pronounced against the poets in his second and third books.[m] The Platonic Sokrates here not only animadverts upon poetry, but extends his disapprobation to other imitative arts, such as painting. He attacks the process of imitation generally, as false and deceptive; pleasing to ignorant people, but perverting their minds by phantasms which they mistake for realities. The work of the imitator is not merely not reality, but is removed from it by two degrees. What is real is the Form or Idea: the one conceived object denoted by each appellative name common to many particulars. There is one Form or Idea, and only one, known by the name of Bed; another by the name of Table.[n] When the carpenter constructs a bed or a table, he fixes his contemplation on this Form or Idea, and tries to copy it. What he constructs, however, is not the true, real, existent, table, which

Tenth Book—Censure of the poets is renewed—Mischiefs of imitation generally, as deceptive—Imitation from imitation.

---

[k] Plato, Republic, ix. p. 591 D. καὶ τὸν ὄγκον τοῦ πλήθους οὐκ, ἐκπληττόμενος ὑπὸ τοῦ τῶν πολλῶν μακαρισμοῦ, ἄπειρον αὐξήσει, ἀπέραντα κακὰ ἔχων—᾽Αλλ᾽ ἀποβλέπων γε, πρὸς τὴν ἐν αὑτῷ πολιτείαν, καὶ φυλάττων μή τι παρακινῇ αὐτοῦ τῶν ἐκεῖ διὰ πλῆθος οὐσίας ἢ δι᾽ ὀλιγότητα, οὕτω κυβερνῶν προσθήσει καὶ ἀναλώσει τῆς οὐσίας, καθ᾽ ὅσον ἂν οἷός τ᾽ ῇ.

[l] Plato, Republic, ix. p. 592.

[m] Plato, Republic, x. p. 607 B. The language here used by Plato seems to imply that his opinions adverse to poetry had been attacked and required defence.

[n] Plato, Republic, x. p. 596 A-B. Βούλει οὖν ἐνθένδε ἀρξώμεθα ἐπισκοποῦντες, ἐκ τῆς εἰωθυίας μεθόδου; εἶδος γάρ πού τι ἓν ἕκαστον εἰώθαμεν τίθεσθαι περὶ ἕκαστα τὰ πολλά, οἷς ταὐτὸν ὄνομα ἐπιφέρομεν — θῶμεν δὴ καὶ νῦν ὅτι βούλει τῶν πολλῶν· οἷον, εἰ θέλεις πολλαί πού εἰσι κλῖναι καὶ τράπεζαι—᾽Αλλ᾽ ἰδέαι γέ πού περὶ ταῦτα τὰ σκεύη δύο, μία μὲν κλίνης, μία δὲ τραπέζης.

alone exists in nature, and may be presumed to be made by
the Gods[o]—but a something like the real existent table: not
true Ens, but only quasi-Ens:[p] dim and indistinct, as compared with the truth, and standing far off from the truth.
Next to the carpenter comes the painter, who copies not the
real existent table, but the copy of that table made by the
carpenter. The painter fixes his contemplation upon it, not
as it really exists, but simply as it appears: he copies an
appearance or phantasm, not a reality. Thus the table will
have a different appearance, according as you look at it from
near or far—from one side or the other: yet in reality it
never differs from itself. It is one of these appearances that
the painter copies, not the reality itself. He can in like
manner paint any thing and every thing, since he hardly
touches any thing at all—and nothing whatever except in
appearance. He can paint all sorts of craftsmen and their
works—carpenters, shoemakers, &c.—without knowledge of
any one of their arts.[q]

The like is true also of the poets. Homer and the trage-

Censure of Homer—He is falsely ex-tolled as edu-cator of the Hellenic world. He and other poets only deceive their hearers. dians give us talk and affirmations about everything:
government, legislation, war, medicine, husbandry,
the character and proceedings of the Gods, the
habits and training of men, &c. Some persons even
extol Homer as the great educator of the Hellenic
world, whose poems we ought to learn by heart as
guides for education and administration.[r] But Homer, Hesiod,
and the other poets, had no real knowledge of the multifarious
matters which they profess to describe. These poets know
nothing except about appearances, and will describe only
appearances, to the satisfaction of the ignorant multitude.[s]
The representations of the painter, reproducing only the appearances to sense, will be constantly fallacious and deceptive,
requiring to be corrected by measuring, weighing, counting—
which are processes belonging to Reason.[t] The lower and the

---

[o] Plato, Republic, x. p. 597 B-D.
μία μὲν ἡ ἐν τῇ φύσει οὖσα, ἣν φαῖμεν
ἂν, ὡς ἐγῷμαι, θεὸν ἐργάσασθαι.

[p] Plato, Republic, x. p. 597 A. οὐκ
ἂν τὸ ὂν ποιοῖ, ἀλλὰ τι τοιοῦτον οἷον τὸ
ὄν, ὂν δὲ οὔ.

[q] Plato, Republic, x. p. 598 B-C.

[r] Plato, Republic, p. 606 E.

[s] Plato, Republic, x. pp. 600-601 C.
τοῦ μὲν ὄντος οὐδὲν ἐπαΐει, τοῦ δὲ φαινο-
μένου. P. 602 B. οἷον φαίνεται καλὸν
εἶναι τοῖς πολλοῖς τε καὶ μηδὲν εἰδόσι,
τοῦτο μιμήσεται.

[t] Plato, Republic, x. pp. 602-603.

higher parts of the mind are here at variance; and the painter addresses himself to the lower, supplying falsehood as if it were truth. The painter does this through the eye, the poet through the ear.[u]

In the various acts and situations of life a man is full of contradictions. He is swayed by manifold impulses, often directly contradicting each other. Hence we have affirmed that there are in his mind two distinct principles, one contradicting the other: the emotional and the rational.[x] When a man suffers misfortune, emotion prompts him to indulge in extreme grief, and to abandon himself like a child to the momentary tide. Reason, on the contrary, exhorts him to resist, and to exert himself immediately in counsel to rectify or alleviate what has happened, adapting his conduct as well as he can to the actual throw of the dice which has befallen him.[y] Now it is these vehement bursts of emotion which lend themselves most effectively to the genius of the poet, and which he must work up to please the multitude in the theatre: the state of rational self-command can hardly be described so as to touch their feelings. We see thus that the poet, like the painter, addresses himself to the lower department of the mind, exalting the emotional into preponderance over the rational— the foolish over the wise—the false over the true.[z] He introduces bad government into the mind, giving to pleasure and pain the sceptre over reason. Hence we cannot tolerate the poet, in spite of all his swe⟩ts and captivations. We can only permit him to compose hymns for the Gods and encomiums for good men.[a]

This quarrel between philosophy and poetry (continues the

The poet chiefly appeals to emotions—Mischief of such eloquent appeals, as disturbing the rational government of the mind.

[u] Plato, Republic, x. p. 603 B.

[x] Plato, Republic, x. p. 603 C. μυρίων τοιούτων ἐναντιωμάτων ἅμα γιγνομένων ἡ ψυχὴ γέμει ἡμῶν—ἐναντίας δὲ ἀγωγῆς γιγνομένης ἐν τῷ ἀνθρώπῳ περὶ τὸ αὐτὸ ἅμα δύο τινέ φαμεν ἐν αὐτῷ ἀναγκαῖον εἶναι.

[y] Plato, Republic, x. p. 604. Τῷ βουλεύεσθαι περὶ τὸ γεγονὸς, καὶ ὥσπερ ἐν πτώσει κύβων πρὸς τὰ πεπτωκότα τίθεσθαι τὰ ἑαυτοῦ πράγματα, ὅπῃ ὁ λόγος αἱρεῖ βέλτιστ' ἂν ἔχειν, ἀλλὰ μὴ προσπταίσαντας, καθάπερ παῖδας, ἐχο-

μένους τοῦ πληγέντος ἐν τῷ βοᾶν διατρίβειν, &c.

[z] Plato, Republic, x. p. 605.

[a] Plato, Republic, x. pp. 605-606-607. τὸν μιμητικὸν ποιητὴν φήσομεν κακὴν πολιτείαν ἰδίᾳ ἑκάστου τῇ ψυχῇ ἐμποιεῖν, τῷ ἀνοήτῳ αὐτῆς χαριζόμενον —εἰ δὲ τὴν ἡδυσμένην μοῦσαν παραδέξει ἐν μέλεσιν ἢ ἔπεσιν, ἡδονή σοι καὶ λύπη βασιλεύσετον ἀντὶ νόμου τε καὶ τοῦ κοινῇ ἀεὶ δόξαντος εἶναι βελτίστου λόγου.

Platonic Sokrates) is of ancient date.[b] I myself am very

Ancient quarrel between philosophy and poetry— Plato fights for philosophy, though his feelings are strongly enlisted for poetry.
sensible to the charms of poetry, especially that of Homer. I should be delighted if a case could be made out to justify me in admitting it into our city. But I cannot betray the cause of what seems to me truth. We must resist our sympathies and preferences, when they are incompatible with the right government of the mind.[c]

To maintain the right government and good condition of

Immortality of the soul affirmed and sustained by argument— Total number of souls always the same.
the soul or mind is the first of all considerations : and will be seen yet farther to be such, when we consider that it is immortal and imperishable. Of this Plato proceeds to give a proof,[d] concluding with a mythical sketch of the destiny of the soul after death. The soul being immortal (he says), the total number of souls is and always has been the same—neither increasing nor diminishing.[e]

I have proved (the Platonic Sokrates concludes) in the

Recapitulation—The Just Man will be happy, both from his justice and from its consequences, both here and hereafter.
preceding discourse, that Justice is better, in itself and intrinsically, than Injustice, quite apart from consequences in the way of reward and honour : that a man for the sake of his own happiness ought to be just, whatever may be thought of him by Gods or men—even though he possessed the magic ring of Gyges. Having proved this, and having made out the intrinsic superiority of justice to injustice, we may now take in the natural consequences and collateral bearings of both. We have hitherto reasoned upon the hypothesis that the just man was mistaken for unjust, and treated accordingly—that the unjust man found means to pass himself off for just, and to attract to himself the esteem and the rewards of justice.[f] But this hypothesis concedes too much, and we must now take back the concession. The just man will be happier than the unjust, not simply from the intrinsic working of justice on his own mind, but also from the exterior consequences of justice. He will be favoured and rewarded both by Gods and

---

[b] Plato, Republic, x. p. 607 B.
παλαιά τις διαφορὰ φιλοσοφίᾳ τε καὶ ποιητικῇ.
[c] Plato, Republic, x. pp. 607-608.

[d] Plato, Republic, x. pp. 609-610.
[e] Plato, Republic, x. p. 611 A.
[f] Plato, Republic, x. p. 612 B-C.

men.   Though he may be in poverty, sickness, or any other apparent state of evil, he may be assured that the Gods will compensate him for it by happiness either in life or after death.[g]   And men too, though they may for a time be mistaken about the just and the unjust character, will at last come to a right estimation of both.   The just man will finally receive honour, reward, and power, from his fellow-citizens: the unjust man will be finally degraded and punished by them.[h]   And after death, the reward of the just man, as well as the punishment of the unjust, will be far greater than even during life.

This latter position is illustrated at some length by the mythe with which the Republic concludes, describing the realm of Hades, with the posthumous condition and treatment of the departed souls.

[g] Plato, Republic, x. pp. 612-613.   [h] Plato, Republic, x. p. 613 C-D.

CHAPTER XXXIV.

REPUBLIC—REMARKS ON ITS MAIN THESIS.

THE preceding Chapter has described, in concise abstract,
Summary of the preceding chapter. that splendid monument of Plato's genius, which
passes under the name of the Πολιτεία or Republic.
It is undoubtedly the grandest of all his compositions ; including in itself all his different points of excellence. In the
first Book, we have a subtle specimen of negative Dialectic,—
of the Sokratic cross-examination or Elenchus. In the second
Book, we find two examples of continuous or Ciceronian
pleading (like that ascribed to Protagoras in the dialogue
called by his name), which are surpassed by nothing in
ancient literature, for acuteness and ability in the statement
of a case. Next, we are introduced to Plato's most sublime
effort of constructive ingenuity, in putting together both the
individual man and the collective City : together with more
information (imperfect as it is even here) about his Dialectic
or Philosophy, than any other dialogue furnishes. The ninth
Book exhibits his attempts to make good his own thesis
against the case set forth in his own antecedent counter-
pleadings. The last Book concludes with a highly poetical
mythe, embodying a Νεκυία shaped after his own fancy,—and
the outline of cosmical agencies afterwards developed, though
with many differences, in the Timæus. The brilliancy of the
Republic will appear all the more conspicuous, when we come
to compare it with Plato's two posterior compositions : with the
Pythagorean mysticism and theology of the Timæus—or with
the severe and dictatorial solemnity of the Treatise De Legibus.

The title borne by this dialogue—the Republic or Polity—
Title of the Republic, of ancient date, but only a partial indi-cation of its contents. whether affixed by Plato himself or not, dates at
least from his immediate disciples, Aristotle among
them.[a] This title hardly presents a clear idea either
of its proclaimed purpose or of its total contents.

[a] See Schleiermacher, Einleitung zum Staat, p. 63 seq. ; Stallbaum, Proleg.
p. lviii. seq.

The larger portion of the treatise is doubtless employed in expounding the generation of a commonwealth generally: from whence the author passes insensibly to the delineation of a Model-Commonwealth—enumerating the conditions of aptitude for its governors and guardian-soldiers, estimating the obstacles which prevent it from appearing in the full type of goodness—and pointing out the steps whereby, even if fully realised, it is likely to be brought to perversion and degeneracy. Nevertheless the avowed purpose of the treatise is, not to depict the ideal of a commonwealth, but to solve the questions, What is Justice? What is Injustice? Does Justice, in itself and by its own intrinsic working, make the just man happy, apart from all consequences, even though he is not known to be just, and is even treated as unjust, either by Gods or men? Does Injustice, under the like hypothesis, (*i. e.* leaving out all consideration of consequences either from Gods or from men), make the unjust man miserable? The reasonings respecting the best polity, are means to this end—intermediate steps to the settlement of this problem. We must recollect that Plato insists strongly on the parallelism between the individual and the state: he talks of "the polity" or Republic in each man's mind, as of that in the entire city.[b]

The Republic, or Commonwealth, is introduced by Plato as being the individual man "writ large," and there-fore more clearly discernible and legible to an observer.[c] To illustrate the individual man, he begins by describing (to use Hobbes's language) the great Leviathan called a "Commonwealth or State, in Latin Civitas, which is but an artificial man, though of greater stature and strength than the natural, for whose protection and defence it was intended."[d] He pursues in much detail this parallel between the individual and the commonwealth, as well as

Parallelism between the Common-wealth and the Individual.

[b] Plato, Repub. ix. p. 591 E. ἀπο-βλέπων πρὸς τὴν ἐν αὐτῷ πολιτείαν. x. p. 608. περὶ τῆς ἐν αὐτῷ πολιτείας δεδιότι, &c.

[c] Plato, Republic, ii. p. 368 D.

"New presbyter is but old priest writ large." —(Milton.)

[d] This is the language of Hobbes. Preface to the Leviathan. In the same treatise (Part ii. ch. 17, pp. 157-158,

Molesworth's ed.) Hobbes says :— " The only way to erect such a common power as may be able to defend men from the invasion of foreigners and the injury of one another, is to confer all their power and strength upon one man or one assembly of men, that may reduce all their wills by plurality of voices to one will: which is as much as to say, to appoint one

between the component parts and forces of the one, and those of the other. The perfection of the commonwealth (he represents) consists in its being One :[e] an integer or unit, of which the constituent individuals are merely functions, each having only a fractional, dependant, relative existence. As the commonwealth is an individual on a large scale, so the individual is a commonwealth on a small scale ; in which the constituent fractions, Reason,—Energy or Courage,—and many-headed Appetite,—act each for itself and oppose each other. It is the tendency of Plato's imagination to bestow vivid reality on abstractions, and to reason upon metaphorical analogy as if it were close parallelism. His language exaggerates both the unity of the commonwealth, and the partibility of the individual, in illustrating the one by comparison with the other. The commonwealth is treated as capable of happiness or misery as an entire Person, apart from its component individuals :[f] while on the other hand, Reason, Energy, Appetite, are described as distinct and conflicting Persons, packed up in the same wrapper and therefore looking like One from the outside, yet really distinct, each acting and suffering by and for itself: like the charioteer and his two horses, which form the conspicuous metaphor in the Phædrus.[g] We are thus told, that though the man is apparently One, he is in reality Many or multipartite: though the perfect Commonwealth is apparently Many, it is in reality One.

Of the parts composing a man, as well as of the parts com-

Each of them a whole, composed of parts distinct in function, and unequal in merit. posing a commonwealth, some are better, others worse. A few are good and excellent; the greater number are low and bad; while there are intermediate gradations between the two. The perfection of a commonwealth, and the perfection of an individual man, is attained when each part performs its own appropriate function and no more,—not interfering with the rest. In

---

man or assembly of men to bear their person. This is more than consent or concord : *it is a real unity of them all in one and the same person,* made by covenant of every man with every man. This done, the multitude so united in one person, is called a Commonwealth, in Latin Civitas. This is the genera-

tion of that great Leviathan," &c.

[e] Plato, Republic, iv. p. 423.

[f] Plato, Republic, iv. pp. 420-421.

[g] Plato, Republic, ix. p. 588, x. p. 604, iv. pp. 436-441.

ὥστε τῷ μὴ δυναμένῳ τὰ ἐντὸς ὁρᾷν, ἀλλὰ τὸ ἔξω μόνον ἔλυτρον ὁρῶντι, ἐν ζῷον φαίνεσθαι, ἄνθρωπον.

the commonwealth there are a small number of wise Elders
or philosophers, whose appropriate function it is to look out
for the good or happiness of the whole; and to controul the
ordinary commonplace multitude, with a view to that end.
Each of the multitude has his own special duty or aptitude,
to which he confines himself, and which he executes in subordination to the wise or governing Few.   And to ensure such
subordination, there are an intermediate number of trained,
or disciplined Guardians; who employ their force under the
orders of the ruling Few, to controul the multitude within,
as well as to repel enemies without.   So too in the perfect
man, Reason is the small but excellent organ whose appropriate function is, to controul the multitude of desires and to
watch over the good of the whole: the function of Energy or
Courage is, while itself obeying the Reason, to assist Reason
in maintaining this controul over the Desires: the function of
each several desire is to obey, pursuing its own special end in
due harmony with the rest.

The End to be accomplished, and with reference to which
Plato tests the perfection of the means is, the happiness of the entire commonwealth,—the happiness
of the entire individual man.   In order to be happy,
a commonwealth or an individual man, must be at
once wise, brave, temperate, just.   There is however this difference between the four qualities.   Though all
four are essential, yet wisdom and bravery belong only to
separate fractions of the commonwealth and separate fractions
of the individual: while justice and temperance belong equally
to all the fractions of the commonwealth and all the fractions
of the individual.   In the perfect commonwealth, Wisdom or
Reason is found only in the One or Few Ruling Elders:—
Energy or Courage only in the Soldiers or Guardians: but
Elders, Guardians, and the working multitude, alike exhibit
Justice and Temperance.   All are just, inasmuch as each
performs his appropriate business: all are temperate, inasmuch as all agree in recognising what is the appropriate
business of each fraction—that of the Elders is, to rule—that
of the others is, to obey.   So too the individual: he is wise
only in his Reason, brave only in his Energy or Courage:

[marginal note:] End proposed by Plato. Happiness of the commonwealth. Happiness of the Individual. Conditions of happiness.

but he is just and temperate in his Reason, Courage, and Appetites alike—each of these fractions acting in its own sphere under proper relations to the rest. In fact, according to the definitions given by Plato in the Republic, justice and temperance are scarce at all distinguishable from each other— and must at any rate be inseparable.

Now in regard to the definition here given by Plato of Justice, which is the avowed object of his Treatise, we may first remark that it is altogether peculiar to Plato; and that if we reason about Justice in the Platonic sense, we must take care not to affirm of it predicates which might be true in a more usual acceptation of the word. Next, that even adopting Plato's own meaning of Justice, it does not answer the purpose for which he produces it—viz.: to provide reply to the objections, and solution for the difficulties, which he had himself placed in the mouths of Glaukon and Adeimantus.

Peculiar view of Justice taken by Plato.

These two speakers (in the second Book) have advanced the position (which they affirm to be held by every one, past and present)—That justice is a good thing or a cause of happiness to the just agent—not in itself or separately, since the performance of just acts is more or less onerous and sometimes painful, presenting itself in the aspect of an obligation, but—because of its consequences, as being indispensable to procure for him some ulterior good, such as esteem and just treatment from others. Sokrates on the other hand declares justice to be good, or a cause of happiness, to the just agent, most of all in itself—but also, additionally, in its consequences: and injustice to be bad, or a cause of misery to the unjust agent, on both grounds also.

Pleadings of Glaukon and Adeimantus.

Suppose (we have seen it urged by Glaukon and Adeimantus) that a man is just, but is mis-esteemed by the society among whom he lives, and believed to be unjust. He will certainly be hated and ill-used by others, and may be ill-used to the greatest possible extent—impoverishment, scourging, torture, crucifixion. Again, suppose a man to be unjust, but to be in like manner misconceived, and treated as if he were just. He will receive from others golden opinions, just dealing, and goodwill, producing to him comfortable consequences : and he will obtain, besides, the profits of injustice. Evidently, under these supposed circumstances, the just man will be miserable, in spite of his justice : the unjust man will, to say the least, be the happier of the two.

Moreover (so argues Glaukon), all fathers exhort their sons to be just, and forbid them to be unjust, admitting that justice is a troublesome obligation, but insisting upon it as indispensable to avert evil consequences and procure good. So also poets and teachers. All of them assume that justice is not inviting for itself, but only by reason of its consequences : and that injustice is in itself easy and inviting, were it not for mischievous consequences and penalties more than countervailing the temptation. All of them either anticipate, or seek to provide, penalties to be inflicted in case the agent commits injustice, and not to be inflicted if he continues just : so that the treatment which he receives afterwards shall be favourable, or severe, conditional upon his own conduct. Such treatment may emanate either from Gods or from men : but in either case, it is assumed that the agent shall be known, or shall seem, to be what he really is : that the unjust agent shall seem, or be known, to be unjust—and that the just shall seem also to be what he is.

It is against this doctrine that the Platonic Sokrates in the Republic professes to contend. To refute it, he sets forth his own explanation, wherein justice consists. How far, or with what qualifications, the Sophists inculcated the doctrine (as various commentators tell us) we do not know. But Plato himself informs us that it was current and received in society, before Protagoras and Prodikus were born : taught by parents to their children, and by poets in their compositions generally circulated.[h] Moreover, Sokrates himself (in the Platonic Apology) recommends virtue on the ground of its remunerative consequences to the agent, in the shape of wealth and other good things.[i] Again, the Xenophontic

The arguments which they enforce were not invented by the Sophists, but were the received views anterior to Plato.

---

[h] Plato, Republic, ii. pp. 363-364.
[i] Plato, Apolog. Sokrat. p. 30 B.
λέγων ὅτι οὐκ ἐκ χρημάτων ἀρετὴ γίγνεται, ἀλλ᾽ ἐξ ἀρετῆς χρήματα καὶ τἆλλα ἀγαθὰ τοῖς ἀνθρώποις καὶ ἰδίᾳ καὶ δημοσίᾳ.

Xenophon in the Cyropædia puts the following language into the mouth of the hero Cyrus, in addressing his officers (Cyrop. i. 5, 9). Καίτοι ἔγωγε οἶμαι, οὐδεμίαν ἀρετὴν ἀσκεῖσθαι ὑπ᾽ ἀνθρώπων, ὡς μηδὲν πλέον ἔχωσιν οἱ

Sokrates, as well as Xenophon himself, agree in the same general doctrine: presenting virtue as laborious and troublesome in itself, but as being fully requited by its remunerative consequences in the form of esteem and honour, to the attainment of which it is indispensable. In the memorable Choice of Heraklês, that youth is represented as choosing a life of toil and painful self-denial, crowned ultimately by the attainment of honourable and beneficial results—in preference to a life of easy and inactive enjoyment.[k]

We see thus that the doctrine which the Platonic Sokrates impugns in the Republic, is countenanced elsewhere by Sokratic authority. It is, in my judgment, more true than that which he opposes to it. The exhortations and orders of parents to their children, which he condemns—were founded upon views of fact and reality more correct than those which the Sokrates of the Republic would substitute in place of them.

Let us note the sentiment in which Plato's creed here originates. He desires, above every thing, to stand forward as the champion and panegyrist of justice—as the enemy and denouncer of injustice. To praise justice, not in itself, but for its consequences—and to blame injustice in like manner—appears to him disparaging and insulting to justice.[1] He is not satisfied with showing that the just man benefits others by his justice, and that the unjust man hurts others by his injustice: he admits

Argument of Sokrates to refute them. Sentiments in which it originates. Panegyric on Justice.

ἐσθλοὶ γενόμενοι τῶν πονηρῶν· ἀλλ' οἵτε τῶν παραύτικα ἡδονῶν ἀπεχόμενοι, οὐχ ἵνα μηδέποτε εὐφρανθῶσι, τοῦτο πραττουσιν, ἀλλ' ὡς διὰ ταύτην τὴν ἐγκράτειαν πολλαπλάσια εἰς τὸν ἔπειτα χρόνον εὐφρανούμενοι, οὕτω παρασκευάζονται, &c.

The love of praise is represented as the prominent motive of Cyrus to the practice of virtue (i. 5, 12, i. 2, 1).

Compare also Xenophon, Cyropæd. ii. 3, 5-15, vii. 5, 82, and Xenophon, Economic. xiv. 5-9; Xenophon, De Venatione, xii. 15-19.

[k] Xenophon, Memorab. ii. 1, 19-20, &c. We read in the 'Works and Days' of Hesiod, 287 :—

Τὴν μέντοι κακότητα καὶ ἵλαδον ἔστιν
ἑλέσθαι
'Ρηϊδίως· λείη μὲν ὁδός, μάλα δ' ἐγγύθι ναίει.

Τῆς δ' ἀρετῆς ἱδρῶτα θεοὶ προπάροιθεν
ἔθηκαν
'Αθάνατοι, μακρὸς δὲ καὶ ὄρθιος οἶμος
ἐπ' αὐτήν,
Καὶ τρηχὺς τοπρῶτον· ἐπὴν δ' εἰς
ἄκρον ἵκηαι,
'Ρηϊδίη δ' ἤπειτα πέλει, χαλεπή περ
ἐοῦσα.

It is remarkable that while the Xenophontic Sokrates cites these verses from Hesiod as illustrating and enforcing the drift of his exhortation, the Platonic Sokrates cites them as misleading, and as a specimen of the hurtful errors instilled by the poets (Republic, ii. p. 364 D).

[1] Plato, Republic, ii. p. 368 B. δέδοικα γὰρ μὴ οὐδ' ὅσιον ᾖ παραγενόμενον δικαιοσύνῃ κακηγορουμένῃ ἀπαγορεύειν καὶ μὴ βοηθεῖν, &c.

nothing into his calculation, except happiness or misery to the agent himself : and happiness, moreover, inherent in the process of just behaviour—misery inherent in the process of unjust behaviour—whatever be the treatment which the agent may receive from either Gods or men. Justice *per se* (affirms Plato) is the cause of happiness to the just agent, absolutely and unconditionally : injustice, in like manner, of misery to the unjust—*quand même*—whatever the consequences may be either from men or Gods. This is the extreme strain of panegyric suggested by Plato's feeling, and announced as a conclusion substantiated by his reasons. Nothing more thoroughgoing can be advanced in eulogy of justice. " Neither the eastern star nor the western star is so admirable "—to borrow a phrase from Aristotle.[m]

Plato is here the first proclaimer of the doctrine afterwards so much insisted on by the Stoics—the all-sufficiency of virtue to the happiness of the virtuous agent, whatever may be his fate in other respects—without requiring any farther conditions or adjuncts. It will be seen that Plato maintains this thesis with reference to the terms *justice* and its opposite *injustice ;* sometimes (though not often) using the general term *virtue* or wisdom, which was the ordinary term with the Stoics afterwards.

The ambiguous meaning of the word *justice* is known to Plato himself (as it is also to Aristotle). One professed purpose of the dialogue called the Republic is to remove such ambiguity. Apart from the many other differences of meaning (arising from dissentient sentiments of different men and different ages), there is one duplicity of meaning which Aristotle particularly dwells upon.[n] In the stricter and narrower sense, justice comprehends only

Different senses of justice—wider and narrower sense.

---

[m] Aristot. Ethic. Nikom. v. 1, 1129, b. 28. οὐθ' ἕσπερος, οὐθ' ἑῷος οὕτω θαυμαστός.

[n] Aristotel. Ethic. Nikom. v. 2, 1129, a. 25. ἔοικε δὲ πλεοναχῶς λέγεσθαι ἡ δικαιοσύνη καὶ ἡ ἀδικία.—also 1130, a. 3.

διὰ δὲ τὸ αὐτὸ τοῦτο καὶ ἀλλότριον ἀγαθὸν δοκεῖ εἶναι ἡ δικαιοσύνη, μόνη τῶν ἀρετῶν, ὅτι πρὸς ἕτερόν ἐστιν· ἄλλῳ γὰρ τὰ συμφέροντα πράττει, ἢ ἄρχοντι ἢ κοινῷ.

This proposition—that justice is ἀλ-

λότριον ἀγαθὸν—is the very proposition which Thrasymachus is introduced as affirming and Sokrates as combating, in the first book of the Republic.

Compare also Aristotle's Ethica Magna, i. 34, p. 1193, b. 19, where the same explanation of justice is given : also p. 1194, a. 7, where the Republic of Plato is cited, and the principle of reciprocity, as laid down at the end of the second book of the Republic, is repeated.

those obligations which each individual agent owes to others,
and for the omission of which he becomes punishable as unjust—though the performance of them, under ordinary circumstances, carries little positive merit: in another and a larger
sense, justice comprehends these and a great deal more, becoming co-extensive with wise, virtuous, and meritorious character generally. The narrower sense is that which is in
more common use; and it is that which Plato assumes provisionally when he puts forward the case of opponents in the
speeches of Glaukon and Adeimantus. But when he comes
to set forth his own explanation, and to draw up his own case,
we see that he uses the term justice in its larger sense, as the
condition of a mind perfectly well-balanced and well-regulated: as if a man could not be just, without being at the
same time wise, courageous, and temperate. The just man,
described in the counter-pleadings of Glaukon and Adeimantus, would be a person like the Athenian Aristeides: the
unjust man whom they contrast with him, would be one who
maltreats, plunders, or deceives others, or usurps power over
them. But the just man, when Sokrates replies to them and
unfolds his own thesis, is made to include a great deal more:
he is a person in whose mind each of the three constituent
elements is in proper relation of controul or obedience to the
others, so that the whole mind is perfect: a person whose
Reason, being illuminated by contemplation of the Universals
or self-existent Ideas of Goodness, Justice, Virtue, has become
qualified to exercise controul over the two inferior elements:
one of which (Energy) is its willing subordinate and auxiliary—while the lowest of the three (Appetite) is kept in
regulation by the joint action of the two. The just man, so
described, becomes identical with the true philosopher: no
man who is not a philosopher can be just.[o] Aristeides would
not at all correspond to the Platonic idéal of justice. He
would be a stranger to the pleasure extolled by Plato as the
exclusive privilege of the just and virtuous—the pleasure of

---

[o] This is the same distinction as
that drawn by Epiktetus between the
φιλόσοφος and the ἰδιώτης (Arrian,
Epiktet. iii. 19). An ἰδιώτης may be
just in the ordinary meaning of the
word. Aristeides was an ἰδιώτης. The
Greek word ἰδιώτης, designating the
ordinary average citizen, as distinguished from any special or professional training, is highly convenient.

contemplating universal Ideas and acquiring extended knowledge.[p]

The Platonic conception of Justice or Virtue on the one side, and of Injustice or Vice on the other, is self-regarding and prudential. Justice is in the mind a condition analogous to good health and strength in the body—(*mens sana in corpore sano*)—Injustice is a condition analogous to sickness, corruption, impotence, in the body.[q] The body is healthy, when each of its constituent parts performs its appropriate function: it is unhealthy, when there is failure in this respect, either defective working of any part, or interference of one part with the rest. So too in the just mind, each of its tripartite constituents performs its appropriate function—the rational mind directing and controlling, the energetic and appetitive minds obeying such controul. In the unjust mind, the case is opposite: Reason exercises no supremacy; Passion and Appetite, acting each for itself, are disorderly, reckless, exorbitant. To possess a healthy body is desirable for its consequences as a means towards other constituents of happiness; but it is still more desirable in itself, as an essential element of happiness *per se*, *i. e.* the negation of sickness, which would of itself make us miserable. On the other hand, an unhealthy or corrupt body is miserable by reason of its consequences, but still more miserable *per se*, even apart from consequences. In like manner, the just mind blesses the possessor twice: first and chiefly, as bringing to him happiness in itself—next also, as it leads to ulterior happy results:[r] the unjust mind is a curse to its possessor in itself, and apart from results—though it also leads to ulterior results which render it still more a curse to him.

This theory respecting justice and injustice was first introduced into ethical speculation by Plato. He tells us himself (throughout the speeches ascribed to Glaukon and Adeimantus), that no one before him had announced it: that all

Plato's sense of the word Justice or Virtue—self-regarding.

[p] Plato, Republic, ix. pp. 446-447. τῆς δὲ τοῦ ὄντος θέας, οἵαν ἡδονὴν ἔχει, ἀδύνατον ἄλλῳ γεγεῦσθαι πλὴν τῷ φιλοσόφῳ.

[q] Plato, Republic, ix. p. 591 B, iv. p. 444 E.

[r] Plato, Republic, ii. p. 367 D. ἐπειδὴ οὖν ὡμολόγησας τῶν μεγίστων ἀγαθῶν εἶναι δικαιοσύνην, ἃ τῶν τε ἀποβαινόντων ἀπ' αὐτῶν ἕνεκα ἄξια κεκτῆσθαι, πολὺ δὲ μᾶλλον αὐτὰ ἑαυτῶν, &c.

with one accord[s]—both the poets in addressing an audience, and private citizens in exhorting their children—inculcated a different doctrine, enforcing justice as an onerous duty, and not as a self-recommending process: that he was the first who extolled justice in itself, as conferring happiness on the just agent, apart from all reciprocity or recognition either by men or Gods—and the first who condemned injustice in itself, as inflicting misery on the unjust agent, independent of any recognition by others. Here then we have the first introduction of this theory into ethical speculation. Injustice is an internal taint, corruption of mind, which (like bad bodily health) is in itself misery to the agent, however he may be judged or treated by men or Gods: and justice is (like good bodily health) a state of internal happiness to the agent, independent of all recognition and responsive treatment from others.

The Platonic theory, or something substantially equivalent

He represents the motives to it, as arising from the internal happiness of the just agents.

to it under various forms of words, has been ever since upheld by various ethical theorists, from the time of Plato downward.[t] Every one would be glad if it could be made out as true: Glaukon and Adeimantus are already enlisted in its favour, and only demand from Sokrates a decent justification for their belief. Moreover, those who deny its truth incur the reproach of being deficient in love of virtue or in hatred of vice. What is still more remarkable—Plato has been complimented as if his theory had been the first antithesis to what is called the "selfish theory of morals"—a compliment which is certainly noway merited: for Plato's theory is essentially self-regarding.[u] He does not indeed lay his main stress on the retri-

---

[s] Plato, Republic, ii. p. 364 A. πάντες ἐξ ἑνὸς στόματος ὑμνοῦσιν, &c. P. 366 D.

[t] It will be found maintained by Shaftesbury and Hutcheson and impugned by Rutherford in his Essay on Virtue: also advocated by Sir James Mackintosh in his Dissertation on Ethical Philosophy, prefixed to the Encyclopædia Britannica; and controverted, or rather reduced to its proper limits, by Mr. James Mill, in his very acute and philosophical volume, Fragment on Mackintosh, published in 1835, see pp. 174-188 seq.

Sir James indeed uses the word Benevolence where Plato uses that of Justice: he speaks of "the inherent delights and intrinsic happiness of Benevolence," &c.

[u] Stallbaum, Proleg. ad Plat. Rep. p. lvii. "Quo facto deinceps ad gravissimam totius sermonis partem ita transitur, ut inter colloquentes conveniat, justitiæ vim et naturam eo modo esse investigandam, ut emolumentorum et commodorum ex eâ redundantium nulla plané ratio habeatur."

This is not strictly exact, for Plato claims on behalf of justice not only

bution and punishments which follow injustice, because he represents injustice as being itself a state of misery to the unjust agent: nor upon the rewards attached to justice, because he represents justice itself as a state of intrinsic happiness to the just agent.   Nevertheless the motive to performance of justice, and to avoidance of injustice, is derived in his theory (as it is in what is called the selfish theory) entirely from the happiness or misery of the agent himself.   The just man is not called upon for any self-denial or self-sacrifice, since by the mere fact of being just, he acquires a large amount of happiness: it is the unjust man who, from ignorance or perversion, sacrifices that happiness which just behaviour would have ensured to him.   Thus the Platonic theory is entirely self-regarding; looking to the conduct of each separate agent as it affects his own happiness, not as it affects the happiness of others.

So much to explain what the Platonic theory is.   But when we ask whether it consists with the main facts of society, or with the ordinary feelings of men living in society, the reply must be in the negative.

His theory departs more widely from the truth than that which he opposes.

If (says Plato, putting the words into the counterpleading of Adeimantus)—"If the Platonic theory were preached by all of you, and impressed upon our belief from childhood, we should not have watched each other to prevent injustice; since each man would have been the best watch upon himself, from fear lest by committing injustice he should take to his bosom the maximum of evil."[x]

Argument of Adeimantus discussed.

These words are remarkable. They admit of two constructions:—1. If the Platonic theory were true. 2. If the Platonic theory, though not true, were constantly preached and impressed upon every one's belief from childhood.

Understanding the words in the first of these two constructions, the hypothetical proposition put into the mouth of Adeimantus is a valid argument against the theory after-

---

that the performance of it is happy in itself, but also that it entails an independent result of ulterior happiness. But he dwells much less upon the second point; which indeed would be superfluous if the first could be thoroughly established.

[x] Plato, Republic, ii. p. 367 A. εἰ γὰρ οὕτως ἐλέγετο ἐξ ἀρχῆς ὑπὸ πάντων ὑμῶν καὶ ἐκ νέων ἡμᾶς ἐπείθετε, οὐκ ἂν ἀλλήλους ἐφυλάττομεν μὴ ἀδικεῖν, ἀλλ' αὐτὸς αὑτοῦ ἦν ἕκαστος ἄριστος φύλαξ, δεδιὼς μὴ ἀδικῶν τῷ μεγίστῳ κακῷ ξύνοικος ᾖ.

wards maintained by Sokrates. If the theory were conformable to facts, no precautions would need to be taken by men
against the injustice of each other. But such precautions
have been universally recognised as indispensable, and universally adopted. Therefore the Sokratic theory is not conformable to facts. It is not true that the performance of duty
(considered apart from consequences) is self-inviting and self-
remunerative—the contrary path self-deterring and self-puni-
tory—to each individual agent. Plato might perhaps argue
that it would be true, if men were properly educated; and that
the elaborate education which he provides for his Guardians
in the Republic would suffice for this purpose. But even if
this were granted, we must recollect that the producing Many
of his Republic would receive no such peculiar education.

Understanding the words in the second construction, they
would then mean that the doctrine, though not true, ought
to be preached and accredited by the lawgiver as an useful
fiction : that if every one were told so from his childhood,
without ever hearing either doubt or contradiction, it would
become an established creed which each man would believe,
and each agent would act upon : that the effect in reference
to society would therefore be the same as if the doctrine
were true. This is in fact expressly affirmed by Plato in
another place.[y] Now undoubtedly the effect of preaching
and teaching, assuming it to be constant and unanimous, is
very great in accrediting all kinds of dogmas. Plato believed
it to be capable of almost unlimited extension—as we may
see by the prescriptions which he gives for the training of
the Guardians in his Republic. But to persuade every one
that the path of duty and justice was in itself inviting, would
be a task overpassing the eloquence even of Plato, since
every man's internal sentiment would refute it. You might
just as well expect to convince a child, through the declarations and encouragements of his nurse, that the medicine
prescribed to him during sickness was very nice. Every
child has to learn obedience as a necessity, under the authority and sanction of his parents. You may assure him that
what is at first repulsive will become by habit comparatively

y Plato, Legg. ii. pp. 663-664.

easy: and that the self-reproach, connected with evasion of duty, will by association become a greater pain than that which is experienced in performing duty. This is to a great degree true, but it is by no means true to the full extent: still less can it be made to appear true before it has been actually realised. You cannot cause a fiction like this to be universally accredited. A child is compelled to practise justice by the fear of displeasure and other painful consequences from those in authority over him: the reason for bringing this artificial motive to bear upon him, is, that it is essential in the first instance for the comfort and security of others: in the second instance for his own. In Plato's theory, the first consideration is omitted, while not only the whole stress is laid upon the second, but more is promised in regard to the second than the reality warrants.

The opponents whom the Platonic Sokrates here seeks to confute held—That Justice is an obligation in itself onerous to the agent, but indispensable in order to ensure to him just dealing and estimation from others—That injustice is a path in itself easy and inviting to the agent, but necessary to be avoided, because he forfeits his chance of receiving justice from others, and draws upon himself hatred and other evil consequences. This doctrine (argues Plato) represents the advantages of justice to the just agent as arising, not from his actually being just, but from his seeming to be so, and being reputed by others to be so: in like manner, it represents the misery of injustice to the unjust agent as arising, not from his actually being unjust, but from his being reputed to be so by others. The inference which a man will naturally draw from hence (adds Plato) is, That he must aim only at seeming to be just, not at being just in reality: that he must seek to avoid the reputation of injustice, not injustice in reality: that the mode of life most enviable is, to be unjust in reality, but just in seeming—to study the means either of deceiving others into a belief that you are just, or of coercing others into submission to your injustice.[z] This indeed cannot be done unless you are strong or artful: if you are weak or simple-minded, the best thing which you can do is to be just. The weak alone

[z] Plato, Republic, ii. pp. 362-367.

are gainers by justice: the strong are losers by it, and gainers by injustice.[a]

These are legitimate corollaries (so Glaukon and Adeimantus are here made to argue) from the doctrine preached by most fathers to their children, that the obligations of justice are in themselves onerous to the just agent, and remunerative only so far as they determine just conduct on the part of others towards him. Plato means, not that fathers, in exhorting their children, actually drew these corollaries; but that if they followed out their own doctrine consistently, they would have drawn them: and that there is no way of escaping them, except by adopting the doctrine of the Platonic Sokrates— That justice is in itself a source of happiness to the just agent, and injustice a source of misery to the unjust agent—however each of them may be esteemed or treated by others.

Now upon this we may observe, That Plato, from anxiety to escape corollaries which are only partially true, and which, in so far as they are true, may be obviated by precautions—has endeavoured to accredit a fiction misrepresenting the constant phenomena and standing conditions of social life. Among those conditions, reciprocity of services is one of the most fundamental. The difference of feeling which attaches to the services which a man renders, called duties or obligations— and the services which he receives from others, called his rights—is alike obvious and undeniable. Each individual has both duties and rights: each is both an agent towards others, and a patient or sentient from others. He is required to be just towards others, they are required to be just towards him: he in his actions must have regard, within certain limits, to their comfort and security—they in their actions must have regard to his. If he has obligations towards them, he has also rights against them; or (which is the same thing) they have obligations towards him. If punishment is requisite to deter him from doing wrong to them, it is equally requisite to deter them from doing wrong to him. Whoever theorises upon society, contemplating it as a connected scheme or system including different individual agents, must accept this

Marginal note: Reciprocity of rights and duties between men in social life— different feelings towards one and towards the other.

---

[a] Plato, Republic, ii. p. 366 C.

reciprocity as a fundamental condition. The rights and obligations, of each towards the rest, must form inseparable and correlative parts of the theory. Each agent must be dealt with by others according to his works, and must be able to reckon beforehand on being so dealt with:—on escaping injury or hurt, and receiving justice, from others, if he behaves justly towards them. The theory supposes, that whether just or unjust, he will appear to others what he really is, and will be appreciated accordingly.[b]

The fathers of families, whose doctrine Plato censures, adopted this doctrine of reciprocity, and built upon it their exhortations to their children. " Be just to others : without that condition, you cannot expect that they will be just to you." Plato objects to their doctrine, on the ground, that it assumed justice to be onerous to the agent, and therefore indirectly encouraged the evading of the onerous preliminary condition, for the purpose of extorting or stealing the valuable consequent without earning it fairly. Persons acting thus unjustly would efface reciprocity by taking away the antecedent. Now Plato, in correcting them, sets up a counter-doctrine which effaces reciprocity by removing the consequent. His counter-doctrine promises me that if I am just towards others, I shall be happy in and through that single circumstance ; and that I ought not to care whether they behave justly or unjustly towards me. Reciprocity thus disappears. The authoritative terms *right* and *obligation* lose all their specific meaning.

In thus eliminating reciprocity—in affirming that the performance of justice is not an onerous duty, but in itself happiness-giving, to the just agent—Plato contradicts his own theory respecting the genesis and foundation of society. What is the explanation

Plato's own theory, respecting the genesis of society, is based on reciprocity.

---

[b] In a remarkable passage of the Laws Plato sets a far higher value upon correct estimation from others, which in the Republic he depicts under the contemptuous appellation of show or seeming.

Plato, Legg. xii. p. 950 B.

Χρὴ δὲ οὔποτε περὶ σμικροῦ ποιεῖσθαι τὸ δοκεῖν ἀγαθοὺς εἶναι τοῖς ἄλλοις ἢ μὴ δοκεῖν· οὐ γὰρ ὅσον οὐσίας ἀρετῆς ἀπεσφαλμένοι τυγχάνουσιν οἱ πολλοί, τοσοῦτον καὶ τοῦ κρίνειν τοὺς ἄλλους οἱ πονηροὶ καὶ ἄχρηστοι, θεῖον δέ τι καὶ εὔστοχόν ἐστι καὶ τοῖς κακοῖς. ὥστε πάμπολλοι καὶ τῶν σφόδρα κακῶν εὖ τοῖς λόγοις καὶ ταῖς δόξαις διαιροῦνται τοὺς ἀμείνους τῶν ἀνθρώπων καὶ τοὺς χείρους. Διὸ καλὸν ταῖς πολλαῖς πόλεσι τὸ παρακέλευσμά ἐστι, προτιμᾶν τὴν εὐδοξίαν πρὸς τῶν πολλῶν· τὸ μὲν γὰρ ὀρθότατον καὶ μέγιστον, ὄντα ἀγαθὸν ἀληθῶς οὕτω τὸν εὔδοξον βίον θηρεύειν —χωρὶς δὲ μηδαμῶς, τόν γε τέλεον ἄνδρα ἐσόμενον.

which he himself gives (in this very Republic) of the primary
origin of a city? It arises (he says) from the fact, that each
individual among us is not self-sufficing, but full of wants.
All having many wants, each takes to himself others as
partners and auxiliaries to supply them: thus grows up the
aggregation called a city.[c] Each man gives to another, and
receives from another, in the belief that it will be better for
him to do so. It is found most advantageous to all, that each
man shall devote himself exclusively to one mode of production, and shall exchange his produce with that of others.
Such interchange of productions and services is the generating
motive which brings about civic communion.[d] Justice and
injustice will be found in certain modes of carrying on this
useful interchange between each man and the rest.[e]

Here Plato expressly declares the principle of reciprocity to
be the fundamental cause which generates and sustains the
communion called the city. No man suffices to himself:
every man has wants which require supply from others: every
man can contribute something to supply the wants of others.
Justice or injustice have place, according as this reciprocal
service is carried out in one manner or another. Each man
labours to supply the wants of others as well as his own.

This is the primitive, constant, indispensable, bond whereby
society is brought and held together. Doubtless it is not the
only bond, nor does Plato say that it is. There are other
auxiliary social principles besides, of great value and importance: but they presuppose and are built upon the fundamental
principle—reciprocity of need and service—which remains
when we reduce society to its lowest terms; and which is not
the less real as underlying groundwork, though it is seldom
enunciated separately, but appears overlaid, disguised, and
adorned, by numerous additions and refinements. Plato cor-

---

[c] Plato, Republic, ii. p. 369 B-C.
γίγνεται πόλις, ἐπειδὴ τυγχάνει ἡμῶν
ἕκαστος οὐκ αὐτάρκης ἀλλὰ πολλῶν
ἐνδεής—μεταδίδωσι δὴ ἄλλος ἄλλῳ,
εἴ τι μεταδίδωσιν, ἢ μεταλαμβάνει,
οἰόμενος αὐτῷ ἄμεινον εἶναι
—ποιήσει δὲ αὐτὴν (τὴν πόλιν) ὡς
ἔοικεν, ἡ ἡμετέρα χρεία.
[d] Plato, Republic, ii. p. 371 B.
Τί δὲ δή; ἐν αὐτῇ τῇ πόλει πῶς

ἀλλήλοις μεταδώσουσιν ὧν ἂν ἕκαστοι
ἐργάζωνται; ὧν δὴ ἕνεκα καὶ
κοινωνίαν ποιησάμενοι πόλιν
ᾠκίσαμεν.
[e] Plato, Republic, ii. pp. 371-372.
Ποῦ οὖν ἄν ποτε ἐν αὐτῇ (τῇ πόλει)
εἴη ἥ τε δικαιοσύνη καὶ ἡ ἀδικία; Ἐγὼ
οὐκ ἐννοῶ, εἰ μή που ἐν αὐτῶν
τούτων χρείᾳ τινὶ τῇ πρὸς
ἀλλήλους.

rectly announces the reciprocity of need and service as one indivisible, though complex, fact, when looked at with reference to the social communion. Neither of the two parts of that fact, without the other part, would serve as adequate groundwork. Each man must act, not for himself alone, but for others also: he must keep in view the requirements of others, to a certain extent, as well as his own. In his purposes and scheme of life, the two must be steadily combined.

It is clear that Plato—in thus laying down the principle of reciprocity, or interchange of service, as the groundwork of the social union—recognises the antithesis, and at the same time the correlation, between obligation and right. The service which each man renders to supply the wants of others is in the nature of an onerous duty; the requital for which is furnished to him in the services rendered by others *Antithesis and correlation of obligation and right. Necessity of keeping the two ideas together, as the basis of any theory respecting society.* to supply his wants. It is payment against receipt, and is expressly so stated by Plato—which every man conforms to, "believing that he will be better off thereby." Taking the two together, every man is better off; but no man would be so by the payment alone; nor could any one continue paying out, if he received nothing in return. Justice consists in the proper carrying on of this interchange in its two correlative parts.[f]

We see therefore that Plato contradicts his own fundamental principle, when he denies the doing of justice to be an onerous duty, and when he maintains that it is in itself happiness-giving to the just agent, whether other men account him just and do justice to him in return—or not. By this latter doctrine he sets aside that reciprocity of want and service, upon which he had affirmed the social union to rest. The fathers, whom he blames, gave advice in full conformity with

[f] We may remark that Plato, though he states the principle of reciprocity very justly, does not state it completely. He brings out the reciprocity of need and service; he does not mention the reciprocal liability of injury. Each man can do hurt to others: each man may receive hurt from others. Abstinence on the part of each from hurting others, and security to each that he shall not be hurt by others, are necessities quite as fundamental as that of production and interchange.

The reciprocal feeling of security, or absence of all fear of ill-usage from others (τὸ καθ' ἡμέραν ἀδεὲς καὶ ἀνεπιβούλευτον πρὸς ἀλλήλους, to use the phrase of Thucydides iii. 37) is no less essential to social sentiment than the reciprocal confidence that each man may obtain from others a supply of his wants on condition of supplying theirs.

his own principle of reciprocity—when they exhorted their sons to the practice of justice, not as self-inviting, but as an onerous service towards others, to be requited by corresponding services and goodwill from others towards them. If (as he urges) such advice operates as an encouragement to crime, because it admits that the successful tyrant or impostor, who gets the services of others for nothing, is better off than the just man who gets them only in exchange for an onerous equivalent—this inference equally flows from that proclaimed reciprocity of need and service, which he himself affirms to be the generating cause of human society. If it be true (as Plato states) that each individual is full of wants, and stands in need of the services of others—then it cannot be true, that payment without receipt, as a systematic practice, is self-inviting and self-satisfying. That there are temptations for strong or cunning men to evade obligation and to usurp wrongful power, is an undeniable fact. We may wish that it were not a fact: but we gain nothing by denying or ignoring it. The more clearly the fact is stated, the better; in order that society may take precaution against such dangers—a task which has always been found necessary, and often difficult. In reviewing the Gorgias,[g] we found Sokrates declaring, that Archelaus, the energetic and powerful king of Macedonia, who had usurped the throne by means of crime and bloodshed, was thoroughly miserable: far more miserable than he would have been, had he been defeated in his enterprise and suffered cruel punishment. Such a declaration represents the genuine sentiment of Sokrates as to what he *himself* would feel, and what ought to be (in his conviction) the feeling of every one, after having perpetrated such nefarious acts. But it does not represent the feeling of Archelaus himself, nor that of the large majority of bystanders: both to these latter, and to himself, Archelaus appears an object of envy and admiration.[h]

---

[g] See above, ch. xxii. pp. 108-112.

[h] Xenophon, Cyropæd. iii. 3, 52-53. Cyrus says:—

ᾶρ' οὐκ, εἰ μέλλουσι τοιαῦται διάνοιαι ἐγγενήσεσθαι ἀνθρώποις καὶ ἔμμονοι ἔσεσθαι, πρῶτον μὲν νόμους ὑπάρξαι δεῖ τοιούτους, δι' ὧν τοῖς μὲν ἀγαθοῖς ἔντιμος καὶ ἐλευθέριος ὁ βίος παρασκευασθήσεται, τοῖς δὲ κα- κοῖς ταπεινός τε καὶ ἀλγεινὸς καὶ ἀβίωτος ὁ αἰὼν ἐπανακείσεται; Ἔπειτα δὲ διδασκάλους, οἶμαι, δεῖ καὶ ἄρχοντας ἐπὶ τούτοις γενέσθαι, οἴτινες δείξουσί τε ὀρθῶς καὶ διδάξουσι καὶ ἐθίσωσι ταῦτα δρᾶν, ἔστ' ἂν ἐγγένηται αὐτοῖς, τοὺς μὲν ἀγαθοὺς καὶ εὐ- κλεεῖς εὐδαιμονεστάτους τῷ ὄντι νομίζειν, τοὺς δὲ κακοὺς καὶ δυσ-

And it would be a fatal mistake, if the peculiar sentiment of Sokrates were accepted as common to others besides, and as forming a sound presumption to act upon: that is, if, under the belief that no ambitious man will voluntarily bring upon himself so much misery, it were supposed that precautions against his designs were unnecessary. The rational and tutelary purpose of punishment is, to make the proposition true and obvious to all—That the wrong-doer, will draw upon himself a large preponderance of mischief by his wrong-doing. But to proclaim the proposition by voice of herald (which Plato here proposes) as if it were already an established fact of human nature, independent of all such precautions—would be only an unhappy delusion.[i]

The characteristic feature of the Platonic commonwealth is to specialize the service of each individual in that function for which he is most fit. It is assumed, that each will render due service to the rest, and will receive from them due service in requital. Upon this assumption, Plato pronounces that the community will be happy.

Characteristic feature of the Platonic Commonwealth—specialization of services to that function for which each man is fit—will not apply to one individual separately.

Let us grant for the present that this conclusion follows from his premises. He proceeds forthwith to apply it by analogy to another and a different case—the case of the individual man. He presumes complete analogy between the community and an individual.[k] To a certain extent, the analogy is real: but it fails on the main point which Plato's inference requires as a basis. The community, composed of various and differently endowed members, suffices to itself and its own happiness: "the individual is not sufficient to himself, but stands in need of much aid from

---

κλεεῖς ἀθλιωτάτους ἁπάντων ἡγεῖσθαι.

Xenophon here uses language at variance with that of Plato, and consonant to that of the fathers of families whom Plato censures. To create habits of just action, and to repress habits of unjust action, society must meet both the one and the other by a suitable response. Assuming such conditional reciprocity to be realised, you may then persuade each agent that the unjust man, whom society brands with dishonour, is miserable (οἱ κακοὶ καὶ δυσκλεεῖς).

[i] Xenophon, Economic. xiii. 11. Ischomachus there declares :—

Πάνυ γάρ μοι δοκεῖ, ὦ Σώκρατες, ἀθυμία ἐγγίνεσθαι τοῖς ἀγαθοῖς, ὅταν ὁρῶσι τὰ μὲν ἔργα δι' αὐτῶν καταπραττόμενα, τῶν δὲ ὁμοίων τυγχάνοντας ἑαυτοῖς τοὺς μήτε πονεῖν μήτε κινδυνεύειν ἐθέλοντας, ὅταν δέῃ.—also xiv. 9-10.

[k] The parallel between the Commonwealth and the individual is perpetually reproduced in Plato's reasoning. Republic, ii. pp. 368-369, vii. p. 541 B, ix. pp. 577 C-D, 579 E, &c.

others "[1]—a grave fact which Plato himself proclaims as the generating cause and basis of society. Though we should admit therefore, that Plato's commonwealth is perfectly well-constituted, and that a well-constituted commonwealth will be happy—we cannot from thence infer that an individual, however well-constituted, will be happy. His happiness depends upon others as well as upon himself. He may have in him the three different mental varieties of souls, or three different persons—Reason, Energy, Appetite—well tempered and adjusted; so as to produce a full disposition to just behaviour on his part: but constant injustice on the part of others will nevertheless be effectual in rendering him miserable. From the happiness of a community, all composed of just men—you cannot draw any fair inference to that of one just man in an unjust community.

Thus much to show that the parallel between the community and the individual, which Plato pursues through the larger portion of the Republic, is fallacious. His affirmation—That the just man is happy in his justice, *quand même*—in his own mental perfection, whatever supposition may be made as to the community among whom he lives—implies that the just man is self-sufficing: and Plato himself expressly declares that no individual is self-sufficing, Indeed, no author can set forth more powerfully than Plato himself in this very dialogue—the uncomfortable and perilous position of a philosophical individual, when standing singly as a dissenter among a community with fixed habits and sentiments—unphilosophical and anti-philosophical. Such a person (Plato says) is like a man who has fallen into a den of wild beasts: he may think himself fortunate, if by careful retirement and abstinence from public manifestation, he can preserve himself secure and uncorrupted: but his characteristic and superior qualities can obtain no manifestation. The philosopher requires a community suited to his character. Nowhere does any such community (so Plato says) exist at present.[m]

I cannot think, therefore, that the main thesis which Sokrates professes to have established, against the difficulties

---

[1] Plato, Republic, ii. p. 369 B.
[m] Plato, Repub. vi. pp. 494 E, 496 D, 497 B. ὥσπερ εἰς θηρία ἄνθρωπος ἐμπεσών, &c. Compare also ix. p. 592.

raised by Glaukon, is either proved or proveable.   Plato has
fallen into error, partly by exaggerating the paral- Plato has not
lelism between the individual man and the common- made good
his refuta-
tion—the
wealth ; partly by attempting to reason on justice thesis which
and injustice in abstract isolation, without regard to he impugns
is true.
the natural consequences of either—while yet those consequences cannot be really excluded from consideration, when
we come to apply to these terms, predicates either favourable
or unfavourable.   That justice, taken along with its ordinary
and natural consequences, tends materially to the happiness of
the just agent—that injustice, looked at in the same manner,
tends to destroy or impair the happiness of the unjust—these
are propositions true and valuable to be inculcated.   But this
was the very case embodied in the exhortations of the ordinary
moralists and counsellors, whom Plato intends to refute.   He
is not satisfied to hear them praise justice taken along with its
natural consequences : he stands forward to panegyrise justice
abstractedly, and without its natural consequences : nay,
even if followed by consequences the very reverse of those
which are ordinary and natural.[n]   He insists that justice is
eligible and pleasing *per se*, self-recommending : that among
the three varieties of *Bona* (1. That which we choose for
itself and from its own immediate attractions.   2. That which
is in itself indifferent or even painful, but which we choose
from regard to its ulterior consequences.   3. That which we
choose on both grounds, both as immediately attractive and
as ultimately beneficial), it belongs to the last variety : whereas
the opponents whom he impugns referred it to the second.

Here the point at issue between the two sides is expressly
set forth.   Both admit that Justice is a Bonum— Statement
both of them looking at the case with reference only of the real
issue between
to the agent himself.   But the opponents contend, him and his
opponents.
that it is Bonum (with reference to the agent) only through
its secondary effects, and noway Bonum or attractive in its
primary working : being thus analogous to medical treatment
or gymnastic discipline, which men submit to only for the

---

[n] Plato, Republic, ii. p. 367 B.   εἰ | οὐ τὸ δίκαιον φήσομεν ἐπαινεῖν σε, ἀλλὰ
γὰρ μὴ ἀφαιρήσεις ἑκατέρωθεν *i. e.* (both | τὸ δοκεῖν—οὐδὲ τὸ ἄδικον εἶναι ψέγειν,
from justice and from injustice) τὰς | ἀλλὰ τὸ δοκεῖν — καὶ παρακελεύεσθαι
ἀληθεῖς δόξας, τὰς δὲ ψευδεῖς προσθήσεις, | ἄδικον ὄντα λανθάνειν, &c.

sake of ulterior benefits. On the contrary, Plato maintained
that it is good both in its primary and secondary effects : good
by reason of the ulterior benefits which it confers, but still
better and more attractive in its direct and primary effect:
thus combining the pleasurable and the useful, like a healthy
constitution and perfect senses. Both parties agree in recognising justice as a good : but they differ in respect of the
grounds on which, and the mode in which, it is good.

Such is the issue as here announced by Plato himself: and
the announcement deserves particular notice because
the Platonic Sokrates afterwards, in the course of his
argument, widens and misrepresents the issue: ascribing to his opponents the invidious post of enemies
who defamed justice and recommended injustice,
while he himself undertakes to counterwork the advocates of
injustice, and to preserve justice from unfair calumny [o]—thus
professing to be counsel for Justice *versus* Injustice. Now
this is not a fair statement of the argument against which
Sokrates is contending. In that argument, justice was admitted to be a Good, but was declared to be a Good of that
sort which is laborious and irksome to the agent in the primary
proceedings required from him—though highly beneficial and
indispensable to him by reason of its ulterior results: like
medicine, gymnastic discipline, industry,[p] &c. Whether this
doctrine be correct or not, those who hold it cannot be fairly
described as advocates of injustice and enemies of Justice :[q]
any more than they are enemies of medicine, gymnastic
discipline, industry, &c., which they recommend as good and
indispensable, on the same grounds as they recommend justice.

It may suit Plato's purpose, when drawing up an argument
which he intends to refute, to give to it the colour of being a

He himself misrepresents this issue—he describes his opponents as enemies of justice.

[o] Plato, Repub. ii. p. 368 B. δέδοικα γὰρ μὴ οὐδ' ὅσιον ᾖ παραγενόμενον
δικαιοσύνῃ κακηγορουμένῃ ἀπαγορεύειν
καὶ μὴ βοηθεῖν, ἔτι ἐμπνέοντα καὶ δυνάμενον φθέγγεσθαι.

[p] Plato, Republic, ii. pp. 357-358.

[q] In the lost treatise De Republicâ
of Cicero, Philus, one of the disputants,
was introduced as spokesman of the
memorable discourse delivered by Karneades at Rome, said to have been
against Justice, and in favour of Injustice—"patrocinium injustitiæ." Læ-
lius replied to him, as "*Justitiæ de-
fensor.*" The few fragments preserved
do not enable us to appreciate the line
of argument taken by Karneades ; but
as far as we can judge, it seems to have
been very different from that which is
assigned to Glaukon and Adeimantus
in the Platonic Republic. See the
Fragments of the third book De Republicâ in Orelli's edition of Cicero,
pp. 460-467.

panegyric upon injustice : but this is no real or necessary part of the opponent's case. Nevertheless the commentators on Plato bring it prominently forward. The usual programme affixed to the Republic is—Plato, the defender of Justice, against Thrasymachus and the Sophists, advocates and pane- gyrists of Injustice. How far the real Thrasymachus may have argued in the slashing and offensive style described in the first book of the Republic, we have no means of deciding. But the Sophists are here brought in as assumed preachers of injustice, without any authority either from Plato or else- where : not to mention the impropriety of treating the Sophists as one school with common dogmas. Glaukon (as I have already observed) announces the doctrine against which So- krates contends, not as a recent corruption broached by the Sophists, but as the generally received view of Justice : held by most persons, repeated by the poets from ancient times downwards, and embodied by fathers in lessons to their children : Sokrates farther declares the doctrine which he himself propounds to be propounded for the first time.[r]

Over and above the analogy between the just common- wealth and the just individual, we find two additional and independent arguments, to confirm the proof of the Platonic thesis, respecting the happiness of the just man. Plato distributes mankind into three varieties. 1. He in whom Reason is preponderant —the philosopher. 2. He in whom Energy or Courage is preponderant—the lover of dominion and superiority—the ambitious man. 3. He in whom Appetite is preponderant— the lover of money. Plato considers the two last as unjust men, contrasting them with the first, who alone is to be regarded as just.

Farther argu- ments of Plato in sup- port of his thesis. Com- parison of three differ- ent charac- ters of men.

The language of Plato in arguing this point is vague, and requires to be distinguished before we can appreciate the extent to which he has made out his point. At one time, he

---

[r] Plato, Republ. ii. p. 358 B. Οὐ τοίνυν δοκεῖ τοῖς πολλοῖς, ἀλλὰ τοῦ ἐπιπόνου εἴδους, &c. P. 358 C. ἀκούων Θρασυμάχου καὶ μυρίων ἄλλων τὸν δὲ ὑπὲρ τῆς δικαιοσύνης λόγον οὐδενός πω ἀκήκοα ὡς βούλομαι. Pp. 362-363.

λέγουσι δέ που καὶ παρακελεύονται πατέρες τε υἱέσι καὶ πάντες οἵ τινων κηδόμενοι, &c.—τούτοις τε πᾶσι τοῖς λόγοις μάρτυρας τοὺς ποιητὰς ἐπάγονται (p. 364 D) : also p. 366 D.

states his conclusion to the effect—That the man who pursues and enjoys the pleasures of ambition or enrichment, but
only under the conditions and limits which reason prescribes,
is happier than he who pursues them without any such controul, and who is the slave of violent and ungovernable im-
pulses.⁸ This is undoubtedly true.

But elsewhere Plato puts his thesis in another way. He
compares the pleasures of the philosopher, arising from intellectual contemplation and the acquisition of knowledge—with
the pleasures of the ambitious man and the money-lover, in
compassing their respective ends, the attainment of power
and wealth. If you ask (says Plato) each of these three
persons which is the best and most pleasurable mode of life,
each will commend his own: each will tell you that the pleasures of his own mode of life are the greatest, and that those
of the other two are comparatively worthless.ᵗ But though
each thus commends his own, the judgment of the philosopher
is decidedly the most trustworthy of the three. For the
necessities of life constrain the philosopher to have some experience of the pleasures of the other two, while they two are
altogether ignorant of his:—moreover, the comparative estimate must be made by reason and intelligent discussion, which
is his exclusive prerogative. Therefore, the philosopher is
to be taken as the best judge, when he affirms that *his* pleasures are the greatest, in preference to the other two.ᵘ To
establish this same conclusion, Plato even goes a step farther.
No pleasures, except those peculiar to the philosopher, are
perfectly true and genuine, pure from any alloy or mixture
of pain. The pleasures of the ambitious man, and of the
money-lover, are untrue, spurious, alloyed with pain and for
the most part mere riddances from pain—appearing falsely
to be pleasures by contrast with the antecedent pains to
which they are consequent. The pleasures of the philosophic life are not preceded by any pains. They are mental
pleasures, having in them closer affinity with truth and reality
than the corporeal: the matter of knowledge, with which the
philosophising mind is filled and satisfied, comes from the

⁸ Plato, Republic, ix. pp. 586-587.   ᵗ Plato, Republic, ix. p. 581 C-D.
ᵘ Plato, Republic, ix. pp. 582-583.

everlasting and unchangeable Ideas—and is thus more akin to true essence and reality, than the perishable substances which relieve bodily hunger and thirst.[x]

It is by these two lines of reasoning, and especially by the last, that Plato intends to confirm and place beyond dispute the triumph of the just man over the unjust.[y] He professes to have satisfied the requirement of Glaukon, by proving that the just man is happy by reason of his justice—*quand même*—however he may be esteemed or dealt with either by Gods or men. But even if we grant the truth of his premises, no such conclusion can be elicited from them. He appears to be successful only because he changes the terminology and the state of the question. Assume it to be true, that the philosopher, whose pleasures are derived chiefly from the love of knowledge and of intellectual acquisitions, has a better chance of happiness than the ambitious or the money-loving man. This I believe to be true in the main, subject to many interfering causes—though the manner in which Plato here makes it out is much less satisfactory than the handling of the same point by Aristotle after him.[z] But when the point is granted, nothing is proved about the just and the unjust man, except in a sense of those terms peculiar to Plato himself.

His arguments do not go to the point which he professes to aim at.

Nor indeed is Plato's conclusion proved, even in his own sense of the words. He identifies the just man with the philosopher or man of reason—the unjust man with the pursuer of power or wealth. Now, even in this Platonic meaning, the just man or philosopher cannot be called happy *quand même* : he requires, as one condition of his happiness, a certain amount of service, forbearance, and estimation, on the part of his fellows. He is not completely self-sufficing, nor can any human being be so.

The confusion, into which Plato has here fallen, arises mainly from his exaggerated application of the analogy between the Commonwealth and the Indi-

Exaggerated parallelism between the

---

[x] Plato, Republic, ix. pp. 585-586.

[y] Plato, Republic, ix. p. 583 B. Ταῦτα μὲν τοίνυν οὕτω δύ᾽ ἐφεξῆς ἂν εἴη καὶ δὶς νενικηκὼς ὁ δίκαιος τὸν ἄδικον· τὸ δὲ τρίτον—τοῦτ᾽ ἂν εἴη τὸ

μέγιστον καὶ κυριώτατον τῶν πτωμάτων.

[z] Aristot. Ethic. Nikom. i. 5, p. 1095 b, 1096 a, x. 6-9, pp. 1176-1179.

vidual : from his anxiety to find in the individual
something like what he notes as justice in the Commonwealth : from his assimilating the mental attributes of each individual, divisible only in logical abstraction,—
to the really distinct individual citizens whose association forms
the Commonwealth.[a] It is only by a poetical or rhetorical
metaphor that you can speak of the several departments of a
man's mind, as if they were distinct persons, capable of be-
having well or ill towards each other. A single man, considered without any reference to others, cannot be either just
or unjust. "The just man" (observes Aristotle, in another
line of argument), "requires others, towards whom and with
whom he may behave justly."[b] Even when we talk by metaphor of a man being just towards himself, reference to
others is always implied, as a standard with which comparison
is taken.

In the main purpose of the Republic, therefore—to prove
Second argu-
ment of Plato
to prove the
happiness of
the just man
—He now re-
calls his pre-
vious con-
cession, and
assumes that
the just man
will receive
just treat-
ment and
esteem from
others. that the just man is happy in his justice, and the
unjust miserable in his injustice, whatever supposition may be made as to consequent esteem or treatment from Gods or men—we cannot pronounce
Plato to have succeeded. He himself indeed speaks
with triumphant confidence of his own demonstration. Yet we find him at the close of the dialogue
admitting that he had undertaken the defence of a
position unnecessarily difficult. "I conceded to you"
(he says) " for argument's sake that the just man should
be accounted unjust, by Gods as well as men, and that the
unjust man should be accounted just. But this is a concession which I am not called upon to make ; for the real fact
will be otherwise. I now compare the happiness of each,

<hr/>

[a] Plato, Republic, i. pp. 351 C,
352 C. οὐ γὰρ ἂν ἀπείχοντο ἀλλήλων
κομιδῇ ὄντες ἄδικοι, ἀλλὰ δῆλον ὅτι
ἐνῆν τις αὐτοῖς δικαιοσύνη, ἣ αὐτοὺς
ἐποίει μή τοι καὶ ἀλλήλους γε καὶ ἐφ'
οὓς ᾔεσαν ἅμα ἀδικεῖν, δι' ἣν ἔπραξαν ἃ
ἔπραξαν, ὥρμησαν δὲ ἐπὶ τὰ ἄδικα ἀδικίᾳ
ἡμιμόχθηροι ὄντες, &c.
We find the same sentiment in the
Opera et Dies of Hesiod, 275, contrasting human society with animal
life :—

ἰχθύσι μὲν καὶ θηρσὶ καὶ ἄλλοισιν
  πετεηνοῖς
ἔσθειν ἀλλήλους, ἐπεὶ οὐ δίκη ἔστιν
  ἐν αὐτοῖς·
ἀνθρώποισι δ' ἔδωκε (Ζεὺς) δίκην, ἣ
  πολλὸν ἀμείνων
γίνεται.

[b] Aristotel. Ethic. Nikomach. x. 7.
ὁ δίκαιος δεῖται πρὸς οὓς δικαιοπραγήσει,
καὶ μεθ' ὧν.

assuming that each has the reputation and the treatment which he merits from others. Under this supposition, the superior happiness of the just man over the unjust, is still more manifest and undeniable." [c]

Plato then proceeds to argue the case upon this hypothesis, which he affirms to be conformable to the reality. The just man will be well-esteemed and well-treated by men: he will also be favoured and protected by the Gods, both in this life and after this life. The unjust man, on the contrary, will be ill-esteemed and ill-treated by men: he will farther be disapproved and punished by the Gods, both while he lives and after his death. Perhaps for a time the just man may seem to be hardly dealt with and miserable—the unjust man to be prosperous and popular—but in the end, all this will be reversed. [d]

This second line of argument is essentially different from the first. Plato dispatches it very succinctly, in two pages: while in trying to prove the first, and in working out the very peculiar comparison on which his proof rests, he had occupied the larger portion of this very long treatise.

In the first line of argument, justice was recommended as implicated with happiness *per se* or absolutely—*quand même* —to the agent: injustice was discouraged, as implicated with misery. In the second line, justice is recommended by reason of its happy ulterior consequences to the agent: injustice is dissuaded on corresponding grounds, by reason of its miserable ulterior consequences to the agent.

It will be recollected that this second line of argument is the same as that which Glaukon described as adopted by parents and by other monitors, in discourse with pupils. Plato therefore here admits that their exhortations were founded on solid grounds; though he blames them for denying or omitting the announcement, that just behaviour conferred happiness upon the agent by its own efficacy, apart from all consequences. He regards the happiness attained by the just man, through the consequent treatment by men and Gods, as real indeed,—but as only supplemental and secondary, inferior in value to the happiness involved in the just behaviour *per se*.

[c] Plato, Republic, x. pp. 612-613.   [d] Plato, Republic, x. p 613.

In this part of the argument, too, as well as in the former, we are forced to lament the equivocal meaning of the word *justice :* and to recollect the observation of Plato at the close of the first book, that those who do not know what justice is, can never determine what is to be truly predicated of it, and what is not.[e] If by the just man he means the philosopher, and by the unjust man the person who is not a philosopher,— he has himself told us before, that in societies as actually constituted, the philosopher enjoys the minimum of social advantages, and is even condemned to a life of insecurity; while the unphilosophical men (at least a certain variety of them) obtain sympathy, esteem, and promotion.[f]

Now in this second line of argument, Plato holds a totally different language respecting the way in which the just man is treated by society. He even exaggerates, beyond what can be reasonably expected, the rewards accruing to the just man: who (Plato tells us), when he has become advanced in life and thoroughly known, acquires command in his own city if he chooses it, and has his choice among the citizens for the best matrimonial alliances: while the unjust man ends in failure and ignominy, incurring the hatred of every one and suffering punishment.[g] This is noway consistent with Plato's previous description of the position of the philosopher in actual society: yet nevertheless his argument identifies the just man with the philosopher.

Plato appears so anxious to make out a triumphant case in

Dependence of the happiness of the individual on the society in which he is placed.   favour of justice and against injustice, that he forgets not only the reality of things, but the main drift of his own previous reasonings. Nothing can stand out more strikingly, throughout this long and eloquent treatise, than the difference between one society and another: the necessary dependance of every one's lot, partly indeed upon his own character, but also most materially upon the society to which he belongs: the impossibility of affirming any thing generally respecting the result of such and such dispositions in the individual, until you know the society of which he is a member, as well as his place therein. Hence

---

[e] Plato, Republic, i. p. 354 B.

[f] Plato, Republic, vi. pp. 492-494-495-497.

[g] Plato, Republic, x. p. 613 D-E.

arises the motive for Plato's own elaborate construction—a
new society upon philosophical principles. This essentially relative point of view pervades the greater part of
his premises, and constitutes the most valuable part of
them.

Whether the commonwealth as a whole, assuming it to be
once erected, would work as he expects, we will not here
enquire. But it is certain that the commonwealth and the
individuals are essential correlates of each other; and that
the condition of each individual must be criticised in reference
to the commonwealth in which he is embraced. Take any
member of the Platonic Commonwealth, and place him in
any other form of government, at Athens, Syracuse, Sparta,
&c.—immediately his condition, both active and passive, is
changed. Thus the philosophers, for whom Plato assumes
unqualified ascendancy as the cardinal principle in his system,
become, when transferred to other systems, divested of influence, hated by the people, and thankful if they can obtain
even security. "The philosopher" (says Plato) "must have a
community suited to him and docile to his guidance: in communities such as now exist, he not only has no influence as
philosopher, but generally becomes himself corrupted by the
contagion and pressure of opinions around him: this is the
natural course of events, and it would be wonderful if the
fact were otherwise." [h]

After thus forcibly insisting upon the necessary correlation between the individual and the society, as well *Inconsist-*
as upon the variability and uncertainty of justice *ency of af-*
firming gene-
and injustice in different existing societies [i]—Plato *ral positions*
respecting
is inconsistent with himself in affirming, as an uni- *the happiness*
of the just
versal position, that the just man receives the favour *man, in all*
societies
and good treatment of society, the unjust man, *without dis-*
tinction.
hatred and punishment. [k] You cannot decide this until you
know in what society the just man is placed. In order to

---

[h] Plato, Republic, vi. pp. 487-488-
489 B, 497 B-C, 492 C. καὶ φήσειν τὰ
αὐτὰ τούτοις καλὰ καὶ αἰσχρὰ εἶναι, καὶ
ἐπιτηδεύσειν ἅπερ ἂν οὗτοι, καὶ ἔσεσθαι
τοιοῦτον ; Compare also ix. pp. 592 A,
494 A. τοὺς φιλοσοφοῦντας ἄρα ἀνάγκη

ψέγεσθαι ὑπ' αὐτῶν (τοῦ πλήθους). vii.
p. 517 A.

[i] Plato, Republic, v. p. 479, vi. p.
493 C.

[k] Plato, Republic, x. p. 613.

make him comfortable, Plato is obliged to construct an imaginary society suited to him: which would have been unnecessary, if you can affirm that he is sure to be well treated in every society.

There is a sense indeed (different from what Plato intended), in which the proposition is both true, and consistent with his own doctrine about the correlation between the individual and the society. When Plato speaks of the just or the unjust man, to whose judgment does he make appeal? To his own judgment? or to which of the numerous other dissentient judgments? For that there were numerous dissentient opinions on this point, Plato himself testifies: a person regarded as just or unjust in one community, would not be so regarded in another. All this ethical and intellectual discord is fully recognised as a fact, by Plato himself: who moreover keenly felt it, when comparing his own judgment with that of the Athenians his countrymen. Such being the ambiguity of the terms, we can affirm nothing respecting the just or the unjust man absolutely and generally—respecting justice or injustice in the abstract: We cannot affirm any thing respecting the happiness or misery of either, except with reference to the sentiments of the community wherein each is placed. Assuming their sentiments to be known, we may pronounce that any individual citizen who is unjust *relatively to them* (*i. e.* who behaves in a manner which they account unjust), will be punished by their superior force, and rendered miserable: while any one who abstains from such behaviour, and conducts himself in a manner which they account just, will receive from them just dealing, with a certain measure of trust, and esteem. Taken in this relative sense, we may truly say of the unjust man, that he will be unhappy; because displeasure, hatred, and punitory infliction from his countrymen will be quite sufficient to make him so, without any other causes of unhappiness. Respecting the just man, we can only say that he will be happy, so far as exemption from this cause of misery is concerned: but we cannot make sure that he will be happy on the whole, because happiness is a product to which many different conditions, positive and negative, must

Qualified sense in which only this can be done.

concur—while the serious causes of misery are efficacious, each taken singly, in producing their result.

Moreover, in estimating the probable happiness either of the just (especially taking this word *sensu Platonico* as equivalent to *the philosophers*) or the unjust, another element must be included: which an illustrious self-thinking reasoner like Plato ought not to have omitted. Does the internal reason and sentiment of the agent coincide with that of his countrymen, as to what is just and unjust? Is he essentially homogeneous with his countrymen (to use the language of Plato in the Gorgias[1]), a chip of the same block? Or has he the earnest conviction that the commandments and prohibitions which they enforce upon him, on the plea of preventing injustice, are themselves unjust? Is he (like the philosopher described by Plato among societies actually constituted, or like Sokrates at Athens[m]) a conscientious dissenter from the orthodox creed—political, ethical, or æsthetical—received among his fellow-citizens generally? Does he (like Sokrates) believe himself to be inculcating useful and excellent lessons, while his countrymen blame and silence him as a corruptor of youth, and as a libeller of the elders?[n] Does he, in those actions which he performs either under legal restraint or under peremptory unofficial custom, submit merely to what he regards as *civium ardor prava jubentium*, or as *vultus instantis tyranni?*

This is a question essentially necessary to be answered, when we are called upon to affirm the general principle—"That the just man is happy, and that the unjust man is unhappy." Antipathy and ill-treatment will be the lot of any citizen who challenges opinions which his society cherish as consecrated, or professes such as they dislike. Such was the fate of Sokrates himself at Athens. He was indicted as unjust and criminal (Ἀδικεῖ

Question—Whether the just man is orthodox or dissenter in his society? —important in discussing whether he is happy.

Comparison of the position of Sokrates at Athens, with that of his accusers.

---

[1] Plato, Gorgias, p. 513 B. αὐτοφυῶς ὅμοιος τῇ πολιτείᾳ, &c.

[m] Plato, Republic, vi. pp. 496-497. Plato, Gorgias, p. 521 D.

[n] Plato, Gorgias, p. 522 B. ἐὰν δέ τίς με ἢ νεωτέρους φῇ διαφθείροειν ἀπορεῖν ποιοῦντα, ἢ πρεσβυτέρους

κακηγορεῖν λέγοντα πικροὺς λόγους ἢ ἰδίᾳ ἢ δημοσίᾳ, οὔτε τὸ ἀληθὲς ἔξω εἰπεῖν, ὅτι Δικαίως πάντα ταῦτα καὶ λέγω καὶ πράττω, τὸ ὑμέτερον δὴ τοῦτο, ὦ ἄνδρες δικασταί—οὔτε ἄλλο οὐδέν· ὥστε ἴσως ὅ, τι ἂν τύχω, τοῦτο πείσομαι.

Σωκράτης), while his accusers, Anytus and Melêtus, carried away the esteem and sympathy of their fellow-citizens generally, as not simply just men, but zealous champions of justice—as resisting the assailants of morality and religion, of the political constitution, and of parental authority. How vehement was the odium and reprobation which Sokrates incurred from the majority of his fellow-citizens, we are assured by his own Apology[o] before the Dikasts. Now it is to every one a serious and powerful cause of unhappiness, to feel himself the object of such a sentiment. Most men dread it so much, like the Platonic Euthyphron, that they refrain from uttering, or at least are most reserved in communicating, opinions which are accounted heretical among their countrymen or companions.[p] The resolute and free-spoken Sokrates braved that odium; which, aggravated by particular circumstances, as well as by the character of his own defence, attained at last such a height as to bring about his condemnation to death. That he was sustained in this unthankful task by native force of character, conscientious persuasion, and belief in the approbation of the Gods—is a fact which we should believe, even if he himself had not expressly told us so. But to call him *happy*, would be a misapplication of the term, which no one would agree with Plato in making—least of all the friends of Sokrates in the last months of his life. Besides, if we are to call Sokrates happy on these grounds, his accusers would be still happier: for they had the same conscientious conviction, and the same belief in the approbation of the Gods: while they enjoyed besides the sympathy of their countrymen as champions of religion and morality.

In spite of all the charm and eloquence, therefore, which abounds in the Republic, we are compelled to declare that the Platonic Sokrates has not furnished the solution required from him by Glaukon and

Imperfect ethical basis on which Plato has conducted

---

[o] Plato, Apolog. Sokr. pp. 28 A, 37 D.

πολλή μοι ἀπεχθεία γέγονε καὶ πρὸς πολλούς, &c.

[p] Plato, Euthyphron, p. 3 D.

᾽Αθηναίοις γάρ τοι οὐ σφόδρα μέλει, ἄν τινα δεινὸν οἴωνται εἶναι, μὴ μέντοι διδασκαλικὸν τῆς αὑτοῦ σοφίας· ὃν δ' ἂν

καὶ ἄλλους οἴωνται ποιεῖν τοιούτους, θυμοῦνται, εἴτ᾽ οὖν φθόνῳ, εἴτε δι᾽ ἄλλο τι.

Euthyphr. Τούτου μὲν πέρι ὅπως ποτὲ πρὸς ἐμὲ ἔχουσιν, οὐ πάνυ ἐπιθυμῶ πειραθῆναι.

Sokrat. Ἴσως γὰρ σὺ μὲν δοκεῖς σπάνιον σεαυτὸν παρέχειν, καὶ διδάσκειν οὐκ ἐθέλειν τὴν σεαυτοῦ σοφίαν, &c.

Adeimantus: and that neither the first point (ix. p. the discussion in the 580 D) nor the second point, of his conclusion (x. Republic. p. 613) is adequately made out. The very grave ethical problem, respecting the connexion between individual just behaviour and individual happiness, is discussed in a manner too exclusively self-regarding, and inconsistent with that reciprocity which Plato himself sets forth as the fundamental, generating, sustaining, principle of human society. If that principle of reciprocity is to be taken as the starting-point, you cannot discuss the behaviour of any individual towards society, considered in reference to his own happiness, without at the same time including the behaviour of society towards him. Now Plato, in the conditions that he expressly prescribes for the discussion,[q] insists on keeping the two apart; and on establishing a positive conclusion about the first, without at all including the second. He rejects peremptorily the doctrine—"That just behaviour is performed for the good of others, apart from the agent." Yet if society be, in the last analysis (as Plato says that it is), an exchange of services, rendered indispensable by the need which every one has of others—the services which each man renders are rendered *for the good of others,* as the services which they render to him are rendered *for his good.* The just dealing of each man is, in the first instance, beneficial to others: in its secondary results, it is for the most part beneficial to himself.[r] His unjust dealing, in like manner, is, in the first instance, injurious to others: in its secondary results, it is for the most part injurious to himself. Particular acts of injustice may, under certain circumstances, be not injurious, nay even beneficial,

---

[q] Plato, Republic, ii. p. 367.

[r] See the instructive chapter on the Moral Sense, in Mr. James Mill's Analysis of the Phenomena of the Human Mind, ch. xxiii. p. 234.

"The actions from which men derive advantage have all been classed under four titles.—Prudence, Fortitude, Justice, Beneficence. When those names are applied to our own acts, the first two, Prudent and Brave, express acts which are useful *to ourselves* in the first instance: the latter two, Just and Beneficent, express acts which are useful *to others* in the first instance. It is farther to be remarked, that those acts of ours which primarily useful to ourselves, are secondarily useful to others ; and those which are primarily useful to others, are secondarily useful to ourselves. Thus it is by our own prudence and fortitude that we are best enabled to do acts of justice and beneficence to others. And it is by acts of justice and beneficence to others, that we best dispose them to do similar acts to us."

to the unjust agent: but they are certain to be hurtful to others: were it not so, they would not deserve to be branded as injustice. I am required to pay a debt, for the benefit of my creditor, and for the maintenance of a feeling of security among other creditors—though the payment may impose upon myself severe privation: indirectly, indeed, I am benefited, because the same law which compels me, compels others also to perform their contracts towards me. The law (to use a phrase of Aristotle) guarantees just dealing by and towards each.[s] The Platonic Thrasymachus, therefore, is right in so far as he affirms—That injustice is *Malum Alienum*, and justice *Bonum Alienum*,[t] meaning that such is the direct and primary characteristic of each. The unjust man is one who does wrong to others, or omits to render to others a service which they have a right to exact, with a view to some undue profit or escape of inconvenience for himself: the just man is one who abstains from wrong to others, and renders to others the full service which they have a right to require, whatever hardship it may impose upon himself. A man is called just or unjust, according to his conduct towards others.

In considering the main thesis of the Republic, we must

Plato in Republic is preacher, inculcating useful beliefs —not philosopher, establishing scientific theory. State of Just and Unjust Man in the Platonic Commonwealth.

look upon Plato as preacher—inculcating a belief which he thinks useful to be diffused ; rather than as philosopher, announcing general truths of human nature, and laying down a consistent, scientific, theory of Ethics. There are occasions on which even he himself seems to accept this character. " If the fable of Kadmus and the dragon's teeth " (he maintains) " with a great many other stories equally improbable, can be made matters of established faith, surely a doctrine so plausible as mine, about justice and injustice, can be easily taught and accredited."[u] To ensure unanimous acquiescence, Plato would constrain all poets to proclaim and

---

[s] Aristot. Polit. iii. 9, 1280, b. 10. ὁ νόμος συνθήκη, καὶ καθάπερ ἔφη Λυκόφρων ὁ σοφιστὴς, ἐγγυητὴς ἀλλήλοις τῶν δικαίων.

[t] Plato, Republic, ii. p. 367 C. καὶ ὁμολογεῖν Θρασυμάχῳ ὅτι τὸ μὲν δίκαιον, ἀλλότριον ἀγαθὸν, ξύμφερον τοῦ κρείττονος· τὸ δὲ ἄδικον, αὑτῷ μὲν

ξύμφερον καὶ λυσιτελοῦν, τῷ δὲ ἥττονι, ἀξύμφορον.

[u] See Plato, Legg. ii. pp. 663-664. Good and simple people, in the earlier times (says Plato), believed every thing that was told them. They were more virtuous and just then than they are now (Legg. iii. p. 679 C-E).

illustrate his thesis—and would prohibit them from uttering anything inconsistent with it.[x] But these or similar official prohibitions may be employed for the upholding of any creed, whatever it be: and have been always employed, more or less, in every society, for the upholding of the prevalent creed. Even in the best society conceivable under the conditions of human life, assuming an ideal commonwealth in which the sentiments of *just* and *unjust* have received the most systematic, beneficent, and rational embodiments, and have become engraven on all the leading minds—even then Plato's first assertion—That the just man is happy *quand même*—could not be admitted without numerous reserves and qualifications. Justice must still be done by each agent, not as a self-inviting process, but as an obligation entailing more or less of sacrifice made by him to the security and comfort of others. Plato's second assertion—That the unjust man is miserable—would be more near the truth; because the ideal commonwealth is assumed to be one in which the governing body has both the disposition and the power to punish injustice—and the discriminating equanimity, or absence of antipathies, which secures them against punishing anything else. The power of society to inflict misery is far more extensive than its power of imparting happiness. But even thus, we have to recollect that the misery of the unjust person arises not from his injustice *per se*, but from consequent treatment at the hands of others.

Thus much for the Platonic or ideal commonwealth. But when we pass from that hypothesis into the actual world, the case becomes far stronger against the truth of both Plato's assertions. Of actual societies, even the best have many imperfections—the less good, many attributes worse than imperfections:—

Comparative happiness of the two in actual communities. Plato is dissatisfied with it—This is his motive for recasting

---

[x] Plato, Legg. ii. pp. 661-662. Illustrated in the rigid and detailed censorship which he imposes on the poets in the Republic, in the second and third books.

In the Legg., however, Plato puts his thesis in a manner less untenable than in the Republic:—"Neither to do wrong to others, nor to suffer wrong from others; this is the happiest condition" (Legg. ii. p. 663 A). This is a very different proposition from that which is defended in the Republic; where we are called upon to believe, that the man who acts justly will be happy, whatever may be the conduct of others towards him.

society on his own principles. *" ob virtutes certissimum exitium."* The dissenter for the better, is liable to be crucified alongside of the dissenter for the worse : King Nomos will tolerate neither.

Plato as a preacher holds one language : as a philosopher and analyst, another.   When he is exhorting youth to justice,
Confusion between the preacher and the philosopher in the Platonic Republic. or dissuading them from injustice, he thinks himself entitled to depict the lot of the just man in the most fascinating colours, that of the unjust man as the darkest contrast against it—without any careful observance of the line between truth and fiction : the fiction, if such there be, becomes in his eyes a *pia fraus*, excused or even ennobled by its salutary tendency.   But when he drops this practical purpose, and comes to philosophise on the principles of society, he then proclaims explicitly how great is the difference between society as it now stands, and society as it ought to be : how much worse is the condition of the just, how much less bad that of the unjust (in every sense of the words, but especially in the Platonic sense) than a perfect commonwealth would provide.   Between the exhortations of Plato the preacher, and the social analysis of Plato the philosopher, there is a practical contradiction, which is all the more inconvenient because he passes backwards and forwards almost unconsciously, from one character to the other.   The splendid treatise called the Republic is composed of both, in portions not easy to separate.

The difference between the two functions just mentioned—
Remarks on the contrast between ethical theory and ethical precepts. the preceptor, and the theorizing philosopher—deserves careful attention, especially in regard to Ethics.   If I lay down a theory of social philosophy, I am bound to take in all the conditions and circumstances of the problem : to consider the whole position of each individual in society, as an agent affecting the security and comfort of others, and also as a person acted on by others, and having his security and comfort affected by their behaviour : as subject to obligations or duties, in the first of the two characters—and as enjoying rights (*i. e.* having others under obligation to him) in the second.   This reciprocity of service and need—of obligation and right—is the basis of social theory : its two parts are in indivisible correlation : alike

integrant and co-essential. But when a preceptor delivers
exhortations on conduct, it is not necessary that he should
insist equally on each of the two parts. As a general fact of
human nature, it is known that men are disposed *proprio motu*
to claim their rights, but not so constantly or equally disposed
to perform their obligations : accordingly, the preceptor
insists upon this second part of the case, which requires
extraneous support and enforcement—leaving untouched the
first part, which requires none. But the very reason why
the second part needs such support, is, because the performance of the obligation is seldom self-inviting, and often the
very reverse : that is, because the Platonic doctrine misrepresents the reality. The preceptor ought not to indulge
in such misrepresentation : he may lay stress especially upon
one part of the entire social theory, but he ought not to
employ fictions which deny the necessary correlation of the
other omitted part. Many preceptors have insisted on the
performance of obligation, in language which seemed to
imply that they considered a man to exist only for the performance of obligation, and to have no rights at all. Plato
in another way undermines equally the integrity of the
social theory, when he contends, that the performance of
obligations alone, without any rights, is delightful *per se,* and
suffices to ensure happiness to the performer. Herein we
can recognise only a well-intentioned preceptor, narrowing
and perverting the social theory for the purpose of edification
to his hearers.

CHAPTER XXXV.

REPUBLIC—REMARKS ON THE PLATONIC COMMONWEALTH.

In my last Chapter, I discussed the manner in which Plato
had endeavoured to solve the ethical problem urged
upon him by Glaukon and Adeimantus. But this
is not the entire purpose of the Republic. Plato,
drawing the closest parallel between the Commonwealth and the individual, seeks solution of the problem first
in the former; because it is there (he says) written in larger
and clearer letters. He sketches the picture of a perfect
Commonwealth—shows wherein its Justice consists—and
proves, to his own satisfaction, that it will be happy in
and through its justice—*per se*. This picture of a Commonwealth is unquestionably *one* of the main purposes of the
dialogue; serving as commencement—or more properly as
intermediate stage—to the Timæus and Kritias. Most critics
have treated it as if it were the dominant and almost
exclusive purpose. Aristotle, the earliest of all critics, adverts to it in this spirit; numbering Plato or the Platonic
Sokrates among those who, not being practical politicians,
framed schemes for ideal commonwealths, like Phaleas or
Hippodamus. I shall now make some remarks on the political provisions of the Platonic Commonwealth: but first I
shall notice the very peculiar manner in which Plato dis-
covers therein the notions of Justice and Injustice.

*Double pur-
pose of the
Platonic Re-
public—ethi-
cal and poli-
tical.*

The Platonic Sokrates (as I remarked above) lays down
as the fundamental, generating, principle of human
society, the reciprocity of need and service, essentially belonging to human beings: exchange of services is indispensable, because each man has many
wants more than he can himself supply, and thus
needs the services of others: while each also can
contribute something to supply the wants of others.

*Plato recog-
nises the
generating
principle of
human so-
ciety—reci-
procity of
need and ser-
vice. Parti-
cular direc-
tion which
he gives to
this princi-
ple.*

To this general principle Plato gives a peculiar direction.
He apportions the services among the various citizens; and
he provides that each man shall be specialised for the service to which he is peculiarly adapted, and confined to that
alone. No double man [a] is tolerated. How such specialisa-
tion is to be applied in detail among the multitude of cultivators and other producers, Plato does not tell us. Each
is to have his own employment: we know no more. But in
regard to the two highest functions, he gives more information: first, the small cabinet of philosophical Elders,[b] Chiefs, or
Rulers—artists in the craft of governing, who supply pro-
fessionally that necessity of the Commonwealth, and from
whom all orders emanate : next, the body of Guardians,
Soldiers, Policemen, who execute the orders of this cabinet,
and defend the territory against all enemies. Respecting
both of these, Plato carefully prescribes both the education
which they are to receive, and the circumstances under which
they are to live. They are to be of both sexes intermingled,
but to know neither family nor property : they live together
in barrack, and with common mess, receiving subsistence and
the means of decent comfort, but no more, from the producers: respecting sexual relations and births, I shall say
more presently.

When Plato has provided thus much, he treats his city as
already planted and brought to consummation. He *The four car-*
thinks himself farther entitled to proclaim it as per- *dinal virtues are assumed*
fectly good, and therefore as including the four con- *as consti-*
tuting the
stituent elements of Good: that is, as being wise, *whole of Good or Vir-*
brave, temperate, just.[c] He then looks to find *tue, where each of these*
wherein each of these four elements resides: wisdom *virtues re-*
sides.
resides specially in the cabinet of Rulers—courage specially
in the Guardians—temperance and justice, in these two, but

---

[a] Plato, Rep. iii. p. 397 E.

[b] The principle laid down in the
Protagoras will be remembered—εἷς
ἔχων τέχνην πολλοῖς ἱκανὸς ἰδιώταις
(Protag. p. 322 D).

[c] Plato, Repub. iv. pp. 427 D, 428 A.
ᾠκισμένη μὲν τοίνυν, ἦν δ' ἐγώ, ἤδη ἂν
σοι εἴη, ὦ παῖ 'Αρίστωνος, ἡ πόλις—

Οἶμαι ἡμῖν τὴν πόλιν, εἴπερ ὀρθῶς γε
ᾤκισται, τελέως ἀγαθὴν εἶναι.
'Ανάγκη, ἔφη. Δῆλον δὴ, ὅτι σοφή τ'
ἐστὶ καὶ ἀνδρεία, καὶ σώφρων καὶ δικαία.
Δῆλον. Οὐκοῦν, ὅ,τι ἂν αὐτῶν εὕρω-
μεν ἐν αὐτῇ, τὸ ὑπόλοιπον ἔσται τὸ οὐχ
εὑρημένον; &c.

in the producing multitude also. The two last virtues are universal in the Commonwealth. Temperance consists in the harmony of opinion between the multitude and the two higher classes as to obedience : the Guardians are as ready to obey as the Chiefs to command : the multitude are also for the most part ready to obey—but should they ever fail in obedience, the Guardians are prepared to lend their constraining force to the authority of the Chiefs. Having thus settled three out of the four elements of Good, which enumeration he assumes to be exhaustive—Plato assumes that what remains must be Justice. This remainder he declares to be—That each of the three portions of the Commonwealth performs its own work and nothing else: and this is Justice. Justice and Temperance are thus common to all the three portions of the Commonwealth: while Wisdom and Prudence belong entirely to the Chiefs, and Courage entirely to the Guardians.

Here, for the first time in Ethical Theory, Prudence, Courage, Temperance, Justice, are assumed as an exhaustive enumeration of virtues: each distinct from the other three, but all together including the whole of Virtue.[d] Through Cicero and others, these four have come down as the cardinal virtues. From whom Plato derived it, I do not know: not certainly from the historical Sokrates, who resolved the last three into the first.[e] Nor is it indeed in harmony with Plato's own view: for temperance and justice are substantially coincident, in his explanation of them (since he does not recognise the characteristic feature of Justice, as directly tending to the good of a person other than the agent), and the line by which he endeavours to part them is obscure as well as unimportant. Schleiermacher, who admits that the distinction drawn here between Temperance and Justice is altogether forced, sup-

(margin note:) First mention of these, as an exhaustive classification, in ethical theory. Plato effaces the distinction between Temperance and Justice.

---

[d] Plat. Rep. iv. p. 432 B. τὸ δὲ δὴ λοιπὸν εἶδος, δι' ὃ ἂν ἔτι ἀρετῆς μέτεχοι πόλις, τί ποτ' ἂν εἴη; δῆλον γὰρ ὅτι τοῦτό ἐστιν ἡ δικαιοσύνη.
Compare p. 444 D, where he defines Ἀρετή—Ἀρετὴ μὲν ἄρα, ὡς ἔοικεν, ὑγίειά τέ τις ἂν εἴη καὶ κάλλος καὶ εὐεξία ψυχῆς· κακία δὲ, νόσος τε καὶ αἶσχος καὶ ἀσθένεια.

[e] Xenoph. Mem. iii. 9, 4-5. σοφίαν δὲ καὶ σωφροσύνην οὐ διώριζεν, &c.
Compare the discussion of σωφροσύνη, iv. 5, 9-11, where Sokrates enforces the practice of it on the ground that it ensured to a man both more pleasures and greater pleasures, of which he would deprive himself if he were foolish enough to be intemperate.

poses that Plato took up this quadruple classification, because
he found it already established in the common, non-theorising,
consciousness.[f] If this be true, the real distinction between
Justice (as directly bearing on the rights of another person)
and Temperance (as directly concerning only the future happiness of the agent himself), which is one of the most important distinctions in Ethics—must have been already felt,
without being formulated, in the common mind: and Plato,
by retaining the two words, but effacing the distinction between the two, and giving a new meaning to Justice—took a
step in the wrong direction.   He himself however tells us,
that the definition, here given of Justice, is not his own ; but
that he had heard it enunciated by many others before him.[g]
What makes this more remarkable is, That the same definition (to do your own business and not to meddle with other
people's business) is what we read in the Charmidês as delivered respecting Temperance, by Charmides and Kritias :[h]
delivered by them, and afterwards pulled to pieces in cross-
examination by Sokrates.   Herein we see farther proof, how
little distinction Plato drew between Justice and Temperance.

From whomsoever Plato may have derived this ethical
classification—Virtue as a whole, distributed into four varieties—1. Prudence or Knowledge—2. Courage or Energy—
3. Temperance—4. Justice—we find it here placed in the
foreground of his doctrine, respecting both the collective

---

[f] Schleiermacher, Einl. zum Staat,
pp. 25-26. "Dieser Tadel trifft höch-
stens die Aufstellung jener vier zusam-
mengehörigen Tugenden ;   welche
Platon offenbar genug nur mit rich-
tigem praktischen Sinne aus Ehrfurcht
für das Bestehende aufgenommen hat :
wie sie denn schon auf dieselbe Weise
aus dem gemeinen Gebrauch in die
Lehrweise des Sokrates übergegangen
sind."

[g] Plato, Rep. iv. p. 433 A. καὶ
μὴν ὅτι γε τὸ τὰ αὑτοῦ πράττειν καὶ μὴ
πολυπραγμονεῖν δικαιοσύνη ἐστι, καὶ
τοῦτο ἄλλων τε πολλῶν ἀκηκόαμεν, καὶ αὐτοὶ πολλάκις εἰρήκαμεν.
Compare iii. p. 406 E.

[h] See Charmidês, pp. 161-162.
Heindorf observes in his note on this
passage :—" A sophistis ergo vulgata

hæc σωφροσύνης definitio : ad justitiam
quoque ab iisdem ut videtur, translata.
Republ. iv. p. 433 (the passage cited
in note preceding). Quo pertinent illa
Ciceronis, De Officiis, i. 9, 2. Item ad
prudentiam, Aristot. Eth. Nicom. vi. 8.
Philosopho vero hoc tribuit Sokrates,
Gorgias, p. 526)."

The definition given in the Charmidês appears plainly ascribed to
Kritias as its author (p. 162 D).   The
affirmation that it was " a sophistis
vulgata," and afterwards transferred
by these same to Justice, is made
without any authority produced ; and
is expressed in the language usual
with the Platonic commentators, who
treat the Sophists as a philosophica
sect or school.

Commonwealth and the individual man.[1] He professes to understand and explain what they are—to reason upon them all with confidence—and to apply them to very important conclusions.

But let us pause for a moment to ask, how these professions harmonise with the dialogues reviewed in my preceding volumes. No reader will have forgotten the doubts and difficulties, exposed by the Sokratic Elenchus throughout the Dialogues of Search : the confessed inability of Sokrates himself to elucidate them, while at the same time his contempt for the false persuasion of knowledge—for those who talk confidently about matters which they can neither explain nor defend—is expressed without reserve. Now, when we turn to the Hippias Major, we find Sokrates declaring, that no man can affirm, and that a man ought to be ashamed to pretend to affirm, what particular matters are beautiful (fine, honourable) or ugly (mean, base), unless he knows and can explain what Beauty is.[k] A similar declaration appears in the Menon, where Sokrates treats it as absurd to affirm or deny any predicate respecting a Subject, until you have satisfied yourself that you know what the Subject itself is : and where he farther proclaims, that as to Virtue, he does not know what it is, and that he has never yet found any one who *did* know.[l] Such ignorance is stated at the end of the dialogue not less emphatically than at the beginning. Again, respecting the four varieties or parts of Virtue. The first of the four, Prudence—(Wisdom—Knowledge)—has been investigated in the Theætêtus—one of the most elaborate of all the Platonic dialogues : several different explanations of it are proposed by Theætetus, and each is shown by Sokrates to be untenable : the problem remains unsolved at last. As to Courage and Temperance, we have not been more for-

All the four are here assumed as certain and determinate, though in former dialogues they appear indeterminate and full of unsolved difficulties.

---

[1] In some of the Platonic Dialogues these four varieties are not understood as exhausting the sum total of Virtue : ἡ ὁσιότης is included also ; see Lachês, p. 199 D, Protagoras, p. 329 D, Euthyphron, pp. 5-6. Plato does not advert to τὸ ὅσιον in the Republic as a separate constituent, seemingly because on matters of piety he enjoins direct reference to Apollo and the Delphian oracle, Rep. iv. p. 427 B.

[k] Plat. Hipp. Maj. pp. 286 D, 304 C.

[l] Plato, Menon, pp. 71 B-C, 86 B, 100 B.

tunate. The Lachês and Charmidês exhibit nothing but a
fruitless search both for one and for the other. And here the
case is more remarkable; because in the Lachês, one of
the several definitions of Courage, tendered to Sokrates and
refuted by him, is, the very definition of Courage delivered
by him in the Republic as complete and satisfactory : while
in the Charmidês, one of the definitions of Temperance refuted, and even treated as scarcely intelligible, by Sokrates
(τὸ πράττειν τὰ ἑαυτοῦ) is the same as that which Sokrates in
the Republic relies on as a valid definition of Justice.[m]
Lastly, every one who has read the Parmenidês, will remember the acute objections there urged against the Platonic
hypothesis of substantive Ideas, participated in by particulars : of which objections no notice is taken in the Republic,
though so much is said therein about these Ideas, in regard
to the training of the philosophical Chiefs.

If we revert to these passages (and many others which might
be produced) of past dialogues, we shall find no   *Difficulties
means provided of harmonising them with the Re-   *left un-
                                                           *solved, but
public. The logical and ethical difficulties still exist : *overleaped
                                                           *by Plato.
they have never been elucidated : the Republic does not pretend
to elucidate them, but overlooks or overleaps them. In composing it, Plato has his mind full of a different point of view,
to which he seeks to give full effect. While his spokesman
Sokrates was leader of opposition, Plato delighted to arm him
with the maximum of negative cross-examining acuteness : but
here Sokrates has passed over to the ministerial benches, and
has undertaken the difficult task of making out a case in reply
to the challenge of Glaukon and Adeimantus. No new leader
of opposition is allowed to replace him. The splendid constructive effort of the Republic would have been spoiled, if
exposed to such an analytical cross-examination as that which
we read in Menon, Lachês, or Charmidês.

---

[m] See Lachês, p. 195 A. τὴν τῶν
δεινῶν καὶ θαρραλέων ἐπιστήμην,
pp. 196 C-199 A-E—in the cross-
examination of Nikias by Sokrates :
and the question in the cross-examination of Lachês (who has defined Courage to be ἡ φρόνιμος καρτερία) put
by Sokrates—ἡ εἰς τί φρόνιμος; compared with Republic, iv. pp. 429 C,
430 B, 433 C. See also Charmidês,
pp. 161 B, 162 B-C, compared with
Republic, iv. p. 433 B-D.

In remarking upon the Platonic Republic as a political scheme only, we pass from the Platonic point of view to the Aristotelian: that is, to the discussion of Ethics and Politics as separate subjects, though adjoining and partially overlapping each other. Plato conceives the two in intimate union, and even employs violent metaphors to exaggerate the intimacy. Xenophon also conceives them in close conjunction. Aristotle goes farther in separating the two: a great improvement in regard to the speculative dealing with both of them.[n]

Ethical and political theory combined by Plato, treated apart by Aristotle.

If, following the example of Aristotle, we criticise Plato's Republic as a scheme of political constitution, we find that on most points which other theorists handle at considerable length, he is intentionally silent. His project is an outline and nothing more. He delineates fully the brain and heart of the great Leviathan, but leaves the rest in very faint outline. He announces explicitly the purpose of all his arrangements, to obtain happiness for the whole city: by which he means, not happiness for the greatest number of individuals, but for the abstract unity called the City, supposed to be capable of happiness or misery, apart from any individuals, many or few, composing it.[o] Each individual is to do the work for which he is best fitted, contributory to the happiness of the whole—and to do nothing else. Each must be content with such happiness as consists with his own exclusive employment.[p]

Platonic Commonwealth—only an outline—partially filled up.

[n] The concluding chapter of the Nikomachean Ethics contains some striking remarks upon this separation.

[o] Plato, Repub. iv. pp. 420-421. The objection that the Guardians will have no happiness, is put by Plato into the mouth of Adeimantus, but is denied by Sokrates; who, however, says that even if it were true he could not admit it as applicable, since what he wishes is that the entire commonwealth shall be happy. Aristotle (Politic. ii. 5, 1264, 6-15) repeats the objection of Adeimantus, and declares that collective happiness (not enjoyed by some individuals) is impossible. See the valuable chapter on Ideal Models in Politics (vol. ii. ch. xxii.

p. 236 seq.) in Sir George Cornewall Lewis's Treatise on the methods of Observation and Reasoning in Politics. The different ideal models framed by theorists ancient and modern, Plato among the number, are there collected, with judicious remarks in comparing and appreciating them.

[p] Plato, Republic, iv. p. 421 C. He lays down this minute subdivision and speciality of aptitude in individuals as a fundamental property of human nature. Republic, iii. p. 395. καὶ ἔτι γε τούτων φαίνεταί μοι εἰς σμικρότερα κατακεκερματίσθαι ἡ τοῦ ἀνθρώπου φύσις, &c.

Compare Xenophon, Cyropæd. ii. 1, 21, where the same principle is laid

The Chiefs or Rulers are assumed to be both specially qualified and specially trained for the business of governing. Their authority is unlimited: they represent that One Infallible Wise Man, whom Plato frequently appeals to (in the Politikus, Kriton, Gorgias, and other dialogues), but never names. They are a very small number, perhaps only one : the persons naturally qualified being very few, and even they requiring the severest preparatory training. The Guardians, all of them educated up to a considerable point, both obey themselves the orders of these few Chiefs, and enforce obedience upon the productive multitude. Of this last mentioned multitude, constituting numerically almost the whole city, we hear little or nothing : except that the division of labour is strictly kept up among them, and that neither wealth nor poverty is allowed to grow up.[q] How this is to be accomplished, Plato does not point out : nor does he indicate how the mischievous working (*i. e.* mischievous, in his point of view, and as he declares it) of the proprietary and the family relations is to be obviated. His scheme tacitly assumes that separate property and family are to subsist among the great mass of the community, but not among the Guardians : he proclaims explicitly, that if the proprietary relations or the family relations were permitted among the Guardians, entire corruption of their character would ensue.[r] Among the Demos or multitude, he postulates nothing except unlimited submission to the orders of the Rulers enforced through the Guardians. The regulative powers of the Rulers are assumed to be of omnipotent efficacy against every cause of mischief, subject only to one condition—That the purity of the golden breed, together with the Platonic training and discipline, are to be maintained among them unimpaired.

Everything in the Platonic Republic turns upon this elaborate training of the superior class : most of all, the Chiefs or

Absolute rule of a few philosophers— Careful and peculiar training of the Guardians.

---

down. Another passage in the same treatise (Cyropæd. viii. 2, 5) is also interesting. Xenophon there contrasts the smaller towns, where many trades were combined in the same hand and none of the works well performed, with the larger towns, where there was a minuter subdivision of labour, each man doing one work only, and doing it well.

[q] Plato, Republic, iv. p. 421.

[r] Plato, Republic, iii. p. 417.

Rulers—next, the Soldiers or Guardians. Besides this training, they are required to be placed in circumstances which will prevent them from feeling any private or separate interest of their own, apart from or adverse to that of the multitude. "Every man" (says Plato) " will best love those whose advantage he believes to coincide with his own, and when he is most convinced that if they do well, he himself will do well also: if not, not."[s] " The Rulers must be wise, powerful, and affectionately solicitous for the city."

These then are the two circumstances which Plato works out: The Education of the Rulers and Guardians: Their position and circumstances in regard to each other and to the remaining multitude. He does not himself prescribe, or at least he prescribes but rarely, what is to be enacted or ordered. He creates the generals and the soldiers; he relies upon the former for ordering, upon the latter for enforcing, aright.

On this point we may usefully compare him with his contemporary Xenophon. He, like Plato, presents himself to mankind as a preceptor or schoolmaster, rather than as a lawgiver. Most Grecian cities (he remarks) left the education of youth in the hands of parents, and permitted adults to choose their own mode of life, subject only to the necessity of obeying the laws: that is of abstaining from certain defined offences, and of performing certain defined obligations—under penalties if such obedience were not rendered. From this mode of proceeding Xenophon dissents, and commends the Spartan lawgiver Lykurgus for departing from it.[t] To regulate public matters, without regulating the private life of the citizens, appeared to him impossible.[u] At Sparta, the citizen was subject to authoritative regulation, from childhood to old age. In the public education, or in the public drill, he was constantly under

Comparison of Plato with Xenophon— Cyropædia— Œconomicus.

---

[s] Plato, Republic, iii. p. 412 D.

Καὶ μὴν τοῦτό γ᾿ ἂν μάλιστα φιλοῖ, ᾧ ξυμφέρειν ἡγοῖτο τὰ αὐτὰ καὶ ἑαυτῷ, καὶ ὅταν μάλιστα ἐκείνου μὲν εὖ πράττοντος οἴηται ξυμβαίνειν καὶ ἑαυτῷ εὖ πράττειν, μὴ δὲ, τοὐνάντιον ;
Compare v. pp. 463-464.

[t] Xenophon, Rep Lacedæm. i. 2. Λυκοῦργος, οὐ μιμησάμενος τὰς ἄλλας πόλεις, ἀλλὰ καὶ ἐνάντια γνοὺς ταῖς πλείσταις, προέχουσαν εὐδαιμονίᾳ τὴν πόλιν ἀπέδειξεν.

[u] Compare Plato, Legg. vi. p. 780 A.

supervision, going through prescribed exercises. This produced, according to Xenophon, "a city of pre-eminent happiness." He proclaims and follows out the same peculiar principle, in his ideal scheme of society called the Persian laws.
He embodies in the Cyropædia the biography of a model
chief, trained up from his youth in (what Xenophon calls)
the Persian system, and applying the virtues acquired therein
to military exploits and to the government of mankind. The
Persian polity, in which the hero Cyrus receives his training,
is described. Instead of leaving individuals to their own
free will, except as to certain acts or abstinences specifically
enjoined, this polity placed every one under a regimental
training: which both shaped his character beforehand, so as to
make sure that he should have no disposition to commit
offences [x]—and subjected him to perpetual supervision afterwards, commencing with boyhood and continued to old age,
through the four successive stages of boys, youths, mature
men, and elders.

This general principle of combining polity with education,
is fundamental both with Plato and Xenophon; to Both of them
a great degree, it is retained also by Aristotle. The polity with
lawgiver exercises a spiritual as well as a temporal temporal
function. He does not content himself with prohibi- tual.
tions and punishments, but provides for fashioning every
man's character to a predetermined model, through systematic discipline begun in childhood and never discontinued.
This was the general scheme, realised at Sparta in a certain
manner and degree, and idealised both by Plato and Xenophon. The full application of the scheme, however, is
restricted, in all the three, to a select body of qualified
citizens; who are assumed to exercise dominion or headship
over the remaining community.[y]

---

[x] Xenophon, Cyrop. i. 2, 2-6.
Οὗτοι δὲ δοκοῦσιν οἱ νόμοι ἄρχεσθαι
τοῦ κοινοῦ ἀγαθοῦ ἐπιμελούμενοι οὐκ
ἔνθεν ταῖς πλείσταις πόλεσιν ἄρχονται.
Αἱ μὲν γὰρ πλεῖσται πόλεις, ἀφεῖσαι
παιδεύειν ὅπως τις ἐθέλει τοὺς ἑαυτοῦ
παῖδας καὶ αὐτοὺς τοὺς πρεσβυτέρους
ὅπως ἐθέλουσι διάγειν, ἔπειτα προστάτ
τουσιν αὐτοὺς μὴ κλέπτειν. Οἱ δὲ

Περσικοὶ νόμοι προλαβόντες ἐπιμέλονται
ὅπως τὴν ἀρχὴν μὴ τοιοῦτοι ἔσονται οἱ
πολῖται, οἷοι πονηροῦ τινὸς ἢ αἰσχροῦ
ἔργου ἐφίεσθαι. Ἐπιμέλονται δὲ ὧδε.

[y] In Xenophon, all Persians are supposed to be legally admissible to the
public training; but in practice, none
can frequent it constantly except those
whose families can maintain them

Thus far the general conception of Xenophon and Plato is
similar: yet there are material differences between
them. In Xenophon, the ultimate purpose is, to set
forth the personal qualities of Cyrus: to which
purpose the description of the general training of the citizens
is preparatory, occupying only a small portion of the Cyropædia, and serving to explain the system out of which Cyrus
sprang. And the character of Cyrus is looked at in reference
to the government of mankind. Xenophon had seen governments, of all sorts, resisted and overthrown—despotisms,
oligarchies, democracies. His first inference from these facts
is, that man is a very difficult animal to govern:—much
more difficult than sheep or oxen. But on farther reflection
he recognises that the problem is noway insoluble: that a
ruler may make sure of ruling mankind with their own
consent, and of obtaining hearty obedience—provided that he
goes to work in an intelligent manner.[z] Such a ruler is
described in Cyrus; who both conquered many distant and
unconnected nations,—and governed them, when conquered,
skilfully, so as to ensure complete obedience without any
active discontent. The abilities and exploits of Cyrus thus
step far beyond the range of the systematic Persian discipline,
though that discipline is represented as having first formed
both his character and that of his immediate companions.
He is a despot responsible to no one, but acting with so much
sagacity, justice, and benevolence, that his subjects obey him
willingly. His military orders are arranged with the utmost
prudence and calculation of consequences. He promotes the
friends who have gone through the same discipline with himself, to be satraps of the conquered provinces, exacting from
them submission, and tribute-collection for himself, together
with just dealing towards the subjects. Each satrap is required to maintain his ministers, officers, and soldiers around
him under constant personal inspection, with habits of temper-

without labour; nor can any be received into the advanced stages, except
those who have passed through the
lower. Hence none go really through
the training except the Homotimoi.

[z] Xenoph. Cyrop. i. 1, 3. ἤν τις
ἐπισταμένως τοῦτο πράττῃ.

Compare Xenoph. Economic. c. xxi.
where τὸ ἐθελόντων ἄρχειν is declared
to be a superhuman good, while τὸ
ἀκόντων τυραννεῖν is reckoned as a
curse equivalent to that of Tantalus.

ance and constant exercise in hunting.[a] These men and the
Persians generally, constitute the privileged class and the
military force of the empire:[b] the other mass of subjects are
not only kept disarmed, but governed as "*gens tailleables et
corvéables.*" Moreover, besides combining justice and personal
activity with generosity and winning manners, Cyrus does not
neglect such ceremonial artifices and pomp as may impose on
the imagination of spectators.[c] He keeps up designedly not
merely competition but mutual jealousy and ill-will among
those around him. And he is careful that the most faithful
among them shall be placed on his left hand at the banquet,
because that side is the most exposed to treachery.[d]

What is chiefly present to the mind of Xenophon is, a
select fraction of citizens passing their whole lives *Xenophontic*
in a regimental training like that of Lacedæmon : *genius for command—*
uniformity of habits, exact obedience, the strongest *Practical training—*
bodily exercise combined with the simplest nutritive *Sokratic principles applied*
diet, perfect command of the physical appetites and *in Persian training.*
necessities, so that no such thing as spitting or blowing the
nose is seen.[e] The grand purpose of the system, as at
Sparta,[f] is warlike efficiency: war being regarded as the
natural state of man. The younger citizens learn the use of
the bow and javelin, the older that of the sword and shield.
As war requires not merely perfectly trained soldiers, but also
the initiative of a superior individual chief, so Xenophon
assumes in the chief of these men (like Agesilaus at Sparta)
an unrivalled genius for command. The Xenophontic Cyrus
is altogether a practical man. We are not told that he
learnt anything except in common with the rest. Neither he
nor they receive any musical or literary training. The
course which they go through is altogether ethical, gymnastical, and military. Their boyhood is passed in learning

[a] Xenophon, Cyropæd. viii. 6, 1-10.
[b] Xenoph. Cyrop. viii. 1, 43-45, viii.
6, 13, vii. 5, 79, viii. 5, 24. εἰ δὲ σὺ,
ὦ Κῦρε, ἐπαρθεὶς ταῖς παρούσαις τύχαις,
ἐπιχειρήσεις τῶν Περσῶν ἄρχειν ἐπὶ
πλεονεξία, ὥσπερ τῶν ἄλλων,
&c.
[c] Xenop. Cyrop. viii. 1, 40. ἀλλὰ
καὶ καταγοητεύειν ᾤετο χρῆναι αὐτούς.

viii. 3, 1.
[d] Xenop. Cyrop. viii. 2, viii. 4, 3.
[e] Xenop. Cyrop. i. 2, 16, viii. 1, 42,
viii. 8, 8. He insists repeatedly upon
this point.
[f] Plato, Legg. i. p. 626. Plutarch,
Lykurg. 25. Comparo Lykurg. and
Num. c. 4.

justice and temperance,[g] which are made express subjects of teaching by Xenophon and under express masters: Xenophon thus supplies the deficiency so often lamented by the Platonic Sokrates, who remarks that neither at Athens nor elsewhere can he find either teaching or teacher of justice. Cyrus learns justice and temperance along with the rest,[h] but he does not learn more than the rest: nor does Xenophon perform his promise of explaining by what education such extraordinary genius for command is brought about.[i] The superior character of Cyrus is assumed and described, but noway accounted for: indeed his rank and position at the court of Astyages (in which he stands distinguished from the other Persians) present nothing but temptations to indulgence, partially countervailed by wise counsel from his father Kambyses. We must therefore consider Cyrus to be a king by nature, like the chief bee in each hive[k]—an untaught or self-taught genius, in his excellence as general and emperor. He obtains only one adventitious aid peculiar to himself. Being of divine progeny, he receives the special favour and revelations of the Gods, who, in doubtful emergencies, communicate to him by signs, omens, dreams, and sacrifices, what he ought to do and what he ought to leave undone.[l] Such privileged communications are represented as indispensable to the success of a leader: for though it was his duty to learn all that could be learnt, yet even after he had done this, so much uncertainty remained behind, that his decisions were little better than a lottery.[m] The Gods arranged the sequences of

[g] Xenophon, Cyrop. i. 2, 6-8. The boys are appointed to adjudicate, under the supervision of the teacher, in disputes which occur among their fellows. As an instance of this practice, we find the well-known adjudication by young Cyrus, between the great boy and the little boy, in regard to the two coats; and a very instructive illustration it is, of the principle of property (Cyrop. i. 3, 17).

[h] Xenop. Cyrop. i. 3, 16, iii. 3, 35. Cyrus is indeed represented as having taken lessons from a paid teacher in the art τοῦ στρατηγεῖν: but these lessons were meagre, comprising nothing beyond τὰ τακτικά, i. 6, 12-15.

[i] Xenop. Cyrop. i. 1, 6. ποίᾳ τινὶ παιδείᾳ παιδευθεὶς τοσούτῳ διήνεγκεν εἰς τὸ ἄρχειν ἀνθρώπων.

[k] Xenoph. Cyrop. v. 1, 24. The queen-bee is masculine in Xenophon's conception.

[l] Xenoph. Cyrop. viii. 7, 3, iv. 2, 15, iv. 1, 24. Compare Xenoph. Economic. v. 19, 20.

[m] Xenophon. Cyrop. i. 6, 46. Οὕτως ἢ γε ἀνθρωπίνη σοφία οὐδὲν μᾶλλον οἶδε τὸ ἄριστον αἱρεῖσθαι, ἢ εἰ κληρούμενος ὅ, τι λάχοι τοῦτό τις πράττοι. Θεοὶ δὲ ἀεὶ ὄντες πάντα ἴσασι τά τε γεγενημένα καὶ τὰ ὄντα, καὶ ὅ, τι ἐξ ἑκάστου αὐτῶν ἀποβήσεται· καὶ τῶν συμβουλευομένων ἀνθρώπων οἷς

events partly in a regular and decypherable manner, so that a man by diligent study might come to understand them: but they reserved many important events for their own free-will, so as not to be intelligible by any amount of human study. Here the wisest man was at fault no less than the most ignorant: nor could he obtain the knowledge of them except by special revelation solicited or obtained. The Gods communicated such peculiar knowledge to their favourites, but not to every one indiscriminately: for they were under no necessity to take care of men towards whom they felt no inclination.[n] Cyrus was one of the men thus specially privileged: but he was diligent in cultivating the favour of the Gods by constant worship, not merely at times when he stood in need of their revelations, but at other times also: just as, in regard to human friends or patrons, assiduous attentions were requisite to keep up their goodwill.[o]

When it is desired to realise an ideal improvement of society (says Plato),[p] the easiest postulate is to assume a despot, young, clever, brave, thoughtful, temperate, and aspiring, belonging to that superhuman breed which reigned under the presidency of Kronus. Such a postulate is assumed by Xenophon in his hero Cyrus. The Xenophontic scheme, though presupposing a collective training, resolves itself ultimately into the will of an individual, enforcing good regulations, and full of tact in dealing with subordinates. What Cyrus is in campaign and empire, Ischomachus (see the Economica of Xenophon) is in the household: but everything depends on the life of this distinguished individual. Xenophon leads us at once into practice, laying only a scanty basis of theory.

In Plato's Republic, on the contrary, the theory predominates. He does not build upon any individual hero: he constructs a social and educational system, capable of self-perpetuation at least for a considerable   Plato does not build upon an individual hero. Platonic

---

ἂν ἱλέῳ ὦσι, προσημαίνουσιν, ἅ, τε χρὴ ποιεῖν καὶ ἃ οὐ χρή. Εἰ δὲ μὴ πᾶσιν ἐθέλουσι συμβουλεύειν, οὐδὲν θαυμαστόν· οὐ γὰρ ἀνάγκη αὐτοῖς ἔστιν, ὧν ἂν μὴ θέλωσιν, ἐπιμελεῖσθαι.
Compare i. 6, 6-23, also the Me-

morabil. i. 1, 8, where the same doctrine is ascribed to Sokrates.
[n] Xenop. Cyrop. i. 6, 46 ad fin.
[o] Xenop. Cyrop. i. 6, 3-5.
[p] Plato, Legg. iv. pp. 709 E, 710-713.

time.[q]　He describes the generating and sustaining
principles of his system, but he does not exhibit it
in action, by any pseudo-historical narrative : we learn indeed,
that he had intended to subjoin such a narrative, in the
dialogue called Kritias, of which only the commencement
was ever written.[r]　He aims at forming a certain type of
character, common to all the Guardians: superadding new
features so as to form a still more exalted type, peculiar to
those few Elders selected from among them to exercise the
directorial function.　He not only lays down the process of
training in greater detail than Xenophon, but he also gives
explanatory reasons for most of his recommendations.

One prominent difference between the two deserves to be
noticed.　In the Xenophontic training, the ethical, gymnastic, and military, exigencies are carefully provided for : but
the musical and intellectual exigencies are left out.　The
Xenophontic Persians are not affirmed either to learn letters,
or to hear and repeat poetry, or to acquire the knowledge of
any musical instrument.　Nor does it appear, even in the
case of the historical Spartans, that letters made any part of
their public training.　But the Platonic training includes
music and gymnastics as co-ordinate and equally indispensable.　Words or intellectual exercises, come in under the
head of music.[s]　Indeed, in Plato's view, even gymnastics,
though bearing immediately on the health and force of the
body, have for their ultimate purpose a certain action upon
the mind : being essential to the due development of courage,
energy, endurance, and self-assertion.[t]　Gymnastics without

[q] Plato pronounces Cyrus to have
been a good general and a patriot, but
not to have received any right education, and especially to have provided
no good education for his children, who
in consequence became corrupt and degenerate (Legg. iii. 694).　Upon this
remark some commentators of antiquity
founded the supposition of grudge or
quarrel between Plato and Xenophon.
We have no evidence to prove such a
state of unfriendly feeling between the
two, yet it is noway improbable : and
I think it highly probable that the
remark just cited from Plato may have
had direct reference to the Xenophontic

Cyropædia.　When we read the elaborate intellectual training which Plato
prescribes for the rulers in his Republic, we may easily understand that, in
his view, the Xenophontic Cyrus had
received no right education at all.　His
remark moreover brings to view the
defect of all schemes built upon a perfect despot—that they depend upon an
individual life.

[r] Plato, Timæus, pp. 20-26.　Plato,
Kritias, p. 108.

[s] Plato, Republic, ii. p. 376 E.

[t] Plato, Republic, iii. p. 410 B.
πρὸς τὸ θυμοειδὲς τῆς φύσεως βλέπων
κἀκεῖνο ἐγείρων πονήσει μᾶλλον ἢ πρὸς

music produce a hard and savage character, insensible to persuasive agencies, hating discourse or discussion,[u] ungraceful as well as stupid. Music without gymnastics generates a susceptible temperament, soft, tender, and yielding to difficulties, with quick but transient impulses. Each of the two, music and gymnastic, is indispensable as a supplement and corrective to the other.

The type of character here contemplated by Plato deserves particular notice, as contrasted with that of Xenophon. It is the Athenian type against the Spartan. Periklês in his funeral oration, delivered at Athens in the first year of the Peloponnesian war, boasts that the Athenians had already reached a type similar to this— and that too, without any special individual discipline, legally enforced: that they combined courage, ready energy, and combined action—with developed intelligence, the love of discourse, accessibility to persuasion, and taste for the Beautiful. That which Plato aims at accomplishing in his Guardians, by means of a state-education at once musical and gymnastical—Periklês declares to have been already realised at Athens without any state-education, through the spontaneous tendencies of individuals called forth and seconded by the general working of the political system.[x] He compliments his countrymen as having accomplished this object without the unnecessary rigour of a positive state-discipline, and without any other restraints than the special injunctions and prohibitions of a known law. It is this absence of state-discipline to which both Xenophon and Plato are opposed. Both of them follow Lykurgus in proclaiming the insufficiency of mere prohibitions; and in demanding a positive routine of duty to be prescribed

Platonic type of character compared with Xenophontic, is like the Athenian compared with the Spartan.

ἰσχύν, οὐχ ὥσπερ οἱ ἄλλοι ἀθληταὶ ῥώμης ἕνεκα.

[u] Plato, Republ. iii. pp. 410-411. Μισόλογος δὴ, οἶμαι, ὁ τοιοῦτος γίγνεται καὶ ἄμουσος, καὶ πειθοῖ μὲν διὰ λόγων οὐδὲν ἔτι χρῆται, βίᾳ δὲ καὶ ἀγριότητι ὥσπερ θηρίον πρὸς πάντα διαπράττεται, καὶ ἐν ἀμαθίᾳ καὶ σκαιότητι μετὰ ἀρρυθμίας καὶ ἀχαριστίας ζῇ.

[x] Thucydid. ii. 38-39-40. The comparison between this speech and the third book of Plato's Re-

public, (pp. 401-402-410-411) is very interesting. The words of Periklês, φιλοκαλοῦμεν γὰρ μετ᾽ εὐτελείας καὶ φιλοσοφοῦμεν ἄνευ μαλακίας, taken along with the chapter preceding, mark that concurrent development of τὸ φιλόσοφον and τὸ θυμοειδὲς which Plato provides, and the avoidance of those defects which spring from the separate and exclusive cultivation of either.

by authority, and enforced upon individuals through life. In regard to end, Plato is more in harmony with Periklês: in regard to means, with Xenophon.

Plato's views respecting special laws and criminal procedure generally are remarkable. He not only manifests that repugnance towards the Dikastery—which is common to Sokrates, Xenophon, Isokrates, and Aristophanes—but he excludes it almost entirely from his system, as being superseded by the constant public discipline of the Guardians.

It is to be remembered that these propositions of Plato *Professional* have reference, not to an entire and miscellaneous *soldiers are* community, but to a select body called the Guardians, *the proper* *modern stan-* required to possess the bodily and mental attributes *dard of com-* *parison with* of soldiers, policemen, and superintendants. The *the regula-* *tions of Plato* standard of comparison in modern times, for the *and Xeno-* *phon.* Lykurgean, Xenophontic, or Platonic, training, is to be sought in the stringent discipline of professional soldiers; not in the general liberty, subject only to definite restrictions, enjoyed by non-military persons. In regard to soldiers, the Platonic principle is now usually admitted—that it is not sufficient to enact articles of war, defining what a soldier ought to do, and threatening him with punishment in case of infraction—but that, besides this, it is indispensable to exact from him a continued routine of positive performances, under constant professional supervision. Without this preparation, few now expect that soldiers should behave effectively when the moment of action arrives. This is the doctrine applied by Plato and Xenophon to the whole life of the citizen.

Music and Gymnastic are regarded by Plato mainly as *Music and* they bear upon and influence the emotional character *gymnastic—* *multifarious* of his citizens. Each of them is the antithesis, and *and varied* *effects of* at the same time the supplement, to the other. *music.* Gymnastic tends to develope exclusively the courageous and energetic emotions:—anger and the feeling of power—but no others. Whereas music (understood in the Platonic sense) has a far more multifarious and varied agency: it may develope either those, or the gentle and tender emotions,

according to circumstances.[y] In the hands of Tyrtæus and
Æschylus, it generates vehement and fearless combatants: in
the hands of Euripides and other pathetic poets, it produces
tender, amatory, effeminate natures, ingenious in talk but
impotent for action.[z]

In the age of Plato, Homer and other poets were extolled as
the teachers of mankind, and as themselves possessing
universal knowledge. They enjoyed a religious respect, being supposed to speak under divine inspiration, and to be the privileged reporters or diviners of a forgotten past.[a] They furnished the most interesting portion of
that floating mass of traditional narrative respecting Gods,
Heroes, and ancestors, which found easy credence both as
matter of religion and as matter of history: being in full harmony with the emotional preconceptions, and uncritical
curiosity, of the hearers. They furnished likewise exhortation
and reproof, rules and maxims, so expressed as to live in the
memory—impressive utterance for all the strong feelings of
the human bosom. Poetry was for a long time the only form
of literature. It was not until the fifth century B.C. that prose
compositions either began to be multiplied, or were carried to
such perfection as to possess a charm of their own calculated to
rival the poets, who had long enjoyed a monopoly as purveyors

(margin note: Great influence of the poets and their works on education.)

---

[y] Plato, Republic, ii. p. 376 B-C.
If we examine Plato's tripartite classification of the varieties of soul or mind,
as it is given both in the Republic and
in the Timæus (1. Reason, in the
cranium. 2. Energy, θυμὸς, in the
thoracic region. 3. Appetite, in the
abdominal region)—we shall see that
it assigns no place to the gentle, the
tender, or the æsthetical emotions.
These cannot be properly ranked either
with energy (θυμὸς) or with appetite
(ἐπιθυμία). Plato can find no root for
them except in reason or knowledge,
from which he presents them as being
collateral derivatives — a singular
origin. He illustrates his opinion by
the equally singular analogy of the
dog, who is gentle towards persons
whom he *knows*, fierce towards those
whom he does not *know*; so that
gentleness is the product of *knowledge*.

[z] See the argument between Æs-

chylus and Euripides in the Ranæ of
Aristophanes, 1043-1061-1068.

[a] Aristophan. Ranæ, 1053. Æschylus is made to say:—
ἀλλ' ἀποκρύπτειν χρὴ τὸ πονηρὸν τόν
  γε ποιητήν,
καὶ μὴ παράγειν μηδὲ διδάσκειν· τοῖς
  μὲν γὰρ παιδαρίοισιν
ἐστὶ διδάσκαλος ὅστις φράζει, τοῖσιν δ'
  ἡβῶσι ποιηταί.
πάνυ δὴ δεῖ χρηστὰ λέγειν ἡμᾶς.
Compare the words of Pluto which
conclude the Ranæ, 1497.
  Plato, Republic, x. p. 598 D. ἐπειδὴ
τινων ἀκούομεν ὅτι οὗτοι (Homer and
the poets) πάσας μὲν τέχνας ἐπίστανται,
πάντα δὲ τἀνθρώπεια τὰ πρὸς ἀρετὴν
καὶ κακίαν, καὶ τά γε θεῖα, &c. : also
Plato, Legg. vii. pp. 810-811 ; Ion, pp.
536 A, 541 B; Xenoph. Memor. iv.
2, 10; and Sympos. iii. 6, where we
learn that Nikeratus could repeat by
heart the whole Iliad and Odyssey.

for æsthetical sentiment and fancy. Rhetors, Sophists, Philosophers, then became their competitors; opening new veins of intellectual activity,[b] and sharing, to a certain extent, the pædagogic influence of the poets—yet never displacing them from their traditional function of teachers, narrators, and guides to the intelligence, as well as improving ministers to the sentiments, emotions, and imagination, of youth. Indeed many Sophists and Rhetors presented themselves not as superseding,[c] but as expounding and illustrating, the poets. Sokrates also did this occasionally, though not upon system.[d]

It is this educational practice—common to a certain extent among Greeks, but more developed at Athens than elsewhere [e]

[b] Plato, Legg. vii. p. 810. ὅλους ποιητὰς ἐκμανθάνοντας, &c.

[c] It was to gain this facility that Kritias and Alkibiades, as Xenophon tells us, frequented the society of Sokrates, who (as Xenophon also tells us) "handled persons conversing with him just as he pleased" (Memor. i. 2, 14-18).

A speaker in one of the Orations of Lysias (Orat. viii. Κακολογιῶν, s. 12) considers this power of arguing a disputed case as one of the manifestations τοῦ φιλοσοφεῖν — Καὶ ἐγὼ μὲν ᾤμην φιλοσοφοῦντας αὐτοὺς περὶ τοῦ πράγματος ἀντιλέγειν τὸν ἐνάντιον λόγον· οἱ δ' ἄρα οὐκ ἀντέλεγον ἀλλ' ἀντέπραττον.

Compare the curious oration of Demosthenes against Lakritus, where the speaker imputes to Lakritus this abuse of argumentative power, as having been purchased by him at a large price from the teaching of Isokrates the Sophist, pp. 928-937·938.

[d] Xenoph. Memorab. i. 2, 57-60.

[e] The language of Plato is remarkable on this point. Republic, ii. p. 376 E. Τίς οὖν ἡ παιδεία; ἢ χαλεπὸν εὑρεῖν βελτίω τῆς ὑπὸ τοῦ πολλοῦ χρόνου εὑρημένης; ἐστὶ δέ που ἡ μὲν ἐπὶ σώμασι γυμναστική, ἡ δ' ἐπὶ ψυχῇ μουσική—and a striking passage in the Kriton (p. 50 D), where education in μουσικὴ and γυμναστικὴ is represented as a positive duty on the part of fathers towards their sons.

About the multifarious and indefinite province of the Muses, comprehending all παιδεία and λόγος, see Plutarch, Sympos. Problem. ix. 14, 2-3, p. 908-

909. Also Plutarch, De Audiendis Poetis, p. 31 F, about the many diverse interpretations of Homer: especially those by Chrysippus and Kleanthes.

The last half of the eighth Book of Aristotle's Politica, contains remarkable reflections on the educational effects of music, showing the refined distinctions which philosophical men of that day drew respecting the varieties of melody and rhythm. Aristotle adverts to music as an agency not merely for παιδεία but also for κάθαρσις (viii. 7, 1341, b. 38); to which last Plato does not advert. Aristotle also notices various animadversions by musical critics upon some of the dicta on musical subjects in the Platonic Republic (καλῶς ἐπιτιμῶσι καὶ τοῦτο Σωκράτει τῶν περὶ τὴν μουσικήν τινες, 1342, b. 23)—perhaps Aristoxenus: also 1342, a. 32. That the established character and habits of music could not be changed without leading to a revolution, ethical and political, in the minds of the citizens—is a principle affirmed by Plato, not as his own, but as having been laid down previously by Damon the celebrated musical instructor (Repub. iii. p. 424 C).

The following passage about Luther is remarkable :—

"Après avoir essayé de la théologie, Luther fut décidé par les conseils de ses amis, à embrasser l'étude du droit qui conduisait alors aux postes les plus lucratifs de l'État et de l'Église. Mais il ne semble pas s'y être jamais livré avec gout. Il aimait bien mieux la belle littérature, et surtout la musique. C'était son art de prédilection. Il la

—which Plato has in his mind, when he draws up the out-
line of a musical education for his youthful Guar- Plato's idea of the pur-
dians.   He does not intend it as a scheme for foster- pose which poetry and
ing the highest intellectual powers, or for exalting music *ought*
men into philosophers—which he reserves as an to serve in education.
ulterior improvement, to be communicated at a later period
of life, and only to a chosen few—the large majority being
supposed incapable of appropriating it.   His musical training (co-operating with the gymnastical) is intended to form
the character of the general body of Guardians: to implant
in them from early childhood a peculiar vein of sentiments,
habits, emotions and emotional beliefs, ethical esteem and
disesteem, love and hatred, &c., to inspire them (in his own
phrase) with love of the beautiful or honourable.

   It is in this spirit that he deals with the traditional, popular,
almost consecrated, poetical literature which pre- He declares war against
vailed around him.   He undertakes to revise and most of the
recast the whole of it.   Repudiating avowedly the traditional and conse-
purpose of the authors, he sets up a different point crated poetry, as mischiev-
of view by which they are to be judged.   The con- ous.
test of principle, into which he now enters, subsisted (he tells
us) long before his time: a standing discord between the
philosophers and the poets.[f]   The poet is an artist[g] whose
aim is to give immediate pleasure and satisfaction: appealing
to æsthetical sentiment, feeding imagination and belief, and
finding embodiment for emotions, religious or patriotic, which
he shares with his hearers: the philosopher is a critic, who
lays down authoritatively deeper and more distant ends which
he considers that poetry *ought to* serve, judging the poets
according as they promote, neglect, or frustrate those ends.
Plato declares the end which he requires poetry to serve in

cultiva toute sa vie et l'enseigna à ses
enfans.   Il n' hésite pas à déclarer que
la musique lui semble le premier des
arts, après la théologie.   La musique
(dit il) est l'art des prophètes : c'est
le seul qui, comme la théologie, puisse
calmer les troubles de l'ame et mettre
le diable en fuite.   Il touchait du luth,
jouait de la flûte." (*Michelet*, Memoires
de Luther, écrits par lui même, pp. 4-5,
Paris, 1835.)

   [f] Plato, Republ. x. p. 607 B. παλαία
τις διαφορὰ φιλοσοφίᾳ τε καὶ ποιητικῇ,
&c.

   [g] Plato, Republ. x. p. 607 A-C.
τὴν ἡδυσμένην Μοῦσαν—ἢ πρὸς ἡδονὴν
ποιητικὴ καὶ μίμησις, &c.

   Compare also Leges ii. p. 655 D seq.,
about the μουσικῆς ὀρθότης.

the training of his Guardians. It must contribute to form the
ethical character which he approves: in so far as it thus contributes, he will tolerate it, but no farther. The charm and
interest especially, belonging to beautiful poems, is not only
no reason for admitting them, but is rather a reason (in his
view) for excluding them.[h] The more beautiful a poem is, the
more effectively does it awaken, stimulate, and amplify, the
emotional forces of the mind : the stronger is its efficacy in
giving empire to pleasure and pain, and in resisting or over-
powering the rightful authority of Reason. It thus directly
contravenes the purpose of the Platonic education—the formation of characters wherein Reason shall effectively controul
all the emotions and desires.[i.] Hence he excludes all the
varieties of imitative poetry :—that is, narrative, descriptive,
or dramatic poetry. He admits only hymns to the Gods and
panegyrics upon good citizens :— probably also didactic,
gnomic, or hortative, poetry of approved tone. Imitative
poetry is declared objectionable farther, not only as it exaggerates the emotions, but on another ground—that it fills the

[h] It is interesting to read in the first book of Strabo (pp. 15-19-25-27, &c.) the controversy which he carries on with Eratosthenes, as to the function of poets generally, and as to the purpose of Homer in particular. Eratosthenes considered Homer, and the other poets also, as having composed verses to please and interest, not to teach—ψυχαγωγίας χάριν, οὐ διδασκαλίας. Strabo (following the astronomer Hipparchus) controverts this opinion; affirming that poets had been the earliest philosophers and teachers of mankind, and that they must always continue to be the teachers of the multitude, who were unable to profit by history and philosophy. Strabo has the strongest admiration for Homer, not merely as a poet but as a moralising teacher. While Plato banishes Homer from his commonwealth, on the ground of pernicious ethical influence, Strabo claims for Homer the very opposite merit, and extols him as the best of all popular teachers — ἡ δὲ ποιητικὴ δημωφελεστέρα καὶ θέατρα πληροῦν δυναμένη· ἡ δὲ δὴ τοῦ Ὁμήρου διαφερόντως—"Ατε δὴ πρὸς τὸ παιδευτικὸν εἶδος ἀναφέρων τοὺς μύθους ὁ

ποιητὴς ἐφρόντισε πολὺ μέρος τἀληθοῦς (Strabo, i. p. 20). The contradiction between Plato and Strabo is remarkable. Compare the beginning of Horace's Epistle, i. 2. In the time of Strabo (more than three centuries after Plato's death) there existed an abundant prose literature on matters of erudition, history, science, philosophy. The work of instruction was thus taken out of the poet's hands ; yet Strabo cannot bear to admit this. In the age of Plato the prose literature was comparatively small. Alexandria and its school did not exist: the poets covered a far larger portion of the entire ground of instruction.
As a striking illustration of the continued and unquestioning faith in the ancient legends, we may cite Galen ; who, in a medical argument against Erasistratus, cites the cure of the daughters of Prœtus by Melampus as an incontestable authentic fact in medical evidence ; putting to shame Erasistratus, who had not attended to it in his reasoning (Galen, De Atrā Bile, T. v. p. 132, Kühn).

[i] Plato, Republic, x. pp. 606-607, iii. p. 387 B.

mind with false and unreal representations; being composed
by men who have no real knowledge of their subject, though
they pretend to a sort of fallacious omniscience, and talk
boldly about every thing.[k]

Even hymns to the Gods, however, may be composed in
many different strains, according to the conception *Strict limits imposed by Plato on poets.*
which the poet entertains of their character and at-
tributes. The Homeric Hymns which we now possess could not be acceptable to Plato. While denouncing
much of the current theological poetry, he assumes a censorial authority, in his joint character of Lykurgus and
Sokrates,[l] to dictate what sort of poetical compositions shall
be tolerated among his Guardians. He pronounces many of
the tales in Homer and Hesiod to be not merely fictions, but
mischievous fictions: not fit to be circulated, even if they had
been true.

Plato admits fiction, indeed, along with truth as an instru-
ment for forming the character. Nay, he draws *His view of the purposes of fiction—little distinction between fiction and truth. His censures upon Homer and the tragedians.*
little distinction between the two, as regards par-
ticular narratives. But the point upon which he
specially insists, is, that all the narratives in circulation, true or false, respecting Gods and Heroes,
shall ascribe to them none but qualities ethically
estimable and venerable. He condemns Homer and Hesiod as
having misrepresented the Gods and Heroes, and as having
attributed to them acts inconsistent with their true character,
like a painter painting a portrait unlike to the original.[m] He
rejects in this manner various tales told in these poems respecting Zeus, Hêrê, Hephæstus—the fraudulent rupture of

[k] Plato, Republic, x. pp. 598-599.
When Plato attacks the poets so
severely on the ground of their departure from truth and reality, and
their false representations of human
life—the poets might have retorted,
that Plato departed no less from truth
and reality in many parts of his Republic, and especially in his panegyric
upon Justice ; not to mention the
various mythes which we read in Republic, Phædon, Phædrus, Politikus,
&c.

Plato's fictions are indeed ethical,
intended to serve a pædagogic purpose ;
Homer's fictions are æsthetical, addressed to the fancy and emotions.
But it is not fair in Plato, the
avowed champion of useful fiction, to
censure the poets on the ground of
their departing from truth.

[l] Plutarch, Sympos. Quæst. viii. 2,
2, p. 719.
'Ο Πλάτων, ἅτε δὴ τῷ Σωκράτει τὸν
Λυκοῦργον ἀναμιγνύς, &c.

[m] Plato, Republic, ii. p. 377 E.

the treaty between the Greeks and Trojans by Pandarus, at the instigation of Zeus and Athênê—the final battle of the Gods, in the Iliad[n]—the transformations of Proteus and Thetis, and the general declaration in the Odyssey that the Gods under the likeness of various strangers visit human cities as inspectors of good and bad behaviour[o]—the dream sent by Zeus to deceive Agamemnon (in the second book of the Iliad) and the charge made by Thetis in Æschylus against Apollo, of having deceived her and killed her son Achilles[p]— the violent amorous impulse of Zeus, in the fourteenth book of the Iliad—the immoderate laughter among the Gods, when they saw the lame Hephæstus busying himself in the service of the banquet. Plato will not permit the realm of Hades to be described as odious and full of terrors, because the Guardians will thereby learn to fear death.[q] Nor will he tolerate the Homeric pictures of heroes or semi-divine persons, like Priam or Achilles, plunged in violent sorrow for the death of friends and relatives :—since a thoroughly right-minded man, while he regards death as no serious evil to the deceased, is at the same time most self-sufficing in character, and least in need of extraneous sympathy.[r]

---

[n] Plato, Repub. ii. p. 379. Plutarch observes about Chrysippus — ὅτι τῷ θεῷ καλὰς μὲν ἐπικλήσεις καὶ φιλανθρώπους ἀεὶ, ἄγρια δ' ἔργα καὶ βάρβαρα καὶ Γαλατικὰ προστίθησιν (De Stoicorum Repugnant. c. 32, p. 1049 B).

[o] Plato, Republ. ii. p. 380. Plato in the beginning of his Sophistês treats this doctrine of the appearances of the Gods with greater respect. Lucretius argues that the Gods, being in a state of perfect happiness and exempt from all want, cannot change; Lucret. v. 170, compared with Plato, Rep. ii. p. 381 B.

[p] Plato, Republ. ii. pp. 380-381-383.

[q] Plato, Republ. iii. p. 386. Maximus Tyrius (Diss. xxiv. c. 5) remarks, that upon the principles here laid down by Plato, much of what occurs in the Platonic dialogues respecting the erotic vehemence and enthusiasm of Sokrates ought to be excluded from education.

[r] Plato, Republic, iii. p. 387. ὁ ἐπιεικὴς ἀνὴρ τῷ ἐπιεικεῖ, οὗπερ καὶ ἑταῖρός ἐστι, τὸ τεθνάναι οὐ δεινὸν

ἡγήσεται—Οὐκ ἄρα ὑπέρ γε ἐκείνου ὡς δεινόν τι πεπονθότος ὀδύροιτ' ἄν— Ἀλλὰ μὴν—ὁ τοιοῦτος μάλιστα αὐτὸς αὐτῷ αὐτάρκης πρὸς τὸ εὖ ζῆν καὶ διαφερόντως τῶν ἄλλων, ἥκιστα ἑτέρου προσδεῖται—Ἥκιστ' ἄρα αὐτῷ δεινὸν στερηθῆναι υἱέος, ἢ ἀδέλφου, ἢ χρημάτων, ἢ ἄλλου του τῶν τοιούτων, &c.

The doctrine of Epikurus, as laid down by Lucretius (iii. 844-920), coincides here with that of Plato :—

Tu quidem ut es letho sopitus, sic eris ævi
Quod superest, cunctis privatus' doloribus
  ægris :
At nos horrifico cinefactum te prope busto
Insatiabiliter deflebimus, æternumque
Nulla dies nobis mœrorem pectore demet.
Illud ab hoc igitur quærendum est, quid sit
  amari
Tantopere, ad somnum si res redit atque
  quietem
Cur quisquam æterno possit tabescere luctu ?

Plato insists, not less strenuously than Lucretius, upon preserving the minds of his Guardians from the frightful pictures of Hades, which terrify all hearers—φρίττειν δὴ ποιεῖ

These and other condemnations are passed by Plato upon the current histories respecting Gods, and respecting heroes the sons or immediate descendants of Gods. He entirely forbids such histories, as suggesting bad examples to his Guardians. He prohibits all poetical composition, except under his own censorial supervision. He lays down, as a general doctrine, that the Gods are good; and he will tolerate no narrative which is not in full harmony with this predetermined type. Without giving any specimens of approved narratives — which he declares to be the business not of the lawgiver, but of the poet—he insists only that all poets shall conform in their compositions to his general standard of orthodoxy.[s]

Type of character prescribed by Plato, to which all poets must conform, in tales about Gods and Heroes.

Applying such a principle of criticism, Plato had little difficulty in finding portions of the current mythology offensive to his ideal type of goodness. Indeed he might have found many others, yet more offensive to it than some of those which he has selected.[t] But the extent of his variance with the current views reveals itself still more emphatically, when he says that the Gods are not to be represented as the cause of evil things to us, but only of good things. Most persons (he says) consider the Gods as causes of all things, evil as well as good: but this is untrue:[u] the Gods dispense only the good things, not the evil; and the good things are few in number compared with the evil. Plato therefore

ὡς οἷόν τε πάντας τοὺς ἀκούοντας, iii. p. 387 :—

"metus ille foras praeceps Acheruntis agendus Funditus, humanam qui vitam turbat ab imo" (iii. 38).

[s] Compare also Plato de Legg. x. p. 886 C, xii. p. 941 B.

[t] As one example, Plato cites the story in the Iliad, that Achilles cut off his hair as an offering to the deceased Patroklus, after his hair had been consecrated by vow to the river Spercheius (Rep. iii. p. 391). If we look at the Iliad (xxiii. 150) we find that the vow to the Spercheius had been originally made by Peleus, conditionally upon the return of Achilles to his native land. Now Achilles had been

already forewarned that he would never return thither, consequently the vow to Spercheius was void, and the execution of it impracticable.

Plato does not disbelieve the legend of Hippolytus; the cruel death of an innocent youth, brought on by the Gods in consequence of the curse of his father Theseus (Legg. xi. p. 931 B).

[u] Plato, Republ. ii. p. 379 D. Οὐδ' ἄρα ὁ θεὸς, ἐπειδὴ ἀγαθὸς, πάντων ἂν εἴη αἴτιος, ὡς οἱ πολλοὶ λέγουσιν, ἀλλ' ὀλίγων μὲν τοῖς ἀνθρώποις αἴτιος, πολλῶν δὲ ἀναίτιος· πολὺ γὰρ ἐλάττω τἀγαθὰ τῶν κακῶν ἡμῖν. Καὶ τῶν μὲν ἀγαθῶν οὐδένα ἄλλον αἰτιατέον, τῶν δὲ κακῶν ἄλλ' ἄττα δεῖ ζητεῖν τὰ αἴτια, ἀλλ' οὐ τὸν θεόν.

requires the poet to ascribe all good things to the Gods and to no one else; but to find other causes, apart from the Gods, for sufferings and evils. But if the poet chooses to describe sufferings as inflicted by the Gods, he must at the same time represent these sufferings as a healing penalty or real benefit to the sufferers.[x]

The principle involved in these criticisms of Plato deserves notice, in more than one point of view.

That which he proposes for his commonwealth is hardly less than a new religious creed, retaining merely old names of the Gods and old ceremonies. He intends it to consist of a body of premeditated fictitious stories, prepared by poets under his inspection and controul. He does not set up any pretence of historical truth for these stories, when first promulgated: he claims no traditionary evidence, no divine inspiration, such as were associated more or less with the received legends, in the minds both of those who recited and of those who heard them. He rejects these legends, because they are inconsistent with his belief and sentiment as to the character of the Gods. Such rejection we can understand :— but he goes a step farther, and directs the coinage of a new body of legends, which have no other title to credence, except that they are to be in harmony with his belief about the general character of the Gods, and that they will produce a salutary ethical effect upon the minds of his Guardians. They are deliberate fictions, the difference between fact and fiction being altogether neglected: they are pious frauds, constructed upon an authoritative type, and intended for an orthodox purpose. The exclusive monopoly of coining and circulating

Marginal note: Position of Plato as an innovator on the received faith and traditions. Fictions indispensable to the Platonic Commonwealth.

---

[x] Plato, Rep. ii. p. 380 B. Plutarch Consolat. ad Apollonium (107 c. 115 E), citation from Pindar—ἐν παρ' ἐσθλὸν πήματα σύνδυο δαίονται βροτοῖς Ἀθάνατοι—πολλῷ γὰρ πλείονα τὰ κακά· καὶ τὰ μὲν (sc. ἀγαθὰ) μόγις καὶ διὰ πολλῶν φροντίδων κτώμεθα, τὰ δὲ κακὰ, πάνυ ῥαδίως.

In the Sept. cont. Thebas of Æschylus, Eteokles complains of this doctrine as a hardship and unfairness to the chief. If (says he) we defend the city successfully, our success will be ascribed to the Gods; if, on the contrary, we fail, Eteokles alone will be the person blamed for it by all the citizens :—

Εἰ μὲν γὰρ εὖ πράξαιμεν, αἰτία θεῶν·
Εἰ δ' αὖθ', ὃ μὴ γένοιτο, συμφορὰ τύχοι,
Ἐτεοκλέης ἂν εἷς μόνος κατὰ πτόλιν
Ὑμνοῖθ' ὑπ' ἀστῶν φροιμίοις πολυρρόθοις
Οἰμώγμασιν θ'—(v. 4).

fictions is a privilege which Plato exacts for himself as founder, and for the Rulers, after his commonwealth is founded.[y] All the narrative matter circulating in his community is to be prepared with reference to his views, and stamped at his mint. He considers it not merely a privilege, but a duty of the Rulers, to provide and circulate fictions for the benefit of the community, like physicians administering wholesome medicines.[z] This is a part of the machinery essential to his purpose. He remarks that it had already been often worked successfully by others, for the establishment of cities present or past. There had been no recent example of it, indeed, nor will he guarantee the practicability of it among his own contemporaries. Yet unless certain fundamental fictions can be accredited among his citizens, the scheme of his commonwealth must fail. They must be made to believe that they are all earthborn and all brethren; that the earth which they inhabit is also their mother: but that there is this difference among them—the Rulers have gold mingled with their constitution, the other Guardians have silver, the remaining citizens have brass or iron. This bold fiction must be planted as a fundamental dogma, as an article of unquestioned faith, in the minds of all the citizens, in order that they may be animated with the proper sentiments of reverence towards the local soil as their common mother—of universal mutual affection among themselves as brothers—and of deference, on the part of the iron and brazen variety, towards the gold and

---

[y] Plato, Republ. iii. p. 389 B; compare ii. p. 382 C.

Dähne (Darstellung der Jüdisch Alexandrin. Religions Philosophie, i. pp. 48-56) sets forth the motives which determined the new interpretations of the Pentateuch by the Alexandrine Jews, from the translators of the Septuagint down to Philo. In the view of Philo there was a double meaning: the literal meaning, for the vulgar: but also besides this, there was an allegorical, the real and true meaning, discoverable only by sagacious judges. Moses (he said) gave the literal meaning, though not true, πρὸς τὴν τῶν πολλῶν διδασκαλίαν. Μανθανέτωσαν οὖν τοιοῦτοι τὰ ψευδῆ, δι' ὧν ὠφεληθήσονται, εἰ μὴ δύνανται δι'

ἀληθείας σωφρονίζεσθαι (Philo, Quæst. in Genesin ap. Dähne, p. 50). Compare also Philo on the κανόνες καὶ νόμοι τῆς ἀλληγορίας, Dähne, pp. 60-68.

Herakleitus (Allegoriæ Homericæ ed. Mehler, 1851) defends Homer warmly against the censorial condemnation of Plato. Herakleitus contends for an allegorical interpretation, and admits that it is necessary to find one. He inveighs against Plato in violent terms. Ἐρρίφθω δὲ καὶ Πλάτων ὁ κόλαξ. &c.

Isokrates (Orat. Panathen. s. 22-28) complains much of the obloquy which he incurred, because some opponents alleged that he depreciated the poets, especially Homer and Hesiod.

[z] Plato, Repub. iii. pp. 389 B, 414 C.

silver. At least, such must be the established creed of all the other citizens except the few Rulers. It ought also to be imparted, if possible, to the Rulers themselves: but *they* might be more difficult to persuade.[a]

Plato fully admits the extreme difficulty of procuring a first introduction and establishment for this new article of faith, which nevertheless is indispensable to set his commonwealth afloat. But if it can be once established, there will be no difficulty at all in continuing and perpetuating it.[b] Even as to the first commencement, difficulty is not to be confounded with impossibility: for the attempt has already been made with success in many different places, though there happens to be no recent instance.

Difficulty of procuring first admission for fictions. Ease with which they perpetuate themselves after having been once admitted.

We learn hence to appreciate the estimate which Plato formed of the ethical and religious faith, prevalent in the various societies around him. He regards as fictions the accredited stories respecting Gods and Heroes, which constituted the matter of religious belief among his contemporaries; being familiarised to all through the works of poets, painters, and sculptors, as well as through votive offerings, such as the robe annually worked by the women of Athens for the Goddess Athênê. These fictions he supposes to have originally obtained credence either through the charm of poets and narrators, or through the deliberate coinage of an authoritative lawgiver; presupposing in the community a vague emotional belief in the Gods—invisible, quasi-human agents, of whom they knew nothing distinct—and an entire ignorance of recorded history, past as well as present. Once received into the general belief, which is much more an act of emotion than of reason, such narratives retain their hold

---

[a] Plato, Republic, iii. p. 414 C. Τίς ἂν οὖν ἡμῖν μηχανὴ γένοιτο τῶν ψευδῶν τῶν ἐν δέοντι γιγνομένων, ὧν νῦν δὴ ἐλέγομεν, γενναῖόν τι ἐν ψευδομένους πεῖσαι, μάλιστα μὲν καὶ αὐτοὺς τοὺς ἄρχοντας—εἰ δὲ μή, τὴν ἄλλην πόλιν ; Ποῖον τι ; Μηδὲν καινὸν, ἀλλὰ Φοινικικόν τι, πρότερον μὲν ἤδη πολλαχοῦ γεγονός, ὥς φασιν οἱ ποιηταὶ καὶ ἡμᾶς πεπείκασιν—ἐφ' ἡμῶν δὲ οὐ γεγονὸς οὐδ' οἶδα εἰ γενόμενον ἂν, πεῖσαι δὲ συχνῆς πειθοῦς ; Compare De Legib. pp. 663-664.

[b] Plato, Republ. iii. p. 415 D. Τοῦτον οὖν τὸν μῦθον ὅπως ἂν πεισθεῖεν, ἔχεις τινὰ μηχανήν ; Οὐδαμῶς, ὅπως γ' ἂν αὐτοὶ οὗτοι· ὅπως μέντ' ἂν οἱ τούτων υἱεῖς καὶ οἱ ἔπειτα οἵ τ' ἄλλοι ἄνθρωποι οἱ ὕστερον.

both by positive teaching and by the self-operating transmission of this emotional faith to each new member of the community, as well as by the almost entire absence of criticism: especially in earlier days, when men were less intelligent but more virtuous than they are now (in Plato's time)—when among their other virtues, that of unsuspecting faith stood conspicuous, no one having yet become clever enough to suspect falsehood.[c]   This is what Plato assumes as the natural mental condition of society, to which he adapts his improvements. He disapproves the received fictions, not because they are fictions, but because they tend to produce a mischievous ethical effect, from the acts which they ascribe to the Gods and Heroes.   These acts were such, that many of them (he says) even if they had been true, ought never to be promulgated.   Plato does not pretend to substitute truth in place of fiction; but to furnish a better class of fictions in place of a worse.[d]   The religion of the Commonwealth, in his view, is to furnish fictions and sanctions to assist the moral and political views of the lawgiver, whose duty it is to employ religion for this purpose.[e]

We read in a poetical fragment of Kritias (the contem-

[c] Plato, Legg. iii. p. 679 C-E.
ἀγαθοὶ μὲν δὴ διὰ ταῦτά τε ἦσαν καὶ διὰ τὴν λεγομένην εὐήθειαν· ἃ γὰρ ἤκουον καλὰ καὶ αἰσχρὰ, εὐήθεις ὄντες ἡγοῦντο ἀληθέστατα λέγεσθαι καὶ ἐπείθοντο· ψεῦδος γὰρ ὑπονοεῖν οὐδεὶς ἠπίστατο διὰ σοφίαν, ὥσπερ τανῦν, ἀλλὰ περὶ θεῶν τε καὶ ἀνθρώπων τὰ λεγόμενα ἀληθῆ νομίζοντες ἔζων κατὰ ταῦτα—τῶν νῦν ἀτεχνότεροι μὲν καὶ ἀμαθέστεροι—εὐηθέστεροι δὲ καὶ ἀνδρειότεροι καὶ ἅμα ·σωφρονέστεροι καὶ ξύμπαντα δικαιότεροι.

[d] Plato, Legg. ii. p. 663 E.
This carelessness about historical matter of fact, as such—is not uncommon with ancient moralists and rhetoricians.   Both of them were "apt to treat history not as a series of true matters of fact, exemplifying the laws of human nature and society, and enlarging our knowledge of them for future inference—but as if it were a branch of fiction, to be handled so as to please our taste or improve our morality.   Dionysius of Halikarnassus,

blaming Thucydides for the choice of his subject, goes so far as to say, that the Peloponnesian war, a period of ruinous discord in Greece, ought to have been left in oblivion, and never to have passed into history" (Dion. H. ad Cn. Pomp. de Præc. Histor. Judic. p. 768, Reisk.).

See a note at the beginning of chap. 38 of my 'History of Greece.'

[e] Sext. Empiric. adv. Mathematicos, ix. 54, p. 562. Compare Polybius, vi. 56; Dionys. Hal. ii. 13; Strabo, i. p. 19.

These three, like Plato, consider the matters of religious belief to be fictions prescribed by the lawgiver for the purpose of governing those minds which are of too low a character to listen to truth and reason.   Strabo states, more clearly than the other two, the employment of μῦθοι by the lawgiver for purposes of education and government; he extends this doctrine to πᾶσα θεολογία ἀρχαϊκή—πρὸς τοὺς νηπιόφρονας (p. 19).

porary of Plato, though somewhat older) an opinion advanced
—that even the belief in the existence of the Gods
sprang originally from the deliberate promulgation
of lawgivers, for useful purposes.   The opinion of
Plato is not exactly the same, but it is very analogous: for he holds that all which the community believe, respecting the attributes and acts of
the Gods, must consist of fictions, and that accordingly it is essential for the lawgiver to determine what the
accredited fictions in his own community shall be : he must
therefore cause to be invented and circulated such as conduce
to the ethical and political results which he himself approves.
Private citizens are forbidden to tell falsehood ; but the lawgiver is to administer falsehood, on suitable occasions, as a
wholesome medicine.[f]

Views enter-
tained by
Kritias and
others, that
the religious
doctrines
generally be-
lieved had
originated
with law-
givers, for
useful pur-
poses.

Plato lays down his own individual preconception respecting the characters of the Gods, as orthodoxy for his Republic :
directing that the poets shall provide new narratives conformable to that type.   What is more, he establishes a peremptory
censorship to prevent the circulation of any narratives dissenting from it.   As to truth or falsehood, all that he himself
claims is that his general preconception of the character of
the Gods is true, and worthy of their dignity ; while those
entertained by his contemporaries are false ; the particular
narratives are alike fictitious in both cases.   Fictitious as
they are, however, Plato has fair reason for his confident
assertion, that if they could once be imprinted on the minds
of his citizens, as portions of an established creed, they would
maintain themselves for a long time in unimpaired force and
credit.   He guards them by the artificial protection of a censorship, stricter than any real Grecian city exhibited : over and
above the self-supporting efficacy, usually sufficient without
farther aid, which inheres in every established religious creed.

---

[f] Plato, Republ. iii. p. 389 B. ἐν
φαρμάκου εἴδει. Compare De Legg. ii.
p. 663 D.
   Eusebius enumerates this as one of
the points of conformity between Plato
and the Hebrew records; in which,
Eusebius says, you may find number-
less similar fictions (μύρια τοιαῦτα),
such as the statements of God being
jealous or angry or affected by other
human passions, which are fictions
recounted for the benefit of those who
require such treatment (Euseb. Præ-
par. Evan. xii. 31).

Chap. XXXV.   THEOLOGY OF PLATO.   189

The points upon which Plato here chiefly takes issue with his countrymen, are—the general character of the Gods—and the extent to which the. Gods determine the lot of human beings. He distinctly repudiates as untrue, that which he declares to be the generally received faith: though in other parts of his writings, we find him eulogising the merit of uninquiring faith — of that age of honest simplicity when every one believed what was told him from his childhood, and when no man was yet clever enough to suspect falsehood.[g]

Main points of dissent between Plato and his countrymen, in respect to religious doctrine.

The discord on this important point between Plato and the religious faith of his countrymen, deserves notice the rather, because the doctrines in the Republic are all put into the mouth of Sokrates, and are even criticised by Aristotle under the name of Sokrates.[h] Most people, and among them the historical Sokrates, believed in the universal agency of the Gods.[i] No—(affirms Plato) the Gods are good beings, whose nature is inconsistent with the production of evil: we must therefore divide the course of events into two portions, referring the good only to the Gods and the evil to other causes. Moreover—since the evil in the world is not merely considerable, but so considerable as greatly to preponderate over good, we must pronounce that most things are produced by these other causes (not farther particularised by Plato) and comparatively few things by the Gods. Now Epikurus (and some contemporaries[k] of Plato even before Epikurus) adopted these

Theology of Plato compared with that of Epikurus—Neither of them satisfied the exigencies of a believing religious mind of that day.

[g] Plato, Legg. iii. p. 679; compare x. p. 887 C, xi. p. 913 C.
So again in the Timæus (p. 40 E), he accepts the received genealogy of the Gods, upon the authority of the sons and early descendants of the Gods. These sons must have known their own fathers; we ought therefore "to follow the law and believe them" (ἐπομένους τῷ νόμῳ πιστευτέον) though they spoke without either probable or demonstrative proof (ἀδύνατον οὖν θεῶν παισὶν ἀπιστεῖν, καίπερ ἄνευ τε εἰκότων καὶ ἀναγκαίων ἀποδείξεων λέγουσιν).
That which Plato here enjoins to be believed is the genealogy of Hesiod and other poets, though he does not expressly name the poets. Julian in his remark on the passage (Orat. vii. p. 237) understands the poets to be meant, and their credibility to be upheld, by Plato—καὶ τοιαῦτα ἕτερα ἐν Τιμαίῳ· πιστεύειν γὰρ ἁπλῶς ἀξιοῖ καὶ χωρὶς ἀποδείξεως λεγομένοις, ὅσα ὑπὲρ τῶν θεῶν φασὶν οἱ ποιηταί. See Lindau's note on this passage in his edition of the Timæus, p. 62.
[h] Aristotel. Politic. ii. 1, &c. Compare the second of the Platonic Epistles, p. 314.
[i] Ζεὺς παναίτιος, πανεργέτας, &c. Æschyl. Agamem. 1453. Xenophon, Memorab. i. 1, 8-9.
[k] Plato, Legg. x. pp. 899 D, 888 C.

same premisses as to the preponderance of evil—but drew a different inference. They inferred that the Gods did not interfere at all in the management of the universe. Epikurus conceived the Gods as immortal beings living in eternal tranquillity and happiness; he thought it repugnant to their nature to exchange this state for any other—above all, to exchange it for the task of administering the universe, which would impose upon them endless vexation without any assignable benefit. Lastly, the preponderant evil, visibly manifested in the universe, afforded to his mind a positive proof that it was not administered by them.[1]

Comparing the two doctrines, we see that Plato, though he did not reject altogether, as Epikurus did, the agency of the Gods in the universe,—restricted it here nevertheless so as to suit the ethical exigencies of his own mind. He thus discarded so large a portion of it, as to place himself, or rather his spokesman Sokrates, in marked hostility with the received religious faith. If Melêtus and Anytus lived to read the Platonic Republic (we may add, also the dialogue called Euthryphron), they would probably have felt increased persuasion that their indictment against Sokrates was well-grounded:[m] since he stood proclaimed by the most eminent of his companions as an innovator in matters of religion, and as disbelieving a very large portion of what was commonly received by pious Athenians. With many persons, it

He intimates that there were no inconsiderable number of persons who then held the doctrine, compare p. 891 B.

[1] Lucretius, R. N. ii. 180, v. 167-196, vi. 68 :—

Nequaquam nobis divinitus esse creatam
Naturam rerum, quæ tantâ 'st prædita culpâ—
   ii. 1092 :—
Nam—proh sancta Deûm tranquillâ pectora pace,
Quæ placidum degunt ævum, vitamque serenam—
Quis regere Immensi summam, quis habere profundi
Indu manu validas potis est moderanter habenas?

[m] Xenoph. Memorab. i. 1. Ἀδικεῖ Σωκράτης, οὕς μὲν ἡ πόλις νομίζει θεούς, οὐ νομίζων, ἕτερα δὲ καινὰ δαιμόνια εἰσφέρων· ἀδικεῖ δὲ καὶ τοὺς νέους διαφθείρων.

This was the form of the indictment against Sokrates. The Republic of Plato certainly shows ground for the first part of it. Sokrates did not introduce new names and persons of Gods, but he preached new views about their characters and agency, and (what probably would cause the greatest offence) he emphatically blames the received views. The Republic of Plato here embodies what we read in the Platonist Maximus Tyrius (ix. 8) as the counter-indictment of Sokrates against the Athenian people —ἡ δὲ Σωκράτους κατὰ 'Αθηναίων γραφή—'Αδικεῖ ὁ 'Αθηναίων δῆμος, οὓς μὲν Σωκράτης νομίζει θεούς, οὐ νομίζων, ἕτερα δὲ καινὰ δαιμόνια ἐπεισφέρων— 'Αδικεῖ δὲ ὁ δῆμος καὶ τοὺς νέους διαφθείρων.

was considered a species of sacrilege to disbelieve any narrative which had once been impressed upon them respecting the Gods or the divine agency: the later Pythagoreans laid it down as a canon, that this was never to be done.[n]

Now the Gods, as here conceived by Plato conformably to his own ethical exigencies, are representatives of abstract goodness, or of what he considers as such[o]— but they are nothing else. They have no other human emotions: they are invoked for the purposes of the schoolmaster and the lawgiver, to distribute prizes, and inflict chastisements, on occasions which Plato thinks suitable. But Gods with these restricted functions were hardly less at variance with the current religious belief than the contemplative, theorising, Gods of Aristotle— or the perfectly tranquil and happy Gods of Epikurus. The Gods of the popular faith were not thus specialised types, embodiments of one abstract, ethical, idea. They were concrete personalities, many-sided and many-coloured, endowed with great variety of dispositions and emotions: having sympathies and antipathies, preferences and dislikes, to persons, places, and objects: sensitive on the score of attention paid to themselves, and of offerings tendered by men, jealous of any person who appeared to make light of them, or to put himself upon a footing of independence or rivality: connected with particular men and cities by ties of family and residence.[p]

Plato conceives the Gods according to the exigencies of his own mind —complete discord with those of the popular mind.

[n] Jamblichus, Vit. Pythag. c. 138-148. Adhortatio ad Philosophiam, p. 324, ed. Kiessling. See chapt. xxxvii. of my 'History of Greece,' p. 345, last edit.

[o] Plato, Republic, ii. p. 379.

In the sixteenth chapter of my 'History of Greece' (see p. 504 seq.) I have given many remarks on the ancient Grecian legends, and on the varying views entertained in ancient times respecting them, considered chiefly in reference to the standard of historical belief. I here regard them more as matters of religious belief and emotion.

[p] Nowhere is the relation between men and the Gods, and the all-covering variety of divine agency, in ancient Grecian belief, more instructively illustrated than in the Hippolytus of Euripides. Hippolytus, a youth priding himself on piety and still more upon inexorable continence (1140-1365), is not merely the constant worshipper of the goddess Artemis, but also her companion; she sits with him, hunts with him; he hears her voice and converses with her: he knows her presence by the divine odour, though he does not see her (σύνθακε, συγκύναγε, 1093-1391-87). But he disdains to address a respectful word to Aphroditè, or to yield in any way to her influence, though he continually passes by her statue which stands at his gates; he even speaks of her in disparaging terms (13-101). Aphroditè becomes deeply indignant with him, not because he is devoted to

They corresponded with all the feelings of the believer; with
his hopes and fears, his joys and sorrows, his pride or his
shame, his love or preference towards some persons or institutions, his hatred and contempt for others. They were sometimes benevolent, sometimes displeased and unpropitious,
according to circumstances. They were indeed believed to
interfere for the protection of what the believer accounted
innocence or merit, and for the avenging of what he called
wrong. But this was only one of many occasions on which
they interfered. They dispensed alternately evil and good,
out of the two casks mentioned in that Homeric verse ꝗ
which Plato so emphatically censures. Nay, it was as much
a necessity of the believer's imagination to impute marked
and serious suffering to the envy or jealousy of the Gods, as
good fortune and prosperity to their kindness. Such a turn
of thought is not less visible in Herodotus, Xenophon, Demosthenes, Lykurgus, &c., than in Homer and the other
poets whom Plato rebukes. Moreover it is frequently expressed or implied in the answers or admonitions delivered
from oracles.ʳ

Artemis, but because he neglects and
despises herself (20): for the Gods
take offence when they are treated
with disrespect, just as men do (6-94).
His faithful attendant laments this
misguided self-sufficiency, and endeavours in vain to reason his master
out of it (see the curious dialogue
87-120, also 445). Aphrodité accordingly resolves to punish Hippolytus
for this neglect by inspiring Phædra,
his step-mother, with an irresistible
passion for him : she foresees that this
will prove the destruction of Phædra
as well as of Hippolytus, but no such
consideration can be allowed to
countervail the necessity of punishing
her enemies. She accordingly smites
Phædra with love-sickness, which,
since Phædra will not reveal the cause,
the chorus ascribes to the displeasure
and visitation of some unknown
divinity, Pan, Hekatê, Kybelê, &c.
(142-238). The course of this beautiful
drama is well known : Aphrodité
proves herself a Goddess and something more (359) : Phædra and Hippolytus both perish ; Theseus is struck

down with grief and remorse (1402) ;
while Artemis, who appears at the end
to console the dying Hippolytus and
reprove Theseus, laments that it was
not in her power, according to the
established etiquette among the Gods,
to interpose for the protection of Hippolytus against the anger of Aphrodité,
but promises to avenge him by killing
with her unerring arrows some marked
favourite of Aphrodité (1327-1421).
"Non esse curæ Diis securitatem
nostram, esse ultionem."—Tacitus.

ꝗ Homer, Iliad xxiv. 525.

ʳ The opinion is memorable, which
Herodotus puts into the mouth of the
wisest and best man of his age—Solon.
Ὦ Κροῖσε, ἐπιστάμενόν με τὸ θεῖον πᾶν
ἐὸν φθονερόν τε καὶ ταραχῶδες, ἐπειρω-
τᾷς με τῶν ἀνθρωπηΐων πραγμάτων
πέρι ; (Herod. i. 32). Krœsus was
overtaken by a terrible divine judgment because he thought himself the
happiest of men (i. 34). The Gods
strike at persons of high rank and
position ; they do not suffer any one
except themselves to indulge in self-
exaltation (vii. 10). Herodotus ascribes

When therefore the Platonic Sokrates in this treatise affirms authoritatively, — and affirms without any proof—his restricted version of the agency of the Gods, calling upon his countrymen to reject all that large portion of their religious belief, which rested upon the assumption of a wider agency, as being unworthy of the real attributes of the Gods,—he would confirm, in the minds of ordinary Athenians, the charge of culpable innovation in religion, preferred against him by his accusers. To set up à priori a certain type (either Platonic or Epikurean) of what the Gods *must* be, different from what they were commonly believed to be,—and then to disallow, as unworthy and incredible, all that was inconsistent with this type, including a full half of the narratives consecrated in the emotional belief of the public—all this could not but appear as "impious rationalism," on the part of "the Sophist Sokrates." [s]   It would be not less repugnant to the feelings of ordinary Greeks, and would appear not more conclusive to their reason, than the arguments of rationalizing critics upon many narratives of the Old Testament appear to orthodox readers of modern times—when these critics disallow as untrue many acts therein ascribed to God, on the ground that such acts are unworthy of a just and good being.

Repugnance of ordinary Athenians, in regard to the criticism of Sokrates on the religious legends.

the like sentiment to another man distinguished for prudence—Amasis king of Egypt (iii. 40-44-125). Compare Pausanias, ii. 33 and Æschyl. Pers. 93, Supplices, 388, Hermann. Herodotus and Pausanias, proclaim the envy and jealousy of the Gods more explicitly than other writers. About the usual disposition to regard the jealousy of the Gods as causing misfortunes and suffering, see Thucyd. ii. 54, vii. 77 ; especially when a man by rash speech or act brings grave misfortune on himself, he is supposed to be under a misguiding influence by the Gods, expressed by Herodotus in the remarkable word θεοβλαβής (Herodot. i. 127, viii. 137 ; Xenoph. Hellen. vi. 4, 3 ; Soph. Œd. Kol. 371). The poverty in which Xenophon found himself when he quitted the Cyreian army, is ascribed by himself, at the suggestion of the prophet Eukleides, to his having omitted to sacrifice to Zeus Meilichius

during the whole course of the expedition and retreat. The next day Xenophon offered an ample sacrifice to this God, and good fortune came upon him immediately afterwards ; he captured Asidates the Persian, receiving a large ransom, with an ample booty, and thus enriched himself (Xenop. Anab. vii. 8, 4-23). Compare about θεῶν φθόνος; Pindar, Pyth. x. 20-44 ; Demosthenes cont. Timokratem, p. 738 ; Naegelsbach, Die Nach-Homerische Theologie der Griechen, pp. 330-335.

[s] Æschines cont. Timarch. Σωκράτη τὸν σοφιστὴν—

Lucretius, i. 82.

Illud in his rebus vereor, ne forté rearis Impia te rationis inire elementa, viamque Endogredi sceleris—

Plato, in Leges, v. 738 B, recognises the danger of disturbing the established and accredited religious φῆμαι, as well as the rites and ceremonies.

Though the Platonic Sokrates, repudiating most of the narratives believed respecting Gods and Heroes, as being
immoral and suggesting bad examples to the hearers,
proposes to construct a body of new fictions in place
of them—yet, if we turn to the Clouds of Aristophanes, we shall find that the old fashioned and unphilosophical Athenian took quite the opposite view. He
connected immoral conduct with the new teaching, not with
the old: he regarded the narratives respecting the Gods as
realities of an unrecorded past, not as fictions for the purposes
of the training-school: he did not imagine that the conduct of
Zeus, in chaining up his father Kronus, was a proper model to
be copied by himself or any other man: nay, he denounced
all such disposition to copy, and to seek excuse for human
misconduct in the example of the Gods, as abuse and profana-
tion introduced by the sophistry of the freethinkers.[t] In his
eyes, the religious traditions, were part and parcel of the established faith, customs and laws of the state ; and Sokrates, in

Aristophanes connects the idea of immorality with the freethinkers and their wicked misinterpretations.

[t] Aristophan. Nubes, 358. λεπ-
τοτάτων λήρων ἱερεῦ—885, γνώμας
καινὰς ἐξευρίσκων.
1381.—
ὡς ἡδὺ καινοῖς πράγμασιν καὶ δεξιοῖς
ὁμιλεῖν,
καὶ τῶν καθεστώτων νόμων ὑπερφρονεῖν
δύνασθαι.
(894. Ἄδικος Λόγος.)—
Πῶς δῆτα δίκης οὔσης, ὁ Ζεὺς
οὐκ ἀπόλωλεν, τὸν πατέρ' αὑτοῦ
δήσας; (Δίκ'-Λογος) αἰβοῖ, τουτὶ καὶ δὴ
χωρεῖ τὸ κακόν· δότε μοι λεκάνην.
1061.—
μοιχὸς γὰρ ἢν τύχης ἁλοὺς, τάδ' ἀντε-
ρεῖς πρὸς αὐτὸν,
ὡς οὐδὲν ἠδίκηκας· εἶτ' εἰς τὸν Δί'
ἐπανενεγκεῖν,
κἄκεινος ὡς ἥττων ἔρωτός ἐστι καὶ
γυναικῶν.
While Aristophanes introduces the
freethinker as justifying unlawful acts
by the example of Zeus, Plato (in the
dialogue called Euthyphron) represents
Euthyphron as indicting his father for
murder, and justifying himself by the
analogy of Zeus: Euthyphron being a
very religious man, who believed all
the divine matters commonly received,
and more besides (p. 6). This exhibits
the opposition between the Platonic
and the Aristophanic point of view.
In the Eumenides of Æschylus (632),

these Goddesses reproach Zeus with
inconsistency, after chaining up his
old father Kronus, in estimating so
highly the necessity of avenging Agamemnon's death, as to authorise Orestes
to kill Klytæmnestra.
An extract from Butler's Analogy,
in reply to the objections offered by
Deists against the Old Testament, will
serve to illustrate the view which pious
Athenians took of those ancient narratives which Plato censures. Butler
says: " It is the province of Reason to
judge of the morality of the Scriptures ;
i. e. not whether it contains things different from what we should have expected from a wise, just, and good
Being, but whether it contains things
plainly contradictory to Wisdom, Justice, or Goodness; to what the light
of nature teaches us about God. And
I know of nothing of the sort objected
against Scripture, unless in such objections as are formed upon the supposition that the constitution of nature is
contradictory to wisdom, justice, or
goodness: which most certainly it is
not. Indeed there are some particular
precepts in Scripture, given to particular persons, requiring actions which
would be immoral and vicious, were it
not for such precepts. But it is easy
to see that all these are of such a kind,

discrediting the traditions, set himself up as a thinker above the laws.   As to this feature, the Aristophanic Sokrates in the

as that the precept changes the whole nature of the case and of the action : and both constitutes and shows *that* not to be immoral which, prior to the precept, must have appeared and really been so ; which may well be, since none of these precepts are contrary to immutable morality.   If it were commanded to cultivate the principles, and act from the spirit, of treachery, ingratitude, or cruelty, the command would not alter the nature of the case or of the action, in any of these instances.   But it is quite otherwise in precepts, which require only the doing an external action : for instance, taking away the life or property of any.   For men have no right to either, but what arises solely from the gift of God : when this grant is revoked, they cease to have any right to either : and when this revocation is made known, as surely it may be, it must cease to be unjust to deprive them of either.   And though a course of external acts which, without command, would be immoral, must make an immoral habit—yet a few detached commands have no such natural tendency.

" I thought proper to say thus much of the few Scripture precepts requiring, not vicious actions, but actions which would have been vicious but for such precepts : because they are sometimes weakly urged as immoral, and great weight is laid upon objections drawn from them.   But to me there seems no difficulty at all in these precepts but what arises from their being offences—*i.e.* from their being liable to be perverted, as indeed they are, to serve the most horrid purposes, by wicked, designing men : and perhaps to mislead the weak and enthusiastic.   And objections from this head are not objections against Revelation, but against the whole notion of Religion, as a trial, and against the whole constitution of Nature." (Butler's Analogy, Part. ii. ch. 3. p. 236.)

I do not here propose to examine the soundness of this argument (which has been acutely discussed in a good pamphlet by Miss Hennell—' Essay on the Sceptical Tendency of Butler's Analogy,' p. 15, John Chapman, 1859).   It appeared satisfactory to an able reasoner like Butler : and believers at Athens would have found satisfaction

in similar arguments, when the narratives in which they believed were pronounced by Sokrates mischievous and incredible, as imputing to the Gods unworthy acts.   For example—Zeus and Athênê instigate Pandarus to break the sworn truce between the Greeks and Trojans : Zeus sends Oneirus, or the Dream-God, to deceive Agamemnon (Plat. Rep. ii. pp. 379-383).   Here are acts (the orthodox reasoner would say) which would be immoral if it were not for the special command : but Agamemnon and the Greeks had no right to life or property, much less to any other comforts or advantages, except what arose from the gift of the Gods.   Now the Gods, on this particular occasion, thought fit to revoke the right which they had granted, making known such revocation to Pandarus ; who, accordingly, in that particular case, committed no injustice in trying to kill Menelaus, and in actually wounding him.   The Gods did not give any general command " to cultivate the spirit and act upon the principles " of perjury and faithlessness : they merely licensed the special act of Pandarus— *hic et nunc*—by making known to him that they had revoked the right of the Greeks to have faith observed with them, at that particular moment.   When any man argues—" Pandarus was instigated by Zeus to break faith : therefore faithlessness is innocent and authorised : therefore *I* may break faith "—this is " a perversion by wicked and designing men for a horrid purpose, and can mislead only the weak and enthusiastic."

Farther, If the Gods may by special mandates cause the murder or impoverishment of particular men by other men to be innocent acts, without sanctioning any inference by analogy— much more may the same be said respecting the acts of the Gods among themselves, which Sokrates censures, viz. their quarrels, violent manifestations by word and deed, amorous gusts, hearty laughter, &c.   These too are particular acts, not intended to lead to consequences in the way of example.   The Gods have not issued any general command, " Be quarrelsome, be violent," &c.   If they are quarrelsome themselves on particular occasions, they have a right to be so ; just as they

Clouds, and the Platonic Sokrates in the Republic, perfectly agree—however much they differ in other respects.

In reviewing the Platonic Republic, I have thought it ne-

Heresies ascribed to Sokrates by his own friends—Unpopularity of his name from this circumstance. cessary to appreciate the theological and pædagogic doctrines, not merely with reference to mankind in the abstract, but also as they appeared to the contemporaries among whom they were promulgated.

To all the abovementioned restrictions imposed by Plato

Restrictions imposed by Plato upon musical modes and reciters. upon the manifestation of the poet, both as to thoughts, words, and manner of recital—we must add those which he provides for music in its limited sense: the musical modes and instruments, the varieties of rhythm. He allows only the lyre and the harp, with the panspipe for shepherds tending their flocks. He forbids both the flute and all complicated stringed instruments. Interdicting the lugubrious, passionate, soft, and convivial, modes of music, he tolerates none but the Dorian and Phrygian, suitable to a sober, resolute, courageous, frame of mind: to which also all the rhythm and movement of the body is to be adapted.[u] Each particular manifestation of speech, music, poetry, and painting, having a natural affinity

have a right to take away any man's life or property whenever they choose: but *you* are not to follow their example, and none but wicked men will advise you to do so.

To those believers who denounced Sokrates as a freethinker (Plat. Euthyp. p. 6 A) such arguments would probably appear satisfactory. "*Sunt Superis sua jura*" is a general principle, flexible and wide in its application. Of arguments analogous to those of Butler, really used in ancient times by advocates who defended the poets against censures like those of Plato, we find an illustrative specimen in the Scholia on Sophokles. At the beginning of the Elektra (35-50), Orestes comes back with his old attendant or tutor to Argos, bent on avenging the death of his father. He has been stimulated to that enterprise by the Gods (70). having consulted Apollo at Delphi, and having been directed by him to accomplish it not by armed force but by deceits (δόλοισι κλέψαι, 36). Keeping himself concealed, he sends the old attendant into the house of Ægisthus, with orders to communicate a false narrative that he Orestes is dead, having perished by an accident in the Pythian chariot-race: and he directs the attendant to certify this falsehood by oath (ἄγγελλε δ᾽ ὅρκῳ προστιθείς, 47). Upon which last words the Scholiast observes as follows :—"We must not take captious exception to the poet, as if he were here exhorting men to perjure themselves. For Orestes is bound to obey the God, who commands him to accomplish the whole by deceit ; so that while he appears to be impious by swearing a false oath, he by that very act shows his piety, since he does it in obedience to the God"—μὴ σμικρολόγως τις ἐπιλάβηται, ὡς κελεύοντος ἐπιορκεῖν τοῦ ποιητοῦ· δεῖ γὰρ αὐτὸν πείθεσθαι τῷ θεῷ, τὸ πᾶν δόλῳ πράσσειν παρακελευομένῳ· ὥστε ἐν οἷς δοκεῖ ἐπιορκῶν δυσσεβεῖν, διὰ τούτων εὐσεβεῖ, πειθόμενος τῷ θεῷ.

[u] Plato, Republic, iii. pp. 399-400.

with some particular emotional and volitional state—emanating from it in the mind of the author and suggesting it in other minds—nothing is to be tolerated except what exhibits goodness· and temperance of disposition,—grace, proportion, and decency of external form.[x] Artisans are to observe the like rules in their constructions : presenting to the eye nothing but what is symmetrical. The youthful Guardians, brought up among such representations, will have their minds imbued with correct æsthetical sentiment; they will learn even in their youngest years, before they are competent to give reasons, to love what is beautiful and honourable—to hate what is ugly and mean.[y]

All these enactments and prohibitions have for their purpose the ethical and æsthetical training of the Guardians : to establish and keep up in each individual Guardian, a good state of the emotions, and a proper internal government—that is, a due subordination of energy and appetite to Reason.[z] All these restrictions intended for the emotional training of the Guardians. Their bodies will also be trained by a good and healthy scheme of gymnastics, which will at the same time not only impart to them strength but inspire them with courage. The body is here considered, not (like what we read in Phædon and Philêbus) as an inconvenient and depraving companion to the mind : but as an indispensable co-operator, only requiring to be duly reined.

The Guardians, of both sexes, thus educated and disciplined, are intended to pass their whole lives in the discharge of their duties as Guardians; implicitly obeying the orders of the Few Philosophical chiefs, and quartered in barracks under strict regulations. Among these regulations, there are two in Regulations for the life of the Guardians, especially the prohibition of separate property and family. particular which have always provoked more surprise and comment than any other features in the commonwealth; first, the prohibition of separate property—next, that of separate family—including the respective position of the two sexes.

---

[x] Plato, Repub. iii. pp. 400-401. ὁ τρόπος τῆς λέξεως—τῷ τῆς ψυχῆς ἤθει ἕπεται — προσαναγκαστέον τὴν τοῦ ἀγαθοῦ εἰκόνα ἤθους ἐμποιεῖν.

[y] Plato, Repub. iii. pp. 401-402 A.

[z] Plato, Repub. x. p. 608. περὶ τῆς ἐν αὑτῷ πολιτείας δεδιότι—μέγας ὁ ἀγὼν, μέγας, οὐχ ὅσος δοκεῖ, τὸ χρηστὸν ἢ κακὸν γενέσθαι.

The directions of Plato on these two points not only hang

Purpose of Plato in these regulations. together, but are founded on the same reason and considerations. He is resolved to prevent the growth of any separate interest, affections, or aspirations, in the mind of any individual Guardian. Each Guardian is to perform his military and civil duties to the Commonwealth, and to do nothing else. He must find his happiness in the performance of his duty: no double functions or occupations are tolerated. This principle, important in Plato's view as regards every one, is of supreme importance as applying to the Guardians,[a] in whom resides the whole armed force of the commonwealth and by whom the orders of the Chiefs or Elders are enforced. If the Guardians aspire to private ends of their own, and employ their force for the attainment of such ends, nothing but oppression and ruin of the remaining community can ensue. A man having land of his own to cultivate, or a wife and family of his own to provide with comforts, may be a good economist, but he will never be a tolerable Guardian.[b] To be competent for this latter function, he must neither covet wealth nor be exposed to the fear of poverty: he must desire neither enjoyments nor power, except what are common to his entire regiment. He must indulge neither private sympathies nor private antipathies: he must be inaccessible to all motives which could lead him to despoil or hurt his fellow-citizens the producers. Accordingly the hopes and fears involved in self-maintenance—the feelings of buyer, seller, donor, or receiver—the ideas of separate property, house, wife, or family—must never be allowed to enter into his mind. The Guardians will receive from the productive part of the community a constant provision, sufficient, but not more than sufficient, for their reasonable maintenance. Their residence will be in public barracks and their meals at a common mess: they must be taught to regard it as a disgrace to meddle in any way with gold and silver.[c] Men and women will live all together, or distributed in a few fractional companies, but always in companionship, and under perpetual drill; beginning from the earliest years with both sexes.

[a] Plato, Republ. iv. pp. 421 A-423 D.   [b] Plato, Republ. iii. p. 417 A-B.
[c] Plato, Republ. iii. pp. 416-417.

Boys and girls will be placed from the beginning under the same superintendance ; and will receive the same training, as well in gymnastic as in music. The characters of both will be exposed to the same influences and formed in the same mould. Upon the maintenance of such early, equal, and collective training, especially in music, under the orders of the Elders,—Plato declares the stability of the commonwealth to depend.[d]

The purpose being, to form good and competent Guardians, the same training which will be best for the boys will also be best for the girls. But is it true that women are competent to the function of Guardians ? Is the female nature endued with the same aptitudes for such duties as the male ? Men will ridicule the suggestion (says Plato) and will maintain the negative. They will say that there are some functions for which men are more competent, others for which women are more competent than men : and that women are unfit for any such duty as that of Guardians. Plato dissents from this opinion altogether. There is no point on which he speaks in terms of more decided conviction. Men and women (he says) can perform this duty conjointly, just as dogs of both sexes take part in guarding the flock. It is not true that the female, by reason of the characteristic properties of sex— parturition and suckling—is disqualified for out-door occupations and restricted to the interior of the house.[e] As in the remaining animals generally, so also in the human race. There is no fundamental difference between the two sexes, other than that of the sexual attributes themselves. From that difference no consequences flow, in respect to aptitude for some occupations, inaptitude for others. There are great individual differences between one woman and another, as there are between one man and another: this woman is peculiarly fit for one task, that woman for something else. But speaking of women generally and collectively, there is not a single profession for which they are peculiarly fit, or more fit than men. Men are superior to women in every- thing, in one occupation as well as in another. Yet among

Marginal note: Common life; education, drill, collective life, and duties, for Guardians of both sexes. Views of Plato respecting the female character and aptitudes.

---

[d] Plato, Republ. iv. pp. 423-424 D-425 A-C.   [e] Plato, Republ. v. p. 451 D.

both sexes, there are serious individual differences, so that many women, individually estimated, will be superior to many men: no women will equal the best men, but the best women will equal the second-best men, and will be superior to the men below them.[f] Accordingly, in order to obtain the best Guardians, selection must be made from both sexes indiscriminately. For ordinary duties, both will be found equally fit: but the heaviest and most difficult duties, those which require the maximum of competence to perform, will usually devolve upon men.[g]

Those who maintain (continues Plato) that because women are different from men, therefore the occupations of the two ought to be different—argue like vexatious disputants who mistake verbal distinctions for real: who do not enquire what is the formal or specific distinction indicated by a name, or whether it has any essential bearing on the matter under discussion.[h] Long-haired men are different from bald-heads: but shall we conclude, that if the former are fit to make shoes, the latter are unfit? Certainly not: for when we enquire into the formal distinction con-

His arguments against the ordinary doctrine.

---

[f] See this remarkable argument— Republ. v. pp. 453-456 — γυναῖκες μέντοι πολλαὶ πολλῶν ἀνδρῶν βελτίους εἰς πολλά· τὸ δὲ ὅλον ἔχει ὡς σὺ λέγεις —Οὐδὲν ἄρα ἐστὶν ἐπιτήδευμα τῶν πόλιν διοικούντων γυναικὸς διότι γυνὴ, οὐδ' ἀνδρὸς διότι ἀνήρ — ἀλλ' ὁμοίως διεσπαρμέναι αἱ φύσεις ἐν ἀμφοῖν τοῖν ζώοιν, καὶ πάντων μὲν μετέχει γυνὴ ἐπιτηδευμάτων κατὰ φύσιν, πάντων δὲ ἀνήρ· ἐπὶ πᾶσι δὲ ἀσθενέστερον γυνὴ ἀνδρός (p. 455 D). It would appear (from p. 455 C) that those who maintained the special fitness of women for certain occupations and their special unfitness for others, cited, as examples of occupations in which women surpassed men, weaving and cookery. But Plato denies this emphatically as a matter of fact; pronouncing that women were inferior to men (i. e. the best women to the best men) in weaving and cookery no less than in other things. We should have been glad to know what facts were present to his mind as bearing out such an assertion, and what observations were open to him of weaving as performed by males. In Greece, weaving was the occupation of women

very generally, whether exclusively or not we can hardly say; in Phœnicia, during the Homeric times, the finest robes are woven by Sidonian women (Iliad vi. 289) : in Egypt, on the contrary, it was habitually performed by men, and Herodotus enumerates this as one of the points in which the Egyptians differed from other countries (Herodot. ii. 35 ; Soph. Œdip. Col. 340, with the Scholia, and the curious citation contained therein from the Βαρβαρικὰ of Nymphodorus). The process of weaving was also conducted in a different manner by the Egyptians. Whether Plato had seen finer webs in Egypt than in Greece we cannot say.

[g] Plato, Republ. v. p. 457 A.

[h] Plato, Republic, v. p. 454 A. διὰ τὸ μὴ δύνασθαι κατ' εἴδη διαιρούμενοι τὸ λεγόμενον ἐπισκοπεῖν, ἀλλὰ κατ' αὐτὸ τὸ ὄνομα διώκειν τοῦ λεχθέντος τὴν ἐναντίωσιν, ἔριδι, οὐ διαλέκτῳ, πρὸς ἀλλήλους χρώμενοι. P. 455 B. ἐπεσκεψάμεθα δὲ οὐδ' ὁπηροῦν, τί εἶδος τὸ τῆς ἑτέρας καὶ τῆς αὐτῆς φύσεως, καὶ πρὸς τί τεῖνον ὡριζόμεθα τότε, ὅτε τὰ ἐπιτηδεύματα ἄλλη φύσει ἄλλα, τῇ δὲ αὐτῇ τὰ αὐτὰ, ἀπεδίδομεν.

noted by these words, we find that it has no bearing upon such handicraft processes. So again the formal distinction implied by the terms *male, female,* in the human race as in other animals, lies altogether in the functions of sex and procreation.[i] Now this has no essential bearing on the occupations of the adult; nor does it confer on the male, fitness for one set of occupations—on the female, fitness for another. Each sex is fit for all, but the male is most fit for all: in each sex there are individuals better and worse, and differing one from another in special aptitudes. Men are competent for the duties of Guardians, only on condition of having gone through a complete musical and gymnastical education. Women are competent also, under the like condition; and are equally capable of profiting by the complete education. Moreover, the chiefs must select for those duties the best natural subjects. The total number of such is very limited: and they must select the best that both sexes afford.[k]

The strong objections, generally entertained against thus assigning to women equal participation in the education and functions of the Guardians, were enforced by saying—That it was a proceeding contrary to Nature. But Plato not only denies the validity of this argument: he even retorts it upon the objectors, and affirms that the existing separation of functions between the two sexes is contrary to Nature, and that his proposition alone is conformable thereunto.[l] He has shown that the specific or formal distinction of the two has no essential bearing on the question, and therefore that no argument can be founded upon it. The specific or formal characteristic, in the case of males, is doubtless superior, taken abstractedly: yet in particular men it is embodied or manifested with various degrees of perfection, from very good to very bad. In the case of females, though inferior abstractedly, it is in its best particular embodiments equal to all except the best males, and superior to all such as are inferior to the best.

Opponents appealed to Nature as an authority against Plato. He invokes Nature on his own side against them.

[i] Plato, Republ. v. p. 455 C-D.
[k] Plato, Republic, v. p. 456.
[l] Plato, Republ. v. p. 456 C. Οὐκ ἄρα ἀδύνατά γε, οὐδὲ εὐχαῖς ὅμοια, ἐνομοθετοῦμεν, ἐπείπερ κατὰ φύσιν ἐτίθεμεν τὸν νόμον· ἀλλὰ τὰ νῦν παρὰ ταῦτα γιγνόμενα παρὰ φύσιν μᾶλλον, ὡς ἔοικε, γίγνεται.

Accordingly, the true dictate of Nature is, not merely that females *may be* taken, but that they *ought to be* taken, conjointly with males, under the selection of the Rulers, to fulfil the most important duties in the Commonwealth. The select females must go through the same musical and gymnastic training as the males. He who ridicules them for such bodily exercises, prosecuted with a view to the best objects, does not know what he is laughing at. "For this is the most valuable maxim which is now, or ever has been, proclaimed—What is useful, is honourable. What is hurtful, is base." [m]

Plato now proceeds to unfold the relations of the sexes as intended to prevail among the mature Guardians, after all have undergone the public and common training from their earliest infancy. He conceives them as one thousand in total number, composed of both sexes in nearly equal proportion : since they are to be the best individuals of both sexes, the male sex, superior in formal characteristic, will probably furnish rather a greater number than the female. It has already been stated that they are all required to live together in barracks, dining at a common mess-table, with clothing and furniture alike for all. There is no individual property or separate house among them : the collective expence, in a comfortable but moderate way, is defrayed by contributions from the producing class. Separate families are unknown : all the Guardians, male and female, form one family, and one only : the older are fathers and mothers of all the younger, the younger are sons and daughters of all the older : those of the same age are all alike brothers and sisters of each other : those who, besides being of the same age, are within the limits of the nuptial age and of different sexes, are all alike husbands and wives of each other. [n] It is the principle of the Platonic Common-

Marginal note: Collective family relations and denominations among the Guardians.

---

[m] Plato, Republ. v. p. 457. Ὁ δὲ γελῶν ἀνὴρ ἐπὶ γυμναῖς γυναιξί, τοῦ βελτίστου ἕνεκα γυμναζομέναις, ἀτελῆ τοῦ γελοίου σοφίας δρέπων καρπόν, οὐδὲν οἶδεν, ὡς ἔοικεν, ἐφ' ᾧ δ γελᾷ οὐδ' ὅ, τι πράττει· κάλλιστα γὰρ δὴ τοῦτο καὶ λέγεται καὶ λελέξεται, ὅτι τὸ μὲν ὠφέλιμον, καλόν — τὸ δὲ βλαβερόν, αἰσχρόν.

[n] Plato, Republic, v. p. 457 C. τὰς γυναῖκας ταύτας τῶν ἀνδρῶν τούτων πάντων πάσας εἶναι κοινάς, ἰδίᾳ δὲ μηδενὶ μηδεμίαν συνοικεῖν· καὶ τοὺς παῖδας αὖ κοινούς, καὶ μήτε γονέα ἔκγονον εἰδέναι τὸν αὑτοῦ μήτε παῖδα γονέα.

wealth that the affections implied in these family-words, instead of being confined to one or a few exclusively, shall be expanded so as to embrace all of appropriate age.

But Plato does not at all intend that sexual intercourse shall take place between these men and women promiscuously, or at the pleasure of individuals. On the contrary, he expressly denounces and interdicts it.[o] A philosopher who has so much general disdain for individual impulse or choice, was not likely to sanction it in this particular case. Indeed it is the special purpose of his polity to bring impulse absolutely under the controul of reason, or of that which he assumes as such. This purpose is followed out in a remarkable manner as to procreation. What he seeks as lawgiver is, to keep the numbers of the Guardians nearly stationary, with no diminution and scarcely any increase:[p] and to maintain the breed pure, so that the children born shall be as highly endowed by nature as possible. To these two objects the liberty of sexual intercourse is made subservient. The breeding is regulated, like that of noble horses or dogs by an intelligent proprietor: the best animals of both sexes being brought together, and the limits of age fixed beforehand.[q] Plato prescribes, as the limits of age, from twenty to forty for females—from thirty to fifty-five, for males—when the powers of body and mind are at the maximum in both. All who are younger as well as all who are older, are expressly forbidden to meddle in the procreation *for the city*: this being a public function.[r] Between the ages above named, couples will be invited to marry in such numbers as the Rulers may consider expedient for ensuring a supply of offspring sufficient and not more than sufficient—having regard to wars, distempers, or any other recent causes of mortality.[s]

Restrictions upon sexual intercourse— Purposes of such restrictions.

[o] Plato, Republ. v. p. 458 E. ἀτάκτως μὲν μίγνυσθαι ἀλλήλοις ἢ ἄλλο ὁτιοῦν ποιεῖν οὔτε ὅσιον ἐν εὐδαιμόνων πόλει οὔτ᾽ ἐάσουσιν οἱ ἄρχοντες.

[p] Plato, Republic, v. p. 460 A. τὸ δὲ πλῆθος τῶν γάμων ἐπὶ τοῖς ἄρχουσι ποιήσομεν, ἵν᾽ ὡς μάλιστα διασώζωσι τὸν αὐτὸν ἀριθμὸν τῶν ἀνδρῶν, πρὸς πολέμους τε καὶ νόσους καὶ πάντα τὰ τοιαῦτα ἀποσκοποῦντες, καὶ μήτε μεγάλη ἡμῖν ἡ πόλις μήτε σμικρὰ γίγνηται.

[q] Plato, Repub. v. p. 459.

[r] This is his phrase, repeated more than once—τίκτειν τῇ πόλει, γεννᾷν τῇ πόλει—τῶν εἰς τὸ κοινὸν γεννήσεων (pp. 460-461).

What Lucan observes about Cato of Utica, is applicable to the Guardians of the Platonic Republic:—

"Venerisque huic maximus usus Progenies: Urbi pater est, Urbique maritus." (ii. 388).

[s] Plato, Republ. v, p. 460 A.

There is no part of the Platonic system in which individual choice is more decidedly eliminated, and the intervention of the Rulers made more constantly paramount than this, respecting the marriages: and Plato declares it to be among the greatest difficulties which they will have to surmount. They will establish festivals, in which they bring together the brides and bridegrooms, with hymns, prayer, and sacrifices, to the Gods: they will determine by lot what couples shall be joined, so as to make up the number settled as appropriate: but.they will arrange the sortition themselves so cleverly, that what appears.chance to others will be a result to them predetermined. The best men will thus always be assorted with the best women, the inferior with the inferior: but this will appear to every one, except themselves, the result of chance.[t] Any young man (of thirty and upwards) distinguished for bravery or excellence will be allowed to have more than one wife; since it is good not merely to recompense his merit, but also to multiply his breed.[u]

Regulations about marriages and family.

In the seventh month, or in the tenth month, after the ceremonial day, offspring will be born from these unions. But the children, immediately on being born, will be taken away from their mothers, and confided to nurses in an appropriate lodgment. The mothers will be admitted to suckle them, and wet-nurses will also be provided, as far as necessary: but the period for the mother to suckle will be abridged as much as possible, and all other trouble required for the care of infancy will be undertaken, not by her, but by the nurses. Moreover the greatest precautions will be taken that no mother shall know her own child: which is considered to be practicable, since many children will be born at nearly the same time.[x] The children in infancy will be examined by the Rulers and other good judges, who will determine how many of them are sufficiently well constituted to promise fitness for the duties of Guardians. The children of the good and vigorous couples, except in any case of bodily deformity, will be brought up and placed under the public training for

---

[t] Plato, Republ. v. p. 460.
[u] Plato, Republ. v. pp. 460 B, 468 C. In the latter passage it even appears

that he is allowed to make a choice.
[x] Plato, Republ. v. pp. 460 D, 461 D.

Guardians: the unpromising children, and those of the inferior couples, being regarded as not fit subjects for the public training, will be secretly got rid of, or placed among the producing class of the commonwealth.[y]

What Plato here understands by marriage, is a special, solemn, consecrated, coupling for the occasion, with a view to breed for the public. It constitutes no permanent bond between the two persons coupled: who are brought together by the authorities under a delusive sortition, but who may perhaps never be brought together at any future sortition, unless it shall please the same authorities. The case resembles that of a breeding stud of horses and mares, to which Plato compares it: nothing else is wanted but the finest progeny attainable. But this, in Plato's judgment, is the most important of all purposes: his commonwealth cannot maintain itself except under a superior breed of Guardians. Accordingly, he invests his marriages with the greatest possible sanctity. The religious solemnities accompanying them are essential to furnish security for the goodness of the offspring. Any proceeding, either of man or woman, which contravenes the provisions of the rulers on this point, is peremptorily forbidden: and any child, born from unauthorised intercourse without the requisite prayers and sacrifices, is considered as an outcast. Within the limits of the connubial age, all persons of both sexes hold their procreative powers exclusively at the disposition of the lawgiver. But after that age is past, both men and women may indulge in intercourse with whomsoever they please, since they are no longer in condition to procreate for the public. They are subject only to this one condition: not to produce any children, or if perchance they do, not to bring them up.[z] There is moreover one restriction upon the personal liberty of intercourse, after the connubial limits of age. No intercourse is permitted between father and daughter, or

Procreative powers of individual Guardians required to be held at the disposal of the rulers, for purity of breed.

---

[y] Compare Republic, v. pp. 459 D, 460 C, 461 C, with Timæus, p. 19 A. In Timæus, where the leading doctrines of the Republic are briefly recapitulated, Plato directs that the children considered as unworthy shall be secretly distributed among the remaining community, *i. e.* not among the Guardians: in the Republic itself, his language, though not clear, seems to imply that they shall be exposed and got rid of.

[z] Plato, Republ. v. p. 461 C.

between mother and son. But how can such restriction be enforced, since no individual paternity or maternity is recognised in the commonwealth? Plato answers by admitting a collective paternity and maternity. Every child born in the seventh month or in the tenth month after a couple have been solemnly wedded, will be considered by them as their son or daughter, and will consider himself as such.[a]

Besides all these direct provisions for the purity of the breed of Guardians, which will succeed (so Plato anticipates) in a large majority of cases—the Rulers will keep up an effective supervision of detail, so as to exclude any unworthy exception, and even to admit into the Guardians any youth of very rare and exceptional promise who may be born among the remaining community. For Plato admits that there may be accidental births both ways: brass and iron may by occasional accident give birth to gold or silver—and *vice versâ*.

It is in this manner that Plato constitutes his body of Guardians: one thousand adult persons of both sexes,[b] in nearly equal numbers, together with a small proportion of children — the proportion of these latter must be very small, since the total number is not allowed to increase. His end here is to create an intimate and equal sympathy among them all, like that between all the members of the same bodily organism: to abolish all independent and exclusive sympathies of particular parts: to make the city One and Indivisible—a single organism, instead of many distinct conterminous organisms: to provide that the causes of pleasure and pain shall be the same to all, so that a man shall have no feeling of mine or thine, except in reference to his own body and that of another, which Plato notes as the greatest good—instead of each individual struggling apart for his own objects and rejoicing on occasions when his neighbour sorrows, which Plato regards as the greatest evil.[c] All

Marginal note: Purpose to create an intimate and equal sympathy among all the Guardians, but to prevent exclusive sympathy of particular members.

---

[a] Plato, Republ. v. p. 461 D.

[b] This number of 1000 appears stated by Aristotle (Politic. ii. 6, p. 1265, a. 9), and is probably derived from Republic, iv. p. 423 A; though that passage appears scarcely sufficient to prove that Plato meant to declare the number 1000 as peremptory. However the understanding of Aristotle himself on the point is one material evidence to make us believe that this is the real construction intended by Plato.

[c] Plato, Republic, v. pp. 462-463-464 D. διὰ τὸ μηδένα ἴδιον ἐκτῆσθαι πλὴν τὸ σῶμα, τὰ δὲ ἄλλα κοινά. Compare Plato, Legg. v. p. 739 C.

standing causes of disagreement or antipathy among the
Guardians are assumed to be thus removed.   But if any two
hotheaded youths get into a quarrel, they must fight it out on
the spot.   This will serve as a lesson in gymnastics:—subject
however to the interference of any old man as by-stander,
whom they as well as all other young men are bound implicitly to obey.[d]   Moreover all the miseries, privations,
anxiety, and dependance, inseparable from the life of a poor
man under the system of private property, will disappear
entirely.[e]

Such are the main features of Plato's Republic, in reference
to his Guardians.   They afford a memorable example of that
philosophical analysis, applied to the circumstances of man
and society, which the Greek mind was the first to conceive
and follow out.   Plato lays down his ends with great distinctness, as well as the means whereby he proposes to attain
them.   Granting his ends, the means proposed are almost
always suitable and appropriate, whether practicable or
otherwise.

The Platonic scheme is communism, so far as concerns the
Guardians; but not communism in reference to the
entire Commonwealth.   In this it falls short of his
own ideal, and is only a second best: the best of all
would be, in his view, a communion that should pervade all
persons and all acts and sentiments, effacing altogether the
separate self.[f]   Not venturing to soar so high, he confined his
perfect communion to the Guardians.   Moreover his communism differs from modern theories in this.   They contemplate individual producers and labourers, handing over the
produce to be distributed among themselves by official authority; they contemplate also a regulation not merely of distribution, but of reserved capital and productive agency, under
the same authority.   But the Platonic Guardians are not producers at all.   Everything which they consume is found for
them.   They are in the nature of paid functionaries, exempted
from all cares and anxiety of self-maintenance, either present
or future.   They are all comfortably provided, without hopes

(margin note:) Platonic scheme— partial communism.

---

[d] Plato, Republic, v. pp. 464-465.
[e] Plato, Republ. v. p. 465 C.
[f] See Plato, De Legibus, v. p. 739 D.

The Republic is *second best;* that which appears sketched in the treatise De Legibus is *third best.*

of wealth or fear of poverty: moreover they are all equally comfortable, so that no sentiment can grow up among them, arising from comparison of each other's possessions or enjoyments. Among such men and women, brought up from infancy as Plato directs, the sentiment of property, with all the multifarious associations derived from it, would be unknown. No man's self-esteem, no man's esteem of others, would turn upon it.

In this respect, the remaining members of the city, apart from the Guardians, and furnishing all the subsistence of the Guardians, are differently circumstanced. They are engaged in different modes of production, each exclusively in one mode. They exchange, buy, and sell, with each other: there exist therefore among them gradations of strength, skill, perseverance, frugality, and good luck—together with the consequent gradations of wealth and poverty. The substance or capital of the Commonwealth is maintained altogether by the portion of it which is extraneous to the Guardians; and among that portion there is no communism. The maintenance of the Guardians is a tax which these men have to pay: but after paying it, they apply or enjoy the rest of their produce as they please, subject to the requirements of the Rulers for public service.[g]

Nevertheless we are obliged to divine what Plato means about the condition of the producing classes in his Commonwealth. He himself tells us little or nothing about them; though they must constitute the large numerical majority. And this defect is in him the less excusable, since he reckons them as component members of his Commonwealth; while Aristotle, in his ideal commonwealth, does not reckon them as component members or citizens, but merely as indispensable adjuncts, in the same manner as slaves. All that we know about the producers in the Platonic Commonwealth is, that each man is to have only one business—that for which he is most fit:—and that all are to be under the administration of the Rulers through the Guardians.

[g] Aristotle, in his comments upon the Platonic Republic (Politic. ii. 5, p. 1262, b. 42 seq.), advances arguments, just in themselves, in favour of individual property, and against community of property. But these arguments have little application to the Republic.

The enlistment of soldiers, apart from civilians, and the holding of them under distinct laws and stricter discipline, is a practice familiar to modern ideas, though it had little place among the Greeks of Plato's day. There prevailed also in Egypt[h] and in parts of Eastern Asia, from time immemorial, a distinction of castes: one caste being soldiers, invested with the defence of the country, and enjoying certain lands by the tenure of such military service: but in other respects, private proprietors like the rest—and receiving no special discipline, training, or education. In Grecian ideas, military duties were a part, but only a part, of the duties of a citizen. This was the case even at Sparta. Though in practice, the discipline of that city tended in a preponderant degree towards military aptitude, yet the Spartan was still a citizen, not exclusively a soldier.

Soldiership as a separate profession has acquired greater development in modern times.

It was from the Spartan institutions (and the Kretan, in many respects analogous) that the speculative political philosophers in Greece usually took the point of departure for their theories. Not only Plato did so, but Xenophon and Aristotle likewise. The most material fact which they saw before them at Sparta was, a public discipline both strict and continued, which directed the movements of the citizens, and guided their thoughts and feelings, from infancy to old age. To this supreme controul the private feelings, both of family and property, though not wholly suppressed, were made to bend: and occasionally in a way quite as remarkable as any restrictions proposed by either Plato or Xenophon.[i] Moreover, the Spartan institutions were of immemorial antiquity; believed to have been suggested or sanctioned originally by Apollo and the Delphian oracle, as the Kretan institutions were by Zeus.[k] They had lasted longer than other Hellenic institutions without forcible subversion: they obtained universal notice, admiration, and deference, throughout Greece. It was this conspicuous fact which emboldened the Grecian

Spartan institutions—great impression which they produced upon speculative Greek minds.

---

[h] Aristot. Politic. vii. 10. Herodot. ii. 164. Plato alludes (Timæ. 24 A) to the analogy of Egyptian castes.

[i] See Xenophon, Hellenic. vi. 4, 16,

the account of what passed at Sparta after the battle of Leuktra, related also in my 'History of Greece,' chap. 78, vol. x. p. 253.

[k] Plato, Legg. i. pp. 632 D, 634 A.

theorists to postulate for the lawgiver that unbounded controul, over the life and habits of citizens, which we read not
merely in the Republic of Plato but in the Cyropædia of
Xenophon, and to a great degree even in the Politica of Aristotle.   To an objector, who asked them how they could possibly expect that individuals would submit to such unlimited
interference, they would have replied — " Look at Sparta.
You see there interference, as constant and rigorous as that
which I propose, endured by the citizens not only without
resistance, but with a tenacity and long continuance such as
is not found among other communities with more lax regulations.   The habits and sentiments of the Spartan citizen are
fashioned to these institutions.   Far from being anxious to
shake them off, he accounts them a necessity as well as an
honour."   This reply would have appeared valid and reasonable, in the fourth century before the Christian era.   And it
explains—what, after all, is the most surprising circumstance
to a modern reader—the extreme boldness of speculation, the
ideal omnipotence, assumed by the leading Grecian political
theorists : much even by Aristotle, though his aspirations were
more limited and practical—far more by Xenophon—most of
all by Plato.   Any theorist, proceeding avowedly κατ᾽ εὐχὴν,
considered himself within bounds when he assumed to himself
no greater influence than had actually been exercised by
Lykurgus.

    Assuming such influence, however, he intended to employ
it for ends approved by himself: agreeing with
Lykurgus in the general principle of forming the
citizen's character by public and compulsory discipline, but not agreeing with him in the type of
character proper to be aimed at.   Xenophon departs
least from the Spartan type : Aristotle and Plato greatly
more, though in different directions.   Each of them applies
to a certain extent the process of abstraction and analysis
both to the individual and to the community : considering
both of them as made up of component elements working
simultaneously either in co-operation or conflict.   But in Plato
the abstraction is carried farthest : the wholeness of the individual Guardian is completely effaced, so that each consti-

Plans of these speculative minds compared with Spartan— Different types of character contemplated.

tutes a small fraction or wheel of the real Platonic whole—the Commonwealth. The fundamental Platonic principle is, that each man shall have one function, and one only: an extreme application of that which political economists call the division of labour. Among these many different functions, one, and doubtless the most difficult as well as important, is that of directing, administering, and defending the community: which is done by the Guardians and Rulers. It is to this one function that all Plato's treatise is devoted: he tells us how such persons are to be trained and circumstanced. What he describes, therefore, is not properly citizens administering their own affairs, but commanders and officers watching over the interests of others: a sort of military *bureaucracy*, with chiefs at its head, directing as well as guarding a multitude beneath them. And what mainly distinguishes the Platonic system, is the extreme abstraction with which this public and official character is conceived: the degree to which the whole man is merged in the performance of his official duties: the entire extinction within him of the old individual Adam—of all private feelings and interests.

Both in Xenophon and in Aristotle, as well as at Sparta, the citizen is subjected to a public compulsory training, severe as well as continuous: but he is still a citizen as well as a functionary. He has private interests as well as public duties:—a separate home, property, wife, and family. Plato, on the contrary, contends that the two are absolutely irreconcileable: that if the Guardian has private anxieties for his own maintenance, private house and lands to manage, private sympathies and antipathies to gratify—he will become unfaithful to his duties as Guardian, and will oppress instead of protecting the people.[1] You must choose between the two (he says): you cannot have the self-caring citizen and the public-minded Guardian in one.[m]

Plato carries abstraction farther than Xenophon or Aristotle.

Looking to ideal perfection, I think Plato is right. If the Rulers and Guardians have private interests of their own, those interests will corrupt more or less the

Anxiety shown by Plato for the

---

[1] Plato, Republic, iii. pp. 416-417.
[m] See the contrary opinion asserted by Nikias in his speech at Athens, Thucyd. vi. 9.

discharge of their public duties. The evil may be
mitigated, by forms of government (representative
and other arrangements), which make the continuance of power dependant upon popular estimation
of the functionaries: but it cannot be abolished. Neither
Xenophon, nor Aristotle, nor the Spartan system, provided
any remedy for this difficulty. They scarcely even recognise
the difficulty as real. In all the three, the proportion of
trained citizens to the rest of the people, would be about the
same (so far as we can judge) as the proportion of the
Platonic Guardians to the Demos or rest of the people. Bnt
when we look to see what security either of the three systems
provide for good behaviour on the part of citizens towards
non-citizens, we find no satisfaction; nor do they make it, as
Plato does, one prominent object of their public training.
Plato shows extreme anxiety for the object; as is proved by
his sacrificing, in order to ensure it, all the private sources of
pleasure to his Guardians. Aristotle reproaches him with doing
this, so as to reduce the happiness of his Guardians to nothing:
but Plato, from his own point of view, would not admit the
justice of such reproach, since he considers happiness to be
derived from and proportional to, the performance of duty.

This last point must be perpetually kept in mind, in
following Plato's reasoning. But though he does
not consider himself as sacrificing the happiness of
his Guardians to their duty, we must give him
credit for anxiety, greater than either Aristotle or
Xenophon has shown, to ensure a faithful discharge
of duty on the part of the Guardians towards the rest of the
people. In Aristotle's theory,[n] the rest of the people are set
aside as not members of the Commonwealth, thus counting as
a secondary and inferior object in his estimation; while the
citizens, who alone are members, are trained to practise
virtue for its own sake and for their own happiness. In
Plato's theory, the rest of the people are not only proclaimed
as members of the Commonwealth,[o] but are the ultimate and

[n] Aristotle, Politic. vii. 9, p. 1328,
b, 40, p. 1329, a. 25.
[o] Aristot. Politic. ii. 5, p. 1264, a.
12-26, respecting the Platonic Commonwealth, καίτοι σχεδὸν τόγε πλῆθος

τῆς πόλεως τὸ τῶν ἄλλων πολιτῶν
γίγνεται πλῆθος, &c.
Ποιεῖ γὰρ (Plato) τοὺς μὲν φύλακας
οἷον φρουροὺς, τοὺς δὲ γεωργοὺς καὶ
τοὺς τεχνίτας καὶ τοὺς ἄλλους, πολίτας.

capital objects of all his solicitude.   It is in protecting,
governing, and administering them, that the lives of the
Rulers and Guardians are passed.   Though they (the remaining people) receive no public training, yet Plato intends
them to reap all the benefit of the laborious training bestowed on the Guardians.   This is a larger and more generous conception of the purpose of political institutions, than
we find either in Aristotle or in Xenophon.

There is however another objection, which seems grave
and well founded, advanced by Aristotle against *Objection
urged by*
the Platonic Republic.   He remarks that it will be *Aristotle
against the*
not one city, but two cities, with tendencies more *Platonic Republic, that*
or less adverse to each other :[p] that the Guar- *it will be
two cities.*
dians, educated under the very peculiar training *Spiritual
pride of the*
and placed under the peculiar relations prescribed *Guardians —
contempt for*
to them, will form one city—while the remaining *the Demos.*
people, who have no part either in the one or the other, but
are private proprietors with separate families—will form
another city.   I do not see what reply the Platonic Republic
furnishes to this objection.   Granting full success to Plato in
his endeavours to make the Guardians One among themselves, we find nothing to make them One with the remaining people, nor to make the remaining people One with
them.[q]   On the contrary, we observe such an extreme
divergence of sentiment, character, pursuit, and education, as
to render mutual sympathy very difficult, and to open fatal
probabilities of mutual alienation: probabilities hardly less,
than if separate proprietary interests had been left to subsist
among the Guardians.   This is a source of mischief which
Plato has not taken into his account.   The entire body of
Guardians cannot fail to carry in their bosoms a sense of
extreme pride in their own training, and a proportionally
mean estimate of the untrained multitude alongside of them.

[p] Aristotel. Politic. ii. 5, p. 1264, a. 24.
ἐν μιᾷ γὰρ πόλει δύο πόλεις ἀναγκαῖον
εἶναι, καὶ ταύτας ὑπεναντίας ἀλλήλαις.
The most forcible of the objections
urged by Aristotle against the Platonic
Republic, are those contained in this
chapter respecting the relations between the Guardians and the rest of
the community.

[q] The oneness, which Plato proclaims as belonging to his whole city,
belongs in reality only to the body of
Guardians; of whom he sometimes
speaks as if they were the whole city,
which however is not his real intention, see Republic, v. p. 462.

The sentiment of the gold and silver men, towards the brass and iron men, will have in it too much of contempt to be consistent with civic fraternity : like the pride of the Twice-Born Hindoo Brahmin, when .comparing himself with the lower Hindoo castes : or like that of the Pythagorean brotherhood, who "regarded the brethren as equal to the blessed Gods, but held all the rest to be unworthy of any account."[r] The Spartan training appears to have produced a similar effect upon the minds of the citizens who went through it. And indeed such an effect appears scarcely avoidable, under the circumstances assumed by Plato. He himself is proud of his own ideal training, so as to ascribe to those who receive it a sentiment akin to that of the Olympic victors ; while he employs degrading analogies to signify the pursuits and enjoyments of the untrained multitude, who are assimilated to the appetite or lower element in the organism, existing only as a mutinous crew necessary to be kept down.[s] That spiritual pride, coupled with spiritual contempt, should be felt by the Guardians, is the natural result ; as it is indeed the essential reimbursement to their feelings, for the life of drill and self-denial which Plato imposes upon them. And how, under such a sentiment, the two constituent elements in his system are to be competent to work out his promised result of mutual happiness, he has not shown.[t]

---

[r] Τοὺς μὲν ἑταίρους ἦγεν ἴσους μακά-
ρεσσι θεοῖσιν,
Τοὺς δ᾽ ἄλλους ἡγεῖτ᾽ οὔτ᾽ ἐν λόγῳ
οὔτ᾽ ἐν ἀριθμῷ.

[s] Plato, Republ. v. 465 D.
Aristotle says (in the Nikom. Ethics, i. 5) when discussing the various ideas entertained about happiness—Οἱ μὲν οὖν πολλοὶ παντελῶς ἀνδραποδώδεις φαίνονται βοσκημάτων βίον προαιρούμενοι. This is much the estimation which the Platonic Guardians would be apt to form respecting the Demos.

[t] The foregoing remarks are an expansion, and a sequel, of Aristotle's objection against the Platonic Republic —That it is not One City, but two discordant cities in that which is nominally One. I must however add that the same objection may be urged against the Xenophontic constitution of a city ; and also, in substance, even against the

proposition of Aristotle himself for the same purpose. Xenophon, in his Cyropædia, proposes a severe, life-long drill and discipline, like that of the Spartans: from which indeed he does not formally exclude any citizens, but which he announces to be actually attended only by the wealthy, since they alone can afford to attend continuously and habitually, the poorer men being engaged in the cares of maintenance. All the functions of the state, civil and military, are performed exclusively by those who go through the public discipline. We have here the two cities in One, which Aristotle objects to in Plato; with the consequent loss of civic fraternity between them. And when we look to that which Aristotle himself suggests, we find him evading the objection by a formal sanction of the very mischief upon which the objection is founded. He puts the husbandmen and artisans

In explanation of the foregoing remarks, I will add that Plato fails in his purpose not from the goodness of the training which he provides for his select Few, but from leaving the rest of his people without any training—without even so much as would enable them properly to appreciate superior training in the few who obtain it—without any powers of self-defence or self-helpfulness. His fundamental postulate—That every man shall do only one thing—when applied to the Guardians, realises itself in something great and considerable: but when applied to the ordinary pursuits of life, reduces every man to a special machine, unfit for any other purpose than its own. Though it is reasonable that a man should get his living by one trade, and should therefore qualify himself peculiarly and effectively for that trade—it is not reasonable that he should be altogether impotent as to every thing else: nor that his happiness should consist, as Plato declares that it ought, exclusively in the performance of this one service to the commonwealth. In the Platonic Republic, the body of the people are represented not only as without training, but as machines rather than individual men. They exist partly as producers to maintain, partly as governable matter to obey, the Guardians; and to be cared for by them.

Plato's scheme fails, mainly because he provides no training for the Demos.

Aristotle, when speaking about the citizens of his own ideal commonwealth (his citizens form nearly the same numerical proportion of the whole population, as the Platonic Guardians) tells us—" Since the End for which the entire City exists is One, it is obviously necessary that the education of all the citizens should be one and the same, and that the care of such education should be a public duty—not left in private

Principle of Aristotle— That every citizen belongs to the city, not to himself— applied by Plato to women.

altogether out of the pale of his city, which is made to include the disciplined citizens or Guardians alone. His city may thus be called One, inasmuch as it admits only homogeneous elements, and throws out all such as are heterogeneous: but he thus avowedly renounces as insoluble the problem which Plato and Xenophon try, though unsuccessfully, to solve. If there be discord and alienation among the constituent members of the Platonic and Xenophontic city—there will subsist the like feelings, in Aristotle's proposition, between the members of the city and the outlying, though indispensable, adjuncts. There will be the same mischief in kind, and probably exaggerated in amount: since the abolition of the very name and idea of fellow-citizen tends to suppress altogether an influence of tutelary character, however insufficient as to its force.

hands as it is now, for a man to teach his children what he thinks fit. Public exigencies must be provided for by public training. Moreover, we ought not to regard any of the citizens as belonging to himself, but all of them as belonging to the city: for each is a part of the city: and nature prescribes that the care of each part shall be regulated with a view to the care of the whole."[u]

The broad principle thus laid down by Aristotle is common to him with Plato, and lies at the bottom of the schemes of polity imagined by both. Each has his own way of applying it.

Plato clearly perceives that it cannot be applied with consistency and effect, unless women are brought under its application as well as men. And to a great extent, Aristotle holds the same opinion too. While commending the Spartan principle, that the character of the citizen must be formed and upheld by continued public training and discipline—Aristotle blames Lykurgus for leaving the women (that is, a numerical half of the city) without training or discipline; which omission produced (he says) very mischievous effects, especially in corrupting the character of the men. He pronounces this to be a serious fault, making the constitution inconsistent and self-contradictory, and indeed contrary to the intentions of Lykurgus himself; who had tried to bring the women under public discipline as well as the men, but was forced to desist by their strenuous opposition.[x] Such remarks from Aristotle are the more remarkable, since it appears as matter of history, that the maidens at Sparta (though not the married women) did to a great extent go

---

[u] Aristotel. Politic. viii. 1, p. 1337, a. 21. Ἐπεὶ δ᾽ ἓν τὸ τέλος τῇ πόλει πάσῃ, φανερὸν ὅτι καὶ τὴν παιδείαν μίαν καὶ τὴν αὐτὴν ἀναγκαῖαν εἶναι πάντων, καὶ ταύτης τὴν ἐπιμέλειαν εἶναι κοινήν, καὶ μὴ κατ᾽ ἰδίαν· ὃν τρόπον νῦν ἕκαστος ἐπιμελεῖται τῶν αὑτοῦ τέκνων ἰδίᾳ τε καὶ μάθησιν ἣν ἂν δόξῃ διδάσκων. Ἅμα δὲ οὐδὲ χρὴ νομίζειν αὐτὸν αὑτοῦ εἶναι τῶν πολιτῶν, ἀλλὰ πάντας τῆς πόλεως· ἡ δ᾽ ἐπιμέλεια πέφυκεν ἑκάστου μορίου βλέπειν πρὸς τὴν τοῦ ὅλου ἐπιμέλειαν.

[x] Aristotel. Politic. ii. 7, p. 1269, b. 12. Ἔτι δὲ, ἡ περὶ τὰς γυναῖκας ἄνεσις, καὶ πρὸς τὴν προαίρεσιν τῆς

πολιτείας βλαβερὰ, καὶ πρὸς εὐδαιμονίαν πόλεως—῾Ωστ᾽ ἐν ὅσαις πόλεσι φαύλως ἔχει τὸ περὶ τὰς γυναῖκας, τὸ ἥμισυ τῆς πόλεως δεῖ νομίζειν ἀνομοθέτητον. ῞Οπερ ἐκεῖ (at Sparta) συμβέβηκεν· ὅλην γὰρ τὴν πόλιν ὁ νομοθέτης εἶναι βουλόμενος καρτερικὴν, κατὰ μὲν τοὺς ἄνδρας φανερός ἐστι τοιοῦτος ὤν, ἐπὶ δὲ τῶν γυναικῶν ἐξημέληκε, &c.Τὰ περὶ τὰς γυναῖκας ἔχοντα μὴ καλῶς ἔοικεν οὐ μόνον ἀπρέπειάν τινα ποιεῖν τῆς πόλεως αὐτῆς καθ᾽ αὑτὴν, ἀλλὰ συμβάλλεσθαί τι πρὸς τὴν φιλοχρηματίαν.

Plato has a similar remark, Legg. vi. pp. 780-781.

through gymnastic exercises along with the young men.[y] These exercises, though almost a singular exception in Greece, must have appeared to Aristotle very insufficient. What amount or kind of regulation he himself would propose for women, he has not defined. In his own ideal commonwealth, he lays it down as alike essential for men and women to have their bodies trained and exercised so as to be adequate to the active duties of free persons (as contrasted with the harder preparation requisite for the athletic contests, which he disapproves), but he does not go into further particulars.[z] The regulations which he proposes, too, with reference to marriage generally and to the maintenance of a vigorous breed of citizens, show, that he considered it an important part of the lawgiver's duty to keep up by positive interference the physical condition both of males and females.[a]

In principle therefore, Aristotle agrees with Plato,[b] as to the propriety of comprehending women as well as men under

[y] Stallbaum (in his note on Plato, Legg. i. p. 638 C, τὴν τῶν γυναικῶν παρ' ὑμῖν ἄνεσιν) observes—"Lacænarum licentiam, quum ex aliis institutis patriis, tum ex gymnicarum exercitationum usu repetendam, Plato carpit etiam infrà," &c. This is a mistake. Plato does not blame the gymnastic exercises of the Spartan maidens: the four passages to which Stallbaum refers do not prove his assertion. They even countenance the reverse of that assertion. Plato approves of gymnastic and military exercises for maidens in the Laws, and for all the female Guardians in the Republic.

Stallbaum also refers to Aristotle as disapproving the gymnastic exercises of the Spartan maidens. I cannot think that this is correct. Aristotle does indeed blame the arrangements for women at Sparta, but not, as I understand him, because the women were subjected to gymnastic exercise; his blame is founded on the circumstance that the women were not regulated, but left to do as they pleased, while the men were under the strictest drill. This I conceive to be the meaning of γυναικῶν ἄνεσις. Euripides indeed has a very bitter passage condemning the exercises of the Spartan maidens, but neither Plato

nor Aristotle shared this view.

Respecting the Spartan maidens and their exercises, see Xenophon, Republ. Laced. i. 4; Plutarch, Lykurg. c. 14.

[z] Aristotel. Politic. vii. 16, p. 1335, b. 8. Πεπονημένην μὲν οὖν ἔχειν δεῖ τὴν ἕξιν, πεπονημένην δὲ πόνοις μὴ βιαίοις, μηδὲ πρὸς ἕνα μόνον, ὥσπερ ἡ τῶν ἀθλητῶν ἕξις, ἀλλὰ πρὸς τὰς τῶν ἐλευθέρων πράξεις. Ὁμοίως δὲ δεῖ ταῦτα ὑπάρχειν ἀνδράσι καὶ γυναιξί. Compare also i. 8, near the end of the first book.

[a] Aristotel. Politic. vii. 16, p. 1335 a. 20, b. 15.

[b] If we take the sentence from Aristotle's Politics, cited in a note immediately preceding, to the effect that all the citizens belonged to the city, and that each was a part of the city (viii. 1, p. 1337. a. 28) in conjunction with another passage in the Politics (i. 3, p. 1254, a. 10)—Τό τε γὰρ μόριον, οὐ μόνον ἄλλου ἐστὶ μόριον, ἀλλὰ καὶ ὅλως ἄλλου—it is difficult to see how he can, consistently with these principles, assign to his citizens any individual self-regarding agency. Plato denies all such to his Guardians, and in so doing he makes deductions consistent with the principles of Aristotle, who lays down his principles too absolutely for the use which he afterwards makes of them.

public training and discipline : but he does not follow out the principle with the same consistency.   He maintains the Platonic Commonwealth to be impossible.[c]

If we go through the separate objections which Aristotle advances as justifying his verdict, we shall find them altogether inadequate for the purpose.   He shows certain inconveniences and difficulties as belonging to it,—which are by no means all real, but which, even conceding them in full force, would have to be set against the objections admitted by himself to bear against other actual societies, before we can determine whether they are sufficiently weighty to render the scheme to which they belong impossible.   The Platonic commonwealth, and the Aristotelian commonwealth, are both of them impossible, in my judgment, for the same reason : that all the various communities of mankind exist under established customs, beliefs, and sentiments, in complete discordance with them : and that we cannot understand from whence the force is to come, tending and competent to generate either of these two new systematic projects.   Both of them require a simultaneous production of many reciprocally adapted elements : both therefore require an express initiative force, exceptional and belonging to some peculiar crisis—something analogous to Zeus in Krete, and to Apollo at Sparta.   This is alike true of both : though the Platonic Republic, departing more widely from received principles and sentiments than the Aristotelian, would of course require a more potent initiative.[d] In the treatises of the two philosophers, each explains and vindicates the principles of his system, without including in the hypothesis any specification of a probable source from whence it was to acquire its first start.   Where is the motive, operative, demiurgic force, ready to translate such an idea into reality ?[e]   But if we assume that either of them had once

Aristotle declares the Platonic Commonwealth impossible—In what sense this is true.

---

[c] Aristotel. Polit. ii. 3, p. 1269, b. 29. φαίνεται δ' εἶναι πάμπαν ἀδύνατος ὁ βίος.

[d] Plato indeed in one place tells us that a single despot becoming by inspiration or accident a philosopher, and having an obedient city, would accomplish the primary construction of his commonwealth (Republ. vi. p. 502 B).   That despot (Plato supposes) will send away all the population of his city above ten years old, and will train up the children in the Platonic principles (vii. pp. 540-541).

This is little better than an εὐχή, whatever Plato may say to deprecate the charge of uttering εὐχάς, p. 540 D.

[e] Aristotel. Metaphys. A. p. 991,

begun, there is no reason why it might not have continued. The causes which first brought about the Spartan constitution and discipline must have been very peculiar, though we have no historical account what they were. At any rate they never occurred a second time; for no second Sparta was ever formed, in spite of the admiration inspired by the first. If Sparta had never been actually established, and if Aristotle had read a description of it as a mere project, he would probably have pronounced it impracticable:[f] though when once brought into reality, it proved eminently durable. In like manner the laws, customs, beliefs, and feelings, prevalent in Egypt—which astonished so vehemently Herodotus and other observing Greeks— would have been declared to be impossible, if described simply in project: yet when once established, they were found to last longer without change than those of other nations.

The Platonic project is submitted, however, not to impartial judges comparing different views on matters yet un- The real im- determined, but to hearers with a canon of criticism already fixed and anti-Platonic "*animis consuetudine imbutis.*" It appears impossible, because it contradicts sentiments conceived as fundamental and consecrated, respecting the sexual and family relations. The supposed impossibility is the mode of expressing strong disapprobation and repugnance: like that which Herodotus describes as manifested by the Greeks on one side and by the

The real impossibility of the Platonic Commonwealth, arises from the fact that discordant sentiments are already established.

---

a. 22. Τί γάρ ἐστι τὸ ἐργαζόμενον, πρὸς τὰς ἰδέας ἀποβλέπον;

We find Aristotle arguing, in the course of his remarks on the Platonic Republic, that it is useless now to promulgate any such novelties; a long time has elapsed, and such things would already have been found established if they had been good (Politic. ii. 5, p. 1264, a. 2). This would have applied (somewhat less in degree, yet with quite sufficient force) to the ideal commonwealth of Aristotle himself, as well as to that of Plato.

Because such institutions have never yet been established anywhere as those proposed by Plato or Aristotle, you cannot fairly argue that they would not be good, or that they would not stand if established. What you may fairly argue is, that they are not at all likely to be established; no originat-

ing force will be forthcoming adequate to the first creation of them. Existing societies have fixed modes of thinking and feeling on social and political matters; each moves in its own groove, and the direction in which it will henceforward move will be a consequence and continuance of the direction in which it is already moving, by virtue of powerful causes now in operation. New originating force is a very rare phenomenon. Overwhelming enemies or physical calamities may destroy what exists, but they will not produce any such innovations as those under discussion.

f Plato himself makes this very remark in the Treatise De Legibus (viii. p. 839 D) in defending the practicability of some of the ordinances therein recommended.

Indians on the other—when Darius, having asked each of them at what price they would consent to adopt the practice of the other respecting the mode of treating the bodies of deceased parents, was answered by a loud cry of horror at the mere proposition.[g] The reasons offered to prove the Platonic project impossible, are principally founded upon the very sentiment above adverted to, and derive all their force from being associated with it. Such is the character of many among the Aristotelian objections.[h] The real, and the truly forcible, objection consists in the sentiment itself. If that be deeply rooted in the mind, it is decisive. To those who feel thus, the Platonic project would be both intolerable and impossible.

But we must recollect that it is these very sentiments, *Plato has strong feelings of right and wrong about sexual intercourse, but referring to different objects.* which Plato impugns and declares to be inapplicable to his Guardians: so that an opponent who, not breaking off at once with the cry of horror uttered by the Indians to Darius, begins to discuss the question with him, is bound to forego objections

[g] Herodot. iii. 38. οἱ δὲ, ἀμβώσαντες μέγα, εὐφημέειν μιν ἐκέλευον.

Plato, in a remarkable passage of the Leges (i. 638 B), deprecates and complains of this instantaneous condemnation without impartial hearing of argument on both sides.

[h] See the arguments urged by Aristotle, Politic. ii. 4, p. 1262, a. 25 et seq. His remarks upon the fictions which Plato requires to be impressed on the belief of his Guardians are extremely just. There are, however, several objections urged by him which turn more upon the Platonic language than upon the Platonic vein of thought, and which, if judged by Plato from his own point of view, would have appeared admissions in his favour rather than objections. In reply to Plato, whose aim it is that all or many of the Guardians shall say *mine* in reference to the same persons or the same things, and not in reference to different persons and different things, Aristotle contends that the word *mine* will not then designate any such strong affection as it does now, when it is special, exclusive, and concentrated on a few persons or things; that each Guardian, having many persons whom he called *brother* and many persons whom he called *father*, would not feel

towards them as persons now feel towards brothers and fathers; that the affection by being disseminated would be weakened, and would become nothing more than a "*diluted friendship*" — φιλία ὑδαρής. See Aristot. Politic. ii. 3, p. 1261, b. 22, ii. 4, p. 1262, b. 15.

Plato if called upon for an answer to this reasoning, would probably have allowed it to be just; but would have said that the "diluted friendship" pervading all the Guardians was apt and sufficient for his purpose, as bringing the whole number most nearly into the condition of one organism. Strong exclusive affections, upon whatever founded, between individuals, he wishes to discourage: the hateful or unfriendly sentiments he is bent on rooting out. What he desires to see preponderant, in each Guardian, is a sense of duty to the public: subordinate to that, he approves moderate and kindly affections, embracing all the Guardians; towards the elders as fathers, towards those of the same age as brothers. Aristotle's expression — φιλία ὑδαρής — describes such a sentiment fairly enough. See Republic, v. pp. 462-463. It must be conceded, however, that Plato's *language* is open to Aristotle's objection.

and repugnances springing as corollaries from a basis avowedly denied.   Plato has earnest feelings of right and wrong,
in regard both to the functions of women and to the sexual
intercourse : but his feelings dissent entirely from those
of readers generally.   That is right, in his opinion, which
tends to keep up the excellence of the breed and the proper
number of Guardians, as well as to ensure the exact and
constant fulfilment of their mission : that is wrong, which
tends to defeat or abridge such fulfilment, or to impair the
breed, or to multiply the number beyond its proper limit.
Of these ends the Rulers are the proper judges, not the individual person.   All the Guardians are enjoined to leave the
sexual power absolutely unexercised until the age of thirty
for men, of twenty for women—and then only to exercise it
under express sanction and authorisation, according as the
Rulers may consider that children are needed to keep up
the legitimate number.

Marriage is regarded as holy, and celebrated under solemn
rites—all the more because both the ceremony is originated,
and the couples selected, by the magistrate, for the most important public purpose : which being fulfilled, the marriage
ceases and determines.   It is not celebrated with a view to
the couple themselves, still less with a view to establish
any permanent exclusive attachment between them : which
object Plato not only does not contemplate, but positively
discountenances : on the same general principle as the Catholic Church forbids marriage to priests : because he believes that it will create within them motives and sentiments
inconsistent with the due discharge of their public mission.

It is clear that among such a regiment as that which Plato
describes in his Guardians, a sentiment would grow
up, respecting the intercourse of the sexes, totally
different from that which prevailed elsewhere around
him.   The Platonic restriction upon that intercourse (until the ulterior limits of age) would be far
more severe : but it would be applied with reference
to different objects.   Instead of being applied to enforce the
exclusive consecration of one woman to one man, choosing
each other or chosen by fathers, without any limit on the

*Different
sentiment
which would
grow up in
the Platonic
Common-
wealth re-
specting the
sexual rela-
tions.*

multiplication of children,—and without any attention to
the maintenance or deterioration of the breed—it would be
directed to the obtaining of the most perfect breed and of
the appropriate number, leaving the Guardians, female as
well as male, free from all permanent distracting influences
to interfere with the discharge of their public duties. In
appreciating the details of the Platonic community, we must
look at it with reference to this form of sexual morality;
which would generate in the Guardians an appreciation of
details consistent with itself, both as to the women and as to
the children. The sentiment of obligation, of right and
wrong, respecting the relations of the sexes, is everywhere
very strong; but it does not everywhere attach to the same
acts or objects. The important obligation for a woman never
to show her face in public, which is held sacred through so
large a portion of the Oriental world, is noway recognised
in the Occidental: and in Plato's time, when mankind were
more disseminated among small independent communities,
the divergence was yet greater than it is now. The Spartans
were not induced, by the censures or mockery of persons in
other Grecian cities,[1] to suppress the gymnastic exercises
practised by their maidens in conjunction with the young
men : nor is Plato deterred by the ridicule or blame which
others may express, from proclaiming his conviction, that the
virtue of his female Guardians is the same as that of the
male—consisting in the faithful performance of their duty as
Guardians, after going through all the requisite training,
gymnastic and musical. And he follows this up by the
general declaration, one of the most emphatic in all his
writings, "The best thing which is now said or ever has been
said, is, that what is profitable is honourable—and what is
hurtful, is base." [k]

[1] Euripid. Andromach. 598.
The criticisms of Xenophon in the
first chapter of his treatise, De Laced.
Republ., exhibit a point of view on
many points analogous to that of Plato
respecting the female sex.

[k] Plato, Republ. v. p. 457. Ἀπο-
δυτέον δὴ ταῖς τῶν φυλάκων γυναιξὶν,
ἐπείπερ ἀρετὴν ἀντὶ ἱματίων ἀμφιέ-
σονται, καὶ κοινωνητέον πολέμου τε καὶ
τῆς ἄλλης φυλακῆς τῆς περὶ τὴν πόλιν,
καὶ οὐκ ἄλλα πρακτέον· τούτων δ' αὐτῶν τὰ ἐλαφρότερα ταῖς γυναιξὶν ἢ τοῖς
ἀνδράσι δοτέον, διὰ τὴν τοῦ γένους
ἀσθένειαν. Ὁ δὲ γελῶν ἀνὴρ ἐπὶ γυμναῖς γυναιξί, τοῦ βελτίστου ἕνεκα
γυμναζομέναις, ἀτελῆ τοῦ γελοίου σοφίας δρέπων καρπόν, οὐδὲν οἶδεν, ὡς
ἔοικεν, ἐφ' ᾧ γελᾷ οὐδ' ὅ,τι πράττει.
Κάλλιστα γὰρ δὴ τοῦτο καὶ λέγεται καὶ λελέξεται, ὅτι τὸ μὲν
ὠφέλιμον, καλὸν—τὸ δὲ βλαβερὸν, αἰσχρόν.

Plato in truth reduces the distinction between the two sexes to its lowest terms: to the physical difference in regard to procreation—and to the general fact, that the female is every way weaker and inferior to the male; while yet, individually taken, many women are superior to many men, and both sexes are alike improveable by training. He maintains that this similarity of training and function is the real order of Nature, and that the opposite practice, which insists on a separation of life and functions between the sexes, is unnatural:[1] which doctrine he partly enforces by the analogy of the two sexes in other animals.[m] Aristotle disputes this reasoning altogether: declaring that Nature prescribes a separation of life and functions between the two sexes—that the relation of man to woman is that of superiority and command on one side, inferiority and obedience on the other, like the relation between father and child, master and slave, though with a difference less in degree—that virtue in a man, and virtue in a woman, are quite different, imposing diverse obligations.[n] It shows how little stress can be laid on arguments based on the word *Nature*, when we see two such distinguished thinkers completely at issue as to the question, what Nature indicates, in this important case. Each of them decorates by that name the rule which he himself approves; whether actually realised anywhere, or merely recommended as a reform of something really existing. In this controversy, Aristotle had in his favour the actualities around him, against Plato: but Aristotle himself is far from always recognising experience and practice as authoritative interpreters of the dictates of Nature, as we may see by his own ideal commonwealth.

What Nature prescribes in regard to the relations of the two sexes —Direct contradiction between Plato and Aristotle.

How strongly Plato was attached to his doctrines about the capacity of women—how unchanged his opinion continued about the mischief of separating the training and functions of the two sexes, and of confining women to indoor occupations, or to what he calls

Opinion of Plato respecting the capacities of women, and the training proper for women, are

---

[1] Plato, Republic, v. pp. 456 C, 466 D. τὰ νῦν παρὰ ταῦτα γιγνόμενα παρὰ φύσιν μᾶλλον, &c.

[m] Compare a similar appeal to the analogy of animals, as proving the

ἔρωτας ἀῤῥένων to be unnatural, Plato, Legg. viii. p. 836 C.

[n] Aristotel. Politic. i. 13, p. 1260, a. 20-30.

maintained in the Leges, as well as in the Republic. Ancient legends harmonising with this opinion.

" a life of darkness and fear "[o]—may be seen farther by his Treatise De Legibus. Although in that treatise he recedes (perforce and without retracting) from the principles of his Republic, so far as to admit separate properties and families for all his citizens—yet he still continues to enjoin public gymnastic and military training, for women and men alike; and he still opens, to both sexes alike, superintending social functions to a great extent, as well as the privilege of being honoured by public hymns after death, in case of distinguished merit.[p] Respecting military matters he speaks with peculiar earnestness. That women are perfectly capable of efficient military service, if properly trained, he proves not only by the ancient legends, but also by facts actual and contemporary, the known valour of the Scythian and Sarmatian women. Whatever doubts persons may have hitherto cherished (says Plato), this is now established matter of fact:[q] the cowardice and impotence of women is not less disgraceful in itself than detrimental to the city, as robbing it of one-half of its possible force.[r] He complains bitterly of the repugnance felt even to the discussion of this proposition.[s] Most undoubtedly, there were ancient legends which tended much to countenance his

---

[o] Plato, Legg. vi. p. 781 D. εἰθισμένον γὰρ δεδοικὸς καὶ σκοτεινὸν ζῆν, &c.

[p] Plato, Legg. vii. pp. 795 C, 796 C, 802 A.

[q] Plato, Legg. vii. pp. 804-805-806. ἀκούων γὰρ δὴ μύθους παλαιοὺς πέπεισμαι, τὰ δὲ νῦν, ὡς ἔπος εἰπεῖν, οἶδα ὅτι μυριάδες ἀναρίθμητοι γυναικῶν εἰσὶ τῶν περὶ τὸν Πόντον, ἃς Σαυρομάτιδας καλοῦσιν, αἷς οὐχ ἵππων μόνον ἀλλὰ καὶ τόξων καὶ τῶν ἄλλων ὅπλων κοινωνία καὶ τοῖς ἀνδράσιν ἴση προστεταγμένη ἴσως ἀσκεῖται. We may doubt whether Plato knew anything of the brave and skilful Artemisia queen of Halikarnassus, who so greatly distinguished herself in the expedition of Xerxes against Greece (Herod. vii. 99, viii. 87), and, indeed, whether he had ever read the history of Herodotus. His argument might have been strengthened by another equally pertinent example, if he could have quoted the original letter addressed by the Emperor Aurelian to the Roman Senate, attesting the courage, vigour, and prudence, of Zenobia queen of Palmyra. Trebellius Pollio, Vitæ Triginta Tyrannorum in Histor. August. p. 198. "Audio, P. C., mihi objici, quod non virile munus impleverim, Zenobiam triumphando. Næ, illi qui me reprehendunt, satis laudarent, si scirent qualis est illa mulier, quam prudens in consiliis, quam constans in dispositionibus, quam erga milites gravis, quam larga cum necessitas postulet, quam tristis cum severitas poscat. Possum dicere illius esse quod Odenatus Persas vicit, et Ctesiphontem usque fugato Sapore pervenit. Possum asserere, tanto apud Orientales et Ægyptiorum populos timori mulierem fuisse, ut se non Arabes, non Sarraceni, non Armeni, commoverent. Nec ego illi vitam conservassem, nisi eam scissem multum Romanæ Reipublicæ profuisse, cum sibi vel liberis suis Orientis servaret imperium."

[r] Plato, Legg. vii. pp. 813-814.

[s] Plato, Legg. vi. p. 781 D.

opinion. The warlike Amazons, daughters of Arês, were among the most formidable forces that had ever appeared on earth; they had shown their power once by invading Attica and bringing such peril on Athens, that it required all the energy of the great Athenian hero Theseus to repel them. We must remember that these stories were not only familiarised to the public eye in conspicuous painting and sculpture, but were also fully believed as matters of past history.[t] Moreover the Goddess Athênê, patroness of Athens, was the very impersonation of intelligent terror-striking might—constraining and subduing Arês[u] himself: the Goddess Enŷo presided over war, no less than the God Arês:[v] lastly Artemis, though making war only on wild beasts, was hardly less formidable in her way—indefatigable as well as rapid in her movements—and unerring with her bow, as Athênê was irresistible with her spear. Here were abundant examples in Grecian legend, to embolden Plato in his affirmations respecting the capacity of the female sex for warlike enterprise and laborious endurance.

The two Goddesses, Athênê and Artemis, were among the few altogether insensible to amorous influences and to the inspirations of Aphroditê: who is the object of contemptuous sarcasm on the part of Athênê, and of repulsive antipathy on the part of Artemis.[x] This may supply an illustration for the Republic of Plato. As far as one can guess what the effect of his *In a Commonwealth like the Platonic, the influence of Aphroditê would probably have been reduced to a minimum.* institutions would have been, it is probable that the influence of Aphroditê would have been at its minimum among his Guardians of both sexes: as it was presented in the warlike dramas of Æschylus.[y] There would have been everything to deaden it, with an entire absence of all provocatives. The

---

[t] Plutarch, Theseus, c. 27; Æschylus, Eumenid. 682; Isokrates, Panegyr. ss. 76-78. How popular a subject the Amazons were for sculptors, we learn from the statement of Pliny (xxxiv. 8, 19) that all the most distinguished sculptors executed Amazons; and that this subject was the only one upon which a direct comparison could be made between them.

[u] Homer, Iliad xv. 123.

[v] Homer, Iliad v. 333-592.

[x] Homer, Hymn. ad Venerem. 10;

Iliad v. 425; Euripid. Hippolyt. 1400-1420.

Athênê combined the attributes of φιλοπόλεμος and φιλόσοφος. Plato, Timæus, p. 24 D; compare Kritias, p. 109 D.

[y] See Aristophan. Ranæ, 1042.

Eurip. Μὰ Δΐ οὐδὲ γὰρ ἦν τῆς Ἀφροδίτης οὐδέν σοι.

Æschyl. Μηδέ γ' ἐπείη. Ἀλλ' ἐπί σοί τοι καὶ τοῖς σοῖσιν πολλὴ πολλοῦ 'πικάθοιτο.

muscular development, but rough and unadorned bodies, of females — the indiscriminate companionship, with perfect identity of treatment and manners, between the two sexes from the earliest infancy—the training of both together for the same public duties, the constant occupation of both throughout life in the performance of those duties, under unceasing official supervision—the strict regulation of exercise and diet, together with the monastic censorship on all poetry and literature—the self-restraint, equal and universal, enforced as the characteristic feature and pride of the regiment, and seconded by the jealous espionage of all over all, the more potent because privacy was unknown — such an assemblage of circumstances would do as much as circumstances could do to starve the sexual appetite, to prevent it from becoming the root of emotional or imaginative associations, and to place it under the full controul of the lawgiver for purposes altogether public.   Such was probably Plato's intention : since he more generally regards the appetites rather as enemies to be combated and extirpated so far as practicable— than as sources of pleasure, yet liable to accompaniments of pain—requiring to be regulated so as to exclude the latter and retain the former.

The public purposes, with a view to which Plato sought to controul the sexual appetite in his Guardians, were three, as I have already stated. 1. To obtain from each of them individually, faithful performance of the public duties, and observance of the limits, prescribed by his system.   2. To ensure the best and purest breed.   3. To maintain unaltered the same total number, without excess or deficiency.

Other purposes of Plato—limitation of number of Guardians—common to Aristotle also.

The first of these three purposes is peculiar to the Platonic system.   The two last are not peculiar to it.   Aristotle recognises them[z] as ends, no less than Plato, though he does not approve Plato's means for attaining them.   In reference to the limitation of number, Aristotle is even more pronounced than Plato.   The great evil of over-population forced itself upon these . philosophers ; living as both of them did among

Law of population expounded by Malthus—Three distinct checks to population—alternative open between preventive and positive.

<hr>

z Aristotel. Politic. vii. 16.

small communities, each with its narrow area hedged in by others—each liable to intestine dispute, sometimes caused, always aggravated, by the presence of large families and numerous poor freemen—and each importing bought slaves as labourers. To obtain for their community the quickest possible increase in aggregate wealth and population, was an end which they did not account either desirable or commendable. The stationary state, far from appearing repulsive or discouraging, was what they looked upon as the best arrangement[a] of things. A mixed number of lots of land, indivisible and inalienable, is the first principle of the Platonic community in the treatise De Legibus. Not to encourage wealth, but to avert, as far as possible, the evils of poverty and dependance, and to restrain within narrow limits the proportion of the population which suffered those evils—was considered by Plato and Aristotle to be among the gravest problems for the solution of the statesman.[b] Consistent with these conditions, essential to security and tranquillity, whatever the form of government might be, there was only room for the free population then existing: not always for that (seeing that the proportion of poor citizens was often uncomfortably great), and never for any sensible increase above that. If all the children were born and brought up, that it was possible for adult couples to produce, a fearful aggravation of poverty, with all its accompanying public troubles and sufferings, would have been inevitable.[c] Accordingly both Plato (for the Guardians in the Republic) and Aristotle agree in opinion that a limit must be fixed upon the number of children which each couple

[a] Compare the view (not unlike though founded on different reasons) of the stationary state taken by Mr. John Stuart Mill, in a valuable chapter of his Principles of Political Economy, Book iv. cap. 6. He says (s. 2, p. 319):—"The best state for human nature is that in which, while no one is poor, no one desires to be richer, nor has any reason to fear being thrust back by the efforts of others to push themselves forward." This would come near to the views of Plato and Aristotle.

[b] See a striking passage in Plato, Legg. v. pp. 742-743. He speaks of rich men as they are spoken of in some verses of the Gospels — a very rich man can hardly be a good man. Wealth and poverty are both of them evils, p. 744 D. Republ. iv. p. 421.

Pheidon the Corinthian, an ancient lawgiver (we do not know when or where), prescribed an unchangeable number both of lots (of land) and of citizens, but the lots were not to be all equal. Aristotel. Politic. ii. 6, p. 1265, b. 14.

[c] Aristot. Politic. ii. 6, p. 1265, b. 10. Τὸ δὲ ἀφεῖσθαι (τὴν τεκνοποΐιαν ἀόριστον) καθάπερ ἐν ταῖς πλείσταις πόλεσιν, πενίας ἀναγκαῖον αἴτιον γίνεσθαι τοῖς πολίταις· ἡ δὲ πενία, στάσιν ἐμποιεῖ καὶ κακουργίαν. Compare ibid. ii. 7, p. 1266, b. 8.

is permitted to introduce. If any objector had argued that each couple, by going through the solemnity of marriage acquired a natural right to produce as many children as they could, and that others were under a natural obligation to support those children—both philosophers would have denied the plea altogether. But they went even farther. They considered procreation as a duty which each citizen owed to the public, in order that the total of citizens might not fall below the proper minimum—yet as a duty which required controul, in order that the total might not rise above the proper maximum.[d] Hence they did not even admit the right of each couple to produce as many children as their private means could support. They thought it necessary to impose a limit on the number of children in every family, binding equally on rich and poor : the number prescribed might be varied from time to time, as circumstances indicated. As the community could not safely admit more than a certain aggregate of births, these philosophers commanded all couples indiscriminately, the rich not excepted, to shape their conduct with a view to that imperative necessity.

Plato in his Republic (as I have already mentioned) assumes for his Archons the privilege of selecting (by a pretended sortition) the couples through whom the legitimate amount of breeding shall be accomplished : in the semi-Platonic commonwealth (De Legibus), he leaves the choice free, but prescribes the limits of age, rendering marriage a peremptory duty between twenty and thirty-five years of age, and adding some emphatic exhortations, though not peremptory enactments, respecting the principles which ought to guide individual choice.[e] In the same manner too he deals with procreation : recognising the

---

[d] Aristotel. Politic. vii. 16, p. 1335, b. 28-38. λειτουργεῖν πρὸς τεκνοποιΐαν —ἀφεῖσθαι δεῖ τῆς εἰς τὸ φανερὸν γεννήσεως.
Plato, Republic, v. pp. 460-461. τίκτειν τῇ πόλει—γεννᾶν τῇ πόλει— τῶν εἰς τὸ κοινὸν γεννήσεων.

[e] Plato, Legg. vi. pp. 772-773-774. The wording is characteristic of the view taken by these philosophers, and of the extent to which they subordinated individual sentiment to public considerations. κατὰ παντὸς εἷς ἔστω μῦθος γάμου—τὸν γὰρ τῇ πόλει δεῖ ξυμφέροντα μνηστεύειν γάμον ἕκαστον,

ἀλλ' οὐ τὸν ἥδιστον αὐτῷ—φέρεται δέ πως ἀεὶ κατὰ φύσιν πᾶς πρὸς τὸν ὁμοιότατον αὐτῷ, &c. P. 773 B. In marriage (he says) the natural tendency is that like seeks like ; but it is good for the city that like should be coupled to unlike, rich to poor, hasty tempers with sober tempers, &c., in order that the specialties may be blended together and mitigated. He does not pretend to embody this in a written law, but directs the authorities to obtain it as far as they can by exhortation. P. 773 E. Compare the Politikus, p. 311.

necessity of imposing a limit on individual discretion, yet not
naming that limit by law, but leaving it to be enforced according to circumstances by the magistrates : who (he says),
by advice, praise, and censure, can apply either effective restraints on procreation, or encouragements if the case requires.[f]
Aristotle blames this guarantee as insufficient : he feels so
strongly the necessity of limiting procreation, that he is not
satisfied unless a proper limit be imposed by positive law.
Unless such a result be made thoroughly sure (he says), all
other measures of lawgivers for equalising properties, or avert-
ing poverty and the discontents growing out of it—must fail
in effect.[g]   Aristotle also lays it down as a part of the duty of
the lawgiver to take care that the bodies of the children
brought up shall be as good as possible : hence he prescribes
the ages proper for marriage, and the age after which no
parents are to produce any more children.[h]

The paramount necessity of limiting the number of children
born in each family, here enforced by Plato and Aristotle—rests
upon that great social fact which Malthus so instructively expounded at the close of the last century. Malthus, enquiring
specially into the law of population, showed upon what conditions the increase of population depends, and what were the
causes constantly at work to hold it back—checks to population. He ranged these causes under three different heads,
though the two last are multiform in detail. 1. Moral or prudential restraint—the preventive check. 2. Vice, and 3. Misery
—the two positive checks. He farther showed that though

[f] Plato, Legg. v. p. 740 D. πορίζετω
μηχανὴν ὅτι μάλιστα, ὅπως αἱ πεντα-
κισχίλιαι καὶ τετταράκοντα οἰκήσεις
ἀεὶ μόνον ἔσονται· καὶ γὰρ ἐπισχέ-
σεις γενέσεως, οἷς ἂν εὔρους εἴη
γένεσις, καὶ τοὐνάντιον ἐπιμέλειαι καὶ
σπουδαὶ πλήθους γεννημάτων εἰσὶν, &c.

[g] Aristotel. Politic. ii. 6, p. 1264,
a. 38, ii. 7, p. 1266, b. 10, vii. 16.
Aristotle has not fully considered
all that Plato says, when he blames
him for inconsistency in proposing to
keep properties equal, without taking
pains to impose and maintain a constant limit on offspring in families.
Ἄτοπον δὲ καὶ τὸ τὰς κτήσεις ἰσάζοντα
(Plato), τὸ περὶ τὸ πλῆθος τῶν πολιτῶν
μὴ κατασκευάζειν, ἀλλ' ἀφεῖναι τὴν
τεκνοποιίαν ἀόριστον, &c.

What Plato really directs is stated
in my text and in my note immediately
preceding.
[h] Aristotel. Politic. vii. 16, p. 1334,
b. 39. εἴπερ οὖν ἀπ' ἀρχῆς τὸν νομο-
θέτην ὁρᾶν δεῖ, ὅπως βέλτιστα τὰ
σώματα γένηται τῶν τρεφομένων, πρῶτον μὲν ἐπιμελητέον περὶ τὴν σύζευξιν
πότε καὶ ποίους τινὰς ὄντας χρὴ ποιεῖσθαι πρὸς ἀλλήλους τὴν γαμικὴν ὁμι-
λίαν, &c. He names thirty-seven as
the age proper for a man, eighteen for
a woman, to marry. At the age of
fifty-five a man becomes unfit to pro-
create for the public, and none of his
children are to appear (ἀφεῖσθαι τῆς
εἰς τὸ φανερὸν γεννήσεως, vii. 16, p.
1335, b. 36).

the aggregate repressive effect of these three causes is infallible and inevitable, determined by the circumstances of each given society—yet that mankind might exercise an option through which of the three the check should be applied : that the effect of the two last causes was in inverse proportion to that of the first—in other words, that the less there was of prudential restraint limiting the number of births, the more there must be of vice or misery, under some of their thousand forms, to shorten the lives of many of the children born—and *é converso,* the more there was of prudential restraint, the less would be the operation of the other checks tending to shorten life.

Three distinct facts—preventive restraint, vice, and misery— having nothing else in common, are arranged under one general head by Malthus, in consequence of the one single common property which they possess— that of operating as checks to population. To him, that one common property was the most important of all, and the most fit to be singled out as the groundwork of classification, having reference to the subject of his enquiry. But Plato and Aristotle looked at the subject in a different point of view. They had present to their minds the same three facts, and the tendency of the first to avert or abate the second and third : but as they were not investigating the law of population, they had nothing to call their attention to the one common property of the three. They did not regard vice and misery as causes tending to keep down population, but as being in themselves evils; enemies among the worst which the lawgiver had to encounter, in his efforts to establish a good political and social condition—and enemies which he could never successfully encounter, without regulating the number of births. Such regulation they considered as an essential tutelary measure to keep out disastrous poverty. The inverse proportion, between regulated or unregulated number of births on the one hand, and diminution or increase of poverty on the other, was seen as clearly by Aristotle and Plato as by Malthus.

But these two Greek philosophers ordain something yet more remarkable. Having prescribed both the age of marriage and the number of permitted births, so

[margin note:] Plato and Aristotle saw the same law as Malthus, but arranged the facts under a different point of view.

[margin note:] Regulations of Plato and Aristotle as to number of

as to ensure both vigorous citizens and a total com- births, and new-born children.
patible with the absence of corrupting poverty—
they direct what shall be done if the result does not correspond to their orders. Plato in his Republic (as I have already
stated) commands that all the children born to his wedded
couples shall be immediately consigned to the care of public
nurses—that the offspring of the well-constituted parents
shall be brought up, that of the ill-constituted parents not
brought up—and that no children born of parents after the
legitimate age shall be brought up.[1] Aristotle forbids the
exposure of children, wherever the habits of the community
are adverse to it : but if after any married couple have had
the number of children allowed by law, the wife should again
become pregnant, he directs that abortion shall be procured
before the commencement of life or sense in the fœtus : after
such commencement, he pronounces abortion to be wrong.[k]
On another point Plato and Aristotle agree : both of them
command that no child born crippled or deformed shall be
brought up :[1] a practice actually adopted at Sparta under the
Lykurgean institutions, and even carried farther, since no
child was allowed to be brought up until it had been inspected
and approved by the public nurses.[m]

We here find both these philosophers not merely per-
mitting, but enjoining—and the Spartan legislation, Such regulations disap-
more admired than any in Greece, systematically proved and forbidden by
realising—practices which modern sentiment re- modern sentiment—
pudiates and punishes. Nothing can more strikingly Variability of ethical senti-
illustrate—what Plato and Aristotle have them- ment as to objects ap-
selves repeatedly observed[n]—how variable and in- proved or disapproved.

---

[1] Plato, Republ. v. pp. 459 D, 460 C, 461 C.

[k] Aristotel. Politic. vii. 16, 10, p. 1335, b. 20. Compare Plato, Theætêt. 149 C.
Περὶ δὲ ἀποθέσεως καὶ τροφῆς τῶν γιγνομένων, ἔστω νόμος, μηδὲν πεπηρω-μένον τρέφειν· διὰ δὲ πλῆθος τέκνων, ἐὰν ἡ τάξις τῶν ἐθῶν κωλύῃ, μηδὲν ἀποτίθεσθαι τῶν γιγνομένων· ὥρισται γὰρ δὴ τῆς τεκνοποιίας τὸ πλῆθος, ἐὰν δέ τισι γίγνηται παρὰ ταῦτα συνδυασ-θέντων, πρὶν αἴσθησιν ἐγγενέσθαι καὶ ζωὴν, ἐμποιεῖσθαι δεῖ τὴν ἄμβλωσιν· τὸ γὰρ ὅσιον καὶ τὸ μὴ, διωρισμένον τῇ αἰσθήσει καὶ τῷ ζῆν ἔσται. For the text of this passage I have followed

Bekker and the Berlin edition. As to the first half of the passage there are some material differences in the text and in the MSS. ; some give ἐθνῶν instead of ἐθῶν, and ὡρίσθαι γὰρ δεῖ instead of ὥρισται γὰρ δή.

[1] Plato, Republic, v. p. 460 C. τὰ δὲ τῶν χειρόνων (τέκνα), καὶ ἐάν τι τῶν ἑτέρων ἀνάπηρον γίγνηται, ἐν ἀπορρήτῳ τε καὶ ἀδήλῳ κατακρύψουσιν ὡς πρέπει. Aristot. ut suprà, ἔστω νόμος, μηδὲν πεπηρωμένον τρέφειν, &c.

[m] Plutarch, Lykurgus, c. 16.

[n] Aristotel. Politic. viii. 2, p. 1337, b. 2. Περὶ δὲ τῶν πρὸς ἀρετὴν, οὐδέν ἐστιν ὁμολογούμενον· καὶ γὰρ τὴν

determinate is the *matter* of ethical sentiment, in different
ages and communities, while the *form* of ethical sentiment
is the same universally : how all men agree subjectively,
in that which they feel—disapprobation and hatred of wrong
and vice, approbation and esteem of right and virtue—yet
how much they differ objectively, as to the acts or persons
which they designate by these names and towards which
their feelings are directed.   It is with these emotions as
with the other emotions of human nature : all men are
moved in the same manner, though in different degree, by
love and hatred—hope and fear—desire and aversion—sympathy and antipathy—the emotions of the beautiful, the sublime, the ludicrous: but when we compare the objects, acts,
or persons, which so move them, we find only a very partial
agreement, amidst wide discrepancy and occasionally strong
opposition.[o]   The present case is one of the strongest opposition.   Practices now abhorred as wrong, are here directly
commanded by Plato and Aristotle, the two greatest authorities of the Hellenic world : men differing on many points
from each other, but agreeing in this : men not only of lofty
personal character, but also of first-rate intellectual force, in
whom the ideas of virtue and vice had been as much developed
by reflection as they ever have been in any mind : lastly, men
who are extolled by the commentators as the champions of
religion and sound morality, against what are styled the unprincipled cavils of the Sophists.

ἀρετὴν οὐ τὴν αὐτὴν πάντες τιμῶσιν·
ὥστ' εὐλόγως διαφέρονται καὶ πρὸς τὴν
ἄσκησιν αὐτῆς.
   Ethica Nikomach. i. 3, p. 1094,
b. 15. Τὰ δὲ καλὰ καὶ τὰ δίκαια, περὶ
ὧν ἡ πολιτικὴ σκοπεῖται, τοσαύτην ἔχει
διαφορὰν καὶ πλάνην, ὥστε δοκεῖν νόμῳ
μόνον εἶναι, φύσει δὲ μή.
   [o] The extraordinary variety and
discrepancy of approved and consecrated customs prevalent in different
portions of the ancient world, is instructively set forth in the treatise of
the Syrian Christian Bardisanes, in
the time of the Antonines. A long
extract from this treatise is given in
Eusebius, Præparat. Evang. vi. 10;
it has been also published by Orelli,
annexed to his edition (Zurich, 1824)
of the argument of Alexander of

Aphrodisias, De Fato, p. 202. Compare Euseb. Hist. Eccles. iv. 30.
   Bardisanes is replying to the arguments of astrologers and calculators of
nativities, who asserted the uniform
and uncontrollable influence of the
heavenly bodies, in given positions,
over human conduct. As a proof that
mankind are not subject to any such
necessity, but have a large sphere of
freewill (αὐτεξούσιον), he cites these
numerous instances of diverse and contradictory institutions among different
societies. Several of the most conspicuous among these differences relate
to the institutions concerning sex and
family, the conduct and occupations
held obligatory in men and women, &c.
   Compare Sextus Empiric. Pyrrhon.
Hypotyp. iii. s. 198 scqq.

It is, in my judgment, both curious and interesting to study the manner in which these two illustrious men— Plato and Aristotle—dealt with the problem of popu- lation. Grave as that problem is in all times, it was peculiarly grave among the small republics of antiquity. Neither of them were disposed to ignore or overlook it: nor to impute to other causes the consequences which it produces: nor to treat as in- different the question, whether poor couples had a greater or less family, to share subsistence already scanty for themselves. Still less were these philosophers disposed to sanction the short-sighted policy of some Hellenic statesmen, who under a mistaken view of increasing the power of the state, proclaimed encouragement and premium simply to the multiplication of male births, without any regard to the comfort and means of families. Both Plato and Aristotle saw plainly, that a married couple, by multiplying their offspring, produced serious effects not merely upon their own happiness but upon that of others besides : up to a certain limit, for good—beyond that limit, for evil. Hence they laid it down, that procreation ought to be a rational and advised act, governed by a forecast of those consequences—not a casual and unforeseen result of present impulse. The same preponderance of reason over impulse as they prescribed in other cases, they endeavoured to enforce in this. They regarded it too, not simply as a branch of prudence, but as a branch of duty; a debt due by each citizen to others and to the commonwealth. It was the main purpose of their elaborate political schemes, to produce a steady habit and course of virtue in all the citizens : and they considered every one as greatly deficient in virtue, who refused to look forward to the consequences of his own pro- creative acts—thereby contributing to bring upon the state an aggravated measure of poverty, which was the sure parent of discord, sedition, and crime. That the rate of total increase should not be so great as to produce these last-mentioned effects—and that the limit of virtue and prudence should be made operative on all the separate families—was in their judgment one of the most important cares of the lawgiver.

We ought to disengage this general drift and purpose,

Plato and Aristotle re- quired sub- ordination of impulse to reason and duty—they applied this to the pro- creative im- pulse, as to others.

common both to Plato and Aristotle, on the subject of population, from the various means—partly objectionable, partly impossible to be enforced—whereby they intended to carry the purpose into effect.

I pass from Plato's picture of the entire regiment of

Training of the few select philosophers to act as chiefs. Guardians, under the regulations above described— to his description of the special training whereby the few most distinguished persons in the regiment (male or female, as the case may be) are to be improved, tested, and exalted to the capacity of philosophers; qualified to act as Rulers or Chiefs.[p] These are the two marked peculiarities of Plato's Republic. The Guardians are admirable as instruments, but have no initiative of their own: we have now to find the chiefs from whom they will receive it. How are philosophers to be formed? None but a chosen Few have the precious gold born with them, empowering them to attain this elevation. To those Few, if properly trained, the privilege and right to exercise command belongs, by Nature. For the rest, obedience is the duty prescribed by Nature.[q]

I have already given, in Chap. XXXIII., a short summary

Comprehensive curriculum for aspirants to philosophy— consummation by means of Dialectic. of the peculiar scientific training which Sokrates prescribes for ripening these heroic aspirants into complete philosophers. They pass years of intellectual labour, all by their own spontaneous impulse, over and above the full training of Guardians. They study Arithmetic, Geometry, Stereometry, Astronomy, Acoustics, &c., until the age of thirty: they then continue in the exercise of Dialectic, with all the test of question and answer, for five years longer: after which they enter upon the duties of practice and administration, succeeding ultimately to the position of chiefs if found competent. It is assumed that this long course of study, consummated by Dialectic, has operated within them that great mental revolution which Plato calls, turning the eye from the shadows in the cave to the realities

---

[p] Plato, Repub. v. p. 473, vi. p. 503 B. τοὺς ἀκριβεστάτους φύλακας φιλοσόφους δεῖ καθιστάναι.

[q] Plato, Repub. v. p. 474 B. τοῖς μὲν προσήκει φύσει, ἅπτεσθαί τε φιλοσοφίας, ἡγεμονεύειν τ᾽ ἐν πόλει· τοῖς δ᾽

ἄλλοις μήτε ἅπτεσθαι, ἀκολουθεῖν τε τῷ ἡγουμένῳ.

P. 476 B.   σπάνιοι ἂν εἶεν, vi. 503, vii. 535. They are to be ἐκ τῶν προκρίτων πρόκριτοι, vii. 537 D.

of clear daylight: that they will no longer be absorbed in the sensible world or in passing phenomena, but will become familiar with the unchangeable Ideas or Forms of the intelligible world, knowable only by intellectual intuition. Reason has with them been exalted to its highest power: not only strengthening them to surmount all intellectual difficulties and to deal with the most complicated conjunctures of practice—but also ennobling their dispositions, so as to overcome all the disturbing temptations and narrow misguiding prejudices inherent in the unregenerate man. Upon the perfection of character, emotional and intellectual, imparted to these few philosophers, depends the Platonic Commonwealth.

The remarks made by Plato on the effect of this preparatory curriculum, and on the various studies composing it, are highly interesting and instructive—even when they cannot be defended as exact. Much of what he so eloquently enunciates respecting philosophy and the philosophical character, is in fact just and profound, whatever view we may take as to Universals: whether we regard them (like Plato) as the only Real Entia, cognizable by the mental eye, and radically disparate from particulars—or whether we hold them to be only general Concepts, abstracted and generalised more or less exactly from particulars. The remarks made by Plato on the educational effect produced by Arithmetic and the other studies, are valuable and suggestive. Even the discredit which he throws on observations of fact, in Astronomy and Acoustics—the great antithesis between him and modern times—is useful as enabling us to enter into his point of view.[r]

Valuable remarks on the effects of these preparatory studies.

---

[r] Plato, Rep. vii. p. 529 C-D.
The manner in which Plato here depreciates astronomical observation is not easily reconcileable with his doctrine in the Timæus. He there tells us that the rotations of the Nous (intellective soul) in the interior of the human cranium, are cognate or analogous to those of the cosmical spheres, but more confused and less perfect: our eyesight being expressly intended for the purpose, that we might contemplate the perfect and unerring rotations of the cosmical spheres, so as to correct thereby the disturbed rota-

tions in our own brain (Timæus, pp. 46-47).
Malebranche shares the feeling of Plato on the subject of astronomical observation. Recherche de la Vérité, Lib. iv. a. iii. vol. ii. p. 219, ed. 1772.
"Car enfin qu'y a-t-il de grand dans la connoissance des mouvemens des planètes? et n'en savons nous pas assez présentement pour régler nos mois et nos années? Qu'avons nous tant à faire de savoir, si Saturne est environné d'un anneau ou d'un grand nombre de petites lunes, et pourquoi prendre parti là-dessus? Pourquoi se

But his point of view in the Republic differs materially
from that which we read in other dialogues: especially in two ways.

Differences
between the
Republic and
other dia-
logues—no
mention of
reminiscence,
nor of the
Elenchus.
First, The scientific and long-continued Quadrivium, through which Plato here conducts the student
to philosophy, is very different from the road to
philosophy as indicated elsewhere. Nothing is here said about
reminiscence—which, in the Menon, Phædon, Phædrus, and
elsewhere, stands in the foreground of his theory, as the engine
for reviving in the mind Forms or Ideas. With these Forms
it had been familiar during a prior state of existence, but they
had become buried under the sensible impressions arising
from its conjunction with the body. Nor do we find in the
Republic any mention of that electric shock of the negative
Elenchus, which (in the Theætêtus, Sophistês, and several
other dialogues) is declared indispensable for stirring up the
natural mind not merely from ignorance and torpor, but even
from a state positively distempered—the false persuasion of
knowledge.

Different
view taken
by Plato in
the Republic
about Dia-
lectic—and
different
place assign-
ed to it.
Secondly, following out this last observation, we perceive another discrepancy yet more striking, in the directions
given by Plato respecting the study of Dialectic. He
prescribes that it shall upon no account be taught
to young men: and that it shall come last of all in
teaching, only after the full preceding Quadrivium.
He censures severely the prevalent practice of applying it to
young men, as pregnant with mischief. Young men (he says)
brought up in certain opinions inculcated by the lawgiver, as
to what is just and honourable, are interrogated on these subjects, and have questions put to them. When asked, What is
the just and the honourable, they reply in the manner which
they have learnt from authority: but this reply, being exposed
to farther interrogatories, is shown to be untenable and inconsistent, such as they cannot defend to their own satisfaction.
Hence they lose all respect for the established ethical creed,

glorifier d'avoir prédit la grandeur
d'une éclipse, où l'on a peut-être mieux
rencontré qu'un autre, parcequ' on a été
plus heureux? Il y a des personnes
destinées, par l'ordre du Prince, à
observer les astres; contentons nous
de leurs observations. Nous devons
être pleinement satisfaits sur une matière qui nous touche si peu, lorsqu' ils
nous font partie de leurs découvertes."

which however stands opposed in their minds to the seductions of immediate enjoyment; yet they acquire no new or better conviction in its place. Instead of following an established law, they thus come to live without any law.[s] Besides, young men when initiated in dialectic debate, take great delight in the process, as a means of exposing and puzzling the respondent. Copying the skilful interrogators whom they have found themselves unable to answer, they interrogate others in their turn, dispute everything, and pride themselves on exhibiting all the negative force of the Elenchus. Instead of employing dialectic debate for the discovery of truth, they use it merely as a disputatious pastime, and thus bring themselves as well as philosophy into discredit.[t]

Accordingly, we must not admit (says Plato) either young men, or men of ordinary untrained minds, to dialectic debate. We must admit none but mature persons, of sedate disposition, properly prepared: who will employ it not for mere disputation, but for the investigation of truth.[u]

Now the doctrine thus proclaimed, with the grounds upon which it rests—That dialectic debate is unsuitable and prejudicial to young men—distinctly contradict both the principles laid down by himself elsewhere, and the frequent indications of his own dialogues: not to mention the practice of Sokrates as described by Xenophon. In the Platonic Parmenidês and Theætêtus, the season of youth is expressly pronounced to be that in which dialectic exercise is not merely appropriate, but indispensable to the subsequent attainment of truth.[x] Moreover, Plato puts into the mouth of

Contradiction with the spirit of other dialogues—Parmenidês, &c.

---

[s] Plato, Republic, vii. pp. 538–539. ὅταν τὸν οὕτως ἔχοντα ἐλθὸν ἐρώτημα ἔρηται, τί ἐστι τὸ καλὸν, καὶ ἀποκρινά-μενον ὃ τοῦ νομοθετοῦ ἤκουεν ἐξελεγχῇ ὁ λόγος, καὶ πολλάκις καὶ πολλαχῇ ἐλέγχων εἰς δόξαν καταβαλῇ ὡς τοῦτο οὐδὲν μᾶλλον καλὸν ἢ αἰσχρόν, καὶ περὶ δικαίου ὡσαύτως καὶ ἀδίκου, καὶ ἃ μάλιστα ἦγεν ἐν τιμῇ, &c.

[t] Plato, Republ. vii. p. 539 B.

[u] Plato, Republ. vii. p. 539 D.

[x] Plato, Parmenidês, pp. 135 D, 137 B. Theætêt. 146 A. Proklus, in his Commentary on the Parmenidês (p. 778, Stallbaum), adverts to the passage of the Republic here discussed, and endeavours to show

that it is not inconsistent with the Parmenidês. He states that the exhortation to practise dialectic debate in youth, as the appropriate season, must be understood as specially and exclusively addressed to a youth of the extraordinary mental qualities of Sokrates; while the passage in the Republic applies the prohibition only to the general regiment of Guardians. But this justification is noway satisfactory; for Plato in the Republic makes no exception in favour of the most promising Guardians. He lays down the position generally. Again, in the Parmenidês, we find the encouragement to dialectic debate ad-

Parmenides a specimen intentionally given to represent that dialectic exercise which will be profitable to youth. The specimen is one full of perplexing, though ingenious, subtleties; ending in establishing, by different trains of reasoning, the affirmative, as well as the negative, of several distinct conclusions. Not only it supplies no new positive certainty, but it appears to render any such consummation more distant and less attainable than ever.[y] It is therefore eminently open to the censure which Plato pronounces, in the passage just cited from his Republic, against dialectic as addressed to young men. The like remark may be made upon the numerous other dialogues (though less extreme in negative subtlety than the Parmenidês), wherein the Platonic Sokrates interrogates youths (or interrogates others, in the presence of youths) without any positive result: as in the Theætêtus, Charmidês, Lysis, Alkibiadês, Hippias, &c., to which we may add the conversations of the Xenophontic Sokrates with Euthydemus and others.[z]

In fact, the Platonic Sokrates expressly proclaims himself Contradiction with the character and declarations of Sokrates. (in the Apology as well as in the other dialogues just named) to be ignorant and incapable of teaching anything. His mission was to expose the ignorance of those, who fancy that they know without really knowing: he taught no one anything, but he cross-examined every one who would submit to it, before all the world, and in a manner especially interesting to young men. Sokrates mentions that these young men not only listened with delight, but tried to imitate him as well as they could, by cross-examining others in the same manner:[a] and in mentioning the fact, he expresses neither censure nor regret, but satisfaction in the thought that the chance would be thereby increased, of exposing that false persuasion of knowledge which prevailed so widely everywhere. Now Plato, in the passage just cited

---

dressed not merely to the youthful Sokrates, but to the youthful Aristoteles (p. 137 B). Moreover, we are not to imagine that all the youths who are introduced as respondents in the Platonic dialogues are implied as equal to Sokrates himself, though they are naturally represented as superior and promising subjects. Compare Plato, Sophistês, p. 217 E; Politikus, p. 257 E.

[y] Plato, Parmenid. p. 166 ad fin. εἰρήσθω τοίνυν τοῦτό τε καὶ ὅτι, ὡς ἔοικεν, ἐν εἴτ' ἔστιν, εἴτε μὴ ἔστιν, αὐτό τε καὶ τἆλλα καὶ πρὸς αὑτὰ καὶ πρὸς ἄλληλα πάντα πάντως ἔστι τε καὶ οὐκ ἔστι, καὶ φαίνεται τε καὶ οὐ φαίνεται. Ἀληθέστατα.

[z] Xenophon, Memorab. iv. 2.

[a] Plato, Apolog. Sokrat. c. 10, p. 23 D, c. 22, p. 33 C, c. 27, p. 37 E, c. 30, p. 39 C.

from the Republic, blames this contagious spirit of cross-examination on the part of young men, as a vice which proved the mischief of dialectic debate addressed to them at that age. He farther deprecates the disturbance of "those opinions which they have heard from the lawgiver respecting what is just and honourable." But it is precisely these opinions which, in the Alkibiadês, Menon, Protagoras, and other dialogues, the Platonic Sokrates treats as untaught, if not unteachable:— as having been acquired, no man knew how, without the lessons of any assignable master and without any known period of study:—lastly, as constituting that very illusion of false knowledge without real knowledge, of which Sokrates undertakes to purge the youthful mind, and which must be dispelled before any improvement can be effected in it.[b]

We thus see, that the dictum forbidding dialectic debate with youth—cited from the seventh book of the Republic, which Plato there puts into the mouth of Sokrates—is decidedly anti-Sokratic; and anti-Platonic, in so far as Plato represents Sokrates. It belongs indeed to the case of Melêtus and Anytus, in their indictment against Sokrates before the Athenian dikastery. It is identical with their charge against him, of corrupting youth, and inducing them to fancy themselves superior to the authority of established customs and opinions heard from their elders.[c] Now the Platonic Sokrates is here made to declare explicitly, that dialectic debate addressed to youth does really tend to produce this effect:—to render them lawless, immoral, disputatious. And when we find him forbidding all such discourse at an earlier age than thirty years—we remark as a singular coincidence, that this is the exact prohibition which Kritias and Charikles actually imposed upon Sokrates himself, during the shortlived dominion of the Thirty Oligarchs at Athens.[d]

The matter to which I here advert, illustrates a material

The remarks here made upon the effect of Dialectic upon youth coincide with the accusation of Melêtus against Sokrates.

---

[b] Plato, Sophist. p. 230.

[c] Xenophon, Memorab. i. 2, 19-49. Compare Aristophanes, Nubes, 1042-1382.

[d] Xenophon, Memorab. i. 2, 33-38.

Isokrates complains that youthful students took more delight in disputa-tion than he thought suitable; nevertheless he declares that youth, and not mature age, is the proper season for such exercises, as well as for Geometry and Astronomy (Orat. xii. Panathen. s. 29-31, p. 239).

distinction between some writings of Plato as compared with others, and between different points of view which his mind took on at different times. In the Platonic Apology, we find Sokrates confessing his own ignorance, and proclaiming himself to be isolated among an uncongenial public falsely persuaded of their own knowledge. In several other dialogues, he is the same : he cannot teach anything, but can only cross-examine, test, and apply the spur to respondents. But the Republic presents him in a new character. He is no longer a dissenter amidst a community of fixed, inherited, convictions.[e] He is himself in the throne of King Nomos : the infallible authority, temporal as well as spiritual, from whom all public sentiment emanates, and by whom orthodoxy is determined. Hence we now find him passing to the opposite pole ; taking up the orthodox, conservative, point of view, the same as Melêtus and Anytus maintained in their accusation against Sokrates at Athens. He now expects every individual to fall into the place, and contract the opinions, prescribed by authority ; including among those opinions deliberate ethical and political fictions, such as that about the gold and silver earthborn men. Free-thinking minds, who take views of their own, and enquire into the evidence of these beliefs, become inconvenient and dangerous. Neither the Sokrates of the Platonic Apology, nor his negative Dialectic, could be allowed to exist in the Platonic Republic.

Contrast between the real Sokrates, as a dissenter at Athens, and the Platonic Sokrates, framer and dictator of the Platonic Republic.

One word more must be said respecting a subject which figures conspicuously in the Republic—the Idea or Form of Good. The chiefs alone (we read) at the end of their long term of study, having ascended gradually from the phenomena of sense to intellectual contemplation and familiarity with the unchangeable Ideas—will come to discern and embrace the highest of all Ideas—the Form of Good :[f] by the help of which alone, Justice, Temperance, and the other virtues, become useful and profitable.[g] If the Archons do not know how and why just and honourable things are good, they will not be fit

Idea of Good —The Chiefs alone know what it is— If they did not they would be unfit for their functions.

---

for their duty.[h]   In regard to Good (Plato tells us) no man is satisfied with mere appearance.   Here every man desires and postulates that which is really good : while as to the just and the honourable, many are satisfied with the appearance, without caring for the reality.[i]

Plato proclaims this Real Good, as distinguished from Apparent Good, to be the paramount and indispensable object of knowledge, without which all other knowledge is useless.   It is that which every man divines to exist, yearns for, and does everything with a view to obtain: but which he misses, from not knowing where to seek ; missing also along with it that which gives value to other acquisitions.[k]   What then is this Real Good—the Noumenon, Idea, or Form of Good?

What is the Good? Plato does not know; but he requires the Chiefs to know it. Without this the Republic would be a failure.

This question is put by Glaukon to Sokrates, with much emphasis, in the dialogue of the Republic.   But unfortunately it remains unanswered.   Plato declines all categorical reply ; though the question is one, as he himself emphatically announces, upon which all the positive consequences of his philosophy turn.[l]   He conducts us to the chamber wherein this precious and indispensable secret is locked up, but he has

[h] Plato, Republic, vi. p. 506 A.

[i] Plato, Republic, vi. p. 505 D.

[k] Plato, Republic, vi. p. 505 A-E. Ὁ δὴ διώκει μὲν ἅπασα ψυχὴ καὶ τούτου ἕνεκα πάντα πράττει, ἀπομαντευομένη τί εἶναι, ἀποροῦσα δὲ καὶ οὐκ ἔχουσα λαβεῖν ἱκανῶς τί ποτ᾽ ἐστὶν οὐδὲ πίστει χρήσασθαι μονίμῳ, οἵᾳ καὶ περὶ τᾶλλα, διὰ τοῦτο δὲ ἀποτυγχάνει καὶ τῶν ἄλλων εἴτι ὄφελος ἦν, &c.

[l] Certainly when we see the way in which Plato deals with the ἰδέα ἀγαθοῦ, we cannot exempt him from the criticism which he addresses to others, vi. p. 493 E. ὡς δὲ ἀγαθὰ καὶ καλὰ ταῦτα τῇ ἀληθείᾳ, ἤδη πώποτε τοῦ ἤκουσας αὐτῶν λόγον διδόντος οὐ καταγέλαστον;

We may illustrate this procedure of Plato by an Oriental fable, cited in an instructive Dissertation of M. Ernest Renan.

"Aristoteles primum sub Almamuno (813-833, A.D.) arabicè factus est. Somniumque effictum à credulis hominibus : vidisse Almamunum in somno virum aspectu venerabili, solio insi-dentem; mirantem Almamuuum quæsivisse, quisnam ille esset? responsum, Aristotelem esse. Quo audito, Chalifam ab eo quæsivisse, Quidnam Bonum esset? respondisse Aristotelem : Quod sapientiores probarent. Quærenti Chalifæ quid hoc esset? Quod lex divina probat — dixisse. Interroganti porro illi, Quid hoc? Quod omnes probarent—respondisse : *neque alii ultra quæstioni respondere voluisse.* Quo somnio permotum Almamunum à Græcorum imperatore veniam petiisse, ut libri philosophici in ipsius regno quærerentur : hujusque rei gratiâ viros doctos misisse." Ernest Renan, De Philosophiâ Peripateticâ apud Syros, commentatio Historica, p. 57 ; Paris, 1852.

Among the various remarks which might be made upon this curious dream, one is, that Bonum is always determined as having relation to the appreciative apprehension of some mind — the Wise Men, the Divine Mind, the Mind of the general public. *Bonum* is that which some mind or

no key to open the door. In describing the condition of other men's minds—that they divine a Real Good—Αὐτὸ-ἀγαθὸν or Bonum *per se*—do everything in order to obtain it, but puzzle themselves in vain to grasp and determine what it is[m]—he has unconsciously described the condition of his own.

minds conceive and appreciate as such. The word has no meaning except in relation to some apprehending Subject.

[m] Plato, Republ. vi. p. 505 E. ἀπομαντευομένη τι εἶναι, ἀποροῦσα δὲ καὶ οὐκ ἔχουσα λαβεῖν ἱκανῶς τί ποτ' ἐστὶν, &c.

The remarks of Aristotle in impugning the Platonic ἰδέαν ἀγαθοῦ are very instructive, Ethic. Nikom. i. 1096-1097 ; Ethic. Eudem. i. 1217-1218.

He maintains that there exists nothing corresponding to the word ; and that even if it did exist, it would neither be πρακτὸν nor κτητὸν ἀνθρώπῳ. Aristotle here looks upon Good as being essentially relative or phenomenal : he understands τὸ ἁπλῶς ἀγαθὸν to mean τὸ ἀγαθὸν τὸ φαινόμενον τῷ σπουδαίῳ (Eth. Nik. iii. 1113, b. 16-32). But he does not uniformly adhere to this meaning.

CHAPTER XXXVI.

TIMÆUS AND KRITIAS.

THOUGH the Republic of Plato appears as a substantive composition, not including in itself any promise of an Persons and scheme of the Timæus and Kritias. intended sequel—yet the Timæus and Kritias are introduced by Plato as constituting a sequel to the Republic. Timæus the Pythagorean philosopher of Lokri, the Athenian Kritias, and Hermokrates, are now introduced, as having been the listeners while Sokrates was recounting his long conversation of ten Books, first with Thrasymachus, next with Glaukon and Adeimantus. The portion of that conversation, which described the theory of a model commonwealth, is recapitulated in its main characteristics: and Sokrates now claims from the two listeners some requital for the treat which he has afforded to them. He desires to see the citizens, whose training he has described at length, and whom he has brought up to the stage of mature capacity—exhibited by some one else as living, acting, and affording some brilliant evidence of courage and military discipline.[a] Kritias undertakes to satisfy his demand, by recounting a glorious achievement of the ancient citizens of Attica, who had once rescued Europe from an inroad of countless and almost irresistible invaders, pouring in from the vast island of Atlantis in the Western Ocean. This exploit is supposed to have been performed nearly 10,000 years before; and though lost out of the memory of the Athenians themselves, to have been commemorated and still preserved in the more ancient records of Sais in Egypt, and handed down through Solon by a family tradition to Kritias. But it is agreed between Kritias and Timæus,[b] that before the former enters upon his quasi-historical or mythical recital about the invasion from

---

[a] Plato, Timæus, p. 20 B.   [b] Plato, Timæus, p. 27 A.

Atlantis, the latter shall deliver an expository discourse, upon
a subject very different and of far greater magnitude. Unfortunately the narrative promised by Kritias stands before us
only as a fragment. There is reason to believe that Plato
never completed it.[c] But the discourse assigned to Timæus
was finished, and still remains, as a valuable record of ancient
philosophy.

For us, modern readers, the Timæus of Plato possesses a
species of interest which it did not possess either for
the contemporaries of its author, or for the ancient
world generally. We read in it a system—at least
the sketch of a system—of universal philosophy, the
earliest that has come to us in the words of the author
himself. Among the many other systems, anterior or simultaneous—those of Thales and the other Ionic philosophers, of
Herakleitus, Pythagoras, Parmenides, Empedokles, Anaxagoras, Demokritus—not one remains to us as it was promulgated
by its original author or supporters. We know all of them
only in fragments and through the criticisms of others: fragments always scanty—criticisms generally dissentient, often
harsh, sometimes unfair, introduced by the critic to illustrate
opposing doctrines of his own. Here, however, the Platonic
system is made known to us, not in this fragmentary and half-
attested form, but in the full exposition which Plato himself
deemed sufficient for it. This is a remarkable peculiarity.

The Timæus is the earliest ancient physical theory, which we possess in the words of its author.

Timæus is extolled by Sokrates as combining the character
of a statesman with that of a philosopher: as being
of distinguished wealth and family in his native
city (the Epizephyrian Lokri), where he had exercised the leading political functions :—and as having attained
besides, the highest excellence in science, astronomical as well
as physical.[d] We know from other sources (though Plato omits
to tell us so, according to his usual undefined manner of designating contemporaries) that he was of the Pythagorean
school. Much of the exposition assigned to him is founded on
Pythagorean principles, though blended by Plato with other

Position and character of the Pythagorean Timæus.

[c] Plutarch, Solon, c. 33.
Another discourse appears to have
been contemplated by Plato, to be
delivered by Hermokrates after Kritias
had concluded (Plato, Timæus, p.
20 A ; Kritias, p. 108). But nothing
of this was probably ever composed.
[d] Plato, Timæus, pp. 20 A, 27 A.

doctrines, either his own or borrowed elsewhere. Timæus undertakes to requite Sokrates by giving a discourse respecting "The Nature of the Universe;" beginning at the genesis of the Kosmos, and ending with the constitution of man.[e] This is to serve as an historical or mythical introduction to the Platonic Republic recently described; wherein Sokrates had set forth the education and discipline proper for man when located as an inhabitant of the earth. Neither during the exposition of Timæus, nor after it, does Sokrates make any remark. But the commencement of the Kritias (which is evidently intended as a second part or continuation of the Timæus) contains, first, a prayer from Timæus that the Gods will pardon the defects of his preceding discourse and help him to amend them—next an emphatic commendation bestowed by Sokrates upon the discourse: thus supplying that recognition which is not found in the first part.[f]

In this Hymn of the Universe (to use a phrase of the rhetor Menander[g] respecting the Platonic Timæus) the prose of Plato is quite as much the vehicle of poetical imagination as the hexameters of Hesiod, Empedokles, or Parmenides. The Gods and Goddesses, whom Timæus invokes at the commencement,[h] supply him with superhuman revelations, like the Muses to Hesiod, or the Goddess of Wisdom to Parmenides. Plato expressly recognises the multiplicity of different statements current, respecting the Gods and the generation of the Universe. He claims no superior credibility for his own. He professes to give us a new doctrine, not less probable than the numerous dissentient opinions already advanced by others, and more acceptable to his own mind. He bids us be content with such a measure of probability, because the limits of our human nature preclude any fuller approach to certainty.[i] It

Poetical imagination displayed by Plato. He pretends to nothing more than probability. Contrast with Sokrates, Isokrates, Xenophon.

---

[e] Plato, Timæus, p. 27 A.   ἔδοξε γὰρ ἡμῖν Τίμαιον μὲν, ἅτε ἀστρονομικώτατον ἡμῶν καὶ περὶ φύσεως τοῦ παντὸς εἰδέναι μάλιστα ἔργον πεποιημένον, πρῶτον λέγειν ἀρχόμενον ἀπὸ τῆς τοῦ κόσμου γενέσεως, τελευτᾶν δὲ εἰς τὴν ἀνθρώπου φύσιν.

[f] Plato, Kritias, p. 108 B.

[g] Menander, De Encomiis, i. 5, p. 39. Compare Karsten, De Empedoclis

Vitâ, p. 72; De Parmenidis Vitâ, p. 21.

[h] Plato, Timæus, p. 27 D; Hesiod, Theogon. 22-35-105.

[i] Plato, Timæus, pp. 29 D, 28 D, 59 C-D, 68 C, 72 D.   κατ᾽ ἐμὴν δόξαν —παρὰ τῆς ἐμῆς ψήφου, p. 52 D. In many parts of the dialogue he repeats that he is delivering his *own opinion*—that he is affirming what is probable. In the Phædon, however,

is important to note the modest pretensions here unreservedly announced by Plato as to the conviction and assent of hearers :—so different from the confidence manifested in the Republic, where he hires a herald to proclaim his conclusion— and from the overbearing dogmatism which we read in his Treatise De Legibus, where he is providing a catechism for the schooling of citizens, rather than proofs to be sifted by opponents. He delivers, respecting matters which he admits to be unfathomable, the theory most in harmony with his own religious and poetical predispositions, which he declares to be as probable as any other yet proclaimed. The Xenophontic Sokrates, who disapproved all speculation respecting the origin and structure of the Kosmos, would probably have granted this equal probability, and equal absence of any satis- factory grounds of preferential belief—both to Plato on one side and to the opposing theorists on the other. And another intelligent contemporary, Isokrates, would probably have con- sidered the Platonic Timæus as one among the same class of unprofitable extravagancies, to which he assigns the theories of Herakleitus, Empedokles, Alkmæon, Parmenides, and others.[k] Plato himself (in the Sophistês)[l] characterises the theories of these philosophers as fables recited to an audience

we find that εἰκότες λόγοι are set aside as deceptive and dangerous, Phædon, p. 92 D. In the remarkable passage of the Timæus, p. 48 C-D, Plato inti- mates that he will not in the present discourse attempt to go to the bottom of the subject—τὴν μὲν περὶ ἀπάντων εἴτε ἀρχὴν εἴτε ἀρχὰς εἴτε ὅπη δοκεῖ τούτων πέρι, τὸ νῦν οὐ ῥητέον—but that he will confine himself to εἰκότες λόγοι— τὸ δὲ κατ᾽ ἀρχὰς ῥηθὲν διαφυλάττων, τὴν τῶν εἰκότων λόγων δύναμιν, πειράσομαι μηδενὸς ἧττον εἰ- κότα, μᾶλλον δὲ καὶ ἔμπροσθεν ἀπ᾽ ἀρ- χῆς περὶ ἑκάστων καὶ ξυμπάντων λέγειν.

What these *principia* are, which Plato here keeps in the background, I do not clearly understand. Susemihl (Entwickelung der Plat. Phil. ii. p. 405) and Martin (Études sur le Timée, ii. p. 173, note 56) have both given elucidations of this passage, but neither of them appear to me satisfactory. Simplikius says :— Ὁ Πλάτων τὴν φυσιολογίαν εἰκοτολογίαν ἔλεγεν εἶναι, ᾧ καὶ Ἀριστοτέλης συμμαρτυρεῖ, Schol.

Aristot. Phys. 325, a. 23, Brandis.

[k] Isokrates, De Permutatione, Or. xv. s. 287-288-304. ἡγοῦμαι γὰρ τὰς μὲν τοιαύτας περιττολογίας ὁμοίας εἶναι ταῖς θαυματοποιίαις ταῖς οὐδὲν μὲν ὠφελούσαις, ὑπὸ δὲ τῶν ἀνοήτων πε- ριστάτοις γιγνομέναις.

τοὺς δὲ τῶν μὲν ἀναγκαίων ἀμελοῦν- τας, τὰς δὲ τῶν παλαιῶν σοφιστῶν τερατολογίας ἀγαπῶντας, φιλοσο- φεῖν φασί.

Compare another passage of Iso- krates, the opening of Orat. x. En- comium Helenæ ; in which latter passage he seems plainly to notice one of the main ethical doctrines advanced by Plato, though he does not mention Plato's name, nor indeed the name of any living person.

[l] Plato, Sophist. pp. 242-243. Μῦθόν τινα ἕκαστος αὐτῶν φαίνεται διηγεῖσθαι παισὶν ὡς οὖσιν ἡμῖν· ὁ μὲν, ὡς τρία τὰ ὄντα, πολεμεῖ δὲ ἀλλήλοις ἐνίοτε αὐτῶν ἄττα πη, τότε δὲ καὶ φίλα γιγνόμενα γάμους τε καὶ τόκους καὶ τροφὰς τῶν ἐκγόνων παρέχεται.

of children, without any care to ensure a rational comprehension and assent. *They* would probably have made the
like criticism upon his Timæus. While he treats it as fable
to apply to the Gods the human analogy of generation and
parentage—they would have considered it only another variety
of fable, to apply to them the equally human analogy of constructive fabrication or mixture of ingredients. The language
of Xenophon shows that he agreed with his master Sokrates
in considering such speculations as not merely unprofitable,
but impious.[m] And if the mission from the Gods—constituting
Sokrates Cross-Examiner general against the prevailing fancy
of knowledge without the reality of knowledge—drove him to
court perpetual controversy with the statesmen, poets, and
Sophists of Athens; the same mission would have compelled
him, on hearing the sweeping affirmations of Timæus, to apply
the test of his Elenchus, and to appear in his well-known
character of confessed[n] but inquisitive ignorance. The Platonic
Timæus is positively anti-Sokratic. It places us at the opposite
or dogmatic pole of Plato's character.[o]

Timæus begins by laying down the capital distinction between—1. Ens or the Existent, the eternal and un- Fundamental
distinction
changeable, the world of Ideas or Forms, apprehended between Ens
and Fientia.

---

[m] Xenophon, Memorab. i. 1, 11-14.
Οὐδεὶς δὲ πώποτε Σωκράτους οὐδὲν
ἀσεβὲς οὐδὲ ἀνόσιον οὔτε πράττοντος
εἶδεν οὔτε λέγοντος ἤκουσεν· οὐδὲ
γὰρ περὶ τῆς τῶν πάντων φύσεως,
ἧπερ τῶν ἄλλων οἱ πλεῖστοι, διελέγετο,
σκοπῶν ὅπως ὁ καλούμενος ὑπὸ
τῶν σοφιστῶν κόσμος ἔχει, καὶ
τίσιν ἀνάγκαις ἕκαστα γίγνεται τῶν
οὐρανίων· ἀλλὰ καὶ τοὺς φροντίζοντας
τὰ τοιαῦτα μωραίνοντας ἀπεδείκνυε.

Lucretius, i. 80 :—
" Illud in his rebus vereor, ne forté rearis
Impia te rationis inire elementa, viamque
Endogredi sceleris," &c.

The above cited passage of Xenophon shows that the term Κόσμος was
in his time a technical word among
philosophers, not yet accepted in that
meaning by the general public. The
aversion to investigation on the Kosmos, on the ground of impiety, entertained by Sokrates and Xenophon,
is expressed by Plato in the Leges
(vii. 821 A) in the following words of
the principal speaker,—Τὸν μέγιστον

θεὸν καὶ ὅλον τὸν κόσμον φαμὲν οὔτε
ζητεῖν δεῖν οὔτε πολυπραγμονεῖν .τὰς
αἰτίας ἐρευνῶντας· οὐ γὰρ οὐδ' ὅσιον
εἶναι· τὸ δ' ἔοικε πᾶν τούτου τοὐνάντιον
γιγνόμενον ὀρθῶς ἂν γίγνεσθαι. This
last passage is sometimes cited as if
the word φαμὲν expressed the opinion
of the principal speaker, or of Plato
himself—which is a mistake; φαμὲν
here expresses the opinion which the
principal speaker is about to con-
trovert.

[n] See above vol. i. ch. vii. of the
present work, where the Platonic
Apology is reviewed.

[o] "Quocirca Timæus non dialecticé
disserens inducitur, sed loquitur ut
hierophanta, qui mundi arcana aliunde
accepta grandi ac magnificâ oratione
pronunciat : quin etiam quæ experi-
entiæ suspicionem superant, mythorum
ac symbolorum involucris obtegit,
eoque modo quam ea certa sint, legen-
tibus non obscuré significat."—Stallbaum, Prolegg. ad Platon. Timæum,
c. iv. p. 37.

only by mental conception or Reason, but the object of infallible cognition.   2. The Generated and Perishable—the
sensible, phenomenal, material world—which never really
exists, but is always appearing and disappearing; apprehended
by sense, yet not capable of becoming the object of cognition,
nor of anything better than opinion or conjecture.   The
Kosmos, being a visible and tangible body, belongs to this
last category.   Accordingly, it can never be really known:
no true or incontestable propositions can be affirmed respecting it: you can arrive at nothing higher than opinion and
probability.

Plato seems to have had this conviction, respecting the uncertainty of all affirmations about the sensible world or any
portions of it, forcibly present to his mind.

He next proceeds to assume or imply, as postulates, his
eternal Ideas or Forms—a coeternal chaotic matter
or indeterminate Something—and a Demiurgus or
Architect to construct, out of this chaos, after contemplation of the Forms, copies of them as good as
were practicable in the world of sense.   The exposition begins with these postulates.   The Demiurgus
found all visible matter, not in a state of rest, but
in discordant and irregular motion.   He brought it out of
disorder into order.   Being himself good (says Plato), and
desiring to make everything else as good as possible, he transformed this chaos into an orderly Kosmos.[p]   He planted in
its centre a soul spreading round, so as to pervade all its
body—and reason in the soul: so that the Kosmos became
animated, rational—a God.

Postulates of Plato. The Demiurgus—The Eternal Id as—Chaotic Materia or Fundamentum. The Kosmos is a living being and a God.

The Demiurgus of Plato is not conceived as a Creator,[q] but
as a Constructor or Artist.   He is the God Promê-
theus, conceived as pre-kosmical, and elevated to
the primacy of the Gods; instead of being subordinate to Zeus, as depicted by Æschylus and others.
He represents provident intelligence or art, and
beneficent purpose, contending with a force superior

The Demiurgus not a Creator The Kosmos arises from his operating upon the random movements of Necessity. He cannot controul ne-

---

p Plato, Timæus, pp. 29-30.

q "The notion of absolute Creation
is unknown to Plato, as it is to all

Grecian and Roman antiquity "
(Brandis, Gesch. der Griech. Rom.
Philos. vol. ii. part 2, p. 306).

cessity—he
only per-
suades.

and irresistible, so as to improve it as far as it will
allow itself to be improved.[r] This pre-existing superior force Plato denominates Necessity—"the erratic, irregular,
random, causality," subsisting prior to the intervention of the
Demiurgus; who can only work upon it by persuasion, but
cannot coerce or subdue it.[s] The genesis of the Kosmos thus
results from a combination of intelligent force with the
original, primordial Necessity; which was persuaded, and consented, to have its irregular agency regularised up to a certain
point, but no farther. Beyond this limit the systematising
arrangements of the Demiurgus could not be carried; but
all that is good or beautiful in the Kosmos was owing to
them.

We ought here to note the sense in which Plato uses the
word Necessity. This word is now usually understood as denoting what is fixed, permanent, unalterable, knowable beforehand. In the Platonic Timæus it
means the very reverse:—the indeterminate, the inconstant,
the anomalous, that which can neither be understood nor pre-
dicted. It is Force, Movement, or Change, with the negative
attribute of not being regular, or intelligible, or determined
by any knowable antecedent or condition—*Vis consili expers.*
It coincides, in fact, with that which is meant by *Freewill*, in
the modern metaphysical argument between Freewill and
Necessity: it is the undetermined or self-determining, as contrasted with that which depends upon some given deter-

<small>Meaning of Necessity in Plato.</small>

<hr>

<small>[r] The verbs used by Plato to describe the proceedings of the Demiurgus are ξυνετεκταίνετο, ξυνέστησε, ξυνεκεράσατο, ἐμηχανήσατο, &c. and such like.

[s] Plato, Timæus, pp. 47-48. ἐπιδείκται τὰ διὰ νοῦ δεδημιουργημένα· δεῖ δὲ καὶ τὰ δι' ἀνάγκης γιγνόμενα τῷ λόγῳ παραθέσθαι. Μεμιγμένη γὰρ οὖν ἡ τοῦδε τοῦ κόσμου γένεσις ἐξ ἀνάγκης τε καὶ νοῦ ξυστάσεως ἐγεννήθη· νοῦ δὲ ἀνάγκης ἄρχοντος τῷ πείθειν αὐτὴν τῶν γιγνομένων τὰ πλεῖστα ἐπὶ τὸ βέλτιστον ἄγειν, ταύτῃ κατὰ ταῦτά τε δι' ἀνάγκης ἡττωμένης ὑπὸ πειθοῦς ἔμφρονος, οὕτω κατ' ἀρχὰς ξυνίστατο τόδε τὸ πᾶν. Εἴ τις οὖν ᾗ γέγονε, κατὰ ταῦτα ὄντως ἐρεῖ, μικτέον καὶ τὸ τῆς πλανωμένης εἶδος αἰτίας, ᾗ φέρειν

πέφυκεν. Compare p. 56 B. ὅπηπερ ἡ τῆς ἀνάγκης ἑκοῦσα πεισθεῖσά τε φύσις ὑπεικε, pp. 68 E, 75 B, 30 A.

Τέχνη δ' ἀνάγκης ἀσθενεστέρα μακρῷ says Prometheus in Æschylus (P. V. 514. He identifies Ἀνάγκη with the Μοῖραι: and we read in Herodotus i. 91 of Apollo as trying to persuade the Fates to spare Croesus, but obtaining for him only a respite of three years—οὐκ οἷόν τε ἐγένετο παραγαγεῖν μοίρας, ὅσον δὲ ἐνέδωκαν αὐται, ἤνυσατο καὶ ἐχαρίσατό οἱ. This is the language used by Plato about Ἀνάγκη and the Demiurgus. A valuable exposition of the relati ns believed to subsist between the Gods and Μοῖρα is to be found in Naegelsbach, Homerische Theologie chap. iii. pp. 113-131).</small>

mining conditions, known or knowable. The Platonic Necessity [t] is identical with the primeval Chaos, recognised in the Theogony or Kosmogony of Hesiod. That poet tells us that Chaos was the primordial Something: and that afterwards came Gæa, Eros, Uranus, Nyx, Erebus, &c., who intermarried, males with females, and thus gave birth to numerous divine persons or kosmical agents—each with more or less of definite character and attributes. By these supervening agencies, the primeval Chaos was modified and regulated, to a greater or less extent. The Platonic Timæus starts in the same manner as Hesiod, from an original Chaos. But then he assumes also, as coæval with it, but apart from it, his eternal Forms or Ideas: while, in order to obtain his kosmical agents, he does not have recourse, like Hesiod, to the analogy of intermarriages and births, but employs another analogy equally human and equally borrowed from experience—that of a Demiurgus or constructive professional artist, architect, or carpenter; who works upon the model of these Forms, and introduces regular constructions into the Chaos. The antithesis present to the mind of Plato is that between disorder or absence of order, announced as Necessity,—and order or regularity, represented by the Ideas.[u] As the mediator between these two primeval opposites, Plato assumes Nous, or Reason, or artistic skill personified in his Demiurgus: whom he calls essentially good—meaning thereby that he is the regularising agent by whom order, method, and symmetry, are copied from the Ideas and partially realised among the intractable data of Necessity. Good is something which Plato in other works often talks about, but never determines: his language implies sometimes that he knows what it is, sometimes that he does not know. But so far as we can understand him, it means order, regularity, symmetry,

[t] In the Symposion (pp. 195 D, 197 B) we find Eros panegyrised as having amended and mollified the primeval empire of Ἀνάγκη.

The Scholiast on Hesiod, Theogon. 119 gives a curious metaphysical explanation of Ἔρος, mentioned in the Hesiodic text—τὴν ἐγκατεσπαρμένην φυσικῶς κινητικὴν αἰτίαν ἑκάστῳ τῶν ὄντων, καθ᾽ ἣν ἐφίεται ἕκαστος τοῦ

εἶναι.

[u] In the Philêbus, p. 23 C-D, these three are recognised under the terms: —1. Πέρας. 2. Ἄπειρον. 3. Αἰτία— τῆς ξυμμίξεως τούτων πρὸς ἄλληλα τὴν αἰτίαν.

Compare a curious passage of Plutarch, Symposiacon. viii. 2, p. 719 E, illustrating the Platonic phrase—τὸν θεὸν ἀεὶ γεωμετρεῖν.

proportion—by consequence, what is ascertainable and predictable.[x] I will not say that Plato means this always and exclusively, by Good: but he seems to mean so in the Timæus. Evil is the reverse. Good or regularity is associated in his mind exclusively with rational agency. It can be produced, he assumes, only by a reason, or by some personal agent analogous to a reasonable and intelligent man. Whatever is not so produced, must be irregular or bad.

These are the fundamental ideas which Plato expands into a detailed Kosmology. The first application which he makes of them is, to construct the total Kosmos. The total is here the logical Prius, or anterior to the parts in his order of conception. The Kosmos is one vast and comprehensive animal: just as in physiological description, the leading or central idea is, that of the animal organism as a whole, to which each and all the parts are referred. The Kosmos is constructed by the Demiurgus according to the model of the Αὐτοζῷον,[y]—(the Form or Idea of Animal—the eternal Generic or Self-Animal,)—which comprehends in itself the subordinate specific Ideas of different sorts of animals. This Generic Idea of Animal comprehended four of such specific Ideas: 1. The celestial race of animals, or Gods, who occupied the heavens: 2. Men. 3. Animals living in air—Birds. 4. Animals living on land or in water.[z] In order that the Kosmos might approach near to its model the Self-Animal, it was required to contain all these four species. As there was but one Self-Animal, so there could only be one Kosmos.

Marginal note: Process of demiurgic construction —The total Kosmos comes logically first, constructed on the model of the Αὐτο-ζῶον.

We see thus, that the primary and dominant idea, in Plato's mind, is, not that of inorganic matter, but that of organized and animated matter—life or soul embodied. With him, biology comes before physics.

The body of the Kosmos was required to be both visible and tangible: it could not be visible without fire: it could

---

[x] Plato, Timæus, p. 30 A. Compare the Republic, vi. p. 506, Philêbus, pp. 65-66, and the investigation in the Euthydêmus, pp. 279-293, which ends in no result.

[y] Plato, Timæus, p. 30 D.

[z] Plato, Timæus, pp. 39-40. ἧπερ

οὖν νοῦς ἐνούσας ἰδέας τῷ ὃ ἔστι ζῷον, οἷαί τε ἔνεισι καὶ ὅσαι, καθορᾷ, τοιαύτας καὶ τοσαύτας διενοήθη δεῖν καὶ τόδε σχεῖν. Εἰσὶ δὲ τέτταρες, μία μὲν οὐρόδνιον θεῶν γένος, ἄλλη δὲ πτηνὸν καὶ ἀερόπορον, τρίτη δὲ ἔνυδρον εἶδος, πέζον δὲ καὶ χερσαῖον τέταρτον.

not be tangible without something solid, nor solid without earth. But two things cannot be well put together by themselves, without a third to serve as a bond of connection : and that is the best bond which makes them One as much as possible. Geometrical proportion best accomplishes this object. But as both Fire and Earth were solids and not planes, no one mean proportional could be found between them. Two mean proportionals were necessary. Hence the Demiurgus interposed air and water, in such manner, that as fire is to air, so is air to water: and as air is to water, so is water to earth.[a] Thus the four elements, composing the body of the Kosmos, were bound together in unity and friendship. Of each of the four, the entire total was used up in the construction : so that there remained nothing of them apart, to

---

[a] Plato, Tim. pp. 31-32. The comment of Macrobius on this passage (Somn. Scip. i. 6, p. 30) is interesting, if not conclusive. But the language in which Plato lays down this doctrine about mean proportionals is not precise, and has occasioned much difference of opinion among commentators. Between two solids (he says) (that is, solid numbers, or numbers generated out of the product of three factors) no one mean proportional can be found. This is not universally true. The different suggestions of critics to clear up this difficulty will be found set forth in the elaborate note of M. Martin (Études sur le Timée, vol. 1. note xx. pp. 337-345`, who has given what seems a probable explanation. Plato (he supposes) is speaking only of prime numbers and their products. In the language of ancient arithmeticians *linear numbers, par excellence* or properly so-called, were the prime numbers, measurable by unity only ; *plane numbers* were the products of two such linear numbers or prime numbers ; *solid numbers* were the products of three such. Understanding solid numbers in this restricted sense, it will be perfectly true that between any two of them you can never find *any one* solid number or any whole number which shall be a mean proportional, but you can always find *two* solid numbers which shall be mean proportionals. One mean proportional will never be sufficient. On the contrary, one mean proportional will be sufficient between two plane numbers (in the restricted sense) when these numbers are squares, though not if they are not squares. It is therefore true, that in the case of two *solid* numbers (so understood) one such mean proportional will never be sufficient, while two can always be found ; and that between two *plane* numbers (so understood) one such mean proportional will in certain cases be sufficient and may be found. This is what is present to Plato's mind, though in enunciating it he does not declare the restriction under which alone it is true. M. Boeckh (Untersuchungen über das Kosmische System des Platon, p. 17) approves of Martin's explanation. At the same time M. Martin has given no proof that Plato had in his mind the distinction between prime numbers and other numbers, for his references in p. 338 do not prove this point ; moreover, the explanation assumes such very loose expression, that the phrase of M. Cousin in his note (p. 334) is, after all, perfectly just :—" Platon n'a pas songé à donner à sa phrase une rigueur mathématique :" and the more simple explanation of M. Cousin (though Martin rejects it as unworthy) may perhaps include all that is really intended. "Si deux surfaces peuvent être unies par un seul terme intermédiaire, il faudra deux termes intermédiaires pour unir deux solides : et l'union sera encore plus parfaite si la raison des deux proportions est la même."

hurt the Kosmos from without, nor anything as raw material for a second Kosmos.[b]

The Kosmos was constructed as a perfect sphere, rounded, because that figure both comprehends all other figures, and is, at the same time, the most perfect, and most like to itself.[c] The Demiurgus made it perfectly smooth on the outside, for various reasons.[d] First, it stood in no need of either eyes or ears, because there was nothing outside to be seen or heard. Next, it did not want organs of respiration, inasmuch as there was no outside air to be breathed :—nor nutritive and excrementory organs, because its own decay supplied it with nourishment, so that it was self-sufficing, being constructed as its own agent and its own patient.[e] Moreover the Demiurgus did not furnish it with hands, because there was nothing for it either to grasp or repel—nor with legs, feet, or means of standing, because he assigned to it only one of the seven possible varieties of movement.[f] He gave to it no other movement except that of rotation in a circle, in one and the same place : which is the sort of movement that belongs most to reason and intelligence, while it is impracticable to all other figures except the spherical.[g]

The Kosmos, one and only-begotten, was thus perfect as to

(margin note: Body of the Kosmos, perfectly spherical—its rotations.)

---

[b] Plat. Timæ. p. 32 E.

[c] Plato, Timæus, p. 33 B. κυκλοτερὲς αὐτὸ ἐτορνεύσατο, &c.

[d] Plato, Timæus, p. 33 D. λεῖον δὲ δὴ κύκλῳ πᾶν ἔξωθεν αὐτὸ ἀπηκριβοῦτο, πολλῶν χάριν, &c.
Aristotle also maintains that the sphericity of the Kosmos is so exact that no piece of workmanship can make approach to it, De Cœlo, ii. p. 287, b. 15.

[e] Plato, Timæus, p. 33 E. On this point the Platonic Timæus is not Pythagorean, but the reverse. The Pythagoreans recognised extraneous to the Kosmos, τὸ ἄπειρον πνεῦμα or τὸ κενόν. The Kosmos was supposed to inhale this vacuum, which penetrating into the interior, formed the separating interstices between its constituent parts (Aristotel. Physic. iv. p. 213, b. 22).

[f] Plato, Timæus, p. 34 A. ἐπὶ δὲ τὴν περίοδον ταύτην, ἅτ᾽ οὐδὲν ποδῶν δέον, ἀσκελὲς καὶ ἄπουν αὐτὸ ἐγέννησεν.
Plato reckons six varieties of rectilinear motion, neither of which was assigned to the Kosmos — forward, backward, upward, downward, to the right, to the left.

[g] Plat. Tim. p. 34 A. κίνησιν γὰρ ἀπένειμεν αὐτῷ τὴν τοῦ σώματος οἰκείαν, τῶν ἑπτα τὴν περὶ νοῦν καὶ φρόνησιν μάλιστα οὖσαν. This predicate respecting circular motion belongs to Plato and not to Aristotle ; but Aristotle makes out, in his own way, a strong case to show that circular motion must belong to the Πρῶτον σῶμα, as being the first among all varieties of motion, the most dignified and privileged, the only one which can be for ever uniform and continuous, Aristot. Physic. ix. p. 265, a. 15 ; De Cœlo, i. pp. 269-270, ii. p. 284, a. 10.

its body, including all existent bodily material,—smooth, even,
round, and equidistant from its centre to all points
of the circumference.[h] The Demiurgus put together at the same time its soul or mind; which he
planted in the centre and stretched throughout its
body in every direction,—so as not only to reach the
circumference, but also to enclose and wrap it round externally. The soul, being intended to guide and govern the
body, was formed of appropriate ingredients, three distinct
ingredients mixed together: 1. The Same—The Identical—
The indivisible, and unchangeable essence of Ideas. 2. The
Different—The Plural—The divisible essence of bodies or of
the elements. 3. A third compound, formed of both these
ingredients melted into one.—These three ingredients—
Same, Different, Same and Different in one,—were blended
together in one compound, to form the soul of the Kosmos:
though the Different was found intractable and hard to conciliate.[i] The mixture was divided, and the portions blended
together, according to a scale of harmonic numerical proportion complicated and difficult to follow.[k] The soul of the
Kosmos was thus harmonically constituted. Among its constituent elements, the Same, or Identity, is placed in an even
and undivided rotation of the outer or sidereal sphere of the
Kosmos,—while the Different, or Diversity, is distributed
among the rotations, all oblique, of the seven interior or planetary spheres—that is, the five planets, Sun, and Moon.
The outer sphere revolved towards the right: the interior
spheres in an opposite direction towards the left. The rotatory

[h] Plat. Tim. p. 31 A. εἷς ὅδε μονογενὴς οὐρανος, &c.
[i] Plat. Tim. p. 35 A. Ταὐτὸν—τὸ
ἀμέριστον — θάτερον — τὸ μεριστὸν —
τρίτον ἐξ ἀμφοῖν οὐσίας εἶδος.
[k] Plato, Timæus, pp. 35-36. The
pains which were taken by commentators in antiquity to expound and
interpret this numerical scale may be
seen especially illustrated in Plutarch's
Treatise, De Animæ Procreatione in
Timæo, pp. 1012-1030, and the Epitome which follows it. There were
two fundamental τετρακτύες or qua-
ternions, one on a binary, the other on
a ternary scale of progression, which

were arranged by Krantor (Plutarch,
p. 1027 E) in the form of the letter Λ,
as given in Macrobius (Somn. Scip.
i. 6, p. 35). The in-
tervals between these
figures are described by
Plato as filled up by in-
tervening harmonic fractions, so as to
constitute an harmonic or musical
diagram or scale of four octaves and a
major sixth, Boeckh's Untersuch. p. 19.
M. Boeckh has expounded this at
length in his Dissert. Ueber die Bildung
der Welt-Seele im Timäos. Other expositors after him.

force of the Same (of the outer Sphere) being not only one and
undivided, but connected with and dependant upon the solid
revolving axis which traverses the diameter of the Kosmos—
is far greater than that of the divided spheres of the Different;
which, while striving to revolve in an opposite direction,
each by a movement of its own—are overpowered and carried
along with the outer sphere, though the time of revolution,
in the case of each, is more or less modified by its own inherent counter-moving force.[1]

In regard to the constitution of the kosmical soul, we must
note, that as it is intended to know Same, Different, and
Same and Different in one—so it must embody these three
ingredients in its own nature: according to the received
axiom. Like knows like—Like is known by like.[m]　Thus
began, never to end, the rotatory movements of the living
Kosmos or great kosmical God.　The invisible soul of the
Kosmos, rooted at its centre and stretching from thence so
as to pervade and enclose its visible body, circulates and
communicates, though without voice or sound, throughout its
own entire range, every impression of identity and of difference which it encounters either from essence ideal and indivisible, or from that which is sensible and divisible.　Information is thus circulated, about the existing relations between
all the separate parts and specialties.[n]　Reason and Science
are propagated by the Circle of the The Same: Sense and
Opinion, by those of the Different.　When these last-mentioned Circles are in right movement, the opinions circulated
are true and trustworthy.

---

[1] Plato, Timæus, p. 36 C. τὴν μὲν
οὖν ἔξω φορὰν ἐπεφήμισεν εἶναι τῆς
ταὐτοῦ φύσεως, τὴν δ' ἐντὸς, τῆς
θατέρου. τὴν μὲν δὴ ταὐτοῦ κατὰ
πλευρὰν ἐπὶ δέξια περιήγαγε, τὴν δὲ
θατέρου κατὰ διάμετρον ἐπ' ἀρίστερα.

For the meaning of κατὰ πλευρὰν
and κατὰ διάμετρον, referring to the
equator and the ecliptic, see the explanation and diagram in Boeckh,
Untersuchungen, p. 25, also in the
note of Stallbaum.　The allusion in
Plato to the letter χῖ is hardly intelligible without both a commentary
and a diagram.

[m] Aristotel. De Animâ, i. 2, 7, i. 3,

11, (pp. 404, b. 16-406 b. 26) with
Trendelenburg's note, pp. 227-253;
Stallbaum, not. ad Timæum, pp. 136-
157. See also the interpretation of
Plato's opinion by Krantor, as given
in Plutarch, De Animæ Procreatione
in Timæo, p. 1012 E. We learn from
Plutarch, however, that the passage
gave much trouble to commentators.

[n] Plato, Timæus, pp. 36-37. λέγει
κινουμένη διὰ πάσης ἑαυτῆς, ὅτῳ τ' ἄν
τι ταὐτὸν ᾖ, καὶ ὅτου ἂν ἕτερον, πρὸς
ὅ, τι τε μάλιστα καὶ ὅπῃ καὶ ὅπως καὶ
ὅποτε ξυμβαίνει κατὰ τὰ γιγνόμενά τε
πρὸς ἕκαστον ἕκαστα εἶναι καὶ πάσχειν,
καὶ πρὸς τὰ κατὰ ταὐτὰ ἔχοντα ἀεί.

With the rotations of the Kosmos, began the course of
Regular or
measured
Time—began
with the
Kosmos. Time—years, months, days, &c. Anterior to the
Kosmos, there was no time : no past, present, and
future: no numerable or mensurable motion or
change. The Ideas are eternal essences, without fluctuation
or change : existing *sub specie æternitatis*, and having only a
perpetual present, but no past or future.[o] Along with them
subsisted only the disorderly, immeasurable, movements of
Chaos. The nearest approach which the Demiurgus could
make in copying these Ideas, was, by assigning to the Kosmos
an eternal and unchanging motion, marked and measured
by the varying position of the heavenly bodies. For this
purpose, the sun, moon, and planets, were distributed among
the various portions of the circle of Different: while the fixed
stars were placed in the Circle of the Same, or the outer
Circle, revolving in one uniform rotation and in unaltered
position in regard to each other. The interval of one day
was marked by one revolution of this outer or most rational
Circle:[p] that of one month, by a revolution of the moon: that
of one year, by a revolution of the sun. Among all these
sidereal and planetary Gods the Earth was the first and oldest.
It was packed close round the great axis which traversed the

[o] Plato, Timæus, pp. 37-38. Lassalle, in his copious and elaborate explanation of the doctrine of Herakleitus (Die Philosophie Herakleitos des Dunkeln, Berlin, 1858, vol. ii. p. 210, s. 26), represents this doctrine of Plato respecting Time as " durch und durch heraklitisch." To me it seems quite distinct from, or rather the inversion of, that which Lassalle himself sets down as the doctrine of Herakleitus. Plato begins with τὸ ἀΐδιον or αἰώνιον, an eternal sameness or duration, without succession, change, generation, or destruction,—this passes into perpetual succession or change, with frequent generation and destruction. Herakleitus, on the other hand, recognises for his primary or general law perpetual succession, interchange of contraries, generation and destruction ; this passes into a secondary state, in which there is temporary duration and sameness of particulars— the flux being interrupted.

The ideal λόγος or law of Herakleitus is that of unremitting process, flux, revolution, implication of Ens with Non-Ens : the real world is an imperfect manifestation of this law, because each particular clings to existence, and thereby causes temporary halts in the process. Now Plato's starting point is τὸ αἰώνιον τὸ ἀεὶ ὡσαύτως ἔχον τὸ ὄντως ὄν: the perishable world of sense and particulars is the world of process, and is so far degenerate from the eternal uniformity of primordial Ens. See Lassalle, pp. 39-292-319.

[p] Plato, Timæus, p. 39 B. ἡ τῆς μιᾶς καὶ φρονιμωτάτης κυκλήσεως περίοδος. Plato remarks that there was a particular interval of time measured off and designated by the revolution of each of the other planets, but that these intervals were unnoticed and unknown by the greater part of mankind.

centre of the Kosmos, by the turning of which axis the outer circle of the Kosmos was made to revolve, generating night and day. The Earth regulated the movement of this great kosmical axis, and thus became the determining agent and guarantee of night and day.[q]

It remained for the Demiurgus,—in order that the Kosmos might become a full copy of its model the Generic Animal or Idea of Animal,—to introduce into it those various species of animals which that Idea contained. He first peopled it with Gods: the eldest and earliest of whom was the Earth, planted in the centre as sentinel over night and day: next the fixed stars, formed for the most part of fire, and annexed to the circle of the Same or the exterior circle, so as to impart to it light and brilliancy. Each star was of spherical figure and had two motions,—one, of uniform rotation peculiar to itself,—the other, an uniform forward movement of translation, being carried along with the great outer circle in its general rotation round the axis of the Kosmos.[r] It is thus that the sidereal orbs, animated beings eternal and divine, remained constantly turning round in the same relative position: while the sun, moon, and planets, belonging to the inner circles of the Different, and trying to revolve by their own effort in the opposite direction to the outer sphere, be-

Divine tenants of the Kosmos. Primary and Visible Gods—Stars and Heavenly Bodies.

[q] My explanation of this much controverted sentence differs from that of previous commentators. I have given reasons for adopting it in a separate Dissertation ('Plato and the Rotation of the Earth,' Murray), to which I here refer. In that Dissertation I endeavoured to show cause for dissenting from the inference of M. Boeckh; who contends that Plato cannot have believed in the diurnal rotation of the Earth, because he (Plato) explicitly affirms the diurnal rotation of the outer celestial sphere, or Aplanes. These two facts nullify each other, so that the effect would be the same as if there were no rotation of either. My reply to this argument was, in substance, that though the two facts really are inconsistent—the one excluding the other—yet we cannot safely conclude that Plato must have perceived the inconsistency; the more so as Aristotle certainly did not perceive it. To hold incompatible doctrines without being aware of the incompatibility, is a state of mind sufficiently common even in the present advanced condition of science, which I could illustrate by many curious examples if my space allowed. It must have been much more common in the age of Plato than it is now.

Batteux observes (Traduction et Remarques sur Ocellus Lucanus, ch. iv. p. 116):—"Il y a un maxime qu'on ne doit jamais perdre de vue en discutant les opinions des Anciens: c'est de ne point leur prêter les conséquences de leurs principes, ni les principes de leurs conséquences."

As a general rule, I perfectly subscribe to the soundness of this admonition.

[r] Plato, Timæus, p. 40.

came irregular in their own velocities and variable in their relative positions.[s] The complicated movements of these planetary bodies, alternately approaching and receding— together with their occultations and reappearances, full of alarming prognostic as to consequences—cannot be described without having at hand some diagrams or mechanical illustrations to refer to.[t]

Such were all the primitive Gods visible and generated[u] by the Demiurgus, to preside over and regulate the Kosmos. By them are generated, and from them are descended, the remaining Gods.

Secondary and generated Gods— Plato's dictum respecting them. His acquiescence in tradition.

Respecting these remaining Gods, however, Plato holds a different language. Instead of speaking in his own name and delivering his own convictions, as he had done about the Demiurgus and the kosmical Gods—with the simple reservation, that such convictions could be proclaimed only as probable and not as demonstratively certain—he now descends to the Sokratic platform of confessed ignorance and incapacity. "The generation of these remaining Gods" (he says) "is a matter too great for me to understand and declare. I must trust to those who have spoken upon the subject before me—who were, as they themselves said, offspring of the Gods, and must therefore have well known their own fathers. It is impossible to mistrust the sons of the Gods. Their statements indeed are unsupported either by probabilities or by necessary demonstration; but since they here profess to be declaring family traditions, we must obey the law and believe.[x] Thus then let it stand and be proclaimed, upon

---

[s] Plato, Timæus, p. 40 C. ὃσ' ἀπλανῆ τῶν ἄστρων ζῶα θεῖα ὄντα καὶ ἀΐδια, &c.

[t] Plato, Timæus, p. 40 D. τὸ λέγειν ἄνευ διόψεως τούτων αὖ τῶν μιμημάτων, μάταιος ἂν εἴη πόνος. Plato himself here acknowledges the necessity of diagrams: the necessity was hardly less in the preceding part of his exposition.

[u] Plato, Timæ. p. 40 D. θεῶν ὁρατῶν καὶ γεννητῶν.

[x] Plato, Timæus, pp. 40-41. Περὶ δὲ τῶν ἄλλων δαιμόνων εἰπεῖν καὶ γνῶναι τὴν γένεσιν μεῖζον ἢ καθ' ἡμᾶς, πειστέον δὲ τοῖς εἰρηκόσιν ἔμπροσθεν, ἐκγόνοις μὲν θεῶν οὖσιν, σαφῶς δέ που

τούς γε αὐτῶν προγόνους εἰδόσιν· ἀδύνατον οὖν θεῶν παισὶν ἀπιστεῖν, καίπερ ἄνευ τε εἰκότων καὶ ἀναγκαίων ἀποδείξεων λέγουσιν, ἀλλ' ὡς οἰκεῖα φάσκουσιν ἀπαγγέλλειν, ἑπομένους τῷ νόμῳ πιστευτέον. Οὕτως οὖν κατ' ἐκείνους ἡμῖν ἡ γένεσις περὶ τούτων τῶν θεῶν ἐχέτω καὶ λεγέσθω.

So, too, in the Platonic Epinomis, attached as an appendix to the Treatise De Legibus, we find (p. 984) Plato—after arranging his quintuple scale of elemental animals (fire, æther, air, water, earth), the highest and most divine, being the stars or visible Gods,

their authority, respecting the generation of the remaining
Gods. The offspring of Uranus and Gæa were, Okeanus and
Tethys: from whom sprang Phorkys, Kronus, Rhea, and
those along with them. Kronus and Rhea had for offspring
Zeus, Hêrê, and all those who are termed their brethren:
from whom too, besides, we hear of other offspring. Thus
were generated all the Gods, both those who always conspicuously revolve, and those who show themselves only when
they please." [y]

The passage above cited serves to illustrate both Plato's
own canon of belief, and his position in regard to his countrymen. The question here is, about the
Gods of tradition and of the popular faith : with the paternity
and filiation ascribed to them, by Hesiod and the other poets,
from whom Greeks of the fifth and fourth centuries B.C.
learnt their Theogony.[z] Plato was a man both competent
and willing to strike out a physical theology of his own, but
not to follow passively in the track of orthodox tradition.
I have stated briefly what he has affirmed about the kosmical
Gods (Earth, Stars, Sun, Planets) generated or constructed
by the Demiurgus as portions or members of the Kosmos:
their bodies, out of fire and other elements,—their souls out
of the Forms or abstractions called Identity and Diversity;
while the entire Kosmos is put together after the model of
the Generic Idea or Form of Animal. All this, combined
with supposed purposes, and fancies of arithmetical proportion dictating the proceedings of the Demiurgus, Plato

Remarks on Plato's Canon of Belief.

the lowest being man, and the three
others intermediate between the two;
after having thus laid out the scale,
he leaves to others to determine,
ὅπῃ τις ἐθέλει, in which place Zeus,
Hêrê, and the other Gods, are to be
considered as lodged. He will not
contradict any one's feeling on that
point; he strongly protests (p. 985 D)
against all attempts on the part of the
lawgiver to innovate (καινοτομεῖν) in
contravention of ancient religious tradition (This is what Aristophanes in
the Nubes, and Melêtus before the
Dikasts, accuse Sokrates of doing.),
but he denounces harshly all who will
not acknowledge with worship and
sacrifice the sublime divinity of the

Sun, Moon, Stars, and Planets.
The Platonic declaration given here
—ἐπομένους τῷ νόμῳ πιστευτέον—is
illustrated in the lines of Euripides,
Bacchæ, 202,—

οὐδὲν σοφιζόμεσθα τοῖσι δαίμοσιν·
πατρίους παραδοχάς, ἅς θ' ὁμήλικας
χρόνῳ
κεκτήμεθ', οὐδεὶς αὐτὰ καταβαλεῖ λόγος,
οὐδ' ἢν δι' ἄκρων τὸ σοφὸν εὕρηται
φρενῶν.

[y] Plato, Timæ. p. 41 A. ἐπεὶ δ'
οὖν πάντες ὅσοι τε περιπολοῦσι φανερῶς,
καὶ ὅσοι φαίνονται καθ' ὅσον ἂν ἐθέλωσι,
θεοὶ γένεσιν ἔσχον.
[z] Herodot. ii. 53.

does not hesitate to proclaim on his own authority and as his own belief—though he does not carry it farther than probability.

But while the feeling of spontaneous belief thus readily arises in Plato's mind, following in the wake of his own constructive imagination and ethical or æsthetical sentiment (*fingunt simul creduntque*)—it does not so readily cleave to the theological dogmas in actual circulation around him. In the generation of Gods from Uranus and Gæa—which he as well as other Athenian youths must have learnt when they recited Hesiod with their schoolmasters—he can see neither proof nor probability : he can find no internal ground for belief.[a] He declares himself incompetent : he will not undertake to affirm any thing upon his own judgment : the mystery is too dark for him to penetrate. Yet on the other hand, though it would be rash to affirm, it would be equally rash to deny. Nearly all around him are believers, at least as well satisfied with their creed as he was with the uncertified affirmations of his own Timæus. He cannot prove them to be wrong, except by appealing to an ethical or æsthetical sentiment which they do not share. Among the Gods said to be descended from Uranus and Gæa, were all those to whom public worship was paid in Greece,—to whom the genealogies of the heroic and sacred families were traced,— and by whom cities as well as individuals believed themselves to be protected in dangers, healed in epidemics, and enlightened on critical emergencies through seasonable revelations and prophecies. Against an established creed thus avouched, it was dangerous to raise any doubts. Moreover Plato could not have forgotten the fate of his master Sokrates ;[b] who was indicted both for not acknowledging the Gods whom the city

---

[a] The remark made by Condorcet upon Buffon is strikingly applicable to Plato :—" On n'a reproché à M. de Buffon que ses hypothèses. Ce sont aussi des espèces de fables—mais des fables produites par une imagination active qui a besoin de créer, et non par une imagination passive qui cède à des impressions étrangeres " (Condorcet, Éloge de Buffon, ad fin.).

Αὐτοδίδακτός δ' εἰμι, θεὸς δέ μοι ἐν
   φρεσὶν οἴμας
Παντοίας ἐνέφυσεν—
            (Homer, Odyss. xxii. 347).—
the declaration of the bard Phemius.
[b] Xenoph. Memor. i. 1. Ἀδικεῖ
Σωκράτης, οὓς μὲν ἡ πόλις νομίζει
θεοὺς, οὐ νομίζων, ἕτερα δὲ καινὰ δαιμόνια εἰσφέρων.
   The word δαιμόνια may mean matters, or persons, or both together.

acknowledged, and for introducing other new divine matters
and persons.   There could be no doubt that Plato was guilty
on this latter count : prudence therefore rendered it the more
incumbent on him to guard against being implicated in the
former count also.   Here then Plato formally abnegates his
own self-judging power, and submits himself to orthodox authority.   " It is impossible to doubt what we have learnt from
witnesses, who declared themselves to be the offspring of the
Gods, and who must of course have known their own family
affairs.   We must obey the law and believe."   In what proportion such submission, of reason to authority, embodied the
sincere feeling of Pascal and Malebranche, or the irony of
Bayle and Voltaire, we are unable to determine.[c]

Having thus, during one short paragraph, proclaimed his
deference, if not his adhesion, to inspired traditions, *Address and
order of the
Demiurgus to
the generated
Gods.*
Plato again resumes the declaration of his own beliefs and his own book of Genesis, without any farther
appeal to authority, and without any intimation that he is
touching on mysteries too great for his reason.   When these
Gods, the visible as well as the invisible,[d] had all been constructed or generated, he (or Timæus) tells us that the
Demiurgus addressed them and informed them that they
would be of immortal duration—not indeed in their own
nature, but through his determination : that to complete the
perfection of the newly-begotten Kosmos, there were three
other distinct races of animals, all mortal, to be added : that
he could not himself undertake the construction of these three,
because they would thereby be rendered immortal, but that
he confided such construction to them (the Gods) : that he
would himself supply, for the best of these three new races, an
immortal element as guide and superintendant, and that they

---

[c] M. Martin supposes Plato to speak
ironically, or with a prudent reserve,
Études sur le Timée, ii. p. 146.

What Plato says here about the
Gods who bore personal names, and
were believed in by the contemporary
public—is substantially equivalent to
the well-known profession of ignorance
enunciated by the Sophist Protagoras,
introduced by him at the beginning of
one of his treatises.   Περὶ δὲ θεῶν
οὔτε εἰ εἰσιν, οὔθ᾽ ὁποῖοί τινές εἰσιν,
δύναμαι λέγειν· πολλὰ γάρ ἐστι τὰ
κωλύοντά με (Sextus Emp. adv.
Mathem. ix. 56) ; a declaration which,
circumspect as it was, (see the remark
of the sillographer Timon in Sextus),
drew upon him the displeasure of the
Athenians, so that his books were
burnt, and himself forced to leave the
city.

[d] Plato, Timæus, p. 41 A.

were to join along with it mortal and bodily accompaniments, to constitute men and animals; thus imitating the power which he had displayed in the generation of themselves.[e]

After this address (which Plato puts into the first person, in Homeric manner), the Demiurgus compounded to-gether, again and in the same bowl, the remnant of the same elements out of which he had formed the kosmical soul, but in perfection and purity greatly inferior. The total mass thus formed was distributed into souls equal in number to the stars. The Demiurgus placed each soul in a star of its own, carried it round thus in the kosmical rotation, and explained to it the destiny intended for all. For each alike there was to be an appointed hour of birth, and of conjunction with a body, as well as with two inferior sorts or varieties of soul or mind. From such conjunction would follow, as a necessary consequence, implanted sensibility and motive power, with all its accompaniments of pleasure, pain, desire, fear, anger, and such like. These were the irra-tional enemies, which the rational and immortal soul would have to controul and subdue, as a condition of just life. If it succeeded in the combat so as to live a good life, it would return after death to the abode of its own peculiar star. But if it failed, it would have a second birth into the inferior nature and body of a female : if, here also, it continued to be evil, it would be transferred after death to the body of some inferior animal. Such transmigration would be farther con-tinued from animal to animal, until the rational soul should acquire thorough controul over the irrational and turbulent. When this was attained, the rational soul would be allowed to return to its original privilege and happiness, residing in its own peculiar star.[f]

Preparations for the construction of man. Conjunction of three souls and one body.

It was thus that the Demiurgus confided to the recently-generated Gods the task of fabricating both mortal bodies, and mortal souls, to be joined with these immortal souls in their new stage of existence—and of guiding and governing the new mortal animal in the best manner, unless in so far as the

---

[e] Plato, Timæus, p. 41 C. τρέπεσθε κατὰ φύσιν ὑμεῖς ἐπὶ τὴν τῶν ζώων δημιουργίαν, μιμούμενοι τὴν ἐμὴν δύνα- μιν περὶ τὴν ὑμετέραν γένεσιν.

[f] Plato, Timæus, p. 42 B-D.

latter should be the cause of mischief to himself. The Demiurgus decreed and proclaimed this beforehand, in order (says Plato) that he might not himself be the cause of any of the evil which might ensue[g] to individual men.

Accordingly the Gods, sons of the Demiurgus, entered upon the task, trying to imitate their father. Borrowing from the Kosmos portions of the four elements, with engagement that what was borrowed should one day

Proceedings of the generated Gods—they fabricate the cranium, as miniature

[g] Plato, Timæus, p. 42 D-E. Διαθεσμοθετήσας δὲ πάντα αὐτοῖς ταῦτα, ἵνα τῆς ἔπειτα εἴη κακίας ἀναίτιος,—παρέδωκε θεοῖς σώματα πλάττειν θνητὰ, τό τε ἐπίλοιπον ὅσον ἔτ᾽ ἦν ψυχῆς ἀνθρωπίνης δέον προσγενέσθαι, τοῦτο καὶ πάνθ᾽ ὅσα ἀκόλουθα ἐκείνοις ἀπεργασαμένους ἄρχειν, καὶ κατὰ δύναμιν ὅ,τι κάλλιστα καὶ ἄριστα τὸ θνητὸν διακυβερνᾶν ζῶον, ὅ,τι μὴ κακῶν αὐτὸ ἑαυτῷ γίγνοιτο αἴτιον.

We have here the theory, intimated but not expanded by Plato, that man is, by misconduct or folly, the cause of all the evil suffered on earth. That the Gods are not the cause of any evil, he tells us in Republ. ii. p. 379. It seems, however, that he did not remain satisfied with the theory of the Timæus, because we find a different theory in the treatise De Legibus (x. p. 896 E)—two kosmical souls, one good, the other evil.

Moreover, the recital of the Timæus itself (besides another express passage in it, pp. 86 D-87 A) plainly contradicts the theory, that man is the cause of his own sufferings and evil. The Demiurgus himself is described as the cause, by directing immortal souls to be joined with mortal bodies. The Demiurgus had constructed a beautiful Kosmos, with perfect and regular rotations—with the Gods, sidereal, planetary, and invisible—and with immortal souls distributed throughout the stars and earth, understanding and appreciating the cosmical rotations. So far all is admirable and faultless. But he is not satisfied with this. He determines to join each of these immortal souls with two mortal souls and with a mortal body. According to Plato's own showing, the immortal soul incurs nothing but corruption, disturbance, and stupidity, by such junction: as Empedokles and Herakleitus had said before, Plutarch, Solert.

Animal. 7, p. 964 E. It is at first deprived of all intelligence (ἄνους) from this stupefaction it gradually but partially recovers; yet nothing short of the best possible education and discipline will enable it to contend, and even then imperfectly, against the corruption and incumbrance arising out of its companion the body; lastly, if it should contend with every success, the only recompense which awaits it is to be re-transferred to the star from whence it came down. What reason was there for removing the immortal soul from its happy and privileged position, to be degraded by forced companionship with an unworthy body and two inferior souls? The reason assigned is, that the Demiurgus required the Kosmos to be enlarged into a full and exact copy of the Αὐτόζωον or Generic Animal, which comprehended four subordinate varieties of animals; one of them good (the Gods)—the other three inferior and corrupt, Men, Birds, Fishes. But here, according to Plato's own exposition, it was the Demiurgus himself and his plan that was at fault. What necessity was there to copy the worst parts of the Generic Animal as well as the best? The Kosmos would have been decidedly better, though it might have been less complete, without such unenviable accompaniments. When Plato constructs his own community, (Republic and Legg.) he does not knowingly train up defective persons, or prepare the foundation for such, in order that every variety of character may be included. We may add here, that according to Plato himself, Νοῦς (intelligence or reason) belongs not to all human beings, but only to a small fraction of them (Timæus, p. 51 E). Except in these few, the immortal soul is therefore irrecoverably debased by its union with the body.

of the Kos-
mos, with the
rational soul
rotating
within it. be paid back, they glued them together, and fastened them by numerous minute invisible pegs into one body. Into this body, always decaying and requiring renovation, they introduced the immortal soul, with its double circular rotations—the Circles of the Same and of the Diverse: embodying it in the cranium, which was made spherical in exterior form like the Kosmos, and admitting within it no other motion but the rotatory. The head, the most divine portion of the human system, was made master; while the body was admitted only as subject and ministerial. The body was endowed with all the six varieties of motive power, forward, backwards—upward, downward—to the right, to the left.[h] The phenomena of nutrition and sensation began. But all these irregular movements, and violent multifarious agitations, checked or disturbed the regular rotations of the immortal soul in the cranium, perverting the arithmetical proportion, and harmony belonging to them. The rotations of the Circles of Same and Diverse were made to convey false and foolish affirmation. The soul became utterly destitute of intelligence, on being first joined to the body, and for some time afterwards.[i] But in the course of time the violence of these disturbing currents abates, so that the rotations of the Circles in the head can take place with more quiet and regularity. The man then becomes more and more intelligent. If subjected to good education and discipline, he will be made gradually sound and whole, free from corruption: but if he neglect this precaution, his life remains a lame one, and he returns back to Hades incomplete and unprofitable.[k]

The Gods, when they undertook the fabrication of the body, The cranium is mounted on a tall body—six varieties of motion—organs of sense. Vision—Light. foresaw the inconvenience of allowing the head—with its intelligent rotations, and with the immortal soul enclosed in it—to roll along the ground, unable to get over a height, or out of a hollow.[l] Accordingly they mounted it upon a tall body; with arms and

[h] Plato, Timæus, pp. 43 B, 44 D.
Plato supposes an etymological connection between αἰσθήσεις and ἀΐσσω, p. 43 C.
[i] Plato, Timæus, p. 44 B. καὶ διὰ δὴ πάντα ταῦτα τὰ παθήματα, κατ' ἀρχάς τε ἄνους ψυχὴ γίγνεται τὸ πρῶ-

τον, ὅταν εἰς σῶμα ἐνδεθῇ θνητόν.
[k] Plato, Timæus, p. 44 C.
[l] Plato, Timæus, p. 44 E. ἵν' οὖν μὴ κυλινδούμενον ἐπὶ γῆς, ὕψη τε καὶ βάθη παντοδαπὰ ἐχούσης, ἀποροῖ τὰ μὲν ὑπερβαίνειν, ἔνθεν δὲ ἐκβαίνειν, ὄχημ' αὐτῷ τοῦτο καὶ εὐπορίαν ἔδοσαν.

legs as instruments of movement, support, and defence.   They caused the movements to be generally directed forward and not backward; since front is more honourable and more commanding than rear.   For the same reason, they placed the face, with the organs of sense, in the fore part of the head. Within the eyes, they planted that variety of fire which does not burn, but is called light, homogeneous with the light without.   We are enabled to see in the daytime, because the light within our eyes pours out through the centre of them, and commingles with the light without.   The two, being thus confounded together, transmit movements from every object which they touch, through the eye inward to the soul; and thus bring about the sensation of sight.   At night no vision takes place: because the light from the interior of our eyes, even when it still comes out, finds no cognate light in the air without, and thus becomes extinguished in the darkness.   All the light within the eye would thus have been lost, if the Gods had not provided a protection: they contrived the eyelids which drop and shut up the interior light within.   This light being prevented from egress, diffuses itself throughout the interior system, and tranquillises the movements within so as to bring on sleep: without dreams, if all the movements are quenched—with dreams, corresponding to the movements which remain, if there are any such.[m]

Such are the auxiliary causes (continues Plato), often mis-

---

[m] Plato, Timæus, p. 45. The theory of vision here given by Plato is interesting.   A theory, similar in the main, had been propounded by Empedoklês before him.   Aristotel. De Sensu, p. 437 b.; Theophrast. De Sensu, cap. 5-9, p. 88 of Philipson's Ὕλη Ἀνθρωπίνη.   Aristotle himself impugns the theory.   It is reported and discussed in Galen, De Hippocratis et Platonis Dogmat. vii. 5, 6, p. 619 seqq. ed Kühn.

The different theories of vision among the ancient philosophers anterior to Aristotle are thus enumerated by E. H. von Baumhauer (De Sententiis Veterum Philosophorum Græcorum de Visu, Lumine, et Coloribus, Utrecht, 1843, p. 137):—"De videndi modo tres apud antiquos primarias theorias invenimus: et primam quidem, emanatione lucis ex oculis ad corpora externa,

ejusque reflexu ad oculos (Pythagorei, Alcmæon): alteram emanationibus e corporibus, quæ per oculos veluti per canales ad animum penetrent (Eleatici, Heraclitus, Gorgias): quam sententiam Anaxagoras et Diogenes Apolloniates eatenus mutarunt, quod dicerent pupillam quasi speculum esse quod imagines acceptas ad animum rejiciat.   Tertia theoria, orta è conjunctione duarum priorum, statuebat tam ex oculis quam è corporibus emanationes fieri, et ambarum illarum concursu visum effici, quum conformata imago per meatus ad animum perveniat (Empedocles, Protagoras, Plato).   Huic sententiæ etiam Democritus annumerari potest; qui eam planè secundum materiam, ut dicunt, exposuit."

The theory of Plato is described in the same treatise, pp. 106-112.

taken by others for principal causes, which the Gods employed
Principal advantages of sight and hearing. Observations of the rotation of the Kosmos. to bring about sight. In themselves, they have no
regularity of action : for nothing can be regular in
action without mind and intelligence.[n] But the
most important among all the advantages of sight is,
that it enables us to observe and study the rotations
of the Kosmos and of the sidereal and planetary bodies. It
is the observed rotations of days, months, and years, which
impart to us the ideas of time and number, and enable us to
investigate the universe. Hence we derive philosophy, the
greatest of all blessings. Hence too we learn to apply the
celestial rotations as a rule and model to amend the rotations
of intelligence in our own cranium—since the first are regular
and unerring, while the second are disorderly and changeful.[o]
It was for the like purpose, in view to the promotion of philosophy, that the Gods gave us voice and hearing. Both discourse and musical harmony are essential for this purpose.
Harmony and rhythm are presents to us, from the Muses, not,
as men now employ them, for unreflecting pleasure and recreation—but for the same purpose of regulating and attuning
the disorderly rotations of the soul, and of correcting the ungraceful and unmeasured movements natural to the body.[p]

At this point of the exposition, the Platonic Timæus breaks
The Kosmos is product of joint action of Reason and Necessity. The four visible and tangible elements are not primitive. off the thread, and takes up a new commencement.
Thus far (he says) we have proceeded in explaining
the part of Reason or Intelligence in the fabrication
of the Kosmos. We must now explain the part of
Necessity: for the genesis of the Kosmos results
from co-operation of the two. By Necessity (as has
been said before) Plato means random, indeterminate, chaotic,
pre-existent, spontaneity of movement or force: spontaneity
(ἡ πλανωμένη αἰτία) upon which Reason works by persuasion
up to a certain point, prevailing upon it to submit to some
degree of fixity and regularity.[q] Timæus had described the
body of the Kosmos as being constructed by the Demiurgus

---

[n] Plato, Timæus, p. 46 D-E.
[o] Plato, Timæus, pp. 47 B-C, 90 C.
[p] Plato, Timæus, p. 47 D. ἡ δε
ἁρμονία—ξύμμαχος ὑπὸ Μουσῶν δέδοται
—καὶ ῥυθμὸς αὖ—ὑπὸ τῶν αὐτῶν ἐδόθη.

Here we see Plato, in the usual Hellenic vein, particularising the functions and attributes of the different
Gods and Goddesses.
[q] Plato, Timæus, p. 48 A.

out of the four elements: thus assuming fire, air, earth, water, as pre-existent. But he now corrects himself, and tells us that such assumption is unwarranted. We must (he remarks) give a better and fuller explanation of the Kosmos. No one of these four elements is either primordial, or permanently distinct and definite in itself.

The only primordial reality is, an indeterminate, all-recipient *fundamentum*: having no form or determination of its own, but capable of receiving any form or determination from without.

In the second explanation now given by Plato of the Kosmos and its genesis, he assumes this invisible *fundamentum* (which he had not assumed before) as " the mother or nurse of all generation." He assumes, besides, the eternal Forms or Ideas, to act upon it and to bestow determination or quality. These Forms fulfil the office of father: the offspring of the two is—the generated, concrete, visible, objects,[r] imitations of the Forms or Ideas, begotten out of this mother. How the Ideas act upon the Materia Prima, Plato cannot well explain: but each Form stamps an imitation or copy of itself upon portions of the common *Fundamentum*.[s]

Forms or Ideas and Materia Prima—Forms of the Elements—Place, or Receptivity.

But do there really exist any such Forms or Ideas—as Fire *per se*, the Generic Fire—Water *per se*, the Generic Water, invisible and intangible?[t] Or is this mere unfounded speech? Does there exist nothing really anywhere, beyond the visible objects which we see and touch?[u]

We must assume (says Plato, after a certain brief argument which he himself does not regard as quite complete) the Forms or Ideas of Fire, Air, Water, Earth, as distinct and self-existent, eternal, indestructible, unchangeable—neither visible nor tan-

[r] Plato, Timæus, p. 51 A. τὴν τοῦ γεγονότος ὁρατοῦ καὶ πάντως αἰσθητοῦ μητέρα καὶ ὑποδοχήν.

[s] Plato, Timæus, pp. 50-51. τυπωθέντα ἀπ' αὐτῶν τρόπον τινὰ δύσφραστον καὶ θαυμαστόν. P. 51 A. ἀνόρατον εἶδός τι καὶ ἄμορφον. πανδεχὲς, μεταλαμβανον δὲ ἀπορώτατά πη τοῦ νοητοῦ καὶ δυσαλωτότατον.

[t] Plato, Timæus, p. 51 C.

[u] Ueberweg, in a learned Dissertation, Ueber die Platonische Weltseele (pp. 52-53), seeks to establish a greater distinction between the Phædrus, Phædon, and Timæus, in respect to the way in which Plato affirms the separate substantiality of Ideas, than the language of the dialogues warrants. He contends that the separate substantiality of the Platonic Ideas is more peremptorily affirmed in the Timæus than in the Phædrus. But this will not be found borne out if we look at Phædrus, p. 247, where the

gible, but apprehended by Reason or Intellect alone—neither
receiving anything else from without, nor themselves moving
to anything else. Distinct from these—images of these, and
bearing the same name—are the sensible objects called Fire,
Water, &c.—objects of sense and opinion—always in a state
of transition—generated and destroyed, but always generated
in some place and destroyed out of some place. There is to
be assumed, besides, distinct from the two preceding—as a
third *fundamentum*—the place or receptacle in which these
images are localised, generated, and nursed up. This Place,
or formless primitive receptivity, is indestructible, but out of
all reach of sense, and difficult to believe in, inasmuch as it
is only accessible by a spurious sort of ratiocination.[x]

Anterior to the construction of the Kosmos, the Forms or

Primordial
Chaos—
Effect of
intervention
by the De-
miurgus.

Ideas of the four elements had already begun to act
upon this primitive recipient or receptacle, but in a
confused and irregular way. Neither of the four could
impress itself in a special and definite manner: there
were some vestiges of each, but each was incomplete: all were
in stir and agitation, yet without any measure or fixed rule.
Thick and heavy, however, were tending to separate from thin
and light, and each particle thus tending to occupy a place of
its own.[y] In this condition (the primordial moving chaos of the
poets and earlier philosophers), things were found by the Demiurgus, when he undertook to construct the Kosmos. There was
no ready-made Fire, Water, &c. (as Plato had assumed at the
opening of the Timæus), but an agitated *imbroglio* of all, with
the portions tending to separate from each other, and to ag-

---

affirmation is quite as peremptory as
that in the Timæus; correlating too,
as it does in the Timæus, with Νοῦς
as the contemplating subject. Indeed
the point may be said to be affirmed
more positively in the Phædrus, because the ὑπερουράνιος τόπος is assigned to the Ideas, while in the
Timæus all τόπος or local existence is
denied to them (p. 52 B-C). Sensible
objects are presented in the Phædrus
as faint resemblances of the archetypal
Ideas (p. 250 C), just as they are in
the Timæus: on the other hand, τὸ
μεταλαμβάνειν τοῦ νοητοῦ occurs in the
Timæus (p. 51 A), equivalent to τὸ
μετέχειν, which Ueberweg states to be

discontinued.

[x] Plato, Timæus, p. 52 B. αὐτὸ δὲ
μετ' ἀναισθησίας ἁπτὸν λογισμῷ τινὶ
νόθῳ, μόγις πιστόν.

[y] Plato, Timæus, pp. 52-53. τὰ
τέτταρα γένη σειόμενα ὑπὸ τῆς δεξα-
μένης, κινουμένης αὐτῆς οἷον ὀργάνου
σεισμὸν παρέχοντος, τὰ μὲν ἀνομοιότατα
πλεῖστον αὐτὰ ἀφ' αὑτῶν ὁρίζειν, τὰ δ'
ὁμοιότατα μάλιστα εἰς ταὐτὸν ξυνωθεῖν·
διὸ δὴ καὶ χώραν ταῦτα ἄλλα ἄλλην
ἴσχειν, πρὶν καὶ τὸ πᾶν ἐξ αὐτῶν διακοσ-
μηθὲν γενέσθαι. P. 57 C. διέστηκε
μὲν γὰρ τοῦ γένους ἑκάστου τὰ πλήθη
κατὰ τόπον ἴδιον διὰ τῆς δεχομένης
κίνησιν. P. 58 C.

glomerate each in a place of its own. The Demiurgus brought these four elements out of confusion into definite bodies and regular movements. He gave to each a body, constructed upon the most beautiful proportions of arithmetic and geometry, as far as this was possible.[z]

Respecting such proportions, the theory which Plato here lays out is admitted by himself to be a novel one; but it is doubtless borrowed, with more or less modification, from the Pythagoreians. Every solid body is circumscribed by plane surfaces: every plane surface is composed of triangles : all triangles are generated out of two—the right-angled isoskeles triangle—and the right-angled scalene or oblong triangle. Of this oblong there are infinite varieties: but the most beautiful is a right-angled triangle, having the hypotenuse twice as long as the lesser of the two other sides.[a] From this sort of oblong triangle are generated the tetrahedron or pyramid—the octahedron—and the eikosihedron: from the equilateral triangle is generated the cube. The cube, as the most stable and solid, was assigned by the Demiurgus for the fundamental structure of earth: the pyramid for that of fire: the octahedron for that of air: the eikosihedron for that of water. The purpose was that the four should be in continuous geometrical proportion : as Fire to Air, so Air to Water: as Air to Water, so Water to Earth. Lastly, the Dodekahedron was assigned as the basis of structure for the spherical Kosmos itself or universe.[b] Upon

Marginal note: Geometrical theory of the elements—fundamental triangles—regular solids.

[z] Plato, Timæus, p. 53. τὸ δὲ ᾖ δυνατὸν ὡς κάλλιστα ἄριστά τε ἐξ οὐχ οὕτως ἐχόντων τὸν θεὸν αὐτὰ ξυνιστάναι, παρὰ πάντα ἡμῖν, ὡς, ἀεὶ, τοῦτο λεγόμενον ὑπαρχέτω.
This is the hypothesis pervading all the Timæus—construction the best and finest which the case admitted. The limitations accompany the assumed purpose throughout.

[a] Plato, Timæus, pp. 53-54. ἀηθεῖ λόγῳ δηλοῦν.

[b] That Plato intended, by this elaborate geometrical construction, to arrive at a continuous geometrical proportion between the four elements, he tells us (p. 30 A-B), adding the qualifying words κάθοσον ἦν δυνατόν. M. Boeckh, however (De Platonicâ Corporis Mundani Fabricâ, pp. viii.-

xxvi.), has shown that the geometrical proportion cannot be properly concluded from the premises assumed by Plato :—" Platonis elementorum doctrinam et parum sibi constare, neque omnibus numeris absolutam esse, immo multis incommodis laborare, et divini ingenii lusui magis quam disciplinæ severitati originem debere fatebimur; nec profundiorem et abstrusiorem naturæ cognitionem in eâ sitam esse suspicabimur—in quem errorem etiam Joh. Keplerus, summi ingenii homo, incidit."
Respecting the Dodekahedron, see Zeller, Gesch. der Philos. ii. p. 513, ed. 2nd. There is some obscurity about it. In the Epinomis (p. 981 C) Plato gives the Æther as a fifth element, besides the four commonly

this arrangement each of the three elements—fire, water, air—passes into the other; being generated from the same radical triangle. But earth does not pass into either of the three (nor either of these into earth), being generated from a different radical triangle. The pyramid, as thin, sharp, and cutting, was assigned to fire as the quickest and most piercing of the four elements: the cube, as most solid and difficult to move, was allotted to earth, the stationary element. Fire was composed of pyramids of different size, yet each too small to be visible by itself, and becoming visible only when grouped together in masses: the earth was composed of cubes of different size, each invisible from smallness: the other elements in like manner, each from its respective solid,[c] in exact proportion and harmony, as far as Necessity could be persuaded to tolerate. All the five regular solids were thus employed in the configuration and structure of the Kosmos.[d]

Such was the mode of formation of the four so-called elemental bodies.[e] Of each of the four, there are diverse species or varieties: and that which distinguishes one variety of the same element from another variety is, that the constituent triangles, though all similar, are of different magni-

known and recited in the Timæus. It appears that Philolaus, as well as Xenokrates, conceived the Dodekahedron as the structural form of Æther (Schol. ad Aristot. Physic. p. 427, a. 16, Brandis): and Xenokrates expressly says, that Plato himself recognised it as such. Zeller dissents from this view, and thinks that nothing more is meant than the implication, that the Dodekahedron can have a sphere described round it more readily than any of the other figures named.

Opponents of Plato remarked that he κατεμαθηματικεύσατο τὴν φύσιν, Schol. ad Aristot. Metaph. A. 985, b. 23, p. 539, Brandis. Aristotle devotes himself in many places to the refutation of the Platonic doctrine on this point, see De Cœlo, iii. 8, 306-307, and elsewhere.

[c] Plato, Timæus, p. 56 C. ὅπηπερ ἡ τῆς Ἀνάγκης ἑκοῦσα πεισθεῖσά τε φύσις ὑπεῖκε.

[d] Plato, Timæus, pp. 55-56.

[e] Plato, Timæus, p. 57 C. ὅσα ἄκρατα καὶ πρῶτα σώματα.

The Platonist Attikus (ap. Eusebium, Præp. Ev. xv. 7) blames Aristotle for dissenting from Plato on this point, and for recognising the celestial matter as a fifth essence distinct from the four elements. Plato (he says) followed both anterior traditions and self-evident sense (τῇ περὶ αὐτὰ ἐναργείᾳ) in admitting only the four elements, and in regarding all things as either compounds or varieties of these. But Aristotle, thinking to make parade of superior philosophical sagacity, προσκατηρίθμησε τοῖς φαινομένοις τέτταρσι σώμασι τὴν πέμπτην οὐσίαν, πάνυ μὲν λαμπρῶς καὶ φιλοδώρως τῇ φύσει χρησάμενος, μὴ συνιδὼν δὲ, ὅτι οὐ νομοθετεῖν δεῖ φυσιολογοῦντα, τὰ δὲ τῆς φύσεως ἐξιστορεῖν. This last precept is what we are surprised to read in a Platonist of the third century B.C. "When you are philosophising upon Nature, do not lay down the law, but search out the real facts of Nature." It is truly Baconian: it is justly applicable as a caution to Aristotle, against whom Atticus directs it; but it is still more eminently applicable to Plato, against whom he does not direct it.

tudes. The diversity of these combinations, though the primary triangles are similar, is infinite : the student of Nature must follow it out, to obtain any probable result.[f]

Plato next enumerates the several varieties of each element—fire, water, earth.[g] He then proceeds to mention the attributes, properties, affections, &c., of each: which he characterises as essentially relative to a sentient Subject : nothing being absolute except the constituent geometrical figures. You cannot describe these attributes (he says) without assuming (what has not yet been described) the sensitive or mortal soul, to which they are relative.[h] Assuming this provisionally, Plato gives account of Hot and Cold, Hard and Soft, Heavy and Light, Rough and Smooth, &c.[i] Then he describes, first, the sensations of pleasure and pain, common to the whole body—next those of the special senses, sight, hearing, smell, taste, touch.[k] These descriptions are very curious and interesting. I am compelled to pass them

Varieties of each element.

---

[f] Plato, Timæus, p. 57 D.

[g] Plato, Timæus, pp. 58-61 C.

[h] Plato, Timæus, p. 61 C. Πρῶτον μὲν οὖν ὑπάρχειν αἴσθησιν δεῖ τοῖς λεγομένοις (γένεσιν) ἀεί· σαρκὸς δὲ, καὶ τῶν περὶ σάρκα γένεσιν, ψυχῆς δὲ ὅσον θνητὸν, οὔπω διεληλύθαμεν. Τυγχάνει δὲ οὔτε ταῦτα χωρὶς τῶν περὶ τὰ παθήματα ὅσα αἰσθητικὰ, οὔτ' ἐκεῖνα ἄνευ τούτων δυνατὰ ἱκανῶς λεχθῆναι· τὸ δὲ ἅμα σχεδὸν οὐ δυνατόν. Ὑποθετέον δὴ πρότερον θάτερα, τὰ δὲ ὕστερα ὑποτεθέντα ἐπάνιμεν αὖθις. Ἵνα οὖν ἐξῆς τὰ παθήματα λέγηται τοῖς γένεσιν, ἔστω πρότερα ἡμῖν τὰ περὶ σῶμα καὶ ψυχὴν ὄντα.

[i] Plato, Tim. pp. 62-64 B. Demokritus appears to have held on this point an opinion approaching to that of Plato. See Demo. Frag. ed. Mullach, pp. 204-215 ; Aristot. Metaph. i. p. 985, b. 15 ; De Sensu, s. 62-65 : Sextus Empiric. adv. Math. vii. 135.

Περὶ μὲν οὖν βαρέος καὶ κούφου καὶ σκληροῦ καὶ μαλακοῦ, ἐν τούτοις ἀφορίζει—τῶν δ' ἄλλων αἰσθητῶν οὐδενὸς εἶναι φύσιν, ἀλλὰ πάντα πάθη τῆς αἰσθήσεως ἀλλοιουμένης. We may remark that Plato includes hardness and softness, the different varieties of resistance, among the secondary or relative qualities of matter; all that he seems to conceive as absolute are extension and figure, the geometrical conception of matter. In the view of most modern philosophers, resistance is

considered as the most obviously and undeniably *absolute* of all the attributes of matter, as that which serves to prove that matter itself is absolute. Dr. Johnson refuted the doctrine of Berkeley by knocking a stick against the ground ; and a similar refutation is adopted in words by Reid and Stewart (see Mill's System of Logic, Book vi. ad finem, also Book i. ch. 3, s. 7-8). To me the fact appealed to by Johnson appears an evidence in favour of Berkeley's theory, rather than against it. The Resistant (ὃ παρέχει προσβολὴν καὶ ἐπαφήν τινα, Plato, Sophist. p. 246 A) can be understood only as a correlate of something which is resisted : the fact of sense called Resistance is an indivisible fact, involving the implication of the two. In the first instance it is the resistance experienced to our own motions (A. Bain, The Senses and the Intellect, pp. 371-372, 1st ed.), and thus involves the feeling of our own spontaneous muscular energy.

The Timæus of Plato is not noticed by Sir W. Hamilton in his very learned and instructive Dissertation on the Primary and Secondary Qualities of Body (notes to his edition of Reid's Works, p. 826), though it bears upon his point more than the Theætêtus, which he mentions.

[k] Plato, Timæus, pp. 65-69 E.

over by want of space, and shall proceed to the statements
respecting the two mortal souls and the containing organism—
which belong to a vein more analogous to that of the other
Platonic dialogues.

The Demiurgus, after having constructed the entire Kosmos, together with the generated Gods, as well as
Necessity would permit—imposed upon these Gods
the task of constructing Man : the second-best of the
four varieties of animals whom he considered it necessary to include in the Kosmos.   He furnished to
them as a basis an immortal rational soul (diluted
remnant from the soul of the Kosmos) ; with which they were
directed to combine two mortal souls and a body.[1]   They
executed their task as well as the conditions of the problem
admitted.   They were obliged to include in the mortal souls
pleasure and pain, audacity and fear, anger, hope, appetite,
sensation, &c., with all the concomitant mischiefs.   By such
uncongenial adjuncts the immortal rational soul was unavoid-
ably defiled.   The constructing Gods however took care to
defile it as little as possible.[m]   They reserved the head as
a separate abode for the immortal soul : planting the mortal
soul apart from it in the trunk, and establishing the neck as
an isthmus of separation between the two.   Again the mortal
soul was itself not single but double : including two divisions,
a better and a worse.   The Gods kept the two parts separate ;
placing the better portion in the thoracic cavity nearer to
the head, and the worse portion lower down, in the abdominal
cavity : the two being divided from each other by the diaphragm, built across the body as a wall of partition: just as
in a dwelling-house, the apartments of the women are separated from those of the men.   Above the diaphragm and near
to the neck, was planted the energetic, courageous, contentious, soul; so placed as to receive orders easily from the
head, and to aid the rational soul in keeping under constraint
the mutinous soul of appetite, which was planted below the
diaphragm.[n]   The immortal soul[o] was fastened or anchored

Construction
of man—
imposed by
the Demi-
urgus upon
the secondary
Gods. Triple
Soul. Dis-
tribution
thereof in
the body.

[1] Plato, Tim. p. 69 C.
[m] Plato, Tim. p. 69 D.   ξυγκερασά-
μενοι τ' αὐτὰ ἀναγκαίως τὸ θνητὸν
γένος ξυνέθεσαν.   καὶ διὰ ταῦτα δὴ

σεβόμενοι μιαίνειν τὸ θεῖον, ὅτι μὴ πᾶσα
ἦν ἀνάγκη, &c.
[n] Plato, Timæus, pp. 69-70.
[o] Plato, Timæus, p. 73 B-D.

in the brain, the two mortal souls in the line of the spinal
marrow continuous with the brain: which line thus formed
the thread of connection between the three. The heart was
established as an outer fortress for the exercise of influence
by the immortal soul over the other two. It was at the same
time made the initial point of the veins,—the fountain from
whence the current of blood proceeded to pass forcibly through
the veins round to all parts of the body. The purpose of this
arrangement is, that when the rational soul denounces some
proceeding as wrong (either on the part of others without, or
in the appetitive soul within), it may stimulate an ebullition
of anger in the heart, and may transmit from thence its exhortations and threats through the many small blood channels
to all the sensitive parts of the body; which may thus be
rendered obedient everywhere to the orders of our better
nature.[p]

In such ebullitions of anger, as well as in moments of im-
minent danger, the heart leaps violently, becoming Functions of the heart and lungs. Thoracic soul.
overheated and distended by excess of fire. The
Gods foresaw this, and provided a safeguard against
it by placing the lungs close at hand with the windpipe and
trachea. The lungs were constructed soft and full of internal
pores and cavities like a sponge; without any blood,[q]—but
receiving, instead of blood, both the air inspired through the
trachea, and the water swallowed to quench thirst. Being
thus always cool, and soft like a cushion, the lungs received
and deadened the violent beating and leaping of the heart;
at the same time that they cooled down its excessive heat,
and rendered it a more equable minister for the orders of
reason.[r]

The third or lowest soul, of appetite and nutrition, was
placed between the diaphragm and the navel. This Abdominal Soul—diffi-culty of con-trouling it—functions of the liver.
region of the body was set apart like a manger for
containing necessary food; and the appetitive soul

---

[p] Plato, Timæus, p. 70 B-C.

[q] Plato, Timæus, p. 70 D. τὴν τοῦ
πλεύμονος ἰδέαν ἐνεφύτευσαν, πρῶτον
μὲν μαλακὴν καὶ ἄναιμον, εἶτα σήραγ-
γας ἐντὸς ἔχουσαν οἷον σπόγγου κατα-
τετρημένας.
Aristotle notices this opinion as

held by some persons (not naming
Plato), but impugns it as erroneous.
He affirms that the lungs have more
blood in them than any of the other
viscera, Histor. Animal. i. 17, p. 496, b.
1-8; De Respirat. c. 15, p. 478, a. 13.
[r] Plato, Timæus, p. 70.

was tied up to it like a wild beast; indispensable indeed for the continuance of the race, yet a troublesome adjunct, and therefore placed afar off, in order that its bellowings might disturb as little as possible the deliberations of the rational soul in the cranium, for the good of the whole. The Gods knew that this appetitive soul would never listen to reason, and that it must be kept under subjection altogether by the influence of phantoms and imagery. They provided an agency for this purpose in the liver, which they placed close upon the abode of the appetitive soul.[s] They made the liver, compact, smooth, and brilliant, like a mirror reflecting images:—moreover, both sweet and bitter on occasions. The thoughts of the rational soul were thus brought within view of the appetitive soul, in the form of phantoms or images exhibited on the mirror of the liver. When the rational soul is displeased, not only images corresponding to this feeling are impressed, but the bitter properties of the liver are all called forth. It becomes crumpled, discoloured, dark and rough; the gall bladder is compressed; the veins carrying the blood are blocked up, and pain as well as sickness arise. On the contrary, when the rational soul is satisfied, so as to send forth mild and complacent inspirations,—all this bitterness of the liver is tranquillised, and all its native sweetness called forth. The whole structure becomes straight and smooth; and the images impressed upon it are rendered propitious. It is thus through the liver, and by means of these images, that the rational soul maintains its ascendancy over the appetitive soul; either to terrify and subdue, or to comfort and encourage it.[t]

Moreover, the liver was made to serve another purpose. It was selected as the seat of the prophetic agency; which the Gods considered to be indispensable, as a refuge and aid for the irrational department of man. Though this portion of the soul had no concern with sense or reason, they would not shut it out altogether

The liver is made the seat of the prophetic agency. Function of the spleen.

---

[s] Plato, Timæus, p. 71 A. εἰδότες δὲ αὐτὸ ὡς λόγου μὲν οὔτε ξυνήσειν ἔμελλεν, εἴτε πῃ καὶ μεταλάμβανοι τινὸς αὖ τῶν αἰσθήσεων, οὐκ ἔμφυτον αὐτῷ τὸ μέλειν τινῶν ἔσοιτο λόγων, ὑπό τε εἰδώλων καὶ φαντασμάτων νυκτός τε καὶ μεθ' ἡμέραν μάλιστα ψυχαγωγή-σοιτο, τούτῳ δὴ θεὸς ἐπιβουλεύσας αὐτῷ τὴν τοῦ ἥπατος ἰδέαν ξυνέστησε.

[t] Plato, Timæus, p. 71 C-D.

from some glimpse of truth. The revelations of prophecy were accordingly signified on the liver, for the instruction and within the easy view of the appetitive soul: and chiefly at periods when the functions of the rational soul are suspended—either during sleep, or disease, or fits of temporary extacy. For no man in his perfect senses comes under the influence of a genuine prophetic inspiration. Sense and intelligence are often required to interpret prophecies, and to determine what is meant by dreams or signs or prognostics of other kinds: but such revelations are received by men destitute of sense. To receive them, is the business of one class of men: to interpret them, that of another. It is a grave mistake, though often committed, to confound the two. It was in order to furnish prophecy to man, therefore, that the Gods devised both the structure and the place of the liver. During life, the prophetic indications are clearly marked upon it: but after death they become obscure and hard to decypher.[u]

The spleen was placed near the liver, corresponding to it on the left side, in order to take off from it any impure or excessive accretions or accumulations, and thus to preserve it clean and pure.[x]

Such was the distribution of the one immortal and the two mortal souls, and such the purposes by which it was dictated. We cannot indeed (says Plato) proclaim this with full assurance as truth, unless the Gods would confirm our declarations. We must take the risk of affirming what appears to us probable—and we shall proceed with this risk yet further.[y] The following is the plan and calculation according to which it was becoming that our remaining bodily frame should be put together.

The Gods foresaw that we should be intemperate in our appetite for food and drink, and that we should thus Length of the intestinal canal, in order that food bring upon ourselves many diseases injurious to life.

---

[u] Plato, Timæus, pp. 71-72.

ἱκανὸν δὲ σημεῖον, ὡς μαντικὴν ἀφροσύνῃ θεὸς ἀνθρωπίνῃ δέδωκεν· οὐδεὶς γὰρ ἔννους ἐφάπτεται μαντικῆς ἐνθέου καὶ ἀληθοῦς.

[x] Plato, Timæus, p. 72 D.

[y] Plato, Timæus, p. 72 E.

τὸ μὲν ἀληθὲς, ὡς εἴρηται, θεοῦ ξυμφήσαντος τότ' ἂν οὕτω μόνως διϊσχυριζοίμεθα· τό γε μὴν εἰκὸς ἡμῖν εἰρῆσθαι καὶ νῦν καὶ ἔτι μᾶλλον ἀνασκοποῦσι διακινδυνευτέον τὸ φάναι—καὶ πεφάσθω. ἐκ δὴ λογισμοῦ τοιοῦδε ξυνίστασθαι μάλιστ' ἂν αὐτὸ πάντων πρέποι.

might not be
frequently
needed. To mitigate this mischief, they provided us with a great length of intestinal canal, but twisted it round so as to occupy but a small space, in the belly. All the food which we introduce remains thus a long time within us, before it passes away. A greater interval elapses before we need fresh supplies of food. If the food passed away speedily, so that we were constantly obliged to renew it, and were therefore always eating—the human race would be utterly destitute of intelligence and philosophy. They would be beyond the controul of the rational soul.[z]

Bone and flesh come next to be explained. Both of them Bone—Flesh
—Marrow. derive their origin from the spinal marrow: in which the bonds of life are fastened, and soul is linked with body—the root of the human race. The origin of the spinal marrow itself is special and exceptional. Among the triangles employed in the construction of all the four elements, the Gods singled out the very best of each sort. Those selected were combined harmoniously with each other, and employed in the formation of the spinal marrow, as the universal seed ground ($\pi\alpha\nu\sigma\pi\epsilon\rho\mu\iota\alpha\nu$) for all the human race. In this marrow the Gods planted the different sorts of souls; distributing and accommodating the figure of each portion of marrow to the requirements of each different soul. For that portion (called the encephalon, as being contained in the head) which was destined to receive the immortal soul, they employed the spherical figure and none other: for the remaining portion, wherein the mortal soul was to be received, they employed a mixture of the spherical and the oblong. All of it together was called by the same name *marrow*, covered and protected by one continuous bony case, and established as the holding ground to fasten the whole extent of soul with the whole extent of body.[a]

Plato next explains the construction of ligaments and flesh Nails—
Mouth—
Teeth.
Plants pro-
duced for
nutrition of
man. —of the mouth, tongue, teeth, and lips : of hair and nails.[b] These last were produced with a long-sighted providence: for the Gods foresaw that the lower animals would be produced from the degeneration

[z] Plato, Timæus, p. 73 A.   [a] Plato, Timæus, p. 73 C-D.
                    [b] Plato, Tim. pp. 75-76.

of man, and that to them nails and claws would be absolutely
indispensable: accordingly, a sketch or rudiment of nails was
introduced into the earliest organisation of man.[c]   Nutrition
being indispensable to man, the Gods produced for this purpose plants (trees, shrubs, herbs, &c.)—with a nature cognate
to that of man, but having only the lowest of the three
human souls.[d]   They then cut ducts and veins throughout
the human body, in directions appropriate for distributing
the nutriment everywhere.   They provided proper structures
(here curiously described) for digestion, inspiration, and expiration.[e]   The constituent triangles within the body, when
young and fresh, overpower the triangles, older and weaker,
contained in the nutritive matters swallowed, and then appropriate part of them to the support and growth of the body: in
old age, the triangles within are themselves overpowered, and
the body decays.   When the fastenings, whereby the triangles in the spinal marrow have been fitted together, are
worn out and give way, they let go the fastenings of the soul
also.   The soul, when thus released in a natural way, flies
away with delight.   Death in this manner is pleasurable:
though it is distressing, when brought on violently, by disease
or wounds.[f]

Here Plato passes into a general survey of diseases and
the proper treatment of them.   "As to the source   General view
from whence diseases arise" (he says) "this is a matter   of Diseases
and their
evident to every one.   They arise from unnatural   Causes.
excess, deficiency, or displacement, of some one or more of
the four elements (fire, air, water, earth) which go to compose the body."[g]   If the element in excess be fire, heat and
continuous fever are produced: if air, the fever comes on
alternate days: if water (a duller element) it is a tertian
fever: if earth, it is a quartan—since earth is the dullest and
most sluggish of the four.[h]

Having dwelt at considerable length on the distempers of

---

[c] Plat. Tim. p. 76 E. ὅθεν ἐν ἀνθρώποις εὐθὺς γιγνομένοις ὑπετυπώ-
σαντο τὴν τῶν ὀνύχων γένεσιν.
[d] Plat. Tim. p. 77 B-C.
[e] Plat. Tim. pp. 78-79.
[f] Plat. Tim. p. 81.

[g] Plat. Tim. p. 81 E. τὸ δὲ τῶν
νόσων ὅθεν ξυνίσταται, δῆλόν που καὶ
παντί.
[h] Plat. Tim. p. 86 A. τὸ δὲ γῆς,
τέταρτον ὂν, νωθέστατον τούτων.

the body, the Platonic Timæus next examines those of the

Diseases of mind—wickedness is a disease—no man is voluntarily wicked. soul, which proceed from the condition of the body.[i] The generic expression for all distemper of the soul is, irrationality—unreason—absence of reason or intelligence. Of this there are two sorts—madness and ignorance. Intense pleasures and pains are the gravest cause of madness.[k] A man under either of these two influences—either grasping at the former, or running away from the latter, out of season—can neither see nor hear any thing rightly. He is at that moment mad and incapable of using his reason. When the flow of sperm round his marrow is overcharged and violent, so as to produce desires with intense throes of uneasiness beforehand and intense pleasure when satisfaction arrives,—his soul is really distempered and irrational, through the ascendancy of his body. Yet such a man is erroneously looked upon in general not as distempered, but as wicked voluntarily, of his own accord. The truth is, that sexual intemperance is a disorder of the soul arising from an abundant flow of one kind of liquid in the body, combined with thin bones or deficiency in the solids. And nearly all those intemperate habits which are urged as matters of reproach against a man—as if he were bad willingly,—are urged only from the assumption of an erroneous hypothesis. No man is bad willingly, but only from some evil habit of body and from wrong or perverting treatment in youth; which is hostile to his nature, and comes upon him against his own will.[l]

Again, not merely by way of pleasures, but by way of Badness of mind arises from body. pains also, the body operates to entail evil or wickedness on the soul. When acid or salt phlegm—when bitter and bilious humours—come to spread through the body, remaining pent up therein, without being able to escape by exhalation,—the effluvia which ought to have been exhaled from them become confounded with the rotation of the soul, producing in it all manner of distempers. These

---

[i] Plato, Timæus, p. 86 B. Καὶ τὰ μὲν περὶ τὸ σῶμα νοσήματα ταύτῃ ξυμβαίνει γινόμενα, τὰ δὲ περὶ ψυχὴν διὰ σώματος ἕξιν τῇδε.

[k] Plato, Timæus, p. 86 B. νόσον

μὲν δὴ ψυχῆς ἄνοιαν ξυγχωρητέον. Δύο δ' ἀνοίας γένη, τὸ μὲν, μανίαν, τὸ δ' ἀμαθίαν.

[l] Plato, Timæus, p. 86 C-D.

effluvia attack all the three different seats of the soul, occasioning great diversity of mischiefs according to the part attacked—irascibility, despondency, rashness, cowardice, forgetfulness, stupidity. Such bad constitution of the body serves as the foundation of ulterior mischief. And when there supervene, in addition, bad systems of government and bad social maxims, without any means of correction furnished to youth through good social instruction—it is from these two combined causes, both of them against our own will, that all of us who are wicked become wicked. Parents and teachers are more in fault than children and pupils. We must do our best to arrange the bringing up, the habits, and the instruction, so as to eschew evil and attain good.[m]

After thus describing the causes of corruption, both in body and mind, Plato adverts to the preservative and corrective agencies applicable to them. Between the one and the other, constant proportion and symmetry must be imperatively maintained. When the one is strong, and the other weak, nothing but mischief can ensue.[n] Mind must not be exercised alone, to the exclusion of body; nor body alone, without mind. Each must be exercised, so as to maintain adequate reaction and equilibrium against the other.[o] We ought never to let the body be at rest: we must keep up within it a perpetual succession of moderate shocks, so that it may make suitable resistance against foreign causes of movement, internal and external.[p] The best of all movements is, that which is both in itself and made by itself: analogous to the self-continuing rotation both of the Kosmos and of the rational soul in our cranium.[q] Movement in itself, but by an external agent, is less good. The worst of all is, movement neither in itself nor by itself. Among these three sorts of movement, the first is, Gymnastic: the second, propulsion backwards and forwards in a swing, gestation in a carriage: the third is, purgation or

Preservative and healing agencies against disease—well-regulated exercise, of mind and body proportionally.

---

[m] Plato, Timæus, p. 87 A-C.
[n] Plat. Tim. pp. 87-88 A.
[o] Plat. Tim. p. 88 C.
[p] Plat. Tim. p. 88 D-E.
[q] Plat. Tim. p. 89 A. τῶν δ' αὖ

κινήσεων, ἡ ἐν ἑαυτῷ ὑφ' ἑαυτοῦ, ἀρίστη κίνησις μάλιστα γὰρ τῇ διανοητικῇ καὶ τῇ τοῦ παντὸς κινήσει ξυγγενής· ἡ δ' ὑπ' ἄλλου χείρων.

medicinal disturbance.[r] This last is never to be employed, except in extreme emergencies.

We must now indicate the treatment necessary for mind

Treatment
proper for
mind alone,
apart from
body—supre-
macy of the
rational soul
must be cul-
tivated.

alone, apart from body. It has been already stated, that there are in each of us three souls, or three distinct varieties of soul; each having its own separate place and special movements. Of these three, that which is most exercised must necessarily become the strongest: that which is left unexercised, unmoved, at rest or in indolence,—will become the weakest. The object to be aimed at is, that all three shall be exercised in harmony or proportion with each other. Respecting the soul in our head, the grandest and most commanding of the three, we must bear in mind, that it is this which the Gods have assigned to each man as his own special Dæmon or presiding Genius. Dwelling as it does in the highest region of the body, it marks us and links us as akin with heaven—as a celestial and not a terrestrial plant, having root in heaven and not in earth. It is this encephalic or head-soul, which, connected with and suspended from the divine soul of the Kosmos, keeps our whole body in its erect attitude. Now if a man neglects this soul, directing all his favour and development towards the two others (the energetic or the appetitive),—all his judgments will infallibly become mortal and transient, and he himself will be degraded into a mortal being, as far as it is possible for man to become so. But if he devotes himself to study and meditation on truth, exercising the encephalic soul more than the other two—he will assuredly, if he seizes truth,[s] have his mind filled with immortal and divine judgments, and will become himself immortal, as far as human nature admits of it. Cultivating as he does systematically the divine element within him, and having his in-dwelling Genius decorated as perfectly as possible, he will be eminently well-inspired or happy.[t]

---

[r] Plat. l. c. δευτέρα δὲ, ἡ διὰ τῶν αἰωρήσεων.

Foes, in the Œconomia Hippocratica 'v. Αἰώρα, gives information about these *pensiles gestationes*, upon which the ancient physicians bestowed much attention.

[s] Plato, Timæus, p. 90 C. ἄν περ ἀληθείας ἐφάπτηται.

[t] Plato, Timæus, p. 90 B-D.

ἔχοντά

The mode of cultivating or developing each soul is the same—to assign to each the nourishment and the movement which is suitable to it. Now the movements which are kindred and congenial to our divine encephalic soul, are—the rotations of the Kosmos and the intellections traversing the kosmical soul. It is these that we ought to follow and study. By learning and embracing in our minds the rotations and proportions of the Kosmos, we shall assimilate the comprehending subject to the comprehended object, and shall rectify that derangement of our own intracranial rotations, which was entailed upon us by our birth into a body. By such assimilation, we shall attain the perfection of the life allotted to us, both at present and for the future.[u]

We must study and understand the rotations of the Kosmos—this is the way to amend the rotations of the rational soul.

We have thus—says the Platonic Timæus in approaching his conclusion—gone through all those matters which we promised at the beginning, from the first construction of the Kosmos to the genesis of man. We must now devote a few words to the other animals. All of these derive their origin from man, by successive degradations. The first transition is from man into woman. Men whose lives had been characterised by cowardice or injustice, were after death and in their second birth born again as women. It was then that the Gods planted in us the sexual impulse, reconstructing the bodily organism with suitable adjustment, on the double pattern, male and female.[x]

Construction of women, birds, quadrupeds, fishes, &c., all from the degradation of primitive man.

Such was the genesis of women, by a partial transformation and diversification of the male structure.

We next come to birds; who are likewise a degraded birth

ἔχοντά τε αὐτὸν εὖ μάλα κεκοσμημένον τὸν δαίμονα ξύνοικον ἐν αὐτῷ, διαφερόντως εὐδαίμονα εἶναι.
It is hardly possible to translate this play upon the word εὐδαίμων.
[u] Plato, Timæus, pp. 90 D, 91 C-D. The phrase of Plato in describing the newly introduced mode of procreation —ὡς εἰς ἄρουραν τὴν μήτραν ἀόρατα ὑπὸ σμικρότητος καὶ ἀδιάπλαστα ζῷα κατασπείραντες—is remarkable, as it might be applied to the spermatozoa,

which nevertheless he cannot have known.
[x] Plat. Tim. p. 91 D. Whoever compares the step of marked degeneration here indicated—in passing from men to women—with that which is affirmed by Plato in the fifth book of the Republic about the character, attributes, and capacities of women, will recognise a marked difference between the two.

or formation, derived from one peculiar mode of degeneracy
in man: hair being transmuted into feathers and wings.
Birds were formed from the harmless, but light, airy, and
superficial men; who, though carrying their minds aloft to the
study of kosmical phenomena, studied them by visual observation and not by reason, foolishly imagining that they had discovered the way of reaching truth.[y]

The more brutal land animals proceeded from men totally
destitute of philosophy, who neither looked up to the heavens
nor cared for celestial objects: from men making no use whatever of the rotations of their encephalic soul, but following
exclusively the guidance of the lower soul in the trunk.
Through such tastes and occupations, both their heads and
their anterior limbs became dragged down to the earth by the
force of affinity. Moreover, when the rotations of the encephalic soul, from want of exercise, became slackened and fell
into desuetude, the round form of the cranium was lost, and
converted into an oblong or some other form. These men
thus degenerated into quadrupeds and multipeds: the Gods
furnishing a greater number of feet in proportion to the
stupidity of each, in order that its approximations to earth
might be multiplied. To some of the more stupid, however,
the Gods gave no feet nor limbs at all; constraining them to
drag the whole length of their bodies along the ground, and
to become Reptiles.[z]

Out of the most stupid and senseless of mankind, by still
greater degeneracy, the Gods formed Fishes or Aquatic
Animals:—the fourth and· lowest genus, after Men, Birds,
Land-Animals. This race of beings, from their extreme
want of mind, were not considered worthy to live on earth, or
to respire thin and pure air. They were condemned to respire
nothing but deep and turbid water, many of them, as oysters
and other descriptions of shellfish, being fixed down at the
lowest depth or bottom.[a]

It is by such transitions (concludes the Platonic Timæus)
that the different races of animals passed originally, and
still continue to pass, into each other. The interchange is

[y] Plato, Timæus, p. 91 E.   [z] Plato, Timæus, pp. 91-92.
[a] Plato, Timæus, p. 92 B.

determined by the acquisition or loss of reason or irrationality.[b]

The vast range of topics, included in this curious exposition, is truly remarkable : Kosmogony or Theogony, Large range
First Philosophy, Physics (resting upon Geometry of topics introduced in
and Arithmetic), Zoology, Physiology, Anatomy, the Timæus.
Pathology, Therapeutics, mental as well as physical. Of all
these, I have not been able to furnish more than scanty illustrations : but the whole are well worthy of study, as the conjectures of a great and ingenious mind in the existing state of
knowledge and belief among the Greeks : and all the more
worthy, because they form in many respects a striking contrast with the points of view prevalent in more recent times.

The position and functions of the Demiurgus, in the
Timæus, form a peculiar phase in Grecian philo- The Demi-
sophy, and even in the doctrine of Plato himself : for Platonic
the theology and kosmology of the Timæus differ Timæus—
how con-
considerably from what we read in the Phædrus, ceived by
other philo-
Politikus, Republic, Leges, &c. The Demiurgus is sophers of
the same
presented in Timæus as a personal agent, pre-kos- century.
mical and extra-kosmical : but he appears only as initiating :
he begets or fabricates, once for all, a most beautiful Kosmos
(employing all the available material, so that nothing more
could afterwards be added). The Kosmos, having body and
soul, is itself a God, but with many separate Gods resident
within it, or attached to it. The Demiurgus then retires,
leaving it to be peopled and administered by the Gods thus
generated, or by its own soul. His acting and speaking is
recounted in the manner of the ancient mythes : and many
critics, ancient as well as modern, have supposed that he is
intended by Plato only as a mythical personification of the
Idea Boni : the construction described being only an ideal
process, like the generation of a geometrical figure.[c]　What-

---

[b] Plato, Timæus, p. 92 B. καὶ κατὰ
ταῦτα δὴ πάντα τότε καὶ νῦν δια-
μείβεται τὰ ζῶα εἰς ἄλληλα,
νοῦ καὶ ἀνοίας ἀποβολῇ καὶ κτήσει
μεταβαλλόμενα.

[c] Stallbaum, Proleg. ad Timæum,
p. 47.

Zeller, Platonische Studien, pp. 207-
215 ; also his Geschichte der Grie-
chisch-Philosophie, vol. ii. p. 508 seq.
ed. 2nd ; and Susemihl, Genetische
Entwicklung der Platon. Philosophie,
vol. ii. pp. 322-340. Ueberweg, Ueber
die Platon. Welt-seele, p. 69, Brandis ;

ever may have been Plato's own intention, in this last sense
his hypothesis was interpreted by his immediate successors,
Speusippus and Xenokrates, as well as by Eudêmus.[d] Aristotle in his comments upon Plato takes little notice of the
Demiurgus : the hypothesis (of a distinct personal constructive
agent) did not fit into his *principia* of the Kosmos, and he probably ranked it among those mythical modes of philosophising
which he expressly pronounces to be unworthy of serious
criticism.[e] Various succeeding philosophers also, especially
the Stoics, while they insisted much upon Providence, conceived this as residing in the Kosmos itself, and in the divine
intra-kosmical agencies.

But though the idea of a pre-kosmic Demiurgus found little
favour among the Grecian schools of philosophy, before the

Gesch. der Griech. Philos. ii. cx. pp.
357-365.
    A good note of Ast (Platon's Leben
und Schriften, p. 363 seq.) illustrates the
analogy between the Platonic Timæus
and the old Greek cosmogonic poems.
    [d] Respecting Speusippus and Xeno-
krates, see Aristotel. De Cœlo, i. 10,
pp. 279-280, with Scholia, 487, b. 37,
488, b. 15-489, a. 10, Brandis. Respecting Eudemus, Krantor, Eudorus,
and the majority of the Platonic followers, see Plutarch, De Animæ Procreatione in Timæo, 1012 D, 1013 A,
1015 D, 1017 B, 1028 B.
    Plutarch reasons against them ; but
he recognises their interpretation as
the predominant one.
    See also the view ascribed to Speu-
sippus and the Pythagoreans by Aristotle (Metaphys. Λ. 1072, a. 1, b. 30).
    [e] Proklus ad Platon. Tim. ii. pp.
138 E, 328, ed. Schn. ἢ γὰρ μόνος ἢ
μάλιστα, Πλάτων τῇ ἀπὸ τοῦ προνο-
οῦντος αἰτίᾳ κατεχρήσατο, φησὶν ὁ Θεόφραστος, τοῦτό γε καλῶς αὐτῷ μαρτυ-
ρῶν, and another reference to Theophrastus, in Pro. p. 417, p. 177, also pp.
118 E, 279, Schn. Ἀριστοτέλης μὲν
οὖν τὴν ἐν τῷ δημιουργῷ τάξιν οὐκ οἶδεν
—ὁ δὲ Πλάτων Ὀρφεῖ συνεπόμενος ἐν
τῷ δημιουργῷ πρῶτον εἶναί φησι τὴν
τάξιν, καὶ τὸ πρὸ τῶν μερῶν ὅλον. For
farther coincidences between the Platonic Timæus and Orpheus (ὁ θεόλο-
γος) see Proklus ad Timæ. pp. 233-
235, Schn. The passage of Aristotle
respecting those who blended mythe

and philosophy is remarkable, Metaphys. B. 1000, a. 9-20. Οἱ μὲν οὖν περὶ
Ἡσίοδον, καὶ πάντες ὅσοι θεολόγοι,
μόνον ἐφρόντισαν τοῦ πιθανοῦ τοῦ πρὸς
αὑτούς, ἡμῶν δὲ ὠλιγώρησαν—Ἀλλὰ
περὶ μὲν τῶν μυθικῶς σοφιζομένων οὐκ
ἄξιον μετὰ σπουδῆς σκοπεῖν· παρὰ δὲ
τῶν δι' ἀποδείξεως λεγόντων δεῖ πυν-
θάνεσθαι διερωτῶντας, &c. About those
whom Aristotle calls οἱ μεμιγμένοι
(partly mythe, partly philosophy) see
Metaphys. N. 1091, b. 8.
    Compare, on Aristotle's non-recogni-
tion of the Platonic Demiurgus, a
remarkable note of Prantl, ad Aristot.
Physica, viii. p. 524, also p. 478, in
his edition of that treatise, Leipsic,
1854. Weisse speaks to the same
effect in his translation of the Physica
of Aristotle, pp. 350-356, Leips. 1829.
    Lichtenstädt, in his ingenious work,
(Ueber Platon's Lehren auf dem Gebiete
der Natur-Forschung und der Heil-
kunde, Leipsic, 1826), ranks several
of the characteristic tenets of the
Timæus as only mythical : the pre-
existent Chaos, the divinity of the
entire Kosmos, even the metempsy-
chosis, though it is affirmed most
directly,—see pp. 24, 46, 48, 86, &c.
How much of all this Plato intended
as purely mythical, appears to me
impossible to determine. I agree with
the opinion of Ueberweg, that Plato
did not draw any clear line in his own
mind between the mythical and the
real.—Ueber die Platonisch. Weltseele,
pp. 70-71.

ЧАП. XXXVI.

Christian era—it was greatly welcomed among the Hellenising Jews at Alexandria, from Aristobulus (about B. C. 150) down to Philo. It formed the suitable point of conjunction, between Hellenic and Judaic speculation. The marked distinction drawn by Plato between the Demiurgus, and the constructed or generated Kosmos, with its in-dwelling Gods—provided a suitable place for the Supreme God of the Jews, degrading the Pagan Gods in comparison. The Timæus was compared with the book of Genesis, from which it was even affirmed that Plato had copied. He received the denomination of the atticising Moses : Moses writing in Attic Greek.[f] It was thus that the Platonic Timæus became the medium of transition, from the Polytheistic theology which served as philosophy among the early ages of Greece, to the omnipotent Monotheism to which philosophy became subordinated after the Christian era.

Ad pted and welc med by the Alexandrine Jews, as a parall l to the Mosaic Genesis.

Of the vast outline sketched in the Timæus, no part illustrates better the point of view of the author, than what is said about human anatomy and physiology. The human body is conceived altogether as subservient to an ethical and æsthetical teleology : it is like the Praxitelean statue of Eros[g]) a work adapted to an archetypal model in Plato's own heart—his emotions, preferences, antipathies.[h]   The leading idea in

Physiol gy of the Platonic Timæus—subordinate to Plato s views of ethical teleology. Tr ple soul—each soul at once material and mental.

[f] The learned work of Gfrörer— —Philo und die Jüdisch-Alexandrin. Theosophie—illustrates well this coalescence of Platonism with the Pentateuch in the minds of the Hellenising Jews at Alexandria. " Aristobulus maintained, 150 years earlier than Philo, that not only the oldest Grecian poets, Homer, Hesiod, Orpheus, &c., but also the most celebrated thinkers, especially Plato, had acquired all their wisdom from a very old translation of the Pentateuch " (Gfrörer, i. p. 308, also ii. 111-118). The first form of Grecian philosophy which found favour among the Alexandrine Jews was the Platonic : — " since a Jew could not fail to be pleased—besides the magnificent style and high moral tone—with a certain likeness between the Oriental Kosmogonies and the Timæus, the favourite treatise of all Theosophists," see p. 72. Compare the same work,

pp. 78-80-167-184-314.
Philo calls Sokrates ἀνὴρ παρὰ Μωϋσεῖ τὰ προτέλεια τῆς σοφίας ἀναδιδαχθείς : he refers to the terminology of the Platonic Timæus Gfrörer, 308-327-328 .
Eusebius Præp. Ev. ix. 6, xi. 10), citing Aristobulus and Numenius, says Τί γὰρ ἐστι Πλάτων, ἤ Μωϋσὴς ἀττικίζων ; Compare also the same work, xi. 16-25-29, and xiii. 18, where the harmony between Plato and Moses, and the preference of the author for Plato over other Greek philosophers, are earnestly declared.
See also Vacherot, Histoire Critique de l'École d'Alexandrie, vol. i. pp. 110-163-319-335.
[g] Πραξιτέλης ὃν ἔπασχε διηκρίβωσεν Ἔρωτα
ἐξ ἰδίης ἕλκων ἀρχέτυπον κραδίης— Anthologia .
[h] Plato says (Tim. p. 53 E that in investigat ng the fundamental con-

his mind is, What purposes would be most suitable to the presumed character of the Demiurgus, and to those generated Gods who are assumed to act as his ministers? The purposes which Plato ascribes, both to the one and to the others, emanate from his own feelings: they are such as he would himself have aimed at accomplishing, if he had possessed demiurgic power: just as the Republic describes the principles on which he would have constituted a Commonwealth, had he been lawgiver or Oekist. His inventive fancy depicts the interior structure, both of the great Kosmos and of its little human miniature, in a way corresponding to these sublime purposes. The three souls, each with its appropriate place and functions, form the cardinal principle of the organism:[1] the unity of which is maintained by the spinal marrow in continuity with the brain; all the three souls having their roots in different parts of this continuous line. Neither of these three souls is immaterial, in the sense which that word now bears: even the encephalic rational soul—the most exalted in function, and commander of the other two—has its own extension and rotatory motion: as the kosmical soul has also, though yet more exalted in its

figuration of the elements you must search for the most beautiful: these will of course be the true ones. Again, p. 72 E, ἐκ δὴ λογισμοῦ τοιοῦδε ξυνίστασθαι μάλιστ' ἂν αὐτῷ πάντων πρέποι. Galen applies an analogous principle of reasoning to explain the structure of apes, whom he pronounces to be a caricature of man. Man having a rational and intelligent soul, Nature has properly attached to it an admirable bodily organism; with equal propriety she has assigned to the ape a ridiculous bodily organism, because he has a ridiculous soul—λέξειεν ἂν ἡ φύσις, γελοίῳ τὴν ψυχὴν ζώῳ γελοίαν ἐχρῆν δοθῆναι σώματος κατασκευήν (De Usu Partium, i. c. 13, pp. 80-81, iii. 16, p. 284, xiii. 2, p. 126, xv. 8, p. 252, Kühn).

[1] Respecting a view analogous to that of Plato, M. Littré observes, in his Proleg. to the Hippokratic treatise Περὶ Καρδίης (Œuvres d'Hippocrate T. ix. p. 77):—"Deux fois l'auteur s'occupe des fins de la structure (du cœur) et admire avec quelle habileté elles sont atteintes. La première, c'est

à-propos des valvules sigmöides: il est instruit de leur usage, qui est de fermer le cœur du côté de l'artère: et dèslors, son admiration ne se méprend pas, quand il fait remarquer avec quelle exactitude ils accomplissent leur office. Mais elle se méprend quand. se tournant vers les oreillettes, elle loue la main de l'artiste habile qui les a si bien arrangées pour s uffler l'air dans le cœur. Ces déceptions de la téléologie sont perpétuelles dans l'histoire de la science: à chaque instant, on s'est extasié devant des structures que l'imagination seule appropriait à certaines fonctions. 'Cet optimisme' (dit Condorcet dans son Fragment sur l'Atlantide) 'qui consiste à trouver tout à merveille dans la nature telle qu'on l'invente, à condition d'admirer également ce qu'elle a suivi d'autres combinaisons: cet optimisme de détail doit être banni de la philosophie, dont le but n'est pas d'admirer, mais de connaître: qui, dans l'étude, cherche la vérité, et non des motifs de reconnaissance.'"

endowments. All these souls have material properties, and
are implicated essentially with other material agents :[k] all are
at once material and mental. The encephalic or rational
soul has its share in material properties, while the abdominal
or appetitive soul also has its share in mental properties:
even the liver has for its function to exhibit images impressed by the rational soul, and to serve as the theatre of
prophetic representations.[l]

The Platonic doctrine, of three souls in one organism, de-
rives a peculiar interest from the earnest way in
which it is espoused afterwards by Galen. This last
author represents Plato as agreeing in main doctrines with Hippokrates. He has composed nine distinct Dissertations or Books, for the purpose of upholding their joint
doctrines. But the agreement which he shows between Hippokrates and Plato is very vague, and his own agreement with
Plato is rather ethical than physiological. What is the essence of the three souls, and whether they are immortal or
not, Galen leaves undecided :[m] but that there must be three
distinct souls in each human body, and that the supposition of
one soul only is an absurdity—he considers Plato to have positively demonstrated. He rejects the doctrine of Aristotle, Theophrastus, Poseidonius, and others, who acknowledged only one
soul, lodged in the heart, but with distinct co-existent powers.[n]

So far Galen concurs with Plato. But he connects this triplicity of soul with a physiological theory of his own,
which he professes to derive from, or at least to hold
in common with, Hippokrates and Plato. Galen recognises three ἀρχὰς—principia, beginnings, originating and governing organs—in the body: the
brain, which is the origin of all the nerves, both of

margin notes: Triplicity of the soul—espoused afterwards by Galen.
Admiration of Galen for Plato—his agreement with Plato, and his dissension from Plato—his improved physiology.

---

[k] Proklus could hardly make out
that Plato recognised any ψυχὴν ἀμέ-
θεκτον, ad Tim. ii. pp. 220, 94 A.
[l] Plat. Tim. p. 71 B-C. The criticism of Aristotle (De Partibus Animal.
iv. 2, 676, b. 21) is directed against
this doctrine, but without naming
Plato. But when Aristotle says Οἱ
λέγοντες τὴν φύσιν τῆς χολῆς αἰσθήσεως τινὸς εἶναι σημεῖον, οὐ καλῶς
λέγουσιν, he substitutes the bile in

place of the liver. Plato does not
connect the bile with the liver. In
Aristotle's mind the two are intimately
associated.
[m] Galen, De Fœtuum Formatione,
p. 701, Kühn. Περὶ Οὐσίας τῶν φυσι-
κῶν δυνάμεων, p. 763. Περὶ τῶν τῆς
ψυχῆς Ἠθῶν, p. 773.
[n] Galen, De Hipp. et Plat. Dogm.
iii. pp. 337-347, Kühn, vi. pp. 515-516,
i. p. 200, iv. p. 363, ix. p. 727.

sensation and motion: the heart, the origin of the arteries: the liver, the sanguifacient organ, and the origin of the veins which distribute nourishment to all parts of the body. These three are respectively the organs of the rational, the energetic, and the appetitive soul.°

The Galenian theory here propounded (which held its place in physiology until Harvey's great discovery of the circulation of the blood in the seventeenth century), though proved by fuller investigation to be altogether erroneous as to the liver—and partially erroneous as to the heart—is nevertheless made by its author to rest upon plausible reasons, as well as upon many anatomical facts, and results of experiments on the animal body, by tying or cutting nerves and arteries.ᵖ Its resemblance with the Platonic theory is altogether superficial: while the Galenian reasoning, so far from resembling the Platonic, stands in striking contrast with it.

° Galen, Hip. et Pl. D. viii. pp. 656-657, Kühn. ἐξ ὧν ἐπεραίνετο ἡ τῶν φλεβῶν ἀρχὴ τὸ ἧπαρ ὑπάρχειν· ᾧ πάλιν εἵπετο, καὶ τῆς κοινῆς πρὸς τὰ φυτὰ δυνάμεως ἀρχὴν εἶναι τοῦτο τὸ σπλάγχνον, ἥντινα δύναμιν ὁ Πλάτων ἐπιθυμητικὴν ὀνομάζει. Compare vi. 519-572, vii. 600-601.

The same triplicity of ἀρχαὶ in the organism had been recognised by Erasistratus, later than Aristotle, though long before Galen. Καὶ Ἐρασίστρατος δὲ ὡς ἀρχὰς καὶ στοιχεῖα ὅλου σώματος ὑποτιθέμενος τὴν τριπλοκίαν τῶν ἀγγείων, νεῦρα, καὶ φλέβας, καὶ ἀρτηρίας (Galen, T. iv. p. 375, ed. Basil). See Littré, Introduction aux Œuvres d'Hippocrate, T. i. p. 203.

Plato does not say, as Galen declares him to say, that the appetitive soul has its primary seat or ἀρχὴ in the liver. It has its seat between the diaphragm and the navel; the liver is placed in this region as an outlying fort, occupied by the rational soul, and used for the purpose of controuling the rebellious tendencies of the appetitive soul. Chrysippus (ap. Galen, H. and P. iii. p. 288, K.) stated Plato's doctrine about the τριμερὴς ψυχὴ more simply and faithfully than Galen himself. Compare his words ib. viii. p. 651, vi. p. 519. Galen represents Plato as saying that nourishment is furnished by the stomach first to the liver, to be there made into blood and sent round

the body through the veins (pp. 576-578). This is Galen's own theory (De Usu Partium, iv. p. 268, K.), but it is not to be found in Plato. Whoever reads the Timæus, pp. 77-78, will see that Plato's theory of the conversion of food into blood, and its transmission as blood through the veins, is altogether different. It is here that he propounds his singular hypothesis—the interior network of air and fire, and the oscillating ebb and flow of these intense agencies in the cavity of the abdomen. The liver has nothing to do with the process.

So again Galen (p. 573) puts upon the words of Plato about the heart – πηγὴν τοῦ περιφερομένου σφοδρῶς αἵματος—an interpretation conformable to the Galenian theory, but noway consistent with the statements of the Timæus itself. And he treats the comparison of the cranium and the rotations of the brain within, to the rotations of the spherical Kosmos—which comparison weighed greatly in Plato's mind—as an illustrative simile without any philosophical value (Galen, H. et P. D. ii. 4, p. 230, Kühn; Plato, Tim. pp. 41 B, 90 A).

ᵖ Galen (Hip. Pl. Dogm. ii. p. 233, K.), καίτοι γε ἡμεῖς, ἅπερ ἐπαγγελλόμεθα λόγῳ, ταῦτα ἐπὶ ταῖς τῶν ζώων ἀνατομαῖς ἐπιδεικνύμεν, &c. P. 220. Πόθεν οὖν τοῦτο δειχθήσεται; πόθεν ἄλλοθεν, ἢ ἐκ τῶν ἀνατομῶν;

Anxious as Galen is to extol Plato, his manner of expounding and defending the Platonic thesis is such as to mark the scientific progress realised during the five centuries intervening between the two. Plato himself, in the Timæus, displays little interest or curiosity about the facts of physiology: the connecting principles, whereby he explains to himself the mechanism of the organs as known by ordinary experience, are altogether psychological, ethical, teleological. In the praise which Galen, with his very superior knowledge of the human organism, bestows upon the Timæus, he unconsciously substitutes a new doctrine of his own, differing materially from that of Plato.

I have no space here to touch on the interesting comparisons which might be made between the physiology and pathology of the Timæus—and that which we read in other authors of the same century— Aristotle and the Hippokratic treatises. More than one allusion is made in the Timæus to physicians: and Plato cites Hippokrates in other dialogues with respect.[q] The study and practice of medicine was at that time greatly affected by the current speculations respecting Nature as a whole: accomplished physicians combined both lines of study, implicating kosmical and biological theories:[r] and in the Platonic Timæus, the former might properly be comprised in the latter, since the entire Kosmos is regarded as one animated and rational being. Among the sixty treatises in the Hippokratic collection, composed by different authors, there are material differences—sometimes even positive opposition

Physiology and pathology of Plato —compared with that of Aristotle and the Hippokratic treatises.

[q] Plato, Phædrus, p. 270; Protagoras, p. 311.

[r] See a remarkable passage, Aristotel. De Sensu, 436, a. 21, τῶν ἰατρῶν οἱ φιλοσοφωτέρως τὴν τέχνην μετιόντες, &c.: also De Respiratione, ad finem, 480, b. 21, and Περὶ τῆς καθ' ὕπνον μαντικῆς, i. p. 463, a. 5. τῶν ἰατρῶν οἱ χαρίεντες. Compare Hippokrat. De Aere, Locis, &c., c. 2.

M. Littré observes :—

"La science antique, et par conséquent la médecine qui en formait une branche, est essentiellement synthétique. Platon, dans le Charmide, dit qu'on ne peut guérir la partie sans le tout. Le philosophe avait pris cette idée à l'enseignement médical qui se donnait de son temps: cet enseignement partait donc du tout, de l'ensemble. Nous en avons la preuve dans le livre même du Pronostic, qui nous montre d'une manière frappante comment la composition des écrits particuliers se subordonne à la conception générale de la science. Ce livre, tel qu'Hippocrate l'a composé, ne pouvait se faire qu'à une époque où la médecine conservait encore l'empreinte des doctrines encyclopédiques qui avaient constitué le fond de tout l'enseignement oriental." (Littré, Œuvres D'Hippocrate, T. ii. p. 96. Argument préfixé to the Prognostic.)

—both of doctrine and spirit. Some of them are the work
of practitioners, familiar with the details of sickness and
bodily injuries, as well as with the various modes of treatment:
others again proceed from pure theorists, following out some
speculative dogmas more or less plausible, but usually vague
and indeterminate. It is to one of this last class of treatises
that Galen chiefly refers, when he dwells upon the agreement
between Plato and Hippokrates.[s] This is the point which the
Platonic Timæus has in common with both Hippokrates and
Aristotle. But on the other hand, Timæus appears entirely
wanting in that element of observation, and special care about
matters of fact, which these two last-mentioned authors very
frequently display, even while confusing themselves by much
vagueness of dogmatising theory. The Timæus evinces no
special study of matters of fact: it contains ingenious and
fanciful combinations, dictated chiefly from the ethical and
theological point of view, but brought to bear upon such
limited amount of knowledge as an accomplished man of

[s] He alludes especially to the Hippokratic treatise Περὶ Φύσιος ἀνθρώπου,
see De Hipp. et Plat. Dogm. viii. pp.
674-710, ed Kühn.

In the valuable Hippokratic composition—Περὶ Ἀρχαίης Ἰητρικῆς—(vol.
i. pp. 570-636, ed. Littré) the author
distinguished ἰητροί, properly so-called,
from σοφισταί, who merely laid down
general principles about medicine.
He enters a protest against the employment, in reference to medicine, of
those large and indefinite assumptions
which characterised the works of
Sophists or physical philosophers such
as Empedokles (pp. 570-620, Littré).
"Such compositions," he says, "belong
less to the medical art than to the art
of literary composition"—ἐγὼ δὲ τού-
τεων μὲν ὅσα τινὶ εἴρηται σοφιστῇ ἢ
ἰητρῷ, ἢ γέγραπται περὶ φύσιος, ἧσσον
νομίζω τῇ ἰατρικῇ τέχνῃ προσήκειν ἢ
τῇ γραφικῇ (p. 620). Such men cannot (he says) deal with a case of actual
sickness: they ought to speak intelligible language—γνωστὰ λέγειν τοῖσι
δημότῃσι (p. 572). Again, in the
Treatise De Aere, Locis, et Aquis,
Hippokrates defends himself against
the charge of entering upon topics
which are μετεωρόλογα (vol. ii. p. 14,
Littré).

The Platonic Timæus would have
been considered by Hippokrates as
the work of a σοφιστής. It was composed not for professional readers alone,
but for the public—ἐπίστασθαι ἐς ὅσον
εἰκὸς ἰδιώτην—(Hippokrat. Περὶ Πα-
θῶν, vol. vi. p. 208, Littré).

The Hippokratic treatises afford
evidence of an established art, with
traditions of tolerably long standing,
a considerable medical literature, and
even much oral debate on medical
subjects — ἐνάντιον ἀκροατέων (Hipp.
Περὶ Νούσων, vol. vi. pp. 140-142-
150, Littré). Ὅς ἂν περὶ ἰήσιος ἐθέλῃ
ἐρωτᾶν τε ὀρθῶς καὶ ἐρωτῶντι ἀποκρίνεσθαι, καὶ ἀντιλέγειν ὀρθῶς, ἐνθυ-
μέεσθαι χρὴ τάδε—Ταῦτα ἐνθυμηθέντα
διαφυλάσσειν δεῖ ἐν τοῖσι λόγοισιν·
ὅ,τι ἂν δέ τις τούτων ἁμαρτάνῃ, ἢ
λέγων ἢ ἐρωτῶν ἢ ἀποκρινόμενος,—
ταύτῃ φυλάσσοντα χρὴ ἐπιτίθεσθαι ἐν
τῇ ἀντιλογίῃ.

The method, which Sokrates and
Plato applied to ethical topics, was
thus applied by others to medicine
and medical dogmas. How the dogmas
of the Platonic Timæus would have
fared, if scrutinised with oral interrogations in this spirit, by men even far
inferior to Sokrates himself in acuteness—I will not say.

Plato's day could hardly fail to acquire without special study. In the extreme importance which it assigns to diet, regimen, and bodily discipline, it agrees generally with Hippokrates: but for the most part, the points of contrast are more notable than those of agreement.

From the glowing terms in which Plato describes the architectonic skill and foresight of those Gods who put together the three souls and the body of man, we should anticipate that the fabric would be perfect, and efficacious for all intended purposes, in spite of interruptions or accidents. But Plato, when he passes from purposes to results, is constrained to draw a far darker picture. He tells us that the mechanism of the human body will work well, only so long as the juncture of the constituent triangles is fresh and tight: after that period of freshness has passed, it begins to fail.[t] But besides this, there exist a formidable catalogue of diseases, attacking both body and mind: the cause of which (Plato says) "is plain to every one:" they proceed from excess, or deficiency, or displacement, of some one among the four constituent elements of the human body.[u] If we enquire why the wise Constructors put together their materials in so faulty a manner, the only reply to be made is, that the counteracting hand of Necessity was too strong for them. In the Hesiodic and other legends respecting anthropogony we find at least a happy commencement, and the deterioration gradually supervening after it. But Plato opens the scene at once with all the suffering reality of the iron age—

Contrast between the admiration of Plato for the constructors of the Kosmos, and the defective results which he describes.

> Πλείη μὲν γὰρ γαῖα κακῶν, πλείη δὲ θάλασσα·
> Νοῦσοι δ' ἀνθρώποισιν ἐφ' ἡμέρῃ ἠδ' ἐπὶ νυκτὶ
> Αὐτόματοι φοιτῶσι—[v]

When Plato tells us that most part of the tenants of earth, air, and water—all women, birds, quadrupeds, reptiles, and fishes—are the deteriorated representatives of primitive men, constructed at the beginning with

Degeneration of the real tenants of Earth from their primitive type.

---

[t] Plat. Tim. pp. 81-89 B.

[u] Plat. Tim. p. 82. δῆλόν που καὶ παντί.

[v] Compare what Plato says in Republic, ii. p. 379 C about the prodigious preponderance of κακὰ over ἀγαθὰ in the life of man.

the most provident skill, but debased by degeneracy in various directions—this doctrine (somewhat analogous to the theory of Darwin with its steps inverted) indicates that the original scheme of the Demiurgus, though magnificent in its *ensemble* with reference to the entire Kosmos, was certain from the beginning to fail in its details. For we are told that the introduction of birds, quadrupeds, &c., as among the constituents of the Auto-zôon, was an essential part of the original scheme.[x] The constructing Gods, while forming men upon a pure non-sexual type (such as that invoked by the austere Hippolytus) exempt from the temptations of the most violent appetite,[y] foresaw that such an angelic type could not maintain itself:—that they would be obliged to reconstruct the whole human organism upon the bi-sexual principle, introducing the comparatively lower type of woman:—and that they must make preparation for the still more degenerate varieties of birds and quadrupeds, into which the corrupt and stupid portion of mankind would sink.[z] Plato does indeed tell us, that the primitive non-sexual type had the option of maintaining itself; and that it perished by its own fault alone.[a] But since we find that not one representative of it has been able to hold his ground :—and since we also read in Plato, that no man is willingly corrupt, but that corruption and stupidity of mind are like fevers and other diseases, under which a man suffers against his own consent[b] :—we see that the option was surrounded with insurmountable difficulties : and that the steady and continued degradation, under which the human race has sunk from its original perfection into the lower endowments of the animal world, can be ascribed only to the impracticability of the original scheme : that is, in other words, to the obstacles interposed by implacable Necessity, frustrating the benevolent purposes of the Constructors.

However, all these details, attesting the low and poor actual condition of the tenants of earth, water, and air—and

---

[x] Plat. Tim. p. 41 B-C.

[y] Eurip. Hippol. 615 ; Medea, 573 ; Milton, Paradise Lost, x. 888.

χρῆν ἄρ' ἄλλοθέν ποθεν βροτοὺς
παῖδας τεκνοῦσθαι, θῆλυ δ' οὐκ εἶναι
γένος·
χοὕτως ἂν οὐκ ἦν οὐδὲν ἀνθρώποις κακόν.

[z] Plat. Tim. p. 76 D. ὡς γάρ, ποτε ἐξ ἀνδρῶν γυναῖκες καὶ τἆλλα θήρια γενήσοιντο, ἠπίσταντο οἱ ξυνιστάντες ἡμᾶς, &c. Compare pp. 90 E, 91.

[a] Plat. Tim. p. 42.

[b] Plat. Tim. pp. 86-87.

forming so marked a contrast to the magnificent description of the Kosmos as a whole, with the splendid type of men who were established at first alone in its central region—all these are hurried over by Plato, as unwelcome accompaniments which he cannot put out of sight. They have their analogies even in the kosmical agencies: there are destructive kosmical forces, earthquakes, deluges, conflagrations, &c., noticed as occurring periodically, and as causing the almost total extinction of different communities.[c] Though they must not be altogether omitted, he will nevertheless touch them as briefly as possible.[d] He turns aside from this, the shameful side of the Kosmos, to the sublime conception of it with which he had begun, and which he now builds up again in the following poetical doxology—the concluding words of the Timæus:—

Close of the Timæus. Plato turns away from the shameful results, and reverts to the glorification of the primitive types.

" Let us now declare that the discourse respecting the Universe is brought to its close. This Kosmos, having received its complement of animals, mortal and immortal, has become greatest, best, most beautiful and most perfect: a visible animal comprehending all things visible—a perceivable God the image of the cogitable God: this Uranus, one and only begotten."[e]

[c] Plato, Timæus, pp. 22, 23. Legg. iii. 677. Politikus, pp. 272, 273.

[d] Plat. Tim. p. 90 E. τὰ γὰρ ἄλλα ζῷα ᾗ γέγονεν αὖ, διὰ βραχέων ἐπιμνηστέον, ὅ, τι μή τις ἀνάγκη μηκύνειν· οὕτω γὰρ ἐμμετρότερός τις ἂν αὑτῷ δόξειε περὶ τοὺς τούτων λόγους εἶναι.

[e] Plat. Tim. p. 92 C. Καὶ δὴ καὶ τέλος περὶ τοῦ παντὸς νῦν ἤδη τὸν λόγον φῶμεν ἔχειν· θνητὰ γὰρ καὶ ἀθάνατα ζῷα λαβὼν καὶ ξυμπληρωθεὶς ὅδε ὁ κόσμος, οὕτω ζῷον ὁρατὸν τὰ ὁρατὰ περιέχον, εἰκὼν τοῦ νοητοῦ θεὸς αἰσθητός, μέγιστος καὶ ἄριστος κάλλιστός τε καὶ τελεώτατος γέγονεν,— εἷς οὐρανὸς ὅδε, μονογενὴς ὤν. ·

Weh! Weh!
Du hast sie zerstört,
Die schöne Welt,
Mit mächtiger Faust;
Sie stürzt, sie zerfällt!
Ein Halb-Gott hat sie zerschlagen!
Wir tragen
Die Trümmern ins Nichts hinüber,
Und klagen
Ueber die verlorne Schöne!
Mächtiger
Der Erdensöhne,
Prächtiger
Baue sie wieder,
In deinem Busen baue sie auf!

(The response of the Geister-Chor, in Goethe's Faust, after the accumulated imprecations uttered by Faust in his despair.)

KRITIAS.

The dialogue Kritias exists only as a fragment, breaking off abruptly in the middle of a sentence. The ancient Platonists found it in the same condition, and it probably was never finished. We know however the general scheme and purpose for which it was destined.

Kritias: a fragment.

The procemium to the Timæus introduces us to three persons[a]:—Kritias and Hermokrates, along with Sokrates. It is to them (as we now learn) that Sokrates had on the preceding day recited the Republic: a fourth hearer having been present besides, whom Sokrates expects to see now, but does not see—and who is said to be absent from illness. In requital for the intellectual treat received from Sokrates, Timæus delivers the discourse which we have just passed in review: Kritias next enters upon his narrative or exposition, now lying before us as a fragment: and Hermokrates was intended to follow it up with a fourth discourse, upon some other topic not specified. It appears as if Plato, after having finished the Republic as a distinct dialogue, conceived subsequently the idea of making it the basis of a Tetralogy, to be composed as follows: 1. *Timæus:* describing the construction of the divine Kosmos, soul and body—with its tenants divine and human; "the diapason ending full in man"—but having its harmony spoiled by the degeneration of man, and the partial substitution of inferior animals. 2. *Republic:* Man in a constituted

Procemium to Timæus. Intended Tetralogy for the Republic. The Kritias was third piece in that Tetralogy.

---

[a] Plato, Tim. p. 17 B-C. εἶς, δύο, τρεῖς· ὁ δὲ δὴ τέταρτος ἡμῖν, ὦ φίλε Τίμαιε, ποῦ, τῶν χθὲς μὲν δαιτυμόνων, τὰνῦν δ' ἑστιατόρων ;

These are the words with which the Platonic Sokrates opens this dialogue. Proklus, in his Commentary on the Timæus (i. pp. 5-10-14, ed. Schneider), notices a multiplicity of insignificant questions raised by the ancient Platonic critics upon this exordium. The earliest whom he notices is Praxiphanes, the friend of Theophrastus, who blamed Plato for the absurdity of making Sokrates count aloud one, two, three, &c. Porphyry replied to him at length.

We see here that the habit of commenting on the Platonic dialogues began in the generation immediately after Plato's death, that is, the generation of Demetrius Phalereus.

Whom does Plato intend for the fourth person, unnamed and absent? Upon this point the Platonic critics indulged in a variety of conjectures, suggesting several different persons as intended. Proklus (p. 14, Schn.) remarks upon these critics justly—ὡς οὔτε ἄξια ζητήσεως ζητοῦντας, οὔτ' ἀσφαλές τι λέγοντας. But the comments which he proceeds to cite from his master Syrianus are not at all more instructive : pp. 15-16, Sch.).

society, administered by a few skilful professional Rulers, subject to perfect ethical training, and fortified by the most
tutelary habits. 3. *Kritias*: this perfect society, exhibited in
energetic action, and under pressure of terrible enemies.
4. *Hermokrates*—subject unknown : perhaps the same society,
exhibited under circumstances calculated to try their justice
and temperance, rather than their courage. Of this intended
tetralogy the first two members alone exist: the third was
left unfinished : and the fourth was never commenced. But
the Republic appears to me to have been originally a distinct
composition. An afterthought of Plato induced him to rank
it as second piece in a projected tetralogy.[b]

The subject embraced by the Kritias is traced back to an
unfinished epic poem of Solon, intended by that
poet and lawgiver to celebrate a memorable exploit
of Athenian antiquity, which he had heard from the
priests of the Goddess Neïth or Athênê at Sais in
Egypt. These priests (Plato tells us) treated the
Greeks as children, compared with the venerable
antiquity of their own ancestors : they despised the short backward reckoning of the heroic genealogies at Athens or Argos.
There were in the temple of Athênê at Sais records of past
time for 9000 years back : and among these records was one,
of that date, commemorating a glorious exploit, of the Athenians as they then had been, unknown to Solon or any of his
countrymen.[c] The Athens, of 9000 years anterior to Solon,

Subject of the Kritias. Solon and the Egyptian priests. Citizens of Platonic Republic are identified with ancient Athenians.

---

[b] Socher (Ueber Platon's Schriften,
pp. 370-371) declares the fragment of
the Kritias now existing to be spurious
and altogether unworthy of Plato.
His opinion appears to me unfounded,
and has not obtained assent; but his
arguments are as good as those upon
which other critics reject so many
other dialogues. He thinks the Kritias
an inferior production : therefore it
cannot have been composed by Plato.
Socher also thinks that the whole
allusion, made by Plato in this dialogue
to Solon, is a fiction by Plato himself.
That the intended epic about Atlantis
would have been Plato's own fiction, I
do not doubt, but it appears to me that
Solon's poems (as they then existed,
though fragmentary) must have contained allusions to Egyptian priests

with whom he had conversed in Egypt,
and to their abundance of historical
anecdote (Plutarch, Solon, c. 26-31).
It is not improbable that Solon did
leave an unfinished Egyptian poem.

[c] Plato, Timæus, pp. 22-23. The
great knowledge of past history (real
or supposed) possessed by the Egyptian
priests, and the length of their back
chronology, alleged by themselves to
depend upon records preserved from a
period of 17000 years, are well known
from the interesting narrative of
Herodotus (ii. 37-43-77-145)—μνήμην
ἐπασκέοντες (the priests of Egypt)
ἀνθρώπων πάντων μάλιστα, λογιώτατοί
εἰσι μακρῷ τῶν ἐγὼ ἐς διάπειραν ἀφικό-
μην—καὶ ταῦτα ἀτρεκέως φασὶν ἐπίστασθαι, αἰεί τε λογιζόμενοι, καὶ αἰεὶ
ἀπογραφόμενοι τὰ ἔτεα. Herodotus

had been great, powerful, courageous, admirably governed, and distinguished for every kind of virtue.[d] Athênê, the presiding Goddess both of Athens and of Sais, had bestowed upon the Athenians a salubrious climate, fertile soil, a healthy breed of citizens, and highly endowed intelligence. Under her auspices, they were excellent alike in war and in philosophy.[e] The separation of professions was fully realised among them, according to the principle laid down in the Republic as the only foundation for a good commonwealth. The military class, composed of both sexes, was quartered in barrack on the akropolis; which was at that time more spacious than it had since become—and which possessed then, in common with the whole surface of Attica, a rich soil covering that rocky bottom to which it had been reduced in the Platonic age, through successive deluges.[f] These soldiers, male and female, were maintained by contributions from the remaining community: they lived in perpetual drill, having neither separate property nor separate families, nor gold nor silver: lastly, their procreation was strictly regulated, and their numbers kept from either increase or diminution.[g] The husbandmen and the artisans were alike excellent in their respective professions, to which they were exclusively confined:[h] Hephæstus being the partner of Athênê in joint tutelary presidency, and joint occupation of the central temple on the akropolis. Thus admirably administered, the Athenians were not only powerful at home, but also chiefs or leaders of all

(ii. 143) tells us that the Egyptian priests at Thebes held the same language to the historian Hekatæus, as Plato here says that they held to Solon, when he talked about Grecian antiquity in the persons of Phorôneus and Niobê. Hekatæus laid before them his own genealogy—a dignified list of sixteen ancestors, beginning from a God—upon which they out-bid him with a counter-genealogy (ἀντεγενεαλόγησαν) of 345 chief priests, who had succeeded each other from father to son. Plato appears to have contracted great reverence for this long duration of unchanged regulations in Egypt, and for the fixed, consecrated, customs, with minute subdivision of professional castes and employments: the hymns,

psalmody, and music, having continued without alteration for 10,000 years (literally 10,000—οὐχ ὡς ἔπος εἰπεῖν μυριοστόν, ἀλλ' ὄντως, Plat. Legg. ii. p. 656 E).

[d] Plato, Timæus, p. 23 C-D.

[e] Plato, Tim. p. 24 C. ἅτε οὖν φιλοπόλεμος τε καὶ φιλόσοφος ἡ θεὸς οὖσα, &c., p. 23 C.

[f] Plato, Kritias, pp. 110 C, 112 B-D.

[g] Plato, Krit. p. 112 D. πλῆθος δὲ διαφυλάττοντες ὅ, τι μάλιστα ταὐτὸν ἑαυτῶν εἶναι πρὸς τὸν ἀεὶ χρόνον ἀνδρῶν καὶ γυναικῶν, &c.

[h] Plato, Krit. p. 111 E. ὑπὸ γεωργῶν μὲν ἀληθινῶν καὶ πραττόντων αὐτὸ τοῦτο, γῆν δὲ ἀρίστην καὶ ὕδωρ ἀφθονώτατον ἐχόντων, &c. p. 110 C.

the cities comprised under the Hellenic name: chiefs by the voluntary choice and consent of the subordinates. But the old Attic race by whom these achievements had been performed, belonged to a former geological period: they had perished, nearly all, by violent catastrophe—leaving the actual Athenians as imperfect representatives.

Such was the enviable condition of Athens and Attica, at a period 9400 years before the Christian era. The Platonic Kritias takes pains to assure us that the statement was true, both as to facts and as to dates: that he had heard it himself when a boy of ten years old, from his grandfather Kritias, then ninety years old, whose father Dropides had been the intimate friend of Solon: and that Solon had heard it from the priests at Sais, who offered to show him the contemporary record of all its details in their temple archives.[i] Kritias now proposes to repeat this narrative to Sokrates, as a fulfilment of the wish expressed by the latter to see the citizens of the Platonic Republic exhibited in full action and movement. For the Athenians of 9000 years before, having been organised on the principles of that Republic, may fairly be taken as representing its citizens. And it will be more satisfactory to Sokrates to hear a recital of real history than a series of imagined exploits.[k]

Plato professes that what he is about to recount is matter of history, recorded by Egyptian priests.

Accordingly, Kritias proceeds to describe, in some detail, the formidable invaders against whom these old Athenians had successfully contended: the inhabitants of the vast island Atlantis (larger than Libya and Asia united), which once occupied most of the space now filled by the great ocean westward of Gades and the pillars of Heraklês. This prodigious island was governed by ten kings of a common ancestry: descending respectively from ten sons (among whom Atlas was first-born and chief) of the God Poseidon by the indigenous Nymph Kleito.[l] We read an imposing description of its large population and abundant produce of every kind: grain for man,

Description of the vast island of Atlantis and its powerful kings.

---

[i] Plat. Tim. pp. 23 E, 24 A-D. τὸ δ' ἀκριβὲς περὶ πάντων ἐφεξῆς εἰσαῦθις κατὰ σχολήν, αὐτὰ τὰ γράμματα λα-

βόντες, διέξιμεν.
[k] Plat. Tim. p 26 D-E.
[l] Plat. Kritias, pp. 113-114.

pasture for animals, elephants being abundant among them :[m] timber and metals of all varieties : besides which the central city, with its works for defence, and its artificial canals, bridges, and harbour, is depicted as a wonder to behold.[n] The temple of Poseidon was magnificent and of vast dimensions, though in barbaric style.[o] The harbour, surrounded by a dense and industrious population, was full of trading vessels, arriving with merchandise from all quarters.[p]

The Atlantid kings, besides this great power and prosperity at home, exercised dominion over all Libya as far as Egypt, and over all Europe as far as Tyrrhenia. The corrupting influence of such vast power was at first counteracted by their divine descent and the attributes attached to it: but the divine attributes became more and more adulterated at each successive generation, so that the breed was no longer qualified to contend against corruption. The kings came to be intoxicated with wealth, full of exorbitant ambition and rapacity, reckless of temperance or justice. The measure of their iniquity at length became full; and Zeus was constrained to take notice of it, for the purpose of inflicting the chastisement which the case required.[q] He summoned a meeting of the Gods, at his own Panoptikon in the centre of the Kosmos, and there addressed them.

Corruption and wickedness of the Atlantid people.

At this critical moment the fragment called Kritias breaks off. We do not know what was the plan which Plato (in the true spirit of the ancient epic) was about to put into the mouth of Zeus, for the information of the divine agora. We learn only that Plato intended to recount an invasion of Attica, by an army of Atlantids almost irresistible : and the glorious repulse thereof by Athens and her allies, with very inferior forces. The tale would have borne much resemblance to the Persian invasion of Greece, as recounted by Herodotus : but Plato, while employing the same religious agencies which that historian puts in the foreground, would probably have invested them with a more ethical character, and would have arranged

Conjectures as to what the Platonic Kritias would have been— an ethical epic in prose.

---

[m] Plat. Krit. p. 114 E.
[n] Plat. Krit. p. 115 D. εἰς ἔκπληξιν μεγέθεσι κάλλεσι τε ἔργων ἰδεῖν, &c.
[o] Plat. Krit. p. 116 D-E.
[p] Plat. Krit. p. 117 E.
[q] Plat. Krit. p. 121.

the narrative so as to illustrate the triumph of philosophical Reason and disciplined Energy, over gigantic, impetuous, and reckless Strength. He would have described in detail the heroic valour and endurance of the trained Athenian Soldiers, women as well as men: and he would have embodied the superior Reason of the philosophical Chiefs not merely in prudent orders given to subordinates, but also in wise discourses[r] and deliberations such as we read in the Cyropædia of Xenophon. We should have had an edifying epic in prose, if Plato had completed his project. Unfortunately we know only two small fractions of it: first the introductory prologue (which I have already noticed)—lastly, the concluding catastrophe. The conclusion was, that both the victors and the vanquished disappeared altogether, and became extinct. Terrific earthquakes, and not less terrific deluges, shook and overspread the earth. The whole military caste of Attica were, in one day and night, swallowed up into the bowels of the earth (the same release as Zeus granted to the just Amphiaraus)[s] and no more heard of: while not only the population of Atlantis, but that entire island itself, was submerged beneath the Ocean. The subsidence of this vast island has rendered navigation impossible; there is nothing in the Atlantic Ocean but shallow water and mud.[t]

The epic of Plato would thus have concluded with an appalling catastrophe of physical agencies or divine prodigies, (such as that which we read at the close of the Æschylean Prometheus[u]) under which both the contending parties perished. These gigantic outbursts of kosmical forces, along with the other facts, Plato affirms to have been recorded in the archives of the Egyptian priests. He wishes us to believe that the whole transaction is historical. As to particular narratives, the line between truth and fiction was obscurely drawn in his mind.

Plato represents the epic Kritias as matter of recorded history.

---

[r] Plat. Tim. p. 19 C-E. κατά τε τὰς ἐν τοῖς ἔργοις πράξεις καὶ κατὰ τὰς ἐν τοῖς λόγοις διερμηνεύσεις.

[s] Apollodorus, iii. 6, 6; Pausanias, ix. 8, 2.

[t] Plat. Tim. p. 25 C-D. σεισμῶν ἐξαισίων καὶ κατακλυσμῶν γενομένων, μιᾶς ἡμέρας καὶ νυκτὸς χαλεπῆς ἐπελθούσης, &c. ἄπορον καὶ ἀδιερευνύητον

γέγονε τὸ ἐκεῖ πέλαγος, &c.

Respecting the shallow and muddy water of the Atlantic and its unnavigable character, as believed in the age of Plato, see a long note in my 'History of Greece' (ch. xviii. vol. iii. p. 381).

[u] Æschyl. Prom. 1086.

Another remark here deserving of notice is, That in this epic of the Kritias, Plato introduces the violent and destructive kosmical agencies (earthquakes, deluges, and the like) as frequently occurring, and as one cause of the periodical destruction of many races or communities. It is in this way that the Egyptian priest is made to explain to Solon the reason why no long-continued past records were preserved in Attica, or anywhere else, except in Egypt.[x] This last-mentioned country was exempt from such calamities : but in other countries, the thread of tradition was frequently broken, because the whole race (except a few) were periodically destroyed by deluges or conflagrations, leaving only a few survivors miserably poor, without arts or letters. The affirmation of these frequent destructions stands in marked contradiction with the chief thesis announced at the beginning of the Timæus—viz. the beauty and perfection of the Kosmos.

[x] Plato, Tim. pp. 22 C-D, 23 B-C.

CHAPTER XXXVII.

LEGES AND EPÍNOMIS.

The Dialogue, entitled Leges—De Legibus—The Laws— distributed into twelve books, besides its Appendix the Epinomis, and longer than any other of the Platonic compositions—is presented to us as held in Krete during a walk from the town of Knossus to the temple of Zeus under Mount Ida—between three elderly persons: Megillus, a Spartan—Kleinias, a Kretan of Knossus—and an Athenian who bears no name, but serves as the principal expositor and conductor. That this dialogue was composed by Plato after the Republic, we know from the express deposition of Aristotle: that it was the work of Plato's old age— probably the last which he ever composed, and perhaps not completely finished at his death—is what we learn from the scanty amount of external evidence accessible to us. The internal evidence, as far as it goes, tends to bear out the same conclusion, and to show that it was written during the last seven years of his life, when he was more than seventy years of age.[a]

Leges, the longest of Plato's works—Persons of the dialogue.

---

[a] The allusions of Aristotle to Plato as the author of the Laws, after the Republic, occur in Politica, ii. b. 1264, b. 26, 1267, b. 5, 1271, b. 1, 1274, b. 9. According to Diogenes Laertius (v. 22) Aristotle had composed separate works Τὰ ἐκ Νόμων Πλάτωνος γ—Τὰ ἐκ της Πολιτείας β.

Plutarch (De Isid. et Osir. p. 370 E) ascribes the composition of the Laws to Plato's old age. In the Προλεγό-μενα εἰς τὴν Πλάτωνος φιλοσοφίαν, it is said that the treatise was left un-finished at his death, and completed afterwards by his disciple the Opuntian Philippus — (Hermann's Edition of Plato's Works, vol. vi. p. 218)—Diog. Laert. iii. 37.

See the learned Prolegomena of Stallbaum, who collects all the information on this subject, and who gives his own judgment (p. lxxxi.) respecting the tone of senility pervading the Leges, in terms which deserve the more attention as coming from so un-qualified an admirer of Plato :—" To-tum Legum opus nescio quid senile refert, ut profecto etiam hanc ob causam a sene scriptum esse longé verisimil-limum videatur." The allusion in the Laws : i. p. 638 A) to the conquest of the Epizephyrian Lokrians by the Syra-cusans, which occurred in 356 B.C., is pointed out by Boeckh as showing that the composition was posterior to that date (Boeckh, ad Platon. Minoem, pp. 72-73).

It is remarkable that Aristotle, in

All critics have remarked the many and important differ-
Abandon-
ment of
Plato's philo-
sophical pro-
jects prior to
the Leges.
ences between the Republic and the Laws. And it
seems certain, that during the interval which sepa-
rates the two, Plato's point of view must have
undergone a considerable change. We know from
himself that he intended the Kritias as a sequel to the
Timæus and Republic: a portion of the Kritias still exists, as
we have just seen—but it breaks off abruptly, and there is no
ground for believing that it was ever completed. We know
farther from himself that he projected an ulterior dialogue or
exposition, assigned to Hermokrates, as sequel to the Kritias:
both being destined to exhibit in actual working and manifestation, the political scheme, of which the Republic had
described the constituent elements.[b] While the Kritias was
prematurely arrested in its progress towards maturity, the
Hermokrates probably was never born. Yet we know certainly that both the one and the other were conceived by
Plato, as parts of one comprehensive project, afterwards
abandoned. Nay, the Kritias was so abruptly abandoned,
that it terminates with an unfinished sentence: as I have
stated in the last chapter.

To what extent such change of project was brought about
Untoward
circum-
stances of
Plato's later
life—His
altered tone
in regard to
philosophy.
by external circumstances in Plato's life, we cannot
with certainty determine. But we know that there
really occurred circumstances, well calculated to
produce a material change in his intellectual character and point of view. His personal adventures
and experience, after his sixty-first year, and after the death of
the elder Dionysius (B. C. 367), were of an eventful and
melancholy character. Among them were included his two
visits to the younger Dionysius at Syracuse; together with

canvassing the opinions delivered by
the 'Αθηναῖος ξένος in the Laws, cites
them as the opinions of Sokrates
(Politic. ii. 1265, b. 11), who, however,
does not appear at all in the dialogue.
Either this is a lapse of memory on
the part of Aristotle; or else (which I
think very possible) the Laws were
originally composed with Sokrates as
the expositor introduced, the change
of name being subsequently made
from a feeling of impropriety in

transporting Sokrates to Krete, and
from the dogmatising anti-dialectic
tone which pervades the lectures
ascribed to him. Some Platonic expositors regarded the Athenian
Stranger in Leges as Plato himself
(Diogen. L. iii. 52; Schol. ad Leg. 1).
Diogenes himself calls him a πλάσμα
ἀνώνυμον.

[b] Plato, Timæus, pp. 20-27. Plato,
Kritias, p. 108.

the earnest sympathy and counsel which he bestowed on his friend Dion ; whose chequered career terminated, after an interval of brilliant promise, in disappointment, disgrace, and violent death. Plato not only suffered much distress, but incurred more or less of censure, from the share which he had taken, or was at least supposed to have taken, in the tragedy. His own letters remain to attest the fact.[c] Considering the numerous enemies which philosophy has had at all times, we may be sure that such enemies would be furnished with abundant materials for invidious remark—by the entire failure of Plato himself at Syracuse—as well as by the disgraceful proceedings first of Dion, next, of his assassin Kallippus: both of them pupils, and the former a favourite pupil, of Plato in the Academy. The prospect, which accident had opened, of exalting philosophy into active influence over mankind, had been closed in a way no less mournful than dishonourable. Plato must have felt this keenly enough, even apart from the taunts of opponents. We might naturally expect that his latest written compositions would be coloured by such a temper of mind: that he would contract, if not an alienation from philosophy, at least a comparative mistrust of any practical good to come from it: and that if his senile fancy still continued to throw out any schemes of social construction, they would be made to rest upon other foundations, eliminating or reducing to a minimum that ascendancy of the philo-

[c] See especially the interesting and valuable Epistola vii. of Plato; also the life of Dion by Plutarch.

The reader will find a full account of Plato's proceedings in Sicily, and of the adventures of Dion, in chap. 84 of my ' History of Greece.'

The passage of Plato in Leg. iv. 709-710 (alluding to the concurrence and co-operation of a youthful despot, sober-minded and moderate, but not exalted up to the level of philosophy, with a competent lawgiver for the purpose of constructing a civic community, furnished with the best laws) is supposed by K. F. Hermann (System der Platon. Philos. p. 69) and by Zeller (Die Philosoph. der Griechen, vol. ii. p. 310, ed. 2nd.) to allude to the hopes which Plato cherished when he undertook his first visit to the younger

Dionysius at Syracuse. See Epistol. vii. pp. 327 C, 330 A-B, 334 C; Epistol. ii. 311 B.

Such allusion is sufficiently probable. Yet we must remember that the Magnêtic community, described by Plato in the Treatise De Legibus, does not derive its origin from any established despot or prince, but from a general resolution supposed to have been taken by the Kretan cities, and from a Decemviral executive Board of Knossian citizens nominated by them. Kleinias, as a chief member of this Board, solicits the suggestion of laws from the Athenian elder (Legg. iii. p. 702 C. This is more analogous to Plato's subsequent counsel, *after* his attempt to guide the younger Dionysius had failed. See Epistol. vii. p. 337 C-E.

sophical mind, which he had once held to be omnipotent and indispensable.

Comparing the Laws with the earlier compositions of Plato, the difference between them will be found to correspond pretty nearly with the change thus indicated in his point of view. If we turn to the Republic, we find Plato dividing the intelligible world (τὸ νοητὸν) into two sections: the higher, that of pure and absolute Ideas, with which philosophy and dialectics deal—the lower, that of Ideas not quite pure, but implicated more or less with sensible illustration, to which the mathematician applies himself: the chief use of the lower section is said to consist in its serving as preparation for a comprehension of the higher.[d] But in the Laws, this higher or dialectical section—the last finish or crowning result of the teaching process, is left out; while even the lower or mathematical section is wrapped up with theology. Moreover, the teaching provided in the Laws, for the ruling Elders, is presented as something new, which Plato has much difficulty both in devising and in explaining: we must therefore understand him to distinguish it pointedly from the teaching which he had before provided for the Elders in the Republic.[e] Again, literary occupation is now kept down rather than encouraged: Plato is more afraid lest his citizens should have too much of it than too little.[f] As for the Sokratic Elenchus, it is not merely not commended, but it is even proscribed and denounced by implication, since free speech and criticism generally is barred out by the rigorous Platonic censorship. On the other hand, the ethical sentiment in the Leges, with its terms designating the varieties of virtue, is much the same as in other Platonic compositions: the political and social doctrine also, though different in some material points, is yet very analogous on several others. But

(marginal note) General comparison of Leges with Plato's earlier works.

---

[d] See the passages, Plat. Legg. vii. pp. 811 B-819 A. Plato, Republic, vi. pp. 510-511. τὰ δύο τμήματα or εἴδη τοῦ νοητοῦ: vii. p. 534 E. ὥσπερ θριγκὸς τοῖς μαθήμασιν ἡ διαλεκτικὴ ἐπάνω κεῖσθαι.

[e] Plat. Legg. p. 966 D, xii. pp. 968 C-E, 969 A. Compare vii. p. 818 E. In p. 966 D, the study of astronomy is enforced on the ground

that it is one of the strongest evidences of natural theology: in p. 818 C, arithmetic, geometry, and astronomy are advocated as studies, because, without having gone through them, a man cannot become a God, a Dæmon, or a Hero, competent to exercise effective care over mankind. This is altogether different from the Republic.

[f] Plat. Legg. vii. pp. 811 B, 819 A.

these ethical and political doctrines appear in the Laws much more merged in dogmatic theology than in other dialogues. This theology is of Pythagorean character—implicated directly and intimately with astronomy—and indirectly with arithmetic and geometry also.   We have here an astronomical religion, or a religious astronomy, by whichever of the two names it may be called.   Right belief on astronomy is orthodoxy and virtue : erroneous belief on astronomy is heretical and criminal.

In the Timæus, Plato recommended the study of astro- nomy, in order that the rotations of man's soul in his cra- nium, which were from the beginning disturbed and irregular, might become regularised, and assimilated by continued con- templation to the perfect uniformity of the celestial and kosmical movements.[g]   In the Leges, he recommends astro- nomy to be studied, because without it we fall into blas- phemous errors respecting the kosmical movements, and because such kosmical errors are among the three varieties of heresy, to one or other of which the commission of all crimes against society may be traced.[h]   Hence we find Plato, in the city here described, consecrating his astronomical views as a part of the state-religion, and prohibiting dissent from them under the most stringent penalties.   In the general spirit of the Treatise de Legibus, Plato approximates to Xeno- phon and the Spartan model.   He keeps his eye fixed on the perpetual coercive discipline of the average citizen.   This discipline, prescribed in all its details by the lawgiver, in- cludes a modicum of literary teaching equal to all; small in quantity, and rigorously sifted as to quality, through the censorial sieve.   The intellectual and speculative genius of the community, which other Platonic dialogues bring into the foreground, has disappeared from the Treatise de Legibus. We find here no youths pregnant with undisclosed original thought, which Sokrates assists them in bringing forth; such as Theætêtus, Charmidês, Kleinias, and others—pictures among the most interesting which the ancient world presents, and lending peculiar charm to the earlier dialogues.   Not only no provision is made for them, but severe precautions are taken

---

[g] Plato, Timæus, p. 47 B-C.
[h] Plato, Legg. vii. pp. 821 D, 822 C; x. pp. 885 B, 886 E.

against them. Even in the Republic, Plato had banished poets, or had at least forbidden them to follow the free inspirations of the Muse, and had subjected them to censorial controul. But such controul was presumed to be exercised by highly trained speculative and philosophical minds, for the perpetual succession of whom express provision was made. In the Treatise De Legibus, such speculative minds are no longer admitted. Philosophy is interdicted or put in chains as well as poetry. An orthodox religious creed is exalted into exclusive ascendancy. All crime or immorality is ascribed to a departure from this creed.[i] The early communities (Plato tells us[k]), who were simple and ignorant, destitute of arts and letters, but who at the same time believed implicitly all that they heard from their seniors respecting Gods and men, and adopted the dicta of their seniors respecting good and evil, without enquiry or suspicion—were decidedly superior to his contemporaries in all the departments of virtue—justice, temperance, and courage. This antithesis, between virtue and religious faith on the one side, and arts and letters with an inquisitive spirit on the other, presenting the latter as a depraving influence, antagonistic to the former—is analogous to the Bacchæ of Euripides—the work of that poet's old age[l]—and analogous also to the Nubes of Aristophanes, wherein the literary and philosophical teaching of Sokrates is represented as withdrawing youth from the received religious creed, and as leading them by consequence to the commission of fraud and crime.[m]

The submergence and discredit of letters and philosophy, Scene of the Leges, not in Athens, but in Krete. which pervades the dialogue De Legibus, is farther indicated by the personages introduced as conversing. Persons Kretan and In all the other Platonic dialogues, the scene is laid

---

[i] Plato, Legg. ϰ. p. 885 B.
[k] Plato, Legg. iii. p. 679. Compare p. 689 D.
[l] Lobeck, Aglaophamus, p. 623. "Superest fabula (Euripidis) Bacchæ, dithyrambi quam tragediæ similior, totaque ita comparata, ut contra illius temporis Rationalistas scripta videatur; quâ et Bacchicarum religionum sanctimonia commendatur, et rerum divinarum disceptatio ab eruditorum

judiciis ad populi transfertur suffragia:—

σοφὰν δ' ἄπεχε πραπίδα φρένα τε
περισσῶν παρὰ φώτων·
τὸ πλῆθος ὅ, τι τὸ φαυλότατον
ἐνόμισε χρῆταί τε, τόδε τοι λεγοίμαν
(427)."

Compare vv. 200-203 of the same drama.

[m] Aristophan. Nubes, 116-875, &c.

at Athens, and the speakers are educated citizens of Spartan, comparatively illiterate. Athens; sometimes visitors, equally or better educated, from other Grecian cities. Generally, they are either adults who have already acquired some intellectual eminence, or youths anxious to acquire it. Nikias and Laches, Melesias and Lysimachus (in the Lachês), are among the leaders (past or present) of the Athenian public assembly. Anytus (in the Menon) is a man not so much ignorant of letters as despising letters.[n] Moreover Sokrates himself formally disclaims positive knowledge, professing to be only a searcher for truth along with the rest.[o] But the scene of the Laws is laid in Krete, not at Athens: the three speakers are not merely all old men, but frequently allude to their old age. One of them only is an Athenian, to whom the positive and expository duty is assigned: the other two are Megillus, a Spartan, and Kleinias, a Kretan of Knossus. Now both Sparta, and the communities of Krete, were among the most unlettered portions of the Hellenic name. They were not only strangers to that impulse of rhetoric, dialectic, and philosophical speculation which, having its chief domicile at Athens, had become diffused more or less over a large portion of Greece since the Persian war—but they were sparingly conversant even with that old poetical culture, epic and lyric, which belonged to the age of Solon and the Seven Wise Men. The public training of youth at Sparta, equal for all the citizens, included nothing of letters and music, which in other cities were considered to be the characteristics of an educated Greek:[p] though probably individual Spartans, more or fewer, acquired these accomplishments for themselves. Gymnastics, with a slight admixture of simple choric music and a still slighter

---

[n] Tacitus, Dialog. de Orator. c. 2. "Aper, communi eruditione imbutus, contemnebat potius literas quam nesciebat."

Nikias is said to have made his son Nikêratus learn by heart the entire Iliad and Odyssey of Homer; at least this is the statement of Nikêratus himself in the Symposion of Xenophon (iii. 5).

[o] This profession appears even in the Gorgias (p. 506 A) and in the Republic (v. p. 450 D).

[p] See Xenophon, Republ. Laced. c. 2.

Compare the description given by Xenophon in the Cyropædia (1, 2, 6) of the public training of Persian youth, which passage bears striking analogy to his description of the Spartan training. The public διδάσκαλοι are not mentioned as teaching γράμματα, which belong to Athens and other cities, but as teaching justice, temperance, self-command, obedience, bodily endurance, the use of the bow and the javelin, &c.

admixture of poetry and letters, formed the characteristic culture of Sparta and Krete.[q] In the Leges, Plato not only notes the fact, but treats it as indicating a better social condition, compared with Athens and other Greeks—that both Spartans and Kretans were alike unacquainted with the old epic or theological poems (Hesiod, Orpheus, &c.), and with the modern philosophical speculations.[r]

Not simply on this negative ground, but on another positive ground also, Sparta and Krête were well suited to furnish listeners for the Laws.[s] Their gymnastic discipline and military drill, especially the Spartan, were stricter and more continuous than anywhere else in Greece; including toilsome fatigue, endurance of pain, heat, and cold, and frequent conflicts with and without arms between different fractions of citizens. The individual and the family were more thoroughly merged in the community: the citizens were trained for war, interdicted from industry, and forbidden to go abroad without permission: attendance on the public mess-table was compulsory on all citizens: the training of youth was uniform, under official authority: the two systems were instituted, both of them, by divine authority—the Spartan by Apollo, the Kretan by Zeus—Lykurgus and Minos, semi-divine persons, being the respective instruments and mediators. In neither of them was any public criticism tolerated upon the laws and institutions (this is a point capital in Plato's view[t]). No voice was allowed among the young men except that of constant eulogy, extolling the system as not merely excellent but of divine

Gymnastic training, military drill, and public mess, in Krete and Sparta.

[q] Plato, Legg. ii. p. 673 B.

[r] Plato, Legg. x. p. 886 B. εἰσὶν ἡμῖν ἐν γράμμασι λόγοι κείμενοι, οἵ παρ' ὑμῖν οὐκ εἰσὶ δι' ἀρετὴν πολιτείας, ὡς ἐγὼ μανθάνω, οἱ μὲν ἔν τισι μέτροις οἱ δὲ καὶ ἄνευ μέτρων λέγοντες περὶ θεῶν, οἱ μὲν παλαιότατοι, ὡς γέγονεν ἡ πρώτη φύσις οὐρανοῦ τῶν τε ἄλλων, προϊόντες τε τῆς ἀρχῆς οὐ πολὺ θεογονίαν διεξέρχονται, γενόμενοί τε ὡς πρὸς ἀλλήλους ὡμίλησαν. °Α τοῖς ἀκούουσιν εἰ μὲν εἰς ἄλλο τι καλῶς ἢ μὴ καλῶς ἔχει, οὐ ῥᾴδιον ἐπιτιμᾶν παλαιοῖς οὖσι, &c.

[s] Ephorus ap. Strabo, x. 480; Xenophon, Repub. Lac. c. 4·6; Isokrates, Busiris, Orat. xi. s. 19; Aristot. Politic.

ii. capp. 9 and 10, pp. 1270-1271, and viii. 9, p. 1338, b. 15; also chap. vi. of the second part of my 'History of Greece,' with the references there given.

[t] Plato, Legg. i. p. 634 E. ὑμῖν μὲν γάρ, εἴπερ καὶ μετρίως κατεσκεύασται τὰ τῶν νόμων, εἷς τῶν καλλίστων ἂν εἴη νόμων μὴ ζητεῖν τῶν νέων μηδένα ἐᾶν ποῖα καλῶς αὐτῶν ἢ μὴ καλῶς ἔχει, μιᾷ δὲ φωνῇ καὶ ἐξ ἑνὸς στόματος πάντας συμφωνεῖν ὡς πάντα καλῶς κεῖται θέντων θεῶν, καὶ ἐάν τις ἄλλως λέγῃ, μὴ ἀνέχεσθαι τὸ παράπαν ἀκούοντας, &c.

Compare Demosthen. adv. Leptin. p. 489, where a similar affirmation is made respecting Sparta.

origin, and resenting all contradiction: none but an old man was permitted to suggest doubts, and he only in private whisper to the Archon, when no young man was near. Both in Sparta and Krete the public authorities stood forward as the conspicuous, positive, constant, agents; enforcing upon each individual a known type of character and habits. There was thus an intelligible purpose, political and social, as contrasted with other neighbouring societies, in which no special purpose revealed itself.[u] Both Sparta and Krete moreover, had continued in the main unchanged from a time immemorial. In this, as in numerous other points, the two systems were cognate and similar.[x]

Comparing the Platonic Leges with the Platonic Republic the difference between them will be illustrated by the theory laid down in the Politikus. We read therein,[y] that the process of governing mankind well is an art, depending upon scientific principles; *Difference between Leges and Republic, illustrated by reference to the Politikus.*

---

[u] These other cities are what Plato calls αἱ τῶν εἰκῇ πολιτευομένων πολιτεῖαι (Legg. i. p. 635 E), and what Aristotle calls νόμιμα χύδην κείμενα, Polit. vii. 1324, b. 5.

[x] Plato, Legg. i. p. 624, iii. pp. 691 E, 696 A, iii. p. 683. Krete and Sparta, ἀδελφοὶ νόμοι.

K. F. Hermann (in his instructive Dissertation, De Vestigiis Institutorum veterum imprimis Atticorum, apud Platonem de Legibus) represents Sparta and Krete as types of customs and institutions which had once been general in Greece, but had been discontinued in the other Grecian cities. " Hoc imprimis in Lacedæmoniorum et Cretensium Respublicas cadit, quæ cum et antiquissimam Græciæ indolem fidelissimé servasse viderentur et moribus ac disciplinâ publicâ optimé fundatæ essent, non mirum est eas Græco philosopho adeò placuisse ut earum formam et libris de Civitate et Legibus quasi pro fundamento subjiceret " (p. 19, compare pp. 13-15-23) "unde (sc. a legitimis Græcarum civitatum principiis) licet plurimi temporum decursu descivissent atque in alia omnia abiissent, nihil tamen Plato proposuit, nisi quod optimus quisque in Græciâ semper expetierat et persecutus erat," p. 15. I think this view is not correct, though it is adopted

more or less by various critics. Sparta and Krete are not specimens (in my judgment) of what all or most Grecian cities once had been—nor of pure Dorism, as K. O. Müller affirms. On the contrary I believe them to have been very peculiar, Sparta especially. So far they resembled all early Greeks, that neither literature nor luxury had grown up among them. But neither the Syssitia nor the *disciplina publica* had ever subsisted among other Greeks; and these were the two characteristic features of Krete and Sparta, more especially of the latter. They were the two features which arrested Plato's attention, and upon which he brought his constructive imagination to bear; constructing upon one principle in his Republic, and upon a different principle in his Dialogue de Legibus. While he copies these two main features from Sparta, he borrows many or most of his special laws from Athens; but the ends, with reference to which he puts these elements together, are his own. K. F. Hermann, in his anxiety to rescue Plato from the charge of rashness (" temerario ingenii lusu," p. 18), understates Plato's originality.

[y] See above, vol. ii. ch. xxviii. p. 488 seq.

like the art of the physician, the general, the steersman : that
it aims at the attainment of a given End, the well-being of the
governed—and that none except the scientific or artistic
Ruler know either the end or the means of attaining it : that
such rulers are the rarest of all artists, never more than one
or a very few, combining philosophical aptitude with philosophical training : but that when they are found, society
ought to trust and obey their directions without any fixed
law : that no peremptory law can be made to fit all contingencies, and that their art is the only law which they
ought to follow in each particular conjuncture. If no such
persons can be found, good government is an impossibility :
but the next best thing to be done is, to establish fixed laws,
as good as you can, and to ensure that they shall be obeyed
by every one. Now the Platonic Republic aims at realising
the first of these two ideal projects : everything in it turns
upon the discretionary orders of the philosophical King or
Oligarchy, and even the elaborate training of the Guardians
serves only to make them perfect instruments for the execution of those orders. But the Platonic Leges or Treatise on
Laws corresponds only to the second or less ambitious project—a tolerable imitation of the first and best.[z] Instead of
philosophical rulers, one or a few invested with discretionary
power, we have a scheme of political constitution—an alterna-
tion of powers temporary and responsible, an apportionment of
functions and duties—a variety of laws enacted, with magistrates and dikasteries provided to apply them. Plato, or his
Athenian spokesman, appears as adviser and as persuader ;
but the laws must be such as the body of citizens can be persuaded to adopt. There is moreover a scheme of education
embodied in the laws : the individual citizen is placed under
dominion at once spiritual and temporal : but the infallibility
resides in the laws, and authority is exercised over him only
by periodical magistrates who enforce them and determine in
their name. It is the Laws which govern—not philosophical
Artists of King-Craft.

The three first books of the Leges are occupied with general
preliminary discussions on the ends at which laws and poli-

[z] Plato, Politikus, pp. 293 C-297 C.

tical institutions ought to aim—on the means which they ought to employ—and on the ethical effects of various institutions in moulding the character of the citizens. "For private citizens" (the Athenian says), "it is enough to say, in reply to the criticism of strangers, This is the law or custom with us. But what I propose to examine is, the wisdom of the lawgiver from whom the law proceeds." [a] At the end of book three, Kleinias announces that the Kretans are about to found a new colony on a deserted site at one end of the island, and that they have confided to a committee of ten Knossians (himself among the number), the task of establishing a constitution and laws for the colony. He invites the Athenian to advise and co-operate with this committee. In the fourth book, we enter upon the special conditions of this colonial project, to which the constitution and laws must conform. It is not until the fifth book that the Athenian speaker begins to declare what constitutional provisions, and what legal enactments, he recommends. His recommendations are continued throughout all the remaining Treatise—from the fifth book to the twelfth or last. They are however largely interspersed with persuasive addresses, expositions, homilies, and comminations, sometimes of extreme prolixity and vehemence,[b] on various topics of ethics and religion : which indeed occupy a much larger space than the Laws themselves.

Large proportion of preliminary discussions and didactic exhortation in the Leges.

The Athenian speaker avails himself of the privilege of old age to criticise the Spartan and Kretan institutions more freely than is approved by his two companions; who feel bound to uphold against all dissentients the divine origin of their respective polities.[c] On enquiring from them what is the purpose of their peculiar institutions—the Syssitia or public mess-table—the gymnastic discipline—the military drill—he is

Scope of the discussion laid down by the Athenian speaker— The Spartan institutions are framed only for war —This is narrow and erroneous.

---

[a] Plato, Legg. i. p. 637 D. πᾶς γὰρ ἀποκρινόμενος ἐρεῖ θαυμάζοντι ξένῳ, τὴν παρ' αὐτοῖς ἀηθείαν ὁρῶντι, Μὴ θαύμαζε ὦ ξένε· νόμος ἔσθ' ἡμῖν οὗτος, ἴσως δὲ ὑμῖν περὶ αὐτῶν τούτων ἕτερος· ἡμῖν δ' ἐστὶ νῦν οὐ περὶ τῶν ἀνθρώπων τῶν ἄλλων ὁ λόγος, ἀλλὰ περὶ τῶν νομοθετῶν αὐτῶν κακίας τε καὶ ἀρετῆς.

[b] This is what Plato alludes to in the Politikus (p. 304 A) as "rhetoric enlisted in the service of the Ruler,"— ὅση βασιλικῇ κοινωνοῦσα ῥητορεία ξυνδιακυβερνᾷ τὰς ἐν ταῖς πόλεσι πράξεις.

[c] Plato, Legg. i. p. 630 D, ii. p. 667 A.

informed by both, that the purpose is to ensure habits of courage, strength, and skill, with a view to superiority in war over foreign enemies : war being, in their judgment, the usual and natural condition of the different communities into which mankind are distributed.[d] Such is the test according to which they determine the good constitution of a city. But the Athenian—proclaiming as the scope of his enquiry,[e] What is it which is *right or wrong by nature, in laws ?*—will not admit the test as thus laid down. War against foreign enemies (*i. e.* enemies foreign to the city-community) is only one among many varieties of war. There exist other varieties besides:—war among the citizens of the same town—among the constituent villages of the same city-community—among the brethren of the same family—among the constituent elements of the same individual man.[f] Though these varieties of war or discord are of frequent occurrence, they are not the less evils, inconsistent with that *idéal* of the Best which a wise lawgiver will seek to approach.[g] Whenever any of them occur, he ought to ensure to the good and wise elements victory over the evil and stupid. But his *idéal* should be, to obviate the occurrence of war altogether—to adjust harmoniously the relation between the better and worse elements, disposing the latter towards a willing subordination and co-operation with the former.[h] Though courage in war is one indispensable virtue, it stands only fourth on the list— wisdom, justice, and temperance, being before it. *Your* aim is to inculcate not virtue, but only one part of virtue.[i] Many mercenary soldiers, possessing courage in perfection, are unjust, foolish, and worthless in all other respects.[k]

[d] Plato, Legg. i. pp. 625-626. ὅρον τῆς εὖ πολιτευομένης πόλεως, &c.

[e] Plato, Legg. i. p. 627 C. ὀρθότητος τε καὶ ἁμαρτίας πέρι νόμων, ἥ τις ποτ᾽ ἐστὶ φύσει. P. 630 E.

Compare the inquiry in the Kratylus respecting naming, wherein consists the ὀρθότης φύσει τῶν ὀνομάτων. See above, vol. ii. ch. xxix. p. 501 seq.

[f] Plato, Legg. i. p. 626.

[g] Plato, Legg. i. p. 628 D.

[h] Plato, Legg. i. p. 627 E. ὃς ἂν τοὺς μὲν χρηστοὺς ἄρχειν, τοὺς χείρους δ᾽ ἐάσας ζῆν ἄρχεσθαι ἑκόντας ποιήσειε.

The *idéal* which Plato here sets forth coincides mainly with that which Xenophon adopts as his theme both in the Cyropædia and in the Œconomicus (see the beginning of the former and the close of the latter) τὸ ἐθελόντων ἄρχειν.

[i] Aristotle cites and approves this criticism of Plato, ἐν τοῖς Νόμοις, Politic. ii. 9, p. 1271, b. 1. Compare vii. 14, 1333, b. 15.

[k] Plato, Legg. i. p. 630 A. The doctrine—that courage is possessed by many persons who have no other virtue —which is here assigned by Plato to his leading speaker the Athenian, appears

If you wish (says the Athenian to Kleinias) to make out a plenary defence and advocacy of the Kretan system, you ought to do it in the following way:

Our laws deserve the celebrity which they have acquired in Greece, because they make us happy, and provide us with all kinds of good things: both with such as are divine and with such as are human. The divine are, Wisdom or Prudence, Justice, Temperance, Courage: the human are, Health, Beauty, Strength, Activity, Wealth. The human depend upon the divine, are certain to follow them, and are not to be obtained without them. All the regulations and precepts of the lawgiver are directed to the attainment and protection of these ends—to establish among the citizens a moral tone of praise and blame favourable to that purpose. He seeks to inculcate on the citizens a body of sentiment, as to what is honourable and not honourable—such as may guide their pleasures and pains, their desires and aversions—and such as may keep their minds right amidst all the disaster (disease, war, poverty, &c.) as well as the prosperity of life. He next regulates the properties, the acquisitions, and the expenditure of the citizens, together with their relations to each other on these heads, upon principles of justice enforced by suitable penalties. Lastly, he appoints magistrates of approved wisdom and right judgment to enforce the regulations. The cementing authority is thus wisdom, following out purposes of temperance and justice, not of ambition or love of money.

Such is the course of exposition (says the Athenian) which ought to be adopted. Now tell me—In what manner are the objects here defined ensured by the institutions of Apollo and Zeus at Sparta and Krete? You two ought to show me: for I myself cannot discern it.[1]

Principles on which the institutions of a state ought to be defended— You must show that its ethical purpose and working is good.

---

in the Protagoras as advocated by Protagoras and impugned by Sokrates (p. 349 D). But the arguments whereby Sokrates impugns it are (according to Stallbaum) known by Plato himself to be mere captious tricks (laquei dialectici—captiosè et argutè conclusa, ad sophistam illudendum et perturbandum) employed only for the purpose of puzzling and turning into ridicule an eminent Sophist. (See Stallbaum, not. ad loc. and Præf. ad Protag. p. 28.) I have already remarked elsewhere, that I think this supposition alike gratuitous and improbable.

[1] Plato, Legg. i. p. 632.

This passage is of some value, because it gives us, thus

Religious
and ethical
character
postulated
by Plato for
a commu-
nity. early in the Treatise, a brief summary of that which
Plato desiderates in the two systems here noted—
and of that which he intends to supply in his own.
We see that he looks upon a political constitution
and laws as merely secondary and instrumental: that he postulates as the primary and fundamental fabric, a given religious
and ethical character implanted in the citizens: that the lawgiver, in his view, combines the spiritual and temporal
authority, making the latter subordinate to the former, and
determining not merely what laws the citizens shall obey, but
how they shall distribute their approval and aversion—religious, ethical, and æsthetical. It is the lawgiver alone who
is responsible and who is open to praise or censure: for to the
people, of each different community and different system,
established custom is always a valid authority.[m]

We Spartans (says Megillus) implant courage in our citizens
Endurance of
pain enforced
as a part of
the public
discipline at
Sparta. not merely by our public mess-table and gymnastic,
but also by inuring them to support pain and hardship. We cause them to suffer severe pain in the
gymnopædia, in pugilistic contests, and other ways:
we put them to hardships and privations in the Kryptia and
in hunting. We thus accustom them to endurance. Moreover, we strictly forbid all indulgences such as drunkenness.
Nothing of the kind is seen at Sparta, not even at the festival of Dionysus; nothing like the drinking which I have
seen at Athens, and still more at Tarentum.[n]

How is it (says the Athenian) that you deal so differently

[m] Plato, Legg. i. p. 637 D.
[n] Plato, Legg. i. pp. 633 B-637 A.
Plato puts into the mouth of the Athenian a remark that in some other cities (not Sparta or Kretan) these συσσίτια or public mess-tables had been found to lead to intestine sedition and disturbance (p. 636 B). He instances the cases of the Bœotians, the Milesians, and the Thurians. It is much to be lamented that we can-not assign the particular events and conjunctures here adverted to. The Spartan and Kretan Syssitia were daily, compulsory, and universal among the citizens, besides the strictness of

the regulations: under such conditions they were peculiar to these two places, as far as our knowledge goes: the Syssitia in Southern Italy (noticed by Aristotle, Polit. vii. 10, p. 1329 b.) are not known and seemingly unimportant. The Syssitia in Bœotia, &c., may pro-bably have been occasional or period-ical banquets among members of the same tribe, deme, club, or θίασος—and voluntary besides, neither prescribed nor regulated by law. Such meetings might very probably give occasion to disturbances under particular circum-stances.

with pains and pleasures? To make your citizens firm against pain, you expose them designedly to severe pains: Why are not the citizens tested in like manner, in regard to resistance against the seductions of pleasure? if they were kept free from pains, you would have no confidence in their firmness against painful actualities, when any such shall occur. But in regard to pleasures, you are content with simple prohibition. You provide no means for strengthening your citizens against the temptations of pleasure. Are you satisfied that their courage (or self-command) shall be lame or one-sided—good against pains, but not good against pleasures?[o] In determining about laws, the whole enquiry turns upon pleasures and pains, both in the city and in individual dispositions. These are the two natural fountains, from which he who draws such draughts as is proper, obtains happiness: while every one who draws unwisely and out of season, will fail of obtaining happiness.[p]

Besides, as to drunkenness, we must not be too hasty in condemnation of it. We must not pronounce generally respecting any institution without examining the circumstances, persons, regulations, &c., attending it. Drunkenness forbidden at Sparta, and blamed by the Spartan converser. The Athenian proceeds to inquire how far such unqualified prohibition is justifiable. Such hasty praise and censure is very misleading. Many other nations act upon the opposite practice. But I (says Plato) shall not pretend to decide the point by witnesses and authority. I shall adopt another course of investigation, and shall show you, in this particular case, a specimen of the way in which all such institutions ought to be criticised and appreciated.[q]

Plato here digresses[r] from his main purpose to examine the question of drunkenness. He will not allow it to be set aside absolutely and offhand, by a self-justifying ethical sentiment, without reason assigned, defence tendered, accompanying precautions discussed. Upon this, as upon the social functions

[o] Plato, Legg. i. pp. 633-634 A. χωλὴν τὴν ἀνδρίαν.
[p] Plato, Legg. i. p. 636 D-E.
[q] Plato, Legg. i. p. 638 D-E. Τρόπον δὲ ἄλλον ὃν ἐμοὶ φαίνεται δεῖν ἐθέλω λέγειν περὶ αὐτοῦ τούτου, τῆς μέθης, πειρώμενος ἂν ἄρα δύνωμαι τὴν περὶ ἁπάντων τούτων ὀρθὴν μεθόδον ὑμῖν δηλοῦν,

ἐπειδὴ καὶ μύρια ἐπὶ μυρίοις ἔθνη περὶ αὐτῶν ἀμφισβητοῦντα ὑμῖν πόλεσι δυεῖν τῷ λόγῳ διαμάχοιτ' ἄν.
Here Plato (as in the Sophistês, Politikus, and elsewhere) announces that the special inquiry is intended to illustrate a general method.
[r] He himself notes it as a digression, iii. p. 682 E.

proper for the female sex, he is a dissenter from the common view. He selects the subject as a case for exhibiting the proper method of criticism respecting social institutions; not without some consciousness that the discussion, if looked at in itself (like the examples of scientific classification or diæresis in the Sophistês and Politikus), would appear unduly prolonged.[s]

To illustrate his peculiar views[t] on the subject of drunken-

Description of Sokrates in the Symposion—his self-command under abundant potations.

ness, we may refer to the picture of Sokrates which he presents in the Symposion, more especially in the latter half of that dialogue, after the appearance of Alkibiades. In this dialogue the occasion is supposed to be festive and joyous. Eros is in the ascendant, and is made the subject of a panegyric by each of the guests in succession. Sokrates partakes in the temper of the society, proclaiming himself to be ignorant of all other matters except those relating to Love.[u] In all the Platonic writings there is hardly any thing more striking than the panegyric upon Eros there pronounced by Sokrates, blending the idea of love with that of philosophical dialectics, and refining the erotic impulse into an enthusiastic aspiration for that generation of new contemplative power, by the colloquial intercourse of two minds reciprocally stimulating each other, which brings them at last into a clear view of the objects of the ideal or intelligible world. Until the appearance of Alkibiades, little wine is swallowed, and the guests are perfectly sober. But Alkibiades, being intoxicated when he first comes in, becomes at once the prominent character of the piece. He is represented as directing the large wine-cooler to be filled with wine (about four pints), first swallowing the whole himself, then ordering it to be filled again for Sokrates, who does the like: Alkibiades observing, "Whatever quantity of wine you prescribe to Sokrates, he will drink it without becoming drunk."[x] Alkibiades then, instead of panegyrising Eros,

[s] Plato, Legg. i. pp. 642 A, 645 D. Compare the Politikus, pp. 264 A-286 C-E.

[t] Aristotle especially notes this as one among the peculiarities of Plato (Politic. ii. 9, 20).

[u] Plato, Symp. p. 177 D. ἐγὼ ὃς οὐδέν φημι ἄλλο ἐπίστασθαι ἢ τὰ ἐρωτικά, &c. P. 198 D. ἔφην εἶναι δεινὸς τὰ ἐρωτικά.

[x] Plato, Symp. pp. 213-214.

undertakes to pronounce a panegyric on Sokrates : proclaiming that nothing shall be said but what is true, and being relieved from all reserve by his drunken condition.[y]   In this panegyric he describes emphatically the playful irony of Sokrates, and the magical influence exercised by his conversation over young men.   But though Sokrates thus acquired irresistible ascendancy over others, himself (Alkibiades) included, no one else acquired the least hold over Sokrates. His will and character, under a playful exterior, were self-sufficing and self-determining; independent of influences from without, to such a degree as was almost insulting to any one who sought either to captivate or oblige him.[z]   The self-command of Sokrates was unshaken either by seduction on one side, or by pain and hardship on the other.   He faced danger with a courage never surpassed; he endured hunger, fatigue, the extremities of heat and cold, in a manner such as none of his comrades in the army could parallel.[a]   He was indifferent to the gratifications of love, even when they were presented to him in a manner the most irresistible to Grecian imagination; while at festive banquets, though he did not drink of his own accord, yet if the society imposed obligation to do so, he outdid all in respect to quantity of wine.   No one ever saw Sokrates intoxicated.[b]   Such is the tenor of the panegyric pronounced by Alkibiades upon Sokrates.   A general drinking-bout closes the Symposion, in which Sokrates swallows large draughts of wine along with the rest, but persists all the while in his dialectic cross-examination, with unabated clearness of head.   One by one the guests drop asleep, and at daybreak Sokrates alone is left awake.   He rises and departs, goes forthwith to the Lykeum, and there passes the whole day in his usual colloquial occupation, without being at all affected by the potations of the preceding night.[c]

---

[y] Plato, Symp. pp. 214-215-217 E.
[z] Plato, Symp. pp. 219 C, 222 A, τῆς Σωκράτους ὑπερηφανίας.
[a] Plato, Symp. p. 220.
[b] Plato, Symp. p. 220 A.
What has been here briefly recapitulated will be found in my twenty-fourth chapter, vol. ii. pp. 225-226 seq.

[c] Plato, Sympos. p. 223. Compare what Plato puts into the mouth of Sokrates in the Protagoras (p. 347 D) : well educated men will carry on a dialectic debate with intelligence and propriety, "*though they may drink ever so much wine*,"—κἂν πάνυ πολὺν οἶνον πίωσιν.

I have thus cited the Symposion to illustrate Plato's view
Sokrates—
an ideal of
self-com-
mand, both
as to pain
and as to
pleasure.
of the ideal of character. The self-command of Sokrates is tested both by pain and by pleasure. He
resists both of them alike and equally : under the
one as well as under the other, his reason works
with unimpaired efficacy, and his deliberate purposes are pursued with unclouded serenity. This is not because he keeps
out of the way of temptation and seduction : on the contrary,
he is frequently exposed to situations of a tempting character,
and is always found superior to them.

Now Plato's purpose is, to impart to his citizens the cha-
Trials for
testing the
self-controul
of the citizen,
under the
influence of
wine. Dio-
nysiac ban-
quets, under
a sober pre-
sident.
racter which he here ascribes to Sokrates, and to
make them capable of maintaining unimpaired the
controul of reason against the disturbances both of
pain and pleasure. He remarks that the Spartan
training kept in check the first of these two enemies,
but not the second. He thinks that the citizen
ought to be put through a regulated system of trials for measuring and testing his competence to contend with pleasure,
as the Spartans provided in regard to pain. The Dionysiac
festivals[d] afforded occasions of applying these trials of pleasure, just as the Gymnopædia at Sparta were made to furnish
deliberate inflictions of pain. But the Dionysiac banquets
ought to be conducted under the superintendence of a discreet president, himself perfectly sober throughout the whole
ceremony. All the guests would drink largely of wine, and
each would show how far and how long he could resist its
disturbing tendencies. As there was competition among the
youths at the Gymnopædia, to show how much pain each
could endure without flinching—honour being shown to those
who endured most, and most successfully—so there would be
competition at the Dionysia to prove how much wine each
could bear without having his reason and modesty overset.
The sober president would decide as judge. Each man's self-
command, as against seductive influences, would be strengthened by a repetition of such trials, while proof would be
afforded how far each man could be counted on.[e]

[d] Plato, Legg. i. pp. 650 A, 637 A, 633 D.

[e] Plato, Legg. i. pp. 647 D-E-649 D. Compare the Republic, iii. pp. 412-

This is one mode in which the unmeasured potations (common throughout the Grecian cities, with the exception of Sparta and Krete) might under proper regulation be rendered useful for civic training.   But there is another mode also, connected with the general musical and gymnastical training of the city.   Plato will not allow Dionysus—and wine, the special gift of that God to mankind—to be censured as absolutely mischievous.[f]

In developing this second topic, he is led into a general theory of ethical and æsthetical education for his city.   This happens frequently enough in the desultory manner of the Platonic dialogues.   We are sometimes conducted from an incidental and outlying corollary, without warning and through a side door, into the central theory from which it ramifies.   The practice is noway favourable to facility of comprehension, but it flows naturally from the unsystematic and spontaneous sequence of the dialogue.

Education of youth consists mainly in giving proper direction to their pleasures and pains—their love and their hatred.   Young persons are capable only of emotions, well or ill directed: in this consists their virtue or vice.   At that age they cannot bear serious teaching: they are incapable of acquiring reason, or true, firm opinions, which constitute the perfection of the mature man: indeed, if a man acquires these even when old, he may be looked on as fortunate.[g] The young can only have their emotions cultivated so as to conform to reason: they may thus be made to love what reason, personified in and enforced by the lawgiver, enjoins—and to hate what reason forbids—but without knowing wherefore.

The gifts of Dionysus may, by precautions, be rendered useful—Desultory manner of Plato.

Theory of ethical and æsthetical education— Training of the emotions of youth through the influence of the Muses, Apollo, and Dionysus. Choric practice and ceremonies.

413, where the same general doctrine is enforced.

[f] Plato, Legg. ii. p. 672 A.

[g] Plato, Legg. ii. pp. 653-659 D-E. παιδεία μὲν ἔσθ᾽ ἡ παίδων ὁλκή τε καὶ ἀγωγὴ πρὸς τὸν ὑπὸ τοῦ νόμου λόγον ὀρθὸν εἰρημένον καὶ τοῖς ἐπιεικεστάτοις καὶ πρεσβυτάτοις δι᾽ ἐμπειρίαν ξυνδεδογμένον, ὡς νόμος ὀρθός ἐστιν· ἵν᾽ οὖν ἡ ψυχὴ τοῦ παιδὸς μὴ ἐναντία χαίρειν καὶ λυπεῖσθαι ἐθίζηται τῷ νόμῳ καὶ τοῖς ὑπὸ τοῦ νόμου πεπεισμένοις, ἀλλὰ ξυνέπηται χαίρουσά τε καὶ λυπουμένη τοῖς αὐτοῖς τούτοις οἷσπερ ὁ γέρων, τούτων ἕνεκα, ἃς ᾠδὰς καλοῦμεν, ὄντως μὲν ἐπῳδαὶ ταῖς ψυχαῖς αὗται νῦν γεγονέναι, πρὸς τὴν τοιαύτην ἣν λέγομεν ξυμφωνίαν ἐσπουδασμέναι, διὰ δὲ τὸ σπουδὴν μὴ δύνασθαι φέρειν τὰς τῶν νέων ψυχάς, παιδιαί τε καὶ ᾠδαὶ καλεῖσθαι καὶ πράττεσθαι, &c.

Unfortunately the hard realities of life are perpetually giving a wrong turn to the emotions. To counteract and correct this, the influence of the Muses, of Apollo, and of Dionysus, are indispensable: together with the periodical festivals of which these Deities are respectively presidents and auxiliaries. Their influence is exercised through the choric ceremony—music, singing, dancing, blended together. Every young man is spontaneously disposed to constant indeterminate movement and exercise of various kinds—running, jumping, speaking, &c. This belongs to man in common with the young of other animals: but what is peculiar to man exclusively is, the sense of rhythm and harmony, as well as of the contrary, in these movements and sounds. Such rhythm and harmony, in song and dance united, is expressed by the chorus at the festivals, in which the Muses and Apollo take part along with the assembled youth. Here we find the only way of properly schooling the emotions.[h] The unschooled man is he who has not gone through a good choric practice; which will require that the matter which he sings shall be good and honourable, while the movements of his frame and the tones of his voice must be rhythmical and graceful. Such choric practice must be universal among the citizens, distributed into three classes: youths, mature men, elders.[i]

But what *is* the good and honourable—or the bad and dishonourable? We must be able to settle this point:—

Music and dancing—imitation of the voice and movements of brave and virtuous men. Youth must be taught to take delight in this.

otherwise we cannot know how far the chorus complies with the conditions abovenamed. Suppose a brave man and a coward in the face of danger: the gestures and speech of the former will be strikingly different from those of the latter. So with other virtues and vices. Now the manifestations, bodily and mental, of the virtuous man, are beautiful and honourable: those of the vicious man, are ugly and base. These are the *really beautiful*,—the same universally, or what ought to be beautiful to all: this *is* the standard of rectitude in music. But they do not always *appear* beautiful to all. There is

---

[h] Plato, Legg. ii. pp. 654-660 A.

[i] This triple distribution of classes for choric instruction and practice is borrowed from Spartan customs, Plutarch, Lykurgus, 21; Schol. ad Legg. p. 633 A.

great diversity in the tastes and sentiments of different persons : what appears to one man agreeable and pleasurable, appears to another disgusting or indifferent.[k] Such diversity is either in the natural disposition, or in the habits acquired. A man's pleasure depends upon the former, his judgment of approbation on the latter. If both his nature, and his acquired habits coincide with the standard of rectitude, he will both delight in what is really beautiful, and will approve it as beautiful. But if his nature be in discordance with the standard, while his habits coincide with that standard—he will approve of what is honourable, but he will take no delight in it : he will delight in what is base, but will at the same time disapprove it as base. He will however be ashamed to proclaim his delight before persons whom he respects, and will never indulge himself in the delightful music except when he is alone.[1]

To take delight in gestures or songs which are manifestations of bad qualities, produces the same kind of mischievous effect upon the spectator as association with bad men in real life. His character becomes assimilated to the qualities in the manifestations of which he delights, although he may be ashamed to commend them. This is a grievous corruption, arising from bad musical and choric exhibitions, which the lawgiver must take care to prevent. He must not allow poets to exhibit what they may prefer or may think to be beautiful. He must follow the practice of Egypt, where both the music and the pictorial type has been determined by the Gods or by divine lawgivers from immemorial antiquity, according to the standard of natural rectitude—and where the government allows neither poet nor painter to innovate or depart from this consecrated type.[m] Accordingly, Egyptian compositions of the present day are exactly like what they were ten thousand years ago : neither more nor less beautiful. The lawgiver must follow this example, and fix the type of his musical and choric exhibitions ; forbidding all innovation introduced on the plea

Bad musical exhibitions and poetry forbidden by the lawgiver. Songs and dances must be consecrated by public authority. Prizes at the musical festivals to be awarded by select judges.

---

[k] Plato, Legg. p. 655 B.   [1] Plato, Legg. pp. 655-656.
[m] Plato, Legg. ii. pp. 656-657.

of greater satisfaction either to the poet or to the audience.
In the festivals where there is competition among poets, the
prize must not be awarded by the pleasure of the auditors,
whose acclamations tend only to corrupt and pervert the
poets. The auditors ought to hear nothing but what is
better than their own characters, in order that their tastes
may thus be exalted. The prize must be awarded according
to the preference of a few elders—or better still, of one single
elder—eminent for excellent training and virtue. This judge
ought not to follow the taste of the auditors, but to consider
himself as their teacher and improver.[n]

Such is the exposition, given by the Athenian speaker, re-

The Spartan
and Kretan
agree with
the Athenian,
That poets
must be kept
under a strict
censorship.
But they do
not agree as
to what the
poets are
required to
conform to.
specting the characteristic function, and proper regulating principles, of choric training (poems learnt,
music and dancing) for the youth. The Spartan and
Kretan cordially concur with him: especially with
that provision which fixes and consecrates the old
established type, forbidding all novelties and spontaneous inspiration of the poets. They claim this compulsory orthodoxy, tolerating no dissent from the
ancient and consecrated canon of music and orchestic, as the
special feature of their two states; as distinguishing Sparta
and Krete from other Hellenic cities, which were invaded with
impunity by novel compositions of every variety.[o]

The Athenian is thus in full agreement with his two companions, on the general principle of subjecting the poets to
an inflexible censorship. But the agreement disappears,
when he comes to specify the dogmas which the poets are
required to inculcate in their hymns. While complimenting
his two friends upon their enforcement of an exclusive canon,
he proceeds to assume that of course there can be but
ONE canon;—that there is no doubt what the dogmas contained in it are to be. He then unfolds briefly the Platonic
ethical creed. "You Spartans and Kretans" (he says)[p] "of
course constrain your poets to proclaim that the just and
temperate man is happy, whether he be tall, strong, and rich
—or short, feeble, and poor: and that the bad man is wretched

<hr>
[n] Plato, Legg. ii. pp. 659 A, 668 A.   [o] Plato, Legg. ii. p. 660 C-D.
                  [p] Plato, Legg. ii. p. 660 E.

and lives in suffering, though he be richer than Midas, and
possessor besides of every other advantage in life.   Most
men appreciate falsely good and evil things.   They esteem as
good things, health, beauty, strength, perfect sight and hearing, power, long life, immortality : they account the contrary
to be bad things.   But you and I take a different view.[q]   We
agree in proclaiming, that all these so-called good things are
good only to the just man.   To the unjust man, we affirm
that health, strength, perfection of senses, power, long life,
&c., are not good, but exceedingly bad.   This, I presume, is
the doctrine which you compel your poets to proclaim, and
no other—in suitable rhythm and harmony.[r]   You agree with
me in this, do you not?"

"We agree with you" (replies Kleinias) "on some of your
affirmations, but we disagree with you wholly on others."

"What?" (says the Athenian.)   "Do you disagree with me
when I affirm, that a man healthy, rich, strong, powerful,
fearless, long-lived, exempt from all the things commonly reputed to be evils, but at the same time unjust and exorbitant
—when I say that such a man is not happy, but miserable?"

"We *do* disagree with you when you affirm this," answers
the Kretan.

"But will you not admit that such a man lives basely or
dishonourably?"

"Basely or dishonourably.—Yes, we grant it."

"What then—do you not grant farther, that he lives badly,
disagreeably, disadvantageously, to himself?"

"No.   We cannot possibly grant you that," — replies
Kleinias.

"Then" (says the Athenian) "you and I are in marked
opposition.[s]   For to me what I have affirmed appears as

[q] Plato, Legg. ii. p. 661 C. ὑμεῖς
δὲ καὶ ἐγώ που τάδε λέγομεν, ὡς ταῦτά
ἐστι ξύμπαντα δικαίοις μὲν καὶ ὁσίοις
ἄνδρασιν ἄριστα κτήματα, ἀδίκοις δὲ
κάκιστα ξύμπαντα, ἀρξάμενα ἀπὸ τῆς
ὑγιείας.

[r] Plato, Legg. ii. p. 661 D. Ταῦτα
δὴ λέγειν οἶμαι τοὺς παρ' ὑμῖν ποιητὰς
πείσετε καὶ ἀναγκάσετε, &c.

[s] Plato, Legg. ii. p. 662 A-B. ἢ
τοῦτο μὲν ἴσως ἂν ξυγχωρήσαιτε, τό γε

αἰσχρῶς (ζῆν);   Κλεινίας. Πάνυ μὲν
οὖν.   'Αθηναῖος. Τί δὲ, τὸ καὶ κακῶς;
Κλειν. Οὐκ ἂν ἔτι τοῦθ' ὁμοίως.
'Αθην. Τί δὲ; τὸ καὶ ἀηδῶς καὶ μὴ
ξυμφερόντως αὐτῷ;   Κλειν. Καὶ πῶς
ἂν ταῦτά γ' ἔτι ξυγχωροῖμεν;   'Αθην.
"Οπως ; εἰ θεὸς ἡμῖν, ὡς ἔοικεν, ὦ φίλοι,
δοίη τις συμφωνίαν, ὡς νῦν γε σχεδὸν
ἀπᾴδομεν ἀπ' ἀλλήλων.   'Εμοὶ γὰρ δὴ
φαίνεται ταῦτα οὕτως ἀναγκαῖα, ὡς οὐδὲ
Κρήτη νῆσος σαφῶς.

necessary as the existence of Krete is indisputable. If I were
Ethical creed lawgiver, I should force the poets and all the citi-
laid down by
the Athenian zens to proclaim it with one voice: and I should
—Poets re-
quired to punish most severely every one[t] who affirmed that
conform to it. there could be any wicked men who lived agreeably, or that there could be any course advantageous or
profitable, which was not at the same time the most just.
These and other matters equally at variance with the opinions received among Kretans, Spartans, and mankind
generally—I should persuade my citizens to declare unani-
mously.—For let us assume for a moment your opinion, and
let us ask any lawgiver or any father advising his son.—You
say that the just course of life is one thing, and that the
agreeable course is another; I ask you which of the two is
the happiest? If you say that the agreeable course is the
happiest, what do you mean by always exhorting me to be
just? Do you wish me not to be happy?[u] If on the contrary you tell me that the just course of life is happier than
the agreeable, I put another question—What is this Good
and Beautiful which the lawgiver extols as superior to pleasure, and in which the just man's happiness consists? What
good *can* he possess, apart from pleasure?[x] He obtains praise
and honour:—Is *that* good, but disagreeable—and would the
contrary, infamy, be agreeable? A life in which a man
neither does wrong to others nor receives wrong from others,—
is *that* disagreeable, though good and honourable—and would
the contrary life be agreeable, but dishonourable? You will
not affirm that it is.[y]

"Surely then, my doctrine—which regards the pleasurable,
the just, the good, and the honourable, as indissolubly connected,—has at least a certain force of persuasion, if it has
nothing more, towards inducing men to live a just and holy
life: so that the lawgiver would be both base and wanting to
his own purposes, if he did not proclaim it as a truth. For no

<hr/>

[t] Plato, Legg. ii. p. 662 C. ζημίαν τε ὀλίγου μεγίστην ἐπιτιθείην ἂν, εἴ τις ἐν τῇ χώρᾳ φθέγξαιτο ὡς εἰσί τινες ἄνθρωποι πονηροὶ μὲν, ἡδέως δὲ ζῶντες, &c.·

[u] Plato, Legg. ii. p. 662 D-E.

[x] Plato, Legg. ii. p. 662 E. εἰ δ' αὖ

τὸν δικαιότατον εὐδαιμονέστατον ἀποφαίνοιτο βίον εἶναι, ζητοῖ που πᾶς ἂν ὁ ἀκούων, οἶμαι, τί ποτ' ἐν αὐτῷ τὸ τῆς ἡδονῆς κρεῖττον ἀγαθόν τε καὶ καλὸν ὁ νόμος ἐνὸν ἐπαινεῖ; τί γὰρ δὴ δικαίῳ χωριζόμενον ἡδονῆς ἀγαθὸν ἂν γένοιτο;

[y] Plato, Legg. ii. p. 663 A.

one will be willingly persuaded to do anything which does not carry with it in its consequences more pleasure than pain.[z] There is indeed confusion in every man's vision, when he looks at these consequences in distant outline: but it is the duty of the lawgiver to clear up such confusion, and to teach his citizens in the best way he can, by habits, encouraging praises, discourses, &c., how they ought to judge amidst these deceptive outlines. Injustice, when looked at thus in prospect, seems to the unjust man pleasurable, while justice seems to him thoroughly disagreeable. On the contrary, to the just man, the appearance is exactly contrary: to him justice seems pleasurable, injustice repulsive. Now which of these two judgments shall we pronounce to be the truth? That of the just man. The verdict of the better soul is unquestionably more trustworthy than that of the worse. We must therefore admit it to be a truth, that the unjust life is not merely viler and more dishonourable, but also in truth more disagreeable, than the just life."[a]

Such is the course of proof which Plato's Athenian speaker considers sufficient to establish this ethical doctrine. But he proceeds to carry the reasoning a step farther, as follows:— The Spartan and Kretan do not agree with him.

"Nay, even if this were not a true position—as I have just shown it to be—any lawgiver even of moderate worth, if ever he ventured to tell a falsehood to youth for useful purposes, could proclaim no falsehood more useful than this, nor more efficacious towards making them disposed to practise justice willingly, without compulsory force."[b]

"Truth is honourable" (observes the Kretan) "and durable. You will not find it easy to make them believe what you propose."

"Why, it was found easy" (replies the Athenian) "to

---

[z] Plato, Legg. ii. p. 663 B. Οὐκοῦν ὁ μὲν μὴ χωρίζων λόγος ἡδύ τε καὶ δίκαιον καὶ ἀγαθὸν καὶ καλὸν, πιθανός γ' εἰ μηδὲν ἄλλο, πρὸς τό τινα ἐθέλειν ζῆν τὸν ὅσιον καὶ δίκαιον βίον· ὥστε νομοθέτῃ γε αἴσχιστος λόγων καὶ ἐναντιώτατος, ὃς ἂν μὴ φῇ ταῦτα οὕτως ἔχειν· οὐδεὶς γὰρ ἂν ἑκὼν ἐθέλοι πράττειν τοῦτο, ὅτῳ μὴ τὸ χαίρειν τοῦ λυπεῖσθαι πλέον ἕπεται.

[a] Plato, Legg. ii. p. 663 C·D.

[b] Plato, Legg. ii. p. 663 E. Νομοθέτης δ', οὗ τι καὶ σμικρὸν ὄφελος, εἰ καὶ μὴ τοῦτο ἦν οὕτως ἔχον, ὡς καὶ νῦν αὐτὸ ἥρηχ' ὁ λόγος ἔχειν, εἴπερ τι καὶ ἄλλο ἐτόλμησεν ἂν ἐπ' ἀγαθῷ ψεύδεσθαι πρὸς τοὺς νέους, ἔστιν ὅ, τι τούτου ψεῦδος λυσιτελέστερον ἂν ἐψεύσατό ποτε, καὶ δυνάμενον μᾶλλον ποιεῖν μὴ βίᾳ ἀλλ' ἑκόντας πάντα τὰ δίκαια;

make men believe the mythe respecting Kadmus and the
armed men who sprang out of the earth after the sowing of
the dragon's teeth—and many other mythes equally incredible. Such examples show conclusively that the lawgiver
can implant in youthful minds any beliefs which he tries to
implant. He need therefore look to nothing, except to determine what are those beliefs which, if implanted, would be
most beneficial to the city. Having determined this, he will
employ all his machinery to make all his citizens proclaim
these beliefs constantly, with one voice, and without contradiction, in all hymns, stories, and discourses." [c]

" This brings me to my own proposition. My three Choruses (youthful, mature, elderly) will be required to sing
perpetually to the tender minds of children all the honourable and good doctrines which I shall prescribe in detail.
But the sum and substance of them will be—The best life
has been declared by the Gods to be also the most pleasurable, and it *is* the most pleasurable. [d] The whole city—man,
boy, freeman, slave, male, female—will be always singing
this doctrine to itself in choric songs, diversified by the poets
in such manner as to keep up the interest and satisfaction of
the singers." [e]

Here, then, we have the general doctrine, ethical and
social, which is to be maintained in exclusive possession of the voice, ear, and mind, of the Platonic
citizens. The imitative movements of the tripartite
Chorus must be kept in perfect accordance with it: [f]
for all music is imitative, and care must be taken to
imitate the right things in a right manner. To ensure such
accordance, magistrates must be specially chosen as censors
over both poets and singers. But this, in Plato's view, is not
enough. He requires, besides, that the choristers should
themselves understand both what they ought to imitate, and
how it should be imitated. Such understanding cannot be

Chorus of Elders are required to set an example in keeping up the purity of the music prescribed.

[c] Plato, Legg. ii. p. 664 A.
[d] Plato, Legg. ii. p. 664 B.
[e] Plato, Legg. ii p. 665 C.
It will be understood that here, as elsewhere, I give the substance of Plato's reasoning, without binding myself to the translation of the particular words.
[f] Plato, Legg. ii. p. 668 A. Οὐκοῦν μουσικήν γε πᾶσάν φαμεν εἰκαστικήν τε εἶναι καὶ μιμητικήν;

expected from the Chorus of youths—nor even from that of mature men. But it may be expected, and must be required, in the Chorus of Elders: which will thus set an example to the other two, of strict adherence to the rectitude of the musical standard.[g] The purity of the Platonic musical training depends mainly upon the constant and efficacious choric activity of the old citizens.

But how is such activity to be obtained? Old men will not only find it repugnant to their natural dispositions, but will even be ashamed to exhibit themselves in choric music and dance before the younger citizens.

It is here that Plato invokes the aid of wine-drinking and intoxication. The stimulus of wine, drunk by the old men at the Dionysiac banquets, will revive in them a temporary fit of something like juvenile activity, and will supply an antidote to inconvenient diffidence.[h] Under such partial excitement, they will stand forward freely to discharge their parts in the choric exhibitions ; which, as performed by them, will be always in full conformity with the canon of musical rectitude, and will prevent it from becoming corrupted or relaxed by the younger choristers. To ensure however that the excitement shall not overpass due limits, Plato prescribes that the president of the banquet shall be a grave person drinking no wine at all. The commendation or reproof of such a president will sustain the reason and self-command of the guests, at the pitch compatible with full execution of their choric duty.[i] Plato interdicts wine altogether to youths, until 18 years of age—allows it only in small quantities until the age of 40—but permits and even encourages elders above 40 to partake of the full inspiration of the Dionysiac banquets.[k]

This manner of regarding intoxication must probably have occurred to Plato at a time later than the composition of the

The Elders require the stimulus of wine, in order to go through the choric duties with spirit.

---

[g] Plato, Legg. ii. pp. 670 B-D, vi. p. 764 C, vii. p. 812 B.

Aristotle directs that the elders shall be relieved from active participation in choric duties, and confined to the function of judging or criticising, Politic. viii. 6. 1340, b. 38.

[h] Plato, Legg. ii. p. 666 A-C. ἐπί-

κουρον τῆς τοῦ γήρως αὐστηρότητος ἐδωρήσατο (Διόνυσος) οἶνον, φάρμακον, ὥστε ἀνηβᾶν ἡμᾶς — πρῶτον μὲν δὴ διατεθεὶς οὕτως ἄρ' οὐκ ἂν ἔθελοι ἕκαστος προθυμότερόν γε, ἧττον αἰσχυνόμενος—ᾄδειν;

[i] Plato, Legg. ii. p.671.

[k] Plato, Legg. ii. p. 666 A.

Republic, wherein we find it differently handled.[1] It deserves attention as an illustration, both of his boldness in following out his own ethical views, in spite of
the consciousness [m] that they would appear strange to
others—and of the prominent function which he assigns to old
men in this dialogue De Legibus. He condemns intoxication
decidedly, when considered simply as a mode of enjoyment,
and left to the taste of the company without any president or
regulation. But with most moralists such condemnation is
an unreflecting and undistinguishing sentiment. Against this
Plato enters his protest. He considers that intoxication, if
properly regulated, may be made conducive to valuable ends,
ethical and social. Without it the old men cannot be wound
up to the pitch of choric activity; without such activity, constant and unfaltering, the rectitude of the choric system has
no adequate security against corruption: without such security,
the emotional training of the citizens generally will degenerate. Farthermore, Plato takes occasion from drunkenness to
lay down a general doctrine respecting pleasures. Men must
be trained to self-command against pleasures, as they are
against pains, not by keeping out of the way of temptation,
but by regulated exposure to temptations, with motives at
hand to help them in the task of resistance. Both these views
are original and suggestive, like so many others in the Platonic
writings: tending to rescue Ethics from that tissue of rhetorical
and emotional commonplace in which it so frequently ap-

[1] In the Republic (iii. p. 398 E) Plato pronounced intoxication (μέθη) to be most unbecoming for his Guardians. He places it in the same class of defects as indolence and effeminacy. He also repudiates those varieties of musical harmony called *Ionic* and *Lydian*, because they were languid, effeminate, symposiac, or suitable for a drinking society (μαλακαί τε καὶ συμποτικαί, χαλαραί). Various musical critics of the day (τῶν περὶ μουσικήν τινες—we learn this curious fact from Aristotle, Polit. viii. 7, near the end) impugned this opinion of Plato. They affirmed that drunkenness was exciting and stimulating, — not relaxing nor favourable to languor and heaviness: that the effeminate musical modes were not congenial to drunkenness.

When we read the Treatise De Legibus, we observe that Plato altered his opinion respecting μέθη, and had come round to agree with these musical critics. He treats μέθη as exciting and stimulating, not relaxing and indolent; he even applies it as a positive stimulus to wind up the Elders. Moreover, instead of repudiating it absolutely, he defends its usefulness under proper regulations. Perhaps the change of his opinion may have been partly owing to these very criticisms.

[m] Plato, Legg. ii. p. 665 B. Old Philokleon, in the Vespæ of Aristophanes (1320 seq.), under the influence of wine and jovial excitement, is a pregnant subject for comic humour.

pears;—and to keep present before those who handle it, those ideas of an end to be attained, and of discrimination as to means—which are essential to its pretensions as a science.

But the general ethical discussion—which Plato tells us[n] that he introduces to establish premises for his enactment respecting drunkenness—is of greater importance than the enactment itself.   He pre- *General ethical doctrine held by Plato in Leges.* scribes imperatively the doctrine and matter which alone is to be tolerated in his choric hymns or heard in his city.   I have given an abstract (p. 322-326) of the doctrine here laid down and the reasonings connected therewith, because they admit of being placed in instructive comparison with his manner of treating the same subject in other dialogues.

What is the relation between Pleasure, Good, and Happiness?   Pain, Evil, Unhappiness?   Do the names in the first triplet mean substantially the same thing, only looked at in different aspects and under different conditions?   Or do they mean three distinct things, *Pleasure—Good—Happiness—What is the relation between them?* separable and occurring the one without the other?   This important question was much debated, and answered in many different ways, by Grecian philosophers from the time of Sokrates downward—and by Roman philosophers after them. Plato handles it not merely in the dialogue now before us, but in several others—differently too in each: in Protagoras, Gorgias, Republic, Philêbus, &c.[o]

Here, in the dialogue De Legibus (by incidental allusion, too, in some of the Epistles), we have the latest form in which these doctrines about Pleasure, Happiness, Good—and their respective contraries—found expression in Plato's compositions.   Much of the doctrines is *Comparison of the doctrine laid down in Leges.* the same—yet with some material variation.   It is here reasserted, by the Athenian, that the just and temperate man is happy, and that the unjust man is miserable, whatever may befal him: moreover that good things (such as health, strength, sight, hearing, &c.) are good only to the just man, evil to the unjust—while the contrary (such as sickness, weakness, blindness) are good things to the unjust, evil only to the just.   To

[n] Plato, Legg. ii. p. 664 D.
[o] See above, vol. ii. ch. xxii. pp. 128-129.

this position both the Spartan and the Kretan distinctly refuse
their assent: and Plato himself admits that mankind in general
would agree with them in such refusal.[p] He vindicates his
own opinion by a new argument which had not before appeared.
" The just man himself" (he urges), " one who has been fully
trained in just dispositions, will feel it to be as I say: the
unjust man will feel the contrary. But the just man is much
more trustworthy than the unjust: therefore we must believe
what he says to be the truth."[q] Appeal is here made, not to
the Wise Man or Artist, but to the just man: whose sentence
is invested with a self-justifying authority, wherein Plato looks
for his *aliquid inconcussum*. Now it is for philosophy, or for the
true Artist, that this pre-eminence is claimed in the Republic,[r]
where Sokrates declares, that each of the three souls combined in the individual man (the rational or philosophical, in
the head—the passionate or ambitious, between the neck and
the diaphragm—and the appetitive, below the diaphragm) has
its special pleasures ; that each prefers its own ; but that the
judgment of the philosophical man must be regarded as paramount over the other two.[s] Comparing this demonstration in
the Republic with the unsupported inference here noted in the
Leges—we perceive the contrast of the oracular and ethical
character of the latter, with the intellectual and dialectic
character of the former.

Again, here in the Leges, the Athenian puts it to his two
companions, Whether the unjust man, assuming him to possess every imaginable endowment and advantage in life, will
not live, nevertheless, both dishonourably and miserably?
They admit that he will live dishonourably: they deny that
he will live miserably.[t] The Athenian replies by reasserting
emphatically his own opinion, without any attempt to prove
it. Now in the Gorgias, this same issue is raised between
Sokrates and Polus: Sokrates refutes his opponent by a dialectic argument, showing that if the first of the two doctrines
(the living dishonourably—$a i \sigma \chi \rho \hat{\omega} s$) be granted, the second

[p] Plato, Legg. ii. p. 662 C.
[q] Plato, Legg. ii. p. 663 C.
[r] Plato, Repub. ix. pp. 580 E-583 A.
[s] Plato, Repub. ix. p. 583 A. Ἀνάγκη 'ὰ ὁ φιλόσοφός τε καὶ ὁ φιλόλογος

ἐπαινεῖ, ἀληθέστατα εἶναι—κύριος γοῦν
ἐπαινέτης ὢν ἐπαινεῖ τὸν ἑαυτοῦ βίον ὁ
φρόνιμος.
[t] Plato, Legg. ii. p. 662 A.

(the living miserably—κακῶς) cannot be consistently denied.[u] The dialectic of Sokrates is indeed more ingenious than conclusive: but still it *is* dialectic—and thus stands contrasted with the oracular emphasis which is substituted for it in Leges.

Farthermore, the distinction between Pleasure and Good, in the language of the Athenian speaker in the Leges, approximates more nearly to the doctrine of Sokrates in the Protagoras, than to his doctrine in the Gorgias, Philêbus, and Republic. The Athenian proclaims that he is dealing with men, and not with Gods, and that he must therefore recognise the nature of man, with its fundamental characteristics: that no man will willingly do anything from which he does not anticipate more pleasure than pain: that every man desires the maximum of pleasure and the minimum of pain, and desires nothing else: that there neither is nor can be any Good, apart from Pleasure or superior to Pleasure: that to insist upon a man being just, if you believe that he will obtain more pleasure or less pain from an unjust mode of life, is absurd and inconsistent: that the doctrine which declares the life of pleasure and the life of justice to lead in two distinct paths, is a heresy deserving not only censure but punishment.[x] Plato here enunciates, as distinctly as Epikurus did after him, that Pleasures and Pains must be regulated (here regulated by the lawgiver), so that each man

Doctrine in Leges about Pleasure and Good—approximates more nearly to the Protagoras than to Gorgias and Philêbus.

---

[u] Plato, Gorgias, pp. 474 C, 478 E.

[x] Plato, Legg. ii. pp. 662 C-D-E, 663 B.

In v. pp. 732 E to 734, the Athenian speaker delivers τὰ ἀνθρώπινα of the general preface or pröem to his Laws, after having previously delivered τὰ θεῖα (v. pp. 727-732).

Τὰ θεῖα. These are precepts respecting piety to the Gods, and behaviour to parents, strangers, suppliants; and respecting the duty of rendering due honour, first to the mind, next to the body—of maintaining both the one and the other in a sound and honourable condition. Repeated exhortation is given to obey the enactments whereby the lawgiver regulates pleasures and pains: the precepts are also enforced by insisting on the suffering which will accrue to the agent if they be neglected. We also read (what is said also in Gorgias) that the δίκη κακουργίας μεγίστη is τὸ ὁμοιοῦσθαι κακοῖς ἄνδρασιν (p. 728 B).

Τὰ ἀνθρώπινα, which follow τὰ θεῖα, indicate the essential conditions of human character which limit and determine the application of such precepts to man. To love pleasure—to hate pain—are the paramount and indefeasible attributes of man; but they admit of being regulated, and they ought to be regulated by wisdom—the μετρητικὴ τέχνη insisted on by Sokrates in the Protagoras (p. 356 E). Compare Legg. i. p. 636 E, ii. p. 653 A.

may attain the maximum of the former with the minimum of
the latter : and that Good, apart from maximum of pleasure or
minimum of pain accruing to the agent himself,[y] cannot be
made consistent with the nature or aspirations of man.

There is another point too in which the Athenian speaker
Comparison of Leges with Republic and Gorgias. here recedes from the lofty pretensions of Sokrates
in the Republic and the Gorgias. In the second
Book of the Republic, we saw Glaukon and Adeiman-
tus challenge Sokrates to prove that justice, apart from all its
natural consequences, will suffice *per se* to make the just man
happy ;[z] *per se*, that is, even though all the society misconceive his character, and render no justice to him, but heap upon
him nothing except obloquy and persecution. If (Glaukon
urges) you can only recommend justice when taken in conjunction with the requiting esteem and reciprocating justice
from others towards the just agent, this is no recommendation
of justice at all. Your argument implies a tacit admission,
that it will be better still if he can pass himself off as just in
the opinion of others, without really being just himself : and
you must be understood as recommending to him this latter
course—if he can do it successfully. Sokrates accepts the
challenge, and professes to demonstrate the thesis tendered to
him : which is in substance the cardinal dogma afterwards
espoused by the Stoics. I have endeavoured to show (in a
former chapter [a]), that his demonstration is altogether unsuccessful : and when we turn to the Treatise De Legibus, we
shall see that the Athenian speaker recedes from the doctrine
altogether : confining himself to the defence of justice *with*
its requiting and reciprocating consequences, not *without* them.
The just man, as the Athenian speaker conceives him, is one who
performs his obligations towards others, and towards whom
others perform their obligations also : he is one who obtains from
others that just dealing and that esteem which is his due :
and when so conceived, his existence is one of pleasure and
happiness.[b] This is, in substance, the Epikurean doctrine substituted for the Stoic. It is that which Glaukon and Adei-

---

[y] It is among the tests of a well-disciplined army (according to Xenophon, Cyropæd. i. 6, 26) ὅποτε τὸ πείθεσθαι αὐτοῖς ἥδιον εἴη τοῦ ἀπειθεῖν.

[z] Plato, Republic, ii. pp. 359-367.
[a] See above, chap. xxxiv. p. 127 seq.
[b] Plato, Legg. ii. p. 663 A.

mantus in the Republic deprecate as unworthy disparagement
of justice; and which they adjure Sokrates, by his attachment
to justice, to stand up and repel.[c] Now even this, the Epikurean doctrine, is true only with certain qualifications: since
there are various other conditions essential to happiness, over
and above the ethical conditions. Still it is not so utterly at
variance with the truth as the doctrine which Sokrates undertakes to prove, but never does prove, in the Republic.

The last point which I shall here remark in this portion of
the Treatise De Legibus is, the sort of mistrust mani- *Plato here*
fested by Plato of the completeness of his own proof. *mistrusts the goodness of*
Notwithstanding the vehement phrases in which the *his own proof. He falls back*
Athenian speaker proclaims his internal persuasion *upon useful fiction.*
of the truth of his doctrine, while acknowledging at the same
time that not only his two companions, but most other persons
also, took the opposite view [d]—he finds it convenient to reinforce
the demonstration of the expositor by the omnipotent infallibility of the lawgiver. He descends from the region of established truth to that of useful fiction. " Even if the doctrine
(that the pleasurable, the just, the good, and the honourable, are
indissoluble) were not true, the lawgiver ought to adopt it as
an useful fiction for youth, effective towards inducing them to
behave justly without compulsion. The lawgiver can obtain
belief for any fiction which he pleases to circulate, as may be
seen by the implicit belief obtained for the Theban mythe
about the dragon's teeth, and a thousand other mythes equally
difficult of credence. He must proclaim the doctrine as an
imperative article of faith; carefully providing that it shall
be perpetually recited, by one and all his citizens, in the
public hymns, narratives, and discourses, without any voice
being heard to call it in question." [e]

---

[c] Plato, Republ. ii. p. 368 B. δέδοικα γὰρ μὴ οὐδ' ὅσιον ᾖ παραγενόμενον
δικαιοσύνη κακηγορουμένῃ μὴ βοηθεῖν.
[d] Plato, Legg. ii. p. 662 B.
[e] Plato, Legg. ii. pp. 663 B, 664 A.
ἐπ' ἀγαθῷ ψεύδεσθαι πρὸς τοὺς νέους,
&c. So, in the Bacchæ of Euripides
(332), the two old men, Kadmus and
Teiresias, after vainly attempting to
inculcate upon Pentheus the belief in
and the worship of Dionysus, at last

appeal to his prudence, and admonish
him of the danger of unbelief:—

κεἰ μὴ γὰρ ἔστιν ὁ θεὸς οὗτος, ὡς σὺ
    φῇς,
παρὰ σοὶ λεγέσθω, καὶ καταψεύδου
    καλῶς
ὡς ἔστι, Σεμέλη θ' ἵνα δοκῇ θεὸν τεκεῖν,
ἡμῖν τε τιμὴ παντὶ τῷ γένει προσῇ.
ὁρᾶς τὸν Ἀκταίωνος ἄθλιον μόρον;
    —— ὃ μὴ πάθῃς σύ——

Here is a second attempt on the part of Plato, in addition
to that which we have seen in the Republic,[f] to employ deliberate ethical fiction as a means of governing his citizens: first to implant and accredit it—
next to prescribe its incessant iteration by all the
citizens in the choric ceremonies—lastly to consecrate it, and
to forbid all questioners or opponents: all application of the
Sokratic Elenchus to test it.   In this treatise he speaks of the
task as easier to the lawgiver than he had described it to be in
his Republic: in which latter we found him regarding a new
article of faith as difficult to implant, but as easy to uphold if
once it be implanted; while in the Treatise De Legibus both
processes are treated as alike achievable and certain.   The conception of dogmatic omnipotence had become stronger in Plato's
mind during the interval between the two treatises.   Intending
to postulate for himself the complete regulation not merely
of the actions, but also of the thoughts and feelings of his
citizens—intending moreover to exclude free or insubordi-
nate intellects—he naturally looks upon all as docile recipients of any faith which he thinks it right to preach.   When
he appeals, however, as proofs of the facility of his plan, to
the analogy of the numerous mythes received with implicit
faith throughout the world around him—we see how low an
estimate he formed of the process whereby beliefs are generated in the human mind, and of their evidentiary value as
certifying the truth of what is believed.   People believed
what was told them at first by some imposing authority, and
transmitted the belief to their successors, even without the
extraneous support of inquisitorial restrictions such as the
Platonic lawgiver throws round the Magnêtic community in
the Leges.   It is in reference to such self-supporting beliefs
that Sokrates stands forth, in the earlier Platonic compositions, as an enquirer into the reasons on which they rested—
a task useful as well as unpleasant to those whom he questioned—attracting unpopularity as well as reputation to himself.   Plato had then keenly felt the inestimable value of this
Elenchus or examining function personified in his master;
but in the Treatise De Legibus the master has no place, and

(margin note) Deliberate ethical fiction employed as means of governing.

the function is severely proscribed. Plato has come round to the dogmatic pole, extolling the virtue of passive recipient minds who have no other sentiment than that which the lawgiver issues to them. Yet while he postulates in his own city the infallible authority of the lawgiver, and enforces it by penalties, as final and all-sufficient to determine the ethical beliefs of all the Platonic citizens—we shall find in a subsequent book of this Treatise that he denounces and punishes those who generalise this very postulate ; and who declare the various ethical beliefs, actually existing in communities of men, to have been planted each by some human authority— not to have sprung from any unseen oracle called Nature.[g]

Such is the ethical doctrine which Plato proclaims in the Leges, and which he directs to be sung by each Chorus among the three (boys, men, elders), with appropriate music and dancing. It is on the constancy, strictness, and sameness of these choric and musical influences, that he relies for the emotional training of youth. If the musical training be either intermitted or allowed to vary from the orthodox canon—if the theatrical exhibitions be regulated by the taste of the general audience, and not by the judgment of a few discerning censors —the worst consequences will arise : the character of the citizens will degenerate, and the institutions of his city will have no foundation to rest upon.[h] The important effects of music, as an instrument in the hands of the lawgiver for regulating the emotions of the citizens, and especially for inspiring a given emotional character to youth—are among the characteristic features of Plato's point of view, common to both the Republic and the Laws. There is little trace of this point of view either in Xenophon or in Isokrates ; but Aristotle embraces it to a considerable extent. It grew out of the practice and tradition of the Grecian cities, in most of which the literary teaching of youth was imparted by making them read, learn, recite, or chaunt the works of various poets; while the use of the lyre was also taught, together with regulated movements in the dance. The powerful ethical effect of musical teaching

Importance of music and chorus as an engine of teaching for Plato. Views of Xenophon and Aristotle compared.

---

[g] Plato, Legg. x. pp. 889-890.
[h] Plato, Republ. iv. p. 424 C-D; Legg. iii. pp. 700-701.

(even when confined to the simplest choric psalmody and dance), enforced by perpetual drill both of boys and men, upon the unlettered Arcadians—may be seen recognised even by a practical politician like Polybius,[i] who considers it indispensable for the softening of violent and sanguinary tempers : the diversity of the effect, according to the different modes of music employed, is noted by Aristotle,[k] and was indeed matter of common repute. Plato, as lawgiver, postulates poetry and music of his own dictation. He relies upon constant supplies of this wholesome nutriment, for generating in the youth such emotional dispositions and habits as will be in harmony, both with the doctrines which he preaches, and with the laws which he intends to impose upon them as adults. Here (as in Republic and Timæus) he proclaims that the perfection of character consists in willing obedience or harmonious adjustment of the pleasures and pains, the desires and aversions, to the paramount authority of reason or wisdom—or to the rational conviction of each individual as to what is good and honourable. If, instead of obedience and harmony, there be discord—if the individual, though rationally convinced that a proceeding is just and honourable, nevertheless hates it—or if, while convinced that a proceeding is unjust and dishonourable, he nevertheless loves it—such discord is the worst state of stupidity or mental incompetence.[l] We must recollect that

---

[i] Polybius, iv. pp. 20-21, about the rude Arcadians of Kynætha. He ascribes to this simple choric practice the same effect which Ovid ascribes to "ingenuæ artes," or elegant literature generally :—

Ingenuas didicisse fideliter artes
Emollit mores, nec sinit esse feros.

See the remarkable contention between Æschylus and Euripides in Aristophan. Ran. 876 seq., about the function and comparative excellence of poets (also Nubes, 955). Aristophanes, comparing Æschylus with Euripides, denounces music as having degenerated, and poetry as having been corrupted, at Athens. So far he agrees with Plato; but he ascribes this corruption in a great degree to the conversation of Euripides with Sokrates (Ranæ, 1487); and here Plato would not have gone along with him—at least not when Plato composed his earlier dia-

logues—though the ἦθος of the Treatise De Legibus is in harmony with this sentiment. Polybius cites, with some displeasure, the remark of the historian Ephorus, who asserted that musical teaching was introduced among men for purposes of cheating and mystification—ἐπ' ἀπάτῃ καὶ γοητείᾳ παρεισῆχθαι τοῖς ἀνθρώποις, οὐδαμῶς ἁρμόζοντα λόγον αὐτῷ ῥίψας (iv. 20). Polybius considers this an unbecoming criticism.

[k] Aristotle, Polit. viii. c. 4-5-7, p. 1340, a. 10, 1341, a. 15, 1342, a. 30. We see by these chapters how much the subject was discussed in his day.

The ethical and emotional effects conveyed by the sense of hearing, and distinguishing it from the other senses, are noticed in the Problemata of Aristotle, xix. 27-29, pp. 919-920.

[l] Plato, Legg. iii. p. 689 A. ἡ μεγίστη ἀμαθία—ὅταν τῷ τι δόξῃ καλὸν

(according to the postulate of Treatise De Legibus) the rational convictions of each individual, respecting what is just and honourable, are assumed to be accepted implicitly from the lawgiver, and never called in question by any one. There exists therefore only one individual reason in the community—that of the lawgiver, or Plato himself.

Besides all the ethical prefatory matter, above noticed, Plato gives us also some historical and social prefatory matter, not essential to his constructive scheme (which after all takes its start partly from theoretical principles laid down by himself, partly from a supposed opportunity of applying those principles in the foundation of a new colony), but tending to illustrate the growth of political society, and the abuses into which it naturally tends to lapse. There existed in his time a great variety of distinct communities: some in the simplest, most patriarchal, Cyclopian condition, nothing more than families—some highly advanced in civilization, with its accompanying good and evil—some in each intermediate stage between these two extremes.—The human race (Plato supposes) has perhaps had no beginning, and will have no end. At any rate it has existed from an indefinite antiquity, subject to periodical crises, destructive kosmical outbursts, deluges, epidemic distempers, &c.[m] A deluge, when it occurs, sweeps away all the existing communities with their property, arts, instruments, &c., leaving only a small remnant, who, finding shelter on the top of some high mountain not covered with water, preserve only their lives. Society, he thinks, has gone through a countless number of these cycles.[n] At the end of each, when the deluge recedes, each associated remnant has to begin its development anew, from the rudest and poorest condition. Each little family or sept exists at first separately, with a patriarch whom all implicitly obey, and peculiar customs of its own. Several of these septs gradually coalesce

Marginal note: Historical retrospect as to the growth of cities— Frequent destruction of established communities, with only a small remnant left.

ἢ ἀγαθὸν εἶναι, μὴ φιλῇ τοῦτο ἀλλὰ μισῇ, τὸ δὲ πονηρὸν καὶ ἄδικον δοκοῦν εἶναι φιλῇ τε καὶ ἀσπάζηται· ταύτην τὴν διαφωνίαν λύπης τε καὶ ἡδονῆς πρὸς τὴν κατὰ λόγον δόξαν, ἀμαθίαν φημὶ εἶναι τὴν ἐσχάτην. Compare p. 688 A.

[m] Plato, Legg. iii. pp. 677-678, vi. p. 782 A.

[n] Plato, Legg. p. 680 A. τοῖς ἐν τούτῳ τῷ μέρει τῆς περιόδου γεγονόσιν, &c.

together into one community, choosing one or a few law-givers to adjust and modify their respective customs into harmonious order, and submitting implicitly to the authority of such chosen few.[o] By successive coalitions of this kind, operated in a vast length of time,[p] large cities are gradually formed on the plain and on the seaboard. Property and public force is again accumulated; together with letters, arts, and all the muniments of life.

Such is the idea which Plato here puts forth of the natural genesis and development of human society. Having thus arrived at the formation of considerable cities with powerful military armaments, he carries us into the midst of Hellenic legend—the Trojan War, the hostile reception which the victorious heroes found on their return to Greece after the siege, the Return of the Herakleids to Peloponnesus, and the establishment of the three Herakleid brethren, Têmenus, Kresphontês, Aristodêmus, as kings of Argos, Messênê, and Sparta. The triple Herakleid kingdom was originally founded (he affirms) as a mode of uniting and consolidating the force of Hellas against the Asiatics, who were eager to avenge the capture of Troy. It received strong promises of permanence, both from prophets and from the Delphian oracle.[q] But these hopes were frustrated by misconduct on the part of the kings of Argos and Messênê: who, being youths destitute of presiding reason, and without external checks, obeyed the impulse of unmeasured ambition, oppressed their subjects, and broke down their own power.

Historical or legendary retrospect— The Trojan war—The return of the Herakleids.

To conduct a political community well is difficult; for there are inherent causes of discord and sedition which can only be neutralised in their effects, but can never be eradicated. Among the foremost of these inherent causes, Plato numbers the many distinct and conflicting titles to obedience which are found among mankind, all coexistent and co-ordinate. There are seven such titles, all founded in the nature of man and the essential conditions of society:[r]—1. Parents

Difficulties of government —Conflicts about command— Seven distinct titles to command exist among mankind, all equally natural, and liable to conflict.

---

[o] Plato, Legg. iii. p. 681 C-D.
[p] Plato, Legg. iii. p. 683 A. ἐν χρόνῳ τινὸς μήκεσιν ἀπλέτοις.

[q] Plato, Legg. iii. pp. 685-686.
[r] Plato, Legg. iii. p. 690 A-D. ἀξιώματα τοῦ τε ἄρχειν καὶ ἄρχεσ-

over children. 2. Men of high birth and breed (such as the Herakleids at Sparta) over men of low birth. 3. Old over young. 4. Masters over slaves. 5. The stronger man over the weaker. 6. The wiser man over the man destitute of wisdom. 7. The fortunate man, who enjoys the favour of the Gods (one case of this is indicated by drawing of the best lot) over the less fortunate man (who draws an inferior lot).

Of these seven titles to command, coexisting, distinct, and conflicting with each other, Plato pronounces the sixth—that of superior reason and wisdom—to be the greatest, preferable to all the rest, in his judgment: though he admits the fifth —that of superior force—to be the most extensively prevalent in the actual world.[s]

Plato thinks it imprudent to found the government of society upon any one of these seven titles singly and separately. He requires that each one of them shall be checked and modified by the conjoint operation of others. Messêne and Argos were depraved and ruined by the single principle: while Sparta

Imprudence of founding government upon any one of these titles separately— Governments of Argos and Mes-ênê ruined by the

---

θαι, &c. Ὅσα ἔστι πρὸς ἄρχοντας ἀξιώματα καὶ ὅτι πεφυκότα πρὸς ἄλληλα ἐναντίως.

[s] Plato, Legg. iii. p. 690 C.

This enumeration by Plato of seven distinct and conflicting ἀξιώματα τοῦ ἄρχειν καὶ ἄρχεσθαι, deserves notice in many ways. All the seven are *natural*: nature is considered as including multifarious and conflicting titles (compare Xenophon, Memorab. ii. 6, 21), and therefore as not furnishing in itself any justification or ground of preference for one above the rest. The ἀξίωμα of superior force is just as *natural* as the ἀξίωμα of superior wisdom, though Plato himself pronounces the latter to be the greatest; that is— greatest, not φύσει but νόμῳ or τέχνῃ, according to his own rational and deliberate estimation. Plato is not uniform in this view, for he uses elsewhere the phrases φύσει and κατὰ φύσιν as if they specially and exclusively belonged to that which he approves, and furnished a justification for it (see Legg. x. pp. 889-890, besides the Republic and the Gorgias). Again the lot, or the process of sortition, is here described as carrying with it both the preference of the Gods and the

principles of justice (τὸ δικαιότατον εἶναί φαμεν). The Gods determine upon whom the lot should fall—compare Homer, Iliad, vii. 179. This is a remarkable view of the lot, and represents a feeling much diffused among the ancient democracies.

The relation of master and slave counts, in Plato's view, among the natural relations, with its consequent rights and obligations.

The force of εὐτυχία, as a title to command, is illustrated in the speech addressed by Alkibiades to the Athenian assembly, Thucyd. vi. 16-17: he allows it even in his competitor Nikias—ἀλλ' ἔως ἐγώ τε ἔτι ἀκμάζω μετ' αὐτῆς καὶ ὁ Νικίας εὐτυχὴς δοκεῖ εἶναι, ἀποχρήσασθε τῇ ἑκατέρου ἡμῶν ὠφελίᾳ. Compare also the language of Nikias himself, in his own last speech under the extreme distress of the Athenian army in Sicily, Thucyd. vii. 77.

In the Politikus (p. 293 and elsewhere) Plato admits no ἀξίωμα τοῦ ἄρχειν as genuine or justifiable, except Science, Art, superior wisdom, in one or a few Artists of governing; the same in Republic, v. p. 474 C, respecting what he there calls φιλοσοφία.

single princi-
ple—Sparta
avoided it. was preserved and exalted by a mixture of different elements. The kings of Argos and Messênê, irrational youths with nothing to restrain them (except oaths, which they despised), employed their power to abuse and mischief. Such was the consequence of trusting to the exclusive title of high breed, embodied in one individual person. But Apollo and Lykurgus provided better for Sparta. They softened regal insolence by establishing the double line of co-ordinate kings: they introduced the title of old age, along with that of high breed, by founding the Senate of twenty-eight elders: they farther introduced the title of sortition, or something near it, by nominating the annual Ephors. The mixed government of Sparta was thus made to work for good, while the unmixed systems of Argos and Messênê both went wrong.[t] Both the two latter states were in perpetual war with Sparta, so as to frustrate that purpose—union against Asiatics—with a view to which the triple Herakleid kingdom was originally erected in Peloponnesus. Had each of these three kingdoms been temperately and moderately governed, like Sparta, so as to maintain unimpaired the projected triple union—the Persian invasions of Greece by Darius and Xerxes would never have taken place.[u]

Plato casts
Hellenic
legend into
accordance
with his own
political
theories. Such is the way in which Plato casts the legendary event, called the Return of the Herakleids, into accordance with a political theory of his own. That event, in his view, afforded the means of uniting Hellas internally, and of presenting such a defensive combination as would have deterred all invasions from Asia, if only the proper principles of legislation and government had been understood and applied. The lesson to be derived from this failure is, that we ought not to concentrate great authority in one hand; and that we ought to blend together several principles of authority, instead of resorting to the exclusive action of one alone.[x] This lesson deserves attention, as a

---

[t] Plato, Legg. iii. pp. 691-692.
[u] Plato, Legg. iii. p. 692 C-D.
[x] Plato, Legg. iii, p. 693 A. ὡς ἄρα οὐ δεῖ μεγάλας ἀρχὰς οὐδ' αὖ ἀμίκτους νομοθετεῖν. Compare pp. 685-686.
　　Plato here affirms not only that

Messênê and Argos were and had been constantly at war with Sparta, but that they were so at the time of the Persian invasion of Greece—and that Messênê thus hindered the Spartans from assisting the Athenians at Marathon, pp. 692 E, 698 E. His statement

portion of political theory; but I feel convinced that neither Herodotus nor Thucydides would have concurred in Plato's historical views. Neither of them would have admitted the disunion between Sparta, Argos, and Messênê as a main cause of the Persian invasion of Greece.

A lesson—analogous, though not exactly the same—is derived by Plato from the comparison of the Persian with the Athenian government. Persia presents an excess of despotism: Athens an excess of liberty. There are two distinct primordial forms of government—*mother-polities*, Plato calls them—out of which all existing governments may be said to have been generated or diversified. One of these is monarchy, of which the Persians manifest the extreme: the other is democracy, of which Athens manifests the extreme. Both extremes are mischievous. The wise lawgiver must blend and combine the two together in proper proportion. Without such combination, he cannot attain good government, with its three indispensable constituents—freedom, intelligence or temperance, and mutual attachment among the citizens.[y]

that Argos was at least neutral, if not treacherous and philo-Persian, during the invasion of Xerxes, is coincident with Herodotus; but not so his statement that the Lacedæmonians were kept back by the war against Messênê. Indeed at that time the Messenians had no separate domicile or independent station in Peloponnesus. They had been conquered by Sparta long before, and their descendants in the same territory were Helots (Thucyd. i. 101). It is true that there always existed struggling remnants of expatriated Messenians, who maintained the name, and whom Athens protected and favoured during the Peloponnesian war; but there was no independent Messenian government in Peloponnesus until the foundation of the city of Messênê by Epaminondas in 369 B.C., two years after the battle of Leuktra: there had never been any *city* of that name in Peloponnesus before.

Now Plato wrote his Treatise De Legibus *after* the foundation of this city of Messênê and the re-establishment of an independent Messenian community in Peloponnesus. The new city was peopled partly by returning Messenian exiles, partly by enfranchised Helots. It is probable enough that both these classes might be disposed to disguise (as far as they could) the past period of servitude—and to represent the Messenian name and community as never having been wholly effaced in the neighbourhood of Ithômê, though always struggling against an oppressive neighbour. Traditions of this tenor would become current, and Plato has adopted one of them in his historical sketch.

If we look back to what Plato says about the Kretan prophet Epimenides, we shall see that here too he must have followed erroneous traditions. He makes Epimenides contemporary with the invasion of Greece by Darius, instead of contemporary with the Kylonian sacrilege (B.C. 612). When a prophet had got reputation, a great many new prophecies were fathered upon him (as upon Bakis and Musæus) with very little care about chronological consistency. Plato may well have been misled by one of these fictions (Legg. i. p. 642, iii. p. 677).

[y] Plato, Legg. iii. p. 693 B-C. Aristotle (Politic. ii. 6, pp. 1265-1266)

The Persians, according to Plato, at the time when they made their conquests under Cyrus, were not despotic-ally governed, but enjoyed a fair measure of freedom under a brave and patriotic military chief, who kept the people together in mutual attachment. But Cyrus, though a great military chief, had neither received a good training himself, nor knew how to secure it for his own sons.[z] He left them to be educated by the women in the harem, where they were brought up with unmeasured indulgence, acquiring nothing but habits of insolence and caprice. Kambyses became a despot; and after committing great enormities, was ultimately deprived of empire by Smerdis and the Medians. Darius, not a born prince, but an usurper, renovated the Persian empire, and ruled it with as much ability and moderation as Cyrus. But he made the same mistake as Cyrus, in educating his sons in the harem. His son Xerxes became thoroughly corrupted, and ruled despotically. The same has been the case with all the successive kings, all brought up as destined for the sceptre, and morally ruined by a wretched education. The Persian government has been

Cyrus and Darius—Bad training of sons of kings.

alludes to this portion of Plato's doctrine, and approves what is said about the combination of diverse political elements ; but he does not approve the doctrine which declares the two "mother-forms" of government to be extreme despotism or extreme democracy. He says that these two are either no governments at all, or the very worst of governments. Plato gives the same opinion about them, yet he thinks it convenient to make them the starting points of his theory. The objection made by Aristotle appears to be dictated by a sentiment which often influences his theories—Τὸ τέλειον πρότερόν ἐστι τῇ φύσει τοῦ ἀτελοῦς. The perfect is prior in order of nature to the imperfect. He does not choose to take his theoretical point of departure from the worst or most imperfect.

[z] Plato, Legg. p. 694 C. Μαντεύομαι περί γε Κύρου τὰ μὲν ἄλλ' αὐτὸν στρατηγόν τε ἀγαθὸν εἶναι καὶ φιλόπολιν, παιδείας δὲ ὀρθῆς οὐχ ἧφθαι τοπαράπαν.

I think it very probable that these words are intended to record Plato's dissent from the Κύρου Παιδεία of Xenophon. Aulus Gellius (xiv. 3) had read that Xenophon composed the Cyropædia in opposition to the two first books of the Platonic Republic, and that between Xenophon and Plato there existed a grudge (*simultas*) or rivalry ; so also Athenæus, xi. p. 504. It is possible that this may have been the case, but no evidence is produced to prove it. Both of them selected Sokrates as the subject of their descriptions; in so far there may have been a literary competition between them : and various critics seem to have presumed that there could not be *æmulatio* without *simultas*. Each of them composed a Symposion for the purpose of exhibiting Sokrates in his joyous moments. The differences between the two handlings are interesting to notice ; but the evidences which some authors produce, to show that Xenophon in his Symposion alluded to the Symposion of Plato, are altogether uncertain. See the Preface of Schneider to his edition of the Xenophontic Symposion, and his extract from Cornarius.

nothing but a despotism ever since Darius.[a] All freedom of action or speech has been extinguished, and the mutual attachment among the subjects exists no more.[b]

While the Persian government thus exhibits despotism in excess, that of Athens exhibits the contrary mischief—liberty in excess. This has been the growth of the time subsequent to the Persian invasion. At the time when that invasion occurred, the government of Athens was an ancient constitution with a quadruple scale of property, according to which scale political privilege and title to office were graduated : while the citizens generally were then far more reverential to authority, and obedient to the laws, than they are now. Moreover, the invasion itself, being dangerous and terrific in the extreme, was enough to make them obedient and united among themselves, for their own personal safety.[c] But after the invasion had been repelled, the government became altered. The people acquired a great increase of political power, assumed habits of independence and self-judgment, and became less reverential both to the magistrates and to the laws.

Changes for the worse in government of Athens, after the Persian invasion of Greece.

The first department in which this change was wrought at Athens was the department of Music : from whence it gradually extended itself to the general habits of the people. Before the invasion, Music had been distributed, according to ancient practice and under the sanction of ancient authority, under four fixed categories—Hymns, Dirges, Pæans, Dithyrambs.[d] The ancient canons in regard to each were strictly enforced : the musical exhibitions were superintended, and the prizes adjudged by a few highly-trained elders ; while the general body of citizens listened in respectful silence, without uttering a word of acclamation, or even conceiving themselves competent to judge what they heard. Any manifestations on their part were punished by blows from the sticks of the attendants.[e] But this docile submission of the Athenians to

This change began in music, and the poets introduced new modes of composition —they appealed to the judgment of the people, and corrupted them.

[a] Plato, Legg. iii. pp. 694-695.
[b] Plato, Legg. iii. p. 697 D.
[c] Plato, Legg. iii. pp. 698-699.
[d] Plato, Legg. iii. p. 700 A. ὕμνοι —θρῆνοι—παιᾶνες—διθύραμβος.

[e] Plato, Legg. iii. p. 700 B. τὸ δὲ κῦρος τούτων γνῶναί τε καὶ ἅμα γνόντα δικάσαι, ζημιοῦν τε αὖ τὸν μὴ πειθό-μενον, οὐ σύριγξ ἦν οὐδέ τινες ἄμουσοι βοαὶ πλήθους, καθάπερ τὰ νῦν, οὐδ'

authority became gradually overthrown, after the repulse of
the Persians, first in the theatre, next throughout all social
and political life. The originators of this corruption were the
poets: men indeed of poetical genius, but ignorant of the
ethical purpose which their compositions ought to aim at, as
well as of the rightful canons by which they ought to be
guided and limited. These poets, looking to the pleasure of
the audience as their true and only standard, exhibited pieces
in which all the old musical distinctions were confounded together—hymns with dirges, the pæan with the dithyramb,
and the flute with the harp. To such irregular rhythm and
melody, words equally irregular were adapted. The poet
submitted his compositions to the assembled audience, appealing to them as competent judges, and practically declaring them to be such. The audience responded to the appeal.
Acclamation in the theatre was substituted for silence ; and
the judgment of the people became paramount instead of
that pronounced by the enlightened few, according to antecedent custom. Hence the people—having once shaken off
the reverence for authority, and learnt to exercise their own
judgment, in the theatre f—began speedily to do the same on
other matters also. They fancied themselves wise enough to
decide everything for themselves, and contracted a shame-
less disregard for the opinion of better and wiser men. An
excessive measure of freedom was established, tending in its
ultimate consequences to an anarchical or Titanic nature : indifferent to magistrates, laws, parents, elders, covenants, oaths,
and the Gods themselves.g

αὖ κρότοι ἔπαινοι ἀποδίδοντες, ἀλλὰ
τοῖς μὲν γεγονόσι περὶ παιδεύσιν δεδογ-
μένον ἀκούειν ἦν αὐτοῖς μετὰ σιγῆς διὰ
τέλους, παισὶ δὲ καὶ παιδαγωγοῖς καὶ
τῷ πλείστῳ ὄχλῳ ῥάβδου κοσμούσης ἡ
νουθέτησις ἐγένετο.

The testimony here given by Plato
respecting the practice of his own time
is curious and deserves notice : respecting the practice of the times anterior to
the Persian invasion he could have had
no means of accurate knowledge.

f Plato, Legg. iii. p. 701 B. νῦν δὲ
ἦρξε μὲν ἡμῖν ἐκ μουσικῆς ἡ πάντων εἰς
πάντα σοφίας δόξα καὶ παρανομία, ξυνε-
φέσπετο δὲ ἐλευθερία.

g Plato, Legg. iii. p. 701. Ἐφεξῆς

δὴ ταύτῃ τῇ ἐλευθερίᾳ ἡ τοῦ μὴ
ἐθέλειν τοῖς ἄρχουσι δουλεύειν γί-
γνοιτ᾽ ἄν.

The phrase here employed by Plato
affirms inferential tendencies—not facts
realised. How much of the tendencies
had passed into reality at Athens, he
leaves to the imagination of his readers
to supply. It is curious to contrast
the faithless and lawless character of
Athens, here insinuated by Plato, with
the oration of Demosthenes adv. Lep-
tinem (delivered B.C. 355, near upon
the time when the Platonic Leges were
composed), where the main argument
which the orator brings to bear upon
the Dikasts, emphatically and re-

The opinion here expressed by Plato—that the political constitution of Athens was too democratical, and that the changes, (effected by Perikles and others during the half-century succeeding the Persian invasion) whereby it had been rendered more democratical, were mischievous—was held by him in common with a respectable and intelligent minority at Athens. That minority had full opportunity of expressing their disapprobation as we may see by the language of Plato himself; though he commends the Spartans for not allowing any such opportunity to dissenters at Sparta, and expressly prohibits any open expression of dissent in his own community. But his assertion, that the deterioration at Athens was introduced and originated by an innovation in the established canon of music and poetry—is more peculiarly his own. The general doctrine of the powerful revolutionizing effect wrought by changes in the national music, towards subverting the political constitution, was adopted by him from the distinguished musical teacher Damon,[h] the contemporary and companion of Perikles. The fear of such danger to the national institutions is said to have operated on the authorities at Sparta, when they forbade the musical innovations of the poet Timotheus, and destroyed the four new strings which he had just added to the established seven strings of his lyre.[i]

Danger of changes in the national music—declared by Damon, the musical teacher.

peatedly, to induce them to reject the proposition of Leptines, is—τὸ τῆς πόλεως ἦθος ἀψευδὲς καὶ χρηστὸν, οὐ τὸ λυσιτελέστατον πρὸς ἀργύριον σκοποῦν ἀλλά τι καὶ καλὸν πρᾶξαι (p. 461) οὐδ' ὁ πλεῖστος λόγος ἔμοιγε περὶ τῆς ἀτελείας ἔστιν, ἀλλ' ὑπὲρ τοῦ πονηρὸν ἔθος εἰσάγειν τὸν νόμον, καὶ τοιοῦτον δι' οὗ παντ' ἄπιστ' ὅσα ὁ δῆμος δίδωσιν ἔσται, also pp. 500-507, and indeed throughout nearly the whole oration. So also in the other discourses, not only of Demosthenes but of the other orators also—good faith, public and private, and respectful obedience to the laws, are constantly invoked as primary and imperative necessities.

Indeed, in order to find a contradiction to the picture here presented by Plato, of Athenian tendencies since the Persian war, we need not go farther than Plato himself. We have only to read the Menexenus, wherein he professes to describe and panegyrise the achievements of Athens during that very period which he paints in such gloomy colours in the Leges — the period succeeding the Persian invasion. Who is to believe that the people, upon whose virtue he pronounces these encomiums, had thrown off all reverence for good faith, obligation, and social authority? As for the Τιτανικὴ φύσις to which Plato represents the Athenians as approximating, the analogy is principally to be found in the person of the Titan Prométheus, with his philanthropic disposition (see Plato, Menexenus, pp. 243 E, 244 E), and the beneficent suggestions which he imparted to mankind in the way of science and art (Æschyl. Prom. 440-507—Πᾶσαι τέχναι βροτοῖσιν ἐκ Προμηθέως).

[h] Plato, Republ. iv. p. 424 D.

[i] Cicero, De Legib. ii. 15; Pausanias, iii. 12.

Cicero agrees with Plato as to the

Of this general doctrine, however, Plato makes a particular
Plato's aver-
sion to the
tragic and
comic poetry
at Athens. application in the passage now before us, which he
would have found few Athenians, either oligarchical
or democratical, to ratify. What he really condemns is, the tragic and comic poetical representations at
Athens, which began to acquire importance only after the
Persian war, and continued to increase in importance for the
next half century. The greatest revolution which Grecian
music and poetry ever underwent was that whereby Attic
tragedy and comedy were first constituted:—built up by distinguished poets from combination and enlargement of the
simpler pre-existent forms — out of the dithyrambic and
phallic choruses.[k] The first who imparted to tragedy its
grand development and its special novelty of character
was Æschylus — a combatant at Marathon as well as one
of the greatest among ancient poets: after him, Sophokles
carried improvement still farther. It is them that Plato probably means, when he speaks of the authors of this revolution
as men of true poetical genius, but ignorant of the lawful purpose of the Muse—as authors who did not recognise any
rightful canon of music, nor any end to be aimed at beyond
the emotional satisfaction of a miscellaneous audience. The
abundance of dramatic poetry existing in Plato's time must
have been prodigious (a few choice specimens only have descended to us):—while its variety of ingredients and its popularity outshone those four ancient and simple manifestations,
which alone he will tolerate as legitimate. He censures the
innovations of Æschylus and Sophokles as a deplorable triumph
of popular preference over rectitude of standard and purpose.
He tacitly assumes—what Aristotle certainly does not believe,
and what, so far as I can see, there is no ground for believing—
that the earlier audience were passive, showing no marks of
favour or disfavour—and that the earlier poets had higher
aims, adapting their compositions to the judgment of a wise
few, and careless about giving satisfaction to the general

mischievous tendency of changes in
the national music.

[k] Aristotle, Poetic. c. 4, p. 1449 a.

The ethical repugnance expressed
by Plato against the many-sided and
deceptive spirit of tragic and comic

compositions, is also expressed in the
censure said to have been pronounced
by Solon against Thespis, when the
latter first produced his dramas (Plutarch, Solon, 29; Diogen. Laert. i. 59).

audience. This would be the practice in the Platonic city·
but it never was the practice at Athens. We may surely
presume that Æschylus stood distinguished from his predecessors not by desiring popularity more, but by greater success in attaining it: and that he attained it partly from his
superior genius, partly from increasing splendour in the
means of exhibition at Athens. The simpler early compositions had been adapted to the taste of the audience who heard
them, and gave satisfaction for the time; until the loftier
genius of Æschylus and the other great constructive dramatists
was manifested.

However Plato—while he tolerates no poetry except in so
far as it produces ethical correction or regulation of
the emotions, and blames as hurtful the poet who
simply touches or kindles emotion—is in a peculiar
manner averse to dramatic poetry, with its diversity
of assumed characters and its obligation of giving
speech to different points of view. His aversion had been
exhibited before, both in the Republic and in the Gorgias:[1]
but it reappears here in the Treatise De Legibus, with this
aggravating feature—that the revolution in music and poetry
is represented as generating cause of a deteriorated character
and an ultra-democratical polity of Athens. This (as I have
before remarked) is a sentiment peculiar to Plato. For undoubtedly, oligarchical politicians (such as Thucydides, Nikias,
Kritias), who agreed with him in disliking the democracy,
would never have thought of ascribing what they disliked to
such a cause as alteration in the Athenian music and poetry.
They would much more have agreed with Aristotle,[m] when
he attributes the important change both in the character and
polity of the Athenian people after the Persian invasion, to

This aversion peculiar to himself, not shared either by oligarchical politicians, or by other philosophers.

---

[1] Plato, Republ. iii. pp. 395-396, x.
p. 605 B; Gorgias, p. 502 B; Legg.
iv. p. 719 B.

Aristotle takes a view of tragedy
quite opposed to that of Plato: he
considers it as calculated to purge or
purify the emotions of fear, compas-
sion, &c. (Aristot. Poet. c. 13. Compare Politic. viii. 7, 9). Unfortunately
the Poetica exist only as a fragment, so
that his doctrine about καθαρσις is

only declared and not fully developed.

Rousseau (in his Lettre à d'Alembert
Sur les Spectacles, p. 33 seq.) impugns
this doctrine of Aristotle, and condemns theatrical representations, partly
with arguments similar to those of
Plato, partly with others of his own.

[m] Aristotel. Politic. v. 4, p. 1304, a.
20, ii. 12, p. 1274, a. 12, viii. 6, 1340,
a. 30.

the events of that invasion itself—to the heroic and universal
efforts made by the citizens, on shipboard as well as on land,
against the invading host—and to the necessity for continuing those efforts by organising the confederacy of Delos.
Hence arose a new spirit of self-reliance and enterprise—or
rather an intensification of what had already begun after the
expulsion of Hippias and the reform by Kleisthenes—which
rendered the previous constitutional forms too narrow to give
satisfaction.[n] The creation of new and grander forms of
poetry may fairly be looked upon as one symptom of this
energetic general outburst: but it is in no way a primary or
causal fact, as Plato wishes us to believe. Nor can Plato himself have supposed it to be so, at the time when he composed
his Menexenus: wherein the events of the post-Xerxeian
period are presented in a light very different from that in
which he viewed them when he wrote his Leges—presented
with glowing commendations on his countrymen.

The long ethical prefatory matter[o] which we have gone
through, includes these among other doctrines—
1. That the life of justice, and the life of pleasure,
are essentially coincident. 2. That Reason, as declared by the lawgiver, ought to controul all our passions and
emotions. 3. That intoxication, under certain conditions, is an
useful stimulus to elderly men. 4. That the political constitution of society ought not to be founded upon one single
principle of authority, but upon a combination of several.
5. That the extreme of liberty, and the extreme of despotism,
are both bad.[p]

Doctrines of Plato in this prefatory matter.

Of these five positions, the two first are coincident with
the doctrines of the Republic: the third is not
coincident with them, but indirectly in opposition to
them: the fourth and fifth put Plato on a standing
point quite different from that of the Republic, and
different also from that of the Xenophontic Cyropædia. In
the Cyropædia, all government is strictly personal: the sub-

Compared with those of the Republic and of the Xenophontic Cyropædia.

---

[n] Herodot. v. 78.
[o] What Aristotle calls τοῖς ἔξωθεν
λόγοις, in reference to the Republic of
Plato (Aristotel. Politic. ii. 36, p. 1264,

b. 39).
[p] Compare on this point Plato's
Epistol. viii. pp. 354-355, where this
same view is enforced.

jects both obey willingly, and are rendered comfortable, because of the supreme and manifold excellence of one person—
their chief, Cyrus—in every department of practical administration, civil as well as military.   In the Platonic Republic,
the government is also personal: to this extent—that Plato
provides neither political checks, nor magistrates, nor laws,
nor judicature: but aims only at the perfect training of the
Guardians, and the still more elaborate and philosophical
training of those few chief or elder Guardians, who are to
direct the rest.   He demands only a succession of these philosophers, corresponding to the regal Artist sketched in the
Politikus: and he leaves all ulterior directions to them.
Upon their perfect dispositions and competence, all the weal
or woe of the community depends.   All is personal government; but it is lodged in the hands of a few philosophers,
assumed to be superexcellent, like the one chief in the Xenophontic Cyropædia.   When however we come to the Leges,
we find that Plato ceases to presume upon such supreme personal excellence.   He drops it as something beyond the limit
of human attainment, and as fit only for the golden or
Saturnian age.[q]   He declares that power, without adequate
restraints, is a privilege with which no man can be trusted.[r]
Nevertheless the magistrates must be vested with sufficient
power: since excess of liberty is equally dangerous.   To steer
between these two rocks,[s] you want not only a good despot
but a sagacious lawgiver.   It is he who must construct a constitutional system, having regard to the various natural foundations of authority in the minds of the citizens.   He must
provide fixed laws, magistrates, and a competent judicature:
moreover, both the magistrates and the judicature must be
servants of the law, and nothing beyond.[t]   The lawgiver must
frame his laws with singleminded view, not to the happiness
of any separate section of the city, but to that of the whole.
He must look to the virtue of the whole, in its most compre-

[q] Plato, Legg. iv. pp. 713-714.
[r] Plato, Legg. iii. p. 687 E-iv. p.
713 B, ix. p. 875 C.
[s] Plato, Legg. iv. pp. 710-711.
[t] Plato, Legg. iv. p. 715 D.   τοὺς δ'
ἄρχοντας λεγομένους νῦν ὑπηρέτας τοῖς

νόμοις ἐκάλεσα, οὔ τι καινοτομίας ὀνομάτων ἕνεκα, ἀλλ'.   It appears us if
this phrase, calling "magistrates the
servants or ministers of the law," was
likely to be regarded as a harsh and
novel metaphor.

hensive sense, and to all good things, ranked in their triple subordination and their comparative value—that is, First the good things belonging to the mind—Secondly, Those belonging to the body—Thirdly, Wealth and External acquisitions.[u]

We now enter upon this constructive effort of Plato's old *Constructive scheme— Plato's new point of view.* age. That a political constitution with fixed laws (he makes the Athenian say) and with magistrates acting merely as servants of the laws, is the only salvation for a city and its people—this is a truth which every man sees most distinctly in his old age, though when younger he was very dull in discerning it.[x] Probably enough what we here read represents the change in Plato's own mind: the acquisition of a new point of view, which was not present to him when he composed his Republic.

Here the exposition assumes a definite shape. The Kretan *New colony to be founded in Krete—its general conditions.* Kleinias apprises his Athenian companion, that the Knossians with other Kretans are about to establish a new colony on an unsettled point in Krete; and that himself with nine others are named commissioners for framing and applying the necessary regulations. He invites the co-operation of the Athenian :[y] who accordingly sets himself to the task of suggesting such laws and measures as are best calculated to secure the march of the new Magnêtic settlement towards the great objects defined in the preceding programme.

The new city is to be about nine English miles from the sea. The land round it is rough, poor, and without any timber for shipbuilding; but it is capable of producing all supplies absolutely indispensable, so that little need will be felt of importation from abroad. The Athenian wishes that the site were farther from the sea. Yet he considers the general conditions to be tolerably good; inasmuch as the city need not become commercial and maritime, and cannot have the means of acquiring much gold and silver—which is among the greatest evils that can befall a city, since it corrupts justice

---

[u] Plato, Legg. iv. pp. 707 B, 714 B, iii. p. 697 A.
[x] Plato, Legg. iv. p. 715 E. Νέος μὲν γὰρ ὢν πᾶς ἄνθρωπος τὰ τοιαῦτα ἀμβλύτατα αὐτὸς αὐτοῦ ὁρᾷ, γέρων δὲ ὀξύτατα.

Compare vii. pp. 819 D-821 D, for marks of Plato's old age and newly acquired opinions.
[y] Plato, Legg. iii. p. 702 C.

and goodness in the citizens.[z] The settlers are all Greeks, from various towns of Krete and Peloponnesus. This (remarks the Athenian) is on the whole better than if they came from one single city. Though it may introduce some additional chance of discord, it will nevertheless render them more open-minded and persuadeable for the reception of new institutions.[a]

The Athenian declares that he will not merely promulgate peremptory laws, but will recommend them to the citizens by prologues or hortatory discourses.

The colonists being supposed to be assembled in their new domicile and ready for settlement, Plato, or his Athenian spokesman, addresses to them a solemn exhortation, inculcating piety towards the Gods, celestial and subterranean, as well as to the Dæmons and Heroes—and also reverence to parents.[b] He then intimates that, though he does not intend to consult the settlers on the acceptance or rejection of laws, but assumes to himself the power of prescribing such laws as he thinks best for them—he nevertheless will not content himself with promulgating his mandates in a naked and peremptory way. He will preface each law with a proëm or prologue (*i. e.* a string of preliminary recommendations): in order to predispose their minds favourably, and to obtain from them a willing obedience.[c] He will employ not command only, but persuasion along with or antecedent to command: as the physician treats his patients when they are freemen, not as he sends his slaves to treat slave-patients, with a simple compulsory order.[d] To begin with an introductory proëm or prelude, prior to the announcement of the positive law, is (he says) the natural course of proceeding. It is essential to all artistic vocal performances: it is carefully studied and practised both by the rhetor and the musician.[e] Yet in spite of this analogy, no lawgiver has ever yet been found to prefix proëms to his laws: every one has contented himself with issuing peremptory commands.[f] Here then Plato undertakes to set the example of prefixing such prefatory

[z] Plato, Legg. iv. p. 705.

[a] Plato, Legg. iv. p. 708.

[b] Plato, Legg. iv. pp. 716-718.

[c] Plato, Legg. iv. pp. 718-719-723.

[d] Plato, Legg. iv. p. 720. This is a curious indication respecting the medical profession and practice at Athens.

[e] Plato, Legg. iv. pp. 722 D-723 D. *τῷ τε ῥήτορι καὶ τῷ μελῳδῷ καὶ τῷ νομοθέτῃ τὸ τοιοῦτον ἑκάστοτε ἐπιτρεπτέον.*

[f] Plato, Legg. iv. p. 722 B-E. The *προοίμια δημηγορικά* of Demosthenes are well known.

introductions. The nature of the case would prescribe that
every law, every speech, every song, should have its suitable
proëm : but such prolixity would be impolitic. A discretion
must be entrusted to the lawgiver, as it is to the orator and
the musician. Proëms or prologues must be confined to the
great and important laws.[g]

General character of these prologues— didactic or rhetorical homilies.
Accordingly, from hence to the end of the Treatise De
Legg., Plato proceeds upon the principle here laid
down. He either prefixes a prologue to each of his
laws—or blends the law with its proëm—or gives
what may be called a proëm without a law, that is a
string of hortatory or comminatory precepts. There are
various points (he says) on which the lawgiver cannot propose
any distinct and peremptory enactment, but must confine
himself to emphatic censure[h] and declaration of opinion, with
threats of displeasure on the part of the Gods : the rather as
he cannot hope to accomplish his public objects, without the
largest interference with private habits—nor without bringing
his regulations to bear upon individual life, where positive
law can hardly reach.[i] The Platonic prologues are sometimes
expositions of the reasons of the law—i. e. of the dangers
which it is intended to ward off, or the advantages to be
secured by it. But far more frequently, they are morsels of
rhetoric—lectures, discourses, or homilies—addressed to the
emotions and not to the reason, insisting on the ethical and
religious point of view, and destined to operate with persuasive
or intimidating effect upon an uninstructed multitude.[k]

Great value set by Plato himself upon these prologues. They
It seems that Plato took credit to himself for what he
thought a beneficial innovation, in thus blending persuasive exhortation with compulsory command. His
assurance, that no Grecian lawgiver had ever done

[g] Plato, Legg. iv. p. 723 C-D.
About τὰ τῶν νόμων προοίμια, compare
what Plato says about his communications with the younger Dionysius,
shortly after his (Plato's) second arrival
at Syracuse, Plato, Epistol. iii. p.
316 A.

[h] Cicero (De Legg. ii. 6) professes
to follow Plato in this practice of prefixing proëms to his Laws. He calls
the proëm an encomium upon the law

which in most cases it is—"ut prius-
quam ipsam legem recitem, de ejus
legis laude dicam."

[i] Plato, Legg. vi. p. 780 A.

[k] Plato, Legg. iv. p. 722 B. πρὸς
τούτῳ δὲ οὐδεὶς ἔοικε διανοηθῆναι πώποτε τῶν νομοθετῶν, ὡς ἐξὸν δυοῖν
χρῆσθαι πρὸς τὰς νομοθεσίας, πειθοῖ καὶ
βίᾳ, καθ' ὅσον οἷόν τε ἐπὶ τὸν ἄπειρον
παιδείας ὄχλον τῷ ἑτέρῳ χρῶνται μόνον.

so before, is doubtless trustworthy :[1] though we may are to serve as type for remark that the confusion of the two has been the all poets— No one is general rule with Oriental lawgivers—the Hindoos, allowed to contradict the Jews, the Mahommedan Arabs, &c.   But with them. him the innovation serves a farther purpose.   He makes it the means of turning rhetoric to account; and of enlisting in his service, as lawgiver, not only all the rhetoric but all the poetry, in his community.   His Athenian speaker is so well satisfied with these prologues, that he considers them to possess the charm of a poetical work, and suspects them to have been dictated by inspiration from the Gods.[m]   He pronounces them the best and most suitable compositions for the teaching of youth, and therefore prescribes that teachers shall cause the youth to recite and learn them, instead of the poetical and rhetorical works usually employed.   He farther enjoins that his prologues shall serve as type and canon whereby all other poetical and rhetorical compositions shall be tried.   If there be any compositions in full harmony and analogy with this type, the teachers shall be compelled to learn them by heart, and teach them to pupîls.   Any teacher refusing to do so shall be dismissed.[n]   Nor shall any poet be allowed to compose and publish works containing sentiments contradictory to the declaration of the lawgiver.[o]

As a contrast to this view of Plato in his later years, it is interesting to turn to that which he entertained in Contrast of an earlier part of his life, in the Gorgias and the Leges with Gorgias and Phædrus, respecting rhetoric.   In the former dia- Phædrus. logue, Gorgias is recognised as a master of the art of persuasion, especially as addressed to a numerous audience, and respecting ethical questions, What is just, and what is unjust? Sokrates, on the contrary, pointedly distinguishes persuasion from teaching—discredits simple persuasion, without teach-

---

[1] The testimony of Plato shows that the προοίμια τῆς νομοθεσίας ascribed to Zaleukus and Charondas (Diodor. xii. 12-20) are composed by authors later than his time, and probably in imitation of his προοίμια : which indeed is probable enough on other grounds. See Heyne, Opuscula, vol. ii. ; Prolus. i. vi., De Zaleuci et Charondæ Legibus.

Cicero read the proëms ascribed to Zaleukus and Charondas as genuine (Legg. ii. 6), so did Diodôrus, xii. 17-20 ; Stobæus, Serm. xlii.

[m] Plato, Legg. vii. p. 811 C. οὐκ ἄνευ τινὸς ἐπιπνοίας θεῶν, ἔδοξαν δ' οὖν μοι πυντάπασι ποιήσει τινὶ προσομοίως εἰρῆσθαι.

[n] Plato, Legg. vii. p. 811 D-E.

[o] Plato, Legg.

ing, as merely deceptive—and contends that rhetorical discourse addressed to a multitude, upon such topics, can never
convey any teaching.[p]　But in the Leges we find that the art
of persuasion has risen greatly in Plato's estimation.　Whether
it be a true art, or a mere unartistic knack, he now recognises its efficacy in modifying the dispositions of the uninstructed multitude, and announces himself to be the first
lawgiver who will employ it systematically for that purpose.
He combines the seductions of the rhetor with the unpalat-
able severities of the lawgiver: the two distinct functions of
Gorgias and his brother the physician Herodikus, when
Gorgias accompanied his brother to visit suffering patients,
and succeeded by force of rhetoric in overcoming their repugnance to the cutting and burning indispensable for cure.[q]
Again, in the Phædrus, Plato treats the art of persuasion,
when applied at once to a mixed assemblage of persons, either
by writing or discourse, as worthless and unavailing.[r]　He
affirms that it makes no durable impression on the internal
mind of the individuals: the same discourse will never suit
all.　Individuals differ materially in their cast of mind;
moreover, they differ in opinion upon ethical topics (just and
unjust) more than upon any other.　Some men are open to
persuasion by topics which will have no effect on others.
Accordingly you must go through a laborious discrimination:
first, you must discriminate generally the various classes of
minds and the various classes of discourse—next, you must
know to which classes of minds the individuals of the multitude before you belong.　You must then address to each mind
the mode of persuasion specially adapted to it.　The dialectic
philosopher is the only one who possesses the true art of persuasion.　Such was Plato's point of view in the Phædrus.　I
need hardly point out how completely it is dropped in his
Leges: wherein he pours persuasion into the ears of an indiscriminate multitude, through the common channel of a rhetorical lecture, considering it of such impressive efficacy as to
justify the supposition of inspiration from the Gods.[s]

[p] Plato, Gorgias, pp. 454-456.
[q] Plato, Gorgias, p. 456 B.
[r] Plato, Phædrus, pp. 263 A, 271-272.273 E-275 E-276 A-277 C.

[s] Zeller, in his 'Platonische Studien' (pp. 66-72-88, &c.), insists much on the rhetorical declamatory prolixity visible throughout the Treatise De Legibus,

After this unusual length of preliminaries, Plato enters on the positive regulation of his colony. As to the worship of the Gods, he directs little or nothing of his own authority. The colony must follow the advice of the oracles of Delphi, Dodona, and Ammon—together with any consecrated traditions, epiphanies, or inspirations from the Gods belonging to the spot— as to the Gods who shall be publicly worshipped, and the suitable temples and rites. Only he directs that to each portion of the territory set apart for civil purposes, some God, Dæmon, or Hero, shall be specially assigned as Patron,[t] with a chapel

Regulations for the new colony— About religious worship, the oracles of Delphi and Dodona are to be consulted.

as quite at variance with the manner of Plato in his earlier and better dialogues, and even as specimens of what Plato there notes as the rhetorical or sophistical manner. He expresses his surprise that the Athenian should be made to ascribe such discourses to the inspiration of the Gods (p. 107). Zeller enumerates these and many other dissimilarities in the Treatise De Legibus, as compared with other Platonic dialogues, as premises to sustain his conclusion that the treatise is not by Plato. In my judgment they do not bear out that conclusion (which indeed Zeller has since renounced in his subsequent work); but they are not the less real and notable, marking the change in Plato's own mind.

How poor an opinion had Plato of the efficacy of the νουθετητικὸν εἶδος λόγων at the time when he composed the Sophistès (p. 230)! What a superabundance of such discourse does he deliver in the Treatise De Legibus, taking especial pride in the peculiarity!

[t] Plato, Legg. v. p. 738 C-D. ὅπως ἂν ξύλλογοι ἑκάστων τῶν μερῶν κατὰ χρόνους γιγνόμενοι τοὺς προσταχθέντας —μετὰ θυσιῶν.

That such "ordained seasons" for meetings and sacrifices should be punctually attended to—was a matter of great moment, on religious no less than on civil grounds. It was with a view to that object principally that each Grecian city arranged its calendar and its system of intercalation. Plato himself states this (vii. p. 809 D).

Sir George Lewis, in his Historical Survey of the Astronomy of the Ancients, adverts to the passage of Plato here cited, and gives a very instructive picture of the state of the Hellenic world as to Calendar and computation of time (see p. 19; also the greater part of chapter i. of his valuable work). The object of all the cities was to adjust lunar time with solar time by convenient intercalations, but hardly any two cities agreed in the method of doing so. Different schemes of intercalation and periods (trietèric, octaetèric, enneadekaetèric) were either adopted by civic authority or suggested by private astronomers, such as Kleostratus and Meton. The practical dissonance and confusion was great, and the theoretical dissatisfaction also.

Now in this dialogue De Legibus, Plato recognises both the importance of the object and the problem to be solved, yet he suggests no means of his own for solving it. He makes no arrangement for the calendar of his new Magnêtic city. I confess that this is to me a matter of some surprise. To combine an exertion of authority with an effort of arithmetical calculation, is in his vein; and the exactness of observances as respects the Gods, in harmony with the religious tone of the treatise, depended on some tolerable solution of the problem.

We may perhaps presume that Plato refused to deal with the problem because he considered it as mathematically insoluble. Days, months, and years are not exactly commensurable with each other. In the Timæus, (p. 36 C) Plato declares that the rotation of the Circle of the Same, or the outermost sidereal sphere, upon which the succession of day and night depends, is according to the side of a parallelogram (κατὰ πλευράν)—while

and precinct wherein all meetings of the citizens of the district shall be held, whether for religious ceremonies, or for recreation, or for political duties.

Plato requires for his community a fixed and peremptory total of 5040 citizens, never to be increased, and never to be diminished: a total sufficient, in his judgment, to defend the territory against invaders, and to lend aid on occasion to an oppressed neighbour. He distributes the whole territory into 5040 lots of land, each of equal value, assigning one lot to each citizen. Each lot is assumed to be sufficient for the maintenance of a family of sober habits, and no more. The total number (5040) is selected because of the great variety of divisors by which it may be divided without remainder.[u]

Perpetuity of number of citizens, and of lots of land, one to each, inalienable and indivisible.

We thus see that Plato, in laying down his fundamental principle (ὑπόθεσιν), recognises separate individual property

the rotations of the Moon and Sun (two of the seven branches composing the Circle of the Different) are according to the diagonal thereof (κατὰ διάμετρον) : now the side and the diagonal represented the type of incommensurable magnitudes among the ancient reasoners. It would appear also that he considers the rotations of the Moon and Sun to be incommensurable with each other, both of them being members included in the Circle of the Different.

Since an exact mathematical solution was thus unattainable, Plato may probably have despised a merely approximative solution, sufficient for practical convenience—to which last object he generally pays little attention. He might also fancy that even the attempt to meddle with the problem betokened that confusion of the incommensurable with the commensurable, which he denounces in this very treatise (vii. pp. 819-820).

[u] Plato, Legg. v. pp. 737-738, vi. p. 771 C.

Aristotle declares this total of 5040 to be extravagantly great, inasmuch as it would require an amount of territory beyond the scale which can be reckoned upon for a Grecian city, to maintain so many unproductive persons, including not merely the 5040 adult citizens, but also their wives,

children, and personal attendants, none of whom would take part in any productive industry (Politic. ii. 6, p. 1265, b. 16).

The remark here cited indicates the small numerical scale upon which the calculations of a Greek politician were framed. But we can hardly be surprised at it, seeing that the new city is intended for the island of Krete, where none even of the existing cities were considerable. Moreover Aristotle had probably present to his mind the analogy of Sparta. The Spartan citizens were in a situation more analogous to the 5040 than any other Grecian residents. But the Spartan citizens could not have been near so numerous as 5040 at that time ; not even one-fifth of it—Aristotle tells us, Politic. ii. 9, 1270, a. 31. Aristotle goes on to remark on the definition given by Plato of the size and value of each lot of land sufficient for the citizen and his family to live σωφρόνως : it ought to be (says Aristotle) σωφρόνως καὶ ἐλευθερίως. These are the two modes of excellence, and the only two, which a man can display in the use of his property (1265, a. 35). But this change would only aggravate the difficulty as to the total area of land required for the 5040. Compare the remark of Aristotle on the scheme of Hippodamus, Polit. ii. 8, 1268, a. 42.

and separate family among his citizens: both of which had been strenuously condemned and strictly excluded, in respect to the Guardians of his Republic. But he admits the principle only with the proviso that there shall be a peremptory limit to number of citizens, to individual wealth, and to individual poverty: moreover, even with this proviso, he admits it only as a second-best, because mankind will not accept and are not sufficiently exalted to work out, what is in itself the best. He reasserts the principle of the Republic, that separate property and separate family are both essentially mischievous: that all individuality, either of interest or sympathy or sentiment, ought to be extinguished as far as possible.[x] Though constrained against his will to renounce this object, he will still approximate to it as near as he can in his second-best. Moreover, he may possibly, at some future time (D. V.), propose a third-best. When once departure from the genuine standard is allowed, the departure may be made in many different ways.

Plato reasserts his adherence to the principle of the Republic, though the repugnance of others hinders him from realising it.

This declaration deserves notice as attesting the undiminished adhesion of Plato to the main doctrines of his Republic. The point here noted is one main difference of principle between the Treatise De Legibus and the Republic: the enactment of written fundamental laws, with prologues serving as homilies to be preached to the citizens, is another. Both of them are differences of principle: each gives rise to many subordinate differences or corollaries.[y]

---

[x] Plato, Legg. v. pp. 739-740, vii. p. 807 B.

[y] Plato, Legg. v. p. 739 E. ἦν δὲ νῦν ἡμεῖς ἐπικεχειρήκαμεν, εἴη τε ἂν γενομένη πως ἀθανασίας ἐγγύτατα καὶ ἡ μία δευτέρως· τρίτην δὲ μετὰ ταῦτα, ἐὰν θεὸς ἐθέλῃ, διαπερανούμεθα. Upon this passage K. F. Hermann observes: —"Hæc enim est quam ordine tertiam uppellat Plato, quæ Aristoteli, Politic. iv. 1, 2, ἐξ ὑποθέσεως πολιτεία dicitur: quod tamen nolim ita accipi, ut à nonnullis factum est, ut hanc quoque olim singulari scripto persecuturum fuisse philosophum credamus, quasi tribus exemplis absolvi rerum publicarum formas censuisset: innumeræ enim pro singularum nationum et urbium for-

tunâ esse possunt," &c. (De Vestigiis Institutorum Atticorum ap. Platon. De Legg. p. 16).

That Plato *did* intend to compose a *third* work upon an analogous subject appears to me clear from the words,— but it does not at all follow that he thought that three varieties would exhaust all possibility. Upon this point I dissent from Hermann, and also upon his interpretation of Aristotle's phrase ἡ ἐξ ὑποθέσεως πολιτεία. Aristotle distinguishes three distinct varieties of end which the political constructor may propose to himself:— 1. τὴν πολιτείαν τὴν ἁπλῶς ἀρίστην, τὴν μάλιστα κατ᾽ εὐχήν. 2. Τὴν ἐκ τῶν ὑποκειμένων ἀρίστην. 3. Τὴν ἐξ

Each citizen proprietor shall hold his lot of land, not as his

Regulations about land, successions, marriages, &c. The number of citizens must not be allowed to increase. own, but as part and parcel of the entire territory, which, taken as a whole, is Goddess and Mistress— conjointly with all the local Gods and Heroes—of the body of citizens generally. No citizen shall either sell or otherwise alienate his lot, nor divide it, nor trench upon its integrity. The total number of lots, the integrity of each lot, and the total number of citizens, shall all remain consecrated in perpetuity, without increase or diminution. Each citizen in dying shall leave one son as successor to his lot: if he has more than one, he may choose which of them he will prefer. The successor so chosen shall maintain the perpetuity of worship of the Gods, reverential rites to the family and deceased ancestors, and obligations towards the city.[z] If the citizen has other sons, they will be adopted into the families of other citizens who happen to be childless: if he has daughters, he will give them out in marriage, but without any dowry. Such family relations will be watched over by a special board of magistrates: with this peremptory condition, that they shall on no account permit either the number of citizen proprietors, or the number of separate lots, to depart from the consecrated 5040.[a] Each

---

ὑποθέσεως ἀρίστην. Now K. F. Hermann here maintains, and Boeckh had already maintained before him (ad Platonis Minoem et de Legibus, pp. 66-67), that the city sketched in Plato's treatise De Legibus coincides with No. 2 in Aristotle's enumeration, and that the projected τρίτη in Plato coincides with No. 3—τὴν ἐξ ὑποθέσεως. I differ from them here. There is no ground for presuming that what Plato puts *third* must also be put by Aristotle *third*. I think that the Platonic city De Legibus corresponds to No. 3 in Aristotle and not to No. 2. It is a city ἐξ ὑποθέσεως, not ἐκ τῶν ὑποκειμένων ἀρίστη. Plato borrows little or nothing from τὰ ὑποκείμενα, and almost everything from his own ὑπόθεσις or assumed principle, which in this case is the fixed number of the citizens as well as of the lots of land, the imposition of a limit on each man's proprietary acquisitions, and the recognition of separate family establishments subject to these limits. This is the

ὑπόθεσις of Plato's second city, to which all his regulations of detail are accommodated: it is substituted by him (unwillingly, because of the repugnance of others) in place of the ὑπόθεσις of his first city or the Republic, which ὑπόθεσις is perfect communism among the φύλακες, without either separate property or separate family. This last is Plato's ἁπλῶς ἀρίστη.

[z] Plato, Legg. v. p. 740 A-B.

[a] Plato, Legg. v. pp. 740 D-742 C. Aristotle remarks that in order to attain the object which Plato here proclaims, restriction ought to be imposed on τεκνοποιΐα. No citizen ought to be allowed to beget more than a certain number of children. He observes that this last-mentioned restriction, if imposed alone and without any others, would do more than all the rest to maintain the permanent 5040 lots, and that without this no other restrictions could be efficacious (Polit. ii. 6, 1265, a. 37, 1266, b. 9).

citizen's name, and each lot of land, will be registered on tablets of cypress wood. These registers will be preserved in the temples, in order that the magistrates may be able to prevent fraud.[b]

The city, with its appropriate accessories, shall be placed as nearly as possible in the middle of the territory. The akropolis, sacred to Hestia and Athênê, will be taken as a centre from whence twelve radiating lines will be drawn to the extremity of the territory, so as to distribute the whole area into twelve sections, not all equal in magnitude, but equalised in value by diminishing the area in proportion to superior goodness of land. The total number of citizens will be distributed also into twelve sections, of 420 each $\left(\frac{5040}{12}\right)$, among whom the lots of land contained in each twelfth will be apportioned. This duodecimal division, the fundamental canon of Plato's municipal arrangements, is a sanctified present from the Gods, in harmony with the months and with the kosmical revolutions.[c] Each twelfth, land and citizens together, will be

Position of the city and akropolis—Distribution of the territory and citizens into twelve equal sections or tribes.

Plato concurs in this opinion, though he trusts to prudence and the admonition of elders for bringing about this indispensable limitation of births in a family, without legal prohibition. I have already touched upon this matter in my review of Plato's Republic. See above—chap. xxxv. p. 226 seq.

The νόμοι θετικοὶ of Philolaus at Thebes, regulating τὴν παιδοποιίαν with a view to keep the lots of land unchanged, are only known by the brief allusion of Aristotle, Polit. ii. 12, 1274, b. 4.

[b] Plato, Legg. v. p. 741 D. κυπαριτ-τίνας μνήμας, &c.

[c] Plato, Legg. vi. p. 771 B. Plato here reckons the different numerical divisions adopted in different cities as being all both natural and consecrated, but he considers his own as the most fortunate and right. He insists much upon the importance of symmetrical distribution, with definite numerical ratio, in all the departments of life: in the various civil subdivisions of the Tribe, such as Phratries, Dêmes, Villages — in the arrangements of the citizens for military service, τάξεις καὶ ἀγωγάς—in the coins, weights and measures—in the modulations of the voice, and in the direction of movements either rectilinear or rotatory. (Whoever looks at Aristophanes, Aves, 1010 seq., will see all such regularity and symmetry derided in the person of Meton.) Nay, he enjoins that all the vessels made for common use shall be exact fractions or exact multiples of each other. This will make it necessary for all the citizens to learn elementary arithmetic, which Plato considers to be of essential value, not only for practical use but as a stimulus to the dormant intelligence. On this point he notes the Egyptians and Phenicians as standing higher than the Greeks (vii. p. 818), but as applying their superior arithmetical knowledge only to a mean and disgraceful thirst for wealth. Against this last defect Plato reckons upon guarding his citizens by other precautions, while he encourages in them the learning of arithmetic (Legg. v. p. 747). Plato here speaks of the Egyptians and Phenicians, much as the Jews have been spoken of in later times. And it is curious that he seems to consider their peculiarities of character as referable to their local domicile. He maintains that one place is intrinsic-

constituted a Tribe, and will be consecrated to some God (determined by lot) whose name it will bear, and at whose altar two monthly festivals will be celebrated : one for the tribe, the other for the entire city. The tribes are peremptorily equal in respect to number of citizens; but care shall also be taken to make them as nearly equal as possible in respect to registered property : that is, in respect to property other than land, which each citizen brings with him to the settlement, and which will all be recorded (as well as the land) in the public registers.[d] The lot of land assigned to each citizen will include a portion near the centre, and a portion near the circumference : the most central portion being coupled with the most outlying, and so on in order. Each citizen will thus have two separate residences :[e] one nearer to the city, the other more distant from it.

Plato would be glad if he were able to establish among all the citizens, equality not merely of landed property, but of all other property besides. This, however, he recognises his inability to exact. The colonists will bring with them moveable property — some more, some less: and inequality must be tolerated up to a certain limit. Each citizen is allowed to possess moveable property as far as four times the value of his lot of land, but no more. The maximum of wealth possessed by any citizen will thus be equal to five times the value of his lot of land: the minimum of the poorest citizen will be the lot of land itself, which cannot, under the worst circumstances, be alienated or diminished. If any citizen shall in any way acquire property above the maximum here named, he is directed to make it over to the city and to the Gods. In case of disobedience, he may be indicted before the Nomophylakes; and if found guilty, shall be disgraced, excluded from his share of public distributions, and condemned to pay twice as much—half being assigned as recompense to the prosecutor.[f] The public register kept by the magistrates, in which is enrolled all the property of every kind belonging to

Moveable property—Inequality therein reluctantly allowed, as far as four to one, but no farther.

---

ally different from another in respect to producing good and bad characters; some places are even privileged by θεία ἐπίπνοια καὶ δαιμόνων λήξεις, &c.

[d] Plato, Legg. v. p. 745.
[e] Plato, Legg. v. p. 745, vi. p. 771 D.
[f] Plato, Legg. v. pp. 744-745, vi. p. 754 E.

each citizen, will enable them to enforce this regulation, and will be farther useful in all individual suits respecting money.

In the public census of the city, the citizens will be distributed into four classes, according to their different scales of property. The richest will be four minæ: the other three, two and one minæ respectively. Direct taxation will be assessed upon them according to the difference of wealth: to which also a certain reference will be had in the apportionment of magistracies, and in the regulation of the voting privilege.[g] *Census of the citizens— four classes, with graduated scale of property. No citizen to possess gold or silver. No loans or interest. No debts enforced by law.*

By this determination of a maximum and minimum, coupled with a certain admitted preference to wealth in the assignment of political power, Plato considers that he has guarded against the intestine dissensions and other evils likely to arise from inequality of property. He accounts great poverty to be a serious cause of evil; yet he is very far from looking upon wealth as a cause of good. On the contrary, he proclaims that great wealth is absolutely incompatible either with great virtue or great happiness.[h] Accordingly, while he aims at preserving every individual citizen from poverty, he at the same time disclaims all purpose of making his community either richer or more powerful.[i] He forbids every private citizen to possess gold and silver. The magistrates must hold a certain stock of it in reserve, in case of public dealing with foreign cities; but they will provide for the daily wants of the community by a special cheap currency, having no value beyond the limits of the territory.[k] Moreover, Plato prohibits all loans on interest. He refuses to enforce by law the restoration even of a deposit. He interdicts all dowry or marriage portion with daughters.[l]

How is the Platonic colony to be first set on its march, and by whom are its first magistrates to be named? By the inhabitants of Knôssus, its mother city—replies Plato. The Knossians will appoint a provisional Board of two hundred: half from their own citizens, half from the elders and most respected *Board of thirty-seven Nomophylakes—general supervisors of the laws and their execution—how elected.*

g Plato, Legg. v. p. 744 B, vi. p. 754 E.   i Plato, Legg. v. p. 742 D.
h Plato, Legg. v. pp. 742 E, 743 A,   k Plato, Legg. v. p. 742 A.
744 E.   l Plato, Legg. v. p. 742 C.

men among the colonists themselves.[m] This Board will choose
the first Nomophylakes, consisting of thirty-seven persons,
half Knossians, half colonists. These Nomophylakes are intended as a Council of State, and will be elected by the
citizens in the following way, when the colony is once in full
march:—All the citizens who perform or have performed
military service, either as hoplites or cavalry, will be electors.
They will vote by tablets laid upon the altar, and inscribed
with the name both of the voter himself and of the person
whom he prefers. First, three hundred persons will be chosen
by the majority of votes according to this process. Next,
out of these three hundred, one hundred will be chosen by a
second process of the same kind. Lastly, out of these one
hundred, thirty-seven will be chosen by a third similar process, but with increased solemnity: these thirty-seven will constitute the Board of Nomophylakes, or Guardians of the Laws.[n]
No person shall be eligible for Guardian until he has attained
the age of fifty. When elected, he shall continue to serve
until he is seventy, and no longer: so that if elected at sixty, he
will have ten years of service.[o] The duties of this Board will
be to see that all the laws are faithfully executed: in which
function they will have superintendance over all special magistrates and officers.

For the office of General and Minister of War, three persons
shall be chosen by show of hands of the military
citizens. It shall be the duty of the Nomophylakes
to propose three names for this office: but other
citizens may also propose different names, and the
show of hands will decide. The three Generals, when chosen,
shall propose twelve names as Taxiarchs, one for each tribe:
other names may also be proposed, and the show of hands of
each tribe will determine.[p]

Military commanders—General council of 360—complicated mode of election.

A Council shall be annually chosen, consisting of 360
members, ninety from each of the four proprietary scales in
the Census. The mode of electing this Council is highly
complicated. First, Plato provides that 360 Councillors shall
be chosen out of the first (or richest) class, and as many out

[m] Plato, Legg. vi. pp. 752 D, 754 C.
[n] Plato, Legg. vi. p. 753 C-D.
[o] Plato, Legg. vi. p. 755 A.
[p] Plato, Legg. vi. p. 755 E.

of the second class, by universal suffrage, every citizen being compelled to give his vote : then that 360 Councillors shall be chosen out of the third class, by universal suffrage, but under this condition, that the three richest classes are compelled to vote, while the fourth class may abstain from voting if they please : next, that 360 Councillors shall be chosen out of the fourth class, still by universal suffrage, but with liberty to the third and fourth classes to abstain from voting, while the first and second classes are compelled to vote. Out of the four batches, of 360 names from each class, 180 names from each class are to be chosen by universal suffrage compulsory on all. This last list of 180 names is to be reduced, by drawing lots, to 90 from each class, or 360 in all : who constitute the Council for the year.[q]

Here the evident purpose of Plato is to obtain in the last result a greater number of votes from the rich than from the poor, without absolutely disfranchising the poor. Where the persons to be voted for are all of the richer classes, there the poor are compelled to come and vote as well as the rich : where the persons to be voted for are all of the poorer class, there the rich are compelled to vote, while the poor are allowed to stay away. He seems to look on the vote, not as a privilege which citizens will wish to exercise, but as a duty which they must be compelled by fine to discharge. This is (as Aristotle calls it) an oligarchical provision. It exhibits Plato's mode of attaining the end stated by Livy as proposed in the Servian constitution at Rome, and the end contemplated (without being announced) by the framers of most other political constitutions recorded in history—" *Gradus facti, ut neque exclusus quisquam suffragio videretur, et vis omnis penes primores esset.*"[r]   Plato defends it by distinguishing two sorts of

Character of the electoral scheme— Plato's views about wealth —he caters partly for the oligarchical sentiment, partly for the democratical.

[q] Plato, Legg. vi. p. 756. Compare Aristot. Polit. ii. 6, p. 1266, a. 14.

The passage of Plato is not perspicuous. It appears to me to have been misunderstood by some commentators, who suppose that only 90 βουλευταὶ are to be chosen out of each census in the original voting (see Schneider's Comment. on the passage of Aristotle above alluded to, p. 99).

The number originally chosen from each class must be 360, because it is directed, in the final process, to be reduced first (by election) to 180 from each class, and next (by sortition) to 90 from each class.

[r] Livy i. 43.

Aristotle characterises these regulations of the Platonic community as oligarchical, and remarks that this is equality : one, complete and undistinguishing, in which all the citizens are put upon a level : the other, in which the good and able citizen is distinguished from the bad and incapable citizen, so that he acquires power and honour in proportion to his superior merit.[s] This second sort of equality Plato approves, pronouncing it to be political justice. But such defence tacitly assumes that superiority in wealth, as between the four classes of his census, is to count as evidence of, or as an equivalent for, superior merit : an assumption doubtless received by many Grecian politicians, and admitted in the general opinion of Greece—but altogether at variance with the declared judgment of Plato himself as to the effect of wealth upon the character of the wealthy man. The poorest citizen in the Platonic community must have his lot of land, which Plato considers sufficient for a sober-minded family : the richest citizen can possess only five times as much : and all receive the same public instruction. Here, therefore, there can be no presumption of superior merit in the richer citizen as compared with the poorer, whatever might be said about the case as it stood in actual Grecian communities. We see that Plato in this case forgets his own peculiar mode of thought, and accommodates himself to received distinctions, without reflecting that the principles of *his* own political system rendered such distinctions inapplicable. He bows to the oligarchical sentiment of his contemporaries, by his preferential encouragement to the votes of the rich : he bows to the democratical sentiment, when he consents to employ to a small extent the principle of the lot.[t]

Of this annually-chosen Council, one twelfth part only (or thirty Councillors) will be in constant session in the city : each of their sessions lasting for one month, and the total thus covering the year. The remaining eleven twelfths will be attending to their private

Meetings of council— other magistrates— Agoranomi— Astynomi, &c.

---

in contradiction to the principle with which Plato set out—that it ought to be a compound of monarchy and democracy. Aristotle understands this last principle somewhat differently from what Plato seems to have intended (Politic. ii. 6, 1266, a. 10).

[s] Plato, Legg. vi. p. 757 A-B.

Compare a like distinction drawn between two sorts of ἰσότης in Isokrates, Areiopagitic. Orat. vii. s. 23-24 ; also Aristotel. Politic.

[t] Plato, Legg. vi. p. 757 E. διὸ δὴ τῷ τοῦ κλήρου ἴσῳ ἀνάγκη προσχρήσασθαι, δυσκολίας τῶν πολλῶν ἕνεκα, &c.

affairs, except when special necessities arise. The Council will have the general superintendence of the city, and controul over all meetings of the citizens.[u] Provision is made for three magistrates called Astynomi, to regulate the streets, roads, public buildings, water-courses, &c.: and for five Agoranomi, to watch over the public market with its appertaining temples and fountains, and to take cognisance of disputes or offences occurring therein. None but citizens of the two richest classes of the census are eligible as Astynomi or Agoranomi: first, twice the number required are chosen by public show of hands—next, half of the number so chosen are drawn off by lot. In regard to the show of hands, Plato again decrees, that all citizens of the two richer classes shall be compelled to take part in it, under fine: all citizens of the two poorer classes may take part if they choose, but are not compelled.[x] By this provision, as before, Plato baits for the oligarchical sentiment: by the partial use of the lot, for the democratical.

The defence of the territory is entrusted to the Agronomi, five persons selected from each of the twelve tribes, *Defence of the territory —rural police —Agronomi, &c.* making sixty in all; and assisted by sixty other junior subordinates, selected by the five Agronomi (those of each tribe choosing twelve) from their respective tribes. Each of these companies of seventeen will be charged with the care of one of the twelve territorial districts, as may be determined by lot. Each will then pass by monthly change from one district to another, so as to make the entire circuit of the twelve districts in one year, going round in an easterly direction or to the right: each will then make the same circuit backward, during a second year, in a westerly direction or to the left.[y] Their term of service will be two years in all, during which all of them will have become familiarly acquainted with every portion of the territory. A public mess will be provided for these companies, and each man among them will be held to strict continuity of service. Their

---

[u] Plato, Legg. vi. p. 758 C-D.
[x] Plato, Legg. vi. pp. 763-764.
[y] Plato, Legg. vi. p. 760 D. τοὺς τῆς χώρας τόπους μεταλλάττοντας ἀεὶ τῶν ἐξῆς τόπων ἑκάστου μηνὸς ἡγεῖσθαι τοὺς φρουράρχους ἐπὶ δέξια κύκλῳ· τὸ

δ' ἐπιδέξια γιγνέσθω τὸ πρὸς ἔω.
In reference to omens and auguries the Greek spectator looked towards the north, so that he had the east on his right hand.

duties will be, not merely to keep each district in a condition
of defence against a foreign enemy, but also to improve its
internal condition: to facilitate the outflow of water where
there is too much, and to retard it where there is too little:
to maintain, in the precincts sacred to the Gods, reservoirs of
spring-water, partly as ornament, partly also as warm baths
(for the heating of which large stocks of dry wood must be
collected)—to benefit the old, the sick, and the overworked
husbandman.[z] Farthermore, these Agronomi will adjudicate
upon disputes and offences among the rural population, both
slave and free. If they abuse their trust, they will be account-
able, first to the assembled citizens of the district, next to the
public tribunals in the city.

Plato considers that these Agronomi will go through hard
Comparison with the Lacedæmonian Kryptia. work during their two years of service, inasmuch as
they will have no slaves, and will have to do every-
thing for themselves: though in the performance of
any public work, they are empowered to put in requisition
both men and cattle from the neighbourhood.[a] He pronounces it to be a salutary discipline for the young men,
whom he admonishes that an apprenticeship in obedience is
indispensable to qualify them for command, and that exact
obedience to the laws and magistrates will be their best title
to posts of authority when older.[b] Moreover, he insists on
the necessity that all citizens should become minutely acquainted with the whole territory: towards which purpose he
encourages young men in the exercise of hunting. He compares (indirectly) his moveable guard of Agronomi to the
Lacedæmonian Krypti, who maintained the police of Laconia,
and kept watch over the Helots:[c] though they are also the

[z] Plato, Legg. vi. p. 761 A-D.
Agreeable and refreshing combinations of springs with shady trees near
the precincts of the Gods were frequent. See Xenophon, Hellen. v.
3, 19.
The thermal waters were also generally connected with some precinct of
Hêraklês or Asklêpius.
In some temples it was forbidden to
use this adjoining water except for
sacred rites, Thucyd. iv. 97.
[a] Plato, Legg. vi. pp. 760 E-763 A.
[b] Plato, Legg. vi. p. 762 E.

[c] Plato, Legg. vi. p. 763 A-B. εἴτε
τις κρυπτοὺς εἴτ' ἀγορανόμους εἴθ' ὅ, τι
καλῶν χαίρει, &c. He notes the hard-
ships endured by these Κρυπτοὶ in their
Κρυπτεία, i. p. 633 C.
The phrase seems however to indi-
cate that Plato did not much like to
call his Agronomi by the name of
Κρυπτοί. The duties performed by the
Lacedæmonian Κρυπτοὶ against the
Helots were of the harshest character.
See chap. vi. p. 509 of my 'History of
Greece.' Schömann, Antiq. Jurisp.
Græc. iv. 1-4, p. 111, v. 1, 21, p. 199.

parallel of the youthful Peripoli at Athens, who were employed as Guards for two years round various parts of Attica.

Besides Astynomi and Agoranomi, Plato provides priests for the care of the sacred buildings in the city, and for the service of the Gods. In choosing these priests, as in choosing the other magistrates, election and sortition are to be combined; to satisfy at once the oligarchical and the democratical sentiment. The lot will be peculiarly suitable in a case where priests are to be chosen—because the God may be expected to guide it in a manner agreeable to himself.[d] Plato himself however is not confident on this point, for he enjoins additional precautions: the person chosen must be sixty years old at least, free from all bodily defect, of legitimate birth, and of a family untainted by previous crime. Plato prescribes farther, that laws or canons respecting matters of divine concern shall be obtained from the Delphian oracle : and that certain Exêgêtæ shall be named as authorised interpreters of these canons, as long as they live.[e] Treasurers or stewards shall also be chosen, out of the two richer classes of the census, to administer the landed property and produce belonging to the various temples.[f]

Priests— Exêgêtæ— Property belonging to temples.

In the execution of the duties imposed upon them, the Agoranomi and Astynomi are empowered to fine an offender to the extent of one mina (one hundred drachmæ), each of them separately—and when both sit together, to the extent of two minæ.[g]

Music and Gymnastic.—For each of these, two magisterial functions must be constituted: one to superintend the teaching and training—the other, to preside over the matches and distribution of prizes. In regard to the musical matches, one President must be appointed for the monôdic singleheaded exhibitions, another

Superintendance of Music and Gymnastic. Educational function.

[d] Plato, Legg. vi. p. 749 D.
[e] Plato, Legg. vi. p. 759 E.
[f] Plato, Legg. vi. p. 760 A.
[g] Plat. Legg. vi. p. 764 B.
Here, as in other provisions, Plato copies the practice at Athens, where each individual magistrate was empowered to impose a fine of definite amount (ἐπιβολὴν ἐπιβάλλειν), though we do not know what that amount was. The Proedri could impose a fine as high as one mina, the Senate as high as five minæ (Meier und Schömann, Der Attische Prozess, p. 34).

for the choric exhibitions. The President of the former must be not less than thirty years of age. The President of the latter must be not less than forty years of age. In order to appoint a fit person, the Nomophylakes shall constrain all the citizens whom they believe to be conversant with monôdic or choric matters, to assemble and agree on a preliminary list of ten candidates, who shall undergo a Dokimasy or examination, upon the single point of skill and competency, and no other. If they all pass, recourse shall be had to lot, and the one who draws the first lot shall be President for the year. In regard to the gymnastic matches, of men as well as of horses, the citizens of the three richest classes shall be constrained to come together (those of the fourth class may come, or stay away, as they please), and to fix upon twenty suitable persons; who shall undergo the Dokimasy, and out of whom three shall be selected by lot as Presidents of gymnastic contests for the year.[h]

We observe that in the nomination of Presidents for the musical and gymnastic contests, Plato adopts the same doublefaced machinery as before—To please the oligarchical sentiment by treating the votes of the rich as indispensable, the votes of the poor as indifferent—To please the democratical sentiment by a partial application of the lot. But in regard to the President of musical and gymnastic education or training, he prescribes a very different manner of choice. He declares this to be the most important function in the city. Upon the way in which the Minister of Education discharges his functions, the ultimate character of the citizens will mainly turn. Accordingly, this magistrate must be a man of fifty years of age, father of legitimate children—and, if possible, of daughters as well as sons. He must also be one of the thirty-seven Nomophylakes. He will be selected, not by the votes of the citizens generally, but by the votes of all the magistrates (except the annual Councillors and the Prytanes): such votes being deposited secretly in the temple of Apollo. The person who obtains the most of these secret votes will be submitted to a farther Dokimasy by all the voting magistrates (except the Nomo-

Grave duties of the Minister of Education—precautions in electing him.

phylakes themselves), and will, if approved, be constituted President of musical and gymnastic education for five years.[1]

From the magisterial authority in his city, Plato now passes to the judicial or dikastic. He remarks that no peremptory line of separation can be drawn between the two. Every magistrate exercises judicial functions on some matters: every dikast, on the days when he sits, decides magisterially.[k] He then proceeds to distinguish (as the Attic forum did) between two sorts of causes:—Private, disputes between man and man, where the persons complaining of being wronged are one or a few individuals—Public, where the party wronged or alleged to be wronged is the state.[l]

Judicial duties.

In regard to the private causes, he institutes Tribe-Dikasteries, taken by lot out of the citizens of each tribe, and applied without notice to each particular cause as it comes on, so that no one can know beforehand in what cause he is to adjudicate, nor can any one be solicited or bribed.[m] He institutes farthermore a superior court of appeal, formed every year by the various Boards of Magistrates, each choosing out of its own body the most esteemed member, subject to approval by an ensuing Dokimasy.[n] When one citizen believes himself to be wronged by another, he must first submit the complaint to arbitration by neighbours and common friends. If this arbitration fails to prove satisfactory, he must next bring the complaint before the Tribe-Dikastery. Should their decision prove unsatisfactory, the case may be brought (seemingly by either of the parties) before the superior court of appeal, whose decision will be final. Plato directs that this superior Court shall hold its sittings publicly, in presence of all the Magistrates and all the Councillors, as well as of any other citizen who may choose to attend. The members of the Court are to give their votes openly.[o] Should

Private Causes— how tried.

[i] Plato, Legg. vi. pp. 765-766.
[k] Plato, Legg. vi. p. 767 A.
[l] Plato, Legg. vi. p. 767 B.
This was the main distinction adopted in the Attic law. 1. Complaint, founded upon injury alleged to be done to the interest of some individual—ἀγὼν ἴδιος, δίκη ἰδία, δίκη in the narrow sense. 2. Complaint, founded upon injury alleged to be

done towards some interest not strictly individual—ἀγὼν δημόσιος, δίκη δημοσία, γραφή (Meier und Schömann, Der Attisch. Prozess, p. 162).
[m] Plato, Legg. vi. p. 768 B.
[n] Plato, Legg. vi. p. 767 C-D. γιγνέσθω κοινὸν ἅπασι τοῖς τὸ τρίτον ἀμφισβητοῦσιν ἰδιώταις πρὸς ἀλλήλους.
[o] Plato, Legg. vi. pp. 767 A-D, 768 B. Compare xii. p. 956.

they be suspected of injustice or corruption, they may be impeached before the Nomophylakes; who, if convinced of their guilt, shall compel them to make good the wrong done, and shall impose penalties besides, if the case requires.[p]

In regard to Public Causes, Plato makes unusual concession to a feeling much prevalent in Greece, and especially potent at Athens. Where the wrong done is to the public, he recognises that the citizens generally will not submit to be excluded from the personal cognisance of it: the citizen excluded from that privilege feels as if he had no share in the city.[q] If one citizen accuses another of treason, or peculation, or other wrong towards the public, the accusation shall be originated at first, and decided at last, before the general body of citizens. But after having been originated before this general assembly, the charge must be submitted to an intermediate stage of examination, before three of the principal Boards of Magistrates; who shall sift the allegations of the accuser, as well as the defence of the accused. These commissioners (we must presume) will make a report on the case, which report will be brought before the general assembly; who will then adjudicate upon it finally, and condemn or acquit as they think right.[r]

Public Causes must be tried directly by the citizens—strong feeling among Greeks about this.

This proposition deserves notice. Plato proclaims his disapprobation of the numerous Dikasteries in Athens, wherein the Dikasts sat, heard, and voted—perhaps with applause or murmurs, but with no searching questions of their own—leaving the whole speech to the parties and their witnesses. To decide justly (he says), the judicial authority must not remain silent, but must speak more than the parties, and must undertake the substantial conduct of the enquiry. No numerous assembly—nor even any few, unless they be intelligent—are competent to such a duty: nor even an intelligent few, without much

Plato's way of meeting this feeling—Intermediate inquiry and report by a special Commissioner.

---

p Plato, Legg. vi. p. 767 E.

q Plato, Legg. vi. p. 768 B. ὁ γὰρ ἀκοινώνητος ὢν ἐξουσίας τοῦ συνδικά-ζειν, ἡγεῖται τὸ παράπαν τῆς πόλεως οὐ μέτοχος εἶναι. This is a remarkable indication about the tone of Grecian feeling from a very adverse witness.

r Plato, Legg. vi. p. 768 A. τὴν δὲ βάσανον ἐν ταῖς μεγίσταις ἀρχαῖς τρίσιν, &c.

Here the word βάσανος is used in a much more extended sense than usual, so as to include the whole process of judicial inquiry.

time and patience.[s] To secure such an enquiry on these public causes—as far as is possible consistent with the necessity of leaving the final decision to the general assembly—is the object of Plato's last-mentioned proposition. It is one of the most judicious propositions in his whole scheme.

Plato has now constituted the magistrates and the judicial machinery. It is time to specify the laws which they are to obey and to enforce.[t]

What laws the magistrates are to enforce—Many details must be left to the Nomophylakes.

Plato considers the Nomophylakes (together with another Board called the Nocturnal Council, to be hereafter described) as the permanent representatives of himself: destined to ensure that the grand ethical purpose of the lawgiver shall be constantly kept in view, and to supply what may have been left wanting in the original programme.[u] Especially at the first beginning, provision will be found wanting in many details, which the Nomophylakes will take care to supply. In respect to the choric festivals, which are of so much importance for the training and intercourse of young men and maidens, the lawgiver must trust to the Choric Superintendents and the Nomophylakes for regulating, by their experience, much which he cannot foresee. But an experience of ten years will enable them to make all the modifications and additions required ; and after that period they shall fix and consecrate in perpetuity the ceremonies as they then stand, forbidding all farther change. Neither in that nor in any other arrangement shall any subsequent change be allowed, except on the unanimous requisition of all the magistrates, all the people, and all the oracles of the Gods.[x]

The choric festivals, in which the youths and maidens will take part, both of them naked as far as a sober modesty will allow, present occasions for mutual acquaintance between them, which serves as foundation for marriage.[y] At the age of twenty-five a young man is permitted to marry ; and before the age of thirty-five he is required to marry, under penalty of

Marriage-Laws—Rich husbands to choose poor wives—No dowries—Costly marriage festivals are forbidden.

[s] Plato, Legg. vi. p. 766 E.
[t] Plato, Legg. vi. 768 E.
[u] Plato, Legg. vi. p. 770 C-E.
[x] Plato, Legg. vi. p. 772 C-D.

[y] Plato, Legg. vi. p. 772 C. γυμνοὺς καὶ γυμνὰς μέχριπερ αἰδοῦς σώφρονας ἑκάστων, &c.

fine and disgrace, if he does not.[z] Plato introduces here a discourse, in the form of a prologue to his marriage law, wherein he impresses on young men the general principles according to which they ought to choose their wives. The received sentiment, which disposes a rich youth to choose his wife from a rich family, is (in Plato's view) altogether wrong. Rich husbands ought to assort themselves with poor wives; and in general the characters of husband and wife ought to be opposite rather than similar, in order that the offspring may not inherit the defects of either.[a] The religious ceremonies antecedent to marriage are to be regulated by the Exêgêtæ. A costly marriage feast—and, above all, drunkenness at that feast—are emphatically forbidden. Any offspring begotten when the parent is in this disorderly and insane condition,[b] will probably be vitiated from the beginning. Out of the two residences which every citizen's lot will comprise, one must be allotted to the son when the son marries.[c]

Plato now enters upon his laws respecting property; and

Laws about slavery. Slaves to be well fed, and never treated with cruelty or insolence. The master must not converse with them.

first of all upon the most critical variety of property : that in human beings, or slavery. This he declares to be a subject full of difficulty. There is much difference of opinion on the subject. Some speak of slaves as deserving trust and good treatment, in proof of which various anecdotes of exemplary fidelity on their part are cited : others again regard them as incorrigibly debased, fit for nothing better than the whip and spur, like cattle. Then moreover the modified form of slavery, such as that of the Helots in Laconia, and the Penestæ in Thessaly, has been found full of danger and embarrassment, though the Spartans themselves are well satisfied with it.[d] (It will be recollected that the Helots and

---

[z] Plato, Legg. vi. pp. 772 E, 774 A.
[a] Plato, Legg. vi. p. 773 C-D.
Compare the Politikus, pp. 310-311, where the necessity is insisted on of coupling in marriage two persons of opposite dispositions—τὸ ἀνδρεῖον ἦθος with τὸ κόσμιον ἦθος. There is a natural inclination (Plato says) for the ἀνδρεῖοι to intermarry with each other, and for the κόσμιοι to do the like : but the lawgiver must contend against this.

If this be permitted, each of the breeds will degenerate through excess of its own peculiarity.
[b] Plato, Legg. vi. p. 775.
[c] Plato, Legg. vi. p. 776 A.
[d] Plato, Legg. vi. p. 777. He alludes also to the enslavement of the indigenous population called the Mariandyni, by the Grecian colonists of Herakleia on the southern coast of the Euxine ; and to the disturbances

Penestæ were not slaves bought and imported from abroad, as the slaves in Attica were, but conquered Hellenic communities who had been degraded from freedom into slavery, and from the condition of independent proprietorship into that of tributary tenants or serfs; but with the right to remain permanently on their lands, without ever being sold for exportation.) This form of slavery (where the slaves are of the same race and language, with reciprocal bonds of sympathy towards each other) Plato denounces as especially dangerous. Care must be taken that there shall be among the slaves as little fellowship of language and feelings as possible; but they must be well fed: moreover everything like cruelty and insolence in dealing with them must be avoided, even more carefully than in dealing with freemen. This he prescribes partly for the protection of the slave himself, but still more for the interest of the master: whose intrinsic virtue, or want of virtue, will be best tested by his behaviour as a master. The slaves must be punished judicially, when they deserve it. But the master must never exhort or admonish them, as he would address himself to a freeman: he must never say a word to them, except to give an order: above all, he must abstain from all banter and joking, either with male or female slaves.[e] Many foolish masters indulge in such behaviour, which emboldens the slaves to give themselves airs, and renders the task of governing them almost impracticable.[f]

and disorders which had occurred through movements of the slaves in Southern Italy. Probably this last may be connected with that revolt whereby the Bruttians became enfranchised; but we can make out nothing definite from Plato's language.

[e] Plato, Legg. vi. p. 777 D-E. κολάζειν γε μὴν ἐν δίκῃ δούλους ἀεὶ, καὶ μὴ νουθετοῦντας ὡς ἐλευθέρους θρύπτεσθαι ποιεῖν. Τὴν δὲ οἰκετοῦ πρόσρησιν χρὴ σχεδὸν ἐπίταξιν πᾶσαν γίγνεσθαι, μὴ προσπαίζοντας μηδαμῇ μηδαμῶς οἰκεταῖς, μήτ' οὖν θηλείαις μήτ' ἄρρεσιν.

[f] Aristotle (Polit. vii. p. 1330, a. 27; Œconom. i. p. 1344, b. 18) agrees with Plato as to the danger of having slaves who speak the same language and are of the same tribes, with common lineage and sympathies. He disapproves of anything which tends to impart spirit and independance to the slave's character; and he takes occasion from hence to deduce some objections against various arrangements of the Platonic Republic (Politic. ii. p. 1264. a. 35). These are precautions—πρὸς τὸ μηδὲν νεωτερίζειν. But Aristotle dissents from Plato on another point—where Plato enjoins that the master shall not exhort or admonish his slave, but shall address to him no word except the word of command (Aristot. Politic. i. p. 1260, b. 5). Aristotle says that there is a certain special and inferior kind of ἀρετή which the slave can possess and ought to possess; that this ought to be communicated to him by the admonition and exhortation of the master; and that the master ought to admonish his slaves even more than he admonishes his children. The slave

As to the construction of the city, Plato prescribes that its

Circular form for the city— Temples in the centre— No walls round it. external contour shall be of circular form, encircling the summit of an eminence, with the agora near the centre. The temples of the Gods shall be planted around the agora, and the buildings for gymnasia and schooling, for theatrical representation, for magistrative, administrative, and judicial business, near at hand. Plato follows the example of Sparta in prohibiting any special outer wall for the fortification of the city, which he treats as an indication of weakness and timidity : nevertheless he suggests that the houses constituting the city may be erected on such a plan, and in such connection, as to be equivalent to a fortification.[g] When once the city is erected, the Astynomi or Ædiles are to be charged with the duty of maintaining its integrity and cleanliness.

Plato next proceeds to regulate the mode of life proper for

Mode of life prescribed to new-married couples— They are to take the best care about good procreation for the city. all his new-married couples. He proclaims broadly that large interference with private and individual life is unavoidable; and that no great public reform can be accomplished without it.[h] He points out that this principle was nowhere sufficiently admitted : not even at Sparta, where it was carried farther than anywhere else. Even the Spartans and Kretans adopted the public mess-table only for males, and not for females.[i] In Plato's view, it is essential for both. He would greatly prefer (as announced already in his Republic) that it should be one and the same for both—males and females taking their meals together.

The newly-married couples are enjoined to bestow their

<hr>

requires a certain ἠθικὴν ἀρετὴν, so that he may not be hindered from his duty by ἀκολασία or δειλία : but it is an ἀρετή μικρά : the courage required for the slave is ὑπηρετική, that for the master ἀρχική (ib. p. 1260, a. 22-35). This measure of virtue the master must impart to the slave by exhortation, over and above the orders which he gives as to the performance of work. It would appear, however, that in Aristotle's time there were various persons who denied that there was any ἀρετή belonging to a slave—παρὰ τὰς ὀργανικὰς καὶ διακονικάς (p. 1259, b. 23). Upon this last theory is founded the injunction of Plato which Aristotle here controverts.

What Aristotle says about slaves in the fifth chapter of the first book of his Œconomica, is superior to what he says in the Politica, and superior to anything which we read in the Platonic Treatise De Legibus.

[g] Plato, Legg. vi. pp. 778-779.

[h] Plato, Legg. vi. p. 780 A, vii. p. 790 A.

[i] Plato, Legg. vi. p. 781 A.

best attention upon the production of handsome and well-con-
stituted children: this being their primary duty to Board of superintend-ing matrons.
the city for ten years after their marriage. Their
conduct will be watched by a Board of Matrons, chosen for
the purpose by the Nomophylakes, and assembling every day
in the temple of Eileithuia. In case of any dispute, or unfaithful or unseemly conduct, these Matrons will visit them to
admonish or threaten, if they see reason. Should such interference fail of effect, the Matrons will apprise the Nomophylakes, who will on their parts admonish and censure, and
will at last denounce the delinquents, if still refractory, to the
public authority. The delinquents will then be disgraced,
and debarred from the public ceremonies, unless they can
clear themselves by indicting and convicting their accusers
before the public tribunal.[k]

The age of marriage is fixed at from thirty to thirty-five for
males, from sixteen to twenty for females. The first Age fixed for marriage. During the first ten years the couple are under obliga-tion to pro-create for the city—
ten years after marriage are considered as appropri-
ated to the production of children *for the city*, and
are subject to the strict supervision above mentioned.
If any couple have no offspring for ten years, the
marriage shall be dissolved by authority. After ten Restrictions during these ten years.
years the supervision is suspended, and the couple
are left to themselves. If either of them shall commit an infidelity with another person still under the decennial restriction, the party so offending is liable to the same penalty as if
he were still himself also under it.[l] But if the person with
whom infidelity is committed be not under that restriction,
no penalty will be incurred beyond a certain general discredit, as compared with others whose conduct is blameless,
and who will receive greater honour. However, Plato advises
that nothing shall be said in the law respecting the conduct
of married couples after the period of decennial restriction has
elapsed, unless there be some grave scandal to call attention
to the subject.[m]

[k] Plato, Legg. vi. p. 784.
[l] Plato, Legg. vi. pp. 784-785.
[m] Plato, Legg. vi. p. 785 A. καὶ μετριαζόντων μὲν περὶ τὰ τοιαῦτα τῶν πλειόνων ἀνομοθέτητα σιγῇ κείσθω, ἀκοσμούντων δὲ νομοθετηθέντα ταύτῃ πραττέσθω, &c.

Plato now proceeds to treat about the children just born.

How infants
are to be
brought up—
Nurses—
Perpetual
regulated
movements
—useful for
toning down
violent emo-
tions.

The principle of separate family being admitted in
the Treatise de Legibus, he refrains from promulgating any peremptory laws on this subject, because
it is impossible for the lawgiver or the magistrate to
enter into each private house, and to enforce obedience on such minute and numerous details: while it
would be discreditable for him to command what he could not
enforce, and it would moreover accustom citizens to disobey
the law with impunity. Still, however, Plato[n] thinks it useful
to deliver some general advice, which he hopes that fathers
and mothers will spontaneously follow. He begins with the
infant as soon as born, and even before birth. The mother
during pregnancy is admonished to take regular exercise;
the infant when born must be carried about constantly in the
nurse's arms. The invigorating effects of such gestation are
illustrated by the practice of Athenian cockfighters, who cause
the cocks while under training to be carried about under the
arms of attendants in long walks.[o] Besides that the nurses
(slaves) must be strong women, there must also be more than
one to each infant, in order that he may be sufficiently carried about. He must be kept in swaddling-clothes for the first
two years, and must not be allowed to walk until he is three
years of age.[p] The perpetual movement and dandling, in the
arms of the nurse, produces a good effect not only on the
health and bodily force of the infant, but also upon his emotions.[q] The infant ought to be kept (if it were possible) in
movement as constant and unceasing as if he were on shipboard. Nurses know this by experience, when they lull to
sleep an insomnious child, not by holding him still, but by
swinging him about in their arms, and by singing a ditty. So
likewise the insane and furious emotions inspired by Dionysus
(also by Zeus, by the mother of the Gods, &c.) are appeased

[n] Plato, Legg. vii. pp. 788-790 A.
[o] Plato, Legg. vii. p. 789.
[p] Plato, Legg. vii. pp. 789 E, 790 A.
[q] Plato, Legg. vii. p. 790 D. λάβωμεν τοίνυν τοῦτο οἷον στοιχεῖον ἐπ'
ἀμφότερα σώματος τε καὶ ψυχῆς τῶν
πάνυ νέων, τὴν τιθήνησιν καὶ κίνησιν,

γιγνομένην ὅτι μάλιστα διὰ πάσης νυκτός τε καὶ ἡμέρας, ὡς ἔστι ξύμφορος
ἅπασι μὲν, οὐχ ἥκιστα δὲ τοῖς ὅτι νεω-
τάτοισιν, καὶ οἰκεῖν, εἰ δυνατὸν ἦν, οἷον
ἀεὶ πλέοντας· νῦν δὲ, ὡς ἐγγύτατα
τούτου ποιεῖν δεῖ περὶ τὰ νεογενῆ
παίδων θρέμματα.

by the regulated movement, dance and music, solemnly performed at the ceremonial worship of the God who excited the
emotions.   These are different varieties of fear and perturbation: they are morbid internal movements, which we overpower and heal by muscular and rhythmical movements impressed from without, with appropriate music and religious
solemnities.[r]

To guard the child, during the first three years of his life,
against disturbing fears, or at least to teach him to conquer
them when they may spring up, is to lay the best foundation
of a fearless character for the future.[s]   By extreme indulgence
he would be rendered wayward: by extreme harshness his
spirit would be broken.[t]   A middle course ought to be pursued, guarding him against pains as far as may be, yet at the
same time keeping pleasures out of his reach, especially the
stronger pleasures: thus shall we form in him a gentle and propitious disposition, such as that which we ascribe to the Gods.[u]

The comparison made here by Plato between the effect
produced by these various religious ceremonies upon
the mind of the votary, and that produced by the
dandling of the nurse upon the perturbed child in
her arms, is remarkable.   In both, the evil is the
same—unfounded and irrational fear—an emotional disturbance within: in both, the remedy is the same—regulated
muscular movement and excitement from without: more
gentle in the case of the infant, more violent in the case of
the adult.   Emotion is a complex fact, physical as well as
mental; and the physical aspect and basis of it (known to
Aristotle[x] as well as to Plato) is here brought to view.   To

Margin note: Choric and orchestic movements, their effect in discharging strong emotions.

[r] Plato, Legg. vii. pp. 790-791. δει-
μαίνειν ἔστι που ταῦτ᾽ ἀμφότερα τὰ
πάθη, καὶ ἔστι δείματα δι᾽ ἕξιν φαύλην
τῆς ψυχῆς τινά. Ὅταν οὖν ἔξωθέν τις
προσφέρῃ τοῖς τοιούτοις πάθεσι σεισμὸν,
ἡ τῶν ἔξωθεν κρατεῖ κίνησις προσφερο-
μένη τὴν ἐντὸς φοβερὰν οὖσαν καὶ
μανικὴν κίνησιν, κρατήσασα δὲ γαλήνην
ἡσυχίαν τε ἐν τῇ ψυχῇ φαίνεται ἀπερ-
γασαμένη τῆς περὶ τὰ τῆς καρδίας
χαλεπῆς γενομένης ἑκάστων πηδήσεως.
About the effect of the movement,
bustle, noise, and solemn exhibitions,
&c. of a Grecian festival, in appeasing
the over-wrought internal excitement

of those who took part in it, see Lobeck, Aglaophamus, p. 689.
Compare Euripid. Hippolyt. 141,
where the Chorus addresses the love-
sick Phædra :—

σὺ τὰρ᾽ ἔνθεος, ὦ κούρα
εἴτ᾽ ἐκ Πανὸς εἴθ᾽ Ἑκάτας,
ἢ σεμνῶν Κορυβάντων,
ἢ ματρὸς ὀρείας φοιτᾷς.

also Eurip. Medea, 1172 about Πανὸς
ὀργάς.
[s] Plato, Legg. vii. p. 791 C.
[t] Plato, Legg. vii. p. 791 D.
[u] Plato, Legg. vii. p. 792 C-D.
[x] Aristot. De Animâ, i. 1.

speak the language of modern science (with which their views
here harmonise, in spite of their imperfect acquaintance with
human anatomy), if the energies of the nervous system are
overwrought within, they may be diverted into a new channel
by bodily movements at once strenuous and measured, and
may thus be discharged in a way tranquillising to the emotions. This is Plato's theory about the healing effects of the
choric and orchêstic religious ceremonies of his day. The
God was believed first to produce the distressing excitement
within—then to suggest and enjoin (even to share in) the
ceremonial movements for the purpose of relieving it. The
votary is brought back from the condition of comparative
madness to that of sober reason.[y] Strong emotion of any kind
is, in Plato's view, a state of distemper. The observances here
prescribed respecting wise regulation of the emotions, especially in young children, are considered by Plato as not being
laws in the proper and positive sense, but as the unwritten
customs, habits, rules, discipline, &c., upon which all positive
laws repose and depend. Though they appear to go into
excessive and petty detail, yet unless they be well understood and efficaciously realised, the laws enacted will fail to
attain their purpose.[z]

Pursuant to this view of the essential dependence of *leges*
upon *mores*, Plato continues his directions about the
training of children. From the age of three to six
the child must be supplied with amusements, under a gentle
but sufficient controul. The children of both sexes will meet
daily at the various temples near at hand, with discreet
matrons to preside over them, and will find amusement for
each other. At six years of age the boys and girls will be
separated, and will be consigned to different male and female
tutors. The boys shall learn riding, military exercise, and
the use of the various weapons of war. The girls shall learn
these very same things also, if it be possible. Plato is most

Training of boys and girls.

[y] Plato, Legg. vii. p. 791 A. κατ-
ειργάσατο ἀντὶ μανικῶν ἡμῖν διαθέσεων
ἕξεις ἔμφρονας ἔχειν.
Servius observes (Not. ad Virgil.
Eclog. v. 73) :—" Sané, ut in religioni-
bus saltaretur, hæc ratio est, quod

nullam majores nostri corporis partem
esse voluerunt, quæ non sentiret reli-
gionem. Nam cantus ad animam,
saltatio ad mobilitatem pertinet corporis."
[z] Plato, Legg. vii. p. 793 C-D.

anxious that they should learn, but he fears that the feelings of the community will not tolerate the practice.[a] All the teaching will be conducted under the superintendence of teachers, female as well as male : competent individuals, of both sexes, being appointed to the functions of command without distinction.[b] The children will be taught to use their left hands as effectively as their right.[c] Wrestling shall be taught up to a certain point, to improve the strength and flexibility of the limbs ; but elaborate wrestling and pugilism is disapproved. Imitative dancing, choric movements, and procession, shall also be taught, but always in arms, to familiarise the youth with military details.[d]

Plato now enters upon the musical and literary teaching proper for the youthful portion of his community. Poetry, music, and dancing, as connected with the service and propitiation of the Gods, are in the first instance recreative and amusing; but they also involve serious consequences.[e] It is most important to the community that these exercises should not only be well arranged, but that when arranged they should be fixed by authority, so as to prevent all innovations or deviations by individual taste. Plato here repeats, with emphasis, his commendation of the Egyptian practice to consecrate all the songs, dances, and festive ceremonies, and to tolerate no others whatever.[f] Change is in itself a most serious evil, and change in one department provokes an appetite for change in all. Plato forbids all innovation, even in matters of detail, such as the shape of vessels or articles of furniture.[g] He allows no poet to circulate any ode except such as is in full harmony with the declaration of the lawgiver respecting good and evil. All the old poems must be sifted and weeded. All new hymns and prayers to the Gods, even before they are shown to a single individual, must be examined by Censors above fifty years of age, in order that it may be seen whether the poet knows what he

Marginal note: Musical and literary teaching for youth— Poetry, songs, music, dances, must all be fixed by authority and never changed— Mischief done by poets aiming to please.

---

[a] Plato, Legg. vii. p. 794 B-D.
[b] Plato, Legg. vii. p. 795 D. ἀρχού- σαις τε καὶ ἄρχουσι. P. 806 E.
[c] Plato, Legg. vii. pp. 794-795, 804 D.
[d] Plato, Legg. vii. p. 796 C-D.
[e] Plato, Legg. vii. p. 803 C-E.
[f] Plato, Legg. vii. p. 799.
[g] Plato, Legg. vii. p. 797.

ought to praise or blame, and what he ought to pray for. In
general, the poets do not know what is good and what is evil.
By mistaken prayers—especially for wealth, which the lawgiver discountenances as prejudicial—they may bring down
great mischief upon the city.[h] Different songs must be composed for the two sexes: songs of a bold and martial character
for males—of a sober and quiet character for females.[i] But
the poet must on no account cultivate "the sweet Muse," or
make it his direct aim to produce emotions delightful to the
audience. The sound and useful music will always in the end
become agreeable, provided the pupils hear it from their
earliest childhood, and hear nothing else.[k] Plato censures
the tragic representations exhibited in the Grecian cities (at
Athens, more than anywhere else) as being unseemly, and
even impious, because, close to the altar where sacrifice was
offered to the Gods, choric and dramatic performances of the
most touching and pathetic character were exhibited. The
poet who gained the prize was he who touched most deeply
the tender emotions of the audience, and caused the greatest
flow of tears among them. Now, in the opinion of Plato, the
exhibition of so much human misery, and the communication
of so much sorrowful sympathy, was most unsuitable to the
festival day, and offensive to the Gods. It was tolerable only
on the inauspicious days of the year, and when exhibited by
hired Karian mourners, such as those who wailed loudly at
funerals. The music at the festivals ought to have no emotional character, except that of gentle, kindly, auspicious
cheerfulness.[l]

At ten years old, the boys and girls (who have hitherto
been exercised in recitation, singing, dancing, &c.)
are to learn their letters, or reading and writing.
They will continue this process until thirteen years

Boys and girls to learn letters and the lyre, from ten to thir-

[h] Plato, Legg. vii. pp. 800 A, 801 B, 802 B.
[i] Plato, Legg. vii. p. 802 D-E.
[k] Plato, Legg. vii. p. 802 C. καὶ μὴ παρατιθεμένης τῆς γλυκείας Μούσης.
[l] Plato, Legg. vii. p. 800 B-E. εὐφημία, καὶ τὸ τῆς ᾠδῆς γένος εὔφημον ἡμῖν πάντῃ πάντως ὑπαρχέτω.
This is a remarkable declaration of Plato, condemning the tragic representations at Athens. Compare
Gorgias, p. 501; Republic, x. p. 605: also about the effect on the spectators, Ion, p. 535 E.
The idea of εὐφημία is more negative than positive; it is often shown by silence. The δυσφήμιαι—Sopho. Phil. 11—or βλασφημία, as Plato calls it, are the positive act or ill-omened manifestation, Plato, Phædon, p. 117. ἐν εὐφημίᾳ χρὴ τελευτᾶν.

old.   They will learn the use of the lyre, for three teen years of
years.   The same period and duration is fixed for all age. Masters will teach
of them, not depending at all upon the judgment or the laws and homilies of
preference of the parents.[m]   It is sufficient if they the lawgiver, and licensed extracts from
learn to read and write tolerably, without aiming to the poets.
do it either quickly or very well.   The boys will be marched
to school at daybreak every morning, under the care of a
tutor, who is chosen by the magistrate for the purpose of
keeping them under constant supervision and discipline.[n]
The masters for teaching will be special persons paid for the
duty, usually foreigners.[o]   They will be allowed to teach
nothing except the laws and homilies of the lawgiver, together
with any selections from existing poets which may be in full
harmony with these.[p]   Plato here proclaims how highly he is
himself delighted with his own string of homilies : which are
not merely exhortations useful to be heard, but also have the
charm of poetry, and have been aided by inspirations from the
Gods.[q]   As for the poets themselves, whether serious or
comic, whose works were commonly employed in teaching,
being committed wholly or partially to memory—Plato repudiates them as embodying a large proportion of mischievous
doctrine which his pupils ought never to hear.   Much reading, or much learning, he discountenances as dangerous to
youths.[r]

The teaching of the harp and of music (occupying the three
years from thirteen to sixteen, after the three pre- The teaching
ceding years of teaching letters) will not be suffered is to be simple, and common to both
to extend to any elaborate or complicated combina- sexes.
tions.   The melody will be simple : the measure grave and
dignified.   The imitative movement or dancing will exhibit
only the gestures and demeanour suitable to the virtuous
man in the various situations of life, whether warlike or

---

[m] Plato, Legg. vii. p. 810 A.
[n] Plato, Legg. vii. pp. 808 C, 809 B.
[o] Plato, Legg. vii. pp. 804 D, 813 E.
[p] Plato, Legg. vii. p. 811 E. Any
new poet who wishes to exhibit must
submit his compositions to the Censors.
P. 817 C-D.
[q] Plato, Legg. vii. p. 811 C-D. οὐκ
ἄνευ τινὸς ἐπιπνοίας θεῶν — μάλα
ἡσθῆναι. Stallbaum in his note treats

this as said in jest (*facete* dicit). To
me it seems sober earnest, and quite in
character with the didactic solemnity
of the whole treatise. Plato himself
would have been astonished (I think)
at the note of his commentator.
[r] Plato, Legg. vii. pp. 810-811,
κίνδυνόν φημι εἶναι φέρουσαν τοῖς παισὶ
τὴν πολυμαθίαν. Compare p. 819 A.

pacific:[s] the subject-matter of the songs or hymns will be regulated (as above described) by censorial authority. The practice will be consecrated and unchangeable, under the supervision of a magistrate for education.[t]

All this teaching is imparted to the youth of both sexes: to boys, by male teachers—to girls, by female teachers, both of them paid. The training in gymnastic and military exercises and in arms, is also common to girls and boys.[u] Plato deems it disgraceful that the females shall be brought up timorous and helpless—unable to aid in defending the city when it is menaced, and even unmanning the male citizens by demonstrations of terror.[x]

We next come to arithmetic, geometry, and astronomy.

Rudiments of arithmetic and geometry to be taught. Pláto directs that all his citizens shall learn the rudiments of these sciences—not for the reason urged by most persons, because of the necessities of practical life, (which reason he discards as extravagantly silly, though his master Sokrates was among those who urged it)—but because these are endowments belonging to the divine nature, and because without them no man can become a God, Dæmon, or Hero, capable of watching over mankind.[y] In Egypt elementary arithmetic and geometry were extensively taught to boys—but very little in Greece:[z] though he intimates that both in Egypt, and in the Phenician towns, they were turned only to purposes of traffic, and were joined with sordid dispositions which a good lawgiver ought to correct by other provisions. In

---

[s] Plato, Legg. vii. p. 812 C-D. Still Plato allows the exhibition, under certain conditions, of low, comic, ludicrous dances; yet not by any freemen or citizens, but by slaves and hired persons of mean character. He even considers it necessary that the citizens should see such low exhibitions occasionally, in order to appreciate by contrast the excellence of their own dignified exhibitions. Of two opposites you cannot know the one unless you also learn to know the other—ἄνευ γὰρ γελοίων τὰ σπουδαῖα καὶ πάντων τῶν ἐναντίων τὰ ἐναντία μαθεῖν οὐ δυνατὸν, εἰ μέλλει τις φρόνιμος ἔσεσθαι, ποιεῖν δὲ οὐκ ἂν δυνατὸν ἀμφότερα, &c. (p. 816 E).

[t] Plato, Legg. vii. p. 813 A.

[u] Plat. Legg. vii. pp. 813 C-E, 814-815. πολεμικὴ ὄρχησις—εἰρηνικὴ or ἀπόλεμος ὄρχησις.

[x] Plato, Legg. vii. p. 814 B. See Æschylus, Sept. ad. Thebas, 172-220.

[y] Plato, Legg. vii. p. 818 B-C. οὗτος πάντων τῶν λόγων εὐηθέστατός ἐστι μακρῷ. In interpreting this curious passage we must remember that regularity, symmetry, exact numerical proportion, &c., are the primary characteristics of the divine agents in Plato's view: of Uranus and the Stars, as the first of them, compare Æschyl. Promet. 460.

[z] Plato, Legg. vii. pp. 818 E, 819 B-D. ᾐσχύνθην — ὑπὲρ ἁπάντων τῶν Ἑλλήνων. Compare Legg. v. p. 747 C, and Republic, iv. p. 436 A.

Respecting the distinction between θεοὶ, δαίμονες, ἥρωες, see Nägelsbach, Nach-Homerische Theologie, pp. 104-115.

the Platonic city, both arithmetic and geometry will be taught, so far as to guard the youth against absurd blunders about measurement, and against confusion of incommensurable lines and spaces with commensurable. Such blunders are now often made by Greeks.[a] By a good method, the teaching of these sciences may be made attractive and interesting; so that no force will be required to compel youth to learn.[b]

[a] Plato, Legg. vii. pp. 819 E, 820 A-C.

[b] Plato, Legg. vii. p. 820 D. μετὰ παιδιᾶς ἅμα μανθανόμενα ὠφελήσει. I transcribe here the curious passage which we read a little before.

Plat. Legg. vii. p. 819 B. Τόσαδε τοίνυν ἕκαστα χρὴ φάναι μανθάνειν δεῖν τοὺς ἐλευθέρους, ὅσα καὶ πάμπολυς ἐν Αἰγύπτῳ παίδων ὄχλος ἅμα γράμμασι μανθάνει. Πρῶτον μὲν γὰρ περὶ λογισμοὺς ἀτεχνῶς παισὶν ἐξευρημένα μαθήματα, μετὰ παιδιᾶς τε καὶ ἡδονῆς μανθάνειν· μήλων τέ τινῶν διανομαὶ καὶ στεφάνων πλείοσιν ἅμα καὶ ἐλάττοσιν, ἁρμοττόντων ἀριθμῶν τῶν αὐτῶν—καὶ δὴ καὶ παίζοντες, φιάλας ἅμα χρυσοῦ καὶ χαλκοῦ καὶ ἀργύρου καὶ τοιούτων τινῶν ἄλλων κεραννύντες, οἱ δὲ καὶ ὅλως πως διαδιδόντες, ὅπερ εἶπον, εἰς παιδιὰν ἐναρμόττοντες τὰς τῶν ἀναγκαίων ἀριθμῶν χρήσεις, ὠφελοῦσι τοὺς μανθάνοντας εἴς τε τὰς τῶν στρατοπέδων τάξεις καὶ ἀγωγὰς καὶ στρατείας καὶ εἰς οἰκονομίας αὖ· καὶ πάντως χρησιμωτέρους αὐτοὺς αὑτοῖς καὶ ἐγρηγορότας μᾶλλον ἀνθρώπους ἀπεργάζονται.

The information here given is valuable respecting the extensive teaching of elementary arithmetic as well as of letters among Egyptian boys, far more extensive than among Hellenic boys. The priests especially, in Egypt a numerous order, taught these matters to their own sons (Diodor. i. 81), probably to other boys also. The information is valuable too in another point of view, as respects the *method* of teaching arithmetic to boys : not by abstract numbers, nor by simple effort of memory in the repetition of a multiplication-table, but by concrete examples and illustrations exhibited to sense in familiar objects. The importance of this concrete method, both in facilitating comprehension and in interesting the youthful learner, are strongly insisted on by Plato, as they

have been also by some of the ablest modern teachers of elementary arithmetic : see Professor Leslie's Philosophy of Arithmetic, and Mr. Horace Grant's Arithmetic for Young Children and Second Stage of Arithmetic. The following passage from a work of Sir John Herschel (Review of Whewell's History of Inductive Sciences, in the Quarterly Review, June, 1841) bears a striking and curious analogy to the sentences above transcribed from Plato : —" *Number* we cannot help regarding as an abstraction, and consequently its general properties or its axioms to be of necessity inductively concluded from the consideration of particular cases. And surely this is the way in which children do acquire their knowledge of number, and in which they learn its axioms. The apples and the marbles are put in requisition (μήλων διανομαὶ καὶ στεφάνων, *Plato*), and through the multitude of gingerbread nuts their ideas acquire clearness, precision, and generality."

I borrow the above references from Mr. John Stuart Mill, System of Logic, Book ii. ch. vi. p. 335, ed. 1. They are annexed as a note to the valuable chapters of his work on Demonstration and Necessary Truths, in which he shows that the truths so-called, both in Geometry and Arithmetic, rest upon inductive evidence.

"The fundamental truths of the Science of Number all rest upon the evidence of sense : they are proved by showing to our eyes and to our fingers that any given number of objects, ten balls for example, may by separation and re-arrangement exhibit to our senses all the different sets of numbers, the sum of which is equal to ten. All the improved methods of teaching arithmetic to children proceed upon a knowledge of this fact. All who wish to carry the child's *mind* along with them in learning arithmetic—all who (as Dr. Biber in his remarkable Letters

Astronomy must also be taught up to a certain point, in order that the youth may imbibe correct belief respecting those great Divinities—Hêlios, Selênê, and the Planets—or may at any rate be protected from the danger of unconsciously advancing false affirmations about them, discreditable to their dignity. The general public consider it impious to study the Kosmos and the celestial bodies, with a view to detect the causes of what occurs:[c] while at the same time they assert that the movements of Hêlios and Selênê are irregular, and they call the planets Wanderers. Regular action is (in Plato's view) the characteristic mark of what is good and perfect: irregularity is the foremost of all defects, and cannot without blasphemy be imputed to any of the celestial bodies. Moreover, many persons also assert untruly, that among the celestial bodies the one which is really the slowest mover, moves the fastest—and that the one which is really the fastest mover, moves the slowest. How foolish would it appear (continues Plato) if they made the like mistake about the Olympic runners, and if they selected the defeated competitor, instead of the victor, to be crowned and celebrated in panegyrical odes! How offensive is such falsehood, when applied to the great Gods in the heavens! Each of them has in reality one uniform circular movement, though they appear to have many and variable movements. Our youth must be taught enough of astronomy to guard against such heresies. The study of astronomy up to this point, far from being impious, is indispensable as a safeguard against impiety.[d] Plato intimates that

on Education expresses it) wish to teach numbers and not mere ciphers—now teach it through the evidence of the senses, in the manner we have described " (p. 335).

[c] Plato, Legg. vii. p. 821 A. We must observe that the Athenian (who here represents Plato himself) does not give this repugnance to astronomical study as his own feeling, but, on the contrary, as a prejudice from which he dissents. There is no ground, therefore, so far as this passage is concerned, for the charge of contradiction advanced by Velleius against Plato in

Cicero De Nat. Deor. i. 12, 30.

[d] Plat. Legg. vii. pp. 821 B-822 C. καταψευδόμεθα νῦν, ὡς ἔπος εἰπεῖν, Ἕλληνες πάντες μεγάλων θεῶν, Ἡλίου τε ἅμα καὶ Σελήνης. Περὶ θεῶν τῶν κατ' οὐρανὸν τοὺς γε ἡμετέρους πολίτας καὶ τοὺς νέους τὸ μέχρι τοσούτου μαθεῖν,— μέχρι τοῦ μὴ βλασφημεῖν περὶ αὐτὰ, εὐφημεῖν δὲ ἀεὶ θύοντας καὶ ἐν εὐχαῖς εὐχομένους εὐσεβῶς. The five Planets were distinguished and named, and their periods to a certain extent understood, by Plato; but by many persons in his day the word Planet was understood more generally as com-

these astronomical truths were of recent acquisition, even to himself.[e]

In regard to hunting, Plato thinks that it is a subject on which positive laws are unsuitable or insufficient, and he therefore gives certain general directions which partake of the nature both of advice and of law. The good citizen (he says) is one who not only obeys

Hunting—how far permitted or advised.

prehending all the celestial bodies, sun and moon among them—(except fixed stars) therefore comets also—τὰ μὴ ἐν τῇ αὐτῇ περιφορᾷ ὄντα, Xenoph. Memor. iv. 7, 5, where an opinion is ascribed to Sokrates quite opposed to that which Plato here expresses. See Schaubach, Geschichte der Astronomie, pp. 212-477.

[e] Plato, Legg. vii. pp. 819 D, 821 E. This portion of the Leges is obscure, and would be hardly intelligible if it were not illustrated by a passage in the Timæus (p. 38). Even with such help it is difficult, and has been understood differently by different interpreters. Proklus (in Timæum, pp. 262-263) and Martin (Études sur le Timée, ii. note 36, p. 84) interpret it as alluding to the spiral line (ἕλικα) described by each planet (Sun and Moon are each counted as planets) round the Earth, arising from the combination of the force of the revolving sidereal sphere or Aplanês, carrying all the planets round along with it from East to West, with the countermovement (contrary, but obliquely contrary) inherent in each planet. The spiral movement of each planet, resulting from combination of these two distinct forces, is a regular movement governed by law, though to an observer who does not understand the law the movements appear irregular. Compare Derkyllides ap. Theon Smyrn. c. 41, f. 27, p. 330, ed. Martin.

The point here discussed forms one of the items of controversy between Gruppe and Boeckh, in the recent discussion about Plato's astronomical views. *Gruppe*, Die Kosmischen Systeme der Griechen, pp. 157-168; *Boeckh*, Untersuchungen über das Kosmische System des Platon, pp. 45-57.

Gruppe has an ingenious argument to show that the novelty (παράδοξον) which Plato had in his mind, but was afraid to declare openly because of existing prejudices, was the heliocentric or Copernican system, which he believes to have been Plato's discovery. Boeckh refutes Gruppe's reasoning; and refutes it, in my judgment, completely. He sustains the interpretation given by Proklus and Martin.

Boeckh also illustrates (pp. 35-38-49-54 i, in a manner more satisfactory than Gruppe, the dicta of Plato about the comparative velocity of the Planets (Sun and Moon counted among them).

Plato declares the Moon to be the quickest mover among the planets, and Saturn to be the slowest. On the contrary Demokritus pronounced the Moon to be the slowest mover of all; slower than the Sun, because the Sun was farther from the Earth and nearer to the outermost or sidereal sphere. It was the rotation of this last-mentioned sphere (according to Demokritus) which carried round along with it the Sun, the Moon, and all the planets: the bodies near to it were more forcibly acted upon by its rotation, and carried round more rapidly, than the bodies distant from it—hence the Moon was the least rapid mover of all (Lucretius, v. 615-635. See Sir George Lewis's Historical Survey of the Astronomy of the Ancients, ch. ii. pp. 139-140).

It appears to me probable that Plato, in the severe remarks which he makes on persons who falsely affirmed the quickest mover in the heavens to be the slowest, had in view these doctrines of Demokritus. Plato never once mentions Demokritus by name (see Mullach, Fragment. Demokrit. p. 25); but he is very sparing in mentioning by name *any* contemporaries. It illustrates the difference between the manner of Aristotle and Plato, that Aristotle frequently names Demokritus—seventy-eight times according to Mullach, p. 107—even in the works which we possess.

the positive laws prescribed by the lawgiver, but who also
conforms his conduct to the general cast of the lawgiver's
opinions: practising what is commended therein, abstaining
from what is blamed.[f] Plato commends one mode of hunting—the chace after quadrupeds: yet only with horses, dogs,
javelins, &c., wherein both courage and bodily strength is
improved—but not with nets or snares, where no such result is
produced. He blames other modes—such as fishing and bird-
snaring (especially by night). He blames still more emphatically theft and piracy, which he regards also as various
modes of hunting.[g]

What principally deserves notice here is, the large general
idea which Plato conceives to himself under the term
Hunting, and the number of diverse particulars
comprehended therein. 1. Hunting of quadrupeds;
either with dogs and javelins openly, or with snares, by
stratagem. 2. Hunting of birds, in the air. 3. Hunting of
fishes, in the water. 4. Hunting after the property of other
men, in the city or country. 5. Hunting after men as slaves,
or after other valuables, by means of piratical vessels.
6. Hunting of public enemies, by one army against an opposite one. 7. Hunting of men to conciliate their friendship
or affection, sometimes by fair means, sometimes by foul.[h]

That all these processes—which Plato here includes as so
many varieties of hunting—present to the mind, when they
are compared, a common point of analogy, is not to be
denied. The number of different comparisons which the
mind can make between phenomena, is almost unlimited.
Analogies may be followed from one to another, until at last,
after successive steps, the analogy between the first and the

Large general sense which Plato gives to the word hunting.

[f] Plato, Legg. vii. p. 822 E.
[g] Plato, Legg. vii. pp. 823-824.
[h] Plato, Legg. vii. p. 823. θήρα γὰρ
παμπολύ τι πρᾶγμά ἐστι, περιειλημ-
μένον ὀνόματι σχεδὸν ἑνί—πολλὴ δὲ ἡ
κατὰ φιλίαν θηρεύουσα—ἄγρας ἀνθρώπων κατὰ θάλατταν—κλωπείας ἐν χώρα
καὶ πόλει. Compare the Epinomis,
p. 975 C.
So also in the Sophistês (pp. 221-
222) Plato analyses and distributes the
general idea of θηρευτική : including
under it, as one variety, the hunting
after men by violent means (τὴν βίαιον

θήραν, τὴν ληστικὴν, ἀνδραποδιστικὴν,
τυραννικὴν, καὶ ξύμπασαν τὴν πολε-
μικὴν)—and as another variety, the
hunting after men by persuasive or
seductive means (τὴν πιθανουργικὴν,
ἐρωτικὴν, κολακικήν). In the Memorabilia of Xenophon also (ii. 6, 29-33),
Sokrates expands this same idea—τὴν
θήραν ἀνθρώπων—τὰ τῶν φίλων θηρα-
τικά, &c. Compare also the conversation between Sokrates and Theodotê
(iii. 11, 8-15).—θηρώμενος, ib. i. 2, 24
—and Plato Protag. init.

last becomes faint or imperceptible. Yet the same word, transferred successively from the first to the last, conceals this faintness of analogy and keeps them all before the mind as one. To us, this extension of the word *hunting* to particular cases dissimilar in so many respects, appears more as poetical metaphor: to intelligent Greeks of the Sokratic school, it seemed a serious comparison: and to Plato, with his theory of Ideas, it ought to have presented a Real Idea or permanent One, which alone remained constant amidst an indefinite multitude of fugitive, shadowy, and deceptive, particulars. But though this is the consistent corollary, from Plato's theory of Ideas, he does not so state it in the Treatise De Legibus, and probably he did not so conceive it. Critics have already observed that in this Treatise scarce any mention is made of the theory of Ideas. Plato had passed into other points of view; yet he neither formally renounces the points of view which we find in anterior dialogues, nor takes the trouble of reconciling them with the thoughts of the later dialogues. Whether there exists any Real, Abstract, Idea of Hunting, apart from the particular acts and varieties of hunting—is a question which he does not touch upon. Yet this is the main feature of the Platonic philosophy, and the main doctrine most frequently impugned by Aristotle as Platonic.

Although, in regard to the religious worship of his community, the oracle of Delphi is asked to prescribe what sacrifices are to be offered, and to what Gods— yet the lawgiver will determine the number of such sacrifices and festivals, as well as the times and seasons.[1] Each day in the year, sacrifice will be offered by one of the magistrates to some God or Dæmon. Once in every month, there will be a solemn sacrifice and festival, with matches of music and gymnastics, offered by each tribe to its eponymous God. The offerings to the celestial Gods will be kept distinct from the offerings to the subterranean Gods. Among these last, Pluto will be especially worshipped during the twelfth month of the year. The festivals will be adjusted to the seasons, and there will on proper occasions be festivals for women separately and exclusively.[k]

Number of religious sacrifices to be determined by lawgiver.

---

[1] Plato, Legg. viii. p. 828.   [k] Plato, Legg. viii. p. 828.

Once a month certainly—and more than once, if the magis-
Military muster of the whole citizen population once in each month—men, women, and children. trates command—on occasion of one of these festivals, all the citizen population are ordered to attend in military muster—men, women, and children. They will be brought together in such divisions and detachments as the magistrate shall direct. They will here go through gymnastic and military exercises. They will also have fights, with warlike weapons not likely to inflict mortal wounds, yet involving sufficient danger to test their bravery and endurance: one against one, two against two, ten against ten.[1] The victors will receive honorary wreaths, and public encomium in appropriate songs. Both men and women will take part alike in these exercises and contests, and in the composition of the odes to celebrate the victors.[m]

Such monthly musters, over and above the constant daily gymnastics of the youthful population, are indispensable as preliminary training; without which the citizens cannot fight with efficiency and success, in the event of a real foreign enemy invading the territory.[n] No athlete ever feels himself qualified to contend at the public games without the most laborious special training beforehand. Yet Plato expresses apprehension that his proposal of regular musters for warlike exercises with sham-battles, will appear ridiculous. He states that nothing of the kind existed in any Grecian city, by reason of two great corruptions:—First, the general love of riches and money-getting: Secondly, the bad governments everywhere existing, whether democracy, oligarchy, or despotism— each of which was in reality a faction or party-government, *i. e.* government by one part over another unwilling part.[o]

Plato prescribes that the gymnastic training in his community shall be such as to have a constant reference to war,

[1] Plat. Legg. viii. p. 833 E.
[m] Plat. Legg. viii. p. 829 B-E. Τὰ αὐτὰ δὲ λέγω στρατείας τε περὶ καὶ τῆς ἐν ποιήσεσι παρρησίας γυναιξί τε καὶ ἄνδρασιν ὁμοίως γίγνεσθαι δεῖν.
χρωμένους ὑποκινδύνοις βέλεσι, p. 830 E.
[n] Plat. Legg. viii. p. 830.
[o] Plat. Legg. viii. pp. 831-832.
I read with surprise the declaration of Plato, that no such military training exercises existed *anywhere* in Greece. How is this to be reconciled with the statements of Xenophon in his Treatise on the Republic of the Lacedæmonians, wherein he expressly calls the Spartans τεχνίτας τῶν πολεμίων—or even with the statement of Plato himself about Sparta in the first book of this Treatise De Legibus? Compare Thucyd. v. 69.

and that elaborate bodily excellence, for the purpose simply of obtaining prizes at the public games, shall be discouraged. There will be foot-races, for men, for boys, and for young women up to twenty years of age— the men always running in full panoply.[p] Horse-racing is permitted, but chariot-racing is discountenanced.[q] There will also be practice with the bow and with other weapons of light warfare, in which the young women are encouraged to take part—yet not constrained, in deference to prevalent sentiment.[r]

Gymnastic training must have reference to war, not to athletic prizes.

In regard to sexual intercourse, Plato recognises that the difficulty of regulating it according to the wisdom of the lawgiver is greater in his city than in any actual city, because of the more free and public life of the women. Neither Krete nor Sparta furnish a good example to follow on this point.[s] He thinks however that by causing one doctrine on the subject to be continually preached, and by preventing any other from being even mentioned, the lawgiver may be able so to consecrate this doctrine as to procure for it pretty universal obedience. The lawgiver may thus be able to suppress pæderasty altogether, and to restrict generally the sexual intercourse to that of persons legally married— or to enforce at least the restriction, that the exceptional cases of sexual intercourse departing from these conditions shall be covered with the veil of secrecy.[t] The constant bodily exercises prescribed in the Platonic community will tend to diminish the influence of such appetites in the citizens: while the example of the distinguished prize combatants at the Olympic games, in whose long-continued training strict continence was practised, shows that even more than what Plato anticipates can be obtained, under the stimulus of sufficient motive.[u]

Regulation of sexual intercourse. Syssitia or public mess.

What is here proposed respecting the sexual appetite finds no approbation from Kleinias, since the customs in Krete were

[p] Plat. Legg. viii. p. 833 B-C.
[q] Plat. Legg. viii. p. 834 B.
[r] Plat. Legg. viii. p. 834 C-D.
[s] Plat. Legg. viii. p. 836 B.
[t] Plato, Legg. viii. p. 841.
[u] Plato, Legg. viii. pp. 840 A, 841 A. Compare the remarks which I have

made above in this volume (page 225) respecting the small probable influence of Aphroditê in the Platonic Republic. A like remark may be made, though not so emphatically, respecting the Platonic community in the Leges.

altogether different. But the Syssitia, or public mess-table
for the citizens, are welcomed readily both by the Kretan and
the Spartan. The Syssitia existed both in Krete and at
Sparta; but were regulated on very different principles in one
and in the other. Plato declines to discuss this difference,
pronouncing it to be unimportant. But Aristotle informs us
what it was; and shows that material consequences turned
upon it, in reference to the citizenship at Sparta.[x]

Plato enters now upon the economical and proprietary rules

Regulations
about landed
property—
Boundaries
—Limited
power of
fining by
magistrates.

proper for his community. As there will be neither
gold and silver nor foreign commerce, he is dispensed from the necessity of making laws about
shipments, retailing, interest, mine-digging, col-
lectors of taxes, &c. The persons under his charge
will be husbandmen, shepherds, beekeepers, &c., with those
who work under them, and with the artisans who supply implements to them.[y] The first and most important of all regulations is, the law of Zeus Horius or Terminalis—Not to
disturb or transgress the boundary marks between different
properties. Upon this depends the maintenance of those unalterable *fundi* or lots, which is the cardinal principle of the
Platonic community. Severe penalties, religious as well as
civil, are prescribed for offenders against this rule.[z] Each
proprietor is directed to have proper regard to the convenience
of neighbours, and above all to abstain from annoying or
damaging them, especially in regard to the transit, or retention,
or distribution, of water. To intercept the supply, or corrupt
the quality of water, is a high crime.[a] Regulations are made
about the carrying of the harvest, both of grain and fruit.
Disputes arising upon these points are to be decided by the
magistrates, up to the sum of three minæ: above that sum, by
the public Dikasteries. Many rules of detail will require to
be made by the magistrates themselves with a view to fulfil

---

[x] Plato, Legg. viii. p. 842 B;
Aristot. Politic. ii. 9-10, p. 1271, a. 26,
1272, a. 12. The statement of Aristotle, about the manner in which the
cost of the Kretan Syssitia was provided, while substantially agreeing
with Ephorus (ap. Strabo. x. p. 480),
does not exactly coincide with the

account given by Dosiadas of the
Kretans in Lyktus (ap. Athenæum, iv.
p. 143). Compare Hoeckh, Kreta, vol.
iii. pp. 134-138.

[y] Plato, Legg. viii. pp. 842 D, 846 D.
[z] Plato, Legg. viii. pp. 842-843.
[a] Plat. Legg. viii. pp. 844 A, 845 E.

the purposes of the lawgiver. So soon as the magistrates think that enough of these regulations have been introduced, they will consecrate the system as it stands, rendering it perpetual and unalterable.[b]

Next, Plato passes to the Demiurgi or Artisans. These are all non-citizens or metics : for it is a peremptory law, that no citizen shall be an artisan in any branch. Nor is any artisan permitted to carry on two crafts or trades at once.[c] If any article be imperatively required from abroad, either for implements of war or for religious purposes, the magistrates shall cause it to be imported. But there shall be no retailing, nor reselling with profit, of any article.[d]

Regulations about artisans—Distribution of the annual landed produce.

The distribution of the produce of land shall be made on a principle approaching to that which prevails in Krete.[e] The total produce raised will be distributed into twelve portions, each equivalent to one month's consumption. Each twelfth portion will then be divided into equal thirds. Two of these thirds will be consumed by the citizens, their families, their slaves, and their agricultural animals : the other third will be sold in the market for the consumption of artisans and strangers, who alone are permitted to buy it, all citizens being forbidden to do so. Each citizen will make the apportionment of his own two-thirds among freemen and slaves : a measured quantity shall then be given to each of the working animals.[f] On the first of each month, the sale of barley and wheat will be made in the market-place, and every artisan or stranger will then purchase enough for his monthly consumption : the like on the twelfth of each month, for wine and other liquids — and on the twentieth of each month, for animals and animal products, such as wool and hides. Firewood may be purchased daily by any stranger or artisan, from the proprietors on whose lands the trees grow, and may be resold by him to other artisans : other articles can only be sold at the monthly market-days. The Agoranomi, or regulators of the market, will preside on those days, and will fix

[b] Plat. Legg. viii. p. 846 A-D.
[c] Plato, Legg. viii. p. 846 D-E.
[d] Plato, Legg. viii. p. 847.

[e] Plato, Legg. viii. p. 847 E. ἐγγὺς τῆς τοῦ Κρητικοῦ νόμου.
[f] Plato, Legg. viii. pp. 847-848.

the spots on which the different goods shall be exposed for sale. They will also take account of the quantity which each man has for sale, fixing a certain price for each article. They will then adjust the entries of each man's property in the public registers according to these new transactions. But if the actual purchases and sales be made at any rate different from what is thus fixed, the Agoranomi will modify their entries in the register according to the actual rate, either in plus or in minus. These entries of individual property in the public register will be made both for citizens and resident strangers alike.[g]

It shall be open to any one who chooses, to come and reside

Admission of resident Metics— conditions attached. in the city as a stranger or artisan to exercise his craft, without payment of any fee, simply on condition of good conduct ; and of being enrolled with his property in the register. But he shall not acquire any fixed settlement. After twenty years, he must depart and take away his property. When he departs, the entries belonging to his name, in the proprietary register, shall be cancelled. If he has a son, the son may also exercise the same art, and reside as a metic in the city for twenty years, but no longer ; beginning from the age of fifteen. Any metic who may render special service to the city, may have his term prolonged, the magistrates and the citizens consenting.[h]

Plato now passes to the criminal code of his community :

Offences and penal judicature—Procedure of the Dikasts. the determination of offences, penalties, and penal judicature. Serious and capital offences will be judged by the thirty-seven Nomophylakes, in conjunction with a Board of Select Dikasts, composed of the best among the magistrates of the preceding year.[i] They will hear first the pleading of the accuser, next that of the accused : they will then proceed, in the order of seniority, to put questions to both these persons, sifting the matter of charge. Plato requires them to be active in this examination, and to get at

---

[g] Plato, Legg. viii. pp. 849-850. These regulations are given both briefly and obscurely.

[h] Plato, Legg. viii. p. 850.

[i] Plato, Legg. ix. pp. 855-856. This judicial Board is mentioned also in xi. pp. 926 D, 928 B, 938 B, under the title of τὸ τῶν ἐκκρίτων δικαστήριον— τὸ τῶν ἐκλεκτῶν δικαστήριον. It forms the parallel to the Areiopagus at Athens. See K. F. Hermann, De Vestigiis Institutorum Atticorum apud Platonem De Legg. pp. 45-46, &c.

the facts by mental effort of their own. They will take notes of
the examination, then seal up the tablet, and deposit it upon
the altar of Hestia. On the morrow they will reassemble and
repeat their examination, hearing witnesses and calling for
information respecting the affair. On the third day, again
the like: after which they will deliver their verdict on the
altar of Hestia. Upon this altar two urns will be placed, for
condemnation and acquittal: each Dikast will deposit his
pebble in one or other of these, openly before the accuser and
accused, and before the assembled citizens.[k]

Conformably to the general sentiment announced still more
distinctly in the Republic, Plato speaks here also of penal
legislation as if it were hardly required. He regards it as
almost an insult to assume that any of his citizens can grow
up capable of committing grave crimes, when they have been
subjected to such a training, discipline, and government as he
institutes. Still human nature is perverse: we must provide
for the occurrence of some exceptional criminals among our
citizens, even after all our precautionary supervision: besides,
over and above the citizens, we have metics and slaves to
watch over.[l]

The first and gravest of all crimes is Sacrilege: pillage or
destruction of places or objects consecrated to the Gods. Next comes high treason: either betrayal of the city to foreign enemies, or overthrow of the established laws and government. Persons charged with these crimes shall be tried before the Select Dikasts, or High Court above constituted. If found guilty, they shall be punished either capitally or by such other sentence as the court may award. But no sentence either of complete disfranchisement or of perpetual banishment can be passed against any citizen, because every one of the 5040 lots of land must always remain occupied.[m] Nor can any citizen be fined to any greater extent

[k] Plato, Legg. ix. pp. 855-856.
Compare the procedure before the
Areiopagus at Athens, as described by
Schömann, Antiq. Juris Publici
Graecor. Part v. s. 63, p. 292. It does
not appear that the Areiopagites at
Athens were in the practice of exercis-
ing any such ἀνάκρισις of the parties

before them, as Plato enjoins upon his
ἐκλεκτοὶ δικασταί: though it was competent to the Dikasts at Athens to put
questions if they chose. Meier und
Schömann, Der Attisch. Prozess, p. 718.

[l] Plato, Legg. ix. p. 853 C-D-E.
[m] Plato, Legg. ix. p. 855 C.
Compare the penalties inflicted by

than what he possesses over and above his lot of land. He
may be imprisoned, or flogged, or exposed in the pillory, or
put to do penance in some sacred precinct. But his punishment shall noway extend to his children, unless persons of the
same family shall be condemned to death for three successive
generations. Should this occur, the family shall be held as
tainted. Their lot of land shall be considered vacant, and assigned to some deserving young man of another citizen family.[n]

Theft.—Plato next adverts to theft, and prescribes that the

Theft—
punished by
pœna dupli.
General ex-
hortation
founded by
Plato
upon this
enactment.
punishment for a convicted thief shall be one and
the same in all cases—to compensate the party
robbed to the extent of double the value of the property, or to be imprisoned until he does so.[o] But
upon a question being raised, how far one and the
same *pœna dupli,* neither more nor less, can be properly
applied to all cases of theft, we are carried (according to the
usual unsystematic manner of the Platonic dialogue) into a
general discussion on the principles of penal legislation. We
are reminded that the Platonic lawgiver looks beyond the
narrow and defective objects to which all other lawgivers
have hitherto unwisely confined themselves.[p] He is under
no pressing necessity to legislate at once: he can afford time
for preliminary discussion and exposition: he desires to instruct his citizens respecting right and wrong, as well as to
constrain their acts by penalty.[q] As he is better qualified
than the poets to enlighten them about the just and honourable, so the principles which he lays down ought to have

---

Plato with those which were inflicted
in Attic procedure. Meier und Schömann, Der Attische Prozess, pp. 739-
740 seq. There is considerable difference between the two, arising to a
great degree out of Plato's peculiar
institution about the unalterable number of lots of land (5040) and of citizen
families—as well as out of his fixation
of maximum and minimum of property.
Flogging or beating is prescribed by
Plato, but had no place at Athens:
ἀτιμία was a frequent punishment at
Athens: Plato's substitute for it seems
to be the pillory—τινας ἀμόρφους ἕδρας.
Fine was frequent at Athens as a
punishment: Plato is obliged to employ it sparingly.

[n] Plato, Legg. ix. p. 856 D.

[o] Plato, Legg. ix. p. 857 A, xii. p.
941. The Solonian Law at Athens
provided, that if a man was sued for
theft under the ἰδία δίκη κλοπῆς, he
should be condemned to the *pœna
dupli* and to a certain προστίμημα
besides (Demosthen. cont. Timokrat.
733-736). But it seems that the thief
might be indicted by a γραφή, and
then the punishment might be heavier.
See Aulus Gellius, xi. 18, and chapt.
xi. of my 'History of Greece,' p. 189.

[p] Plato, Legg. ix. p. 857 O. τὰ περὶ
τὴν τῶν νόμων θέσιν οὐδενὶ τρόπῳ πώποτε γέγονεν ὀρθῶς διαπεπονημένα, &c.

[q] Plato, Legg. ix. pp. 857 E, 858 A.

more weight than the verses of Homer or Tyrtæus.[r]   In regard to Justice and Injustice generally, there are points on which Plato differs from the public, and also points on which the public are at variance with themselves.   For example, every one is unanimous in affirming that whatever is just is also beautiful or honourable.   But if this be true, then not only what is justly done, but also what is justly suffered, is beautiful or honourable.   Now the penalty of death, inflicted on the sacrilegious person, is justly inflicted.   It must therefore be beautiful or honourable : yet every one agrees in declaring it to be shocking and infamous.   Here there is an inconsistency or contradiction in the opinions of the public themselves.[s]

But Plato differs from the public on another point also. He affirms all wicked or unjust men to be unwillingly wicked or unjust: he affirms that no man does injustice willingly.[t]   How is he to carry out this maxim in his laws?   He cannot make any distinction (as all existing cities make it) in the penalties prescribed for voluntary injustice, and for involuntary injustice; for he does not recognise the former as real.[u]   He must explain upon what foundation his dissent from the public rests.   He discriminates between *Damnum* and *Injuria*—between Damage or Hurt, and Injustice.   When damage is done, it is sometimes done voluntarily—sometimes, and quite as often, involuntarily. The public call this latter by the name of involuntary injustice; but in Plato's view it is no injustice at all.   Injustice is essentially distinct from damage : it depends on the temper, purpose, or disposition of the agent, not on the result as affecting the patient.   A man may be unjust when he is conferring benefit upon another, as well as when he is doing hurt to another.   Whether the result be beneficial or hurtful, the

Marginal note: All unjust men are unjust involuntarily—No such thing as voluntary injustice. Injustice depends upon the temper of the agent —Distinction between damage and injury.

---

[r] Plato, Legg. ix. pp. 858-859.
[s] Plato, Legg. ix. pp. 859-860. The same argument is employed by Sokrates in the Gorgias, p. 476 E.
[t] Plato, Legg. ix. p. 860 D-E.
[u] Plato, Legg. ix. p. 861 A. ἃ δὴ κατὰ πάσας τὰς πόλεις ὑπὸ νομοθετῶν πάντων τῶν πώποτε γενομένων ὡς δύο εἴδη τῶν ἀδικημάτων ὄντα, τὰ μὲν ἑκούσια, τὰ δὲ ἀκούσια, ταύτῃ καὶ νομοθετεῖται.

The eighth chapter, fifth Book, of Aristotle's Nikomachean Ethics, discusses this question more instructively than Plato.

action will be right or wrong, and the agent just or unjust, according to the condition of his own mind in doing it.[x]

Damage may be voluntary or involuntary—Injustice is shown often by conferring corrupt profit upon another—Purpose of punishment, to heal the distemper of the criminal. The real distinction therefore (according to Plato) is not between voluntary and involuntary injustice, but between voluntary and involuntary damage. Voluntary damage is injustice, but it is not voluntary injustice. The unjust agent, so far forth as unjust, acts involuntarily : he is under the perverting influence of mental distemper. He must be compelled to make good the damage which he has done, or to offer such requital as may satisfy the feelings of the person damaged ; and he must besides be subjected to such treatment as will heal the distemper of his mind, so that he will not be disposed to do farther voluntary damage in future. And he ought to be subjected to this treatment equally, whether his mental distemper (injustice) has shown itself in doing wilful damage to another, or in conferring corrupt profit on another—in taking away another man's property, or in giving away his own property wrongfully.[y] The healing treatment may be different in different cases: discourses addressed, or works imposed—pleasures or pains, honour or disgrace, fine or otherwise. But in all cases the purpose is one and the same—to heal the distemper of his mind, and to make him hate injustice. If he be found incurable, he must be put to death. It is a gain for himself to die, and a still greater gain for society that he should die, since his execution will serve as a warning to others.[z]

*Three distinct causes of misguided proceedings.
1. Painful stimulus.
2. Pleasurable stimulus.
3. Ignorance.* Of misguided or erroneous proceeding there are in the human mind three producing causes, acting separately or conjointly:—1. The painful stimulus— Anger, Envy, Hatred, or Fear. 2. The seductive stimulus of Pleasure or Desire. 3. Ignorance. Ignorance is twofold:—1. Ignorance pure and simple. 2. Ignorance combined with the false persuasion of knowledge. This last again is exhibited under two distin-

---

[x] Plato, Legg. ix. pp. 861-862.

[y] Plato, Legg. ix. p. 862 A-B. οὔτ' εἴ τίς τῳ δίδωσί τι τῶν ὄντων οὔτ' εἰ τοὐνάντιον ἀφαιρεῖται, δίκαιον ἁπλῶς ἢ ἄδικον χρὴ τὸ τοιοῦτον οὕτω λέγειν, ἀλλ' ἐὰν ἤθει καὶ δικαίῳ τρόπῳ χρώ-

μενός τις ὠφελῇ τινά τι ἢ καὶ βλάπτῃ, τοῦτό ἐστι τῷ νομοθέτῃ θεατέον, καὶ πρὸς δύο ταῦτα δὴ βλεπτέον, πρός τε ἀδικίαν καὶ βλαβήν.

[z] Plato, Legg. ix. p. 862 C-E.

guishable cases :—1. When combined with power; and in this
case it produces grave and enormous crimes. 2. When found
in weak persons, children or old men, in which case it produces nothing worse than slight and venial offences, giving
little trouble to the lawgiver.[a]

Now the unjust man (Plato tells us) is he in whose mind
either one or other of the two first causes are paramount, and not controuled by Reason: either Hatred,
Anger, Fear—or else Appetite and the Desire of
Pleasure. What he does under either of these two
stimuli is unjust, whether he damages any one else
or not. But if neither of these two stimuli be prevalent in his mind—if, on the contrary, both of
them are subordinated to the opinion which he
entertains about what is good and right—then *The unjust
man is under
the influence
either of the
first or second
of these
causes, with-
out controul
of Reason.
If he acts un-
der controul
of Reason,
though the
Reason be
bad, he is not
unjust.*
everything which he does is just, even though he falls into
error. If in this state of mind he hurts any one else, it will
be simply *hurt*, not injustice. Those persons are incorrect
who speak of it as injustice, but as involuntary injustice. The
proceedings of such a man may be misguided or erroneous,
but they will never be unjust.[b]

All these three causes may realise themselves in act under
three varieties of circumstances :—1. By open and violent
deeds. 2. By secret, deceitful, premeditated contrivance.
3. By a combination of both the two. Our laws must make
provision for all the three.[c]

Such is the theory here advanced by Plato to reconcile his
views and recommendations in the Leges with a doctrine which he had propounded and insisted upon
elsewhere :—That no man commits injustice voluntarily—That all injustice is involuntary, arising
from ignorance—That every one would be just, if he only *Reasoning of
Plato to save
his doctrine
—That no
man commits
injustice
voluntarily.*
knew wherein justice consists—That knowledge, when it exists

[a] Plato, Legg. ix. p. 863.
Τρίτον μὴν ἄγνοιαν λέγων ἄν τις τῶν
ἁμαρτημάτων αἰτίαν οὐκ ἂν ψεύδοιτο.
[b] Plato, Legg. ix. p. 864 A. τὴν δὲ
τοῦ ἀρίστου δόξαν, ὅπῃ περ ἂν ἔσεσθαι
τοῦτο ἡγήσωνται πόλις εἴτε ἰδιῶταί
τινες, ἐὰν αὐτὴ κρατοῦσα ἐν ψυχῇ δια-

κοσμῇ πάντα ἄνδρα, κἂν σφάλληταί τι,
δίκαιον μὲν πᾶν εἶναι τὸ ταύτῃ πραχθὲν
καὶ τὸ τῆς τοιαύτης ἀρχῆς γιγνόμενον
ὑπήκοον ἑκάστων, καὶ ἐπὶ τὸν ἅπαντα
ἀνθρώπων βίον ἄριστον.
[c] Plato, Legg. ix. p. 864 C.

in the mind, will exercise controul and preponderance over the passions and appetites.[d]

The distinction whereby Plato here proposes to save all inconsistency, is a distinction between misconduct or misguided actions (ἁμαρτήματα, or ἁμαρτανόμενα), and unjust actions (ἀδικήματα). The last of these categories is comprised by him in the first, as one species or variety thereof. That is, all ἀδικήματα are ἁμαρτήματα: but all ἁμαρτήματα are not ἀδικήματα. He reckons three distinct causes of ἁμαρτήματα: two belonging to the emotional department of mind; one to the intellectual. Those ἁμαρτήματα which arise from either of the two first causes are also ἀδικήματα: those which arise from the third are not ἀδικήματα.

This is the distinction which Plato here draws, with a view to save consistency in his own doctrine—at least as far as I can understand it, for the reasoning is not clear. It proceeds upon a restricted definition, peculiar to himself, of the word *injustice*—a restriction, however, which coincides in part with that which he gives of Justice in the Republic,[e] where he treats Justice as consisting in the controul exercised over Passion and Appetite (the emotional department) by Reason (the intellectual): each of the three departments of the soul, or each of the three separate souls, keeping in its own place, and discharging its own appropriate functions. Every act which a man does under the influence of persuasion or opinion of the best, is held by Plato to be *just*—whatever his persuasion may be—whether it be true or false.[f] If he be sincerely persuaded that he is acting for the best, he cannot commit injustice.

Injustice being thus restricted to mean the separate and unregulated action of emotional impulse—and such unregulated action being, as a general fact, a cause of misery to the agent—Plato's view is, that no man is voluntarily unjust: for no man wishes to be miserable. Every man wishes to be happy: therefore

---

[d] Compare Legg. v. p. 731 C; Timæus, p. 86 D; Republic, ix. p. 589 C; Protagoras, pp. 345 D-352 D.

[e] Plato, Republ. iv. pp. 443-444.
[f] Plato, Legg. ix. pp. 863 C, 864 A.

every man wishes to be just: because some controul *It under the influence of Reason, and not of Appetite.* of impulse by reason is absolutely essential to happiness. When once such controul is established, a man becomes just: he no longer commits injustice. But he may still commit misconduct, and very gross misconduct: moreover, this misconduct will be, or may be, voluntary. For though the rational soul be now preponderant and controuling over the emotional (which controul constitutes *justice*), yet the rational soul itself may be imperfectly informed (ignorance simple); or may not only be ignorant, but preoccupied besides with false persuasions and prejudices. Under such circumstances the just man may commit misconduct, and do serious hurt to others. What he does may be done voluntarily, in full coincidence with his own will: for the will postulates only the controul of reason over emotion, and here that condition is fulfilled, the fault lying with the controuling reason itself.

Plato's reasoning here (obscure and difficult to follow) is intended to show that there can be no voluntary *injustice*, but that there is much both of voluntary *misconduct* and voluntary *mischief*. His purpose as lawgiver is to prevent or remedy not only (what he calls) *injustice*, but also misconduct and mischief. *Plato's purpose in the Laws is to prevent or remedy not only injustice but misconduct.* As a remedy for mischief done, he prescribes that the agent thereof shall make full compensation to the sufferer. As an antidote to injustice, he applies his educational discipline as well as his penal and remuneratory treatment, to the emotions, with a view to subdue some and develope others.[g] As a corrective to misconduct in all its branches, he assumes to himself as lawgiver a spiritual power, applied to the improvement of the rational or intellectual man: prescribing what doctrines and beliefs shall be accredited in his city, tolerating no others, and forbidding all contradiction, or dissentient individuality of judgment.[h] He thus ensures that every man's individual reason shall be in harmony with the infallible reason.

[g] Plato, Legg. ix. p. 862 C-D.

[h] K. F. Hermann, in his valuable Dissertation, De Vestigiis Institutorum Veterum, imprimis Atticorum, per Platonis Leges indagandis, Marpurg, 1836, p. 54, says:—"Platonis manum novatricem in iis tantum agnosco, quæ de exilii tempore pro diversis criminum fontibus diverso argutatur: qui quum omnino omnium, nisi fallor, primus in hoc ipso Legum Opere veterem usuque receptam criminum divisionem in

The peculiar sense in which Plato uses the words justice and injustice is perplexing throughout this discussion. The words, as he uses them, coincide only in part with the ordinary meaning. They comprehend more in one direction, and less in another.

Plato now proceeds to promulgate laws in respect to homicide, wounds, beating, &c.

Homicide, however involuntary and unintentional, taints

Varieties of homicide— modes of dealing with them penally. the person by whose hands it is committed. He must undergo purification, partly by such expiatory ceremonies as the Exêgêtæ may appoint, partly by a temporary exile from the places habitually frequented by the person slain: who even after death (according to the doctrine of an ancient fable, which Plato here ratifies[i]), if he saw the homicidal agent among his prior haunts, while the occurrence was yet recent, would be himself disturbed, and would communicate tormenting disturbance to the agent. This latter accordingly is commanded to leave the territory for a year, and to refrain from visiting any of the sacred precincts until he has been purified. If he obeys, the relatives of the person slain shall forgive him; and he shall, after his year's exile, return to his ordinary abode and citizenship. But if he evades obedience, these relatives shall indict him for the act, and he shall incur double penalties. Should the nearest relative, under these circumstances, neglect to indict, he may himself be indicted by any one who chooses, and shall be condemned to an exile of five years.[k]

voluntaria et invita reprehenderit, eaque secundum tres animi partes trifariam distribuerit, ita hic quoque mediam inter imprudentiam et dolum malum iracundiam inseruit, quâ quis motus cædem vel extemplo committeret vel etiam posterius animum suum sanguine expleret."

I do not conceive Plato's reasoning exactly in the same way as Hermann. Plato denies only the reality of ἑκούσια ἀδικήματα: he considers all ἀδικήματα as essentially ἀκούσια. But he does not deny ἑκούσια ἁμαρτήματα (which is the large genus comprehending ἀδικήματα as one species): he recognises both ἁμαρτήματα ἑκούσια and ἁμαρτήματα ἀκούσια. And he considers the ἁμαρτήματα arising from θυμὸς to be

midway between the two. But he also recognises ἁμαρτήματα as springing from the three different sources in the human mind. The two positions are not incompatible; though the whole discussion is obscured by the perplexing distinction between ἁμαρτήματα and ἀδικήματα.

[i] Plato, Legg. ix. pp. 865 A-D. 866 B.

Compare Antiphon. Accus. Cæd. p. 116, and Lobeck, Aglaophamus, p. 301. The old law of Drako is given in substance in Demosthen. adv. Leptin. p. 505. Ἀπενιαυτισμὸς, compulsory year of exile. K. F. Hermann, Griechische Privat Alterthümer, s. 61, not. 23.

[k] Plato, Legg. ix. p. 866.

Plato provides distinct modes of proceeding for this same act of involuntary homicide, under varieties of persons and circumstances—citizens, metics, strangers, slaves, &c. He especially lays it down that physicians, if a patient dies under their hands, they being unwilling—shall be held innocent, and shall not need purification.[1]

After involuntary homicide, Plato passes to the case of homicide committed under violent passion or provocation; which he ranks as intermediate between the involuntary and the voluntary—approaching the one or the other, according to circumstances:[m] according as it is done instantaneously, or with more or less of interval and premeditation. If the act be committed instantaneously, the homicide shall undergo two years' exile: if after time for deliberation, the time of exile must be extended to three years.[n] But if the slain person before his death shall have expressed forgiveness, the case shall be dealt with as one of involuntary homicide.[o] Special enactments are made for the case of a slave killed by a citizen, a citizen killed by a slave, a son killed by his father, a wife by her husband, &c., under the influence of passion or strong provocation. Homicide in self-defence against a previous aggressor is allowed universally.[p]

Thirdly, Plato passes to the case of homicide voluntary, the extreme of injustice, committed under the influence of pleasure, appetite, envy, jealousy, ambition, fear of divulgation of dangerous secrets, &c.—homicide premeditated and unjust. Among all these causes, the chief and most frequent is love of wealth; which gets possession of most men, in consequence of the untrue and preposterous admiration of wealth imbibed in their youth from the current talk and literature. The next in frequency is the competition of ambitious men for power or rank.[q] Whoever has committed homicide upon a fellow-citizen, under these circumstances, shall be interdicted from all the temples and other public

---

[1] Plato, Legg. ix. p. 865 B.
[m] Plato, Legg. ix. p. 867 A. θυμῷ καὶ ὅσοι προπηλακισθέντες λόγοις ἢ καὶ ἀτίμοις ἔργοις μεταξύ που τοῦ τε ἑκουσίου καὶ ἀκουσίου.

[n] Plato, Legg. ix. p. 867 D.
[o] Plato, Legg. ix. p. 869 D.
[p] Plato, Legg. ix. pp. 868-869 C.
[q] Plato, Legg. ix. p. 870.

places, and shall be indicted by the nearest relatives of the
deceased.   If found guilty, he shall be put to death: if he
leave the country to evade trial, he must be banished in perpetuity.   The nearest relative is bound to indict, otherwise
he draws down upon himself the taint, and may himself be
indicted.   Certain sacrifices and religious ceremonies will be
required, in such cases, to accompany the legal procedure.
These, together with the names of the Gods proper to invoke,
will be prescribed by the Nomophylakes, in conjunction with
the prophets and the Exêgêtæ, or religious interpreters.[r]   The
Dikasts before whom such trials will take place are the Nomophylakes, together with some select persons from the magistrates of the past year: the same as in the case of sacrilege
and treason.[s]   The like procedure and penalty will be employed against any one who has contrived the death of another, not with his own hands, but by suborning some third
person: except that this contriver may be buried within the
limits of the territory, while the man whose hands are stained
with blood cannot be buried therein.[t]

For the cases of homicide between kinsmen or relatives,
Plato provides a form of procedure still more
solemn, and a still graver measure of punishment.
He also declares suicide to leave a taint upon the country, which
requires to be purified as the Exêgêtæ may prescribe: unless
the act has been committed under extreme pain or extreme
disgrace.   The person who has killed himself must be buried
apart without honour, not in the regular family-burying
places.[u]   The most cruel mode of death is directed to be inflicted upon a slave who has voluntarily slain, or procured to
be slain, a freeman.   If a slave be put to death without any
fault of his own, but only from apprehension of secrets which
he may divulge, the person who kills him shall be subjected
to the same trial and sentence as if he had killed a citizen.[x]
If any animal, or even any lifeless object, has caused the
death of a man, the surviving relatives must prosecute, and the
animal or the object must be taken away from the country.[y]

*Homicide be-
tween kins-
men.*

[r] Plato, Legg. ix. p. 871.
[s] Plato, Legg. ix. p. 871 D.
[t] Plato, Legg. ix. p. 872 A.
[u] Plato, Legg. ix. p. 873.

[x] Plato, Legg. ix. p. 872 D.
[y] Plato, Legg. ix. p. 873 E.   He
makes exception of the cases in which
death of a man is caused by thunder

Justifiable Homicide.—Some special cases are named in which he who voluntarily kills another, is neverthe- Homicide justifiable— less perfectly untainted.   A housebreaker caught in what cases. in act may thus be rightfully slain: so also a clothes-stealer, a ravisher, a person who attacks the life of any man's father, mother, or children.[z]

Wounds.—Next to homicide, Plato deals with wounds in-flicted: introducing his enactments by a preface on Infliction of the general necessity of obedience to law.[a] Whosoever, wounds. having intended to kill another (except in the special cases wherein homicide is justifiable), inflicts a wound which proves not mortal, is as criminal as if he had killed him. Nevertheless he is not required to suffer so severe a punishment, inasmuch as an auspicious Dæmon and Fortune have interposed to ward off the worst results of his criminal purpose. He must make full compensation to the sufferer, and then be exiled in per-petuity.[b] The Dikastery will decide how much compensation he shall furnish. In general, Plato trusts much to the dis-cretion of the Dikastery, under the great diversity of the cases of wounds inflicted. He would not have allowed so much discretion to the numerous and turbulent Dikasteries of Athens: but he regards his select Dikastery as perfectly trust-worthy.[c] Peculiar provision is made for cases in which the person inflicting the wound is kinsman or relative of the sufferer—also for homicide under the same circumstances. Plato also directs how to supply the vacancy which perpetual banishment will occasion in the occupation of one among the 5040 citizen-lots.[d] If one man wounds another in a fit of passion, he must pay simple, double, or triple, compensation according as the Dikasts may award: he must farther do all the military duty which would have been incumbent on the wounded man, should the latter be disabled.[e] But if the person inflicting the wound be a slave and the wounded man a freeman, the slave shall be handed over to the wounded freeman to deal with as he pleases. If the master of the

---

or some such other missile from the Gods—πλὴν ὅσα κεραυνὸς ἤ τι παρὰ θεοῦ τοιοῦτον βέλος ἰόν.

[z] Plato, Legg. ix. p. 874 C.

[a] Plato, Legg. ix. p. 875.

[b] Plato, Legg. ix. p. 877 A.

[c] Plato, Legg. ix. p. 876 A.

[d] Plato, Legg. ix. p. 877.

[e] Plato, Legg. ix. p. 878 C.

slave will not give him up, he must himself make compensation for the wound, unless he can prove before the Dikastery that the case is one of collusion between the wounded freeman and the slave; in which case the wounded freeman will become liable to the charge of unlawfully suborning away the slave from his master.[f]

Beating.—The laws of Plato on the subject of beating are more peculiar. They are mainly founded in reverence for age. One who strikes a person twenty years older than himself, is severely punished: but if he strikes a person of the same age with himself, that person must defend himself as he can with his own hands—no punishment being provided.[g] For him who strikes his father or mother, the heaviest penalty, excommunication and perpetual banishment, is provided.[h] If a slave strike a freeman, he shall be punished with as many blows as the person stricken directs, nevertheless in such manner as not to diminish his value to his master.[i]

Infliction of blows.

Throughout all this Treatise De Legibus, in regard both to civil and criminal enactments, Plato has borrowed largely from Attic laws and procedure. But in regard to homicide and wounds, he has borrowed more largely than in any other department. Both the general character, and the particular details, of his provisions respecting homicide, are in close harmony with ancient Athenian sentiment, and with the embodiments of that sentiment by the lawgivers Drako and Solon. At Athens, though the judicial procedure generally, as well as the political constitution, underwent great modification between the time of Solon and that of Demosthenes, yet the procedure in the case of homicide remained without any material change. It was of a sanctified character, depending mainly upon ancient religious tradition. The person charged with homicide was not tried before the general body of Dikasts, drawn by lot, but before special ancient tribunals and in certain consecrated places, according to the circum-

Plato has borrowed much from Attic procedure, especially in regard to Homicide— Peculiar view of Homicide at Athens, as to procedure.

---

f Plato, Legg. ix. p. 879 A.
g Plato, Legg. ix. pp. 879-880.
The person who struck first blow was guilty of αἰκία, Demosth. adv.

Euerg. and Mnesibul. pp. 1141-1151.
h Plato, Legg. ix. p. 881.
i Plato, Legg. p. 882 A.

stances under which the act of homicide was charged. The principal object contemplated, was to protect the city and its public buildings against the injurious consequences arising from the presence of a tainted man—and to mollify the posthumous wrath of the person slain. This view of the Attic procedure[k] against homicide is copied by the Platonic. Plato keeps prominently in view the religious bearing and consequences of such an act; he touches comparatively little upon its consequences in causing distress and diminishing the security of life. He copies the Attic law both in the justifications which he admits for homicide, and in the sentence of banishment which he passes against both animals and inanimate objects to whom any man owes his death. He goes beyond the Attic law in the solemnity and emphasis of his details about homicide among members of the same family and relatives: as well as in the severe punishment which he imposes upon the surviving relatives of the person slain, if they should neglect their obligation of indicting.[l] Throughout all this chapter, Plato not only follows the Attic law, but overpasses it, in dealing with homicide as a portion of the Jus Sacrum rather than of the Jus Civile.

In respect to the offence of beating, he does not follow the Attic law, when he permits it between citizens of the same age, and throws the beaten person upon his powers of self-defence. This is Spartan, not Athenian. It is also Spartan when he makes the criminality, in giving blows, to turn upon the want of reverence for age: upon the circumstance, that the person beaten is twenty years older than the beater.[m]

[k] The oration of Demosthenes against Aristokrates treats copiously of this subject, pp. 627-646. εἴργειν τῆς τοῦ παθόντος πατρίδα, δίκαιον εἶναι—ὅσων τῷ παθόντι ζῶντι μετῆν, τούτων εἴργει τὸν δεδρακότα, πρῶτον μὲν τῆς πατρίδος (632-633).

The first of Matthiæ's Dissertations, De Judiciis Atheniensium (Miscellanea Philologica, vol. i. pp. 145-176), collects the information on these matters: and K. F. Hermann (De Vestigiis Institutorum Veterum, præsertim Atticorum, per Platonis De Legibus Libros indagandis, Marpurg, 1836) gives a detailed comparison of Plato's directions with what we know about

the Attic law:—" Ipsas homicidiorum religiones (Plato) ex antiquissimo jure patrio in suum ita transtulit, ut nihil opportunius ad illustranda illius vestigia inveniri posse videatur" (p. 49): "quæ omnia Solonis Draconisve legibus ferè ad verbum eadem inveniuntur" (p. 50). The same about τραύματα ἐκ προνοίας, pp. 58-59.

[l] K. F. Hermann, De Vestigiis, ut suprà, p. 54. Compare Demosthenes adv. Theokrin. p. 1331.

[m] Plato, Legg. ix. p. 879 C. He admits the same provision as to blows between ἥλικες into his Republic (v. p. 464 E).

Compare, about Sparta, Xenophon,

From these various crimes—sacrilege or plunder of holy

Impiety or outrage offered to divine things or places. places, theft, homicide, wounding, beating—Plato passes in the tenth book to insult or outrage (ὕβρις). These outrages (he considers) are essentially the acts of wild young men. Outrage may be offered towards five different subjects. 1. Public temples. 2. Private chapels and sepulchres. 3. Parents. 4. The magistrates, in their dignity or their possessions. 5. Private citizens, in respect of their civic rights and dignity.[n] The tenth book is devoted entirely to the two first-mentioned heads, or to impiety and its alleged sources: the others come elsewhere, not in any definite order.[o]

Plato declares that all impiety, either in word or deed,

All impiety arises from one or other of three heresies. 1. No belief in the Gods. 2. Belief that the Gods interfere very little. 3. Belief that they may be appeased by prayer and sacrifice. springs from one of three heretical doctrines. 1. The heretic does not believe in the Gods at all. 2. He believes the Gods to exist, but believes also that they do not interest themselves about human affairs; or at least that they interfere only to a small extent. 3. He believes that they exist, and that they direct every thing; but that it is perfectly practicable to appease their displeasure, and to conciliate their favour, by means of prayer and sacrifice.[p]

If a person displays impiety, either by word or deed, in

Punishment for these three heretical beliefs, with or without overt act. either of these three ways, he shall be denounced to the archons by any citizen who becomes acquainted with the fact. The archons, on pain of taking the impiety on themselves, shall assemble the dikastery, and put the person accused on trial. If found guilty, he shall be put in chains and confined in one or other of the public prisons. These public prisons are three in number: one in the market-place, for ordinary offenders: a second, called the House of Correction (σωφρονιστήριον), attached to the building in which the Supreme Board of Magistrates hold their nocturnal sittings: a third, known by some designation of solemn

---

Rep. Laced. iv. 5; Cicero, Tusc. Disp. v. 27; Pausanias, iii. 14: Dionys. Halikarnass. Arch. Rom. xx. 2. Λακεδαιμόνιοι ὅτι τοῖς πρεσβυτέροις ἐπέτρεπον τοὺς ἀκοσμοῦντας τῶν πολιτῶν ἐν ὅτῳ δὴ τινι τῶν δημοσίων τόπων ταῖς βακτηρίαις παίειν.

[n] Plato, Legg. x. pp. 884-885.
[o] Treatment of parents comes xi. pp. 930-931.
[p] Plato, Legg. x. p. 885.

penality, in the centre of the territory, but in some savage and desolate spot.^q

Suppose the heretic, under either one of the three heads, to be found guilty of heresy pure and simple—but that his conduct has been just, temperate, unexceptionable, and his social dispositions steadily manifested, esteeming the society of just men, and shunning that of the unjust.^r   There is still danger *(margin: Heretic, whose conduct has been virtuous and faultless, to be imprisoned for five years, perhaps more.)* that by open speech or scoffing he should shake the orthodox belief of others : he must therefore be chained in the House of Correction for a term not less than five years.   During this term, no citizen whatever shall be admitted to see him, except the members of the Nocturnal Council of Magistrates. These men will constantly commune with him, administering exhortations for the safety of his soul and for his improvement. If at the expiration of the five years, he appears to be cured of his heresy and restored to a proper state of mind, he shall be set at liberty, and allowed to live with other proper-minded persons.   But if no such cure be operated, and if he shall be found guilty a second time of the same offence, he shall suffer the penalty of death.^s

Again—the heretic may be found guilty, not of heresy pure and simple in one of its three varieties, but of heresy manifesting itself in bad conduct and with aggravating circumstances.   He may conceal his real *(margin: Heretic with bad conduct —punishment to be inflicted.)* opinion, and acquire the reputation of the best dispositions, employing that reputation to overreach others, and combining dissolute purposes with superior acuteness and intelligence : he may practise stratagems to succeed as a despot, a public orator, a general, or a sophist : he may take up, and will more frequently take up, the profession of a prophet or religious

<hr/>

^q Plato, Legg. x. p. 908. δεσμὸς μὲν οὖν ὑπαρχέτω πᾶσι· δεσμωτηρίων δ' ὄντων ἐν τῇ πόλει τρίων, &c.

Imprisonment included chains round the prisoner's legs.   Sokrates was put in chains during his thirty days' confinement, arising from the voyage of the Theôric ship to Delos (Plat. Phædon, p. 60 B).

^r Plato, Legg. p. 908 B-E. ᾧ γὰρ ἂν, μὴ νομίζοντι θεοὺς εἶναι τὸ παράπαν, ἦθος φύσει προσγένηται δίκαιον, μισοῦν-

τές τε γίγνονται τοὺς κακούς, καὶ τῷ δυσχεραίνειν τὴν ἀδικίαν οὔτε τὰς τοιαύτας πράξεις προσίενται πράττειν, τούς τε μὴ δικαίους τῶν ἀνθρώπων φεύγουσι, καὶ τοὺς δικαίους στέργουσι, &c.

^s Plato, Legg. x. p. 909 A. ἐν τούτῳ δὲ τῷ χρόνῳ μηδεὶς τῶν πολιτῶν αὐτοῖς ἄλλος ξυγγιγνέσθω, πλὴν οἱ τοῦ νυκτερινοῦ ξυλλόγου κοινωνοῦντες, ἐπὶ νουθετήσει τε καὶ τῇ τῆς ψυχῆς σωτηρίᾳ ὁμιλοῦντες.

ritualist or sorcerer, professing to invoke the dead or to command the aid of the Gods by prayer and sacrifice. He may thus try to bring ruin upon citizens, families, and cities.[t] A heretic of this description (says Plato) deserves death not once or twice only, but several times over, if it were possible.[u] If found guilty, he must be kept in chains for life in the central penal prison—not allowed to see any freeman—not visited by any one, except the slave who brings to him his daily rations. When he dies, his body must be cast out of the territory without burial: and any freeman who may assist in burying it, shall himself incur the penalty of impiety. From the day that the heretic is imprisoned, he shall be considered as civilly dead; his children being placed under wardship as orphans.[x]

As a still farther assurance for reaching and punishing these dangerous heretics, Plato enacts—No one shall erect any temple or altar, no one shall establish any separate worship or sacrifice, in his own private precincts. No one shall propitiate the Gods by secret prayer and sacrifice of his own. When a man thinks fit to offer prayer and sacrifice, he must do it at the public temples, through and along with recognised priests and priestesses. If a man keep in his house any sacred object to which he offers sacrifice, the archons shall require him to bring it into the public temples, and shall punish him until he does so. But if he be found guilty of sacrificing either at home or in the public temples, after the commission of any act which the Dikastery may consider grave impiety—he shall be condemned to death.[y]

No private worship or religious rites allowed. Every citizen must worship at the public temples.

In justifying this stringent enactment, Plato not only proclaims that the proper establishment of temples and worship can only be dictated by a man of the highest intelligence, but he also complains of the violent and irregular working of the religious feeling in the minds of individuals. Many men (he says) when sick, or in danger and troubles of what kind soever,

Uncertain and mischievous action of the religious sentiment upon individuals, if not controuled by public authority.

[t] Plato, Legg. x. pp. 908-909.
[u] Plato, Legg. x. p. 908 E. ὧν τὸ μὲν εἰρωνικὸν οὐχ ἑνὸς οὐδὲ δυοῖν ἄξια
θανάτοιν ἁμάρτανον, &c.
[x] Plato, Legg. x. p. 909 C.
[y] Plato, Legg. x. pp. 909-910.

or when alarmed by dreams or by spectres seen in their waking hours, or when calling to mind and recounting similar narratives respecting the past, or when again experiencing unexpected good fortune — many men under such circumstances, and all women, are accustomed to give a religious colour to the situation, and to seek relief by vows, sacrifices, and altars to the Gods. Hence the private houses and villages become full of such foundations and proceedings.[z] Such religious sentiments and fears, springing up spontaneously in the minds of individuals, are considered by Plato to require strict repression. He will allow no religious worship or manifestation, except that which is public and officially authorised.

Such is the Act of Uniformity promulgated by Plato for his new community of the Magnêtes, and such the terrible sanctions by which it is enforced. The lawgiver is the supreme and exclusive authority, spiritual as well as temporal, on matters religious as well as on matters secular. No dissenters from the orthodoxy prescribed by him are admitted. Those who believe more than he does, and those who believe less, however blameless their conduct, are condemned alike to pass through a long solitary imprisonment to execution. Not only the speculations of enquiring individual reason, but also the spontaneous inspirations of religious disquietude or terror, are suppressed and punished.[a]

Intolerant spirit of Plato's legislation respecting uniformity of belief.

We seem to be under a legislation imbued with the persecuting spirit and self-satisfied infallibility of mediæval Catho-

---

[z] Plato, Legg. x. p. 909 E-910 A. ἔθος τε γυναιξὶ διαφερόντως πάσαις καὶ τοῖς ἀσθενοῦσι πάντῃ καὶ κινδυνεύουσι καὶ ἀποροῦσιν, ὅπῃ τις ἂν ἀπορῇ, καθιεροῦν τε τὸ παρὸν ἀεί, καὶ θυσίας εὔχεσθαι καὶ ἱδρύσεις ὑπισχνεῖσθαι θεοῖς, &c.

If, however, we turn back to v. p. 738 C, we shall see that Plato ratifies these καθιερώσεις, when they have once got footing, and rejects only the new ones. The rites, worship, and sacrifices, in his city, are assumed to have been determined by local or oracular inspiration (v. p. 738 B): the orthodox creed is set out by himself.

[a] Plato himself is here the Νόμος Πόλεως, which the Delphian oracle, in its responses, sanctioned as the proper

rule for individual citizens, Xenophon, Memor. iv. 3, 16. Compare iv. 6, 2, and i. 3, 1; Lysias, Or. xxx. 21-26. θύειν τὰ πάτρια—θύειν τὰ ἐκ τῶν κύρβεων, is εὐσεβεία.

See K. F. Hermann, Gottesdienstliche Alterthümer der Griechen, sect. 10; Nägelsbach, Nach-Homerische Theologie, pp. 201-204.

Cicero also enacts, in his Treatise De Legibus (ii. 8-10) :—"Separatim nemo habessit Deos: neve novos, sed ne advenas, nisi publicé adscitos, privatim colunto." Compare Livy, xxxix. 16, about the Roman prohibitions of *sacra externa*. But Cicero does not propose to inflict such severe penalties as Plato.

licism and the Inquisition. The dissenter is a criminal, and among the worst of criminals, even if he do nothing more than proclaim his opinions.[b] How striking is the contradiction be-

[b] Milton, in his Areopagitica, or Argument for Unlicensed Printing (vol. i. p. 149, Birch's edition of Milton's Prose Works), has some strenuous protestations against the rigour of the Platonic censorship in this tenth Book. In the year 1480 Hermolaus Barbarus wrote to George Merula as follows :—"Plato, in Institutione De Legibus, inter prima commemorat, in omni republicâ præscribi curarive oportere, ne cui liceat, quæ composuerit, aut privatim ostendere, aut in usum publicum edere, antequam ea constituti super id judices viderint, nec damnarint. Utinam hodicque haberetur hæc lex : neque enim tam multi scriberent, neque tam pauci bonas litteras discerent. Nam et copiâ malorum librorum offundimur, et omissis eminentissimis auctoribus, plebeios et minutulos consectamur. Et, quod calamitosissimum est, periti juxta imperitique de studiis impuné ac promiscué judicant" (Politiani Opera, 1533, p. 441).

I transcribe the above passage from an interesting article upon Book-Censors, in Beckmann's History of Inventions (vol. iii. p. 93 seq.), where numerous examples are cited of the prohibition, combustion, or licensing of books by authority, from the burning of the work of Protagoras by decree of the Athenian assembly, down to modern times ; illustrating the tendency of different sects and creeds, in proportion as they acquired power, to silence all open contradiction. The Christian Arnobius, at a time when his creed was under disfavour by the Emperors, protests against this practice ; in a liberal and comprehensive phrase which would have much offended Plato (at the time when he wrote the Leges) and Hermolaus :—"Alios audio mussitare indignanter et dicere—oportere statui per Senatum, aboleantur ut hæc scripta, quibus Christiana religio comprobetur et vetustatis opprinatur auctoritas. Nam intercipere scripta, et publicatam velle submergere lectionem, non est Deos defendere, sed veritatis testimonium timere " (Arnob. adv. Gentes, iii. p. 104-iv. p. 152).

"We are told by Eusebius " (Beckmann, p. 96) " that Diocletian caused the sacred Scriptures to be burnt. After the spreading of the Christian religion, the clergy exercised against books that were either unfavourable or disagreeable to them, the same severity which they had censured in the heathens as foolish and prejudicial to their own cause. Thus were the writings of Arius condemned to the flames at the Council of Nice ; and Constantine threatened with the punishment of death those who should conceal them. The clergy assembled at the Council of Ephesus requested the Emperor Theodosius II. to cause the works of Nestorius to be burnt ; and this desire was complied with. The writings of Eutyches shared the like fate at the Council of Chalcedon : and it would not be difficult to collect examples of the same kind from each of the following centuries."

Dr. Vaughan observes, in criticising the virtuous character and sincere persecuting spirit of Sir Thomas More : —" If there be any opinion which it would be just to punish as a crime, it is the opinion which makes it a virtue not to tolerate opinion." (Revolutions in English History, vol. ii. p. 178.)

I find the following striking anecdote in the transactions of the Académie Royale de Belgique, 1862 ; Bulletins, Communications, &c., pp. 156-157 ; Vie et Travaux de *Nicholas Cleynaerts* par M. Thonissen. Cleynaerts (or Clenardus) was a learned Belgian (born 1495–died 1543), professor both at Louvain and at Salamanca, and author of *Grammaticæ Institutiones*, both of the Greek and the Hebrew languages. He acquired, under prodigious difficulties and disadvantages, a knowledge of the Arabic language ; and he employed great efforts to organise a course of regular instruction in that language at Louvain, with a view to the formation of missionaries who would combat the doctrines of Islam.

At Grenada, in Spain (1538), " Clenardus ne réussit pas mieux à arracher aux bûchers de l'inquisition les manuscrits et les livres " (Moorish and Arabic books which had been seized after the conquest of Grenada by the Spaniards)

tween this spirit and that in which Plato depicts the Sokrates of the Phædon, the Apology, and the Gorgias! How fully does Sokrates in the Phædon [c] recognise and respect the individual reason of his two friends, though dissenting from his own! How emphatically does he proclaim, in the Apology and Gorgias, not merely his own individual dissent from his fellow-citizens, but also his resolution to avow and maintain it against one and all, until he should hear such reasons as convinced him that it was untrue! How earnestly does he declare (in the Apology) that he has received from the Delphian God a mission to cross-examine the people of Athens, and that he will obey the God in preference to them: [d] thus claiming to himself that special religious privilege which his accuser Melêtus imputes to him as a crime, and which Plato, in his Magnêtic colony, also treats as a crime, interdicting it under the severest penalties! During the interval of forty-five years (probably) between the trial of Sokrates and the composition of the Leges, Plato had passed from sympathy with the free-spoken dissenter to an opposite feeling—hatred of all dissent, and an unsparing employment of penalties for upholding orthodoxy. I have already remarked on the Republic, and I here remark it again—if Melêtus lived long enough to read the Leges, he would have found his own accusation of Sokrates

" qu'elle avait entassés dans sa succursale de Grenade. Ce fut en vain que Cleynaerts, faisant valoir le but éminemment chrétien qu'il voulait atteindre, prodigua les démarches et les prières, pour se faire remettre ces papiers plus nécessaires à lui qu'à Vulcain. L'inexorable inquisition refusa de lâcher sa proie. Un savant théologien, Jean Martin Silicæus, précepteur de Philippe II., fit cependant entendre à notre compatriote, que ses vœux pourraient être exaucés, s'il consentait à fonder son école, non à Louvain, mais à Grenade, où une multitude de néophytes faisaient semblant de professer le Christianisme, tout en conservant les préceptes de Mahomet au fond du cœur. Mais le linguiste Belge lui fit cette réponse, doublement remarquable à cause du pays et de l'époque où elle fut émise. ' C'est en Brabant, et nullement en Espagne, que je poserai les fondemens

de mon œuvre. Je cherche des compagnons d'armes pour lutter là où la lutte peut être loyale et franche. Les habitans du royaume de Grenade n'oseraient pas me répondre; puisque la terreur de l'inquisition les force à se dire chrétiens. Le combat est impossible, là où personne n'ose assumer le rôle de l'ennemi'——.'' Galen calls for a strict censorship, even over medical books—ad Julianum—Vol. xviii. p. 247 K.

[c] Plato, Apolog. p. 29; Gorgias, p. 472 A-B. καὶ νῦν περὶ ὧν σὺ λέγεις ὀλίγου σοι πάντες συμφήσουσιν ταῦτα 'Αθηναῖοί τε καὶ ξένοι. 'Αλλ' ἐγώ σοι εἶς ὢν οὐχ ὁμολογῶ.

Compare also p. 482 B of the same dialogue, where Sokrates declares his anxiety to maintain consistency with himself, and his indifference to other authority.

[d] Plato, Apol. S. p. 29 D. πείσομαι δὲ μᾶλλον τῷ θεῷ ἢ ὑμῖν, pp. 30 A, 31 D, 33 C.

amply warranted by the enactments and doctrines of the most distinguished Sokratic Companion.[e]

It is true that the orthodoxy which Plato promulgates, and

The persons denounced by Plato as heretics, and punished as such, would have included a majority of the Grecian world.

forbids to be impugned, in the Magnêtic community, is an orthodoxy of his own, different from that which was recognised at Athens; but this only makes the case more remarkable, and shows the deep root of intolerance in the human bosom—esteemed as it frequently is, by a sincere man, among the foremost of his own virtues. Plato marks out three varieties of heresy, punishable by long imprisonment, and subsequent death in case of obstinate persistance. Now under one or other of the three varieties, a large majority of actual Greeks would have been included. The first variety—those who did not believe the Gods to exist—was doubtless confined to a small minority of reflecting men; though this minority (according to Plato[f]), not contemptible even in number, was distinguished in respect to intellectual accomplishments. The second variety—that of those who believed the Gods to exist, but believed them to produce some results only, not all—was more numerous. And the third variety—that of those who believed them to be capable of being appeased or won over by prayer and sacrifice—was the most numerous of all. Plato himself informs us[g] that this last doctrine was proclaimed by the most eminent poets, rhetors, prophets, and priests, as well as by thousands and tens of thousands besides. That prayer and sacrifice were means of appeasing the displeasure or unfavourable dispositions of the Gods—was the general belief of the Grecian

[e] The indictment of Melêtus against Sokrates ran thus—'Ἀδικεῖ Σωκράτης, οὓς μὲν ἡ πόλις νομίζει θεοὺς, οὐ νομίζων, ἕτερα δὲ καινὰ δαιμόνια εἰσηγούμενος· ἀδικεῖ δὲ καὶ τοὺς νέους διαφθείρων· τίμημα, θάνατος (Diogen. Laert. ii. 40; Xenoph. Memor. i. 1). The charge as to introduction of καινὰ δαιμόνια was certainly well founded against Sokrates (compare Plato, Republic, vi. p. 496 C). Whoever was guilty of promulgating καινὰ δαιμόνια, in the Platonic city De Legibus, would have perished miserably long before he reached the age of 70; which Sokrates attained at Athens.

Compare my 'History of Greece,' ch. xxviii.

I have in one passage greatly understated the amount of severity which Plato employs against heretics. I there affirm that he banishes them: whereas the truth is, that he imprisons them, and ultimately, unless they recant, puts them to death.

[f] Plato, Legg. x. p. 886 E. πάμπολλοι. Pp. 888 E, 891 B.

[g] Plato, Legg. x. p. 885 D. νῦν μὲν γὰρ ταῦτα ἀκούοντές τε καὶ τοιαῦθ᾽ ἕτερα τῶν λεγομένων ἀρίστων εἶναι ποιητῶν τε καὶ ῥητόρων καὶ ἄλλων μυριάκις μυρίων, &c.

world, from the Homeric times downwards. The oracles or
individual prophets were constantly entreated to inform peti-
tioners, what was the nature or amount of expiatory ceremony
which would prove sufficient for any specific case; but that
there was *some* sort of expiatory ceremony which would avail,
was questioned by few sincere believers.[h] All these would
have been ranked as heretics by Plato. If the Magnêtic community had become a reality, the solitary cells of the Platonic
Inquisition might have been found to include Anaxagoras,
and most of the Ionic philosophers, under the first head of
heresy; Aristotle and Epikurus under the second; Herodotus
and Nikias under the third. Indeed most of the 5040 Magnêtic colonists must have adjusted anew their canon of orthodoxy in order to satisfy the exigence of the Platonic Censors.

To these severe laws and penalties against heretics, Plato
prefixes a Proëm or Prologue of considerable length,   Proëm or
commenting upon and refuting their doctrines. In   prefatory discourse of
the earlier part of this dialogue he had taken credit   Plato, for these severe
to himself for having been the first to introduce his   laws against heretics.
legal mandates by a prefatory harangue, intended to persuade
and conciliate the persons upon whom the mandate was imposed, and to procure cheerful obedience.[i] For such a purpose the Proëm in the tenth Book would be badly calculated.
But Plato here introduces it with a different view:[k] partly
to demonstrate a kosmical and theological theory, partly to
excite alarm and repugnance in the heretics whom he marks
out and condemns. How many among them might be convinced by Plato's reasonings, I do not know; but the large
majority of them could not fail to be offended and exasperated
by the tone of his Proëm or prefatory discourse. Confessing
his inability to maintain completely the calmness and dignity
of philosophical discussion, he addresses them partly with
passionate asperity, partly with the arrogant condescension of
a schoolmaster lecturing indocile pupils. He describes them

[h] See the sections 23 and 24 of the
Lehrbuch of K. F. Hermann, Über die
Gottesdienstlichen Alterthümer der
Griechen; Herodot. vi. 91; Thucydid.
i. 134.—Respecting Plato's aversion
for Anaxagoras— and the physical philosophers—see Legg. x. 888 E. xii.

967 A., with Stallbaum's notes.
[i] Plato, Legg. iv. pp. 722-723. ἵνα
γὰρ εὐμενῶς καὶ διὰ τὴν εὐμένειαν
εὐμαθέστερον τὴν ἐπίταξιν, ὃ δή ἐστιν
ὁ νόμος, δέξηται ᾧ τὸν νόμον ὁ νομοθέτης
λέγει, &c.
[k] Plato, Legg. x. p. 887 A.

now as hateful and unprincipled men—now as presumptuous
youths daring to form opinions before they are competent,
and labouring under a distemper of reason;[1] and this too,
although he intimates that the first-named variety of heresy
was adopted by most of the physical philosophers; and the
third variety by many of the best poets, rhetors, prophets, and
priests.[m] Such unusual vehemence is justified by Plato on
the ground of a virtuous indignation against the impugners
of orthodox belief. We learn from the Platonic and Xenophontic Apologies, that Melêtus and Anytus, when they accused
Sokrates of impiety before the Dikastery, indulged in the
same invective, announced the same justification, and felt the
same confidence that they were righteous champions of the
national faith against an impious and guilty assailant.

Among the three varieties of heresy, Plato considers the
third to be the worst. He accounts it a greater
crime to believe in indulgent and persuadeable Gods,
than not to believe in any Gods at all.[n] Respecting the entire unbelievers, he acknowledges that a
certain proportion are so from intellectual, not from
moral, default: and that there are, among them,
persons of blameless life and disposition.[o] It must be remembered that the foremost of these unbelievers, and the most
obnoxious to Plato, were the physical astronomers: those
who did not agree with him in recognising the Sun, Moon,
and Stars as animated and divine Beings—those who studied
their movements as if they were mechanical agents. Plato
gives a brief summary of various cosmogonic doctrines professed by these heretics, who did not recognise (he says)
either God, or reason, or art, in the cosmogonic process; but
ascribed to nature, chance, and necessity, the genesis of celestial and terrestrial substances, which were afterwards modified
by human art and reason. Among these matters regulated
by human art and reason, were included (these men said) the
beliefs of each society respecting the Gods and religion,

Marginal note: The third variety of heresy is de-clared to be the worst —the belief in Gods per-suadeable by prayer and sacrifice.

---

[1] Plato, Legg. x. pp. 887 B-E, 888 B, 891 B, 900 B, 907 A-B. καὶ μὴν εἴρηνταί γέ πως σφοδρότερον (οἱ λόγοι) διὰ φιλονεικίαν τῶν κακῶν ἀνθρώπων—προθυμία μὲν δὴ διὰ ταῦτα νεω-

τέρως εἰπεῖν ἡμῖν γέγονε.

[m] Plato, Legg. x. pp. 891 D, 885 D.
[n] Plato, Legg. x. pp. 907 A, 906 B.
[o] Plato, Legg. x. pp. 886 A, 908 B.

respecting political and social arrangements, respecting the just and the beautiful: though there were (they admitted) certain things beautiful by nature, yet not those which the lawgiver declared to be such. Lastly, these persons affirmed (Plato tells us) that the course of life naturally right was, for each man to seize all the wealth, and all the power over others, which his strength enabled him to secure, without any regard to the requirements of the law. And by such teaching they corrupted the minds of youth.[p]

Who these teachers were, whom Plato groups together as if they taught the same doctrine, we do not know. Having no memorials from themselves, we cannot fully trust the description of their teaching given by an opponent: especially when we reflect, that it coincides substantially with the accusation which Melêtus and Anytus urged against Sokrates before the Athenian Dikastery: viz.: that he was irreligious, and that he corrupted youth by teaching them to despise both the laws and their senior relatives—of which corruption Kritias and Alkibiades were cited as examples. Such allegations, when advanced against Sokrates, are noted both by Plato and Xenophon as the stock-topics, always ready at hand for those who wished to depreciate philosophers.[q]

Heretics censured by Plato—Sokrates censured before the Athenian Dikasts.

In so far as these heretics affirmed that right as opposed to wrong, just as opposed to unjust, true belief as opposed to false respecting the Gods, were determined by the lawgiver and not by any other authority—Plato has little pretence for blaming them; because he himself claims such authority explicitly in his Magnetic community, and punishes severely not merely those who disobey his laws in act, but those who contradict his dogmas in speech or argument. Before he proclaims his intended punishments in a penal law, he addresses the heretics in a proëm or prefatory discourse intended to persuade or win them over: a discourse which was the more in-

---

[p] Plato, Legg. x. pp. 889-890.

[q] Plato, Apolog. Sokr. p. 23. τὰ κατὰ πάντων τῶν φιλοσοφούντων πρόχειρα ταῦτα λέγουσιν, ὅτι τὰ μετέωρα καὶ τὰ ὑπὸ γῆς καὶ θεοὺς μὴ νομίζειν καὶ τὸν ἥττω λόγον κρείσσω ποιεῖν. Xenoph. Memor. i. 2, 31. See generally the first two chapters of the Memorabilia, where Xenophon intimates that Sokrates was accused of training youth to a life of lawless and unprincipled ambition and selfishness, and especially of having trained Kritias and Alkibiades.

dispensable, since their doctrines (he tells us) were disseminated everywhere.[r] If he seriously intended to persuade real dissentients, his attempt is certainly a failure: for the premisses on which he reasons are such as would not have been granted by them—nor indeed by many who agreed in the conclusion which he was himself trying to prove.

The theory, here given by Plato, represents merely the state of his own convictions at the time when the Leges were composed. It is a theory of kosmology or universal genesis; different in many respects from what he propounds in the Timæus, since it comprises no mention of the extra-kosmical Demiurgus—nor of the eternal Ideas—nor of the primordial chaotic movements called Necessity—while it contains (what we do not find in the Timæus) the allegation of a twofold or multiple soul pervading the universe—the good soul (one or more), being coexistent and coeternal with others (one or more) that are bad.[s]

Kosmological and Kosmogonical theory announced in Leges.

The fundamental principle which he lays down (in this tenth Book De Legibus) is—That soul or mind is older, prior, and more powerful, than body. Soul is the principle of self-movement, activity, spontaneous change. Body cannot originate any movement or change by itself. It is simply passive, receiving movement from soul, and transmitting movement onward. The movement or change which we witness in the universe could never have begun at first, except through the originating spontaneity of soul. None of the four elements—earth, water, air, or fire—is endowed with any self-moving power.[t] As soul is older and more powerful than body, so the attributes of soul are older and more powerful than those of body: that is, pleasure, pain, desire, fear, love, hatred, volition, deliberation, reason, reflection, judgment true or false—are older and more powerful than heat, cold, heaviness, lightness, hardness, softness, whiteness, sweetness, &c.[u] The attributes and changes of body are all secondary effects, brought about, determined, modified, or suspended, by the prior and primitive attributes and changes of soul. In all things that are moved

Soul—older, more powerful in the universe than Body. Different souls are at work in the universe—the good soul, and the bad soul.

[r] Plato, Legg. x. pp. 890 D, 891 A.
[s] Plato, Legg. x. p. 896 E.
[t] Plato, Legg. x. pp. 894 D, 895 B.

[u] Plato, Legg. x. pp. 896 A, 897 A. The κινήσεις of soul are πρωτουργοί—those of body are δευτερουργοί.

there dwells a determining soul: which is thus the cause of all effects however contrary—good and bad, just and unjust, honourable and base. But it is one variety of soul which works to good, another variety which works to evil.[x] The good variety of soul works under the guidance of Νοῦς or Reason—the bad variety works irrationally.[y] Now which of the two (asks Plato) directs the movements of the celestial sphere, the Sun, Moon, and Stars? Certainly, the good soul, and not the bad. This is proved by the nature and character of their movements: which movements are rotatory in a circle, and exactly uniform and equable. Now among all the ten different sorts of motion or change, rotatory motion in a circle is the one which is most akin or congenial to Reason.[z]

---

[x] Plato, Legg. x. p. 896 E. ψυχὴν δὴ διοικοῦσαν καὶ ἐνοικοῦσαν ἐν ἅπασι τοῖς κινουμένοις.

As an illustration or comment on this portion of Plato De Legibus, Lord Monboddo's *Antient Metaphysics* are instructive. See vol. i. pp. 2-7-9-25. He adopts the distinction between Mind and Body made both in the tenth Book De Legg., and in the Epinomis. He considers that Body and Mind are mixed together in each part of nature; and in the material world never separated: that motion is perpetual; and "Where there is motion there must be something that *moves*. What is *moved* I call Body; what moves I call Mind.

"Under Mind, in this definition, I include:—1. The rational and intellectual. 2. The animal life. 3. That principle in the vegetable, by which it is nourished, grows, and produces its like, and which therefore is called commonly the *vegetable life*. 4. That motive principle which I understand to be in all bodies, even such as are inanimate. This is the distinction between Body and Mind made by Plato in his tenth Book of Laws."

"The Greek word ψυχή denotes the three first kinds I have mentioned, which are not expressed by any one word that I know in English; for the word Mind, that I have used to express them, denotes in common use only the *rational mind* or soul, as it is called. The fourth kind I have mentioned, viz., the *motive principle in all bodies*, is not commonly in Greek

called ψυχή. But Aristotle, in a passage which I shall afterwards quote, says that it is ὥσπερ ψυχή.

(P. 9). "As to the *principle of motion* or *moving principle*, which Aristotle supposes to be in all bodies, it is what he calls *Nature*. He makes Nature also to be the principle of *rest* in bodies; by which I suppose he means, that those bodies which he calls *heavy*, that is, which move towards the centre of the earth, would *rest* if they were there."

(P. 25.) "From the account here given of motion, it is evident that by it the whole business of nature, above, below, and round about us, is carried on. . . . To those who hold that Mind is the first of things, and principal in the Universe, it will not appear surprising, that I have made *moving* or *producing motion* an essential attribute of *Mind*."

In the same Treatise—which exhibits very careful study both of Plato and of Aristotle — Lord Monboddo analyses the ten varieties of motion here recognised by Plato, and shows that it is confused and unsatisfactory. Ancient Metaphysics, vol. i. pp. 23-230-252.

[y] Plato, Legg. x. p. 897 B.

[z] Plato, Legg. x. pp. 897 E-898 A. ᾗ προσέοικε κινήσει νοῦς, τῶν δέκα ἐκείνων κινήσεων τὴν εἰκόνα λάβωμεν — τούτοιν δὴ τοῖν κινήσεοιν τὴν ἐν ἑνὶ φερομένην ἀεὶ περί γέ τι μέσον ἀνάγκη κινεῖσθαι, τῶν ἐντόρνων οὐσῶν μίμημά τι κύκλων εἶναί τε αὐτὴν τῇ τοῦ νοῦ περιόδῳ πάντως ὡς δυνατὸν οἰκειοτάτην τε καὶ ὁμοίαν.

The motion of Reason, and the motion of the stars, is alike rotatory, and the same, and unchangeable—in the same place, round the same centre, and returning into itself. The bad soul, acting without reason, produces only irregular movements, intermittent, and accompanied by constant change of place.[a] Though it is the good variety of soul which produces the celestial rotation, yet there are many distinct and separate souls, all of this same variety, which concur to the production of the result. The Sun, the Moon, and each of the Stars, has a distinct soul inherent in itself or peculiar to its own body.[b] Each of these souls, invested in the celestial substance and in each of the visible celestial bodies, is a God: and thus all things are full of Gods.[c]

In this argument—which Plato tells us that no man will be

Plato's argument is unsatisfactory and inconsistent.

insane enough to dispute,[d] and which he proclaims to be a triumphant refutation of the unbelievers— we find, instead of the extra-kosmical Demiurgus and the pre-kosmical Chaos or Necessity (the doctrine of the Platonic Timæus[e]), two opposing primordial forces both intra-kosmical: the good soul and the bad soul, there being a multiplicity of each. Though Plato here proclaims his conclusion with an unqualified confidence which contrasts greatly with the modest reserve often expressed in his Timæus—yet the conclusion is rather disproved than proved by his own premisses. It cannot be true that all things are full of Gods, since there are two varieties of soul existing and acting, the bad as well as the good : and Plato calls the celestial bodies Gods, as endowed with and moved by good and rational souls. Aristotle in his theory draws a marked distinction between the regularity and perfection of the celestial region, and the irregularity and imperfection of the terrestrial and sublunary : Plato's premisses as here laid out would have called upon him to do the same, and to designate the Kosmos as the theatre of counteracting agencies, partly divine, partly not divine. So he terms it indeed in the Timæus.[f]

[a] Plato. Legg. x. p. 898 B-C.
[b] Plato, Legg. x. p. 898 D.
[c] Plato, Legg. x. p. 899 B. εἶθ, ὅστις ὁμολογεῖ ταῦτα, ὑπομένει μὴ θεῶν εἶναι πλήρη πάντα ;

[d] Plato, Legg. x. p. 899 B. οὐκ ἔστιν οὕτως παραφρονῶν οὐδείς.
[e] Plato, Timæus, pp. 48 A, 69 A-B.
[f] Plato, Timæus, p. 48 A.
The remarks of Zeller, in the second

There is another feature, common both to the Timæus and the Leges, which deserves attention as illustrating Plato's point of view. It is the reverential sentiment with which he regards uniform rotatory movement in the same place. This he pronounces to be the perfect, regular, movement appertaining and congenial to Reason and the good variety of soul. Because the celestial bodies move thus and only thus, he declares them to be Gods. It is this circular rotation which continues with perfect and unchangeable regularity in the celestial sphere of the Kosmos, and also, though imperfect and perturbed, in the spherical cranium of man.[g] Aristotle in his theory maintains unabated the reverence for this mode of motion, as the perfection of reason and regularity. The feeling here noted exercised a powerful and long continued influence over the course of astronomical speculations.

Reverence of Plato for uniform circular rotation.

Having demonstrated to his own full satisfaction, from the regularity of the celestial rotations, that the heavenly bodies are wise and good Gods, and that all things are full of Gods—Plato applies this conclusion to refute the second class of heretics—those who did not believe that the Gods directed all human affairs, the small things as well as the great;[h] that is, the lot of each individual person as well as that of the species or of its component aggregates. He himself affirms that they direct all things. It is incon-

Argument of Plato to confute the second class of heretics.

---

edition of his work, Die Philosophie der Griechen (vol. ii. p. 634 seq.), upon this portion of the Treatise De Legibus, are very acute and instructive. He exposes the fallacy of the attempt made by various critics to explain away the Manichæan doctrine declared in this Treatise, and to reconcile the Leges with the Timæus. The subject is handled in a manner superior to the Platonische Studien of the same author (wherein the Leges are pronounced to be spurious, while in the History of Philosophy Zeller retracts this opinion), though in that work also there is much instruction.—Stallbaum's copious notes on these passages (pp. 188-189-195-207-213 of his edition of Leges) while admitting the discrepancy between Leges and Timæus, furnish what he thinks a satisfactory explanation. One portion of his explanation is, that Plato here accommodates himself " ad captum vulgarem—ad captum civium communem accommodaté et populari ratione explicari." I dissent from this as a matter of fact. I think that the heretics of the second and third class coincide rather with the " captus vulgaris." So Plato himself intimates.

[g] Plato, Timæus, pp. 44 B·47 C.

[h] The language of Plato sometimes implies, that the opponents whom he is controverting disbelieve altogether the intervention of the Gods in human affairs, pp. 899 E, 900 A, 885 B. But the main stress of his argument is directed against those who, admitting the intervention of the Gods in great things, deny it in small, pp. 900 D, 901 A-B-C-D, 902 A-B.

sistent with their attributes of perfect intelligence, power, and
goodness, (he maintains) that they should leave anything
either small or great, without regulation. All good human
administrators, generals, physicians, pilots, &c., regulate all
things small and great, in their respective provinces: the
Gods cannot be inferior to them, and must be held to do
the same. They regulate everything with a view to the happiness of the whole, in which each man has his share and
interest; and each man has his special controuling Deity
watching over his minutest. proceedings, whether the individual sees it or not.[1] Soul, both in its good variety and
its bad variety, is essentially in change from one state to
another, and passes from time to time out of one body into
another. In the perpetual conflict between the good and
the bad variety of soul, according as each man's soul in-
clines to the better or to the worse, the Gods or Fate
exalt it to a higher region or degrade it to a lower. By
this means the Gods do the best they can to ensure triumph
to virtue, and defeat to vice, in the entire Kosmos. This
reference to the entire Kosmos is overlooked by the heretics
who deny the all-pervading management of the Gods.[k]

Plato gives here an outburst of religious eloquence which
Contrary doc- might prove impressive when addressed to fellow-
trine of Plato
in Republic.   believers—but which, if employed for the avowed
purpose of convincing dissentients, would fail of its purpose, as
involving assumptions to which they would not subscribe. As
to the actual realities of human life, past as well as present,
Plato himself always gives a very melancholy picture of them.
" The heaven is full of good things, and also full of things
opposite to good: but mostly of things not good."[1] Moreover, when we turn back to the Republic, we find Plato therein

---

[1] Plato, Legg. x. pp. 902-903 B-C.
[k] This argument is set forth from
p. 903 B to 905 B. It is obscure and
difficult to follow.
[1] Plato, Legg. x. p. 906 A. ἐπειδὴ
γὰρ συγκεχωρήκαμεν ἡμῖν αὐτοῖς εἶναι
μὲν τὸν οὐρανον πολλῶν μεστὸν ἀγαθῶν
εἶναι δὲ τῶν ἐναντίων, πλειόνων δὲ
τῶν μή—μάχη δὴ φαμὲν, ἀθάνατός ἐστιν
ἡ τοιαύτη καὶ φυλακῆς θαυμαστῆς
δεομένη. Ast in his note affirms that

after μὴ is understood ἀγαθῶν. Stallbaum thinks, though with some hesi-
tation, that ἐναντίων is understood
after μή. I agree with Ast.
Compare iii. pp. 676-677, where
Plato states that in the earlier history
of the human race, a countless number
of different societies (μύριαι ἐπὶ μυρίαις)
have all successively grown up and
successively perished, with extinction
of all their comforts and civilization.

expressly blaming a doctrine very similar to what he declares true here in the Leges — as a dangerous heresy, although extensively believed, from the time of Homer downward. " Since God is good " (Plato had there affirmed[m]) " he cannot be the cause of all things, as most men pronounce him to be. He is the cause of a few things, but of most things he is not the cause: for the good things in our lot are much fewer than the evil. We must ascribe all the good things to him, but for the evil things we must seek some other cause, and not God." The confessed imperfection of the actual result[n] was one of the main circumstances urged by those heretics, who denied that all-pervading administration of the Gods which Plato in the Leges affirms.[o] If he undertook to convince them at all, he would have done well to state and answer more fully their arguments, and to clear up the apparent inconsistencies in his own creed.

A similar criticism may be made still more forcibly, upon the demonstration whereby he professes to refute the third and most culpable class of heretics— " Those who believe that the Gods exercise an universal agency, but that they can be persuaded by prayer and conciliated by sacrifice." Here he was treading on dangerous ground: for he was himself a heretic, by his own confession, if compared with Grecian belief generally. Not merely the ordinary public, but the most esteemed and religious persons among the public[p]—poets, rhetors, prophets, and priests—believed the doctrine which he here so vehemently condemns. Moreover it was the received doctrine of the city[q]—that is, it was assumed as the basis of the official and authorised religious manifestations: and the law of the city was recognised by the Delphian oracle[r] as the proper

Argument of Plato to refute the third class of heretics.

---

[m] Plato, Republic, ii. p. 379 C.
Οὐδ᾽ ἄρα ὁ θεὸς, ἐπειδὴ ἀγαθὸς, πάντων ἂν εἴη αἴτιος, ὡς οἱ πολλοὶ λέγουσιν· ἀλλ᾽ ὀλίγων μὲν τοῖς ἀνθρώποις αἴτιος, πολλῶν δὲ ἀναίτιος· πολὺ γὰρ ἐλάττω τἀγαθὰ τῶν κακῶν ἡμῖν· καὶ τῶν μὲν ἀγαθῶν οὐδένα ἄλλον αἰτιατέον, τῶν δὲ κακῶν ἄλλ᾽ ἄττα ζητεῖν δεῖ τὰ αἴτια, ἀλλ᾽ οὐ τὸν θεόν.

[n] Plato, Legg. x. p. 903 B. Πειθώμεν τὸν νεανίαν τοῖς λόγοις—ὧν ἓν καὶ τὸ σὸν, ὦ σχέτλιε, μόριον εἰς τὸ πᾶν ξυντείνει βλέπον ἀεί.

[o] Lucretius, v. 197 :—
Nequaquam nobis divinitus esse paratam
Naturam rerum, tantâ stat prædita culpâ.

[p] Plato, Legg. x. p. 885 D ; Republic, ii. pp. 364-365-366.

[q] Plato, Republic, ii. p. 366 A. αἱ τελεταί αὖ μέγα δύνανται, καὶ οἱ λύσιοι θεοὶ, ὡς μέγισται πόλεις λέγουσι καὶ οἱ θεῶν παῖδες ποιηταὶ καὶ προφῆται τῶν θεῶν γενόμενοι, οἱ ταῦθ᾽ οὕτως ἔχειν μηνύουσι.

[r] Xenophon, Memor. i. 3, 1, iv. 3, 16 ; Cicero, Legg. ii. 16.

422   LEGES.   Chap. XXXVII.

standard of reference for individual enquirers who came there
to ask for information on matters of doubtful religious propriety. In the received Grecian conception of religious worship, prayer and sacrifice were correlative and inseparable:
sacrifice was the gift of man to the Gods, accompanying the
prayer for gifts from the Gods to man, and accounted necessary to render the prayer efficacious.[s] The priest was the
professional person competent and necessary to give advice as
to the details: but as a general principle, it was considered
disrespectful to ask favours from the Gods without tendering
to them some present, suitable to the means of the petitioner.
Plato himself states this view explicitly in his Politikus.[t]

General be-
lief in Greece
about the
efficacy of
prayer and
sacrifice to
appease the
Gods.

Moreover, when a man desired information from the
Gods on any contemplated project or on any grave
matter of doubt, he sought it by means of sacrifice.[u]
Such sacrifice was a debt to the God; and if it remained unpaid, his displeasure was incurred.[x] The
motive for sacrificing to the Gods was thus, not simply to ensure the granting of prayers, but to pay a debt: and thus
either to prevent or to appease the wrath of the Gods. The
religious practice of Greece rested upon the received belief
that the Gods were not merely pleased with presents, but
exacted them as a mark of respect, and were angry if they
were not offered: yet that being angry, their wrath might be
appeased by acceptable presents and supplications.[y] To learn
what proceedings of this kind *were* suitable, a man went to
consult the oracle, the priests, or the Exêgêtæ: in cases
wherein he believed that he had incurred the displeasure of
the Gods by any wrong or omission.[z]

---

[s] See Nägelsbach, Nach-Homerische
Theologie, Part 5, 1, p. 194 seq., where
this doctrine is set forth and largely
illustrated.

In approaching a king, a satrap, or
any other person of exalted position
above the level of ordinary men, it was
the custom to come with a present.
Thucyd. ii. 97; Xenop. Anab. vii.
3, 26; Xenop. Hellen. iii. 1, 10-12.

The great person, to whom the
presents were made, usually requited
them magnificently.

[t] Plato, Politikus, p. 290 D. καὶ μὴν
καὶ τὸ τῶν ἱερέων γένος, ὡς τὸ νόμιμόν
φησι, παρὰ μὲν ἡμῶν δωρεὰς θεοῖς διὰ

θυσιῶν ἐπιστῆμόν ἐστι κατὰ νοῦν ἐκείνοις δωρεῖσθαι, παρὰ δ' ἐκείνων ἡμῖν
εὐχαῖς κτῆσιν ἀγαθῶν αἰτήσασθαι. Compare Euthyphron, p. 14.

[u] Xenophon, Anab. vii. 6, 44;
Euripid. Ion, 234.

[x] Plato, Republic, i. p. 331 B. Compare also Phædon, p. 118, the last
words spoken by Sokrates before his
decease—ὀφείλομεν 'Ασκληπιῷ ἀλεκ-
τρύονα· ἀλλ' ἀπόδοτε καὶ μὴ ἀμελήσητε.

[y] See Nägelsbach, Nach-Homerische
Theologie, pp. 211-213.

[z] See, as one example among a thousand, the proceeding of the Spartan government, Thucyd. i. 134, also ii. 48-54.

Now it is against this latter sentiment—that which recognised the Gods as placable or forgiving [a]—that Plato Incongruities of Plato's own doctrine. declares war as the worst of all heresies.   He admits indeed, implicitly, that the Gods are influenced by prayer and sacrifice; since he directs both the one and the other to be constantly offered up, by the citizens of his Magnêtic city, in this very Treatise.   He even implies that the Gods are too facile and compliant: for in his second Alkibiadês, Sokrates is made to remark that it was dangerous for an ignorant man to pray for specific advantages, because he might very probably bring ruin upon himself by having his prayers granted—

> "Evertêre domos totas, optantibus ipsis,
> Di faciles."

Farthermore Plato does not scruple to notice [b] it as a real proceeding of the Gods, that they executed the prayer or curse of Theseus, by bringing a cruel death upon the blameless youth Hippolytus; which Theseus himself is the first to deplore when he becomes acquainted with the true facts. That the Gods should inflict punishment on a person who did not deserve it, Plato accounts not unworthy of their dignity: but that they should remit punishment in any case where he conceives it to have been deserved, he repudiates with indignation.   Though accessible and easily influenced by prayer and sacrifice from other persons, they are deaf and inexorable to those who have incurred their displeasure by wrong-doing. [c] The prayer so offered is called by Plato a treacherous cajolery, the sacrifice a guilty bribe, to purchase their indulgence. [d] Since, in human affairs, no good magistrate, general, physician, pilot, &c., will allow himself to be persuaded by prayers or presents to betray his trust: much less can we suppose (he argues) the Gods to be capable of such betrayal. [e] The general doctrine, upon which Plato here lays so much

---

[a] The common sentiment is expressed in a verse of Euripides—
Τίνα δεῖ μακάρων ἐκθυσαμένους Εὑρεῖν μόχθων ἀνάπαυλαν—(Fragm. Ino 155); compare Eurip. Hippol. 1323.
[b] Plato, Legg. xi. p. 931 B, iii. p. 687 D. ἀραῖος γὰρ γονεὺς τοῖς ἐκγό-νοις ὡς οὐδεὶς ἕτερος ἄλλοις, δικαιό-τατα.
[c] Plato, Legg. iv. pp. 716-717.
[d] Plato, Legg. x. p. 906 B. θω-πείαις λόγων.
[e] Plato, Legg. x. pp. 906-907.

stress, and the dissent from which he pronounces to be a
capital offence—that the Gods, though persuadeable
by every one else, were thoroughly unforgiving, deaf
to any prayer or sacrifice from one who had done
wrong—is a doctrine from which Sokrates[f] himself
dissented; and to which few of Plato's contemporaries, perhaps hardly even himself, consistently adhered. The argument, upon which Plato rests for convincing all these numerous
dissentients, is derived from his conception of the character
and functions of the Gods. But this, though satisfactory to
himself, would not have been granted by his opponents. The
Gods were conceived by Herodotus as jealous, meddlesome,
intolerant of human happiness beyond a narrow limit, and
keeping all human calculations in a state of uncertainty:[g] in
this latter attribute Sokrates also agreed. He affirmed that
the Gods kept all the important results essentially unpredictable by human study, reserving them for special revelations
by way of prophecy to those whom they preferred. These
were privileged and exclusive communications to favoured
individuals, among whom Sokrates was one:[h] and Plato,
though not made a recipient of the same favour as Sokrates,
declares his own full belief in the reality of such special revelations from the Gods, to particular persons and at particular
places.[i] Aristotle, on the other hand, pronounces action and
construction, especially action in details, to be petty and unworthy of the Gods; whom he regards as employed in per-

Both Herodotus and Sokrates dissented from Plato's doctrine.

---

[f] Xenophon, Memorab. ii. 3, 14.
Σὺ μὲν, ὦ παῖ, ἂν σωφρονῇς, τοὺς μὲν
θεοὺς παραιτήσῃ συγγνώμονάς σοι εἶναι,
εἴτι παρημέληκας τῆς μητρὸς, μή σε καὶ
οὗτοι νομίσαντες, ἀχάριστον εἶναι, οὐκ
ἐθέλωσιν εὖ ποιεῖν.
At the same time, Sokrates maintains
that the Gods accepted sacrifices from
good men with greater favour than
sacrifices from bad men. Xenop. Mem.
i. 3, 3.

[g] Herodotus, i. 32, iii. 40.

[h] Xenop. Mem. i. 8-9. τοὺς γὰρ
θεοὺς, οἷς ἂν ὦσιν ἵλεω, σημαίνειν: also
i. 3, 4, iv. 3, 12; Cyropæd. i. 6, 5-23-
46. θεοὶ ἀεὶ ὄντες πάντα ἴσασι—καὶ
τῶν συμβουλευομένων ἀνθρώπων οἷς ἂν
ἵλεω ὦσι, προσημαίνουσιν ἅ τε χρὴ
ποιεῖν καὶ ἃ οὐ χρή. Εἰ δὲ μὴ πᾶσιν
ἐθέλουσι συμβουλεύειν, οὐδὲν θαυμαστόν·

οὐ γὰρ ἀνάγκη αὐτοῖς ἔστιν, ὧν ἂν μὴ
θέλωσιν, ἐπιμελεῖσθαι.
Solon. Frag. v. 52, ed. Gaisf.:—
Ἄλλον μάντιν ἔθηκεν ἄναξ· ἑκάεργος
Ἀπόλλων
Ἔγνω δ' ἀνδρὶ κακὸν τήλοθεν ἐρχό-
μενον.
See the curious narrative in Herodotus ix. 94 seq. about the prophetic
gifts bestowed on Euenius. The same
narrative attests the full belief prevalent respecting both the displeasure
of the Gods and their placability on
the proper expiation being made. It
conflicts signally in every respect with
the canon of orthodoxy set up by
Plato.
[i] Plato, Legg. v. pp. 738 C, 747 E,
vii. p. 811 D; Republic, vi. pp. 496 C,
499 C.

petual contemplation and theorising, as the only occupation worthy to characterise their blessed immortality.[k] Epikurus and his numerous followers, though not agreeing with Aristotle in regarding the Gods as occupied in intellectual contemplation, agreed with him fully in considering the existence of the Gods as too dignified and enviable to be disturbed by the vexation of meddling with human affairs, or to take on the anxieties of regard for one man, displeasure towards another.

The orthodox religious belief, which Plato imposes upon his 5040 Magnêtic citizens under the severest penalties, would thus be found inconsistent with the general belief, not merely of ordinary Greeks, but also of the various lettered and philosophical individuals who thought for themselves. Most of these latter would have passed, under one of the three heads of Platonic heresy, into the Platonic prison for five years, and from thence either to recantation or death. The arguments which Plato considered so irresistible, that none but silly youth could be deaf to them—did not appear conclusive to Aristotle and other intelligent contemporaries. Plato makes up his own mind what proceedings he thinks worthy and unworthy of the Gods, and then proclaims with confidence as a matter of indisputable fact, that they act conformably. But neither Herodotus, nor Aristotle, would have granted his premisses: they conceived the attributes and character of the Gods differently from him, and differently from each other. And if we turn to the Kratylus of Plato, we find Sokrates there declaring, that men knew nothing about the Gods: that speculations about the Gods were in reality speculations about the opinions of men respecting the Gods.[l]

Such opinions were local, traditional, and dissentient, among the numerous distinct cities and tribes which divided the in-

Great opposition which Plato's doctrine would have encountered in Greece.

---

[k] Aristotle, Ethic. Nikom. x. 8, p. 1178, b. 21. ὥστε ἡ τοῦ θεοῦ ἐνεργεία, μακαριότητι διαφέρουσα, θεωρητικὴ ἂν εἴη.

[l] Plato, Kratylus, pp. 400-401. Περὶ θεῶν οὐδὲν ἴσμεν, οὔτε περὶ αὐτῶν, οὔτε περὶ τῶν ὀνομάτων, ἅττα ποτὲ αὐτοὶ ἑαυτοὺς καλοῦσι — σκοπῶμεν ὥσπερ

προειπόντες τοῖς θεοῖς ὅτι περὶ αὐτῶν οὐδὲν ἡμεῖς σκεψόμεθα, οὐ γὰρ ἀξιοῦμεν οἷοί τε ἂν εἶναι σκοπεῖν, ἀλλὰ περὶ ἀνθρώπων, ἥντινά ποτε δόξαν ἔχοντες ἐτίθεντο αὐτοῖς τὰ ὀνόματα· τοῦτο γὰρ ἀνεμέσητον. Compare also Kratyl. p. 425 B.

habited earth between them in Plato's time.[m] Each of these

Local infalli-
bility was
claimed as a
rule in each
community,
though rarely
enforced with
severity:
Plato both
claims it
more empha-
tically, and
enforces it
more rigor-
ously.

claimed a local infallibility, principally as to religious rites and customs, indirectly also as to dogmas
and creed: and Plato's Magnetic community, if it
had come into existence, would have added one to the
number of distinct varieties. To this general sentiment, deeply rooted in the emotions and unused to
the scrutiny of reason, the philosophers were always
more or less odious, as dissenters, enquirers, and
critics, each on his own ground.[n] At Athens the sentiment
manifested itself occasionally in severe decrees and judicial
sentences against obnoxious freethinkers, especially in the
case of Sokrates. If the Athenians had carried out consistently and systematically the principle involved in their
sentence against Sokrates, philosophy must have been banished
from Athens.[o] The school of Plato could never have been
maintained. But the principle of intolerance was usually left
dormant at Athens: philosophical debate continued active
and unshackled, so that the school of Plato subsisted in the
city without interruption for nearly forty years until his
death. We might have expected that the philosophers, to
whose security toleration of free dissent and debate was
essential, would have upheld it as a general principle against
the public. But here we find the most eminent among them,
at the close of a long life, not only disallowing all liberty of
philosophising to others, and assuming to himself the exclusive right of. dictating the belief, as well as the conduct, of
his imaginary citizens—but also enforcing this exclusive principle with an amount of systematic rigour, which I do not
believe to have been equalled in any actual Grecian city.
This is a memorable fact in the history of Grecian philosophy.
The Stoic Kleanthes, in the century after Plato's death, declared that the Samian astronomer Aristarchus ought to be
indicted for impiety, because he had publicly advocated the

[m] Plato, Politikus, p. 262 E. γένεσιν
ἀπείροις οὖσι καὶ ἀμίκτοις καὶ ἀσυμφώ-
νοις παρ' ἄλληλα. Herodot. iii. 39.
[n] Plato, Euthyphron, p. 3.
[o] See the Apologies both of Plato
and Xenophon. In one of the rhetorical discourses cited by Aristotle,

on the subject of the trial of Sokrates
(seemingly that by the rhetor Theodektês), the point is put thus :—Μέλ-
λετε δὲ κρίνειν, οὐ περὶ Σωκράτους,
ἀλλὰ περὶ ἐπιτηδεύματος, εἰ χρὴ φιλοσοφεῖν (Aristot. Rhetor. ii. 1399, a. 8,
b. 10).

doctrine of the Earth's rotation round the Sun.   Kleanthês
and Plato thus stand out as known examples, among Grecian
philosophers before the Christian era, of that intolerance which
would apply legal penalties against individual dissenters and
competitors.[p]

The eleventh Book of the Treatise De Legibus, and the
larger portion of the twelfth, are devoted to a string   Farther civil
of civil and political regulations for the Magnetic   and political
regulations
community.   Each regulation is ushered in with an   for the Magnêtic com-
munity.   No
expository prologue, often with severe reproof to-   evidence that
Plato had
wards persons committing the various forbidden acts.   studied the
working of
There is little of systematic order in the enumera-   different institutions in
tion of subjects.   In general, we may remark that   practice.
neither here nor elsewhere in the Treatise is there any proof,
that Plato—though doubtless he had visited Italy, Sicily, and
Egypt, perhaps other countries—had taken much pains to
acquaint himself with the practice of human life, or that he
had studied and compared the working of different institutions
in different communities.   His experience seems all derived
from Athenian law and practice: the criticisms and modifications which he applies to it flow from his own sentiment and
theory: from his religious or ethical likings or dislikings.   He
sets up a type of character which he desires to enforce among
his citizens, and which he guards against adulteration by very
stringent interference.   The displeasure of the Gods is constantly appealed to, as a justification for the penalties which
he proposed: sometimes even the current mythes are invoked
as authority, though in other places Plato so greatly dis-
parages them.[q]

Various modes of acquiring property are first forbidden as
illegitimate.   The maxim[r]—"That which you have   Modes of
acquiring
not put down, do not take up"—is rigorously en-   property—
legitimate
forced: any man who finds a buried treasure is pro-   and illegitimate.
hibited from touching it, though he find it by acci-

---

[p] The Platonist and astronomer
Derkyllides afterwards (about 100-
120 A.D.) declares those who affirm the
doctrine, that the earth moves and that
the stars are stationary, to be accursed
and impious—τοὺς δὲ τὰ κινητὰ στή-
σαντας, τὰ δὲ ἀκίνητα φύσει καὶ ἔδρᾳ
κινήσαντας, ὡς παρὰ τὰς τῆς μαντικῆς

ὑποθέσεις, ἀποδιομπεῖται.
Theon Smyrnæus, De Astronomiâ,
ch. 41, p. 328, fol. 26, ed. Martin.
[q] Plato, Legg. xi. p. 913 D.
[r] Plato, ib.   Ἃ μὴ κατέθου, μὴ
ἀνελῇ.   This does not include, however, what has been deposited by a
man's father or grandfather.

dent and though the person who buried it be unknown. If a
man violates this law, every one, freeman or slave, is invited
and commanded to inform against him. Should he be found
guilty, a special message must be sent to the Delphian oracle,
to ask what is to be done both with the treasure and with the
offender. So again, an article of property left on the highway is declared to be under protection of the Goddess or
Dæmon of the Highway: whoever finds and takes it, if he be
a slave, shall be severely flogged by any freeman above thirty
years of age who meets him: if he be a freeman, he shall be
disgraced and shall pay, besides, ten times its value to the
person who left it.[s] These are average specimens of Plato's
point of view and manner of handling offences respecting
property.

The general constitution of Plato's community restricts
Plato's gene-
ral regula-
tions leave
little room
for disputes
about owner-
ship. within comparatively narrow limits the occasions of
proprietary dispute. His 5040 lots of land are all
marked out, unchangeable, and indivisible, each possessed by one citizen. No man is allowed to acquire
or possess moveable property to a greater value than four
times the lot of land: every article of property possessed by
every man is registered by the magistrates. Disputes as to
ownership, if they arise, are settled by reference to this register.[t] If the disputed article be not registered, the possessor
is bound to produce the seller or donor from whom he received
it. All purchases and sales are required to take place in the
public market before the Agoranomi: and all for ready money,
or by immediate interchange and delivery. If a man chooses
to deliver his property, without receiving the consideration, or
in any private place, he does so at his own risk: he has no
legal claim against the receiver.[u] So likewise respecting the

---

[s] Plato, Legg. xi. p. 914. Seemingly, if any man found a treasure
buried in the ground, or a purse lying
on the road without an owner, he was
not considered by most persons dis-
honest if he appropriated it: to do
so was looked upon as an admissible
piece of good luck. See Theophrastus, περὶ Μεμψιμοιρίας. From Plato's
language we gather that the finder
sometimes went to consult the prophets what he should do, p. 913 B

—μήτε τοῖς λεγομένοις μάντεσιν ἀνα-
κοινώσαιμι: his phrase is not very
respectful towards the prophets.
[t] Plato, Legg. xi. p. 914 D.
[u] The same principle is laid down
by Plato, Republic, viii. p. 556 A, and
was also laid down by Charondas
(Theophrast. ap. Stobæum Serm. xliv.
21, p. 204). Aristotle alludes to some
Grecian cities in which it was the established law. K. F. Hermann, Privat-
Alterthümer der Griechen, s. 71, n. 10.

Eranoi or Associations for mutual Succour and Benefit.   Plato gives no legal remedy to a contributor or complainant respecting any matter arising out of these associations.   He requires that every man shall contribute at his own risk: and trust for requital to the honesty or equity of his fellow-contributors.[x]

A remark must here be made upon Plato's refusal to allow any legal redress in such matters as sale on credit, or payments for the purpose of mutual succour and relief.   Such refusal appears to contradict his general manner of proceeding: for his usual practice is, to estimate offences not according to the mischief which they inflict, but according to the degree of wickedness or impiety which he supposes them to imply in the doer.   Now the contributor to an association for mutual succour, who, after paying his contributions for the aid of his associates, finds that they refuse to contribute to his aid when the hour of his necessity arrives—suffers not only heavy calamity but grievous disappointment: which implies very bad dispositions on the part of those who, not being themselves distressed, nevertheless refuse.   Of such dispositions Plato takes no notice in the present case.   He does not expatiate (as he does in many other cases far more trifling and disputable) upon the displeasure of the Gods when they see a man who has been benefited in distress by his neighbour's contributions, refusing all requital at the time of that neighbour's need.   Plato indeed treats it as a private affair between friends.   You do a service to your friend, and you must take your chance whether he will do you a service in return: you must not ask for legal redress, if he refuses: what you have contributed was a present voluntarily given, not a loan lent to be repaid.   This is an intelligible point of view, but it excludes those ethical and sentimental considerations which Plato usually delights in enforcing.[y]   His

Plato's principles of legislation, not consistent—comparison of them with the Attic law about Eranoi.

---

[x] Plato, Legg. xi. p. 915 D-E.

[y] In Xenophon's ideal legislation, or rather. education of the Persian youth, in the Cyropædia, he introduces legal trial and punishment for ingratitude. generally (Cyropæd. i. 2, 7). The Attic judicature took cognizance of neglect or bad conduct towards parents, which Xenophon ranks as a sort of ingratitude—but not of ingratitude towards any one else (Xenoph. Memor. ii. 2, 13). There is an interesting discussion in Seneca (De Beneficiis, iii. 6-18) about the propriety of treating ingratitude as a legal offence.

ethics here show themselves by leading him to turn aside from that which takes the form of a pecuniary contract. It was in this form that the Eranoi or Mutual Assurance Associations were regarded by Attic judicature: that is, they seem to have been considered as a sort of imperfect obligation, which the Dikastery would enforce against any citizen whose circumstances were tolerably prosperous, but not against one in bad circumstances. Such Eranic actions before the Attic Dikastery were among those that enjoyed the privilege of speedy adjudication (ἔμμηνοι δίκαι).[z]

As to property in slaves, Plato allows any owner to lay hold of a fugitive slave belonging either to himself or to any friend. If a third party reclaims the slave as being not rightfully in servitude, he must provide three competent sureties, and the slave will then be set free until legal trial can be had. Moreover, Plato enacts, respecting one who has been a slave, but has been manumitted, that such freedman (ἀπελεύθερος), if he omits to pay "proper attention" to his manumitter, may be laid hold of by the latter, and re-enslaved. Proper attention consists in: 1. Going three times per month to the house of his former master, to tender service in all lawful ways. 2. Not contracting marriage without consulting his former master. 3. Not acquiring so much wealth as to become richer than his former master: if he should do so, the latter may appropriate all that is above the limit. The freedman, when liberated, does not become a citizen, but is only a non-citizen or metic. He is therefore subject to the same necessity as all other metics—of departing from the territory after a residence of twenty years,[a] and of never acquiring more wealth than is possessed by the second class of citizens enrolled in the Schedule.

Marginal note: Regulations about slaves, and about freedmen.

---

[z] Respecting the ἐρανικαὶ δίκαι at Athens, see Heraldus-Animadversiones in Salmasium, vi. 1, p. 407 seq.; Meier und Schömann, Der Attische Prozess, p. 540 seq.; K. F. Hermann, Staats Alterth. s. 146, not. 9.

The word ἔρανος meant very different things—a pic-nic banquet, a club for festive meetings kept up by subscription with a common purse, a contribution made to relieve a friend in distress, carrying obligation on the receiver to requite it if the donor fell into equal distress. This last sense is the prevalent one in the Attic orators, and is brought out well in the passage of Theophrastus — Περὶ Μεμψιμοιρίας. Probably the Attic ἐρανικαὶ δίκαι took cognizance of complaints arising out of ἔρανος in all its senses.

[a] Plato, Legg. xi. p. 915 A-B.

The duties imposed by Plato on the freedman towards his former master—involving a formal recognition at least of the prior dependence, and some positive duties besides—are deserving of remark, as we know so little of the condition or treatment of this class of persons in antiquity.

Regulations are made to provide for the case where a slave, sold by his master, is found to be distempered or mad, or to have committed a murder. If the sale has been made to a physician or a gymnast, Plato holds that these persons ought to judge for themselves about the bodily condition of the slave bought: he therefore grants them no redress. But if the buyer be a non-professional man, he may within one month restore the distempered slave (or within one year, if the distemper be the Morbus Sacer), and may cause a jury of physicians to examine the case. Should they decide the distemper of the slave to be undoubted, the seller must take him back: repaying the full price, if he be a private man—double the price, if he be a professional man, who ought to have known, and perhaps did know, the real condition of the slave sold.[b]

Provisions in case a slave is sold, having a distemper upon him.

In regard to Retail Selling, and to frauds committed either in sale or in barter, Plato provides or enjoins strict regulations. The profession of the retailer, and the function of money as auxiliary to it, he pronounces to be useful and almost indispensable to society, for the purpose of rendering different articles of value commensurable with each other, and of ensuring a distribution suitable to the requirements of individuals. This could not be done without retailers, merchants, hired agents, &c.[c] But though retailing is thus useful, if properly conducted, it slides easily and almost naturally into cheating, lying, extortion, &c., from the love of money inherent in most men. Such abuses must be restrained: at any rate they must not be allowed to corrupt the best part of the community. Accordingly, none of the 5040 citizens will be allowed either to practise retailing, or to exercise any hired function, except under his own senior

Retailers. Strict regulations about them. No citizen can be a retailer.

[b] Plato, Legg. xi. p. 916 B-C.
[c] Plato, Legg. xi. p. 918 B. The like view of retail trade is given in the Republic, ii. p. 371. It indicates just and penetrating social observation, taken in reference to Plato's age.

relatives, and of a dignified character. The discrimination of
what is dignified and not dignified must be made according to
the liking or antipathy of a Court of Honour, composed of such
citizens as have obtained prizes for virtue.[d] None must be permitted to sell by retail except metics or non-citizens; and these
must be kept under strict watch by the Nomophylakes, who,
after enquiring into the details of each article, will fix its price
at such sum as will afford to the dealer a moderate profit.[e]

If there be any fraud committed by the seller (which is
nearly akin to retailing[f]), Plato prescribes severe
penalty. The seller must never name two prices for
his article during the same day. He must declare
his price; and if no one will give it, he must with-
draw the article for the day.[g] He is not allowed to praise his
own articles, or to take any oath respecting them. If he shall
take any oath, any citizen above thirty years of age shall be
held bound to thrash him, and may do so with impunity: such
citizen, if he neglect to thrash the swearer, will himself be
amenable to censure for betraying the laws. If the seller
shall sell a spurious or fraudulent article, the magistrates
must be informed of it by any one cognizant. The informer,
if a slave or a metic, shall be rewarded by having the article
made over to him. If he be a citizen, he will receive the
article, but is bound to consecrate it to the Gods who preside
over the market: if being cognizant he omits to inform, he
shall be proclaimed a wicked man, for defrauding the Gods of
that to which they are entitled. The magistrates, on receiving information, will not only deprive the seller of the
spurious article, but will cause him to be flogged by the herald
in the market-place—one stripe for every drachma contained
in the price demanded. The herald will publicly proclaim
the reason why the flogging is given. Besides this, the

Side note: Frauds committed by sellers—severe punishments on them.

---

[d] Plato, Legg. xi. pp. 918-919. τὸ
δ' ἐλευθερικὸν καὶ ἀνελεύθερον ἀκριβῶς
μὲν οὐ ῥ᾽διον νομοθετεῖν, κρινέσθω γε
μὴν ὑπὸ τῶν τὰ ἀριστεῖα εἰληφότων τῷ
ἐκείνων μίσει καὶ ἀσπασμῷ.

[e] Plato, Legg. xi. p. 920 B-C.

[f] Plato, Legg. xi. p. 920 D. τῆς
κιβδηλείας πέρι, ξυγγενοῦς τούτῳ (κα-
πηλείᾳ) πράγματος, &c.
Plato is more rigorous on these

matters than the Attic law. See K. F.
Hermann, Griech. Privat-Alterthümer,
s. 62.

[g] Plato, Legg. xi. p. 917 B-C. I
do not quite see how this is to be reconciled with Plato's direction that the
prices of articles sold shall be fixed by
the magistrates; but both of the two
are here found.

magistrates will collect and write up in the market-place both regulations of detail for the sellers, and information to put buyers on their guard.[h]

Compare this enactment in Plato with the manner in which the Attic law would have dealt with the like offence. The defrauded buyer would have brought his action before the Dikastery against the fraudulent seller, who, if found guilty, would have been condemned in damages to make good the wrong; perhaps fined besides. The penalties inflicted by the usual course of law at Athens were fine, disfranchisement, civil disability of one kind or other, banishment, confiscation of property: occasionally imprisonment—sometimes, though rarely, death by the cup of hemlock in prison.[i] Except in very rare cases, an accused person might retire into banishment if he chose, and might thus escape any penalty worse than banishment and confiscation of property. But corporal punishment was never inflicted by the law at Athens. The people, especially the poorer citizens, were very sensitive on this point,[k] regarding it as one great line of distinction between the freeman and the slave. At Sparta, on the contrary, corporal chastisement was largely employed as a penalty: moreover the use of the fist in private contentions, by the younger citizens, was encouraged rather than forbidden.[l]

Comparison with the lighter punishment inflicted by Attic law.

Plato follows the analogy of Sparta in preference to that of Athens. Here, as elsewhere, he employs corporal punishment abundantly as a penalty. Here, as elsewhere, he not only prescribes that it shall be inflicted by a public agent under the supervision of magistrates, but also directs it to be administered, against certain offenders, by private unofficial citizens. I believe that this feature of his system would have been more repugnant than any other, to the feelings of all classes of Athenian citizens—to all the different types of character represented by Periklês, Nikias, Kleon, Isokrates, Demosthenes, and Sokrates. Abstinence from manual violence was characteristic of Athenian manners. Whatever

[h] Plato, Legg. xi. p. 917 B-D.

[i] See Meier und Schömann, Der Attische Prozess, B. iv. chap. 13, 740.

[k] See Xenophon, Memorab. i. 2, 58.

[l] Xenophon, Hellen. iii. 3, 11; De Republ. Laced. ii. 8, iv. 6, ix. 5; Aristophanes Aves, 1013.

licence might be allowed to the tongue, it was at least a substitute for the aggressive employment of the arm and hand.
Athens exhibited marked respect for the sanctity of the person
against blows—much equality of dealing between man and
man—much tolerance, public as well as private, of individual
diversity in taste and character—much keenness of intellectual and oral competition, liable to degenerate into unfair
stratagem in political, forensic, professional, and commercial
life, as well as in rhetorical, dialectical, and philosophical exercises. All these elements, not excepting even the first,
were distasteful to Plato. But those who copy the disparaging judgment which he pronounces against Athenian manners, ought in fairness to take account of the point of view
from which that judgment is delivered. To a philosopher
whose ideal is depicted in the two treatises De Republicâ and
De Legibus, Athenian society would appear repulsive enough.
We learn from these two treatises what it was that a great speculative politician of the day desired to establish as a substitute.

Plato next goes on to make regulations about orphans and
Regulations
about Or-
phans and
Guardians:
also about
Testament-
ary Powers. guardians, and in general for cases arising out of
the death of a citizen. The first question present-
ing itself naturally is, How far is the citizen to be
allowed to direct by testament the disposition of his
family and property? What restriction is to be placed upon
his power of making a valid will? Many persons (Plato says)
affirmed that it was unjust to impose any restriction: that the
dying man had a right to make such dispositions as he chose,
for his property and family after his death. Against this view
Plato enters his decided protest. Each man—and still more
each man's property—belongs not to himself, but to his family
and to the city: besides which, an old man's judgment is constantly liable to be perverted by decline of faculties, disease,
or the cajoleries of those around him.[m] Accordingly Plato
grants only a limited liberty of testation. Here, as elsewhere,
he adopts the main provisions of the Attic law, with such
modifications as were required by the fundamental principles

---

[m] Plato, Legg. xi. p. 923 B.
It is to be observed that Plato does
not make any allusion to these misguiding influences operating upon an
aged man, when he talks about the
curse of a father against his son being
constantly executed by the Gods: xi.
p. 931 B.

of his Magnêtic city: especially by the fixed total of 5040 lots or *fundi*, each untransferable and indivisible.   The lot, together with the plant or stock for cultivating it,[n] must descend entire to one son: but the father, if he has more than one son, may determine by will to which of them it shall descend.   If there be any one among the sons whom another citizen (being childless) is disposed to adopt, such adoption can only take place with the father's consent.   But if the father gives his consent, he cannot bequeath his own lot to the son so adopted, because two lots cannot be united in the same possessor.   Whatever property the father possesses over and above his lot and its appurtenances, he may distribute by will among his other sons, in any proportion he pleases.   If he dies leaving no sons, but only daughters, he may select which of them he pleases; and may appoint by will some suitable husband, of a citizen family, to marry her and inherit his lot.   If a citizen (being childless) has adopted a son out of any other family, he must bequeath to that son the whole of his property, except one-tenth part of what he possesses over and above his lot and its appurtenances: this tenth he may bequeath to any one whom he chooses.[o]

If the father dies intestate, leaving only daughters, the nearest relative who has no lot of his own shall marry one of the daughters, and succeed to the lot.   The nearest is the brother of the deceased; next, the brother of the deceased wife (paternal and maternal uncles of the maiden); next, their sons; next, the paternal and maternal uncle of the deceased father, and their sons.   If all these relatives be wanting, the magistrates will provide a suitable husband, in order that the lot of land may not remain unoccupied.[p]   If a citizen die both intestate and childless, two of his nearest unmarried relatives, male and female, shall intermarry and succeed to his property: reckoning in the order of kinship above mentioned.[q]   In thus imposing marriage as a legal obligation

[n] Plato, Legg. xi. p. 923 D.   πλὴν τοῦ πατρῴου κλήρου καὶ τῆς περὶ τὸν κλῆρον κατασκευῆς πάσης.

[o] Plato, Legg. xi. pp. 923-924.   The language of Plato seems to imply that this childless citizen would not be likely to make any will, but that having adopted a son, the son so adopted would hardly be satisfied unless he inherited the whole.

[p] Plato, Legg. xi. pp. 924-925.

[q] Plato, Legg. xi. p. 925 C-D.   These provisions appear to me not very clear.

upon persons in a certain degree of kinship, Plato is aware
that there will be individual cases of great hardship and of repugnance almost insurmountable. He treats this as unavoidable: providing however that there shall be a select judicial
Board of Appeal, before which persons who feel aggrieved by
the law may bring their complaints, and submit their grounds
for dispensation.[r]

These provisions deserve notice as showing how largely
Plato coincides with the prevalent Attic sentiment
respecting family and relationship. He does not
award the slightest preference to primogeniture,
among brothers: he grants to agnates a preference
over cognates: he regards it as a public misfortune that any
house shall be left empty, so as to cause interruption of the
sacred rites of the family: lastly, he ensures that the family,
in default of lineal male heirs, shall be continued by inter-mar-
riage with the nearest relatives—and he especially approves
the marriage of an heiress with her paternal or maternal uncle.
On these points Plato is in full harmony with his countrymen,
though he dissents widely from modern sentiment.

Plato's general coincidence with Attic law and its sentiment.

Respecting tutelage of orphans, he makes careful provision
against abuse, as the Attic law also did: he tries also
to meet the cases of family discord, where father and
son are in bitter wrath against each other. A father
may formally renounce his son, but not without previously obtaining the concurrence of a *conseil de famille*: if
the father has become imbecile with age, and wastes his substance, the son may institute a suit as for lunacy, but not
without the permission of the Nomophylakes.[s] Respecting
disagreement between married couples, ten of the Nomophylakes, together with ten women chosen as supervisors of
marriages, are constituted a Board of reference,[t] to obtain a
reconciliation, if it be possible: but if this be impossible, then

Tutelage of Orphans—Disagreement of Married Couples—Divorce.

[r] Plato, Legg. xi. p. 926 B-D. He directs also (p. 925 A) that the Dikasts shall determine the fit season when these young persons become marriage-able by examining their naked bodies: that is, the males quite naked, the females half naked. A direction seemingly copied from Athenian practice, and illustrating curiously the language of Philokleon in Aristo-phanes, Vesp. 598. See K. F. Her-mann, Vestig. Juris Domestici ap. Pla-tonem cum Græciæ Institutis Compa-rata, p. 27.

[s] Plato, Legg. xi. pp. 928-929.
[t] Plato, Legg. xi. pp. 929-930.

to divorce the couple, and unite each with some more suitable partner.   The lawgiver must keep in view, as far as he can, to obtain from each married couple a sufficiency of children— that is, one· male and one female child from each, whereby the total of 5040 lots may be kept up.[u]   If a husband loses his wife before he has these two children, the law requires him to marry another wife: but if he becomes a widower, having already the sufficiency of children, he is advised not to marry a second wife (who will become stepmother), though not pro- hibited from doing so, if he chooses.   So also, if a woman be- comes a widow, not having the sufficient number of children, she must be compelled to marry again: if she already has the sufficient number, she is directed to remain in the house, and to bring them up.   In case she is still young, and her health requires a husband, her relatives will apply to the Female Supervisors of Marriage, and will make such arrange- ments as may seem advisable.[x]

Against neglect of aged parents by their children, Plato both denounces the most stringent legal penalties, Neglect of parents. and delivers the most emphatic reproofs: commend- ing with full faith the ancient traditional narratives, that the curse of an offended parent against his sons was always executed by the Gods, as in the cases of Œdipus, Theseus, Amyntor, &c.[y]   In the event of lunacy, he directs that the lunatic shall be kept in private custody by his relatives, who will be fined if they neglect the duty.[z]

Hurt or damage, not deadly, done by one man to another. —Plato enumerates two different modes of inflicting damage: —1. By drugs (applied externally or internally), magic, or sorcery.   2. By theft or force.[a]

As to the first mode, if the drug be administered by a phy- sician, he must be put to death: if by one not a Poison— Magic—In- cantations— Severe punishment. physician, the Dikasts will determine the nature of his punishment.   And in the case of magical arts, or incantations, if the person who resorts to them be a prophet

[u] Plato, Legg. xi. p. 930 C.   παίδων δὲ ἱκανότης ἀκριβὴς ἄρρην καὶ θήλεια ἔστω τῷ νόμῳ.

[x] Plato, Legg. xi. p. 930 C.

[y] Plato, Legg. xi. pp. 931-932.

[z] Plato, Legg. xi. p. 934 D.

[a] Plato, Legg. xi. pp. 932 E-933 E. Both these come under the general head ὅσα τις ἄλλος ἄλλον πημαίνει.

or an inspector of prodigies, he must be put to death : another person doing the same will be punished at the discretion of the Dikasts.   Here we see that the prophet is ranked as a professional person (the like appears in Homer) along with the physician,[b]—who must know what he is about, while another person perhaps may not know.   But Plato's own opinion respecting magical incantations is delivered with singular reserve.   He will neither avouch them nor reject them.   He intimates that a man can hardly find out what is true on the subject ; and even if he could, it would be harder still to convince others.   Most men are in serious alarm when they see waxen statuettes hung at their doors or at their family tombs ; and it is useless to attempt to tranquillise them by reminding them that they have no certain evidence on the subject.[c] Here we see how Plato discourages the received legends and the current faith, when he believes them to be hurtful—as contrasted with his vehemence in upholding them when he thinks them useful : as in the case of the paternal curse, and the judgments of the Gods.   The question of their truth is made to depend on their usefulness.[d]   The Gods are made to act exactly as he thinks they ought to act.   They are not merely invoked, but positively counted on, as executioners of Plato's ethical sentences.

Respecting the second mode of damage—by theft or violence—Plato's law forms a striking contrast to that which has been just set forth.   The person who inflicts damage must repay it, or make full compensation for it, to the sufferer : small, if the damage be small—great, if it be great.   Besides this, the guilty person must undergo some farther punishment with a view to correction or reformation.   This will be smaller, if he be young

Punishment is inflicted with a view to future prevention or amendment.

---

[b] Plato, Legg. xi. p. 933 D. ὡς πρῶτον μὲν τὸν ἐπιχειροῦντα φαρμάττειν οὐκ εἰδότα τί δρᾷ, τά τε κατὰ σώματα, ἐὰν μὴ τυγχάνῃ ἐπιστήμων ὢν ἰατρικῆς, τά τε αὖ περὶ τὰ μαγγανεύματα, ἐὰν μὴ μάντις ἢ τερατόσκοπος ὢν τυγχάνῃ.
Homer, Odys. xvii. 383 :—

τῶνδ' οἳ δημιοεργοὶ ἔασιν,
μάντιν, ἢ ἰητῆρα κακῶν, ἢ τέκτονα δούρων,
ἢ καὶ θέσπιν ἀοιδόν, &c.

[c] Plato, Legg. xi. p. 933 A.   ἄν ποτε

ἴδωσί που κήρινα μιμήματα πεπλασμένα. Compare Theokritus, Idyll. ii. 28-59.

See the remarkable narrative of the death of Germanicus in Syria, supposed to have been brought about by the magical artifices wrought under the auspices of Piso (Tacitus, Ann. ii, 69).

[d] Cicero, Legg. i. 7. " Utiles autem esse has opiniones, quis neget, cum intelligat, quam multa firmentur jurejurando," &c.

and seduced by the persuasion of others; but it must be graver, if he be self-impelled by his own desires, fears, wrath, jealousy, &c. Understand, however (adds Plato), that such ulterior punishment is not imposed on account of the past misdeed—for the past cannot be recalled or undone—but on account of the future: to ensure that he shall afterwards hate wrong-doing, and that those who see him punished shall hate it also. The Dikasts must follow out in detail the general principle here laid down.[e]

This passage proclaims distinctly an important principle in regard to the infliction of legal penalties: which principle, if kept in mind, might have led Plato to alter or omit a large portion of the Leges.

Respecting *words of abuse, or revilement,* or insulting derision.—These are altogether forbidden. If used in any temple, market, or public and frequented place, the magistrate presiding must punish the offender forthwith, as he thinks fit: if elsewhere, any citizen by-stander, being older than the offender, is authorised and required to thrash him.[f] No writer of comedy is allowed to ridicule or libel any citizen.

Penalty for abusive words—for libellous comedy. Mendicity forbidden.

Mendicity is strictly prohibited. Every mendicant must be sent away at once, in order that the territory may be rid of such a creature. Every man, who has passed an honest life, will be sure to have made friends who will protect him against the extremity of want.[g]

The rules provided by Plato about witnesses in judicial trials and indictments for perjury, are pretty much the same as those prevalent at Athens: with some peculiarities. Thus he permits a free woman to bear witness, and to address the court in support of a party interested, provided she be above forty years of age. Moreover, she may institute a suit, if she have no husband: but not if

Regulations about witnesses on judicial trials.

[e] Plato, Legg. xi. pp. 933-934. Compare Plato, Protagor. p. 324 B.
[f] Plato, Legg. xi. p. 935 C-D. The Attic law expressly forbade the utterance of abusive words against any individual *in an office or public place* upon any pretence (Lysias, Or. ix. Pro Milite, s. 6-9). Demosthenes (contra Konon. p. 1263) speaks of κακηγορία or λοιδορία as in itself trifling, but as forbidden by the law, lest it should lead to violence and blows.
[g] Plato, Legg. xi. p. 936 C. ὅπως ἡ χώρα τοῦ τοιούτου ζῴου καθαρὰ γίγνηται τὸ παράπαν.

she be married.[h] A slave or a child may bear witness at a trial for murder; provided security be given that they will remain in the city to await an indictment for perjury, if presented against them.

Among Plato's prohibitions, we are not surprised to find one directed emphatically against forensic eloquence, and against those who professed to teach it. Every thing beneficial to man (says he) has its accompanying poison and corruption. Justice is a noble thing, the great civilising agent in human affairs: to aid any one in obtaining justice, is of course a noble thing also. But these benefits are grossly abused by men, who pretend to possess an art, whereby every one may be sure of judicial victory, either as principal or as auxiliary, whether his cause be just or unjust:—and who offer to teach this art to all who pay a stipulated price. Whether this be (as they pretend) a real art, or a mere inartificial knack—it would be a disgrace to our city, and must be severely punished. Whoever gives show of trying to pervert the force of justice in the minds of the Dikasts, or indulges in unseasonable and frequent litigation, or even lends his aid to other litigants—may be indicted by any citizen as guilty of abuse of justice, either as principal or auxiliary. He shall be tried before the Court of Select Judges: who, if they find him guilty, will decide whether he has committed the offence from love of money, or from love of contention and ambitious objects. If from love of contention, he shall be interdicted, for such time as the Court may determine, from instituting any suit at law on his own account as well as from aiding in any suit instituted by others.[i] If from love of money, the citizen found guilty shall

Censure of forensic eloquence, and the teachers of it. Penalties against contentious litigation.

---

[h] Plato, Legg. xi. p. 937 A-B.

It appears that women were not admitted as witnesses before the Athenian Dikasteries. Meier und Schömann, Attisch. Prozess, pp. 667-668. The testimony of slaves was received after they had been tortured; which was considered as a guarantee for truth, required in regard to them but not required in regard to a freeman. The torture is not mentioned in this Platonic treatise. Plato treats a male as *young* up to the age of thirty (compare Xenoph. Memor. i. 2, 35), a female as *young* up to the age of forty (pp. 932 B-C, 961 B).

[i] Plato, Legg. xi. p. 938 B. τιμᾶν αὐτῷ τὸ δικαστήριον ὅσου χρὴ χρόνου τὸν τοιοῦτον μηδενὶ λαχεῖν δίκην μηδὲ ξυνδικῆσαι. I cannot understand why Stallbaum, in his very useful notes on the Leges, observes upon this passage: —" λαγχάνειν δίκην de caussidicis accipiendum, qui caussam aliquam pro aliis in foro agendam ac defendendam suscipiunt." This is the explanation

be capitally punished, the non-citizen shall be banished in perpetuity. Moreover the citizen convicted of committing this offence even from love of contention, if it be a second conviction for the offence, shall be put to death also.[k]

The vague and undefined character of this offence, for which Plato denounces capital punishment, shows how much his penal laws are discharges of ethical antipathy and hostility against types of character conceived by himself—rather than measures intended for application, in which he had weighed beforehand the practical difficulties of singling out and striking the right individual. On this matter *Many of Plato's laws are discharges of ethical antipathy. The antipathy of Melêtus against Sokrates was of the same character.* the Athenian public had the same ethical antipathy as himself; and Melêtus took full advantage of it, when he brought his accusation against Sokrates. We know both from the Apologies of Plato and Xenophon, and from the Nubes of Aristophanes—that Sokrates was rendered odious to the Athenian people and Dikasts, partly as heterodox and irreligious, but partly also as one who taught the art of using speech so as to make the worse appear the better reason. Both Aristophanes and Melêtus would have sympathised warmly with the Platonic law. If there had been any Solonian law to the same effect, which Melêtus could have quoted in his accusatory speech, his case against Sokrates would have been materially strengthened. Especially, he would have had the express sanction of law for his proposition of death as the penalty: a proposition to which the Athenian Dikasts would not have consented, had they not been affronted and driven to it by the singular demeanour of Sokrates himself when before them. It would be irrelevant here to say that Sokrates was not guilty of what was imputed to him: that he never came before the Dikastery until the time of his trial—and that he did not teach "the art of words." If he did not teach it, he was at least believed to teach it, not merely by Aristophanes and by the Athenian Dikasts, but also by intelligent men like Kritias and Chariklês,[l] who knew him perfectly well: while the example of Antiphon shows that a man might be most

---

belonging to ξυνδικῆσαι: λαχεῖν δίκην is the well known phrase for a plaintiff or a prosecutor as principal.

[k] Plato, Legg. xi. pp. 937 E, 938 C.
[l] Xenophon, Memor. i. 2, 31 seq.

acute and efficacious as a forensic adviser, without coming in
person before the Dikastery.[m]   What the defence really makes
us feel is, the indefinite nature of the charge: which is neither
proveable nor disproveable, and which is characterised, both
by Xenophon and in the Platonic Apology, as one of the
standing calumnies against all philosophising men.[n]   Here,
in the Platonic Leges, this same unproveable offence is
adopted and made capital: the Select Platonic Dikasts being
directed to ascertain, not only whether a man has really committed it, but whether he has been impelled to commit it by
love of money, or by love of victory and personal consequence.

The twelfth and last Book of the Treatise De Legibus deals

Penalty for abuse of public trust —wrongful appropria- tion of public money—eva- sion of mili- tary service.

with various cases of obligation, not towards individuals, but towards the public or the city.   Abuse
of trust in the character of a public envoy is declared punishable.   This offence (familiar to us at
Athens through the two harangues of Demosthenes
and Æschines) is invested by Plato with a religious colouring,
as desecrating the missions and commands of Hermês and
Zeus.[o]   Wrongful appropriation of the public money by a
citizen is also made capital.   The penalty is to be inflicted
equally whether the sum appropriated be large or small: in
either case the guilt is equal, and the evidence of wicked disposition the same, for one who has gone through the public
education and training.[p]   This is quite different from Plato's
principle of dealing with theft or wrongful abstraction of
property from private persons: in which case, the sentence of
Plato was, that the amount of damage done, small or great,
should be made good by the offender, and that a certain ulterior penalty should be inflicted sufficient to deter him as well
as others from a repetition.

[m] Thucydid. viii. 68.
[n] Plato, Apol. Sokr. p. 23.
Such was the colloquial power of
Sokrates, in the portrait drawn by
Xenophon (Mem. i. 2, 14), "that he
handled all who conversed with him
just as he pleased—τοῖς δὲ διαλεγο-
μένοις αὐτῷ πᾶσι χρώμενον ἐν τοῖς
λόγοις ὅπως βούλοιτο. Kritias and
Alkibiades (Xenophon tells us) sought
his society for the purpose of strengthening their own oratorical powers as
political men, and of becoming κρείτ-
τονε τῶν συγγιγνομένων (i. 2, 16).

Looked at from the point of view of
opponents, this would be described as
the proceeding of one who himself
both could pervert, and did pervert,
justice—and who taught others to pervert it also.   This was the picture of
Sokrates which the accusers presented
to the Athenian Dikastery; as we may
see by the language of Sokrates himself at the beginning of the Platonic
Apology.
[o] Plato, Legg. xii. p. 941 A.
[p] Plato, Legg. xii. p. 941: compare
xi. p. 934 A.

Provision is farther made for punishing any omission of
military service either by males or females, or any discreditable abandonment of arms.[q] The orders of the military commander must be implicitly and exactly obeyed. The actions
of all must be orderly, uniform, and simultaneous. Nothing
can be more mischievous than that each should act for himself, separately and apart from others. This is especially true
as to war, but it is no less essential as to the proceedings in
peace.[r] Suppression of individuality, and conversion of life
into a perpetual, all-pervading, drill and discipline — is a
favourite aspiration always present to Plato.

A Board of Elders is constituted by Plato, as auditors of
the proceedings of all Magistrates after their term of office.[s]
The mode of choosing these Elders, as well as their duties,
liabilities, privileges, and honours, both during life and after
death, are prescribed with the utmost solemnity.

Plato forbids the parties in any judicial suit from swearing: they will present their case to the court, but
not upon oath. No judicial oath is allowed to be
taken by any one who has a pecuniary interest in the
matter on hand. The Dikasts—the judges in all
public competitions—the Electors before they elect

Oaths. Dikasts, Judges, Electors, are to be sworn; but no parties to a suit, or interested witnesses, can be sworn.

---

[q] Plato, Legg. xii. p. 944. It is
curious to compare this passage of
Plato with the two orations of Lysias
κατὰ Θεομνήστου A and B (Oratt. x.-
xi.). Plato enjoins upon all accusers
the greatest caution and precision in
the terms used to indicate what they
intended to charge upon the accused.
To call a man ῥίψασπις is a more
aggravated offensive designation than
to call him ἀποβολεὺς ὅπλων, which
latter term is more general, and may
possibly be applied to those who have
lost their arms under the pressure of
irresistible necessity, without any disgrace. On the other hand, we read in
Lysias, that the offence which was
punishable under the Attic law was
ὅπλων ἀποβολή, and that to assert
falsely respecting any citizen, τὰ ὅπλα
ἀποβέβληκε, was an ἀπόρρητον or forbidden phrase, which exposed the
speaker to a fine of 500 drachmæ (sect.
1-12). But to assert respecting any
man that he was ῥίψασπις was not
expressly ἀπόρρητον, (compare Lysias
cont. Agorat. Or. xiii. ss. 87-89), and

the speaker might argue (successfully
or not) that he had said nothing
ἀπόρρητον, and was not guilty of legal
κακηγορία.—There is another phrase
in this section of Plato to which I
would call attention. He enumerates
the excusable cases of losing arms as
follows—ὅπυσοι κατὰ κρημνῶν ῥιφέντες
ἀπώλεσαν, ὅπλα ἢ κατὰ θάλασσαν (p.
944 A). Now the cases of soldiers
being thrown down cliffs are, I believe,
unknown until the Phokian prisoners
were so dealt with in the Sacred War,
as sacrilegious offenders against Apollo
and the Delphian temple. Hence we
may probably infer that this was composed after the Sacred War began, B.C.
356. See Diodorus and my 'Hist. of
Greece,' chap. 87, p. 350 seq.

[r] Plato, Legg. xii. pp. 942-945. ἐνί
τε λόγῳ τὸ χωρίς τι τῶν ἄλλων πράττειν διδάξαι τὴν ψυχὴν ἔθεσι μήτε
γιγνώσκειν μήτ' ἐπίστασθαι τὸ παράπαν,
ἀλλ' ἄθροον ἀεὶ καὶ ἅμα καὶ κοινὸν τὸν
βίον ὅ, τι μάλιστα πᾶσι πάντων γίγνεσθαι.

[s] Plato, Legg. xii. pp. 946-948.

444 LEGES. CHAP. XXXVII.

to a public trust—are all to be sworn: but neither the parties
to any cause, nor (seemingly) the witnesses. If oaths were
taken on both sides, one or other of the parties must be per-
jured: and Plato considers it dreadful, that they should go on
living with each other afterwards in the same city. In afore-
time Rhadamanthus (he tells us) used to settle all disputes
simply, by administering an oath to the parties: for in his
time no one would take a false oath : men were then not only
pious, but even sons or descendants of the Gods. But now
(in the Platonic days) impiety has gained ground, and men's
oaths are no longer to be trusted, where anything is to be
gained by perjury.[t]

Strict regulations are provided, as to exit from the Platonic

Regulations about admission of strangers, and foreign travel of citizens. city, and ingress into it. Plato fears contamination to his citizens from converse with the outer world. He would introduce the peremptory Spartan Xene-lasy, if he were not afraid of the obloquy attending
it. He strictly defines the conditions on which the foreigner
will be allowed to come in, or the citizen to go out. No citizen is allowed to go out before he is forty years of age.[u]
Envoys must be sent on public missions ; and sacred legations
(theôries) must be despatched to the four great Hellenic
festivals—Olympic, Pythian, Nemean, and Isthmian. But
private citizens are not permitted to visit even these great
festivals at their own pleasure. The envoys sent must be
chosen and trustworthy men: moreover, on returning, they
will assure their youthful fellow-citizens, that the home institutions are better than anything that can be seen abroad.[x]

Special travellers, between the ages of fifty and sixty, will
also be permitted to go abroad; and will bring back reports to
the Magistrates of what they have observed. Strangers are
admitted into the city or its neighbourhood, under strict supervision ; partly as observers, partly as traders, for the limited
amount of traffic which the lawgiver tolerates.[y] Thus scanty
is the worship which Plato will allow his Magnêtes to pay to
Zeus Xenius.[z] He seems however to take credit for it as
liberal dealing.

[t] Plato, Legg. xii. pp. 948-949.
[u] Plat. Legg. xii. p. 950.
[x] Plat. Legg. xii. p. 951.

[y] Plato, Legg. xii. pp. 952-953.
[z] Plato, Legg. xii. p. 953 E. Τούτοις
δὴ τοῖς νόμοις ὑποδέχεσθαί τε χρὴ

Plato proceeds with various enactments respecting surety- Suretyship—Length of prescription for owner-ship, &c. ship—time of prescription for ownership—keeping men away by force either from giving testimony in court or from contending at the public matches— receiving of stolen goods—private war or alliance on the part of any individual citizen, without the consent of the city— receipt of bribes by functionaries—return and registration of each citizen's property—dedications and offerings to the Gods.[a] No systematic order or classification can be traced in the successive subjects.

In respect to judiciary matters, he repeats (what had before been directed) his constitution of three stages of tri- Judicial trial—three stages. 1. Arbitrators. 2. Tribe-Dikasteries. 3. Select Dikastery. bunals. First, Arbitrators, chosen by both parties in the dispute. From their decision, either party may appeal to the Tribe-Dikasteries, composed of all the citizens of the Tribe or Dême: or at least, com- posed of a jury taken from these. After this, there is a final appeal to the Select Dikastery, chosen among all the Ma- gistrates for the time being.[b] Plato leaves to his successors the regulations of details, respecting the mode of impannelling and the procedure of these Juries.

Lastly come the regulations respecting funerals—the cost, ceremonies, religious proceedings, mode of showing Funerals—proceedings prescribed—expence limited. sorrow and reverence, &c.[c] These are given in con- siderable detail, and with much solemnity of religious exhortation.

We have now reached the close. The city has received its full political and civil outfit: as much legal regula- Conservative organ to keep up the original scheme of the lawgiver. Nocturnal Council for tion as it is competent for the lawgiver to provide at the beginning. One guarantee alone is wanting. Some security must be provided for the continuance

---

πάντας ξένους τε καὶ ξένας καὶ τοὺς αὐτῶν ἐκπέμπειν, τιμῶντας ξένιον Δία, μὴ βρώμασι καὶ θύμασι τὰς ξενηλασίας ποιουμένους, καθάπερ ποιοῦσι νῦν θρέμ- ματα Νείλου, μηδὲ κηρύγμασιν ἀγρίοις. Stallbaum says in his note :—" μὴ βρώ- μασι καὶ θύμασι—peregrinos non ex- pellentes coenis et sacrificiis, h. e. eorum usu iis interdicentes." This surely is not the right explanation. Plato means to say that the Egyptian habits as to

eating and sacrifice were intolerably repulsive to a foreigner. We may see this from κηρύγμασι which follows. The peculiarities of Egypt, which Herodotus merely remarks upon with astonishment, may well have given offence to the fastidious and dictatorial spirit of Plato.

[a] Plato, Legg. xii. pp. 954-956.
[b] Plato, Legg. xii. p. 956.
[c] Plato, Legg. xii. pp. 957-958.

this purpose —how constituted. and durability of the enactments.[d] We must have a special conservative organ, watching over and keeping up the scheme of the original lawgiver. For this function, Plato constitutes a Board, which, from its rule of always beginning its sittings before daybreak, he calls the Nocturnal council. It will comprise ten of the oldest Nomophylakes: all those who have obtained prizes for good conduct or orderly discipline: all those who have been authorised to go abroad, and have been approved on their return. Each of these members will introduce into the Synod one young man of thirty years of age, chosen by himself, but approved by the others.[e] The members will thus be partly old, partly young.

This Nocturnal council is intended as the conservative organ of the Platonic city. It is, in the city, what the soul and head are in an animal. The soul includes Reason: the head includes the two most perfect senses—Sight and Hearing. The fusion, in one, of Reason with these two senses ensures the preservation of the animal.[f] In the Nocturnal council, the old members represent Reason, the young members represent the two superior senses, serving as instruments and means of communication between Reason and the outer world. The Nocturnal council, embracing the agency of both, maintains thereby the life and continuity of the city.[g]

It is the special duty of this council, to serve as a perpetual embodiment of the original lawgiver, and to comprehend as well as to realise the main purpose for which the city was put together. The councillors must keep constantly in view this grand political end, as the pilot keeps in view safe termination of the voyage—as the military commander keeps in view victory, and the physician, recovery of health. Should the physician or the pilot either not know his end or not know the conditions under which it may be attained—his labour will be in vain. So, if there does not exist in the city an authority understanding the great political end and the means (either by laws or human agents) of accomplishing it, the

---

[d] Plato, Legg. xii. p. 960 C-D. Compare Plato, Republ. vi. p. 497 D. ὅτι δέησοί τι ἀεὶ ἐνεῖναι ἐν τῇ πόλει, λόγον ἔχον τῆς πολιτείας τὸν αὐτὸν ὅνπερ καὶ σὺ ὁ νομοθέτης ἔχων τοὺς νόμους ἐτίθης.

[e] Plato, Legg. xii. p. 961 A-B.
[f] Plato, Legg. xii. p. 961 D.
[g] Plato, Legg. xii. pp. 964 D-965 A.

‹city will be a failure. Hence the indispensable necessity
‹ of the Nocturnal council, with members properly taught and
‹ organised.[h]

The great political end must be one, and not many. All
the arrows aimed by the central Conservative organ This Council must keep steadily in view the one great end of the city—
must be aimed at one and the same point.[1] This is
the chief excellence of a well-constituted conserva-
tive authority. Existing cities err all of them in one Mistakes made by existing cities about the right end.
of two ways. Either they aim at one single End, but
that End bad and wrong: or they aim at a variety
of Ends without giving exclusive attention to any one. Survey existing cities: you will find that in one, the great purpose, and the main feature of what passes for justice, is, that
some party or faction shall obtain or keep political power,
whether its members be better or worse than their fellow-
citizens: in a second city, it is wealth—in a third, freedom of
individuals—in a fourth, freedom combined with power over
foreigners. Some cities, again, considering themselves wiser
than the rest, strive for all these objects at once or for a
variety of others, without exclusive attention to any one.[k]
Amidst such divergence and error in regard to the main end,
we cannot wonder that all cities fail in attaining it.

The One End proposed by *our* city is, the virtue of its
citizens. But virtue is fourfold, or includes four The one end of the city is the virtue of its citizens—
varieties—Courage, Prudence, Temperance, Justice.
Our End is and must be One. The medical Reason that property which is common to the four varieties of Virtue—Reason, Courage, Temperance, Justice.
has its One End, Good Health:[1] the stratêgic Rea-
son has its One End—Victory: What is that One
End (analogous to these) which the political Reason
aims at? It must be that in which the four cardinal

---

[h] Plato, Legg. xii. p. 962 A-B. δεῖ
—εἶναί τι τὸ γίγνωσκον ἐν αὑτῷ (the
city) πρῶτον μὲν τοῦτο ὃ λέγομεν, τὸν
σκοπὸν, ὃς τίς ποτε ὁ πολιτικὸς ὢν ἡμῖν
τυγχάνει, ἔπειτα ὅντινα τρόπον δεῖ μετα-
σχεῖν τούτου καὶ τίς αὐτῷ καλῶς ἢ μὴ
συμβουλεύει τῶν νόμων αὐτῶν πρῶτον,
ἔπειτα ἀνθρώπων.

[1] Plato, Legg. xii. p. 962 C. δεῖ δὴ
τούτου (the nocturnal synod) πᾶσαν
ἀρετὴν ἔχειν, ἧς ἄρχει τὸ μὴ πλανᾶσθαι
πρὸς πολλὰ στοχαζόμενον, ἀλλ᾽ εἰς ἓν
βλέποντα πρὸς τοῦτο ἀεὶ τὰ πάντα οἷον
βέλη ἀφιέναι.

[k] Plato, Legg. xii. p. 962 D-E,
Compare Aristot. Eth. Nikom. x. 1180.
a. 26.

[1] Plato, Legg. xii. p. 963 B. νοῦν
γὰρ δὴ κυβερνητικὸν μὲν καὶ ἰατρικὸν
καὶ στρατηγικὸν εἴπομεν εἰς τὸ ἓν ἐκεῖνο
οἷ δεῖ βλέπειν, τὸν δὲ πολιτικὸν ἐλέγ-
χοντες ἐνταῦθ᾽ ἐσμὲν νῦν—Ὦ θαυμάσιε,
σὺ δὲ δὴ ποῖ σκοπεῖς ; τί ποτ᾽ ἐκεῖνό
ἐστι τὸ ἕν, ὃ δὴ σαφῶς ὁ μὲν ἰατρικὸς
νοῦς ἔχει φράζειν, σὺ δ᾽ ὢν δὴ διαφέρων,
ὡς φαίης ἄν, πάντων τῶν ἐμφρόνων, οὐχ
ἕξεις εἰπεῖν ;

virtues—Courage, Prudence, Temperance, Justice—are One,
or coincide: that common property, possessed by all and by
each, which makes them to be virtue, and constitutes the
essential meaning of the name, Virtue. We must know the
four as four, that is, the points of difference between them:
but it is yet more important to know them as One—to discern
the point of essential coincidence and union between them.[m]

To understand thoroughly this unity of virtue, so as to act
The Noc-
turnal Coun-
cil must com-
prehend this
unity of Vir-
tue, explain
it to others,
and watch
that it be
carried out
in detail.
upon it themselves, to explain it to others and to
embody it in all their orders—is the grand requisite
for the supreme Guardians of our city—the Nocturnal council. We cannot trust such a function in
the hands of poets, or of visiting discoursers who
announce themselves as competent to instruct youth.
It cannot be confided to any less authority than the chosen
men—the head and senses—of our city, properly and specially trained to exercise it.[n] Upon this depends the entire
success or failure of our results. Our guardians must be
taught to see that One Idea which pervades the Multiple and
the Diverse:[o] to keep it steadily before their own eyes, and
to explain and illustrate it in discourse to others. They must
contemplate the point of coincidence and unity between
Courage, Prudence, Temperance, Justice: as well as between
the many different things called Beautiful, and the many different things called Good.[p] They must declare whether the
name Virtue, common to all the four, means something One—
or a Whole or Aggregate—or both together.[q] If they cannot
explain to us whether Virtue is Manifold or Fourfold, or in
what manner it is One—they are unfit for their task, and
our city will prove a failure. To know the truth about
these important matters—to be competent to explain and
defend it to others—to follow it out in practice, and to apply
it in discriminating what is well done and what is ill done—

---

[m] Plato, Legg. xii. pp. 963 E-964 A.
[n] Plato, Legg. xii. p. 964 D.
[o] Plato, Legg. xii. p. 965 C. τὸ
πρὸς μίαν ἰδέαν ἐκ τῶν πολλῶν καὶ
ἀνομοίων δυνατὸν εἶναι βλέπειν.
[p] Plato, Legg. xii. pp. 965 D, 966
A-B.
[q] Plato, Legg. xii. p. 965 E.   πρὶν ἂν

ἱκανῶς εἴπωμεν τί ποτ' ἔστιν, εἰς ὃ
βλεπτέον, εἴτε ὡς ἓν, εἴτε ὡς ὅλον,
εἴτε ὡς ἀμφότερα, εἴτε ὅπως ποτε
πέφυκεν· ἢ τούτου διαφυγόντος ἡμᾶς
οἰόμεθά ποτε ἡμῖν ἱκανῶς ἕξειν τὰ πρὸς
ἀρετὴν, περὶ ἧς οὔτε εἰ πολλὰ ἔστ', οὔτ'
εἰ τέτταρα, οὔθ' ὡς ἓν, δυνατοὶ φράζειν
ἐσόμεθα;

these are the imperative and indispensable duties of our Guardians.[r]

Farthermore it is also essential that they should adopt an orthodox religious creed, and should be competent to explain and defend it.   The citizens generally must believe without scrutiny such dogmas as the lawgiver enjoins; but the Guardians must master the proofs of them.[s]   The proofs upon which, in Plato's view, all true piety rests, are two[t] (he here repeats them) :—1. Mind or Soul is older than Body—anterior to Body as a moving power—and invested with power to impel, direct, and controul Body. 2. When we contemplate the celestial rotation, we perceive such extreme exactness and regularity in the movement of the stars (each one of the vast multitude maintaining its relative position in the midst of prodigious velocity of movement) that we cannot explain it except by supposing a Reason or Intelligence pervading and guiding them all.   Many astronomers have ascribed this regular movement to an inherent Necessity, and have hereby drawn upon science reproaches from poets and others, as if it were irreligious.   But these astronomers (Plato affirms) were quite mistaken in excluding Mind and Reason from the celestial bodies, and in pronouncing the stars to be bodies without mind, like earth or stones.   Necessity cannot account for their exact and regular movements: no other supposition is admissible except the constant volition of mind in-dwelling in each, impelling and guiding them towards exact goodness of result.   Astronomy well understood is, in Plato's view, the foundation of true piety.   It is only the erroneous astronomical doctrines which are open to the current imputations of irreligion.[u]

They must also adopt, explain, and enforce upon the citizens, an orthodox religious creed. Fundamental dogmas of such creed.

These are the capital religious or kosmical dogmas which the members of the Nocturnal Council must embrace and expound to others, together with the mathematical and musical teaching suitable to illustrate them.   Application must

---

[r] Plato, Legg. xii. p. 966 B.
[s] Plato, Legg. xii. p. 966 D.
[t] Plato, Legg. xii. p. 967 E.
[u] Plato, Legg. xii. p. 967 A-D. διανοίαις βουλήσεως ἀγαθῶν περὶ τελου-

μένων—μήποτ' ἂν ἄψυχα ὄντα οὕτως εἰς ἀκρίβειαν θαυμαστοῖς λογισμοῖς ἂν ἐχρῆτο, νοῦν μὴ κεκτημένα— τόν τε εἰρημένον ἐν τοῖς ἄστροις νοῦν τῶν ὄντων.

be made of these dogmas to improve the laws and customs of the city, and the dispositions of the citizens.[x]

When this Nocturnal Council, with its members properly trained and qualified, shall be established in the akropolis—symbolising the conjunction of Reason with the head or with the two knowledge-giving senses—the Magnêtic City may securely be entrusted to it, with certainty of an admirable result.[y]

EPINOMIS.

Here closes the dialogue called Leges: somewhat prematurely, since the peculiar training indispensable for these Nocturnal Counsellors has not yet been declared. The short dialogue called Epinomis supplies this defect. It purports to be a second day's conversation between the same trio.

Leges close, without describing the education proper for the Nocturnal Counsellors. *Epinomis* — supplying this defect.

The Athenian—adverting to the circumstances of human life generally, as full of toil and suffering, with few and transient moments of happiness—remarks that none except the wise have any chance of happiness; and that few can understand what real wisdom is, though every one presumes that there must be something of the kind discoverable.[z] He first enumerates what *it is not*. It is not any of the useful arts—husbandry, house-building, metallurgy, weaving, pottery, hunting, &c.: nor is it prophecy, or the understanding of omens: nor any of the elegant arts—music, poetry, painting: nor the art of war, or navigation, or medicine, or forensic eloquence: nor does it consist in the natural endowments of quick wit and good memory.[a] True wisdom is something different from all these. It consists in arithmetic, geometry, astronomy, leading to a full comprehension of the regular movements of the Kosmos—combined with a correct religious creed as to the divine attributes of the Kosmos and its planetary bodies, which are all pervaded and kept in harmonious rotation by

The Athenian declares his plan of education—Arithmetic, Geometry, Astronomy.

[x] Plato, Legg. xii. p. 967 E.
[y] Plat. Legg. xii. p. 969 B.

[z] Plat. Epinom. pp. 973-974.
[a] Plat. Epinom. pp. 975-976.

divine, in-dwelling, soul or mind.[b] It is the God Uranus (or Olympus, or Kosmos), with the visible Gods included therein, who furnishes to us not only the gifts of the seasons and the growth of food, but also varied intelligence, especially the knowledge of number, without which no other knowledge would be attainable.[c] Number and proportion are essential conditions of every variety of art. The regular succession of night and day, and the regularly changing phases of the moon —the comparison of months with the year—first taught us to count, and to observe the proportions of numbers to each other.[d]

The Athenian now enters upon the directly theological point of view, and re-asserts the three articles of orthodoxy which he had laid down in the tenth book of Leges: together with the other point of faith also—That Soul or Mind is older than body: soul is active and ruling—body, passive and subject. An animal is a compound of both. There are five elementary bodies—fire, air, æther, water, earth[e]—which the kosmical soul moulded, in varying proportions, so as to form different animals and plants. Man, animals, and plants, were moulded chiefly of earth, yet with some intermixture of the other elements: the stars were moulded chiefly from fire, having the most beautiful bodies, endowed with divine and happy souls, and immortal, or very long-lived.[f] Next to the stars were moulded the Dæmons, out of æther, and inhabitants of that element: after them, the animals inhabiting air, and Nymphs inhabiting water. These three occupy intermediate place between the stars above and man below.[g] They serve as media of communication between man and the Gods: and also for the diffusion of thought and intelligence

Theological view of Astronomy— Divine Kosmos—Soul more ancient and more sovereign than Body.

---

[b] Plat. Epinom. pp. 976-977.
[c] Plat. Epinom. pp. 977-978.
[d] Plat. Epinom. pp. 978-979.
[e] Plat. Epinom. pp. 980-981. We know, from a curious statement of Xenokrates (see Fragm. of his work Περὶ τοῦ Πλάτωνος βίου, cited by Simplikius, ad Aristot. Physic. p. 427, a. 17, Schol. Brandis), that this quintuple elementary scale was a doctrine of Plato. But it is not the doctrine of the Timæus. The assertion of Xeno-

krates (good evidence) warrants us in believing that Plato altered his views after the composition of Timæus, and that his latest opinions are represented in the Epinomis. Zeller indeed thinks that the dodekahedron in the Timæus might be construed as a fifth element, but this is scarcely tenable. Zeller, Philos. der Griechen, vol. ii. p. 513, ed. 2nd.
[f] Plat. Epinom. pp. 981-982.
[g] Plat. Epinom. pp. 983-984.

among all parts of the Kosmos.[h] The Gods of the ordinary
faith—Zeus, Hêrê, and others—must be left to each person's
disposition, if he be inclined to worship them: but the great
visible Kosmos, and the sidereal Gods, must be solemnly exalted and sanctified, with prayer and the holiest rites.[i] Those
astronomers who ignore this divine nature, and profess to
explain their movements by physical or mechanical forces,
are guilty of grave impiety. The regularity of their movements is a proof of their divine nature, not a proof of the
contrary, as some misguided persons affirm.[k]

Next, the Athenian intimates that the Greeks have ob-
Improving effects of the study of Astronomy in this spirit. tained their astronomical knowledge, in the first
instance, from Egypt and Assyria, but have much
improved upon what they learnt (p. 987): that the
Greeks at first were acquainted only with the three φοραὶ—
the outer or sidereal sphere ('Απλανὴς), the Sun, and the
Moon—but unacquainted with the other five or planetary
φοραὶ, which they first learned from these foreigners, though
not the names of the planets (p. 986): that all these eight
were alike divine, fraternal agents, partakers in the same
rational nature, and making up altogether the divine Κόσμος:
that those who did not recognise all the eight as divine, con-
summately rational, and revolving with perfectly uniform
movement, were guilty of impiety (p. 985 E): that these
kosmical, divine, rational agents taught to mankind arithmetic and the art of numeration (p. 988 B): that soul, or
plastic, demiurgic, cognitive force (p. 981 C), was an older
and more powerful agent in the universe than body—but that
there were two varieties of soul, a good and bad, of which the
good variety was the stronger: the good variety of soul produced all the good movements, the bad variety produced all
the bad movements (p. 988 D, E): that in studying astronomy, a man submitted himself to the teaching of this good
soul and these divine agents, from whom alone he could learn
true wisdom and piety (pp. 989 B-990 A): that this study,
however, must be conducted not with a view to know the
times of rising and setting of different stars (like Hesiod),

---

[h] Plat. Epinom. p. 985.   [i] Plat. Epinom. pp. 984 D-985 D.
[k] Plat. Epinom. pp. 982 D, 983 C.

but to be able to understand and follow the eight περιφοράς (p. 990 B).

To understand these—especially the five planetary and difficult περιφορὰς—arithmetic must also be taught, not in the concrete, but in the abstract (p. 990 C, D), to understand how much the real nature of things is determined by the generative powers and combination of Odd and Even Number. Next, geometry also must be studied, so as to compare numbers with plane and solid figures, and thus to determine proportions between two numbers which are not directly commensurable. The varieties of proportion, which are marvellously combined, must be understood—first arithmetical and geometrical proportions, the arithmetical proportion increasing by equal addition (1+1 = 2), or the point into a line—then the geometrical proportion by way of multiplication ($2 \times 2 = 4$; $4 \times 2 = 8$), or the line raised into a surface, and the surface raised into a cube. Moreover there are two other varieties of proportion (τὸ ἡμιόλιον or sesquialterum, and τὸ ἐπίτριτον or sesquitertium), both of which occur in the numbers between the ratio of 6 to 12 (i. e. 9 is τὸ ἡμιόλιον of 6, or $9 = 6 + \frac{6}{2}$; again, 8 is τὸ ἐπίτριτον of 6, or $8 = 6 + \frac{6}{3}$). This last is *harmonic proportion*, when there are three terms, of which the third is as much greater than the middle, as the middle is greater than the first (3 : 4 : 6)—six is greater than four by one-third of six, while four is greater than three by one-third of three (p. 991 A).

Study of arithmetic and geometry: varieties of proportion.

Lastly, having thus come to comprehend the general forms of things, we must bring under them properly the visible individuals in nature; and in this process interrogation and cross-examination must be applied (p. 991 C). We must learn to note the accurate regularity with which time brings all things to maturity, and we shall find reason to believe that all things are full of Gods (p. 991 D). We shall come to perceive that there is one law of proportion pervading every geometrical figure, every numerical series, every harmonic combination, and all the celestial rotations: one and the

When the general forms of things have thus been learnt, particular individuals in nature must be brought under them.

same bond of union among all (p. 991 E). These sciences, whether difficult or easy, must be learnt: for without them no happy nature will be ever planted in our cities (p. 992 A). The man who learns all this will be the truly wise and happy man, both in this life and after it; only a few men can possibly arrive at such happiness (p. 992 C). But it is these chosen few, who, when they become Elders, will compose our Nocturnal Council, and maintain unimpaired the perpetual purity of the Platonic City.

Such then is the answer given by the Epinomis, to the question left unanswered in the Leges. However unsatisfactory it may appear, to those who look for nothing but what is admirable in Plato—I believe it to represent the latest views of his old age, when dialectic had given place in his mind to the joint ascendancy of theological sentiment and Pythagorean arithmetic.[1]

Question as to education of the Nocturnal Council is answered in the Epinomis.

[1] In connection with the treatise called Epinomis, the question arises, What were the modifications which Plato's astronomical doctrines underwent during the latter years of his life? In what respect did they come to differ from what we read in the Platonic Timæus, where a geocentric system is proclaimed: whether we suppose (as Boeckh and others do) that the Earth is represented as stationary at the centre—or (as I suppose) that the Earth is represented as fastened to the centre of the kosmical axis, and revolving with it. The Epinomis delivers a geocentric system also.

Now it is upon this very point that Plato's opinions are said to have changed towards the close of his life. He came to repent that he had assigned to the Earth the central place in the system; and to conceive that place as belonging properly to something else, some other better (or more powerful) body. This is a curious statement, made in two separate passages by Plutarch, and in one of the two passages with reference to Theophrastus as his witness (Plutarch, Vit. Numæ, c. 11; Platonic. Quæst. 8, p. 1006 C).

Boeckh (Untersuchungen über das Kosmische System des Platon, pp. 144-149) and Martin (Études sur le Timée, ii. 91) discredit the statement ascribed by Plutarch to Theophrastus. But I see no sufficient ground for such discredit. Sir George Lewis remarks very truly (Historical Survey of the Astronomy of the Ancients, p. 143):— "The testimony of Theophrastus, the disciple of Aristotle and nearly his contemporary, has' great weight upon this point. The ground of the opinion alludes to the Pythagorean doctrine mentioned by Aristotle, that the centre is the most dignified place, and that the earth is not the first in dignity among the heavenly bodies. It has no reference to observed phenomena, and is not founded on inductive scientific arguments. The doctrine as to the superior dignity of the central place, and of the impropriety of assigning this most dignified station to the earth—was of Pythagorean origin, and was probably combined with the Philolaic cosmology."

This remark of Sir George Lewis deserves attention, not merely from the proper value which he assigns to the testimony of Theophrastus, but because he confines himself to the exact matter which Theophrastus affirmed; viz., that Plato in his old age came to repent of his own kosmical views on one particular point and on one special ground. Theophrastus does not tell us what it was that Plato supposed to be in the

Assuming that the magistrates of the Nocturnal Council have gone through the course of education prescribed in the Epinomis, and have proved themselves unimpeachable on the score of orthodoxy —will they be able to solve the main problem which he has imposed upon them at the close of the Leges? There, as elsewhere, he proclaims a problem as indispensable to be solved, but does not himself furnish any solution. What is the common property, or point of similarity, between Prudence, Courage, Temperance, Justice—by reason of which each is termed Virtue? What are the characteristic points of difference, by reason of which Virtue sometimes receives one of these names, sometimes another?

Problem which the Nocturnal Council are required to solve, What is the common property of Prudence, Courage, Temperance, Justice, by reason of which each is called Virtue.

centre, after he had become convinced that it was too dignified a place for the earth. Plato *may* have come to adopt the positive opinion of Philolaus (that of a central fire) as well as the negative opinion (that the Earth was not the central body). But we cannot affirm that he *did* adopt either this positive opinion or any other positive opinion upon that point. I take Theophrastus to have affirmed exactly what Plutarch makes him affirm, and no more : that Plato came to repent of having assigned to the earth the central place which did not befit it, and to account the centre the fit place "for some other body better than the Earth," yet without defining what that other body was. If Theophrastus had named what the other body was, surely Plutarch would never have suppressed the specific designation to make room for the vague ἑτέρῳ τινὶ κρείττονι.

There is thus, in my judgment, ground for believing that Plato in his old age (after the publication of the Treatise De Legibus) came to distrust the geocentric dogma which he had previously supported; but we do not know whether he adopted any other dogma in place of it. The geocentric doctrine passed to the Epinomis as a continuation of the Treatise De Legibus. The phrase which Plutarch cites from Theophrastus deserves notice—Θεόφραστος δὲ καὶ προσιστορεῖ τῷ Πλάτωνι πρεσβυτέρῳ γενομένῳ μεταμελεῖν, ὡς οὐ προσήκουσαν ἀποδόντι τῇ γῇ τὴν μέσην

χώραν τοῦ παντός. Plato *repented.* Whoever reads the Treatise De Legibus (especially Books vii. and x.) will see that Plato at that period of his life considered astronomical errors as not merely errors, but heresies offensive to the Gods ; and that he denounced those who supported such errors as impious. If Plato came afterwards to alter his astronomical views, he would *repent* of his own previous views as of a heresy. He came to believe that he had rated the dignity of the Earth too high; and we can see how this change of view may have been occasioned. Earth was looked upon by him, as well as by many others, in two distinct points of view. 1. As a kosmical body, divine, and including τοὺς χθονίους θεούς. 2. As one of the four elements, along with water, air, and fire ; in which sense it was strung together with λίθοι, and had degrading ideas associated with it (Plato, Apol. Sokr. p. 26 D). These two meanings, not merely distinct but even opposed to each other, occur in the very same sentence of De Legibus, x. p. 886 D. The elemental sense of Earth was brought prominently forward by those reasoners whom Plato refutes in Book x.: and the effect of such reasonings upon him was, that though he still regarded Earth as a Deity, he no longer continued to regard Earth as worthy of the kosmical post of honour. At that age, however, he might well consider himself excused from broaching any new positive theory.

The proper way of answering this question has been much
debated, from Plato's day down to the present. It
is one of the fundamental problems of Ethical Philosophy.

The subjective matter of fact, implied by every
one who designates an act or a person as virtuous,
is an approving or admiring sentiment which each
man knows in his own bosom. But Plato assumes
that there is, besides this, an objective connotation: a common
object or property, to which such sentiment refers. What
is that common object? I see no other except that which
is indicated by the principle of Utility: I mean that principle
which points out Happiness and Unhappiness, not merely of
the agent himself, but also of others affected or liable to be
affected by his behaviour, as the standard to which these denominations refer. Courage, Prudence, Temperance, Justice,
all tend to prevention and mitigation of unhappiness, and to
increase of happiness, as well for the agent himself as for the
society surrounding him. The opposite qualities—Timidity,
Imprudence, Intemperance, Injustice—tend with equal certainty either to increase positively the unhappiness of the
agent and of society, or to remove the means for warding it
off or abating it. Indeed there is a certain minimum of all
the four—Courage, Prudence, Temperance, Justice—without
which or below which neither society could hold together,
nor the life of the individual agent himself could be continued.

The only common property is that all of them are essential to the maintenance of society, and tend to promote human security and happiness.

Here then is one answer at least to the question of Plato.
Courage, Prudence, Temperance, Justice—all of
them mental attributes of rational voluntary agents—
have also the common property of being, in a certain
minimum degree, absolutely essential to the life of
the agent and the maintenance of society—and of being,
above that degree, tutelary against the suffering, and beneficial to the happiness, of both. This tutelary or beneficent
tendency is the common objective property signified by the
general term Virtue; and is implicated with the subjective
property before mentioned—the sentiment of approbation.
The four opposite qualities are designated by the general

Tendency of the four opposite quali-ties to lessen human hap-piness.

term Vice or Defect, connoting both maleficent tendency and the sentiment of disapprobation.

This proposition will be farther confirmed, if we look at all the four qualities—Courage, Prudence, Temperance, Justice—in another point of view.   Taking them in their reference to Virtue, each of them belongs to Virtue as a part to the whole,[m] not as one species contradistinguished from and excluding other species. The same person may have, and ought to have, a certain measure of all : he will not be called virtuous unless he has a measure of all.   Excellence in any one will not compensate for the entire absence of the others.

A certain measure of all the four virtues is required. In judging of particular acts instigated by each, there is always a tacit reason to the hurt or benefit in the special case.

A just and temperate man will not be accounted virtuous, if (to use an Aristotelian simile) he be so extravagantly timid as to fear every insect that flits by, or the noise of a mouse.[n] All probability of beneficent results from his agency is effaced by this capital defect : and it is the probability of such results which constitutes his title to be called virtuous.

When we speak of the four as qualities or attributes of men (as Plato does in this treatise, while considering the proper type of character which the lawgiver should aim at forming) we speak of them in the abstract—that is, making abstraction of particular circumstances, and regarding only what is common to most men in most situations.   But in the realities of life these particulars are always present : there is a series of individual agents and patients, acts and sufferings, each surrounded by its own distinct circumstances and situation. Now in each of these situations an agent is held responsible for the consequences of his acts, when they are such as he knows and foresees, or might by reasonable care know and foresee.   An officer who (like Charles XII. at Bender) marches up without necessity at the head of a corporal's guard to attack a powerful hostile army of good soldiers,

---

[m] Compare Plato, Legg. i. p. 629 B, where he describes τὴν ξύμπασαν ἀρετὴν —δικαιοσύνη καὶ σωφροσύνη καὶ φρόνησις εἰς ταὐτὸν ἐλθοῦσα μετ' ἀνδρίας : also pp. 630 C-E, 631 A, where he considers all these as μόρια ἀρετῆς, but φρόνησις as the first of the four

and ἀνδρία as the last.
  See also iii. pp. 688 B, 696 C-D, iv. p. 705 D.
  [n] Aristot. Ethic. Nikomach. vii. 6, p. 1148, a. 8 ; Politic. vii. 1, p. 1323, a. 29.   κἂν ψοφήσῃ μῦς — δεδιὼς τὰς παραπετομένας μύιας.

exhibits the maximum of courage : but his act, far from being commended as virtue, must be blamed as rashness, or pitied as folly. If a friend has deposited in my care a sword or other deadly weapon (to repeat the very case put by Sokrates[o]), justice requires me to give it back to him when he asks for it. Yet if, at the time when he asks, he be insane, and exhibits plain indications of being about to employ it for murderous purposes, my just restoration of it will not be commended as an act of virtue. When we look at these four qualities—Courage, Prudence, Temperance, Justice—not in the abstract, but in reference to particular acts, agents, and situations—we find that before a just or courageous act can be considered to deserve the name of Virtue, there is always a tacit supposition, that no considerable hurt to innocent persons is likely or predictable from it in the particular case. The sentiment of approbation, implied in the name Virtue, will not go along with the act, if in the particular case it produce a certain amount of predictable mischief. This is another property common to all the four attributes of mind—Courage, Prudence, Temperance, Justice :—and forming one of the conditions under which they become entitled to the denomination of Virtue.

In the first books of the Leges, Plato[p] puts forward Courage, Prudence, Temperance, Justice, as the parts or sorts of Virtue : telling us that the natural rectitude of laws consists in promoting, not any one of the four separately, but all the four together in their due subordination. He classifies good things (Bona or Expetenda) in a triple scale of value.[q]

Plato places these four virtues in the highest scale of Expetenda or Bona, on the ground that all the other Bona are sure to flow from them.

First, and best of all, come the mental attributes—which he calls divine—Prudence or Intelligence, Temperance,

<hr/>

[o] Plato, Republic, i. p. 331 C ; Xenoph. Memor. iv. 2, 17 ; Cicero, De Officiis, iii. 25.

[p] Plato, Legg. i. pp. 627 D, 631 A-C.

[q] Plato, Legg. i. p. 631 B-D, iii. p. 697 B. This tripartite classification of Bona differs altogether from the tripartite classification of Bona given at the commencement of the second book of the Republic. But it agrees with that, the "tria genera Bonorum,"

distinguished by Aristotle in the first book of the Nikomachean Ethics (p. 1098, b. 12), among which τὰ περὶ ψυχὴν were κυριώτατα καὶ μάλιστα ἀγαθά. This recognition of "tria genera Bonorum" is sometimes quoted as an opinion characteristic of the Peripatetics : but Aristotle himself declares it to be ancient and acknowledged, and we certainly have it here in Plato.

Justice, and Courage: Second, or second best, come the
attributes of body—health, strength, beauty, activity, manual
dexterity: Third, or last, come the extraneous advantages,
Wealth, Power, Family-Position, &c. It is the duty of the
lawgiver to employ his utmost care to ensure to his citizens
the first description of Bona (the mental attributes)—upon
which (Plato says) the second and third description depend,
so that if the first are ensured, the second and third will be
certain to follow: while· if the lawgiver, neglecting the first,
aims at the second and third exclusively or principally, he
will miss all three.[r] Here we see, that while Plato assigns
the highest scale of value to the mental attributes, he justifies
such preference by assuring us that they are the essential
producing causes of the other sorts of Bona. His assurance
is even given in terms more unqualified than the realities of
life will bear out.

When Plato therefore proclaims it as the great desideratum
for his Supreme Council, that they shall understand
the common relation of the four great mental attributes (Courage, Prudence, Temperance, Justice) to
each other as well as to the comprehensive whole,
Virtue — he fastens their attention on the only
common property which the four can be found to
possess: *i.e.* that they are mental attributes required
in every one for the security and comfort of himself
and of society. To ward off or mitigate the suffering, and to improve the comfort of society, is thus
inculcated as the main and constant End for them to keep
in view. It is their prescribed task, to preserve and carry
forward that which he as lawgiver had announced as his purpose in the beginning of the Leges.

In thus directing the attention of the Council to the common property of the four virtues, Plato enforces upon them the necessity of looking to the security and happiness of their community as the paramount end.

In thus taking leave of Plato, at the close of his longest,
latest, and most affirmative composition, it is satisfactory to be able to express unqualified sympathy
with this main purpose which, as departing lawgiver, he directs his successors to promote. But to these

But he enjoins also - other objectionable ends.

---

[r] Plato, Legg. i. p. 631 C. ἤρτηται
δ' ἐκ τῶν θείων θάτερα, καὶ ἐὰν μὲν
δέχηται τὰ μείζονα πόλις, κτᾶται καὶ
τὰ ἐλάσσονα· εἰ δὲ μὴ, στέρεται ἀμφοῖν.
The same doctrine is declared by

Sokrates in the Platonic Apology, pp.
29-30. λέγων, ὅτι οὐκ ἐκ χρημάτων
ἀρετὴ γίγνεται, ἀλλ' ἐξ ἀρετῆς χρήματα
καὶ τἆλλα ἀγαθὰ τοῖς ἀνθρώποις καὶ
ἰδίᾳ καὶ δημοσίᾳ.

salutary directions, unfortunately, he has attached others noway connected with them except by common feelings of reverence in his own mind—and far less deserving of sympathy. He requires that his own religious belief shall be erected into a peremptory orthodoxy, and that heretics shall be put down by the severest penalties. Now a citizen might be perfectly just, temperate, brave, and prudent—and yet dissent altogether from the Platonic creed. For such a citizen—the counterpart of Sokrates at Athens—no existence would be possible in the Platonic community.

We must farther remark that, even when Plato's ends are *Intolerance of Plato— Comparison of the Platonic community with Athens.* unexceptionable, the amount of interference which he employs to accomplish them is often extravagant. As a Constructor, he carries the sentiment of his own infallibility—which in a certain measure every lawgiver must assume—to an extreme worthy only of the kings of the Saturnian age:[s] manifesting the very minimum of tolerance for that enquiring individual reason, of which his own negative dialogues remain as immortal masterpieces. We trace this intolerance through all the dialogue Leges. Even when he condescends to advise and persuade, he speaks rather in the tone of an encyclical censor, than of one who has before him a reasonable opponent to be convinced. The separate laws proposed by Plato are interesting to read, as illustrating antiquity : but most of them are founded on existing Athenian law. Where they depart from it, they depart as often for the worse as for the better—so far as I can pretend to judge. And in spite of all the indisputable defects, political and judicial, of that glorious city, where Plato was born and passed most of his days—it was, in my judgment, preferable to his Magnêtic city, as to all the great objects of security, comfort, recreation, and enjoyment. Athens was preferable, even for the ordinary citizen : but for the men of free, inquisitive, self-thinking, minds—the dissentient minority, who lived upon that open speech of which Athenian orators and poets boasted—it was a condition of existence: since the Platonic censorship would have tolerated neither their doctrines nor their persons.

[s] Plato, Politikus, pp. 271 E, 275 A-C.

APPENDIX.

Since the commencement of the present century, with its increased critical study of Plato, different and opposite opinions have been maintained by various authors respecting the genuineness or spuriousness of the Treatise De Legibus. Schleiermacher (Platons Werke, I. i. p. 51) admitted it as a genuine work of Plato, but ranked it among the Nebenwerke, or outlying dialogues: i.e. as a work that did not form an item or stepping-stone in the main Platonic philosophical series (which Schleiermacher attempts to lay out according to a system of internal sequence and gradual development), but was composed separately, in general analogy with the later or more constructive portion of that series. On the other hand, Ast (Platons Leben und Schriften, pp. 376-392) distinctly maintains that the Treatise De Legibus is not the composition of Plato, but of one of his scholars and contemporaries, perhaps Xenokrates or the Opuntian Philippus. Ast supports this opinion by many internal grounds, derived from a comparison of the treatise with other Platonic dialogues.

Zeller (in his Platonische Studien, Tübingen. 1839, pp. 1-144) discussed the same question in a more copious and elaborate manner, and declared himself decidedly in favour of Ast's opinion—that the Treatise De Legibus was not the work of Plato, but of one among his immediate scholars. But in his History of Grecian Philosophy (vol. ii. pp. 348-615-641, second edition), Zeller departs from this judgment, and pronounces the Treatise to be a genuine work of Plato—the last form of his philosophy, modified in various ways.

Again, Suckow (in his work, Die Wissenschaftliche und künstlerische Form der Platonischen Schriften, Berlin, 1855, I. pp. 111-118 seq.) advocates Zeller's first opinion—that the Treatise De Legibus is not the work of Plato.

Lastly, Stallbaum, in the Prolegomena prefixed to his edition of the Treatise, strenuously vindicates its Platonic authorship. This is also the opinion of Boeckh and K. F. Hermann; and was, moreover, the opinion of all critics (I believe) anterior to Ast.

To me, I confess, it appears that the Treatise De Legibus is among the best authenticated works of the Platonic collection. I do not know what better positive proof can be tendered than the affirmation of Aristotle in his Politics —distinct and unqualified, mentioning both the name of the author and the title of the work, noting also the relation in which it stood to the Republic, both as a later composition of the same author, and as discrepant on some points of doctrine, analogous on others. This in itself is the strongest *primâ facie* evidence, not to be rebutted, except by some counter testimony, or by some internal mark of chronological impossibility: moreover, it coincides with the consentient belief of all the known ancient authors later than Aristotle— such as Persæus, the Alexandrine critics, Cicero, Plutarch, &c. (Stallbaum, Prolegg. p. xliv.) Aristophanes Grammaticus classified both Leges and Epinomis as Plato's works. The arguments produced in Zeller's Platonische Studien, to show that Aristotle may have been mistaken in his assertion, are of little or no force. Nor will it be material to the present question, even if we concede to Zeller and Suckow another point which they contend for—that the remarks of Aristotle upon Plato's opinions are often inaccurate at least, if not unfair. For here Aristotle is produced in court only as a witness to authenticity.

Among the points raised by Suckow, there is indeed one, which if it were made out, would greatly invalidate, if not counterbalance, the testimony of Aristotle. Suckow construes the passage in the Oration of Isokrates ad Philippum (p. 84, § 16)—ὁμοίως οἱ τοιοῦτοι τῶν λόγων ἄκυροι τυγχάνουσιν ὄντες τοῖς νόμοις καὶ ταῖς πολιτείαις ταῖς ὑπὸ τῶν σοφιστῶν γεγραμμέναις—as if it alluded to the Platonic Republic, and to the Treatise De Legibus ; but as if it implied, at the same time, that the two treatises were not composed by the same author, but by different authors, indicated by the plural σοφιστῶν. If this were the true meaning of Isokrates, we should then have Aristotle distinctly contradicted by another respectable contemporary witness, which would of course much impair the value of his testimony.

But Stallbaum (p. lii.) disputes altogether the meaning ascribed by Suckow to the words of Isokrates, and contends that the plural σοφιστῶν noway justifies the hypothesis of a double authorship. So far, I think, he is decidedly right : and this clears away the only one item of counter-testimony which has yet been alleged against Aristotle as a witness. Stallbaum, indeed, goes a step farther. He contends that the passage above cited from Isokrates is an evidence on his side, and against Suckow : that Isokrates alludes to Plato as author of both Republic and Leges, and thus becomes available as a second contemporary witness, confirming the testimony of Aristotle. This is less certain ; yet perhaps supposable. We may imagine that Isokrates, when he composed the passage, had in his mind Plato pre-eminently—then recently dead at a great age, and the most illustrious of all the Sophists who had written upon political theory. The vague and undefined language in which Isokrates speaks, however, sets forth, by contrast, the great evidentiary value of Aristotle's affirmation, which is distinct and specific in the highest degree, declaring Plato to be the author of Leges.

To contradict this affirmation—an external guarantee of unusual force— Zeller produces a case of internal incredibility. The Legg. cannot be the work of Plato (he argues) because of the numerous disparities and marked inferiority of style, handling, and doctrine, which are very frequently un-Platonic, and not seldom anti-Platonic. Whoever will read the Platonische Studien, will see that Zeller has made out a strong case of this sort, set forth with remarkable ability and ingenuity. Indeed, the strength of the case, as to internal discrepancy, is fully admitted by his opponent Stallbaum, who says, in general terms—" Argumentatio quidem et disserendi ratio, quæ in Legibus regnat, ubi considerata fuerit paullo accuratius, dubitare sanè nemo poterit, quin multa propria ac peculiaria habere judicanda sit, quæ ab aliorum librorum Platonicorum usu et consuetudine longissimé récedant." He then proceeds to enumerate in detail many serious points of discrepancy. See the second part (ch. xv.) of his Prolegomena, prefixed to Book v. Legg., and in Prolegg. to his edition of 1859, pp. lv.-lix. But in spite of such undeniable force of internal improbability, Stallbaum still maintains that the Treatise is really the work of Plato. Of course, he does not admit that the whole of the internal evidence is nothing but discrepancy. He points out also much that is homogeneous and Platonic.

I agree with his conclusion (which is also the subsequent conclusion of Zeller) respecting the authorship of Legg. To me the testimony of Aristotle appears conclusive. But when I perceive how strong are the grounds for doubt, so long as we discuss the question on grounds of internal evidence simply (that is, by comparison with other Platonic dialogues)—while yet such doubts are over-ruled, by our fortunately possessing incontestable authenticating evidence *ab extra*—an inference suggests itself to me, of which Platonic critics seem for the most part unconscious. I mean the great fallibility of reasonings founded simply on internal evidence, for the purpose of disproving authenticity, where we have no external evidence, contemporary or nearly contemporary, to controul them. In this condition are the large majority of the dialogues. I do not affirm that such reasonings are *never* to be trusted; but I consider them eminently fallible. To compare together the various dialogues, indeed, and to number as well as to weigh the various instances of analogy and discrepancy between them, is a process always instructive. It is among the direct tasks and obligations of the critic. But when, after detecting discrepancies, more or less grave and numerous, he proceeds to conclude, that the dialogue in which they occur cannot have been composed by Plato, he steps upon ground full of hypothesis and uncertainty. Who is to fix the limit of admissible divergence between the various compositions of a man like Plato? Who can determine what changes may have taken place in Plato's opinions, or point of view, or intellectual powers—during a long literary life of more than fifty years, which we know only in mere outline? Considering that Plato systematically lays aside his own personal identity, and speaks only under the assumed names of different expositors, opponents, and respondents—which of us can claim to possess a full and exhaustive catalogue of all the diverse phases of Platonism, so as to make sure that some unexpected variety has no legitimate title to be ranked among them?

For my part, I confess that these questions appear to me full of doubt and difficulty. I am often surprised at the confidence with which critics, upon the faith of internal evidence purely and simply, pronounce various dialogues of the Platonic collection to be spurious. A lesson of diffidence may be learnt from the Leges: which, if internal evidence alone were accessible, would stand among the questionable items of the Platonic catalogue—while it now takes rank among the most unquestionable, from the complete external certificate which has been fortunately preserved to us.

Stallbaum, who maintains the authenticity of the Platonic Leges, disallows altogether that of the Epinomis. In his long and learned Prolegg. (vol. iii. p. 441-470), he has gone over the whole case, and stated at length his reasons for this opinion. I confess that his reasons do not satisfy me. If, on the faith of those reasons, I rejected the Epinomis, I should also on the grounds stated by Ast and Zeller reject the Leges. The reasons against the Leges are of the same character and tenor as those against the Epinomis, and scarce at all less weighty. Respecting both of them, it may be shewn that they are greatly inferior in excellence to the Republic and the other masterpieces of the Platonic genius, and that they contain points of doctrine and reasoning different from what we read in other Platonic works. But when, from these premisses, I am called upon to admit that they are not the works of Plato, I cannot assent either about the one or the other. I have already observed that I expect to find among his genuine compositions, some inferior in merit, others dissentient in doctrine—especially in compositions admitted to belong to his oldest age. All critics from Aristophanes down to Tennemann, have admitted the Epinomis as genuine: and when Stallbaum contends that Diogenes mentions doubts on the point entertained even in antiquity—I think he is not warranted by the words of that author, iii. 37: ἔνιοι δέ φασιν, ὅτι Φίλιππος ὁ Ὀπούντιος τοὺς Νόμους αὐτοῦ (Πλάτωνος) μετέγραψεν ὄντας ἐν κηρῷ· τούτου δὲ καὶ τὴν Ἐπινομίδα φασὶν εἶναι. I do not think we can infer from these words anything more than this—that "Philippus transcribed the Epinomis also out of the waxen tablet as he had

transcribed the Leges." The persons (whosoever they were—ἔνιοι) to whom
Diogenes refers, considered Philippus as in part the author of the Νόμοι; because
he had first transcribed them in a legible form from the rough original, and
might possibly have introduced changes of his own in the transcription. If
they had meant to distinguish what he did in respect to the Leges, from what
he did in respect to the Epinomis: if they had meant to assert that he transcribed the Leges, but that he composed the Epinomis as an original addition
of his own; I think they would have employed, not the conjunction καί, but
some word indicating contrast and antithesis.

But even if we concede that the persons here alluded to by Diogenes did
really believe, that the Epinomis was the original composition of Philippus and
not of Plato—we must remember that all the critics of antiquity known to us
believed the contrary—that it was the genuine work of Plato. In particular,
Aristophanes Grammaticus acknowledges it as such; enrolling it in one trilogy
with the Minos and the Leges. The testimony of Aristophanes, and the records
of the Alexandrine Library in his time, greatly outweigh the suspicions of the
unknown critics alluded to by Diogenes; even if we admit that those critics did
really conceive the Epinomis as an actual composition of Philippus.

CHAPTER XXXVIII.

OTHER COMPANIONS OF SOKRATES.

HAVING dwelt at some length on the life and compositions of Plato, I now proceed to place in comparison with him some other members of the Sokratic philosophical family: less eminent, indeed, than the illustrious author of the Republic, yet still men of marked character, ability, and influence.[a] Respecting one of the brethren, Xenophon, who stands next to Plato in celebrity, I shall say a few words separately in my next and concluding chapter.

The ascendancy of Sokrates over his contemporaries was powerfully exercised in more than one way. He brought into vogue new subjects both of indefinite amplitude, and familiar as well as interesting to every one. On these subjects, moreover, he introduced, or at least popularised, a new method of communication, whereby the relation of teacher and learner, implying a direct transfer of ready-made knowledge from the one to the other, was put aside. He substituted an interrogatory process, at once destructive and suggestive, in which the teacher began by unteaching and the learner by unlearning what was supposed to be already known, for the purpose of provoking in the learner's mind a self-operative energy of thought, and an internal generation of new notions. Lastly, Sokrates worked forcibly upon the minds of several friends, who were in the habit of attending him when he talked in the market-place or the palæstra. Some tried to copy his wonderful knack of colloquial cross-examination: how far they did so with success or reputation we do not know: but Xenophon says that several

Side note: Influence exercised by Sokrates over his companions.

---

[a] Dionysius of Halikarnassus contrasts Plato with τὸ Σωκράτους διδασκαλείον πᾶν (De Adm. Vi Dic. Demosthen. p. 956). Compare also Epistol. ad Cn. Pomp. p. 762, where he contrasts the style and phraseology of Plato with that of the Σωκρατικοὶ διάλογοι generally.

of them would only discourse with those who paid them a fee, and that they thus sold for considerable sums what were only small fragments obtained gratuitously from the rich table of their master.[b] There were moreover several who copied the general style of his colloquies by composing written dialogues. And thus it happened that the great master,—he who passed his life in the oral application of his Elenchus, without writing anything,—though he left no worthy representative in his own special career, became the father of numerous written dialogues and of a rich philosophical literature.[c]

Besides Plato and Xenophon, whose works are known to us,

Names of those companions.

we hear of Alexamenus, Antisthenes, Æschines, Aristippus, Bryson, Eukleides, Phædon, Kriton, Simmias, Kebês, &c., as having composed dialogues of this sort. All of them were companions of Sokrates; several among them either set down what they could partially recollect of his conversations, or employed his name as a dramatic speaker of their own thoughts. Seven of these dialogues were ascribed to Æschines, twenty-five to Aristippus, seventeen to Kriton, twenty-three to Simmias, three to Kebês, six to Eukleides, four to Phædon. The compositions of Antisthenes were far more numerous: ten volumes of them, under a variety of distinct titles (some of them probably not in the form of dialogues) being recorded by Diogenes.[d] Aristippus was the first of the line of philosophers

---

[b] Xenophon, Memor. i. 2, 60. ὧν τινὲς μικρὰ μέρη παρ᾽ ἐκείνου προῖκα λαβόντες πολλοῦ τοῖς ἄλλοις ἐπώλουν, καὶ οὐκ ἦσαν ὥσπερ ἐκεῖνος δημοτικοί· τοῖς γὰρ μὴ ἔχουσι χρήματα διδόναι οὐκ ἤθελον διαλέγεσθαι.

[c] We find a remarkable proof how long the name and conception of Sokrates lasted in the memory of the Athenian public, as having been the great progenitor of the philosophy and philosophers of the fourth century B.C. in Athens. It was about 306 B.C., almost a century after the death of Sokrates, that Democharês (the nephew of the orator Demosthenes) delivered an oration before the Athenian judicature for the purpose of upholding the law proposed by Sophokles, forbidding philosophers or Sophists to lecture without a license obtained from the government; which law, passed a year before, had determined

the secession of all the philosophers from Athens until the law was repealed. In this oration Demochares expatiated on the demerits of many philosophers, their servility, profligate ambition, rapacity, want of patriotism, &c., from which Athenæus makes several extracts. Τοιοῦτοί εἰσιν οἱ ἀπὸ φιλοσοφίας στρατηγοί· περὶ ὧν Δημοχάρης ἔλεγεν, —῎Ωσπερ ἐκ θύμβρας οὐδεὶς ἂν δύναιτο κατασκευάσαι λόγχην, οὐδ᾽ ἐκ Σωκρά-τους στρατιώτην ἄμεμπτον.

Demetrius Phalereus also, in or near that same time, composed a Σωκράτους ἀπολογίαν (Diog. La. ix. 37-57). This shows how long the interest in the personal fate and character of Sokrates endured at Athens.

[d] Diogenes Laert. i. 47-61-83, vi. 15; Athenæ. xi. p. 505 C.

Bryson is mentioned by Theopompus ap. Athenæum, xi. p. 508 D. Theopompus, the contemporary of Aristotle

called Kyrenaic or Hedonic, afterwards (with various modifications) Epikurean: Antisthenes, of the Cynics and Stoics: Eukleides, of the Megaric school.   It seems that Aristippus, Antisthenes, Eukleides, and Bryson, all enjoyed considerable reputation, as contemporaries and rival authors of Plato: Æschines, Antisthenes (who was very poor), and Aristippus, are said to have received money for their lectures; Aristippus being named as the first who thus departed from the Sokratic canon.[e]

Æschines the companion of Sokrates did not become (like Eukleides, Antisthenes, Aristippus) the founder of a succession or sect of philosophers.   The few fragments remaining of his dialogues do not enable us to appreciate their merit.   He seems to have employed the name of Aspasia largely as a conversing personage, and to have esteemed her highly.   He also spoke with great admiration of Themistokles.   But in regard to present or recent characters, he stands charged with much bitterness and ill-nature: especially we learn that he denounced the Sophists Prodikus and Anaxagoras, the first on the ground of having taught Theramenes, the second as the teacher of two worthless persons

Æschines— Oration of Lysias against him.

and pupil of Isokrates, had composed an express treatise or discourse against Plato's dialogues, in which discourse he affirmed that most of them were not Plato's own, but borrowed in large proportion from the dialogues of Antisthenes, Aristippus, and Bryson. Ephippus also, the comic writer (of the fourth century B.C., contemporary with Theopompus, perhaps even earlier), spoke of Bryson as contemporary with Plato (Athenæ. xi. 509 C). This is good proof to authenticate Bryson as a composer of "Sokratic dialogues" belonging to the Platonic age, along with Antisthenes and Aristippus : whether Theopompus is correct when he asserts that Plato borrowed *much* from the three, is very doubtful.

Many dialogues were published by various writers, and ascribed falsely to one or other of the *viri Sokratici* : Diogenes (ii. 64) reports the judgment delivered by Panætius, which among them were genuine and which not so. Panætius considered that the dialogues ascribed to Plato, Xenophon, Antisthenes, and Æschines, were genuine ; that those assigned to Phædon and

Eukleides were doubtful ; and that the rest were all spurious. He thus regarded as spurious those of Alexamenus, Kriton, Simmias, Kebês, Simon, Bryson, &c., or he did not know them all. It is possible that Panætius may not have known the dialogues of Bryson ; if he did know them, and believed them to be spurious, I should not accept his assertion, because I think that it is outweighed by the contrary testimony of Theopompus. Moreover, though Panætius was a very able man, our confidence in his critical estimate is much shaken when we learn that he declared the Platonic Phædon to be spurious.

[e] Diogen. Laert. i. 62-65; Athenæus, xi. p. 507 C.

Dion Chrysostom (Orat. lv. De Homero et Socrate, p. 289, Reiske) must have had in his view some of these other Sokratic dialogues, not those composed by Plato or Xenophon, when he alludes to conversations of Sokrates with Lysikles, Glykon, and Anytus; what he says about Anytus can hardly refer to the Platonic Menon.

—Ariphrades and Arignôtus. This accusation deserves greater notice, because it illustrates the odium raised by Melêtus against Sokrates as having instructed Kritias and Alkibiades.[f] Moreover, we have Æschines presented to us in another character, very unexpected in a *vir Socraticus*. An action for recovery of money alleged to be owing, was brought in the Athenian Dikastery against Æschines, by a plaintiff, who set forth his case in a speech composed by the rhetor Lysias. In this speech it is alleged, that Æschines, having engaged in trade as a preparer and seller of unguents, borrowed a sum of money at interest from the plaintiff; who affirms that he counted with assurance upon honest dealing, from a disciple of Sokrates, continually engaged in talking about justice and virtue.[g] But so far was this expectation from being realised, that Æschines had behaved most dishonestly. He repaid neither principal nor interest; though a judgment of the Dikastery had been obtained against him, and a branded slave belonging to him had been seized under it. Moreover, Æschines had been guilty of dishonesty equally scandalous in his dealings with many other creditors also. Farthermore, he had made love to a rich woman seventy years old, and had got possession of her property; cheating and impoverishing her family. His character as a profligate and cheat was well known and could be proved by many witnesses. Such are the allegations against Æschines, contained in the fragment of a lost speech of Lysias, and made in open court by a real plaintiff. How much of them could be fairly proved, we cannot say:

[f] Plutarch, Perikles, c. 24-32 ; Cicero, De Invent. i. 31 ; Athenæus, v. 220. Some other citations will be found in Fischer's collection of the few fragments of Æschines Sokraticus (Leipsic, 1788, p. 68 seq.), though some of the allusions which he produces seem rather to belong to the orator Æschines. The statements of Athenæus, from the dialogue of Æschines called Telaugês, are the most curious. The dialogue contained, among other things, τὴν Προδίκου καὶ 'Αναξαγόρους τῶν σοφιστῶν διαμώκησιν, where we see Anaxagoras denominated a *Sophist* (see also Diodor. xii. 39) as well as Prodikus.

Fischer considers the three Pseudo-Platonic dialogues—Περὶ 'Αρετῆς, Περὶ Πλούτου, Περὶ Θανάτου—as the works of Æschines. But this is noway established.

[g] Athenæus, xiii. pp. 611-612. Πεισθεὶς δ' ὑπ' αὐτοῦ τοιαῦτα λέγοντος, καὶ ἅμα οἰόμενος τοῦτον Αἰσχίνην Σωκράτους γεγονέναι μαθητὴν, καὶ περὶ δικαιοσύνης καὶ ἀρετῆς πολλοὺς καὶ σεμνοὺς λέγοντα λόγους, οὐκ ἂν ποτε ἐπιχειρῆσαι οὐδὲ τολμῆσαι ἅπερ οἱ πονηρότατοι καὶ ἀδικώτατοι ἄνθρωποι ἐπιχειροῦσι πράττειν—

We read also about another oration of Lysias against Æschines—περὶ συκοφαντίας (Diogen. Laert. ii. 63), unless indeed it be the same oration differently described.

but it seems plain at least that Æschines must have been a trader as well as a philosopher. All these writers on philosophy must have had their root and dealings in real life, of which we know scarce anything.

The dialogues known by the title of Sokratic dialogues,[h] were composed by all the principal companions of Sokrates, and by many who were not companions. Yet though thus composed by many different authors, they formed a recognised class of literature, noticed by the rhetorical critics as distinguished for plain, colloquial, unstudied, dramatic execution, suiting the parts to the various speakers: from which general character Plato alone departed —and he too not in all of his dialogues. By the Sokratic authors generally Sokrates appears to have been presented under the same main features: his proclaimed confession of ignorance was seldom wanting: and the humiliation which his cross-questioning inflicted even upon insolent men like Alkibiades, was as keenly set forth by Æschines as by Plato: moreover the Sokratic disciples generally were fond of extolling the Dæmon or divining prophecy of their master.[i] Some

[margin note: Written Sokratic Dialogues—their general character.]

---

[h] Aristotel. ap. Athenæum, xi. p. 505 C; Rhetoric, iii. 16.

Dionys. Halikarnass. ad Cn. Pomp. de Platone, p. 762, Reisk. Τραφεὶs (Plato) ἐν τοῖς Σωκρατικοῖς διαλόγοις ἰσχνοτάτοις οὖσι καὶ ἀκριβεστάτοις, οὐ μείνας δ' ἐν αὐτοῖς, ἀλλὰ τῆς Γοργίου καὶ Θουκυδίδου κατασκευῆς ἐρασθείς: also, De Admir. Vi Dicend. in Demosthene, p. 968. Again in the same treatise De Adm. V. D. Demosth. p. 956. ἡ δὲ ἑτέρα λέξις, ἡ λιτὴ καὶ ἀφελὴς καὶ δοκοῦσα κατασκευήν τε καὶ ἰσχὺν τὴν πρὸς ἰδιώτην ἔχειν λόγον καὶ ὁμοιότητα, πολλοὺς μὲν ἔσχε καὶ ἀγαθοὺς ἄνδρας προστάτας—καὶ οἱ τῶν ἠθικῶν διαλόγων ποιηταί, ὧν ἦν καὶ τὸ Σωκρατικὸν διδασκαλεῖον πᾶν, ἔξω Πλάτωνος, &c.

Dionysius calls this style ὁ Σωκρατικὸς χαρακτήρ, p. 1025. I presume it is the same to which the satirist Timon applies the words:—

Ἀσθενικὴ δὲ λόγων δυὰς ἢ τριάς, ἢ ἔτι πόρσω,
Οἷος Ξεινοφόων, ἵς τ' Αἰσχίνου οὐκ εὐπειθὴς
γράψαι· Diogen. La. ii. 55.

Hermogenes, Phrynichus, Longinus, and some later rhetorical critics of

Greece judged more favourably than Timon about the style of Æschines as well as of Xenophon. See Zeller, Gesch. der Phil. ii. p. 171, sec. ed. And Demetrius Phalereus (or the author of the treatise which bears his name), as well as the rhetor Aristeides, considered Æschines and Plato as the best representatives of the Σωκρατικὸs χαρακτήρ, Demetr. Phaler. De Interpretat. 310; Aristeides, Orat. Platon. i. p. 35; Photius, Cods. 61 and 158; Longinus, ap. Walz. ix. p. 559, c. 2.

An inedited discourse of Michael Psellus, printed by Mr. Cox in his very careful and valuable catalogue of the MSS. in the Bodleian Library, recites the same high estimate as having been formed of Æschines by the chief ancient rhetorical critics: they reckoned him among and alongside of the foremost Hellenic classical writers, as having his own peculiar merits of style—παρὰ μὲν Πλάτωνι, τὴν διαλογικὴν φράσιν, παρὰ δὲ τοῦ Σωκρατικοῦ Αἰσχίνου, τὴν ἐμμελῆ συνθήκην τῶν λέξεων, παρὰ δὲ Θουκυδίδου, &c. See Mr. Cox's Catalogue, pp. 743-745.

[i] Cicero, Brutus, 85, s. 292; De Divinatione, i. 54-122; Aristeides, Orat.

dialogues circulating under the name of some one among the companions of Sokrates, were spurious, and the authorship was a point not easy to determine. Simon, a currier at Athens, in whose shop Sokrates often conversed, is said to have kept memoranda of the conversations which he heard, and to have afterwards published them: Æschines also, and some other of the Sokratic companions, were suspected of having preserved or procured reports of the conversations of the master himself, and of having made much money after his death by delivering them before select audiences.[k] Aristotle speaks of the followers of Antisthenes as unschooled, vulgar men: but Cicero appears to have read with satisfaction the dialogues of Antisthenes, whom he designates as acute though not well-instructed.[l] Other accounts describe his dialogues as composed in a rhetorical style, which is ascribed to the fact of his having received lessons from Gorgias:[m] and Theopompus must have held in considerable estimation the dialogues of that same author, as well as those of Aristippus and Bryson, when he accused Plato of having borrowed from them largely.[n]

Eukleides, Antisthenes, and Aristippus, were all companions and admirers of Sokrates, as was Plato. But none of them

xlv. περὶ Ῥητορικῆς, vol. ii. pp. 24-25; Orat. xlvi. Ὑπὲρ τῶν Τεττάρων, vol. ii. pp. 295-369, ed. Dindorf. It appears by this that some of the dialogues composed by Æschines were mistaken by various persons for actual conversations held by Sokrates. It was argued, that because Æschines was inferior to Plato in ability, he was more likely to have repeated accurately what he had heard Sokrates say.

k Diog. L. ii. 122. He mentions a collection of thirty-three dialogues in one volume, purporting to be reports of real colloquies of Sokrates, published by Simon. But they can hardly be regarded as genuine.

The charge here mentioned is advanced by Xenophon (see a preceding note, Memorab. i. 2, 60) against some persons (τινες), but without specifying names. About Æschines, see Athenæus, xiii. p. 611 C; Diogen. Laert. ii. 62.

l Cicero, Epist. ad Atticum, xii. 38 : —"viri acuti magis quam eruditi," is

the judgment of Cicero upon Antisthenes. I presume that these words indicate the same defect as that which is intended by Aristotle when he says —οἱ Ἀντισθένειοι καὶ οἱ οὕτως ἀπαίδευτοι, Metaphysic. H. 3, p. 1043, b. 24. It is plain too that Lucian considered the compositions of Antisthenes as not unworthy companions to those of Plato (Lucian, adv. Indoctum, c. 27).

m Diogen. Laert. vi. 1. If it be true that Antisthenes received lessons from Gorgias, this proves that Gorgias must sometimes have given lessons gratis; for the poverty of Antisthenes is well known. See the Symposion of Xenophon.

n Theopomp. ap. Athenæ. xi. p. 508. See K. F. Hermann, Ueber Plato's Schriftsteller. motive, p. 300.

An extract, of some length, of a dialogue composed by Æschines between Sokrates and Alkibiades is given by Aristeides, Or. xlvi. Ὑπὲρ τῶν Τεττάρων, vol. ii. pp. 292-294, ed. Dindorf.

were his disciples, in the strict sense of the word: none of them continued or enforced his doctrines, though each used his name as a spokesman. During his lifetime the common attachment to his person formed a bond of union, which ceased at his death. There is indeed some ground for believing that Plato then put himself forward in the character of leader, with a view to keep the body united.[o] We must recollect that Plato though then no more than twenty-eight years of age, was the only one among them who combined the advantages of a noble Athenian descent, opulent circumstances, an excellent education, and great native genius. Eukleides and Aristippus were neither of them Athenians: Antisthenes was very poor: Xenophon was absent on service in the Cyreian army. Plato's proposition however found no favour with the others, and was even indignantly repudiated by Apollodorus: a man ardently attached to Sokrates, but violent and overboiling in all his feelings.[p] The companions of Sokrates, finding themselves unfavourably looked upon at Athens after his death, left the city for a season and followed Eukleides to Megara. How long they stayed there we do not know. Plato is said, though I think on no sufficient authority, to have remained absent from Athens for several years continuously. It seems certain (from an anecdote recounted by Aristotle)[q] that he talked with something like arrogance among the companions of Sokrates; and that Aristippus gently rebuked him, by reminding him how very different had been the language of Sokrates himself. Complaints too were made by contempo-

Relations between the companions of Sokrates— Their proceedings after the death of Sokrates.

---

[o] Athenæus, xi. p. 507 B. from the ὑπομνήματα of the Delphian Hegesander. Who Hegesander was, I do not know: but there is nothing improbable in the anecdote which he recounts.

[p] Plato, Phædon. pp. 59 A, 117 D. Eukleides, however, though his school was probably at Megara, seems to have possessed property in Attica: for there existed, among the orations of Isæus, a pleading composed by that rhetor for some client—Πρὸς Εὐκλείδην τὸν Σωκρατικὸν, ἀμφισβήτησις ὑπὲρ τῆς τοῦ χωρίου λύσεως. Dionys. Hal. Isæus, c. 14. Harpokration—῞Οτι τὰ ἐπικη-

ρυττόμενα: also under some other words by Harpokration and by Pollux, viii. 48.

[q] Aristot. Rhetoric, ii. 24, p. 1398, b. 30.

ἢ ὡς ᾽Αρίστιππος, πρὸς Πλάτωνα ἐπαγγελτικώτερόν τι εἰπόντα, ὡς ᾤετο —ἀλλὰ μὴν ὁ γ᾽ ἑταῖρος ἡμῶν, ἔφη, οὐδὲν τοιοῦτον—λέγων τὸν Σωκράτην.

This anecdote, mentioned by Aristotle, who had good means of knowing, appears quite worthy of belief.

The jealousy and love of supremacy inherent in Plato's temper (τὸ φιλότιμον), were noticed by Dionysius Hal. (Epist. ad Cn. Pompeium, p. 756).

raries, about Plato's jealous, censorious, spiteful, temper. The critical and disparaging tone of his dialogues, notwithstanding the admiration which they inspire, accounts for the existence of these complaints : and anecdotes are recounted, though not verified by any sufficient evidence, of ill-natured dealing on his part towards other philosophers who were poorer than himself.[r] Dissension or controversy on philosophical topics is rarely carried on without some invidious or hostile feeling. Athens, and the *viri Sokratici*, Plato included, form no exception to this ordinary malady of human nature.

It is common for historians of philosophy to speak of a Sokratic school : but this phrase, if admissible at all, is only admissible in the largest and vaguest sense. The effect produced by Sokrates upon his companions was, not to teach doctrine, but to stimulate self-working enquiry, upon ethical and social subjects. Eukleides, Antisthenes, Aristippus, each took a line of his own, not less decidedly than Plato. But unfortunately we have no compositions remaining from either of the three. We possess only brief reports respecting some leading points of their doctrine, emanating altogether from those who disagreed with it: we have besides aphorisms, dicta, repartees, bons-mots, &c., which they are said to have uttered. Of these many are evident inventions; some proceeding from opponents and probably coloured or exaggerated, others hardly authenticated at all. But if they were ever so well authenticated, they would form very insufficient evidence on which to judge a philosopher—much less to condemn him with asperity.[s]

No Sokratic school—each of the companions took a line of his own.

[r] Athenæus, xi. pp. 505-508. Diog. Laert. ii. 60-65, iii. 36.

The statement made by Plato in the Phædon—That Aristippus and Kleombrotus were not present at the death of Sokrates, but were said to be in Ægina —is cited as an example of Plato's illwill and censorious temper (Demetr. Phaler. s. 306). But this is unfair, The statement ought not to be so considered, if it were true : and if not true, it deserves a more severe epithet. We read in Athenæus various other criticisms, citing or alluding to passages of Plato, which are alleged to indicate ill-nature; but many of the passages cited do not deserve the remark.

[s] Respecting these ancient philosophers, whose works are lost, I transcribe a striking passage from Descartes, who complains, in his own case, of the injustice of being judged from the statements of others, and not from his own writings :—

"Quod adeo in hâc materiâ verum est, ut quamvis sæpe *aliquas ex meis opinionibus explicaverim viris acutissimis, et qui me loquente videbantur eas valdé distincté intelligere: attamen cum eas retulerunt, observavi ipsos fere semper illas ita mutavisse, ut pro meis agnoscere amplius non possem.* Quâ occasione posteros hic oratos volo, ut nunquam credant, quidquam à me esse

Philosophy (as I have already observed) aspires to deliver not merely truth, but reasoned truth. We ought to know, not only what doctrines a philosopher maintained, but how he maintained them:—what objections others made against him, and how he replied:—what objections he made against dissentient doctrines, and what replies were made to him. Respecting Plato and Aristotle, we possess such information to a considerable extent: respecting Eukleides, Antisthenes, and Aristippus, we are without it. All their compositions (very numerous, in the case of Antisthenes) have perished.

EUKLEIDES.

Eukleides was a Parmenidean, who blended the ethical point of view of Sokrates with the ontology of Parmenides, and followed out that negative Dialectic which was common to Sokrates with Zeno. Parmenides (I have already said)[t] and Zeno after him, recognised no absolute reality except Ens Unum, continuous, indivisible: they denied all real plurality: they said that the plural was Non-Ens or Nothing, *i. e.* nothing real or absolute, but only apparent, perpetually transient and changing, relative, different as appreciated by one man and by another. Now Sokrates laid it down that wisdom or knowledge of Good, was the sum total of ethical perfection, including within it all the different virtues: he spoke also about the divine wisdom inherent in, or pervading the entire Kosmos or universe.[u] Eukleides blended together the Ens of Parmenides with the Good of Sokrates, saying that the two names designated one and the same thing: sometimes called Good, Wisdom, Intelligence, God, &c., and by other names also, but always one and the same object named and meant. He farther maintained that the opposite of Ens, and the opposite of Bonum

Eukleides of Megara—he blended Parmenides with Sokrates.

---

profectum, quod ipse in lucem non edidero. *Et nullo modo miror absurda illa dogmata, quæ veteribus illis philosophis tribuuntur, quorum scripta non habemus:* nec propterea judico ipsorum cogitationes valdé à ratione fuisse alienas, cum habuerint præstantissima suorum sæculorum ingenia; sed tantum nobis perperam esse relatas." (Descartes, Diss. De Methodo, p. 43.)

[t] See vol. i. ch. i. pp. 20-23.

[u] Xenophon, Memor. i. 4, 17. $\tau \grave{\eta} \nu$ $\grave{\epsilon} \nu$ $\tau \hat{\wp}$ $\pi a \nu \tau \grave{\iota}$ $\phi \rho \acute{o} \nu \eta \sigma \iota \nu$. Compare Plato, Philèbus, pp. 29-30; Cicero, Nat. Deor. ii. 6, 6, iii. 11.

(Non-Ens, Non-Bonum, or Malum) were things non-existent, unmeaning names, Nothing,[x] &c. : *i. e.* that they were nothing really, absolutely, permanently, but ever varying and dependant upon our ever varying conceptions. The One—the All—the Good—was absolute, immoveable, invariable, indivisible· But the opposite thereof was a non-entity or nothing: there was no one constant meaning corresponding to Non-Ens—but a variable meaning, different with every man who used it.

It was in this manner that Eukleides solved the problem

Doctrine of Eukleides about Bonum.

which Sokrates had brought into vogue—What is the Bonum—or (as afterwards phrased) the Summum Bonum? Eukleides pronounced the Bonum to be coincident with the Ens Unum of Parmenides. The Parmenidean thesis, originally belonging to Transcendental Physics or Ontology, became thus implicated with Transcendental Ethics.[y]

Plato departs from Sokrates on the same point. He agrees

The doctrine compared to that of Plato —changes in Plato.

with Eukleides in recognising a Transcendental Bonum. But it appears that his doctrines on this head underwent some change. He held for some time what is called the doctrine of Ideas : transcendental Forms, Entia, Essences : he considered the Transcendental to be essentially multiple, or to be an aggregate—whereas Eukleides had regarded it as essentially One. This is the doctrine which we find in some of the Platonic dialogues. In the Republic, the Idea of Good appears as one of these, though it is declared to be the foremost in rank and the most ascendant in efficacy.[z] But in the later part of his life, and in his lectures (as we learn from Aristotle), Plato came to adopt a different view. He resolved the Ideas into numbers. He regarded them as made up by the combination of two distinct factors :—1. The One—the Essentially One. 2. The Essentially Plural : the Indeterminate Dyad : the Great and

[x] Diog. L. ii. 106. Οὗτος ἓν τὸ ἀγαθὸν ἀπεφήνατο πολλοῖς ὀνόμασι καλούμενον· ὅτε μὲν γὰρ φρόνησιν, ὅτε δὲ θεὸν, καὶ ἄλλοτε νοῦν καὶ τὰ λοιπά. Τὰ δὲ ἀντικείμενα τῷ ἀγαθῷ ἀνῄρει, μὴ εἶναι φάσκων. Compare also vii. 2, 162, where the Megarici are represented as recognising only μίαν ἀρετὴν πολλοῖς ὀνόμασι καλουμένην. Cicero, Academ. ii. 42.

[y] However in the verse of Xenophanes, the predecessor of Parmenides —Οὖλος ὁρᾷ, οὖλος δὲ νοεῖ, οὖλος δέ τ' ἀκούει—the Universe is described as a thinking, seeing, hearing, God—Ἐν καὶ Πᾶν. Sextus, Emp. adv. Mathemat. ix. 144; Xenophon, Fragm. p. 36, ed. Karsten.

[z] Plato, Republic, vi. p. 508 E, vii. p. 517 A.

Little.—Of these two elements he considered the Ideas to be compounded. And he identified the Idea of Good with the essentially One—τὸ ἀγαθὸν with τὸ ἕν: the principle of Good with the principle of Unity: also the principle of Evil with the Indeterminate. But though Unity and Good were thus identical, he considered Unity as logically antecedent, or the subject—Good as logically consequent, or the predicate.[a]

This last doctrine of Plato in his later years (which does not appear in the dialogues, but seems, as far as we can make out, to have been delivered substantially in his oral lectures, and is ascribed to him by Aristotle) was nearly coincident with that of Eukleides. Both of them held the identity of τὸ ἕν with τὸ ἀγαθόν. This one doctrine is all that we know about Eukleides : what consequences he derived from it, or whether any, we do not know. But Plato combined, with this transcendental Unum = Bonum, a transcendental indeterminate plurality: from which combination he considered his Ideas or Ideal Numbers to be derivatives.

Last doctrine of Plato nearly the same as Eukleides.

[a] The account given by Aristotle of Plato's doctrine of Ideas, as held by Plato in his later years, appears in various passages of the Metaphysica, and in the curious account repeated by Aristoxenus (who had often heard it from Aristotle—Ἀριστοτέλης ἀεὶ διηγεῖτο) of the ἀκρόασις or lecture delivered by Plato, De Bono. See Aristoxen. Harmon. ii. p. 30, Meibom. Compare the sixth chapter in this work, Platonic Dialogues, Generally, p. 217. Metaphys. N. 1091, b. 13. τῶν δὲ τὰς ἀκινήτους οὐσίας εἶναι λεγόντων (sc. Plato Schol.) οἱ μὲν φασὶν αὐτὸ τὸ ἕν τὸ ἀγαθὸν αὐτὸ εἶναι· οὐσίαν μέντοι τὸ ἕν αὐτοῦ ᾤοντο εἶναι μάλιστα, which words are very clearly explained by Bonitz in the note to his Commentary, p. 586 : also Metaphys. 987, b. 20, and Scholia, p. 551, b. 20, p. 567, b. 34, where the work of Aristotle, Περὶ Τἀγαθοῦ, is referred to; probably the memoranda taken down by Aristotle from Plato's lecture on that subject, accompanied by notes of his own. In Schol. p. 573 a. 18, it is stated that the astronomer Eudoxus was a hearer both of Plato and of Eukleides.

The account given by Zeller (Gesch. der Philos. ii. p. 453, 2nd ed.) of this latter phase of the Platonic doctrine of Ideas, applies exactly to that which we hear about the main doctrine of Eukleides. Zeller describes the Platonic doctrine as being "Eine Vermischung des ethischen Begriffes vom höchsten Gut, mit dem Metaphysischen des Absoluten : Der Begriff des Guten ist zunächst aus dem menschlichen Leben abstrahirt : er bezeichnet das, was dem Menschen zuträglich ist. So noch bei Sokrates. Plato verallgemeinert ihn nun zum Begriff des Absoluten ; dabei spielt aber seine ursprüngliche Bedeutung noch fortwährend herein, und so entsteht die Unklarheit, dass weder der ethische noch der metaphysische Begriff des Guten rein gefasst wird."

This remark is not less applicable to Eukleides than to Plato, both of them agreeing ·in the doctrine here criticised. Zeller says truly, that the attempt to identify Unum and Bonum produces perpetual confusion. The two notions are thoroughly distinct and independent. It ought not to be called (as he phrases it) "a generalization of Bonum." There is no common property on which to found a generalization. It is a forced conjunction between two disparates.

Eukleides is said to have composed six dialogues, the titles

of which alone remain.   The scanty information which we possess respecting him relates altogether to his negative logical procedure.   Whether he deduced any consequences from his positive doctrine of the Transcendental Ens, Unum, Bonum, we do not know: but he, as Zeno had been before him,[b] was acute in exposing contradictions and difficulties in the positive doctrines of opponents.   He was a citizen of Megara, where he is said to have harboured Plato and the other companions of Sokrates, when they retired for a time from Athens after the death of Sokrates.   Living there as a teacher or debater on philosophy, he founded a school or succession of philosophers who were denominated *Megarici*.   The title is as old as Aristotle, who both names them and criticises their doctrines.[c]   None of their compositions are preserved.   The earliest who becomes known to us is Eubulides, the contemporary and opponent of Aristotle; next Ichthyas, Apollonius, Diodôrus Kronus, Stilpon, Alexinus, between 340-260 B.C.

With the Megaric philosophers there soon become confounded another succession, called Eleian or Eretrian, who trace their origin to another Sokratic man—Phædon.   The chief Eretrians made known to us are Pleistanus, Menedêmus, Asklepiades.   The second of the three acquired some reputation.

The Megarics and Eretrians, as far as we know them,

turned their speculative activity altogether in the logical or intellectual direction, paying little attention to the ethical and emotional field.   Both Antisthenes and Aristippus, on the contrary, pursued the ethical path.   To the Sokratic question, What is the Bonum? Eukleides had answered by a transcendental definition: Antisthenes and Aristippus each gave to it an ethical answer, having reference to human wants and emotions, and

---

[b] Plato, Parmenides, p. 128 C, where Zeno represents himself as taking for his premisses the conclusions of opponents, to show that they led to absurd consequences.   This seems what is meant, when Diogenes says about Eukleides—ταῖς ἀποδείξεσιν ἐνίστατο οὐ κατὰ λήμματα, ἀλλὰ κατ' ἐπιφοράν (ii. 107); Deycks, De Megaricorum

Doctrinâ, p. 34.

[c] Aristot. Metaph. iv. p. 1046, b. 29.

The sarcasm ascribed to Diogenes the Cynic implies that Eukleides was really known as the founder of a *school* —καὶ τὴν μὲν Εὐκλείδου σχολὴν ἔλεγε χολήν (Diog. L. vi. 24)—the earliest mention (I apprehend) of the word σχολὴ in that sense.

to the different views which they respectively took thereof. Antisthenes declared it to consist in virtue, by which he meant an independent and self-sufficing character, confining all wants within the narrowest limits: Aristippus placed it in the moderate and easy pleasures, in avoiding ambitious struggles, and in making the best of every different situation, yet always under the guidance of a wise calculation and self-command. Both of them kept clear of the transcendental: they neither accepted it as Unum et Omne (the view of Eukleides), nor as Plura (the Eternal Ideas or Forms, the Platonic view). Their speculations had reference altogether to human life and feelings, though the one took a measure of this wide subject very different from the other: and in thus confining the range of their speculations, they followed Sokrates more closely than either Eukleides or Plato followed him. They not only abstained from transcendental speculation, but put themselves in declared opposition to it. And since the intellectual or logical philosophy, as treated by Plato, became intimately blended with transcendental hypothesis—Antisthenes and Aristippus are both found on the negative side against its pretensions. Aristippus declared the mathematical sciences to be useless, as conducing in no way to happiness, and taking no account of what was better or what was worse.[d] He declared that we could know nothing except in so far as we were affected by it, and as it was or might be in correlation with ourselves: that as to causes not relative to ourselves, or to our own capacities and affections, we could know nothing about them.[e]

Such were the leading writers and talkers contemporary with Plato, in the dialectical age immediately following on the death of Sokrates. The negative vein greatly preponderates in them, as it does on the

Preponderance of the negative vein in the Platonic age.

---

[d] Aristotel. Metaph. B. 996, a. 32. ὥστε διὰ ταῦτα τῶν σοφιστῶν τινες οἷον Ἀρίστιππος προεπηλάκιζον αὐτὰς (τὰς μαθηματικὰς τέχνας)· ἐν μὲν γὰρ ταῖς ἄλλαις τέχναις—καὶ ταῖς βαναύσοις, οἷον ἐν τεκτονικῇ καὶ σκυτικῇ, διότι βελτίον ἢ χεῖρον λέγεσθαι πάντα, τὰς δὲ μαθηματικὰς οὐθένα ποιεῖσθαι λόγον περὶ ἀγαθῶν καὶ κακῶν.

Aristotle here ranks Aristippus

among the σοφισταί.

Aristippus, in discountenancing φυσιολογίαν, cited the favourite saying of Sokrates, that the proper study of mankind was ὅττι τοι ἐν μεγάροισι κακόν τ' ἀγαθόν τε τέτυκται.

Plutarch, ap. Euseb. Præp. Evang. i. 8.

[e] Sext. Emp. adv. Math. vii. 191; Diog. L. ii. 92.

whole even in Plato—and as it was pretty sure to do, so long as the form of dialogue was employed. Affirmative exposition and proof is indeed found in some of the later Platonic works, carried on by colloquy between two speakers. But the colloquial form manifests itself evidently as unsuitable for the purpose: and we must remember that Plato was a lecturer as well as a writer, so that his doctrines made their way, at least in part, through continuous exposition. But it is Aristotle with whom the form of affirmative continuous exposition first becomes predominant, in matters of philosophy. Though he composed dialogues (which are now lost), and though he appreciates dialectic as a valuable exercise, yet he considers it only as a discursive preparation; antecedent, though essential, to the more close and concentrated demonstrations of philosophy.

Most historians deal hardly with this negative vein.
Harsh manner in which historians of philosophy censure the negative vein. They depreciate the Sophists, the Megarics and Eretrians, the Academics and Sceptics of the subsequent ages—under the title of Eristics, or lovers of contention for itself—as captious and perverse enemies of truth.

I have already said that my view of the importance and
Negative method in philosophy essential to the controul of the affirmative. value of the negative vein of philosophy is altogether different. It appears to me quite as essential as the affirmative. It is required as an antecedent, a test, and a corrective. Aristotle deserves all honour for his attempts to construct and defend various affirmative theories: but the value of these theories depends upon their being defensible against all objectors. Affirmative philosophy, as a body not only of truth but of reasoned truth, holds the champion's belt, subject to the challenge not only of competing affirmants, but of all deniers and doubters. And this is the more indispensable, because of the vast problems which these affirmative philosophers undertake to solve: problems especially vast during the age of Plato and Aristotle. The question has to be determined, not only which of two proposed solutions is the best, but whether either of them is tenable, and even whether any solution at all is attainable by the human faculties: whether there exist positive evidence

adequate to sustain any conclusion, accompanied with adequate replies to the objections against it. The burthen of proof lies upon the affirmant; and the proof produced must be open to the scrutiny of every dissentient.

Among these dissentients or negative dialecticians, Sokrates himself, during his life, stood prominent. In his footsteps followed Eukleides and the Megarics: who, though they acquired the unenviable surname of Eristics or Controversialists, cannot possibly have surpassed Sokrates, and probably did not equal him, in the refutative Elenchus. Of no one among the Megarics, probably, did critics ever affirm, what the admiring Xenophon says about Sokrates—" that he dealt with every one in colloquial debate just as he chose,"—*i. e.* that he baffled and puzzled his opponents whenever he chose. No one of these Megarics probably ever enunciated so sweeping a negative programme, or declared so emphatically his own inability to communicate positive instruction, as Sokrates in the Platonic Apology. A person more thoroughly Eristic than Sokrates never lived. And we see perfectly, from the Memorabilia of Xenophon (who nevertheless strives to bring out the opposite side of his character), that he was so esteemed among his contemporaries. Plato, as well as Eukleides, took up this vein in the Sokratic character, and worked it with unrivalled power in many of his dialogues. The Platonic Sokrates is compared, and compares himself, to Antæus, who compelled every new-comer, willing or unwilling, to wrestle with him.[f]

Note in margin: Sokrates—the most persevering and acute Eristic of his age.

---

[f] Plato, Theætēt. p. 169 A.

Theodorus. Οὐ ῥᾴδιον, ὦ Σώκρατες, σοὶ παρακαθήμενον μὴ διδόναι λόγον, ἀλλ' ἐγὼ ἄρτι παρελήρησα φάσκων σε ἐπιτρέψειν μοι μὴ ἀποδύεσθαι, καὶ οὐχὶ ἀναγκάσειν καθάπερ Λακεδαιμόνιοι· σὺ δέ μοι δοκεῖς πρὸς τὸν Σκίρρωνα μᾶλλον τείνειν. Λακεδαιμόνιοι μὲν γὰρ ἀπιέναι ἢ ἀποδύεσθαι κελεύουσιν, σὺ δὲ κατ' Ἀνταῖόν τί μοι μᾶλλον δοκεῖς τὸ δρᾶμα δρᾶν· τὸν γὰρ προσελθόντα οὐκ ἀνίης πρὶν ἀναγκάσῃς ἀποδύσας ἐν τοῖς λόγοις προσπαλαῖσαι.

Sokrates. Ἄριστα, ὦ Θεόδωρε, τὴν νόσον μου ἀπείκασας· ἰσχυρικώτερος μέντοι ἐγὼ ἐκείνων· μύριοι γὰρ ἤδη μοι Ἡρακλέες τε καὶ Θησέες ἐντυχόντες κάρτεροι πρὸς τὸ λέγειν μάλ' εὖ ξυγκεκόφασιν, ἀλλ' ἐγὼ οὐδέν τι μᾶλλον ἀφίσταμαι. οὕτω τις ἐρὼς δεινὸς ἐνδέδυκε τῆς περὶ ταῦτα γυμνασίας· μὴ οὖν μηδὲ σὺ φθονήσῃς προσανατριψάμενος σαυτόν τε ἅμα καὶ ἐμὲ ὀνῆσαι.

How could the eristic appetite be manifested in stronger language either by Eukleides, or Eubulides, or Diodôrus Kronus, or any of those Sophists upon whom the Platonic commentators heap so many harsh epithets ?

Among the compositions ascribed to Protagoras by Diogenes Laertius (ix. 55), one is entitled Τέχνη Ἐριστικῶν. But if we look at the last chapter of the Treatise De Sophisticis Elenchis, we shall find Aristotle asserting explicitly that there existed no Τέχνη Ἐριστικῶν anterior to his own work the Topica.

Of the six dialogues composed by Eukleides, we cannot

Platonic Par-
menides—its
extreme ne-
gative cha-
racter. speak positively, because they are not preserved. But they cannot have been more refutative, and less affirmative, than most of the Platonic dialogues; and we can hardly be wrong in asserting that they were very inferior both in energy and attraction. The Theætêtus and the Parmenides, two of the most negative among the Platonic dialogues, seem to connect themselves, by the *personnel* of the drama, with the Megaric philosophers: the former dialogue is ushered in by Eukleides, and is, as it were, dedicated to him: the latter dialogue exhibits, as its *protagonistes*, the veteran Parmenides himself, who forms the one factor of the Megaric philosophy, while Sokrates forms the other. Parmenides (in the Platonic dialogue so called) is made to enforce the negative method in general terms, as a philosophical duty coordinate with the affirmative; and to illustrate it by a most elaborate argumentation, directed partly against the Platonic Ideas (here advocated by the youthful Sokrates), partly against his own (the Parmenidean) dogma of Ens Unum. Parmenides adduces unanswerable objections against the dogma of Transcendental Forms or Ideas; yet says at the same time that there can be no philosophy unless you admit it. He reproves the youthful Sokrates for precipitancy in affirming the dogma, and contends that you are not justified in affirming any dogma until you have gone through a bilateral scrutiny of it—that is, first assuming the doctrine to be true, next assuming it to be false, and following out the deductions arising from the one assumption as well as from the other.[g] Parmenides then gives a string of (to remind the reader of what has been already set forth in my twenty-fourth chapter) successive deductions (at great length, occupying the last half of the dialogue)—four pairs of counter-demonstrations or Antinomies—in which contradictory conclusions appear each to be alike proved. He enunciates the final result as follows:—" Whether Unum exists, or does not exist, Unum itself and Cætera, both exist and do not exist, both appear and do not appear, all things and in all ways—both in relation to themselves and in relation to each other." [h]

---

g Plato, Parmen. p. 136.

h Plato, Parmen. p. 166.   ἐν εἴτ' |
ἔστιν, εἴτε μὴ ἔστιν, αὐτό τε καὶ τἄλλα
καὶ πρὸς αὐτὰ καὶ πρὸς ἄλληλα πάντα

If this memorable dialogue, with its concluding string of elaborate antinomies, had come down to us under the name of Eukleides, historians would probably have denounced it as a perverse exhibition of ingenuity, worthy of "that litigious person, who first infused into the Megarians the fury of disputation."[i] But since it is of Platonic origin, we must recognise Plato not only as having divided with the Megaric philosophers the impulse of negative speculation which they had inherited from Sokrates, but as having carried that impulse to an extreme point of invention, combination, and dramatic handling, much beyond their powers. Undoubtedly, if we pass from the Parmenidês to other dialogues, we find Plato very different. He has various other intellectual impulses, an abundant flow of ideality and of constructive fancy, in many distinct channels. But negative philosophy is at least one of the indisputable and prominent items of the Platonic aggregate.

While then we admit that the Megaric succession of philosophers exhibited negative subtlety and vehement love of contentious debate, we must recollect that these qualities were inherited from Sokrates and shared with Plato. The philosophy of Sokrates, who taught nothing and cross-examined every one, was essentially more negative and controversial, both in him and his successors, than any which had preceded it. In an age when dialectic colloquy was considered as appropriate for philosophical subjects, and when long continuous exposition was left to the rhetor—Eukleides established a succession or school[k] which was more distinguished for impugning dogmas of others than for defending dogmas of its own. Schleiermacher and others suppose that Plato in his dialogue Euthy-

The Megarics shared the negative impulse with Sokrates and Plato.

πάντως ἐστί τε καὶ οὐκ ἔστι, καὶ φαίνεταί τε καὶ οὐ φαίνεται—'Αληθέστατα.
See above, vol. i. ch. xxv. pp. 288-318.
[i] This is the phrase of the satirical sillographer Timon, who spoke with scorn of all the philosophers except Pyrrhon :—
'.'Αλλ' οὔ μοι τούτων φλεδόνων μέλει, οὐδὲ μὲν ἄλλου
(Οὐδενὸς, οὐ Φαίδωνος, ὅτις γε μὲν—οὐδ' ἐριδάντεω

Εὐκλείδου, Μεγαρεῦσιν ὃς ἔμβαλε λύσσαν ἐρισμοῦ.
[k] If we may trust a sarcastic bon-mot ascribed to Diogenes the Cynic, the contemporary of the *viri Socratici* and the follower of Antisthenes, the term σχολὴ was applied to the visitors of Eukleides rather than to those of Plato—καὶ τὴν μὲν Εὐκλείδου σχολὴν ἔλεγε, χολὴν, τὴν δὲ Πλάτωνος διατριβὴν, κατατριβήν. Diog. L. vi. 42.

dêmus intends to expose the sophistical fallacies of the Megaric school:[1] and that in the dialogue Sophistês, he refutes the same philosophers (under the vague designation of "the friends of Forms") in their speculations about Ens and Non-Ens. The first of these two opinions is probably true to some extent, though we cannot tell how far: the second of the two is supported by some able critics—yet it appears to me untenable.[m]

Of Eukleides himself, though he is characterised as strongly controversial, no distinct points of controversy have been preserved: but his successor Eubulides is celebrated for various sophisms. He was the contemporary and rival of Aristotle; who, without however expressly naming him, probably intends to speak of him when alluding to the Megaric philosophers generally.[n] Another of the same school, Alexinus (rather later than Eubulides), is also said to have written against Aristotle.

Six sophisms are ascribed to Eubulides. 1. Ὁ ψευδόμενος—

Eubulides—his logical problems or puzzles—difficulty of solving them—many solutions attempted.

Mentiens. 2. Ὁ διαλανθάνων, or ἐγκεκαλυμμένος— the person hidden under a veil. 3. Ἠλέκτρα. 4. Σωρείτης — Sorites. 5. Κερατίνης — Cornutus. 6. Φάλακρος—Calvus. Of these the second is substantially the same with the third; and the fourth the same with the sixth, only inverted.[o]

---

[1] Schleierm. Einleitung to Plat. Euthyd. p. 403 seq.

[m] Schleierm. Introduction to the Sophistês, pp. 134-135.

See Deycks, Megaricorum Doctrina, p. 41 seq. Zeller, Gesch. der Griech. Phil. vol. ii. p. 180 seq., with his instructive note. Prantl, Gesch. der Logik, vol. i. p. 37, and others cited by Zeller.—Ritter dissents from this view, and I concur in his dissent. To affirm that Eukleides admitted a plurality of Ideas or Forms, is to contradict the only one deposition, certain and unequivocal, which we have about his philosophy. His doctrine is that of the Transcendental Unum, Ens, Bonum; while the doctrine of the Transcendental Plura (Ideas or Forms) belongs to Plato and others. Both Deycks and Zeller (p. 185) recognise this as a difficulty. But to me it seems fatal to their hypothesis; which, after all, is only an hypothesis—first originated by Schleiermacher. If it be true

that the Megarici are intended by Plato under the appellation οἱ τῶν εἰδῶν φίλοι, we must suppose that the school had been completely transformed before the time of Stilpon, who is presented as the great opponent of τὰ εἴδη.

[n] Aristokles, ap. Euseb. Præp. Ev. xv. 2. Eubulides is said not merely to have controverted the philosophical theories of Aristotle, but also to have attacked his personal character with bitterness and slander: a practice not less common in ancient controversy than in modern. About Alexinus, Diog. L. ii. 109.

Among those who took lessons in rhetoric and pronunciation from Eubulides, we read the name of the orator Demosthenes, who is said to have improved his pronunciation thereby. Diog. Laert. ii. p. 108. Plutarch, x. Orat. 21, p. 845 C.

[o] Diog. L. ii. pp. 108-109; vii. 82. Lucian Vit. Auct. 22.

1. Cicero, Academ. ii. pp. 30-96.

These sophisms are ascribed to Eubulides, and belonged probably to the Megaric school both before and after him. But it is plain both from the Euthydêmus of Plato, and from the Topica of Aristoteles, that there were many others of similar character; frequently employed in the abundant dialectic colloquies which prevailed at Athens during the fourth and third centuries B.C. Plato and Aristotle handle such questions and their authors contemptuously, under the name of Eristic: but it was more easy to put a bad name upon them, as well as upon the Eleate Zeno, than to elucidate the logical difficulties which they brought to view. Neither Aristotle nor Plato provided a sufficient answer to them: as is proved by the fact, that several subsequent philosophers wrote treatises expressly in reference to them—even philosophers of reputation, like Theophrastus and Chrysippus.[p] How these two latter philosophers performed their task, we cannot say. But the fact, that they attempted the task, exhibits a commendable anxiety to make their logical theory complete, and to fortify it against objections.

It is in this point of view—in reference to logical theory—that the Megaric philosophers have not been fairly appreciated. They, or persons reasoning in their manner, formed one essential encouragement and condition to the formation of any tolerable logical theory. They administered, to minds capable and constructive, that painful sense of contradiction, and shock of perplexity, which Sokrates relied upon as the stimulus to *Real character of the Megaric sophisms, not calculated to deceive, but to guard against deception.*

"Si dicis te mentiri verumque dicis, mentiris. Dicis autem te mentiri, verumque dicis: mentiris igitur." 2, 3. Ὁ ἐγκεκαλυμμένος. You know your father: you are placed before a person covered and concealed by a thick veil: you do not know him. But this person is your father. Therefore you both know your father, and do not know him. 5. Κερατίνης. That which you have not lost, you have: but you have not lost horns; therefore you *have* horns. 4, 6. Σωρείτης—Φάλακρος. What number of grains make a heap—or are many? What number are few? Are three grains few, and four *many?*—or, where will you draw the line between Few and Many? The like question about the hairs on a man's head—How many must he lose before he can be said to have only a few, or to be bald?

[p] Diog. L. v. p. 49; vii. pp. 192-198. Seneca, Epistol. p. 45. Plutarch (De Stoicor. Repugnantiis, p. 1037) has some curious extracts and remarks from Chrysippus; who (he says) spoke in the harshest terms against the Μεγαρικὰ ἐρωτήματα, as having puzzled and unsettled men's convictions without ground—while he (Chrysippus) had himself proposed puzzles and difficulties still more formidable, in his treatise κατὰ Συνηθείας.

mental parturition—and which Plato extols as a lever for raising the student to general conceptions.[q] Their sophisms were not intended to impose upon any one, but on the contrary, to guard against imposition.[r] Whoever states a fallacy clearly and nakedly, applying it to a particular case in which it conducts to a conclusion known upon other evidence not to be true—contributes to divest it of its misleading effect. The persons most liable to be deceived by the fallacy are those who are not forewarned :—in cases where the premisses are stated not nakedly, but in an artful form of words—and where the conclusion, though false, is not known beforehand to be false by the hearer. To use Mr. John Stuart Mill's phrase,[s] the fallacy is a case of apparent evidence mistaken for real evidence: you expose it to be evidence only apparent and not real, by giving a type of the fallacy, in which the conclusion obtained is obviously false: and the more obviously false it is, the better suited for its tutelary purpose. Aristotle recognises, as indispensable in philosophical enquiry, the preliminary wrestling into which he conducts his reader, by means of a long string of unsolved difficulties or puzzles— (ἀπόριαι). He declares, distinctly and forcibly, that whoever attempts to lay out a positive theory, without having before his mind a full list of the difficulties with which he is to grapple, is like one who searches without knowing what he is

---

[q] Plato, Republic. vii. pp. 523 A, 524. τὰ μὲν ἐν ταῖς αἰσθήσεσιν οὐ παρακαλοῦντα τὴν νόησιν εἰς ἐπίσκεψιν ὡς ἱκανῶς ὑπὸ τῆς αἰσθήσεως κρινόμενα —τὰ δὲ παντάπασι διακελευόμενα ἐκείνην ἐπισκέψασθαι, ὡς τῆς αἰσθήσεως οὐδὲ ὑγιὲς ποιούσης—Τὰ μὲν οὐ παρακαλοῦντα, ὅσα μὴ ἐκβαίνει εἰς ἐναντίαν αἴσθησιν ἅμα· τὰ δ' ἐκβαίνοντα, ὡς παρακαλοῦντα τίθημι, ἐπειδὰν ἡ αἴσθησις μηδὲν μᾶλλον τοῦτο ἢ τὸ ἐνάντιον δηλοῖ. Compare p. 524 E: the whole passage is very interesting.

[r] The remarks of Ritter (Gesch. der Philos. ii. p. 139, 2nd ed.) upon these Megaric philosophers are more just and discerning than those made by most of the historians of philosophy—"Doch darf man wohl annehmen, dass sie solche Trugschlüsse nicht zur Taüschung, sondern zur Belehrung für unvorsichtige, oder zur Warnung vor der Seichtigkeit gewöhnlicher Vorstellungsweisen, gebrauchen wollten. So viel ist gewiss, dass die Megariker sich viel mit den Formen des Denkens beschäftigten, vielleicht mehr zur Aufsuchung einzelner Regeln, als zur Begründung eines wissenschaftlichen Zusammenhangs unter ihnen; obwohl auch besondere Theile der Logik unter ihren Schriften erwähnt werden."
This is much more reasonable than the language of Prantl, who denounces "the shamelessness of doctrinarism" (die Unverschämtheit des Doctrinarismus) belonging to these Megarici— "the petulance and vanity which prompted them to seek celebrity by intentional offences against sound common sense," &c. (Gesch. der Logik, pp. 39-40.)

[s] See the first chapter of his book v. on Fallacies, System of Logic, vol. ii.

looking for; without being competent to decide whether what he hits upon as a solution be really a solution or not.[t] Now that enumeration of puzzles which Aristotle here postulates (and in part undertakes, in reference to Philosophia Prima) is exactly what the Megarics and various other dialecticians (called by Plato and Aristotle Sophists) contributed to furnish for the use of those who theorised on Logic.

You may dislike philosophy: you may undervalue, or altogether proscribe, the process of theorising. This is the standing-point usual with the bulk of mankind, ancient as well as modern: who generally dislike all accurate reasoning, or analysis and discrimination of familiar abstract words, as mean and tiresome hairsplitting.[u] But if you admit the business of theorising to be legitimate, useful, and even honourable, you must reckon on free working of independent, individual, minds as the operative force—and on the necessity of dissentient, conflicting manifestations of this common force, as essential conditions to any successful result. Upon no other conditions can you obtain any tolerable body of reasoned truth—or even reasoned *quasi-truth*.

If the process of theorising be admissible, it must include negative as well as affirmative.

Now the historians of philosophy seldom take this view of philosophy as a whole—as a field to which the free antithesis of affirmative and negative is indispensable. They consider true philosophy as represented by Sokrates, Plato, and Aristotle, one or other of them: while the contemporaries of these eminent men are discredited under the name of Sophists, Eristics, or sham-philosophers, sowing tares among the legitimate crop of wheat—or as devils whom the miraculous virtue of Sokrates and Plato is employed in ex-

Logical position of the Megaric philosophers erroneously described by historians of philosophy. Necessity of a complete collection of difficulties.

---

[t] Aristotel. Metaphys. B. 1, p. 994, a. 33.

διὸ δεῖ τὰς δυσχερείας τεθεωρηκέναι πάσας πρότερον, τούτων δὲ χάριν καὶ διὰ τὸ τοὺς ζητοῦντας ἄνευ τοῦ διαπορῆσαι πρῶτον ὁμοίους εἶναι τοῖς ποῖ δεῖ βαδίζειν ἀγνοοῦσιν, καὶ πρὸς τούτοις οὐδ' εἴ ποτε τὸ ζητούμενον εὕρηκεν ἢ μὴ, γιγνώσκειν· τὸ γὰρ τέλος τούτῳ μὲν οὐ δῆλον, τῷ δὲ προηπορηκότι δῆλον.

Aristotle devotes the whole of this Book to an enumeration of ἀπόριαι.

[u] See my account of the Platonic dialogue Hippias Major, vol. i. ch. xi. pp. 382-385. Aristot. Metaphys. A minor, p. 995, a. 9. τοὺς δὲ λυπεῖ τὸ ἀκριβὲς, ἢ διὰ τὸ μὴ δύνασθαι συνείρειν, ἢ διὰ τὴν μικρολογίαν· ἔχει γάρ τι τὸ ἀκριβὲς τοιοῦτον, ὥστε καθάπερ ἐπὶ τῶν συμβολαίων, καὶ ἐπὶ τῶν λόγων ἀνελεύθερον εἶναί τισι δοκεῖ. Cicero (Paradoxa, c. 2) talks of the "minutæ interrogatiunculæ" of the Stoics as tedious and tiresome.

pelling from the Athenian mind. Even the companions of
Sokrates, and the Megarics among them, whom we know
only upon the imperfect testimony of opponents, have
fallen under this unmerited sentence:[x] as if they were destructive agents breaking down an edifice of well-constituted philosophy—no such edifice in fact having ever existed
in Greece, though there were several dissenting lecture rooms
and conflicting veins of speculation promoted by eminent
individuals.

Whoever undertakes, *bonâ fide*, to frame a complete and
defensible logical theory, will desire to have before him a
copious collection of such difficulties, and will consider those
who propound them as useful auxiliaries.[y] If he finds no one
to propound them, he will have to imagine them for himself.

[x] The same charge is put by Cicero
into the mouth of Lucullus against the
Academics :—" Similiter vos (Aca-
demici) quum perturbare, ut illi " (the
Gracchi and others) "rempublicam, sic
vos philosophiam, benè jam constitutam velitis. Tum exortus est, ut in
optimâ republicâ Tiberius Gracchus,
sic Arcesilas, qui constitutam philosophiam everteret."

Even in the liberal and comprehensive history of the Greek philosophy by Zeller (vol. ii. p. 187, ed. 2nd.),
respecting Eukleides and the Megarians ;—" Dagegen bot der *Streit
gegen die geltenden Meinungen* dem
Scharfsinn, der Rechthaberei, und dem
wissenschaftlichen Ehrgeiz, ein uner-
schöpfliches Feld dar, welches denn
auch die Megarischen Philosophen
rüstig ausbeuteten."

If by "die geltenden Meinungen"
Zeller means the *common sense* of the
day—that is, the opinions and beliefs
current among the ἰδιῶται, the working, enjoying, non-theorising public—
it is very true that the Megaric philosophers contended against them : but
Sokrates and Plato contended against
them quite as much ; we see this in
the Platonic Apology, Gorgias, Republic, Timæus, Parmenidês, &c.

If, on the other hand, by "die
geltenden Meinungen" Zeller means
any philosophical or logical theories
generally or universally admitted by
thinking men as valid, the answer is
that there were none such in the fourth
and third centuries B.C.   Various

eminent speculative individuals were
labouring to construct such theories,
each in his own way, and each with
a certain congregation of partisans; but
established theory there was none. Nor
can any theory (whether accepted or
not) be firm or trustworthy, unless it
be exposed to the continued thrusts of
the negative weapon, searching out its
vulnerable points. We know of the
Megarics only what they furnished
towards that negative testing; without
which, however,—as we may learn
from Plato and Aristotle themselves,—
the true value of the affirmative de-
fences can never be measured.

[y] Marbach (Gesch. der Philos. s. 91),
though he treats the Megarics as jesters
(which I do not think they were), yet
adds very justly : "Nevertheless these
puzzles (propounded by the Megarics)
have their serious and scientific side.
We are forced to inquire, how it happens that the contradictions shown up
in them are not merely possible but
even necessary."

Tiedemann and Winckelmann also
both remark that the debaters called
Eristics contributed greatly to the for-
mation of the theory and precepts of
Logic, afterwards laid out by Aristotle.
Winckelmann, Prolegg. ad Platon.
Euthydem. pp. xxiv.-xxxi. Even
Stallbaum, though full of harshness
towards those Sophists whom he de-
scribes as belonging to the school of
Protagoras, treats the Megaric philo-
sophers with much greater respect.
Prolegom. ad Platon. Euthydem. p. 9.

"The philosophy of reasoning" (observes Mr. John Stuart Mill) "must comprise the philosophy of bad as well as of good reasoning."[z] The one cannot be complete without the other. To enumerate the different varieties of apparent evidence which is not real evidence (called Fallacies), and of apparent contradictions which are not real contradictions— referred as far as may be to classes, each illustrated by a suitable type—is among the duties of a logician. He will find this duty much facilitated, if there happen to exist around him an active habit of dialectic debate: ingenious men who really study the modes of puzzling and confuting a well-armed adversary, as well as of defending themselves against the like. Such a habit did exist at Athens: and unless it had existed, the Aristotelian theories on logic would probably never have been framed. Contemporary and antecedent dialecticians, the Megarici among them, supplied the stock of particular examples enumerated and criticised by Aristotle in the Topica:[a] which treatise (especially the last book, De Sophisticis Elenchis) is intended both to explain the theory, and to give suggestions on the practice, of logical controversy. A man who takes lessons in fencing must learn not only how to thrust and parry, but also how to impose on his opponent by feints, and to meet the feints employed against himself: a general who learns the art of war must know how to take advantage of the enemy by effective cheating and treachery (to use the language of Xenophon), and how to avoid being cheated himself. The Aristotelian Topica, in like manner, teach the arts both of dialectic attack and of dialectic defence.[b]

[z] System of Logic, Book v. 1, 1.

[a] Prantl (Gesch. der Logik. vol. i. pp. 43-50), ascribes to the Megarics all or nearly all the sophisms which Aristotle notices in the Treatise De Sophisticis Elenchis. This is more than can be proved, and more than I think probable. Several of them are taken from the Platonic Euthydêmus.

[b] See the remarkable passages in the discourses of Sokrates (Memorab. iii. 1, 6; iv. 2, 15), and in that of Kambyses to Cyrus, which repeats the same opinion—Cyropæd. i. 6. 27 —respecting the amount of deceit,

treachery, the thievish and rapacious qualities required for conducting war against an enemy—(τὰ πρὸς τοὺς πολεμίους νόμιμα, i. 6. 34).

Aristotle treats of Dialectic, as he does of Rhetoric, as an art having its theory, and precepts founded upon that theory. I have already observed, in a former chapter (vol. i. c. xix. pp 543-550), that logical Fallacies are not generated or invented by persons called Sophists, but are inherent liabilities to error in the human intellect; and that the habit of debate affords the only means of bringing them into

The Sophisms ascribed to Eubulidês, looked at from the point of view of logical theory, deserve that attention which they seem to have received. The logician lays down as a rule that no affirmative proposition can be at the same time true and false. Now the first sophism (called *Mentiens*) exhibits the case of a proposition which is, or appears to be, at the same time true and false.[c] It is for the logician to explain how this proposition

Sophisms propounded by Eubulides.
1. Mentiens.
2. The Velled Man.
3. Sorites.
4. Cornutus.

clear daylight, and guarding against being deceived by them. Aristotle gives precepts both how to thrust, and how to parry, with the best effect: if he had taught only how to parry, he would have left out one-half of the art.

One of the most learned and candid of the Aristotelian commentators—M. Barthélemy St. Hilaire—observes as follows (Logique d'Aristote, p. 435, Paris, 1838) respecting De Sophist. Elenchis :—

"Aristote va donc s'occuper de la marche qu'il faut donner aux discussions sophistiques : et ici il serait difficile quelquefois de décider, à la manière dont les choses sont présentées par lui, si ce sont des conseils qu'il donne aux Sophistes, où à ceux qui veulent éviter leurs ruses. Tout ce qui précède, prouve, au reste, que c'est en ce dernier sens qu'il faut entendre la pensée du philosophe. Ceci est d'ailleurs la seconde portion du traité."

It appears to me that Aristotle intended to teach or to suggest both the two things which are here placed in Antithesis — though I do not agree with M. St. Hilaire's way of putting the alternative—as if there were one class of persons, professional Sophists, who fenced with poisoned weapons, while every one except them refrained from such weapons. Aristotle intends to teach the art of Dialectic as a whole; he neither intends nor wishes that any learners shall make a bad use of his teaching; but if they do use it badly, the fault does not lie with him. See the observations in the beginning of the Rhetorica, i. p. 1355, a. 26, and the observations put by Plato into the mouth of Gorgias (Gorg. p. 456 E).

Even in the Analytica Priora (ii. 19, a. 34) (independent of the Topica) Aristotle says:—χρὴ δὲ ὅπερ φυλάττεσθαι παραγγέλλομεν ἀποκρινομένους, αὐτοὺς ἐπιχειροῦντας πειρᾶσθαι λαν-

θάνειν. Investigations of the double or triple senses of words (he says) are useful—καὶ πρὸς τὸ μὴ παραλογισθῆναι, καὶ πρὸς τὸ παραλογίσασθαι, Topica, i. 18, p. 108, a. 26. See also other passages of the Topica where artifices are indicated for the purpose of concealing your own plan of proceeding and inducing your opponent to make answer in the sense which you wish, Topica, i. 2, p. 101, a. 25, vi. 10, p. 148, a. 37, viii. 1, p. 151, b. 23, viii. 1, p. 153, a. 6, viii. 2, p. 154, a. 5, viii. 11, p. 161, a. 24 seq. You must be provided with the means of meeting every sort and variety of objection—πρὸς γὰρ τὸν πάντως ἐνιστάμενον, πάντως ἀντιτακτέον ἐστίν. Topic. v. 4, p. 134, a. 4.

I have already touched on the Topica, in this point of view, as founded upon and illustrating the Megaric logical puzzles (vol. i. ch. vi. pp. 241-243-259).

[c] Theophrastus wrote a treatise in three books on the solution of the puzzle called Ὁ ψευδόμενος (see the list of his lost works in Diogenes L. v. 49). We find also other treatises entitled Μεγαρικὸς ά (which Diogenes cites, vi. 22),—Ἀγωνιστικὸν τῆς περὶ τοὺς ἐριστικοὺς λόγους θεωρίας—Σοφισμάτων ά, β—besides several more titles relating to dialectics, and bearing upon the solution of syllogistic problems. Chrysippus also, in the ensuing century, wrote a treatise in three books, Περὶ τῆς τοῦ ψευδομένου λύσεως (D. L. vii. 197). Such facts show the importance of these problems in their bearing upon logical theory, as conceived by the ancient world. Epikurus also wrote against the Μεγαρικοί (D. L. x. 27).

The discussion of sophisms, or logical difficulties (λύσεις ἀποριῶν), was a favourite occupation at the banquets of philosophers at Athens, on or about 100 B.C. Ἀντίπατρος δὲ ὁ φιλόσοφος, συμπόσιόν ποτε συνάγων, συνέταξε τοῖς

can be brought under his rule—or else to admit it as an exception. Again, the second and third sophisms in the list (the Veiled or Hidden Man) are so contrived as to involve the respondent in a contradiction: he is made to say both that he knows his father, and that he does not know his father. Both the one answer and the other follow naturally from the questions and circumstances supposed. The contradiction points to the loose and equivocal way in which the word *to know* is used in common speech. Such equivocal meaning of words is not only one of the frequent sources of error and fallacy in reasoning, but also one of the least heeded by persons untrained in dialectics; who are apt to presume that the same word bears always the same meaning. To guard against this cause of error, and to determine (or impel others to determine) the accurate meaning or various distinct meanings of each word, is among the duties of the logician: and I will add that the verb *to know* stands high in the list of words requiring such determination—as the Platonic Theætêtus [d] alone would be sufficient to teach us. Farthermore, when we examine what is called the Soritês of Eubulidês, we perceive that it brings to view an inherent indeterminateness of various terms: indeterminateness which cannot be avoided, but which must be pointed out in order that it may not mislead. You cannot say how many grains are *much*—or how many grains make *a heap*. When this want of precision, pervading many words in the language, was first brought to notice in a suitable special case, it would naturally appear a striking novelty. Lastly, the sophism called Κερατίνης or Cornutus, is one of great plausibility, which would probably impose upon most persons, if the question were asked for the first time without any forewarning. It serves to administer a lesson, nowise unprofitable or superfluous, that before you answer a ques-

ἐρχομένοις ὡς περὶ σοφισμάτων ἐροῦσιν (Athenæus, v. 186 C; Plutarch, Non posse suaviter vivi secundum Epicurum, p. 1096 C). De Sanitate Præcepta, c. 20, p. 133 B.

[d] Various portions of the Theætêtus illustrate this Megaric sophism (pp. 165-188). The situation assumed in the question of Eubulidês — having before your eyes a person veiled —

might form a suitable addition to the various contingencies specified in Theætêt. pp. 192-193.

The manner in which the Platonic Sokrates proves (Theæt. 165) that you at the same time see, and do not see, an object before you, is quite as sophistical as the way in which Eubulidês proves that you both know, and do not know, your father.

tion, you should fully weigh its import and its collateral bearings.

The causes of error and fallacy are inherent in the compli-

Causes of error constant—The Megarics were sentinels against them. cation of nature, the imperfection of language, the small range of facts which we know, the indefinite varieties of comparison possible among those facts, and the diverse or opposite predispositions, intellectual as well as emotional, of individual minds. They are not fabricated by those who first draw attention to them.[e] The Megarics, far from being themselves deceivers, served as sentinels against deceit. They planted conspicuous beacons upon some of the sunken rocks whereon unwary reasoners were likely to be wrecked. When the general type of a fallacy is illustrated by a particular case in which the conclusion is manifestly untrue, the like fallacy is rendered less operative for the future.

Of the positive doctrines of the Megarics we know little:

Controversy of the Megarics with Aristotle about Power. Arguments of Aristotle. but there is one upon which Aristotle enters into controversy with them, and upon which (as far as can be made out) I think they were in the right. In the question about Power, they held that the power to do a thing did not exist, except when the thing was actually done: that an architect, for example, had no power to build a house, except when he actually did build one. Aristotle controverts this opinion at some length; contending

---

[e] Cicero, in his Academ. Prior. ii. pp. 28-30, has very just remarks on the obscurities and difficulties in the reasoning process, which the Megarics and others brought to view—and were blamed for so doing, as unfair and captious reasoners — as if they had themselves created the difficulties— "(Dialectica) primo progressu festivé tradit elementa loquendi et ambiguorum intelligentiam concludendique rationem; tum paucis additis venit ad soritas, lubricum sané et periculosum locum, quod tu modo dicebas esse vitiosum interrogandi genus. Quid ergo? *istius vitii num nostra culpa est?* Rerum natura nullam nobis dedit cognitionem finium, ut ullâ in re statuere possimus quatenus. Nec hoc in acervo tritici solum, unde nomen est, sed nullâ omnino in re minutatim interroganti—dives, pauper —clarus, obscurus, sit—multa, pauca, magna, parva, longa, brevia, lata, angusta, quanto aut addito aut dempto certum respondeamus, non habemus. At vitiosi sunt soritæ. Frangite igitur eos, si potestis, ne molesti sint. . . . . Sic me (inquit) sustineo, neque diutius captiosé interroganti respondes. Si habes quod liqueat neque respondes, superbis: si non habes, ne tu quidem percipis."

The principle of the Sorites (ἡ σωριτικὴ ἀπορία—Sextus adv. Gramm. s. 68) though differently applied, is involved in the argument of Zeno the Eleate, addressed to Protagoras—see Simplikius ad Aristot. Physic. 250, p. 423, b. 42, Sch. Brand.; compare chap. ii. of this work, vol. i. p. 98-104.

that there exists a sort of power or cause which is in itself irregular and indeterminate, sometimes turning to the affirmative, sometimes to the negative, to do or not to do;[f] that the architect *has* the *power to build* constantly, though he exerts it only on occasions: and that many absurdities would follow if we did not admit a given power or energy—and the exercise of that power—to be things distinct and separable.[g]

Now these arguments of Aristotle are by no means valid against the Megarics, whose doctrine, though apparently paradoxical, will appear when explained to be no paradox at all, but perfectly true. When we say that the architect has power to build, we do not mean that he has power to do so under all supposable circumstances, but only under certain conditions: we wish to distinguish him from non-professional men, who under those same conditions have no power to build. The architect must be awake and sober: he must have the will or disposition to build:[h] he must be provided with tools and materials, and be secure against destroying enemies. These and other conditions being generally understood, it is unnecessary to enunciate them in common speech. But when we engage in dialectic analysis, the accurate discussion (ἀκριβολογία) indispensable to philosophy requires us to bring under distinct notice, that which the elliptical character of common speech implies without enunciating. Unless these favourable conditions be supposed, the architect is no more able to build than an ordinary non-professional man. Now the Megarics did not deny the distinctive character of the architect, as compared with the non-architect; but they defined more accurately in what it consisted, by restoring the omitted conditions. They went a step farther: they pointed out that whenever the architect

These arguments not valid against the Megarici.

---

[f] Aristot. De Interpret. p. 19, a. 6-20. ὅλως ἔστιν ἐν τοῖς μὴ ἀεὶ ἐνεργοῦσι τὸ δυνατὸν εἶναι καὶ μή, ὁμοίως· ἐν οἷς ἄμφω ἐνδέχεται, καὶ τὸ εἶναι καὶ τὸ μὴ εἶναι, ὥστε καὶ τὸ γενέσθαι καὶ τὸ μὴ γενέσθαι.

[g] Aristot. Metaph. Θ. 3, p. 1046, b. 29. Εἰσὶ δέ τινες, οἵ φασιν, οἷον οἱ Μεγαρικοί, ὅταν ἐνεργῇ, μόνον δύνασθαι, ὅταν δὲ μὴ ἐνεργῇ, μὴ δύνασθαι—οἷον τὸν μὴ οἰκοδομοῦντα οὐ δύνασθαι οἰκοδο-

μεῖν, ἀλλὰ τὸν οἰκοδομοῦντα ὅταν οἰκοδομῇ· ὁμοίως δὲ καὶ ἐπὶ τῶν ἄλλων.

Deycks (De Megaricorum Doctrinâ, pp. 70-71) considers this opinion of the Megarics to be derived from their general Eleatic theory of the Ens Unum et Immotum. But I see no logical connection between the two.

[h] About this condition, implied in the predicate δυνατὸς, see Plato, Hippias Minor, p. 366 D.

finds himself in concert with these accompanying conditions (his own volition being one of the conditions) he goes to work —and the building is produced. As the house is not built, unless he wills to build, and has tools and materials, &c.—so conversely, whenever he has the will to build and has tools and materials, &c., the house is actually built. The effect is not produced, except when the full assemblage of antecedent conditions come together: but as soon as they do come together, the effect is assuredly produced. The accomplishments of the architect, though an essential item, are yet only one item among several, of the conditions necessary to building the house. He has no power to build, except when those other conditions are assumed along with him: in other words, he has no such power except when he actually does build.

Aristotle urges against the Megarics, various arguments, as follows:—1. Their doctrine implies that the architect is not an architect, and does not possess his professional skill,[i] except at the moment when he is actually building.—But the Megarics would have denied that their doctrine did imply this. The architect possesses his art at all times: but his art does not constitute a power of building except under certain accompanying conditions.

His arguments cited and criticised.

2. The Megaric doctrine is the same as that of Protagoras, implying that there exists no perceivable Object, and no Subject capable of perceiving, except at the moment when perception actually takes place.[k]—On this we may observe, that the Megarics coincide with Protagoras thus far, that they bring into open daylight the relative and conditional, which the received phraseology tends to hide. But neither they nor he affirm what is here put upon them. When we speak of a perceivable Object, we mean that which may and will be perceived, *if* there be a proper Subject to perceive it: when we affirm a Subject capable of perception, we mean, one which will perceive, under those circumstances which we call the presence of an Object suitably placed. The Subject and Object are correlates: but it is convenient to have a language

---

[i] Aristot. Metaph. Θ, 3, 1047, a. 2. ὅταν παύσηται (οἰκοδομῶν) οὐχ ἕξει τὴν τέχνην.

[k] Aristot. Metaph. Θ. 3. 1047, a. 8-13.

CHAP. XXXVIII. CONTROVERSY ABOUT POWER. 493

in which one of them alone is introduced unconditionally, while the conditional sign is applied to the correlate: though the matter affirmed involves a condition common to both.

3. According to the Megaric doctrine (Aristotle argues) every man when not actually seeing, is blind; every man when not actually speaking, is dumb.—Here the Megarics would have said that this is a misinterpretation of the terms dumb and blind; which denote a person who cannot speak or see, even though he wishes it. One who is now silent, though not dumb, may speak if he wills it: but his own volition is an essential condition.[1]

4. According to the Megaric doctrine (says Aristotle) when you are now lying down, you have no power to rise: when you are standing up, you have no power to lie down: so that the present condition of affairs must continue for ever unchanged: nothing can come into existence which is not now in being.—Here again, the Megarics would have denied his inference. The man who is now standing up, has power to lie down, *if he wills* to do so—or he may be thrown down by a superior force: that is, he will lie down, *if* some new fact of a certain character shall supervene. The Megarics do not deny that he has power, *if*—so and so: they deny that he has power, without the *if*—that is, without the farther accompaniments essential to energy.

On the whole, it seems to me that Aristotle's refutation of the Megarics is unsuccessful. A given assemblage of condi-

---

[1] The question between Aristotle and the Megarics has not passed out of debate with modern philosophers.

Dr. Thomas Brown observes, in his inquiry into Cause and Effect—"From the mere silence of any one, we cannot infer that he is dumb in consequence of organic imperfection. He may be silent only because he has no desire of speaking, not because speech would not have followed his desire: and it is not with the mere *existence* of any one, but *with his desire of speaking*, that we suppose utterance to be connected. A man who has *no desire of speaking, has in truth*, and in strictness of language, *no power of speaking, when in that state of mind:* since he has not a circumstance which, as immediately

prior, is essential to speech. But since he has that power, as soon as the new circumstance of desire arises—and as the presence or absence of the desire cannot be perceived but in its effects—*there is no inconvenience in the common language*, which ascribes the power, *as if it were possessed at all times, and in all circumstances of mind*, though unquestionably, nothing more is meant than that the desire existing will be followed by utterance." (Brown, Essay on the Relation of Cause and Effect, p. 200.)

This is the real sense of what Aristotle calls τὸ δὲ (λέγεται) δυνατὸν, οἷον δυνατὸν εἶναι βαδίζειν ὅτι βαδίσειεν ἂν, i. e. he will walk *if* he desires to do so (De Interpret. p. 23, a. 9-15).

tions is requisite for the production of any act:—while there
are other circumstances, which, if present at the same
time, would defeat its production. We often find
it convenient to describe a state of things in which
some of the antecedent conditions are present without the
rest: in which therefore the act is not produced, yet would be
produced, if the remaining circumstances were present, and if
the opposing circumstances were absent.[m] The state of things
thus described is the *potential* as distinguished from the
actual: power, distinguished from act or energy: it represents
an incomplete assemblage of the antecedent positive conditions—or perhaps a complete assemblage, but counteracted by
some opposing circumstances. As soon as the assemblage
becomes complete, and the opposing circumstances removed,
the potential passes into the actual. The architect, when he
is not building, possesses, not indeed the full or plenary power
to build, but an important fraction of that power, which will
become plenary when the other fractions supervene, but will
then at the same time become operative, so as to produce the
actual building.[n]

[m] Hobbes, in his Computation or Logic (chaps. ix. and x. Of Cause and Effect. Of Power and Act) expounds this subject with his usual perspicuity. "A Cause simply, or an Entire Cause, is the aggregate of all the ac- cidents, both of the agents, how many soever they be, and of the patient, put together; which, when they are all supposed to be present, it cannot be understood but that the effect is pro- duced at the same instant: and if any one of them be wanting, it cannot be understood but that the effect is not produced " (ix. 3).
"Correspondent to Cause and Effect are power and Act; nay, those and these are the same things, though for divers considerations they have divers names. For whensoever any agent has all those accidents which are neces- sarily requisite for the production of some effect in the patient, then we say that agent has power to produce that effect if it be applied to a patient. In like manner, whensoever any patient has all those accidents which it is requisite it should have for the produc- tion of some effect in it, we say it is in the power of that patient to produce

that effect if it be applied to a fitting agent. Power, active and passive, are parts only of plenary and entire power: nor, except they be joined, can any effect proceed from them. And there- fore these powers are but conditional : namely, the agent has power if it be applied to a patient, and the patient has power if it be applied to an agent. *Otherwise neither of them have power, nor can the accidents which are in them severally be properly called powers :* nor any action be said to be possible for the power of the agent alone or the patient alone."
[n] Aristotle does in fact grant all that is here said in the same book and in the page next subsequent to that which contains his arguments against the Megaric doctrine, Metaphys. Θ. 5, 1048, a. 1-24.
In this chapter Aristotle distinguishes powers belonging to things from powers belonging to persons—powers irrational from powers rational—powers in which the agent acts without any will or choice, from those in which the will or choice of the agent is one item of the aggregate of conditions. He here expressly recognises that the power

The doctrine which I have just been canvassing is expressly cited by Aristotle as a Megaric doctrine, and was therefore probably held by his contemporary Eubulidês.   From the pains which Aristotle takes (in the treatise 'De Interpretatione' and elsewhere) to explain and vindicate his own doctrine about the Potential and the Actual, we may see that it was a theme much debated among the dialecticians of the day.   And we read of another Megaric, Diodorus[o] Kronus, perhaps contemporary (yet probably a little later than Aristotle), as advancing a position substantially the same as that of Eubulidês.   That alone is possible (Diodorus affirmed) which either is happening now, or will happen at some future time.   As, in speaking about facts of an unrecorded past, we know well that a given fact either occurred or did not occur, yet without knowing which of the two is true—and therefore we affirm only that the fact *may* have occurred: so also about the future, either the assertion that a given fact will at some time occur, is positively true, or

Diodôrus Kronus—his doctrine about τὸ δυνατόν.

of the agent, separately considered, is only *conditional ;* that is, conditional on the presence and suitable state of the patient, as well as upon the absence of counteracting circumstances.   But he contends that such absence of counteracting circumstances is plainly implied, and need not be expressly mentioned in the definition.

ἐπεὶ δὲ τὸ δυνατὸν τὶ δυνατόν, καὶ ποτὲ, καὶ πῶς, καὶ ὅσα ἄλλα ἀνάγκη προσεῖναι ἐν τῷ διορισμῷ—

τὸ δυνατὸν κατὰ λόγον ἅπαν ἀνάγκη, ὅταν ὀρέγηται, οὗ τ' ἔχει τὴν δύναμιν καὶ ὡς ἔχει, τοῦτο ποιεῖν· ἔχει δὲ παρόντος τοῦ παθητικοῦ καὶ ὡδὶ ἔχοντος ποιεῖν· εἰ δὲ μὴ, ποιεῖν οὐ δυνήσεται.   τὸ γὰρ μηθενὸς τῶν ἔξω κωλύοντος προσδιορίζεσθαι, οὐδὲν ἔτι δεῖ· τὴν γὰρ δύναμιν ἔχει ὡς ἔστι δύναμις τοῦ ποιεῖν, ἔστι δ' οὐ πάντως, ἀλλ' ἐχόντων πως, ἐν οἷς ἀφορισθήσεται καὶ τὰ ἔξω κωλύοντα· ἀφαιρεῖται γὰρ ταῦτα τῶν ἐν τῷ διορισμῷ προσόντων ἔνια.   The commentary of Alexander Aphr. upon this chapter is well worth consulting (pp. 546-548 of the edition of his commentary by Bonitz, 1847).   Moreover Aristotle affirms in this chapter, that when τὸ ποιητικὸν and τὸ παθητικὸν come together under suitable circumstances the power will certainly pass into act.

Here then, it seems to me, Aristotle concedes the doctrine which the Megarics affirmed; or, if there be any difference between them, it is rather verbal than real.   In fact, Aristotle's reasoning in the third chapter (wherein he impugns the doctrine of the Megarics), and the definition of δυνατὸν which he gives in that chapter (1047, a. 25), is hardly to be reconciled with his reasoning in the fifth chapter.   Bonitz (Notes on the Metaphys. pp. 393-395) complains of the *mira levitas* of Aristotle in his reasoning against the Megarics, and of his omitting to distinguish between *Vermögen* and *Möglichkeit.*   I will not use so uncourteous a phrase; but I think his refutation of the Megarics is both unsatisfactory and contradicted by himself.   I agree with the following remark of Bonitz : — "Nec mirum, quod Megarici, aliis illi quidem in rebus arguti, in hâc autem satis acuti, existentiam τῷ δυνάμει ὄντι tribuere recusarint," &c.

[o] The dialectic ingenuity of Diodorus is powerfully attested by the verse of Ariston, applied to describe Arkesilaus. (Sextus Emp. Pyrrh. Hyp. i. p. 234.)

Πρόσθε Πλάτων, ὄπιθεν Πύῤῥων, μέσσος Διόδωρος.

the assertion that it will never occur, is positively true: the assertion that it may or may not occur some time or other, represents only our ignorance, which of the two is true. That which will never at any time occur, is impossible.

The argument here recited must have been older than *Sophism of Diodorus—* Diodorus, since Aristotle states and controverts it: ʽΟ Κυριεύων. but it seems to have been handled by him in a peculiar dialectic arrangement, which obtained the title of ʽΟ Κυριεύων.[p] The Stoics (especially Chrysippus) in times somewhat later, impugned the opinion of Diodorus, though seemingly upon grounds not quite the same as Aristotle. This problem was one upon which speculative minds occupied themselves for several centuries. Aristotle and Chrysippus maintained that affirmations respecting the past were *necessary* (one necessarily true and the other necessarily false)—affirmations respecting the future, *contingent* (one must be true and the other false, but either might be true). Diodorus held that both varieties of affirmations were equally necessary—Kleanthes the Stoic thought, that both were equally contingent.[q]

It was thus that the Megaric dialecticians, with that fertility of mind which belonged to the Platonic and Aristotelian century, stirred up many real problems and difficulties connected with logical evidence, and supplied matters for discussion which not only occupied the speculative minds of the next four or five centuries, but have continued in debate down to the present day.

The question about the Possible and Impossible, raised be-*Question between Aristotle and Diodorus, depends upon whether universal regularity of sequence be admitted or denied.* tween Aristotle and Diodorus, depends upon the larger question, Whether there are universal laws of Nature or not? whether the sequences are, universally and throughout, composed of assemblages of conditions regularly antecedent, and assemblages of events regularly consequent; though from the number and complication of causes, partly co-operating and

---

[p] Aristot. De Interpret. p. 18, a. pp. 27-38. Alexander ad Aristot. Analyt. Prior. 34, p. 163, b. 34, Schol. Brandis.

[q] Arrian ad Epiktet. ii. p. 19. Upton, in his notes on this passage of Arrian (p. 151) has embodied a very valuable and elaborate commentary by Mr. James

Harris (the great Aristotelian of the 18th century), explaining the nature of this controversy, and the argument called ὁ Κυριεύων.

Compare Cicero, De Fato, c. 7-9. Epistol. Fam. ix. 4.

partly conflicting with each other, we with our limited intelligence are often unable to predict the cause of events in each particular situation. Sokrates, Plato, and Aristotle, all maintained that regular sequence of antecedent and consequent was not universal, but partial only:[r] that there were some agencies essentially regular, in which observation of the past afforded ground for predicting the future—other agencies (or the same agencies on different occasions) essentially irregular, in which the observation of the past afforded no such ground. Aristotle admitted a graduation of causes from perfect regularity to perfect irregularity :—1. The Celestial Spheres, with their included bodies or divine persons, which revolved and exercised a great and preponderant influence throughout the Kosmos, with perfect uniformity; having no power of contraries, i. e. having no power of doing anything else but what they actually did (having ἐνεργεία without δύναμις). 2. The four Elements, in which the natural agencies were to a great degree necessary and uniform, but also in a certain degree otherwise—either always or for the most part uniform (τὸ ὡς ἐπὶ τὸ πολύ)—tending by inherent appetency towards uniformity, but not always attaining it. 3. Besides these there were two other varieties of Causes accidental, or perfectly irregular—Chance and Spontaneity : powers of contraries, or with equal chance of contrary manifestations—essentially capricious, undeterminable, unpredictable.[s] This *Chance* of Aristotle—with one of two contraries sure to turn up, though you could never tell beforehand which of the two—was a conception analogous to what logicians sometimes call an Indefinite Proposition, or to what some grammarians have reckoned as a special variety of genders called the *doubtful gender*. There were thus positive causes of regularity, and positive causes of irregularity, the co-operation or conflict of

---

[r] Xenophon, Memor. i. 1 ; Plato, Timæus, p. 48 A.   ἡ πλανωμένη αἰτία, &c.

[s] Ἡ τύχη—τὸ ὁπότερ' ἔτυχε—τὸ αὐτόματον are in the conception of Aristotle independent Ἀρχαί, attached to and blending with ἀνάγκη and τὸ ὡς ἐπὶ τὸ πολύ. See Physic. ii. 196, b. 11 ; Metaphys. v. 1026-1027.

Sometimes τὸ ὁπότερ' ἔτυχε is spoken

of as an Ἀρχὴ, but not as an αἴτιον, or belonging to ὕλη as the Ἀρχή.   1027, b. 11.   δῆλον ἄρα ὅτι μέχρι τινος βαδίζει ἀρχῆς, αὕτη δὲ οὐκετ' εἰς ἄλλο· ἔσται οὖν ἡ τοῦ ὁπότερ' ἔτυχεν αὐτή, καὶ αἴτιον τῆς γενέσεως αὐτοῦ οὐδέν.

See, respecting the different notions of Cause held by ancient philosophers, my remarks on the Platonic Phædon suprà, vol. ii. ch. xxiii. pp. 182-186.

which gave the total manifestations of the actual universe. The principle of irregularity, or the Indeterminate, is sometimes described under the name of Matter,[t] as distinguishable from, yet co-operating with, the three determinate Causes— Formal, Efficient, Final. The Potential—the Indeterminate— the *May or May not be*—is characterised by Aristotle as one of the inherent principles operative in the Kosmos.

In what manner Diodorus stated and defended his opinion upon this point, we have no information. We know only that he placed affirmations respecting the future on the same footing as affirmations respecting the past: maintaining that our potential affirmation— *May or May not be*—respecting some future event, meant no more than it means respecting some past event, viz. : no inherent indeterminateness in the future sequence, but our ignorance of the determining conditions, and our inability to

Conclusion of Diodōrus —defended by Hobbes— Explanation given by Hobbes.

---

[t] Aristot. Metaph. E. 1027, a. 12, Λ. 1071, a. 10.

ὥστε ἡ ὕλη ἔσται αἰτία, ἡ ἐνδεχομένη παρὰ τὸ ὡς ἐπὶ τὸ πολὺ ἄλλως, τοῦ συμβεβηκότος.

Matter is represented as the principle of irregularity, of τὸ ὁπότερ᾽ ἔτυχε—as the δύναμις τῶν ἐναντίων.

In the explanation given by Alexander of Aphrodisias of the Peripatetic doctrine respecting chance—free-will, the principle of irregularity—τύχη is no longer assigned to the material cause, but is treated as an αἰτία κατὰ συμβεβηκὸς, distinguished from αἰτία προηγούμενα or καθ᾽αὑτά. The exposition given of the doctrine by Alexander is valuable and interesting. See his treatise De Fato, addressed to the Emperor Severus, in the edition of Orelli, Zurich, 1824 (a very useful volume, containing treatises of Ammonius, Plotinus, Bardesanes, &c. on the same subject); also several sections of his Quæstiones Naturales et Morales, ed. Spengel, Munich, 1842, pp. 22-61-65-123, &c. He gives, however, a different explanation of τὸ δυνατὸν and τὸ ἀδύνατον in pp. 62-63, which would not be at variance with the doctrine of Diodorus. We may remark that Alexander puts the antithesis of the two doctrines differently from Aristotle,— in this way. 1. Either all events happen καθ᾽ εἱμαρμένην. 2. Or all events do not happen καθ᾽ εἱμαρμένην, but

some events are ἐφ᾽ ἡμῖν. See De Fato, p. 14 seq. This way of putting the question is directed more against the Stoics, who were the great advocates of εἱμαρμένη, than against the Megaric Diodorus. The treatises of Chrysippus and the other Stoics alter both the wording and the putting of the thesis. We know that Chrysippus impugned the doctrine of Diodorus, but I do not see how.

The Stoic antithesis of τὰ καθ᾽ εἱμαρμένην—τὰ ἐφ᾽ ἡμῖν is different from the antithesis conceived by Aristotle, and does not touch the question about the universality of regular sequence. Τὰ ἐφ᾽ ἡμῖν describes those sequences in which human volition forms one among the appreciable conditions determining or modifying the result : τὰ καθ᾽ εἱμαρμένην includes all the other sequences wherein human volition has no appreciable influence. But the sequence τῶν ἐφ᾽ ἡμῖν is just as regular as the sequence τῶν καθ᾽ εἱμαρμένην : both the one and the other are often imperfectly predictable, because our knowledge of facts and power of comparison is so imperfect.

Theophrastus discussed τὸ καθ᾽ εἱμαρμένην, and explained it to mean the same as τὸ κατὰ φύσιν. φανερώτατα δὲ Θεόφραστος δείκνυσι ταὐτὸν ὂν τὸ καθ᾽ εἱμαρμένην τῷ κατὰ φύσιν (Alexander Aphrodisias ad Aristot. De Animâ, ii.).

calculate their combined working.[u]   In regard to scientific method generally, this problem is of the highest importance: for it is only so far as uniformity of sequence prevails, that facts become fit matter for scientific study.[x]   Consistently with the doctrine of all-pervading uniformity of sequence, the definition of Hobbes gives the only complete account of the Impossible and Possible: *i. e.* an account such as would appear to an omniscient calculator, where *May or May not* merge in *Will or Will not*.   According as each person falls short of or approaches this ideal standard—according to his

[u] The same doctrine as that of the Megaric Diodorus is declared by Hobbes in clear and explicit language (First Grounds of Philosophy, ii. 10, 4-5):—

"That is an impossible act, for the production of which there is no power plenary.   For seeing plenary power is that in which all things concur which are requisite for the production of an act, if the power shall never be plenary, there will always be wanting some of those things, without which the act cannot be produced. Wherefore that act shall never be produced: that is, that act is *impossible*. And every act, which is not impossible, is *possible*. Every act therefore which is possible, shall at some time or other be produced.   For if it shall never be produced, then those things shall never concur which are requisite for the production of it: wherefore that act is *impossible*, by the definition; which is contrary to what was supposed.

"A *necessary act* is that, the production of which it is impossible to hinder: and therefore every act that shall be produced, shall necessarily be produced; for that it shall not be produced is impossible, because, as has already been demonstrated, every possible act shall at some time be produced.   Nay, this proposition—*What shall be shall be*—is as necessary a proposition as this—*A man is a man.*

"But here, perhaps, some man will ask whether those future things which are commonly called *contingents*, are necessary. I say, then, that generally all contingents have their necessary causes, but are called *contingents*, in respect of other events on which they do not depend—as the rain which shall be to-morrow shall be necessary, that is,

from necessary causes: but we think and say, it happens by chance, because we do not yet perceive the causes thereof, though they exist now.   For men commonly call that *casual* or *contingent*, whereof they do not perceive the necessary cause: *and in the same manner they use to speak of things past, when not knowing whether a thing be done or not, they say, It is possible it never was done.*

"Wherefore all propositions concerning future things, contingent or not contingent, as this—It will rain to-morrow, or to-morrow the sun will rise—are either necessarily true or necessarily false: but we call them contingent, because we do not yet know whether they be true or false; whereas their verity depends not upon our knowledge, but upon the foregoing of their causes.   But there are some, who, though they will confess this whole proposition—*To-morrow it will either rain or not rain*—to be true, yet they will not acknowledge the parts of it, as, *To-morrow it will rain*, or *To-morrow it will not rain*, to be either of them true by itself; because (they say) neither this nor that is true *determinately*.   But what is this *true determinately*, but true *upon our knowledge*, or *evidently true?* And therefore they say no more but that it is not yet known whether it be true or not: but they say it more obscurely, and darken the evidence of the truth with the same words by which they endeavour to hide their own ignorance."

[x] The reader will find this problem admirably handled in Mr. John Stuart Mill's System of Logic, Book iii. ch. 21, and Book vi. ch. 2 and 3; also in the volume of Mr. Alexander Bain on the Emotions and the Will, ch. xi. s. 4, p. 546, seq.

knowledge and mental resource, inductive and deductive—
will be his appreciation of what may be or may not be—as of
what may have been or may not have been during the past.
But such appreciation, being relative to each individual mind,
is liable to vary indefinitely, and does not admit of being embodied in one general definition.

Besides the above doctrine respecting Possible and Impossible, there is also ascribed to Diodorus a doctrine respecting
Hypothetical Propositions, which, as far as I comprehend it,
appears to have been a correct one.[y]   He is also said to have
reasoned against the reality of motion, renewing the arguments of Zeno the Eleate.

But if he reproduced the arguments of Zeno, he also employed another, peculiar to himself. He admitted
the reality of *past* motion : but he denied the reality
of *present* motion. You may affirm truly (he said)
that a thing *has been moved :* but you cannot truly
affirm that any thing *is being moved.* Since it was
here before, and is *there* now, you may be sure that
it has been moved : but actual present motion you cannot
perceive or prove. Affirmation in the perfect tense may be
true, when affirmation in the present tense neither is nor ever
was true : thus it is true to say—Helen *had* three husbands
(Menelaus, Paris, Deiphobus) : but it was never true to say—
Helen *has* three husbands, since they became her husbands
in succession.[z] Diodorus supported this paradox by some
ingenious arguments, and the opinion which he denied seems
to have presented itself to him as involving the position of
indivisible minima —atoms of body, points of space, instants
of time. He admitted such minima of atoms, but not of space
or time : and without such admission he could not make intelligible to himself the fact of present or actual motion. He
could find no present *Now* or Minimum of Time ; without

[y] Sextus Emp. Pyrrhon. Hypotyp.
ii. pp. 110-115. ἀληθὲς συνημμένον.
adv. Mathemat. viii. 112. Philo maintained that an hypothetical proposition
was true, if both the antecedent and
consequent were true—"If it be day,
I am conversing." Diodorus denied
that this proposition, as an Hypothetical proposition, was true ; since the
consequent might be false, though the
antecedent were true. An Hypothetical proposition was true only, when,
assuming the antecedent to be true,
the consequent must be true also.

[z] Sextus Emp. adv. Mathemat. x.
pp. 85-101.

Reasonings of Diodōrus—respecting Hypothetical Propositions—respecting Motion. His difficulties about the Now of time.

which neither could any present motion be found.   Plato in the Parmenidês [a] professes to have found this inexplicable moment of transition, but he describes it in terms not likely to satisfy a dialectical mind: and Aristotle, denying that the Now is any portion or constituent part of time, considers it only as a boundary of the past and future.[b]

This opinion of Aristotle is in the main consonant with that of Diodorus; who, when he denied the reality of present motion, meant probably only to deny the reality of *present motion apart from past and future motion.* Herein also we find him agreeing with Hobbes, who denies the same in clearer language.[c]   Sextus Empiricus declares

Motion is always present, past, and future.

---

[a] Plato, Parmenidês, p. 156 D-E. Πότε οὖν μεταβάλλει; οὔτε γὰρ ἑστὸς ἂν οὔτε κινούμενον μετάβαλλοι, οὔτε ἐν χρόνῳ ὄν. (Here Plato adverts to the difficulties attending the supposition of actual μεταβολὴ, as Diodorus to those of actual κίνησις.   Next we have Plato's hypothesis for getting over the difficulties.) Ἆρ᾽ οὖν ἔστι τὸ ἄτοπον τοῦτο, ἐν ᾧ τότ᾽ ἂν εἴη ὅτε μεταβάλλει; Τὸ ποῖον δή; Τὸ ἐξαίφνης· ἡ ἐξαίφνης αὐτὴ φύσις ἄτοπός τις ἐγκάθηται μεταξὺ τῆς κινήσεώς τε καὶ στάσεως, ἐν χρόνῳ οὐδενὶ οὖσα, καὶ εἰς ταύτην δὴ καὶ ἐκ ταύτης τό τε κινούμενον μεταβάλλει ἐπὶ τὸ ἑστάναι καὶ τὸ ἑστὸς ἐπὶ τὸ κινεῖσθαι.

Diodorus could not make out this φύσις ἄτοπος which Plato calls τὸ ἐξαίφνης.

[b] To illustrate this apparent paradox of Diodorus, affirming past motion, but denying present motion, we may compare what is said by Aristotle about the Now or Point of Present Time—that it is not a part, but a boundary between Past and Future.

Aristot. Physic. iv. p. 218, a. 4-10. τοῦ δὲ χρόνου τὰ μὲν γέγονε, τὰ δὲ μέλλει, ἔστι δ᾽ οὐδέν, ὄντος μεριστοῦ· τὸ δὲ νῦν οὐ μέρος—τὸ δὲ νῦν πέρας ἔστι (a. 24) — p. 222, a. 10-20-223, a. 20.   ὁ δὲ χρόνος καὶ ἡ κίνησις ἅμα κατά τε δύναμιν καὶ κατ᾽ ἐνεργείαν.

Which doctrine is thus rendered by Harris in his Hermes, ch. vii. pp. 101-103-105 :—

"Both Points and Nows being taken as Bounds, and not as Parts, it will follow that in the same manner as the same point may be the end of one line and the beginning of another—so the same Now may be the End of one

time, and the beginning of another. . . I say of these two times, that with respect to the *Now*, or Instant which they include, the first of them is necessarily Past time, as being previous to it : the other is necessarily Future, as being subsequent. . .   From the above speculations, there follow some conclusions, which may be called paradoxes, till they have been attentively considered.   In the first place, there cannot (strictly speaking) be any such thing as Time Present.   For if all Time be transient, as well as continuous, it cannot like a line be present altogether, but part will necessarily be gone and part be coming.   If therefore any portion of its continuity were to be present at once, it would so far quit its transient nature, and be Time no longer.   But if no portion of its continuity can be thus present, how can Time possibly be present, to which such continuity is essential ?"

[c] Hobbes, First Grounds of Philosophy, ii. 8. 11.

"That is said to be at rest which, during any time, is in one place; and that to be moved, or to have been moved, which whether it be now at rest or moved, was formerly in another place from that which it is now in.   From which definition it may be inferred, first, that whatsoever is moved *has been* moved: for if it be still in the same place in which it was formerly, it is at rest: but if it be in another place, it *has been* moved, by the definition of moved.   Secondly, that what *is* moved, *will yet be* moved: for that which is moved, leaveth the place where it is, and consequently will be moved still.

Diodorus to have been inconsistent in admitting past motion while he denied present motion.[d]   But this seems not more inconsistent than the doctrine of Aristotle respecting the *Now* of time.   I know, when I compare a child or a young tree with what they respectively were a year ago, that they have grown: but whether they actually are growing, at every moment of the intervening time, is not ascertainable by sense, and is a matter of probable inference only.[e]   Diodorus could not understand present motion, except in conjunction with past and future motion, as being the common limit of the two: but he could understand past motion, without reference to present or future.   He could not state to himself a satisfactory theory respecting the beginning of motion: as we may see by his reasonings distinguishing the motion of a body all at once in its integrity, from the motion of a body considered as proceeding from the separate motion of its constituent atoms—the moving atoms preponderating over the atoms at rest, and determining them to motion,[f] until gradually the whole body came to move.   The same argument re-appears in another example, when he argues—The wall does not fall while its component stones hold together, for then it is still standing: nor yet when they have come apart, for then it *has* fallen.[g]

That Diodorus was a person seriously anxious to solve

Stilpon of Megara—His great celebrity. logical difficulties, as well as to propose them, would be incontestably proved if we could believe the story recounted of him—that he hanged himself because he could not solve a problem proposed by Stilpon in the presence of Ptolemy Soter.[h]   But this story probably grew out of the fact, that Stilpon succeeded Diodorus at Megara, and eclipsed him in reputation.   The celebrity of Stilpon, both at Megara and at Athens (between 320-300 B.C., but his exact

---

Thirdly, that whatsoever is moved, is not in one place during any time, how little soever that may be: for by the definition of rest, that which is in one place during any time, is at rest. . . . From what is above demonstrated—namely, that whatsoever *is* moved, *has also been* moved, and *will be* moved : this also may be collected, That there can be no conception of motion without conceiving past and future time."

[d] Sext. Emp. adv. Mathem. x. pp. 91-97-112-116.

[e] See this point touched by Plato in Philêbus, p. 43 B.

[f] Sext. Emp. adv. Math. x. 113. κίνησις κατ᾽ εἰλικρίνειαν κίνησις καὶ ἐπικράτειαν.   Compare Zeller, Geschichte der Griech. Philos. ii. p. 191, ed. 2nd.

[g] Sext. Emp. adv. Mathem. x. pp. 346-348.

[h] Diog. L. ii. 112.

date can hardly be settled), was equal, if not superior, to that of any contemporary philosopher.   He was visited by listeners from all parts of Greece, and he drew away pupils from the most renowned teachers of the day; from Theophrastus as well as the others.[i]   He was no less remarkable for fertility of invention than for neatness of expression.   Two persons who came for the purpose of refuting him are said to have remained with him as admirers and scholars.   All Greece seemed as it were looking towards him, and inclining towards the Megaric doctrines.[k]   He was much esteemed both by Ptolemy Soter and by Demetrius Poliorkêtes, though he refused the presents and invitations of both: and there is reason to believe that his reputation in his own day must have equalled that of either Plato or Aristotle in theirs.   He was formidable in disputation; but the nine dialogues which he composed and published are characterised by Diogenes as cold.[l]

Contemporary with Stilpon (or perhaps somewhat later) was Menedêmus of Eretria, whose philosophic parentage is traced to Phædon.   The name of Phædon has been immortalised, not by his own works, but by the splendid dialogue of which Plato has made him the reciter. He is said (though I doubt the fact) to have been a native of Elis.   He was of good parentage, a youthful companion of Sokrates in the last years of his life.[m]   After the death of

[i] This is asserted by Diogenes upon the authority of Φίλιππος ὁ Μεγαρικός, whom he cites κατὰ λέξιν.   We do not know anything about Philippus.

Menedêmus, who spoke with contempt of the other philosophers, even of Plato and Xenokrates, admired Stilpon (Diog. L. ii. p. 134).

[k] The phrase of Diogenes is here singular, and must probably have been borrowed from a partisan—ὥστε μικροῦ δεῆσαι πᾶσαν τὴν Ἑλλάδα ἀφορῶσαν εἰς αὐτὸν μεγαρίσαι.   Stilpon, εὑρεσιλογίᾳ καὶ σοφιστείᾳ προῆγε τοὺς ἄλλους—κομψότατος (Diog. L. ii. 113-116).

[l] Diog. L. ii. pp. 119-120.   ψυχροί.

[m] The story given by Diogenes (L. ii. pp. 31-105; compare Aulus Gellius, xi. p. 18), about Phædon's adventures, antecedent to his friendship with Sokrates, is unintelligible to me.

"Phædon was made captive along with his country (Elis), sold at Athens, and employed in a degrading capacity, until Sokrates induced Alkibiades or Kriton, to pay his ransom."   Now, no such event as the capture of Elis, and the sale of its Eupatrids as slaves, happened at that time: the war between Sparta and Elis (described by Xenophon Hellen. iii. p. 3) led to no such result, and was finished, moreover, after the death of Sokrates. Alkibiades had been long in exile.   If, in the text of Diogenes, where we now read Φαίδων, Ἤλειος, τῶν εὐπατριδῶν —we were allowed to substitute Φαίδων Μήλιος, τῶν εὐπατριδῶν—the narrative would be rendered consistent with known historical facts.   The Athenians captured the island of Melos in 415 B.C., put to death the Melians of

Sokrates, Phædon went to Elis, composed some dialogues, and established a succession or sect of philosophers—Pleistanus, Anchipylus, Moschus.   Of this sect Menedêmus,[n] contemporary and hearer of Stilpon, became the most eminent representative, and from him it was denominated Eretriac instead of Eleian.   The Eretriacs, as well as the Megarics, took up the negative arm of philosophy, and were eminent as puzzlers and controversialists.

But though this was the common character of the two, in a logical point of view, yet in Stilpon, as well as Menedêmus, other elements became blended with the logical.   These persons combined, in part at least, the free censorial speech of Antisthenes with the subtlety of Eukleides.   What we hear of Menedêmus is chiefly his bitter, stinging sarcasms, and clever repartees.   He did not, like the Cynic Diogenes, live in contented poverty, but occupied a prominent place (seemingly under the patronage of Antigonus and Demetrius) in the government of his native city Eretria.   Nevertheless he is hardly less celebrated than Diogenes for open speaking of his mind, and carelessness of giving offence to others.[o]

Open speech and licence of censure assumed by Menedêmus.

ANTISTHENES.

Antisthenes, the originator of the Cynic succession of philosophers, was one of those who took up principally the ethical element of the Sokratic discoursing, which the Megarics left out or passed lightly over. He did not indeed altogether leave out the logical element: all his doctrines respecting it, as far as we hear of them, appear to have been on the negative side.   But re-

Antisthenes took up Ethics principally, but with negative Logic intermingled.

---

military age, and sold into slavery the younger males as well as the females (Thucyd. v. 116).   If Phædon had been a Melian youth of good family, he would have been sold at Athens, and might have undergone the adventures narrated by Diogenes.   We know that Alkibiades purchased a female Melian

as slave (Pseudo-Andokides cont. Alkibiad.)

[n] Diog. L. ii. 105-126.   There was a statue of Menedêmus in the ancient stadium of Eretria : Diogenes speaks as if it existed in his time, and as if he himself had seen it (ii. 133).

[o] Diog. L. ii. 129-142.

specting ethics, he laid down affirmative propositions,[p] and delivered peremptory precepts. His aversion to pleasure, by which he chiefly meant sexual pleasure, was declared in the most emphatic language. He had therefore, in the negative logic, a point of community with Eukleides and the Megarics: so that the coalescence of the two successions, in Stilpon and Menedêmus, is a fact not difficult to explain.

The life of Sokrates being passed in conversing with a great variety of persons and characters, his discourses were of course multifarious, and his ethical influence operated in different ways. His mode of life, too, exercised a certain influence of its own.

Antisthenes, and his disciple Diogenes, were in many respects closer approximations to Sokrates than either Plato or any other of the Sokratic companions. The extraordinary colloquial and cross-examining force was indeed a peculiar gift, which Sokrates bequeathed to none of them: but Antisthenes took up the Sokratic purpose of inculcating practical ethics not merely by word of mouth, but also by manner of life. He was not inferior to his master in contentment under poverty, in strength of will and endurance,[q] in acquired insensibility both to pain and pleasure, in disregard of opinion around him, and in fearless exercise of a self-imposed censorial mission. He learnt from Sokrates indifference to conventional restraints and social superiority, together with the duty of reducing wants to a minimum, and stifling all such as were above the lowest term of necessity. To this last point, Sokrates gave a religious colour, proclaiming that the Gods had no wants, and that those who had least came nearest to the Gods.[r] By Antisthenes, these qualities were exhibited in eminent mea-

He copied the manner of life of Sokrates, in plainness and rigour.

---

[p] Clemens Alexandr. Stromat. ii. 20, p. 485, Potter. ἐγὼ δ' ἀποδέχομαι τὸν Ἀφροδίτην λέγοντα κἂν κατατοξεύσαιμι, εἰ λάβοιμι, &c.

Μανείην μᾶλλον ἢ ἡσθείην, Diog. L. vi. 3.

[q] Cicero, de Orator. iii. 17, 62; Diog. L. vi. 2. παρ' οὗ (Sokrates) καὶ τὸ καρτερικὸν λαβὼν καὶ τὸ ἀπαθὲς ζηλώσας κατῆρξε πρῶτος τοῦ κυνισμοῦ: also vi. 15. The appellation of Cynics is said to have arisen from the practice of Antisthenes to frequent the gymnasium called Κυνόσαργες (D. L. vi. 13), though other causes are also assigned for the denomination (Winckelmann, Antisth. Frag. pp. 8–10).

[r] Sokrates had said, τὸ μηδενὸς δεῖσθαι, θεῖον εἶναι· τὸ δὲ ὡς ἐλαχίστων, ἐγγυτάτω τοῦ θείου (Xenophon, Memor. i. 6, 10. Compare Apuleius, Apol. p. 25). Plato, Gorgias, p. 492 E. The same dictum is ascribed to Diogenes (Diog. L. vi. 105).

sure; and by his disciple Diogenes they were still farther exaggerated. Epiktetus, a warm admirer of both, considers them as following up the mission from Zeus which Sokrates (in the Platonic Apology) sets forth as his authority, to make men independent of the evils of life by purifying and disciplining the appreciation of good and evil in the mind of each individual.[s]

Doctrines of Antisthenes exclusively ethical and ascetic. He despised music, literature, and physics.
Antisthenes declared virtue to be the End for men to aim at—and to be sufficient *per se* for conferring happiness; but he also declared that virtue must be manifested in acts and character, not by words. Neither much discourse nor much learning was required for virtue: nothing else need be postulated except bodily strength like that of Sokrates.[t] He undervalued theory even in regard to Ethics: much more in regard to Nature (Physics) and to Logic: he also despised literary, geometrical, musical teaching, as distracting men's attention from the regulation of their own appreciative sentiment, and the adaptation of their conduct to it. He maintained strenuously (what several Platonic dialogues call in question) that virtue both could be taught and must be taught: when once learnt, it was permanent, and could not be eradicated. He prescribed the simplest mode of life, the reduction of wants to a minimum, with perfect indifference to enjoyment, wealth, or power. The reward was, exemption from fear, anxiety, disappointments, and wants: together with the pride of approximation to the Gods.[u] Though Antisthenes thus despised both literature and theory, yet he had obtained a rhetorical education, and had even heard the rhetor Gorgias. He composed a large number of dialogues and other treatises, of which only the titles (very multifarious) are preserved to us.[v] One dialogue, entitled Sathon, was a coarse attack on Plato: several treated of Homer and of other poets, whose verses he seems to have allegorised. Some of his dialogues are also

---

[s] Epiktetus, Dissert. iii. 1, 19-22, iii. 21-19, iii. 24-40-60-69. The whole of the twenty-second Dissertation, Περὶ Κυνισμοῦ, is remarkable. He couples Sokrates with Diogenes more closely than with any one else.
[t] Diog. L. vi. 11.

[u] Diog. L. vi. 102-104.
[v] Diog. L. vi. 1, 15-18. The two remaining fragments—Αἴας, Ὀδυσσεὺς (Winckelmann, Antisth. Fragm. pp. 38-42)—cannot well be genuine, though Winckelmann seems to think them so.

declared by Athenæus to contain slanderous abuse of Alkibiades, and other leading Athenians. On the other hand, the dialogues are much commended by competent judges; and Theopompus even affirmed that much in the Platonic dialogues had been borrowed from those of Antisthenes, Aristippus, and Bryson.[x]

Antisthenes was among the most constant friends and followers of Sokrates, both in his serious and in his playful colloquies.[y] The Symposion of Xenophon describes both of them, in their hours of joviality. The picture, drawn by an author, himself a friend and companion, exhibits Antisthenes (so far as we can interpret caricature and jocular inversion) as poor, self-denying, austere, repulsive, and disputatious—yet bold and free-spoken, careless of giving offence, and forcible in colloquial repartee.[z]

Constant friendship of Antisthenes with Sokrates. —Xenophontic Symposion.

In all these qualities, however, Antisthenes was surpassed by his pupil and successor Diogenes of Sinôpê; whose ostentatious austerity of life, eccentric and fearless character, indifference to what was considered as decency, great acuteness and still greater

Diogenes, successor of Antisthenes —His Cynical perfection —striking effect which he produced.

---

[x] Athenæus, v. 220, xi. 508; Diog. L. iii. 24-35; Phrynichus ap. Photium, cod. 158; Epiktêtus, ii. 16-35. Antisthenes is placed in the same line with Kritias and Xenophon, as a Sokratic writer, by Dionysius of Halikarnassus, De Thucyd. Jud. p. 941. That there was standing reciprocal hostility between Antisthenes and Plato we can easily believe. Plato never names Antisthenes, and if the latter attacked Plato it was under the name of Sathon. How far Plato in his dialogues intends to attack Antisthenes without naming him—is difficult to determine. Probably he does intend to designate Antisthenes as γέρων ὀψιμαθής, in Sophist. 251. Schleiermacher and other commentators think that he intends to attack Antisthenes in Philêbus, Theætêtus, Euthydêmus, &c. But this seems to me not certain. In Philêbus, p. 44, he can hardly include Antisthenes among the μάλα δεινοί περὶ φύσιν. Antisthenes neglected the study of φύσις.

[y] Xenophon, Memor. iii. 11, 17.

[z] Xenophon, Memorab. iii. 11, 17; Symposion, ii. 10, iv. 2-3-44. Plutarch

(Quæst. Symp. ii. 1, 6, p. 632) and Diogenes (Laertius, vi. 1, 15) appear to understand the description of Xenophon as ascribing to Antisthenes a winning and conciliatory manner. To me it conveys the opposite impression. We must recollect that the pleasantry of the Xenophontic Symposion (not very successful as pleasantry) is founded on the assumption, by each person, of qualities and pretensions the direct reverse of that which he has in reality—and on his professing to be proud of that which is a notorious disadvantage. Thus Sokrates pretends to possess great personal beauty, and even puts himself in competition with the handsome youth Kritobulus; he also prides himself on the accomplishments of a good μαστροπός. Antisthenes, quite indigent, boasts of his wealth; the neglected Hermogenes boasts of being powerfully friended. The passage, iv. 57-61, which talks of the winning manners of Antisthenes, and his power of imparting popular accomplishments, is to be understood in this ironical and inverted sense.

power of expression, freedom of speech towards all and against all—constituted him the perfect type of the Cynical sect. Being the son of a money-agent at Sinôpê, he was banished with his father for fraudulently counterfeiting the coin of the city. On coming to Athens as an exile, he was captivated with the character of Antisthenes, who was at first unwilling to admit him, and was only induced to do so by his invincible importunity. Diogenes welcomed his banishment, with all its poverty and destitution, as having been the means of bringing him to Antisthenes,[a] and to a life of philosophy. It was Antisthenes (he said) who emancipated him from slavery, and made him a freeman. He was clothed in one coarse garment with double fold: he adopted the wallet (afterwards the symbol of cynicism) for his provisions, and is said to have been without any roof or lodging—dwelling sometimes in a tub near the Metroon, sometimes in one of the public porticoes or temples: he is also said to have satisfied all his wants in the open day. He here indulged unreservedly in that unbounded freedom of speech, which he looked upon as the greatest blessing of life. No man ever turned that blessing to greater account: the string of repartees, sarcasms, and stinging reproofs, which are attributed to him by Diogenes Laertius, is very long, but forms only a small proportion of those which that author had found recounted.[b]   Plato de-

---

[a] Diog. L. vi. 2, 21-49; Plutarch, Quæst. Sympos. ii. 1, 7; Epiktetus, iii. 22, 67, iv. 1, 114; Dion Chrysostom. Orat. viii.-ix.-x.

Plutarch quotes two lines from Diogenes respecting Antisthenes:—

'Ος με ῥάκη τ' ἤμπισχε κἀξηνάγκασε
Πτωχὸν γενέσθαι καὶ δόμων ἀνάστατον—
οὐ γὰρ ἂν ὁμοίως πιθανὸς ἦν λέγων—
"Ος με σοφὸν καὶ αὐτάρκη καὶ μακάριον
ἐποίησε. The interpretation given of the passage by Plutarch is curious, but quite in the probable meaning of the author. However it is not easy to reconcile with the fact of this extreme poverty another fact mentioned about Diogenes, that he asked fees from listeners, in one case as much as a mina (Diog. L. vi. 2, 67).

[b] Diog. L. v. 18, vi. 2, 69. ἐρωτηθείς, τί κάλλιστον ἐν ἀνθρώποις ἔφη—παρρησία. Among the numerous lost works of Theophrastus (enumerated by

Diogen. Laert. v. 43) one is Τῶν Διογένους Συναγωγὴ, ἄ, a remarkable evidence of the impression made by the sayings of Diogenes upon his contemporaries. Compare Dion Chrysostom, Or. ix. (vol. i. 288 seq. Reisk) for the description of the conduct of Diogenes at the Isthmian festival, and the effect produced by it on spectators.

These smart sayings, of which so many are ascribed to Diogenes, and which he is said to have practised beforehand, and to have made occasions for—ὅτι χρείαν εἴη μεμελετηκώς (Diog. L. vi. 18, vi. 91, vii. 26)—were called by the later rhetors Χρεῖαι. See Hermogenes and Theon, apud Walz, Rhetor. Græc. i. pp. 19-201; Quintilian, i. 9, 4.

Such collections of Ana were ascribed to all the philosophers in greater or less number. Photius, in giving the

scribed Diogenes as Sokrates running mad:[c] and when Diogenes, meeting some Sicilian guests at his house and treading upon his best carpet, exclaimed—" I am treading on Plato's empty vanity and conceit," Plato rejoined—" Yes, with a different vanity of your own." The impression produced by Diogenes in conversation with others, was very powerfully felt both by young and old. Phokion, as well as Stilpon, were among his hearers.[d] In crossing the sea to Ægina, Diogenes was captured by pirates, taken to Krete, and there put up to auction as a slave: the herald asked him what sort of work he was fit for: whereupon Diogenes replied—To command men. At his own instance, a rich Corinthian named Xeniades bought him and transported him to Corinth. Diogenes is said to have assumed towards Xeniades the air of a master: Xeniades placed him at the head of his household, and made him preceptor of his sons. In both capacities Diogenes discharged his duty well.[e] As a slave well treated by his master, and allowed to enjoy great freedom of speech, he lived in greater comfort than he had ever enjoyed as a freeman: and we are not surprised that he declined the offers of friends to purchase his liberation. He died at Corinth in very old age: it is said, at ninety years old, and on the very same day on which Alexander the Great died at Babylon (B.C. 323). He was buried at the gate of Corinth leading to the Isthmus: a monument being erected to his honour, with a column of Parian marble crowned by the statue of a dog.[f]

list of books from which the Sophist Sopater collected extracts, indicates one as Τὰ Διογένους τοῦ Κυνικοῦ 'Αποφθέγματα (Codex 161).

[c] Diog. L. 2, 53. Σωκράτης μαινόμενος. Οἱ δέ φασι τὸν Διογένην εἰπεῖν, Πατῶ τὸν Πλάτωνος τῦφον· τὸν δὲ φάναι, 'Ετέρῳ γε τυφῷ, Διόγενες. The term τῦφος (" vanity, self-conceit, assumption of knowing better than others, being puffed up by the praise of vulgar minds ") seems to have been much interchanged among the ancient philosophers, each of them charging it upon his opponents: while the opponents of philosophy generally imputed it to all philosophers alike. Pyrrho the Sceptic took credit for being the only ἄτυφος: and he is complimented as such by his panegyrist

Timon in the Silli. Aristokles affirmed that Pyrrho had just as much τῦφον as the rest. Eusebius, Præp. Evang. xiv. 18.

[d] Diog. L. vi. 2, 75-76.
[e] Diog. L. vi. 2, 74.
Xeniades was mentioned by Demokritus: he is said to have been a sceptic (Sext. Emp. adv. Mathem. vii. 48-53), at least he did not recognise any κριτήριον.
[f] Diog. L. vi. 2, 77-78.
Diogenes seems to have been known by his contemporaries under the title of ὁ Κύων. Aristotle cites from him a witty comparison under that designation, Rhetoric, iii. 10, 1410, a. 24. καὶ ὁ Κύων (ἐκάλει) τὰ καπηλεῖα, τὰ 'Αττικὰ φιδίτια.

In politics, ethics, and rules for human conduct, Diogenes

Doctrines
and smart
sayings of
Diogenes—
Contempt of
pleasure—
training and
labour re-
quired—in-
difference to
literature and
geometry.

adopted views of his own, and spoke them out freely. He was a freethinker (like Antisthenes) as to the popular religion; and he disapproved of marriage laws, considering that the intercourse of the sexes ought to be left to individual taste and preference.[g] Though he respected the city and conformed to its laws, yet he had no reverence for existing superstitions, or for the received usages as to person, sex, or family. He declared himself to be a citizen of the Kosmos and of Nature.[h] His sole exigency was, independance of life, and freedom of speech: having these, he was satisfied, fully sufficient to himself for happiness, and proud of his own superiority to human weakness. The main benefit which he derived from philosophy (he said) was, that he was prepared for any fortune that might befall him. To be ready to accept death easily, was the sure guarantee of a free and independent life.[i] He insisted emphatically upon the necessity of exercise or training (ἄσκησις) both as to the body and as to the mind. Without this, nothing could be done: by means of it everything might be achieved. But he required that the labours imposed should be directed to the acquisition of habits really useful; instead of being wasted, as they commonly were, upon objects frivolous and showy. The truly wise man ought to set before him as a model the laborious life of Hêraklês: and he would find, after proper practice and training, that the contempt of pleasures would afford him more enjoyment than the pleasures themselves.[k]

Diogenès declared that education was sobriety to the

[g] Diog. L. vi. 2, 72. Cicero, De Nat. Door. i. 13.

[h] Diog. L. vi. 2, 63-71. The like declaration is ascribed to Sokrates. Epiktêtus, i. 9, 1.

[i] Diog. L. vi. 2, 63, 72. μηδὲν ἐλευθερίας προκρίνων. Epiktêtus, iv. 1, 30. Οὕτω καὶ Διογένης λέγει, μίαν εἶναι μηχανὴν πρὸς ἐλευθερίαν—τὸ εὐκόλως ἀποθνήσκειν. Compare iv. 7-28, i. 24, 6.

[k] Diog. L. vi. 2, 70-71. καὶ γὰρ αὐτὴ τῆς ἡδονῆς ἡ καταφρόνησις ἡδυτάτη προμελετηθεῖσα, καὶ ὥσπερ οἱ συνεθισ-

θέντες ἡδέως ζῆν, ἀηδῶς ἐπὶ τοὐνάντιον μετίασιν, οὕτως οἱ τοὐνάντιον ἀσκηθέντες ἥδιον αὐτῶν τῶν ἡδονῶν καταφρονοῦσι. See Lucian, Vitar. Auct. c. 9, about the hard life and the happiness of Diogenes. Compare s. 26 about the τῦφος of Diogenes treading down the different τῦφος of Plato, and Epiktêtus iii. 22, 57. Antisthenes, in his dialogue or discourse called 'Ηρακλῆς, appears to have enforced the like appeal to that hero as an example to others. See Winckelmann, Fragm. Antisthen. pp. 15-18.

young, consolation to the old, wealth to the poor, ornament to
the rich. But he despised much of what was commonly imparted as education—music, geometry, astronomy, &c.: and he
treated with equal scorn Plato and Eukleides.[1] He is said
however to have conducted the education of the sons of his
master Xeniades[m] without material departure from the received
usage. He caused them to undergo moderate exercise (not
with a view to athletic success) in the palæstra, and afterwards
to practise riding, shooting with the bow, hurling the javelin,
slinging, and hunting: he cultivated their memories assidu-
ously, by recitation from poets and prose authors, and even
from his own compositions: he kept them on bread and
water, without tunic or shoes, with clothing only such as was
strictly necessary, with hair closely cut, habitually silent, and
fixing their eyes on the ground when they walked abroad.
These latter features approximate to the training at Sparta
(as described by Xenophon) which Diogenes declared to contrast with Athens as the apartments of the men with those of
the women. Diogenes is said to have composed several dialogues and even some tragedies.[n] But his most impressive
display (like that of Sokrates) was by way of colloquy—
prompt and incisive interchange of remarks. He was one of
the few philosophers who copied Sokrates in living constantly
before the public—in talking with every one indiscriminately
and fearlessly, in putting home questions like a physician to
his patient.[o] Epiktêtus,—speaking of Diogenes as equal, if not
superior, to Sokrates—draws a distinction pertinent and accurate. "To Sokrates" (says he) "Zeus assigned the elenchtic
or cross-examining function: to Diogenes, the magisterial and
chastising function: to Zeno (the Stoic) the didactic and dog-
matical." While thus describing Diogenes justly enough, Epiktêtus nevertheless insists upon his agreeable person and his
extreme gentleness and good-nature:[p] qualities for which

[1] Diog. L. vi. 2, 68-73-24-27.
[m] Diog. L. vi. 2, 30-31.
[n] Diog. L. vi. 2, 80. Diogenes
Laertius himself cites a fact from one
of the dialogues—Pordalus (vi. 2, 20):
and Epiktêtus alludes to the treatise
on Ethics by Diogenes—ἐν τῇ Ἠθικῇ—
ii. 20, 14. It appears however that
the works ascribed to Diogenes were

not admitted by all authors as genuine
(Diog. L. c.).
[o] Dion Chrysost. Or. x.; De Servis,
p. 295 R. Or. ix.; Isthmicus, p. 289 R.
ὥσπερ ἰατροὶ ἀνακρίνουσι τοὺς ἀσθενοῦν-
τας, οὕτως Διογένης ἀνέκρινε τὸν ἄνθρωπον, &c.
[p] Epiktêtus, iii. 21, 19. ὡς Σωκράτει
συνεβούλευε τὴν ἐλεγκτικὴν χώραν

probably Diogenes neither took credit himself, nor received

Admiration of Epiktêtus for Diogenes, especially for his consistency in acting out his own ethical creed.

credit from his contemporaries. Diogenes seems to have really possessed—that which his teacher Antisthenes postulated as indispensable—the Sokratic physical strength and vigour. His ethical creed, obtained from Antisthenes, was adopted by many successors, and (in the main) by Zeno and the Stoics in the ensuing century. But the remarkable feature in Diogenes, which attracts to him the admiration of Epiktêtus, is—that he set the example of acting out his creed, consistently and resolutely, in his manner of life :[q] an example followed by some of his immediate successors, but not by the Stoics, who confined themselves to writing and preaching. Contemporary both with Plato and Aristotle, Diogenes stands to both of them in much the same relation as Phokion to Demosthenes

ἔχειν, ὡς Διογένει τὴν βασιλικὴν καὶ ἐπιπληκτικήν, ὡς Ζήνωνι τὴν διδασκαλικὴν καὶ δογματικήν.

About τὸ ἥμερον καὶ φιλάνθρωπον of Diogenes, see Epiktêtus, iii. 24, 64 ; who also tells us (iv. 11-19), professing to follow the statements of contemporaries, that the bodies both of Sokrates and Diogenes were by nature so sweet and agreeable (ἐπίχαρι καὶ ἡδύ) as to dispense with the necessity of washing.

"Ego certé" (says Seneca, Epist. 108, about the lectures of the eloquent Stoic Attalus) " cum Attalum audirem, in vitia, in errores, in mala vitæ perorantem, sæpé misertus sum generis humani, et illum sublimem altioremque humano fastigio credidi. Ipse regem se esse dicebat : sed plus quam regnare mihi videbatur, cui liceret censuram agere regnantium." See also his treatises De Beneficiis, v. 4-6, and de Tranquillitate Animi (c. 8), where, after lofty encomium on Diogenes, he exclaims -"Si quis de felicitate Diogenis dubitat, potest idem dubitare et de Deorum immortalium statu, an parum beaté degant," &c.

[q] Cicero, in his Oration in defence of Murena (30-61-62) compliments Cato (the accuser) as one of the few persons who adopted the Stoic tenets with a view of acting them out, and who did really act them out—"Hæc homo ingeniosissimus M. Cato, autoribus eruditissimis inductus, arripuit : neque

disputandi causâ, ut magna pars, sed ita vivendi." Tacitus (Histor. iv. 5) pays the like compliment to Helvidius Priscus.

M. Gaston Boissier (Étude sur la Vie et les Ouvrages de Varron, pp. 113-114, Paris, 1861) expresses an amount of surprise which I should not have expected, on the fact that persons adopted a philosophical creed for the purpose only of debating it and defending it, and not of acting it out. But he recognises the fact, in regard to Varro and his contemporaries, in terms not less applicable to the Athenian world : amidst such general practice, Antisthenes, Diogenes, Krates, &c., stood out as memorable exceptions. " Il ne faut pas non plus oublier de quelle manière, et dans quel esprit les Romains lettrés étudiaient la philosophie Grecque. Ils venaient écouter les plus habiles maîtres, connaître les sectes les plus célèbres : mais ils les étudiaient plutôt en curieux, qu'ils ne s'y attachaient en adeptes. On ne les voit guères approfondir un système et s'y tenir, adopter un ensemble de croyances, et y conformer leur conduite. On étudiait le plus souvent la philosophie pour discuter. C'était seulement une matière à des conversations savantes, un exercice et un aliment pour les esprits curieux. Voilà pourquoi la secte Académique étoit alors mieux accueillie que les autres," &c.

in politics and oratory: he exhibits strength of will, insensibility to applause as well as to reproach, and self-acting independence—in antithesis to their higher gifts and cultivation of intellect.   He was undoubtedly next to Sokrates, the most original and unparalleled manifestation of Hellenic philosophy.

Respecting Diogenes and the Cynic philosophers generally, we have to regard not merely their doctrines, but the effect produced by their severity of life.   In this point Diogenes surpassed his master Antisthenes, whose life he criticised as not fully realising the lofty spirit of his doctrine.   The spectacle of man not merely abstaining from enjoyment, but enduring with indifference hunger, thirst, heat, cold, poverty, privation, bodily torture, death, &c., exercises a powerful influence on the imagination of mankind.   It calls forth strong feelings of reverence and admiration in the beholders: while in the sufferer himself also, self-reverence and self-admiration, the sense of power and exaltation above the measure of humanity, is largely developed.   The extent to which self-inflicted hardships and pains have prevailed in various regions of the earth, the long-protracted and invincible resolution with which they have been endured, and the veneration which such practices have procured for the ascetics who submitted to them—are among the most remarkable chapters in history.[r]   The East, especially India, has always been, and still is, the country in which these voluntary endurances have reached their extreme pitch of severity; even surpassing those of the Christian monks in Egypt and Syria, during the fourth and fifth centuries of the Christian era.[s]   When Alexander the Great first opened India to the observation of Greeks, one of the novelties which most surprised him and his followers was, the sight of the Gymnosophists or naked philosophers.   These men were found lying on the ground, either totally uncovered or with nothing but a cloth round the loins; abstaining from all enjoyment, nourishing themselves upon a minimum of coarse vegetables or fruits, careless

Marginal note: Admiration excited by the asceticism of the Cynics —Asceticism extreme in the East— Comparison of the Indian Gymnosophists with Diogenes.

[r] Dion Chrysostom, viii. p. 275, Reisk.

[s] See the striking description in

Gibbon, Decl. and Fall, ch. xxxvii. pp. 253-265.

of the extreme heat of the plain, and the extreme cold of the mountain; and often superadding pain, fatigue, or prolonged and distressing uniformity of posture. They passed their time either in silent meditation or in discourse on religion and philosophy: they were venerated as well as consulted by every one, censuring even the most powerful persons in the land. Their fixed idea was to stand as examples to all, of endurance, insensibility, submission only to the indispensable necessities of nature, and freedom from all other fear or authority. They acted out the doctrine, which Plato so eloquently preaches under the name of Sokrates in the Phædon—That the whole life of the philosopher is a preparation for death: that life is worthless, and death an escape from it into a better state.[t] It is an interesting fact to learn that when Onesikritus (one of Alexander's officers, who had known and frequented the society of Diogenes in Greece), being despatched during the Macedonian march through India for the purpose of communicating with these Gymnosophists, saw their manner of life and conversed with them—he immediately compared them with Diogenes, whom he had himself visited—as well as with Sokrates and Pythagoras, whom he knew by reputation. Onesikritus described to the Gymnosophists the manner of life of Diogenes: but Diogenes wore a threadbare mantle, and this appeared to them a mark of infirmity and imperfection. They remarked that Diogenes was right to a considerable extent; but wrong for obeying convention in preference to nature, and for being ashamed of going naked, as they did.[u]

---

[t] Strabo, xv. 713 A (probably from Onesikritus, see Geier, Fragment. Alexandr. Magn. Histor. p. 379). Πλείστους δ' εἶναι αὐτοῖς λόγους περὶ τοῦ θανάτου· νομίζειν γὰρ δὴ, τὸν μὲν ἐνθάδε βίον ὡς ἂν ἀκμὴν κυομένων εἶναι· τὸν δὲ θάνατον γένεσιν εἰς τὸν ὄντως βίον καὶ τὸν εὐδαίμονα τοῖς φιλοσοφή- σασι· διὸ τῇ ἀσκήσει πλείστῃ χρῆσθαι πρὸς τὸ ἑτοιμοθάνατον· ἀγαθὸν δὲ ἢ κακὸν μηδὲν εἶναι τῶν συμβαινόντων ἀνθρώποις, &c.
This is an application of the doctrines laid down by the Platonic Sokrates in the Phædon, p. 64 A: Κινδυ- νεύουσι γὰρ ὅσοι τυγχάνουσιν ὀρθῶς ἁπτόμενοι φιλοσοφίας, λεληθέναι τοὺς ἄλλους ὅτι οὐδὲν ἄλλο αὐτοὶ ἐπιτη-

δεύουσιν ἢ ἀποθνήσκειν τε καὶ τεθνάναι. Compare p. 67 D. Cicero, Tusc. D. i. 30. Compare Epiktêtus, iv. 1, 30 (cited in a former note) about Diogenes the Cynic. Also Cicero, Tusc. Disp. v. 27; Valerius Maximus, iii. 3, 6; Diogen. L. Prooem. s. 6; Pliny, H. N. vii. 2.
Bohlen observes (Das Alte Indien, ch. ii. pp. 279-289), "It is a remarkable fact that Indian writings of the highest antiquity depict as already existing the same ascetic exercises as we see existing at present: they were even then known to the ancients, who were especially astonished at such fanaticism."
[u] Strabo gives a condensed summary of this report, made by Onesikritus respecting his conversation with the

These observations of the Indian Gymnosophist are a reproduction and an application in practice[x] of the memorable declaration of principle enunciated by Sokrates—" That the Gods had no wants: and that the man who had fewest wants, approximated most nearly to the Gods." This principle is first introduced into Grecian ethics by Sokrates: ascribed to him both by Xenophon and Plato, and seemingly approved by both. In his life, too, Sokrates carried the principle into effect, up to a certain point. Both admirers and opponents attest his poverty, hard fare, coarse clothing, endurance of cold and privation:[y] but he was a family man, with a wife and children to maintain, and he partook occasionally of indulgences which made him fall short of his own ascetic principle. Plato and Xenophon—both of them well-born Athenians, in circumstances affluent, or at least easy, the latter being a knight, and even highly skilled in horses and horsemanship—contented themselves with preaching on the text, whenever they had to deal with an opponent more self-indulgent than themselves;

The precepts and principles laid down by Sokrates were carried into fullest execution by the Cynics.

Indian Gymnosophist Mandanis, or Dandamis (Strabo, xv. p. 716 B): —Ταῦτ' εἰπόντα ἐξερέσθαι (Dandamis asked Onesikritus), εἰ καὶ ἐν τοῖς Ἕλλησι λόγοι τοιοῦτοι λέγοιντο. Εἰπόντος δὲ ('Ονησικρίτου), ὅτι καὶ Πυθαγόρας τοιαῦτα λέγει, κελεύει τε ἐμψύχων ἀπέχεσθαι, καὶ Σωκράτης, καὶ Διογένης, οὗ καὶ αὐτὸς (Onesikritus) ἀκροάσαιτο, ἀποκρίνασθαι (Dandamis), ὅτι τἄλλα μὲν νομίζει φρονίμως αὐτοῖς δοκεῖν, ἐν δ' ἁμαρτάνειν—νόμον πρὸ τῆς φύσεως τιθεμένους· οὐ γὰρ ἂν αἰσχύνεσθαι γυμνοὺς, ὥσπερ αὐτὸν, διάγειν, ἀπὸ λιτῶν ζῶντας· καὶ γὰρ οἰκίαν ἀρίστην εἶναι, ἥτις ἂν ἐπισκευῆς ἐλαχίστης δέηται.

About Onesikritus, Diog. Laert. vi. 75-84; Plutarch, Alexand. c. 65; Plutarch, De Fortunâ Alexandri, p. 331.

The work of August Gladitsch (Einleitung in das Verständniss der Weltgeschichte, Posen, 1841) contains an instructive comparison between the Gymnosophists and the Cynics, as well as between the Pythagoreans and the Chinese philosophers — between the Eleatic sect and the Hindoo philosophers. The points of analogy, both in doctrine and practice, are very numerous and strikingly brought out, pp. 356-377. I cannot, however, agree in his conclusion, that the doctrines and practice of Antisthenes were borrowed, not from Sokrates with exaggeration, but from the Parmenidean theory, and the Vedanta theory of the Ens Unum, leading to negation and contempt of the phenomenal world.

[x] Onesikritus observes, respecting the Indian Gymnosophists, that " they were more striking in act than in discourse" (ἐν ἔργοις γὰρ αὐτοὺς κρείττους ἢ λόγοις εἶναι, Strabo, xv. 713 B); and this is true about the Cynic succession of philosophers, in Greece as well as in Rome. Diogenes Laertius (compare his Procem, s. 19, 20, and vi. 103) ranks the Cynic philosophy as a distinct αἵρεσις: but he tells us that other writers (especially Hippobotus) would not reckon it as an αἵρεσις, but only as an ἔνστασις βίου—practice without theory.

[y] Xenophon, Memor. i. 6, 2-5; Plato, Sympos. 219, 220.

The language of contemporary comic writers, Ameipsias, Eupolis, Aristophanes, &c., about Sokrates—is very much the same as that of Menander a century afterwards about Kratès. Sokrates is depicted as a Cynic in mode of life (Diogen. L. ii. 28; Aristophan. Nubes, 104-362-415).

but made no attempt to carry it into practice.[z] Zeno the
Stoic laid down broad principles of self-denial and apathy:
but in practice he was unable to conquer the sense of shame,
as the Cynics did, and still more the Gymnosophists. Antisthenes, on the other hand, took to heart, both in word and
act, the principle of Sokrates: yet even he, as we know from
the Xenophontic Symposion, was not altogether constant in
rigorous austerity. His successors Diogenes and Krates attained the maximum of perfection ever displayed by the
Cynics of free Greece. They stood forth as examples of endurance, abnegation—insensibility to shame and fear—free-
spoken censure of others. Even they however were not so recognised by the Indian Gymnosophists; who, having reduced
their wants, their fears, and their sensibilities, yet lower, had
thus come nearer to that which they called the perfection of
Nature, and which Sokrates called the close approach to
divinity.[a] When Alexander the Great (in the first year of
his reign, and prior to any of his Asiatic conquests) visited
Diogenes at Corinth, found him lying in the sun, and asked
if there was any thing which he wanted—Diogenes made the
memorable reply—"Only that you and your guards should
stand out of my sunshine." This reply doubtless manifests
the self-satisfied independence of the philosopher. Yet it is
far less impressive than the fearless reproof which the Indian
Gymnosophists administered to Alexander, when they saw
him in the Punjab at the head of his victorious army, after
exploits, dangers, and fatigues almost superhuman, as con-
queror of Persia and acknowledged son of Zeus.[b]

[z] Zeno, though he received instructions from Kratês, was ἄλλως μὲν εὔ-
τονος πρὸς τὴν φιλοσοφίαν, αἰδήμων δὲ
ὡς πρὸς τὴν κυνικὴν ἀναισχυντίαν (Diog.
L. vii. 3).

[a] "Disputare cum Socrate licet, dubitare cum Carneade, cum Epicuro
quiescere, hominis naturam cum Stoicis
vincere, cum Cynicis excedere," &c.
This is the distinction which Seneca
draws between Stoic and Cynic (De
Brevitat. Vitæ, 14). His admiration
for the "seminudus" Cynic Demetrius, his contemporary and companion, was extreme (Epist. 62, and
Epist. 20).

[a] Xenoph. Memor. i. 6, 10 (the passage is cited in a previous note).

The Emperor Julian (Orat. vi. p.
192 Spanh.) says about the Cynics—
ἀπάθειαν γὰρ ποιοῦνται τὸ τέλος, τοῦτο
δὲ ἴσον ἐστὶ τῷ θεὸν γενέσθαι. Dion
Chrysostom (Or. vi. p. 208) says also
about Diogenes the Cynic—καὶ μάλιστα
ἐμιμεῖτο τῶν θεῶν τὸν βίον.

[b] Cicero, Tusc. Disp. v. 32, and the
Anabasis of Arrian, vii. 1-2-3, where
both the reply of Diogenes and that
of the Indian Gymnosophists are reported. Dion Chrysostom (Orat. iv.
p. 145 seq. Reisk) gives a prolix
dialogue between Alexander and
Diogenes. His picture of the effect
produced by Diogenes upon the dif-

Another point, in the reply made by the Indian Gymnosophist to Onesikritus, deserves notice: I mean the antithesis between law (or convention) and nature ($\nu\acute{o}\mu o\varsigma$—$\phi\acute{v}\sigma\iota\varsigma$)—the supremacy which he asserts for Nature over law—and the way in which he understands Nature and her supposed ordinances. This antithesis was often put forward and argued in the ancient Ethics: and it is commonly said, without any sufficient proof, that the Sophists (speaking of them collectively) recognised only the authority of law—while Sokrates and Plato had the merit of vindicating against them the superior authority of Nature. The Indian Gymnosophist agrees with the Athenian speaker in the Platonic treatise De Legibus, and with the Platonic Kallikles in the Gorgias, thus far—that he upholds the paramount authority of Nature. But of these three interpreters, each hears and reports the oracles of Nature differently from the other two: and there are many other dissenting interpreters besides.[c] Which of them are we to follow? And if,

Antithesis between Nature—and Law or Convention—insisted on by the Indian Gymnosophists.

ferent spectators at the Isthmian festival, is striking and probable.

Kalanus, one of the Indian Gymnosophists, was persuaded, by the instances of Alexander, to abandon his Indian mode of life and to come away with the Macedonian army—very much to the disgust of his brethren, who scornfully denounced him as infirm and even as the slave of appetite ($\dot{\alpha}\kappa\acute{o}\lambda\alpha\sigma\tau o\nu$, Strabo, xv. 718). He was treated with the greatest consideration and respect by Alexander and his officers; yet when the army came into Persis, he became sick of body and tired of life. He obtained the reluctant consent of Alexander to allow him to die. A funeral pile was erected, upon which he voluntarily burnt himself in presence of the whole army; who witnessed the scene with every demonstration of military honour. See the remarkable description in Arrian, Anab. vii. 3. Cicero calls him "Indus indoctus et barbarus" (Tusc. Disp. ii. 21); but the impression which he made on Alexander himself, Onesikritus, Lysimachus, and generally upon all who saw him, was that of respectful admiration (Strabo, xv. 715; Arrian, l. c.). One of these Indian sages, who had come into Syria along with the Indian envoys sent by an Indian king

to the Roman Emperor Augustus, burnt himself publicly at Athens, with an exulting laugh when he leaped upon the funeral pile (Strabo, xv. 720 A) —$\kappa\alpha\tau\grave{\alpha}$ $\tau\grave{\alpha}$ $\pi\acute{\alpha}\tau\rho\iota\alpha$ $\tau\tilde{\omega}\nu$ $\text{'}I\nu\delta\tilde{\omega}\nu$ $\H{\epsilon}\theta\eta$.

The like act of self-immolation was performed by the Grecian Cynic Peregrinus Proteus, at the Olympic festival in the reign of Marcus Antoninus, 165 A.D. (See Clinton, Fasti Romani.) Lucian, who was present and saw the proceeding, has left an animated description of it, but ridicules it as a piece of silly vanity. Theagenes, the admiring disciple of Peregrinus, and other Cynics, who were present in considerable numbers—and also Lucian himself—compare this act to that of the Indian Gymnosophists—$o\H{v}\tau o\varsigma$ $\delta\grave{\epsilon}$ $\tau\acute{\iota}\nu o\varsigma$ $\alpha\grave{\iota}\tau\acute{\iota}\alpha\varsigma$ $\H{\epsilon}\nu\epsilon\kappa\epsilon\nu$ $\dot{\epsilon}\mu\beta\acute{\alpha}\lambda\lambda\epsilon\iota$ $\phi\acute{\epsilon}\rho\omega\nu$ $\dot{\epsilon}\alpha\upsilon\tau\grave{o}\nu$ $\epsilon\grave{\iota}\varsigma$ $\tau\grave{o}$ $\pi\tilde{v}\rho$; $\nu\grave{\eta}$ $\Delta\acute{\iota}$, $\H{o}\pi\omega\varsigma$ $\tau\grave{\eta}\nu$ $\kappa\alpha\rho\tau\epsilon\rho\acute{\iota}\alpha\nu$ $\dot{\epsilon}\pi\iota\delta\epsilon\acute{\iota}\xi\eta\tau\alpha\iota$, $\kappa\alpha\theta\acute{\alpha}\pi\epsilon\rho$ $o\grave{\iota}$ $B\rho\alpha\chi\mu\tilde{\alpha}\nu\epsilon\varsigma$ (Lucian, De Morte Peregrini, 25-39, &c.)

[c] Though Seneca (De Brevitate Vit. 14) talks of the Stoics as "conquering Nature, and the Cynics as exceeding Nature," yet the Stoic Epiktêtus considers his morality as the only scheme conformable to Nature (Epiktêt. Diss. iv. 1, 121-128); while the Epikurean Lucretius claims the same conformity for the precepts of Epikurus.

adopting any one of them, we reject the others, upon what grounds are we to justify our preference? When the Gymnosophist points out, that nakedness is the natural condition of man; when he farther infers, that because natural it is therefore right—and that the wearing of clothes, being a departure from nature, is also a departure from right—how are we to prove to him that his interpretation of nature is the wrong one? These questions have received no answer in any of the Platonic dialogues: though we have seen that Plato is very bitter against those who dwell upon the antithesis between Law and Nature, and who undertake to decide between the two.

Reverting to the Cynics, we must declare them to be in one respect the most peculiar outgrowth of Grecian philosophy: because they are not merely a doctrinal sect, with phrases, theories, reasonings, and teachings, of their own—but still more prominently a body of practical ascetics, a mendicant order[d] in philosophy, working upon the by-standers by exhibiting themselves as models of endurance and apathy. These peculiarities seem to have originated partly with Pythagoras, partly with Sokrates—for there is no known prior example of it in Grecian history, except that of the anomalous priests of Zeus at Dodona, called Selli, who lay on the ground with unwashed feet. ' The discipline of Lykurgus at Sparta included severe endurance; but then it was intended to form, and actually did form, good soldiers. The Cynics had no view to military action. They exaggerated the peculiarities of Sokrates, and we should call their mode of life the Sokratic life, if we followed the example

The Greek Cynics—an order of ascetic or mendicant friars.

[d] Respecting the historical connexion between the Grecian Cynics and the ascetic Christian monks, see Zeller, Geschichte der Griech. Philos. ii. p. 241, ed. 2nd.

Homer, Iliad xvi. 235:—

Ζεῦ ἄνα, Δωδωναῖε Πελασγικὲ, τηλόθι ναίων
Δωδώνης μεδέων δυσχειμέρου, ἀμφὶ δὲ Σέλλοι
Σοὶ ναίουσ' ὑποφῆται ἀνιπτόποδες, χαμαιεῦναι.

There is no analogy in 'Grecian history to illustrate this very curious passage: the Excursus of Heyne furnishes no information (see his edition of the Iliad, vol. vii. p. 289) except the general remark:—" Selli—vitam genus et institutum affectabant abhorrens à communi usu, vitæ monachorum mendicantium haud absimile, cum sine vitæ cultu viverent, nec corpus abluerent, et humi cubarent. Ita inter barbaros non modo, sed inter feras gentes ipsas intellectum est, eos qui auctoritatem apud multitudinem consequi vellent, externâ specie, vitæ cultu austeriore, abstinentiâ et continentiâ, oculos hominum in se convertere et mirationem facere debere."

of those who gave names to the Pythagorean or Orphic life, as a set of observances derived from the type of Pythagoras or Orpheus.[e]

Though Antisthenes and Diogenes laid chief stress upon ethical topics, yet they also delivered opinions on logic and evidence.[f]   Antisthenes especially was engaged in controversy, and seemingly in acrimonious controversy, with Plato; whose opinions he impugned in an express dialogue entitled Sathon. *Logical views of Antisthenes and Diogenes —they opposed the Platonic Ideas.*

Plato on his side also attacked the opinions of Antisthenes, and spoke contemptuously of his intelligence, yet without formally naming him.   At least there are some criticisms in the Platonic dialogues (especially in the Sophistês, p. 251) which the commentators pronounce, on strong grounds, to be aimed at Antisthenes: who is also unfavourably criticised by Aristotle.   We know but little of the points which Antisthenes took up against Plato—and still less of the reasons which he urged in support of them.   Both he and Diogenes, however, are said to have declared express war against the Platonic theory of self-existent Ideas.   The functions of general Concepts and general propositions, together with the importance of defining general terms, had been forcibly insisted on in the colloquies of Sokrates; and his disciple Plato built upon this foundation the memorable hypothesis of an aggregate of eternal, substantive realities, called Ideas or Forms, existing separate from the objects of sense, yet affording a certain participation in themselves to those objects:—not discernible by sense, but only by the Reason or understanding.   These bold creations of the Platonic fancy were repudiated by Antisthenes and Diogenes: who are both said to have declared—" We see Man, and we see Horse; but Manness and Horseness we do not see."   Whereunto Plato replied—" You possess that eye

---

[e] Plato, Republic, x. 600 B; Legib. vi. 782 C; Eurip. Hippol. 955; Fragm. Κρῆτες.

See also the citations in Athenæus (iv. pp. 161-163) from the writers of the Attic middle comedy, respecting the asceticism of the Pythagoreans, analogous to that of the Cynics.

[f] Among the titles of the works of Antisthenes, preserved by Diogenes

Laertius (vi. 15), several relate to dialectic or logic.   'Αλήθεια.   Περὶ τοῦ διαλέγεσθαι ἢ ἀντιλογικός.   Σάθων ἢ περὶ τοῦ ἀντιλέγειν, α, β, γ,   Περὶ Διαλέκτου.   Περὶ Παιδείας ἢ περὶ ὀνομάτων, α, β, γ, δ, ε.   Περὶ ὀνομάτων χρήσεως ἢ ἐριστικός, περὶ ἐρωτήσεως καὶ ἀποκρίσεως, &c. &c.

Diogenes Laertius refers to ten τόμοι of these treatises.

by which Horse is seen: but you have not yet acquired that eye by which Horseness is seen."[g]

First protest of Nominalism against Realism.

This debate between Antisthenes and Plato marks an interesting point in the history of philosophy. It is the first protest of Nominalism against the doctrine of an extreme Realism. The Ideas or Forms of Plato (according to many of his phrases, for he is not always consistent with himself) are not only real existences distinct from particulars, but absorb to themselves all the reality of particulars. The real universe in the Platonic theory was composed of Ideas or Forms—such as Manness or Horseness[h] (called by Plato the Αὐτὸ-᾽Ανθρωπος and Αὐτὸ-"Ιππος), of which particular men and horses were only disfigured, transitory, and every-varying photographs. Antisthenes denied what Plato affirmed, and as he affirmed it. Aristotle denied it also; maintaining that genera, species, and attributes, though distinguishable as separate predicates of, or inherencies in, individuals — yet had no existence apart from individuals. Aristotle was no less wanting than Antisthenes, in the intellectual eye required for discerning the Platonic Ideas. Antisthenes is said to have declared these Ideas to be mere thoughts or conceptions (ψιλὰς ἐννοίας): i. e. merely subjective or within the mind, without any object corresponding to them. This is one of the various modes of presenting the theory of Ideas, resorted to even in the Platonic Parmenidês, not by one who opposes that theory, but by one seeking to defend it—viz. by Sokrates, when he is hard pressed by the objections of the

---

[g] Simplikius, ad Aristot. Categ. p. 66, b. 47, 67, b. 18, 68, b. 25, Schol. Brand.; Tzetzes, Chiliad. vii. 606.

τῶν δὲ παλαιῶν οἱ μὲν ἀνῄρουν τὰς ποιότητας τελέως, τὸ ποιὸν συγχωροῦντες εἶναι· ὥσπερ ᾽Αντισθένης, ὅς ποτε Πλάτωνι διαμφισβητῶν — ὦ Πλάτων, ἔφη, ἵππον μὲν ὁρῶ, ἱππότητα δ᾽ οὐχ ὁρῶ· καὶ ὃς εἶπεν, ἔχεις μὲν ᾧ ἵππος ὁρᾶται τόδε τὸ ὄμμα, ᾧ δὲ ἱππότης θεωρεῖται, οὐδέπω κέκτησαι· καὶ ἄλλοι δέ τινες ἦσαν ταύτης τῆς δόξης· οἱ δὲ τινὰς μεν ἀνῄρουν ποιότητας, τινὰς δὲ κατελίμπανον.

᾽Ανθρωπότης occurs p. 68, n. 31. Compare p. 20, n. 2.

The same conversation is reported as having taken place between Diogenes

and Plato, except that instead of ἱππότης and ἀνθρωπότης, we have τραπεζότης and κυαθότης (Diog. L. vi. 53).

We have ζωότης—᾽Αθηναιότης—in Galen's argument against the Stoics (vol. xix. p. 481, Kühn).

[h] We know from Plato himself (Theætêtus, p. 182 A) that even the word ποιότης, if not actually first introduced by himself, was at any rate so recent as to be still repulsive, and to require an apology. If ποιότης was strange, ἀνθρωπότης and ἱππότης would be still more strange. Antisthenes probably invented them, to present the doctrine which he impugned in a dress of greater seeming absurdity.

Eleate against the more extreme and literal version of the theory.[1] It is remarkable, that the objections ascribed to Parmenides against that version which exhibits the Ideas as mere Concepts of and in the mind, are decidedly less forcible than those which he urges against the other versions.

There is another singular doctrine, which Aristotle ascribes to Antisthenes, and which Plato notices and con- futes; alluding to its author contemptuously, but not mentioning his name. Every name (Antis- thenes argued) has its own special reason or mean- ing (οἰκεῖος[k] λόγος), declaring the essence of the thing named, and differing from every other word : you cannot therefore truly predicate any one word of any other, because the reason or meaning of the two is different : there can be no true propositions except identical propositions, in which the predicate is the same with the subject—" man is man, good is good." " Man is good" was an inadmissible propo- sition : affirming different things to be the same, or one thing to be many.[1] Accordingly, it was impossible for two speakers really to contradict each other. There can be no contradiction between them if both declare the essence of the same thing— nor if neither of them declare the essence of it—nor if one speaker declares the essence of one thing, and another speaker that of another. But one of these three cases must happen : therefore there can be no contradiction.[m]

Doctrine of Antisthenes about predi- cation—He admits no other predi- cation but identical.

The works of Antisthenes being lost, we do not know how he himself stated his own doctrine, nor what he said on behalf

---

[1] Plato, Parmenidês, p. 132 B. See vol. ii. chap. xxv. p. 271 of this work.

[k] Diogen. L. vi. 3. Πρῶτός τε ὡρί- σατο (Antisthenes) λόγον εἰπὼν, λόγος ἐστιν ὃ τὸ τί ἦν ἢ ἔστι δηλῶν.

[1] Aristotle, Metaphy. Δ 1024, b. 32, attributes this doctrine to Antisthenes by name; which tends to prove that Plato meant Antisthenes, though not naming him, in Sophist. p. 251 B, where he notices the same doctrine. Compare Philêbus, p. 14 D.

It is to be observed that a doctrine exactly the same as that which Plato here censures in Antisthenes, will be found maintained by the Platonic Sokrates himself, in Plato, Hippias

Major, p. 304 A. See chap. xi. vol. i. p. 378 of the present work.

[m] Aristot. Topic. i. p. 104, b. 20. θέσις δὲ ἔστιν ὑπόληψις παράδοξος τῶν γνωρίμων τινος κατὰ φιλοσοφίαν· οἷον ὅτι οὐκ ἔστιν ἀντιλέγειν, καθάπερ ἔφη Ἀντισθένης.

Plato puts this θέσις into the mouth of Dionysodorus, in the Euthydêmus— p. 286 B; but he says (or makes Sokrates say) that it was maintained by many persons, and that it had been maintained by Protagoras, and even by others yet more ancient.

Antisthenes had discussed it speci- ally in a treatise of three sections, polemical against Plato—Σάθων, ἢ περὶ τοῦ ἀντιλέγειν, α, β, γ (Diog. L. vi. 16).

of it, declaring contradiction to be impossible. Plato sets

The same doctrine asserted by Stilpon, after the time of Aristotle.

aside the doctrine as absurd and silly; Aristotle —since he cites it as a paradox, apt for dialectical debate, where the opinion of a philosopher stood opposed to what was generally received—seems to imply that there were plausible arguments to be urged in its favour.[n] And that the doctrine actually continued to be held and advocated, in the generation not only after Antisthenes but after Aristotle—we may see by the case of Stilpon: who maintained (as Antisthenes had done) that none but identical propositions, wherein the predicate was a repetition of the subject, were admissible: from whence it followed (as Aristotle observed) that there could be no propositions either false or contradictory. Plutarch,[o] in reciting this doctrine of Stilpon (which had been vehemently impugned by the Epikurean Kolôtês), declares it to have been intended only in jest. There is no ground for believing that it was so intended: the analogy of Antisthenes goes to prove the contrary.

Stilpon, however, while rejecting (as Antisthenes had done) the universal Ideas[p] or Forms, took a larger ground of objec-

[n] Aristotle (Met. Δ. 1024) represents the doctrine of Antisthenes, That contradictory and false propositions are impossible—as a consequence deduced from the position laid down—That no propositions except identical propositions were admissible. If you grant this last proposition, the consequence will be undeniable. Possibly Antisthenes may have reasoned in this way: There are many contradictory and false propositions now afloat; but this arises from the way in which predication is conducted. So long as the predicate is different from the subject, there is nothing *in the form of a proposition* to distinguish falsehood from· truth (to distinguish *Theætêtus sedet*, from *Theætêtus volat*—to take the instance in the Platonic Sophistês—p. 263). There ought to be no propositions except identical propositions: the form itself will then guarantee you against both falsehood and contradiction: you will be sure always to give τὸν οἰκεῖον λόγον τοῦ πράγματος. There would be nothing inconsistent in such a pre-

cept: but Aristotle might call it silly (εὐηθῶς), because, while shutting out falsehood and contradiction, it would also shut out the great body of useful truth, and would divest language of its usefulness as a means of communication.

Brandis (Gesch. der Gr. Römisch. Phil. vol. ii. xciii. 1) gives something like this as the probable purpose of Antisthenes—"Nur Eins bezeichne die Wesenheit eines Dinges—die Wesenheit als einfachen Träger des mannichfaltigen der Eigenschaften" (this is rather too Aristotelian)—"zur Abwehr von Streitigkeiten auf dem Gebiete der Erscheinungen." Compare also Ritter, Gesch. Phil. vol. ii. p. 130. We read in the Kratylus, that there were persons who maintained the rectitude of all names: to say that a name was not right, was (in their view) tantamount to saying that it was no name at all, but only an unmeaning sound (Plato, Krat. pp. 429-430).

[o] Plutarch, adv. Kolôten, p.1119 C-D.

[p] Hegel (Geschichte der Griech. Philos. i. p. 123) and Marbach (Ge-

tion. He pronounced them to be inadmissible both as subject and as predicate. If you speak of Man in general (he said) what, or whom, do you mean? You do not mean A or B, or C or D, &c.: that is, you do not mean any one of these more than any other. You have no determinate meaning at all: and beyond this indefinite multitude of individuals, there is nothing that the term can mean. Again, as.to predicates—when you say, *The man runs,* or *The man is good,* what do you mean by the predicate *runs,* or is *good?* You do not mean any thing specially belonging to *man:* for you apply the same predicates to many other subjects: you say *runs,* about a horse, a dog, or a cat—you say *good* in reference to food, medicine, and other things besides. Your predicate, therefore, being applied to many and diverse subjects, belongs not to one of them more than to another: in other words, it belongs to neither: the predication is not admissible.[q]

(marginal note: Nominalism of Stilpon. His reasons against accidental predication.)

schichte der Philos. s. 91) disallow the assertion of Diogenes, that Stilpon ἀνήρει τὰ εἴδη. They maintain that Stilpon rejected the particular affirmations, and allowed only general or universal affirmations. This construction appears to me erroneous.

[q] Diog. L. ii. 113; Plutarch, adv. Kolôten, 1119-1120. εἰ περὶ ἵππου τὸ τρέχειν κατηγοροῦμεν, οὔ φησι (Stilpon) ταὐτὸν εἶναι τῷ περὶ οὗ κατηγορεῖται τὸ κατηγορούμενον—ἑκατέρου γὰρ ἀπαιτούμενοι τὸν λόγον, οὐ τὸν αὐτὸν ἀποδίδομεν ὑπὲρ ἀμφοῖν. Ὅθεν ἁμαρτάνειν τοὺς ἕτερον ἑτέρου κατηγοροῦντας. Εἰ μὲν γὰρ ταὐτόν ἐστι τῷ ἀνθρώπῳ τὸ ἀγαθὸν, καὶ τῷ ἵππῳ τὸ τρέχειν, πῶς καὶ σιτίου καὶ φαρμάκου τὸ ἀγαθὸν, καὶ νὴ Δία πάλιν λέοντος καὶ κυνὸς τὸ τρέχειν, κατηγοροῦμεν· εἰ δ' ἕτερον, οὐκ ὀρθῶς ἄνθρωπον ἀγαθὸν καὶ ἵππον τρέχειν, λέγομεν.

Sextus Empiricus (adv. Mathem. vii. p. 269-282) gives a different vein of reasoning respecting predication,—yet a view which illustrates this doctrine of Antisthenes. Sextus does not require that all predication shall be restricted to identical predication: but he maintains that you cannot define any general word. To define, he says, is to enunciate the essence of that which is defined. But when you define Man—"a mortal, rational animal, capable of reason and knowledge"—you give only certain attributes of Man, which go along with the essence—you do not give the essence itself. If you enumerate even all the accompaniments (συμβεβηκότα), you will still fail to tell me what the essence of Man is; which is what I desire to know, and what you profess to do by your definition. It is useless to enumerate accompaniments, until you explain to me what the essence is which they accompany.

These are ingenious objections, which seem to me quite valid, if you assume the logical subject to be a real, absolute essence, apart from all or any of its predicates. And this is a frequent illusion, favoured even by many logicians. We enunciate the subject first, then the predicate: and because the subject can be conceived after abstraction of this, that, or the other predicates—we are apt to imagine that it may be conceived without *all* or *any* of the predicates. But this is an illusion. If you suppress all predicates, the subject or supposed substratum vanishes along with them: just as the Genus vanishes, if you suppress all the different species of it.

"Sais tu au moins ce que c'est que la matière? Par exemple, cette pierre est grise, et d'une telle forme; elle a ses trois dimensions, elle est pesante et divisible. Eh bien (dit le Sirien), cette

Stilpon (like Antisthenes, as I have remarked above) seems
to have had in his mind a type of predication, similar
to the type of reasoning which Aristotle laid down
in the syllogism: such that the form of the proposition should be itself a guarantee for the truth of
what was affirmed. Throughout the ancient philosophy, especially in the more methodised debates between
the Academics and Sceptics on one side, and the Stoics on
the other—what the one party affirmed and the other party
denied, was, the existence of a Criterion of Truth: some distinguishable mark, such as falsehood could not possibly carry.
To find this infallible mark in propositions, Stilpon admitted
none except identical. While agreeing with Antisthenes, that
no predicate could belong to a subject different from itself, he
added a new argument, by pointing out that predicates applied
to one subject were also applied to many other subjects.

Difficulty of understanding how the same predicate could belong to more than one subject.

chose qui te paraît être divisible, pesante, et grise, me diras tu bien ce que
c'est ? Tu vois bien ce que c'est : mais
le fond de la chose, le connais tu ?
Non, dit l'autre. Tu ne sais donc point
ce que c'est que la matière." (Voltaire,
Micromégas, c. 7.)

" Le fond de la chose"—the Ding
an sich—is nothing but the name itself,
divested of every fraction of meaning :
it is *titulus sine re*. But the name
being familiar, and having been always
used with a meaning, still appears invested with much of the old emotional
associations, even though it has been
stripped of all its meaning by successive
acts of abstraction. If you subtract
from four, $1+1+1+1$, there will remain
zero. But by abstracting, from the subject *man*, all its predicates, real and
possible, you cannot reduce it to zero.
The *name* man always remains, and
appears by old association to carry with
it some meaning—though the meaning
can no longer be defined.

This illusion is well pointed out in a
valuable passage of Cabanis (Du Degré
de Certitude de la Médecine, p. 61):—
" Je pourrois d'ailleurs demander ce
qu'on entend par la nature et les causes
premières des maladies. Nous con-
noissons de leur nature, ce que les
faits en manifestent. Nous savons, par
exemple, que la fièvre produit tels et
tels changemens : ou plutôt, c'est par
ces changemens qu'elle se montre à nos

yeux : c'est *par eux seuls qu'elle existe
pour nous.* Quand un homme tousse,
crache du sang, respire avec peine,
ressent une douleur de côté, a le pouls
plus vite et plus dur, la peau plus
chaude que dans l'état naturel—l'on
dit qu'il est attaqué d'une pleurésie.
Mais qu'est ce donc *qu'une pleurésie ?*
On vous répliquera que c'est une maladie, dans laquelle tous, ou presque
tous, ces accidens se trouvent combinés.
S'il en manque un ou plusieurs, ce n'est
point la pleurésie, du moins la vraie
pleurésie essentielle des écoles. *C'est
donc le concours de ces accidens qui la
constitue.* Le mot *pleurésie ne fait que
les retracer d'une manière plus courte.
Ce mot n'est pas un être par lui-même :*
il exprime une abstraction de l'esprit,
et réveille par un seul trait toutes les
images d'un assez grand tableau.

" Ainsi lorsque, non content de con-
noître une maladie par ce qu'elle offre
à nos sens, par ce qui seul la constitue,
et sans quoi elle n'existeroit pas, *vous
demandez encore ce qu'elle est en elle-
même, quelle est son essence*—c'est
*comme si vous demandiez quelle est
l'essence d'un mot, d'une pure abstraction.* Il n'y a donc pas beaucoup de
justesse à dire, d'un air de triomphe,
que les médecins ignorent même la
nature de la fièvre, sans cesse
ils agissent dans des circonstances, et
manient des instrumens, dont l'essence
leur est inconnue."

Now if the predicates belonged to one, they could not (in his view) belong to the others : and therefore they did not really belong to any. He considered that predication involved either identity or special and exclusive implication of the predicate with the subject.

Stilpon was not the first who had difficulty in explaining to himself how one and the same predicate could be applied to many different subjects. The difficulty had already been set forth in the Platonic Parmenidês.[r] How can the Form (Man, White, Good, &c.) be present at one and the same time in many distinct individuals? It cannot be present as a whole in each : nor can it be divided, and thus present partly in one, partly in another. How therefore can it be present at all in any of them? In other words, how can the One be Many, and how can the Many be One? Of this difficulty (as of many others) Plato presents no solution, either in the Parmenidês or anywhere else.[s] Aristotle alludes to several contemporaries or predecessors who felt it. Stilpon reproduces it in his own way. It is a very real difficulty, requiring to be dealt with by those who lay down a theory of predication, and calling upon them to explain the functions of general propositions, and the meaning of general terms.

Analogous difficulties in the Platonic Parmenidês.

Menedêmus the Eretrian, one among the hearers and admirers of Stilpon, combined even more than Stilpon the attributes of the Cynic with those of the Megaric. He was fearless in character, and uncontrouled in speech, delivering harsh criticisms without regard to offence given : he was also a great master of ingenious dialectic and puzzling controversy.[t] His robust frame, grave

Menedêmus disallowed all negative predications.

---

[r] Plato, Parmenidês, p. 131. Compare also Philêbus, p. 15, and Stallbaum's Proleg. to the Parmenidês, pp. 46-47. The long commentary of Proklus (v. 100-110, pp. 670-682 of the edition of Stallbaum) amply attests the δυσκολίαν of the problem.

The argument of Parmenidês (in the dialogue called Parmenidês) is applied to the Platonic εἴδη and to τὰ μετέχοντα. But the argument is just as much applicable to attributes, genera, species : to all general predicates.

[s] Aristot. Physic. i. 2, 185, b. 26-36.

Lykophron and some others anterior to Aristotle proposed to elude the difficulty, by ceasing to use the substantive verb as copula in predication : instead of saying Σωκράτης ἔστι λευκὸς, they said either Σωκράτης λευκὸς, simply, or Σωκράτης λελεύκωται.

This is a remarkable evidence of the difficulty arising, even in those early days of logic, about the logical function of the copula.

[t] Diog. L. ii. 127-134. ἦν γὰρ καὶ ἐπικόπτης καὶ παῤῥησιαστής.

deportment, and simplicity of life, inspired great respect; especially as he occupied a conspicuous position, and enjoyed political influence at Eretria.   He is said to have thought meanly both of Plato and Xenokrates.   We are told that Menedêmus, like Antisthenes and Stilpon, had doctrines of his own on the subject of predication.   He disallowed all negative propositions, admitting none but affirmative: more-over, even of the affirmative propositions, he disallowed all the hypothetical, approving only the simple and categorical.[u]

It is impossible to pronounce confidently respecting these doctrines, without knowing the reasons upon which they were grounded.   Unfortunately these last have not been trans-mitted to us.   But we may be very sure that there *were* rea-sons, sufficient or insufficient: and the knowledge of those reasons would have enabled us to appreciate more fully the state of the Greek mind, in respect to logical theory, in and before the year 300 B.C.

Another doctrine, respecting knowledge and definition, is ascribed by Aristotle to " the disciples of Anti-sthenes and other such uninstructed persons:" it is also canvassed by Plato in the Theætêtus,[x] without specifying its author, yet probably having Anti-sthenes in view.   As far as we can make out a doc-trine which both these authors recite as opponents, briefly and in their own way, it is as follows:—" Objects must be distinguished into 1. Simple or primary; and 2. Compound or secondary combinations of these simple elements.   This last class, the compounds, may be explained or defined, because you can enumerate the component elements.   By such ana-lysis, and by the definition founded thereupon, you really come to *know* them—describe them—predicate about them. But the first class, the simple or primary objects, can only be perceived by sense and named: they cannot be analysed, de-fined, or known.   You can only predicate about them that they are like such and such other things: e. g. *silver*, you cannot say what it is in itself, but only that it is like tin, or like something else.   There may thus be a *ratio* and a defini-

Marginal notes: Distinction ascribed to Antisthenes between simple and complex objects. Simple objects undefinable.

[u] Diog. L. ii. 134.
[x] Plato, Theætêt. pp. 201-202.   Aristotel. Metaph. H. 1043, b. 22.

tion of any compound object, whether it be an object of perception or of conception : because one of the component elements will serve as Matter or Subject of the proposition, and
the other as Form or Predicate. But there can be no definition of any one of the component elements separately taken :
because there is neither Matter nor Form to become the Subject and Predicate of a defining proposition."

This opinion, ascribed to the followers of Antisthenes, is not
in harmony with the opinion ascribed by Aristotle to Antisthenes himself (viz., That no propositions, except identical
propositions, were admissible) : and we are led to suspect that
the first opinion must have been understood or qualified by
its author in some manner not now determinable. But the
second opinion, drawing a marked logical distinction between
simple and complex Objects, has some interest from the criticisms of Plato and Aristotle: both of whom select, for the
example illustrating the opinion, the syllable—as the compound made up of two or more letters which are its simple
constituent elements.

Plato refutes the doctrine,[y] but in a manner not so much to
prove its untruth, as to present it for a verbal incon- Remarks of
gruity.   How can you properly say (he argues) that Plato on this
doctrine.
you *know* the compound AB, when you know neither A nor
B separately ?   Now it may be incongruous to restrict in this
manner the use of the words *know—knowledge :* but the distinction between the two cases is not denied by Plato.   Antisthenes said—" I feel a simple sensation (A or B) and can
name it, but I do not *know* it: I can affirm nothing about it
in itself, or about its real essence.   But the compound AB
I do know, for I know its essence: I can affirm about it that
it is compounded of A and B, and this is its essence."   Here
is a real distinction : and Plato's argument amounts only to
affirming that it is an incorrect use of words to call the compound *known,* when the component elements are not known.
Unfortunately the refutation of Plato is not connected with
any declaration of his own counter-doctrine, for the Theætêtus
ends in a result purely negative.

Aristotle, in his comment on the opinion of Antisthenes,

Remarks of
Aristotle
upon the
same. makes us understand better what it really is:—
" Respecting simple essences (A or B), I cannot tell
what they really are : but I can tell what they are
like or unlike, *i. e.* I can compare them with other essences,
simple or compound. But respecting the compound AB, I
can tell what it really is: its essence is, to be compounded of
A and B. And this I call *knowing* or *knowledge.*" [z] The distinction here taken by Antisthenes (or by his followers) is
both real and useful : Plato does not contest it : while Aristotle distinctly acknowledges it, only that among the simple
items he ranks both Percepta and Concepta.

Monimus a Syracusan, and Krates a Theban, with his wife

Later Gre-
cian Cynics—
Monimus—
Krates—
Hipparchia. Hipparchia,[a] were successors of Diogenes in the
Cynic vein of philosophy : together with several
others of less note. Both Monimus and Krates are

---

[z] Aristot. Metaphys. H. 1043, b. 24-
32, with the Scholia, p. 774, b. Br.

Mr. J. S. Mill observes, Syst. of
Logic, i. 5, 6, p. 114, ed. 5 :—"There
is still another exceptional case, in
which, though the predicate is the
name of a class, yet in predicating it
we affirm nothing but resemblance :
the class being founded not on resemblance in any given particular, but on
general unanalysable resemblance. The
classes in question are those into which
our simple sensations, or other simple
feelings, are divided. Sensations of
white, for instance, are classed together,
not because we can take them to pieces,
and say, they are alike in this, not alike
in that, but because we feel them to
be alike altogether, though in different
degrees. When therefore I say—The
colour I saw yesterday was a white
colour, or, The sensation I feel is one
of tightness—in both cases the attribute
I affirm of the colour or of the other
sensation is mere resemblance : simple
likeness to sensations which I have had
before, and which have had that name
bestowed upon them. The names of
feelings, like other concrete general
names, are connotative : but they con-
note a mere resemblance. When predicated of any individual feelings, the
information they convey is that of its
likeness to the other feelings which we
have been accustomed to call by the
same name."

[a] Hipparchia was a native of Ma-
roneia in Thrace ; born in a considerable station, and belonging to an opulent family. She came to Athens with
her brother Mêtroklês, and heard both
Theophrastus and Kratês. Both she
and her brother became impressed with
the strongest admiration for Kratês :
for his mode of life, as well as for his
discourses and doctrine. Rejecting various wealthy suitors, she insisted upon
becoming his wife, both against his
will and against the will of her parents.
Her resolute enthusiasm overcame the
reluctance of both. She adopted fully
his hard life, poor fare, and threadbare
cloak. She passed her days in the
same discourses and controversies, indifferent to the taunts which were
addressed to her for having relinquished
the feminine occupations of spinning
and weaving. Diogenes Laertius found
many striking dicta or replies ascribed
to her (ἄλλα μύρια τῆς φιλοσόφου, vi.
96-98). He gives an allusion made to
her by the contemporary comic poet
Menander, who (as I before observed)
handled the Cynics of his time as Aristophanes, Eupolis, &c., had handled
Sokrates—

Συμπεριπατήσεις γὰρ τρίβων᾽ ἔχουσ᾽
ἐμοί,
ὥσπερ Κράτητι τῷ Κυνικῷ ποθ᾽ ἡ γυνὴ,
Καὶ θυγατέρ᾽ ἐξέδωκ᾽ ἐκεῖνος, ὡς ἔφη
αὐτὸς, ἐπὶ πειρᾷ δοὺς τριάκονθ᾽ ἡμέρας.
(vi. 93.)

said to have been persons of wealthy condition,[b] yet their
minds were so powerfully affected by what they saw of Diogenes, that they followed his example, renounced their wealth,
and threw themselves upon a life of poverty; with nothing
beyond the wallet and the threadbare cloak, but with fearless
independence of character, free censure of every one, and
indifference to opinion. " I choose as my country " (said
Krates) " poverty and low esteem, which fortune cannot
assail: I am the fellow-citizen of Diogenes, whom the snares
of envy cannot reach." [c] Krates is said to have admonished
every one, whether they invited it or not: and to have gone
unbidden from house to house for the purpose of exhortation.
His persistence in this practice became so obtrusive that he
obtained the title of " the Door-Opener." [d] This feature,
common to several other Cynics, exhibits an approximation
to the missionary character of Sokrates, as described by himself in the Platonic Apology: a feature not found in any of
the other eminent heads of philosophy—neither in Plato nor
in Aristotle, Zeno, or Epikurus.

Among other hearers of Krates, who carried on, and at the
same time modified, the Cynic discipline, we have to Zeno of Kitium in
mention Zeno, of Kitium in Cyprus, who became Cyprus.
celebrated as the founder of the Stoic sect. In him the Cynic,
Megaric, and Herakleitean tendencies may be said to have
partially converged, though with considerable modifications:[e]
the ascetic doctrines (without the ascetic practices or obtrusive
forwardness) of the Cynics—and the logical subtleties of the
others. He blended them, however, with much of new positive theory, both physical and cosmological. His compositions were voluminous; and those of the Stoic Chrysippus,
after him, were still more numerous. The negative and

[b] Diog. L. vi. 82-88. Μόνιμος ὁ Κύων,
Sext. Emp. adv. Mathem. vii. 48-88.
    About Krates, Plutarch, De Vit. Aere
Alieno, 7, p. 831 F.
    [c] Diog. L. vi. 93. ἔχειν δὲ πατρίδα
ἀδοξίαν καὶ πενίαν ἀνάλωτα τῇ τύχῃ,
καὶ Διογένους εἶναι πολίτης ἀνεπιβού-
λευτου φθόνῳ. The parody or verses
of Krates, about his city of Pera (the
Wallet), vi. 85, are very spirited—
    Πήρη τις πόλις ἔστι μέσῳ ἐνὶ οἴνοπι
        τύφῳ, &c.

Krates composed a collection of philosophical Epistles, which Diogenes pronounces to be excellent, and even to
resemble greatly the style of Plato
(vi. 98).
    [d] Diog. L. vi. 86. ἐκαλεῖτο δὲ θυρε-
πανοίκτης, διὰ τὸ εἰς πᾶσαν εἰσιέναι
οἰκίαν καὶ νουθετεῖν. Compare Seneca,
Epist. 29.
    [e] Numenius ap. Euseb. Præp. Evang.
xiv. 5.

oppugning function, which in the fourth century B.C. had been directed by the Megarics against Aristotle, was in the third century B.C. transferred to the Platonists, or Academy represented by Arkesilaus: whose formidable dialectic was brought to bear upon the Stoic and Epikurean schools—both of them positive, though greatly opposed to each other.

ARISTIPPUS.

Along with Antisthenes, among the hearers and companions of Sokrates, stood another Greek of very opposite dispositions, yet equally marked and original—Aristippus of Kyrênê. The stimulus of the Sokratic method, and the novelty of the topics on which it was brought to bear, operated forcibly upon both, prompting each of them to theorise in his own way on the best plan of life.

Aristippus, a Kyrenean of easy circumstances, having heard of the powerful ascendancy exercised by Sokrates over youth, came to Athens for the express purpose of seeing him, and took warm interest in his conversation.[f] He set great value upon mental cultivation and accomplishments; but his habits of life were inactive, easy, and luxurious. Upon this last count, one of the most interesting chapters in the Xenophontic Memorabilia reports an interrogative lecture addressed to him by Sokrates, in the form of dialogue.[g]

Aristippus—life, character, and doctrine.

Sokrates points out to Aristippus that mankind may be distributed into two classes: 1. Those who have trained themselves to habits of courage, energy, bodily strength, and command over their desires and appetites, together with practice in the actual work of life:—these are the men who become qualified to rule, and who do actually rule. 2. The rest of mankind, inferior in these points, who have no choice but to obey, and who do obey.[h]—Men of the first or ruling

Discourse of Sokrates with Aristippus.

---

[f] Plutarch (De Curiositate, p. 516 A) says that Aristippus informed himself, at the Olympic games, from Ischomachus respecting the influence of Sokrates.

[g] See the first chapter of the Second Book of the Memorabilia.

I give an abstract of the principal points in the dialogue, not a literal translation.

[h] Xen. Mem. ii. 1, pp. 64-67. τὸν μὲν ὅπως ἱκανὸς ἔσται ἄρχειν, τὸν δὲ, ὅπως μηδ' ἀντιποιήσεται ἀρχῆς—τοὺς ἀρχικούς.

class possess all the advantages of life; they perform great
exploits, and enjoy a full measure of delight and happiness,
so far as human circumstances admit. Men of the second
class are no better than slaves, always liable to suffer, and
often actually suffering, ill treatment and spoliation of the
worst kind. To which of these classes (Sokrates asks
Aristippus) do you calculate on belonging—and for which do
you seek to qualify yourself?—To neither of them (replies
Aristippus). I do not wish to share the lot of the subordinate
multitude: but I have no relish for a life of command, with
all the fatigues, hardships, perils, &c., which are inseparable
from it. I prefer a middle course: I wish neither to rule,
nor to be ruled, but to be a freeman: and I consider freedom
as the best guarantee for happiness.[i] I desire only to pass
through life as easily and pleasantly as possible.[k]—Which of
the two do you consider to live most pleasantly, the rulers or
the ruled? asks Sokrates.—I do not rank myself with either
(says Aristippus): nor do I enter into active duties of citizenship anywhere: I pass from one city to another, but everywhere as a stranger or non-citizen.—Your scheme is impracticable (says Sokrates). You cannot obtain security in
the way that you propose. You will find yourself suffering
wrong and distress along with the subordinates[l]—and even
worse than the subordinates: for a stranger, wherever he
goes, is less befriended and more exposed to injury than the
native citizens. You will be sold into slavery, though you
are fit for no sort of work: and your master will chastise you,
until you become fit for work.—But (replies Aristippus) this
very art of ruling, which you consider to be happiness,[m] is
itself a hard life, a toilsome slavery, not only stripped of

---

[i] Xen. Mem. ut suprà. ἀλλ' εἶναί
τίς μοι δοκεῖ μέση τούτων ὁδὸς, ἣν
πειρῶμαι βαδίζειν, οὔτε δι' ἀρχῆς, οὔτε
διὰ δουλείας, ἀλλὰ δι' ἐλευθερίας, ἥπερ
μάλιστα πρὸς εὐδαιμονίαν ἄγει.

[k] Xen. Mem. ut s. ἐμαυτὸν τοίνυν
τάττω εἰς τοὺς βουλομένους ὡς ῥᾷστα
καὶ ἥδιστα βιοτεύειν.

[l] Xen. Mem. l. c. εἰ μέντοι ἐν ἀνθρώποις ὢν μήτε ἄρχειν ἀξιώσεις μήτε
ἄρχεσθαι, μήτε τοὺς ἄρχοντας ἑκὼν
θεραπεύσεις, οἶμαί σε ὁρᾶν, ὡς ἐπί-

στανται οἱ κρείττονες τοὺς ἥττονας καὶ
κοινῇ καὶ ἰδίᾳ κλαίοντας καθίσαντες,
ὡς δούλοις χρῆσθαι.

What follows is yet more emphatic,
about the unjust oppression of rulers,
and the suffering on the part of subjects.

[m] Xen. Mem. l. c. p. 71. Ἀλλὰ
γὰρ, ὦ Σώκρατες, οἱ εἰς τὴν βασιλικὴν
τέχνην παιδευόμενοι, ἣν δοκεῖς μοι σὺ
νομίζειν εὐδαιμονίαν εἶναι.
Compare Memor. ii. 8, 4.

enjoyment, but full of privation and suffering. A man must be a fool to embrace such discomforts of his own accord.—It is that very circumstance, (says Sokrates) that he does embrace them of his own accord—which renders them endurable, and associates them with feelings of pride and dignity. They are the price paid beforehand, for a rich reward to come. He who goes through labour and self-denial, for the purpose of gaining good friends or subduing enemies, and for the purpose of acquiring both mental and bodily power, so that he may manage his own concerns well and may benefit both his friends and his country—such a man will be sure to find his course of labour pleasurable. He will pass his life in cheerful[n] satisfaction, not only enjoying his own esteem and admiration, but also extolled and envied by others. On the contrary, whoever passes his earlier years in immediate pleasures and indolent ease, will acquire no lasting benefit either in mind or body. He will have a soft lot at first, but his future will be hard and dreary.[o]

Sokrates enforces his lecture by reciting to Aristippus the memorable lecture or apologue, which the Sophist Prodikus was then delivering in lofty diction to numerous auditors[p]—the fable still known as the Choice of Hêraklês. Virtue and Pleasure (the latter of the two being here identified with Evil or Vice) are introduced as competing for the direction of the youthful Hêraklês. Each sets forth her case, in dramatic antithesis. Pleasure is introduced as representing altogether the gratification of the corporeal appetites and the love of repose: while Virtue replies by saying, that if youth be employed altogether in pursuing such delights, at the time when the appetites are most vigorous—the result will be nothing but fatal disappointment, accompanied with entire loss of the different and superior pleasures available in mature years and in old age. Youth is the season of labour: the physical appetites must be indulged

Choice of Hêraklês.

---

[n] Xen. Mem. 1. c. p. 72. πῶς οὐκ οἴεσθαι χρὴ τούτους καὶ πονεῖν ἡδέως εἰς τὰ τοιαῦτα, καὶ ζῆν εὐφραινομένους, ἀγαμένους μὲν ἑαυτούς, ἐπαινουμένους δὲ καὶ ζηλουμένους ὑπὸ τῶν ἄλλων;

[o] Xen. Mem. 1. c. p. 73, cited from

Epicharmus:—

μὴ τὰ μαλακὰ μώεο, μὴ τὰ σκλήρ' ἔχῃς.

[p] Xen. Mem. 1. c. p. 74. ἐν τῷ συγγράμματι τῷ περὶ Ἡρακλέους, ὅπερ δὴ καὶ πλείστοις ἐπιδείκνυται—μεγαλειοτέροις ῥήμασιν. P. 81.

sparingly, and only at the call of actual want: accomplishments of body and mind must be acquired in that season, which will enable the mature man to perform in after life great and glorious exploits. He will thus realise the highest of all human delights—the love of his friends and the admiration of his countrymen—the sound of his own praises and the reflexion upon his own deserts. At the price of a youth passed in labour and self-denial, he will secure the fullest measure of mature and attainable happiness.

"It is worth your while, Aristippus" (says Sokrates, in concluding this lecture), "to bestow some reflexion on what is to happen in the latter portions of your life."

This dialogue (one of the most interesting remnants of antiquity, and probably reported by Xenophon from actual hearing) is valuable in reference not only to Aristippus, but also to Sokrates himself. Many recent historians of philosophy describe Sokrates and Plato as setting up an idea of Virtue or Good Absolute (*i. e.* having no essential reference to the happiness or security of the agent or of any one else) which they enforce—and an idea of Vice or Evil Absolute (*i. e.* having no essential reference to suffering or peril, or disappointment, either of the agent or of any one else), which they denounce and discommend—and as thereby refuting the Sophists, who are said to have enforced Virtue and denounced Vice only relatively—*i. e.* in consequence of the bearing of one and the other upon the security and happiness of the agent or of others. Whether there be any one doctrine or style of preaching which can be fairly ascribed to the Sophists as a class, I will not again discuss here: but I believe that the most eminent among them, Protagoras and Prodikus, held the language here ascribed to them. But it is a mistake to suppose that upon this point Sokrates was their opponent. The Xenophontic Sokrates (a portrait more resembling reality than the Platonic) always holds this same language: the Platonic Sokrates not always, yet often. In the dialogue between Sokrates and Aristippus, as well as in the apologue of Prodikus, we see that the devotion of the season of youth to indulgence and inactive gratification of appetite, is blamed as productive of ruinous

Illustration afforded of the views of Sokrates respecting Good and Evil.

consequences—as entailing loss of future pleasures, together
with a state of weakness which leaves no protection against
future suffering; while great care is taken to show, that
though laborious exercise is demanded during youth, such
labour will be fully requited by the increased pleasures and
happiness of after life. The pleasure of being praised, and
the pleasure of seeing good deeds performed by one's self, are
especially insisted on. On this point both Sokrates and
Prodikus concur.[q]

If again we compare the Xenophontic Sokrates with the
Platonic Sokrates, we shall find that the lecture of

Comparison of the Xenophontic Sokrates with the Platonic Sokrates.

the former to Aristippus coincides sufficiently with
the theory laid down by the latter in the dialogue
Protagoras; to which theory the Sophist Protagoras
is represented as yielding a reluctant adhesion. But we shall
find also that it differs materially from the doctrine maintained by Sokrates in the Platonic Gorgias. Nay, if we
follow the argument addressed by the Xenophontic Sokrates
to Aristippus, we perceive that it is in substance similar to
that which the Platonic dialogue Gorgias puts in the mouth
of the rhetor Pôlus and the politician Kalliklês. The Xenophontic Sokrates distributes men into two classes—the rulers
and the ruled: the former strong, well-armed, and well-
trained, who enjoy life at the expense of the submission and
suffering of the latter: the former committing injustice, the
latter enduring injustice. He impresses upon Aristippus the
misery of being confounded with the suffering many, and exhorts him to qualify himself by a laborious apprenticeship for
enrolment among the ruling few. If we read the Platonic
Gorgias, we shall see that this is the same strain in which
Pôlus and Kalliklês address Sokrates, when they invite him
to exchange philosophy for rhetoric, and to qualify himself
for active political life. " Unless you acquire these accomplishments, you will be helpless and defenceless against injury
and insult from others : while, if you acquire them, you will
raise yourself to political influence, and will exercise power

---

[q] Xenop. Mem. l. c. pp. 80-81.   τοῦ
δὲ πάντων ἡδίστου ἀκούσματος, ἐπαίνου
σεαυτῆς, ἀνήκοος εἶ, καὶ τῶν πάντων
ἡδίστου θεάματος ἀθέατος· οὐδὲν γὰρ

πώποτε σεαυτῆς ἔργον καλὸν τεθέασαι.
τὰ μὲν ἡδέα ἐν τῇ νεότητι διαδρα-
μόντες, τὰ δὲ χαλεπὰ ἐς τὸ γῆρας
ἀποθέμενοι.

over others, thus obtaining the fullest measure of enjoyment which life affords: see the splendid position to which the Macedonian usurper Archelaus has recently exalted himself.[r] Philosophy is useful, when studied in youth for a short time as preface to professional and political apprenticeship: but if a man perseveres in it and makes it the occupation of life, he will not only be useless to others, but unable to protect himself; he will be exposed to suffer any injustice which the well-trained and powerful men may put upon him." To these exhortations of Pôlus and Kalliklês Sokrates replies by admitting their case as true matter of fact. " I know that I am exposed to such insults and injuries: but my life is just and innocent. If I suffer, I shall suffer wrong: and those who do the wrong will thereby inflict upon themselves a greater mischief than they inflict upon me. Doing wrong is worse for the agent than suffering wrong."[s]

There is indeed this difference between the Xenophontic Sokrates in his address to Aristippus, and the Platonic Kalliklês in his exhortation to Sokrates: That whereas Kalliklês proclaims and even vindicates it as natural justice and right, that the strong should gratify their desires by oppressing and despoiling the weak— the Xenophontic Sokrates merely asserts such oppression as an actual fact, notorious and undeniable,[t] without either approving or blaming it. Plato, constructing an imaginary conversation with the purpose that Sokrates shall be victorious, contrives intentionally and with dramatic consistency that the argument of Kalliklês shall be advanced in terms so invidious and revolting that no one else would be bold enough to speak it out:[u] which contrivance was the more necessary, as So-

Marginal note: Xenophontic Sokrates talking to Aristippus— Kalliklês in Platonic Gorgias.

---

[r] Plato, Gorgias, pp. 466-470-486.

[s] Plato, Gorgias, pp. 508-509-521-527 C. καὶ ἐασόν τινα σοῦ καταφρονῆσαι ὡς ἀνοήτου, καὶ προπηλακίσαι ἐὰν βούληται, καὶ ναὶ μὰ Δία σύ γε θαρρῶν πατάξαι τὴν ἄτιμον ταύτην πληγήν· οὐδὲν γὰρ δεινὸν πείσει, ἐὰν τῷ ὄντι ἦς καλὸς κἀγαθὸς, ἀσκῶν ἀρετήν.

[t] If we read the conversation alleged by Thucydides (v. 94-105-112) to have taken place between the Athenian generals and the executive council of Melos, just before the siege of that island by the Athenians, we shall see that this same language is held by the Athenian. " You, the Melians, being much weaker, must submit to us who are much stronger; this is the universal law and necessity of nature, which we are not the first to introduce, but only follow out, as others have done before us, and will do after us. Submit—or it will be worse for you. No middle course, or neutrality, is open to you."

[u] Plato, Gorgias, pp. 482-487-492.

krates is made not only to disparage the poets, rhetors, and most illustrious statesmen of historical Athens, but to sustain a thesis in which he admits himself to stand alone, opposed to aristocrats as well as democrats.[x] Yet though there is this material difference in the manner of handling, the plan of life which the Xenophontic Sokrates urges upon Aristippus, and the grounds upon which he enforces it, are really the same as those which Kalliklês in the Platonic Gorgias urges upon Sokrates. " Labour to qualify yourself for active political power "—is the lesson addressed in the one case to a wealthy man who passed his life in ease and indulgence, in the other case to a poor man who devoted himself to speculative debate on general questions, and to cross-examination of every one who would listen and answer. The man of indulgence, and the man of speculation,[y] were both of them equally destitute of those active energies, which were necessary to confer power over others, or even security against oppression by others.

In the Xenophontic dialogue, Aristippus replies to Sokrates

Language held by Aristippus—his scheme of life.

that the apprenticeship enjoined upon him is too laborious, and that the exercise of power, itself laborious, has no charm for him. He desires a middle course, neither to oppress, nor to be oppressed: neither to command, nor to be commanded—like Otanes among the seven Persian conspirators.[z] He keeps clear of political obligation, and seeks to follow, as much as he can, his own individual judgment. Though Sokrates, in the

---

[x] Plato, Gorgias, pp. 472-521.

[y] If we read the treatise of Plutarch, Περὶ Στωϊκῶν ἐναντιωμάτων (c. 2-3, p. 1033 C-D), we shall see that the Stoic writers, Zeno, Kleanthes, Chrysippus, Diogenes, Antipater, all of them earnestly recommended a life of active citizenship and laborious political duty, as incumbent upon philosophers not less than upon others; and that they treated with contempt a life of literary leisure and speculation. Chrysippus explicitly declared οὐδὲν διαφέρειν τὸν σχολαστικὸν βίον τοῦ ἡδονικοῦ, i. e. that the speculative philosopher who kept aloof from political activity, was in substance a follower of Epikurus. Tacitus holds much the same language (Hist. iv. 5) when he says about Helvidius Priscus : — "ingenium il-

lustre altioribus studiis juvenis admodum dedit : non, ut plerique, ut nomine magnifico segne otium velaret, sed quo constantior adversus fortuita, rempublicam capesseret," &c.

The contradiction which Plutarch notes is, that these very Stoic philosophers (Chrysippus and the others) who affected to despise all modes of life except active civic duty—were themselves, all, men of literary leisure, spending their lives away from their native cities, in writing and talking philosophy. The same might have been said about Sokrates and Plato (except as to leaving their native cities), both of whom incurred the same reproach for inactivity as Sokrates here addresses to Aristippus.

[z] Herodot. iii. 80-83.

Xenophontic dialogue, is made to declare this middle course impossible, yet it is substantially the same as what the Platonic Sokrates in the Gorgias aspires to:—moreover the same as what the real Sokrates at Athens both pursued as far as he could, and declared to be the only course consistent with his security.[a] The Platonic Sokrates in the Gorgias declares emphatically that no man can hope to take active part in the government of a country, unless he be heartily identified in spirit with the ethical and political system of the country: unless he not merely professes, but actually and sincerely shares, the creed, doctrines, tastes, and modes of appreciation prevalent among the citizens.[b] Whoever is deficient in this indispensable condition, must be content "to mind his own business and to abstain from active meddling with public affairs." This is the course which the Platonic Sokrates claims both for himself and for the philosopher generally:[c] it is also the course which Aristippus chooses for himself, under the different title of a middle way between the extortion of the ruler and the suffering of the subordinate. And the argument of Sokrates that no middle way is possible—far from refuting Aristippus (as Xenophon says that it did)[d] is founded upon an

[a] Plato, Apol. So. p. 32 A. ἰδιωτεύειν, ἀλλὰ μὴ δημοσιεύειν.

[b] Plato, Gorgias, pp. 510-513. Τίς οὖν ποτ' ἔστι τέχνη τῆς παρασκευῆς τοῦ μηδὲν ἀδικεῖσθαι ἢ ὡς ὀλίγιστα; σκέψαι εἴ σοι δοκεῖ ἥπερ ἐμοί· ἐμοὶ μὲν γὰρ δοκεῖ ἥδε· ἢ αὐτὸν ἄρχειν δεῖν ἐν τῇ πόλει ἢ καὶ τυραννεῖν, ἢ τῆς ὑπαρχούσης πόλεως ἑταῖρον εἶναι; (This is exactly the language which Sokrates holds to Aristippus, Xenop. Memor. ii. 1, 12.)

ὃς ἂν ὁμοηθὴς ὢν, ταὐτὰ ψέγων καὶ ἐπαινῶν, ἐθέλῃ ἄρχεσθαι καὶ ὑποκεῖσθαι τῷ ἄρχοντι—εὐθὺς ἐκ νέου ἐθίζειν αὐτὸν τοῖς αὐτοῖς χαίρειν καὶ ἄχθεσθαι τῷ δεσπότῃ (510 D). οὐ γὰρ μιμητὴν δεῖ εἶναι ἀλλ' αὐτοφυῶς ὅμοιον τούτοις (513 B).

[c] Plato, Gorgias, p. 526 C-D. (Compare Republic, vi. p. 496 D.) ἀνδρὸς ἰδιώτου ἢ ἄλλου τινός, μάλιστα μέν, ἔγωγέ φημι, ὦ Καλλικλεῖς, φιλοσόφου τὰ αὐτοῦ πράξαντος καὶ οὐ πολυπραγμονήσαντος ἐν τῷ βίῳ—καὶ δὴ καὶ ἀντιπαρακαλῶ σε (Sokrates to Kalliklês) ἐπὶ τοῦτον τὸν βίον. Upon these words Routh remarks: "Respicitur inter hæc verba ad Calliclis orationem, quâ rerum civilium tractatio et πολυπραγμοσύνη Socrati persuadentur,"—which is the same invitation as the Xenophontic Sokrates addresses to Aristippus. Again, in Plat. Republ. viii. pp. 549 C, 550 A we read, that corruption of the virtuous character begins by invitations to the shy youth to depart from the quiet plan of life followed by a virtuous father (who τὰ ἑαυτοῦ πράττει) and to enter on a career of active political ambition. The youth is induced, by instigation of his mother and relatives without, to pass from ἀπραγμοσύνη to ἀπραγμοσύνη, which is described as φιλοπραγμοσύνη, which is described as a change for the worse. Even in Xenophon (Memor. iii. 2, 16) Sokrates recognises and jests upon his own ἀπραγμοσύνη.

[d] Xen. Mem. iii. 8, 1. Diogenes L. says (and it is probable enough, from radical difference of character) that Xenophon was adversely disposed to Aristippus. In respect to other persons also, Xenophon puts invidious constructions (for which at any rate no ground is shown) upon their purposes

incorrect assumption: had it been correct, neither literature nor philosophy could have been developed.

The real Sokrates, since he talked incessantly and with every one, must of course have known how to diversify his conversation and adapt it to each listener. Xenophon not only attests this generally,[e] but has preserved the proofs of it in his Memorabilia—real conversations, reported though doubtless dressed up by himself. The conversations which he has preserved relate chiefly to piety and to the duties and proceedings of active life: and to the necessity of controuling the appetites: these he selected partly because they suited his proclaimed purpose of replying to the topics of indictment, partly because they were in harmony with his own *idéal*. Xenophon was a man of action, resolute in mind and vigorous in body, performing with credit the duties of the general as well as of the soldier. His heroes were men like Cyrus, Agesilaus, Ischomachus—warriors, horsemen, hunters, husbandmen, always engaged in active competition for power, glory, or profit, and never shrinking from danger, fatigue, or privation. For a life of easy and unambitious indulgence, even though accompanied by mental and speculative activity —"homines ignavâ operâ et philosophâ sentèntiâ"—he had no respect. It was on this side that the character of Aristippus certainly seemed to be, and probably really was, the most defective. Sokrates employed the arguments the most likely to call forth within him habits of action—to render him πρακτικώτερον.[f] In talking with the presumptuous youth Glaukon, and with the diffident Charmides,[g] Sokrates used language adapted to correct the respective infirmities of each. In addressing Kritias and Alkibiades, he would consider it necessary not only to inculcate self-denial as to appetite, but to repress an exorbitance of ambition.[h] But in dealing with Aristippus, while insisting upon command of appetite and acquirement of active energy, he at the same time endeavours to kindle ambition, and the love of command: he even goes

Marginal note: Diversified conversations of Sokrates, according to the character of the hearer.

in questioning Sokrates: thus, in the dialogue (i. 6)) with the Sophist Antiphon, he says that Antiphon questioned Sokrates in order to seduce away his companions.

[e] Xen. Mem. iv. 1, 2-3.

[f] Xenoph. Memor. iv. 5, 1. ὡς δὲ καὶ πρακτικωτέρους ἐποίει τοὺς συνόντας αὐτῷ, νῦν αὖ τοῦτο λέξω.
[g] Xenoph. Mem. iii. capp. 6 and 7.
[h] Xenoph. Memor. i. 2, 15-18-24.

so far as to deny the possibility of a middle course, and to maintain (what Kritias and Alkibiades[i] would have cordially approved) that there was no alternative open, except between the position of the oppressive governors and that of the suffering subjects. Addressed to Aristippus, these topics were likely to thrust forcibly upon his attention the danger of continued indulgences during the earlier years of life, and the necessity, in view to his own future security, for training in habits of vigour, courage, self-command, endurance.

Xenophon notices briefly two other colloquies between Sokrates and Aristippus. The latter asked Sokrates, "Do you know anything good?" in order (says Xenophon) that if Sokrates answered in the affirmative and gave as examples, health, wealth, strength, courage, bread, &c., he (Aristippus) might show circumstances in which this same particular was evil; and might thus catch Sokrates in a contradiction, as Sokrates had caught him before.[k] But Sokrates (says Xenophon) far from seeking to fence with the question, retorted it in such a way as to baffle the questioner, and at the same time to improve and instruct the by-standers.[l] "Do you ask me if I know anything good for a fever?—No. Or for ophthalmic distemper?—No. Or

Conversation between Sokrates and Aristippus about the Good and Beautiful.

[i] We see from the first two chapters of the Memorabilia of Xenophon (as well as from the subsequent intimation of Æschines, in the oration against Timarchus, p. 173) how much stress was laid by the accusers of Sokrates on the fact that he had educated Kritias and Alkibiades; and how the accusers alleged that his teaching tended to encourage the like exorbitant aspirations in others, dangerous to established authority, traditional, legal, parental, divine. I do not doubt (what Xenophon affirms) that Sokrates, when he conversed with Kritias and Alkibiades, held a very opposite language. But it was otherwise when he talked with men of ease and indulgence without ambition, such as Aristippus. If Melêtus and Anytus could have put in evidence the conversation of Sokrates with Aristippus, many points of it would have strengthened their case against Sokrates before the Dikasts. We read in Xenophon (Mem. i. 2, 58) how the point was made to tell, that

Sokrates often cited and commented on the passage of the Iliad (ii. 188) in which the Grecian chiefs, retiring from the agora to their ships, are described as being respectfully addressed by Odysseus—while the common soldiers are scolded and beaten by him, for the very same conduct: the relation which Sokrates here dwells on as subsisting between οἱ ἀρχικοὶ and οἱ ἀρχόμενοι, would favour the like colouring.

[k] Xenoph. Memor. iii. 8, 1. Both Xenophon and some of his commentators censure this as a captious string of questions put by Aristippus - "captiosas Aristippi quæstiunculas." Such a criticism is preposterous, when we recollect that Sokrates was continually examining and questioning others in the same manner. See in particular his cross-examination of Euthydêmus, reported by Xenophon, Memor. iv. 2: and many others like it, both in Xenophon and in Plato.

[l] Xenoph. Memor. iii. 8, 1. βουλόμενος τοὺς συνόντας ὠφελεῖν.

for hunger?—No. Oh! then, if you mean to ask me, whether
I know anything good, which is good for nothing—I reply,
that I neither know any such thing, nor care to know it."

Again, on another occasion Aristippus asked him—" Do
you know anything beautiful?—Yes; many things.—Are
they all like to each other?—No; they are as unlike as
possible to each other.—How then (continues Aristippus)
can that which is unlike to the beautiful, be itself beautiful?
—Easily enough (replies Sokrates); one man is beautiful for
running; another man, altogether unlike him, is beautiful for
wrestling. A shield, which is beautiful for protecting your
body, is altogether unlike to a javelin, which is beautiful for
being swiftly and forcibly hurled.—Your answer (rejoined
Aristippus) is exactly the same as it was when I asked you
whether you knew anything good.—Certainly (replies Sokrates). Do you imagine, that the Good is one thing, and the
Beautiful another? Do you not know that all things are good
and beautiful in relation to the same purpose? Virtue is not
good in relation to one purpose, and beautiful in relation to
another. Men are called both good and beautiful in reference
to the same ends: the bodies of men, in like manner: and all
things which men use, are considered both good and beautiful,
in consideration of their serving their ends well.—Then (says
Aristippus) a basket for carrying dung is beautiful?—To be
sure (replied Sokrates), and a golden shield is ugly; if the
former be well made for doing its work, and the latter badly.
—Do you then assert (asked Aristippus) that the same things
are both beautiful and ugly?—Assuredly (replied Sokrates);
and the same things are both good and evil. That which is
good for hunger, is often bad for a fever: that which is good
for a fever, is often bad for hunger. What is beautiful for
running, is often ugly for wrestling—and *vice versâ*. All
things are good and beautiful, in relation to the ends which
they serve well: all things are evil and ugly, in relation to
the ends which they serve badly." [m]

These last cited colloquies also, between Sokrates and Aris-
Remarks on
the conversa-
tion—Theory
of Good. tippus, are among the most memorable remains of
Grecian philosophy; belonging to one of the years

preceding 399 B.C., in which last year Sokrates perished. Here (as in the former dialogue) the doctrine is distinctly enunciated by Sokrates—That Good and Evil—Beautiful (or Honourable) and Ugly (or Dishonourable—Base)—have no intelligible meaning except in relation to human happiness and security.   Good or Evil Absolute (*i.e.* apart from such relation) is denied to exist. · The theory of Absolute Good (a theory traceable to the Parmenidean doctrines, and adopted from them by Eukleides) becomes first known to us as elaborated by Plato.   Even in his dialogues it is neither always nor exclusively advocated, but is often modified by, and sometimes even exchanged for, the eudæmonistic or relative theory.

Sokrates declares very explicitly, in his conversation with Aristippus, what *he* means by the Good and the Beautiful: and when therefore in the name of the Good and the Beautiful, he protests against an uncontrolled devotion to the pleasures of sense (as in one of the Xenophontic dialogues with Euthydemus[n]), what he means is, that a man by such intemperance ruins his prospects of future happiness, and his best means of being useful both to himself and others.   Whether Aristippus first learnt from Sokrates the relative theory of the Good and the Beautiful, or had already embraced it before, we cannot say.   Some of his questions, as reported in Xenophon, would lead us to suspect that it took him by surprise : just as we find, in the Protagoras of Plato, that a theory substantially the same, though in dif-

Marginal note: Good is relative to human beings and wants, in the view of Sokrates.

---

[n] Xenoph. Memor. iv. 5.

Sokrates exhorts those with whom he converses to be sparing in indulgences, and to cultivate self-command and fortitude as well as bodily energy and activity. The reason upon which these exhortations are founded is eudæmonistic : that a person will thereby escape or be able to confront serious dangers—and will obtain for himself ultimately greater pleasures than those which he foregoes (Memor. i. 6, 8, ii. 1, 31-33, iii. 12, 2-5). Τοῦ δὲ μὴ δουλεύειν γαστρὶ μηδὲ ὕπνῳ καὶ λαγνείᾳ οἴει τι ἄλλο αἰτιώτερον εἶναι, ἢ τὸ ἕτερα ἔχειν τούτων ἡδίω, ἃ οὐ μόνον ἐν χρείᾳ ὄντα εὐφραίνει, ἀλλὰ καὶ ἐλπίδας παρέχοντα ὠφελήσειν ἀεί; See

also Memor. ii. 4, ii. 10, 4, about the importance of acquiring and cultivating friends, because a good friend is the most useful and valuable of all possessions. Sokrates, like Aristippus, adopts the prudential view of life, and not the transcendental; recommending sobriety and virtue on the ground of pleasures secured and pains averted. We find Plutarch, in his very bitter attacks on Epikurus, reasoning on the Hedonistic basis, and professing to prove that Epikurus discarded pleasures more and greater for the sake of obtaining pleasures fewer and less. See Plutarch, Non posse suaviter vivi secundum Epicurum, pp. 1096-1099.

ferent words, is proposed by the Platonic Sokrates to the Sophist Protagoras: who at first repudiates it, but is compelled ultimately to admit it by the elaborate dialectic of Sokrates.[o] If Aristippus did not learn the theory from Sokrates, he was at any rate fortified in it by the authority of Sokrates; to whose doctrine, in this respect, he adhered more closely than Plato.

Aristippus is recognised by Aristotle[p] in two characters:

Aristippus adhered to the doctrine of Sokrates. both as a Sophist, and as a companion of Sokrates and Plato. Moreover it is remarkable that the doctrine, in reference to which Aristotle cites him as one among the Sophists, is a doctrine unquestionably Sokratic—contempt of geometrical science as useless, and as having no bearing on the good or evil of life.[q] Herein also Aristippus followed Sokrates, while Plato departed from him.

In estimating the character of Aristippus, I have brought

Life and dicta of Aristippus—His type of character. into particular notice the dialogues reported by Xenophon, because the Xenophontic statements, with those of Aristotle, are the only contemporary evidence (for Plato only names him once, to say that he was not present at the death of Sokrates, and was reported to be in Ægina). The other statements respecting Aristippus, preserved by Diogenes and others, not only come from later authorities, but give us hardly any facts; though they ascribe to him a great many sayings and repartees, adapted to a peculiar type of character. That type of character, together with an imperfect notion of his doctrines, is all that we can make out. Though Aristippus did not follow the recommendation of Sokrates, to labour and qualify himself for a ruler, yet both the advice of Sokrates, to reflect and prepare himself for the anxieties and perils of the future—and the spectacle of self-sufficing independence which the character of Sokrates afforded—were probably highly useful to him. Such advice being adverse to the natural tendencies of his mind, impressed upon him forcibly those points of the case which he was most likely to forget; and contributed to form in him that habit of self-command which is a marked feature in his

---

[o] Plato, Protagoras, pp. 351-361.

[p] Aristot. Rhetoric. ii. 24; Meta- physic. B. 996, a. 32.

[q] Xenophon, Memor. iv. 7, 2.

character. He wished (such are the words ascribed to him by Xenophon) to pass through life as easily and agreeably as possible. Ease comes before pleasure: but his plan of life was to obtain as much pleasure as he could, consistent with ease, or without difficulty and danger. He actually realised, as far as our means of knowledge extend, that middle path of life which Sokrates declared to be impracticable.

Much of the advice given by Sokrates, Aristippus appears to have followed, though not from the reasons which Sokrates puts forward for giving it. When Sokrates reminds him that men liable to be tempted and ensnared by the love of good eating, were unfit to command—when he animadverts on the insanity of the passionate lover, who exposed himself to the extremity of danger for the purpose of possessing a married woman, while there were such abundant means of gratifying the sexual appetite without any difficulty or danger whatever[r]—to all this Aristippus assents: and what we read about his life is in perfect conformity therewith. Reason and prudence supply ample motives for following such advice, whether a man be animated with the love of command or not. So again, when Sokrates impresses upon Aristippus that the Good and the Beautiful were the same, being relative only to human wants cr satisfaction—and that nothing was either good or beautiful, except in so far as it tended to confer relief, security, or enjoyment—this lesson too Aristippus laid to heart, and applied in a way suitable to his own peculiar dispositions and capacities.

Aristippus acted conformably to the advice of Sokrates.

The type of character represented by Aristippus is the man who enjoys what the present affords, so far as can be done without incurring future mischief, or provoking the enmity of others—but who will on no account enslave himself to any enjoyment; who always maintains his own self-mastery and independence—and who has prudence and intelligence enabling him to regulate each separate enjoyment so as not to incur preponderant evil in future.[s] This self-mastery and independence

Self-mastery and independence—the great aspiration of Aristippus.

[r] Xen. Mem. ii. 1, 5. καὶ τηλικούτων μὲν ἐπικειμένων τῷ μοιχεύοντι κακῶν τε καὶ αἰσχρῶν, ὄντων δὲ πολλῶν τῶν ἀπολυσόντων τῆς τῶν ἀφροδισιῶν ἐπιθυμίας ἐν ἀδείᾳ, ὅμως εἰς τὰ ἐπικίνδυνα φέρεσθαι, ἆρ' οὐκ ἤδη τοῦτο παντάπασι κακοδαιμονοῦντός ἐστιν; Ἔμοιγε δοκεῖ, ἔφη ('Αρίστιππος).
[s] Diog. L. ii. 67. οὕτως ἦν καὶ ἑλέσθαι καὶ καταφρονῆσαι πολύς.

is in point of fact the capital aspiration of Aristippus, hardly
less than of Antisthenes and Diogenes. He is competent to
deal suitably with all varieties of persons, places, and situations, and to make the best of each—Οὐ γὰρ τοιούτων δεῖ,
τοιοῦτος εἰμ᾿ ἐγώ :[t] but he accepts what the situation presents,
without yearning or struggling for that which it cannot present.[u] He enjoys the society both of the Syracusan despot
Dionysius, and of the Hetæra Lais ; but he will not make
himself subservient either to one or to the other : he conceives himself able to afford, to both, as much satisfaction as
he receives.[x] His enjoyments are not enhanced by the idea
that others are excluded from the like enjoyment, and that
he is a superior, privileged, man : he has no jealousy or antipathy, no passion for triumphing over rivals, no demand for
envy or admiration from spectators. Among the Hetæræ in
Greece were included all the most engaging and accomplished
women—for in Grecian matrimony, it was considered becoming and advantageous that the bride should be young and
ignorant, and that as a wife she should neither see nor know
any thing beyond the administration of her own feminine
apartments and household.[y] Aristippus attached himself to
those Hetæræ who pleased him ; declaring that the charm of
their society was in no way lessened by the knowledge that
others enjoyed it also, and that he could claim no exclusive
privilege.[z] His patience and mildness in argument is much

---

[t] Diog. L. ii. 66. ἦν δὲ ἱκανὸς ἁρ-
μόσασθαι καὶ τόπῳ καὶ χρόνῳ καὶ προ-
σώπῳ, καὶ πᾶσαν περίστασιν ἁρμοδίως
ὑποκρίνασθαι· διὸ καὶ παρὰ Διονυσίῳ
τῶν ἄλλων ηὐδοκίμει μᾶλλον, ἀεὶ τὸ
παρὸν εὖ διατιθέμενος· ἀπέλαυε μὲν γὰρ
ἡδονῆς τῶν παρόντων, οὐκ ἐθήρα δὲ
πόνῳ τὴν ἀπόλαυσιν τῶν οὐ παρόντων.
   Horat. Epistol. i. 17-23 :—
"Omnis Aristippum decuit color et status et
   res,
Tentantem majora, ferè præsentibus æquum."
   [u] Sophokles, Philoktêtes, 1049 (the
words of Odysseus).
   [x] Diog. L. ii. 75. ἐχρῆτο καὶ Λαΐδι
τῇ ἑταίρᾳ· πρὸς οὖν τοὺς μεμφομένους
αὐτῷ ἔφη, Ἔχω Λαΐδα, ἀλλ᾿ οὐκ ἔχομαι·
ἐπεὶ τὸ κρατεῖν καὶ μὴ ἡττᾶσθαι ἡδονῶν,
ἄριστον—οὐ τὸ μὴ χρῆσθαι. ii. 77,
Διονυσίου ποτ᾿ ἐρομένου, ἐπὶ τί ἥκοι.
ἔφη, ἐπὶ τῷ μεταδώσειν ὧν ἔχοι, καὶ
μεταλήψεσθαι ὧν μὴ ἔχοι.

[y] Xenophon, Œconomic. iii. 13, vii.
5, Ischomachus says to Sokrates about
his wife, Καὶ τί ἂν ἐπισταμένην αὐτὴν
παρέλαβον, ἢ ἔτη μὲν οὔπω πεντεκαίδεκα
γεγονυῖα ἦλθε πρὸς ἐμὲ, τὸν δ᾿ ἔμπροσθεν χρόνον ἔζη ὑπὸ πολλῆς ἐπι-
μελείας, ὅπως ὡς ἐλάχιστα μὲν
ὄψοιτο, ἐλάχιστα δ᾿ ἀκούσοιτο,
ἐλάχιστα δὲ ἔροιτο;
   [z] Diog. L. ii. 74. On this point his
opinion coincided with that of Diogenes, and of the Stoics Zeno and
Chrysippus (D. L. vii. 131),—who maintained, that among the wise wives
ought to be in common, and that all
marital jealousy ought to be discarded.
᾿Αρέσκει δ᾿ αὐτοῖς καὶ κοινὰς εἶναι τὰς
γυναῖκας δεῖν παρὰ τοῖς σοφοῖς ὥστε τὸν
ἐντυχόντα τῇ ἐντυχούσῃ χρῆσθαι, καθά
φησι Ζήνων ἐν τῇ Πολιτείᾳ καὶ Χρύσιπ-
πος ἐν τῷ περὶ Πολιτείας, ἀλλ᾿ ἔτι Διογένης δ Κυνικὸς καὶ Πλάτων· πάντας δὲ

commended. The main lesson which he had learnt from philosophy (he said), was self-appreciation—to behave himself with confidence in every man's society : even if all laws were abrogated, the philosopher would still, without any law, live in the same way as he now did.[a] His confidence remained unshaken, when seized as a captive in Asia by order of the Persian satrap Artaphernes : all that he desired was, to be taken before the satrap himself.[b] Not to renounce pleasure, but to enjoy pleasure moderately and to keep desires under controul,—was in his judgment the true policy of life. But he was not solicitous to grasp enjoyment beyond what was easily attainable, nor to accumulate wealth or power which did not yield positive result.[c] While Sokrates recommended, and Antisthenes practised, the precaution of deadening the sexual appetite by approaching no women except such as were ugly and repulsive,[d]—while Xenophon in the Cyropædia,[e] working out the Sokratic idea of the dangerous fascination of beauty, represents Cyrus as refusing to see the captive Pantheia, and depicts the too confident Araspes, (who treats such precaution as exaggerated timidity, and fully trusts his own self-possession) when appointed to the duty of guarding her, as absorbed against his will in a passion which makes him forget all reason and duty—Aristippus has sufficient self-mastery to visit the most seductive Hetæræ without being drawn into ruinous extravagance or humiliating subjugation. We may doubt whether he ever felt even for Lais, a more passionate sentiment than Plato in his Epigram expresses towards the Kolophonian Hetæra Archeanassa.

Aristippus is thus remarkable, like the Cynics Antisthenes and Diogenes, not merely for certain theoretical doctrines, but also for acting out a certain plan of life.[f] We know little or nothing of the real life

Aristippus compared with Antisthenes and Diogenes —

παῖδας ἐπίσης στέρξομεν πατέρων τρόπον, καὶ ἡ ἐπὶ μοιχείᾳ ζηλοτυπία περιαιρεθήσεται. Compare Sextus Emp. Pyrrh. H. iii. 205.

[a] Diog. L. ii. 68. The like reply is ascribed to Aristotle. Diog. L. v. 20; Plutarch, De Profect. in Virtut. p. 80 D.

[b] Diog. L. ii. 79.

[c] Diog. L. ii. 72-74.

[d] Xenoph Memor. i. 3, 11-14; Symposion, iv. 38 ; Diog. L. vi. 3. ('Αντισθένης) ἔλεγε συνεχὲς—Μανείην μᾶλλον ἢ ἡσθείην—καὶ — χρὴ τοιαύταις πλησιάζειν γυναῖξιν, αἱ χάριν εἴσονται.

[e] Xenop. Cyropæd. v. 1.

[f] Sextus Empiricus and others describe this by the Greek word ἀγωγή (Pyrrhon. Hypotyp. i. 150). Plato's beautiful epigram upon Archeanassa is given by Diogenes L. iii. 31. Com-

Points of agreement and disagreement between them. of Aristippus, except what appears in Xenophon. The biography of him (as of the Cynic Diogenes) given by Diogenes Laertius, consists of little more than a string of anecdotes, mostly sayings, calculated to illustrate a certain type of character.[g] Some of these are set down by those who approved the type, and who therefore place it in a favourable point of view—others by those who disapprove it and give the opposite colour.

We can understand and compare the different types of character represented by Antisthenes or Diogenes, and by Aristippus: but we have little knowledge of the real facts of their lives. The two types, each manifesting that marked individuality which belongs to the Sokratic band, though in many respects strongly contrasted, have also some points of agreement. Both Aristippus and Diogenes are bent on individual freedom and independence of character: both of them stand upon their own appreciation of life and its phenomena: both of them are impatient of that servitude to the opinions and antipathies of others, which induces a man to struggle for objects, not because they afford him satisfaction, but because others envy him for possessing them—and to keep off evils, not because he himself feels them as such, but because others pity or despise him for being subject to them: both of them are exempt from the competitive and ambitious feelings, from the thirst after privilege and power, from the sense of superiority arising out of monopolised possession and exclusion of others from partnership. Diogenes kept aloof from political life and civil obligations as much as Aristippus; and would have pronounced (as Aristippus replies to Sokrates in the Xenophontic dialogue) that the task of ruling others, instead of being a prize to be coveted, was nothing better than an onerous and mortifying servitude,[h] not at all less onerous

pare this with the remark of Aristippus—Plutarch, Amatorius, p. 750 E.

That the society of these fascinating Hetæræ was dangerous, and exhaustive to the purses of those who sought it, may be seen from the expensive manner of life of Theodotê, described in Xenophon, Mem. iii. 11, 4.

The amorous impulses or fancies of Plato were censured by Dikæarchus.

See Cicero, Tusc. Disp. iv. 34 with Davies's note.

[g] This is justly remarked by Wendt in his instructive Dissertation, De Philosophiâ Cyrenaicâ, p. 8 (Göttingen, 1841).

[h] It is this servitude of political life, making the politician the slave of persons and circumstances around him, which Horace contrasts with the phi-

because a man took up the burthen of his own accord. These
points of agreement are real: but the points of disagreement
are not less real. Diogenes maintains his free individuality,
and puts himself out of the reach of human enmity, by clothing himself in impenetrable armour: by attaining positive
insensibility, as near as human life permits. This is with
him not merely the acting out of a scheme of life, but also a
matter of pride. He is proud of his ragged garment and
coarse[i] fare, as exalting him above others, and as constituting
him a pattern of endurance: and he indulges this sentiment
by stinging and contemptuous censure of every one. Aristippus has no similar vanity: he achieves his independence
without so heavy a renunciation: he follows out his own plan
of life, without setting himself up as a pattern for others.
But his plan is at the same time more delicate; requiring
greater skill and intelligence, more of manifold sagacity, in
the performer. Horace, who compares the two and gives the
preference to Aristippus, remarks that Diogenes, though professing to want nothing, was nevertheless as much dependent
upon the bounty of those who supplied his wallet with provisions, as Aristippus upon the favour of princes: and that
Diogenes had only one fixed mode of proceeding, while Aristippus could master and turn to account a great diversity of
persons and situations—could endure hardship with patience
and dignity, when it was inevitable, and enjoy the oppor-
tunities of pleasure when they occurred. "To Aristippus
alone it is given to wear both fine garments and rags"—is a
remark ascribed to Plato.[k] In truth, Aristippus possesses in

losophical independence of Aristippus:—

"Ac ne forté roges, quo me duce, quo lare tuter;
Nullius addictus jurare in verba magistri
Quo me cunque rapit tempestas, deferor hos-
    pes.
Nunc agilis fio et mersor civilibus undis,
Virtutis veræ custos rigidusque satelles:
Nunc in Aristippi furtim præcepta relabor,
Et mihi res, non me rebus, subjungere conor."
                                    (Epist. 1, 15.)

So also the Platonic Sokrates
(Theætêt. pp. 172-175) depicts forcibly
the cramped and fettered lives of
rhetors and politicians; contrasting
them with the self-judgment and independence of speculative and philosophical enquirers — ὡς οἰκέται πρὸς

ἐλευθέρους τεθράφθαι—ὁ δὴ τῷ ὄντι ἐν
ἐλευθερίᾳ τε καὶ σχολῇ τεθραμμένος, ὃν
δὴ φιλόσοφον καλεῖς.
  [1] Diog. L. ii. 37. στρέψαντος Ἀντι-
σθένους τὸ διερρωγὸς τοῦ ἱματίου εἰς
τοὐμφανές, 'Ορῶ σοῦ, ἔφη (Σωκράτης)
διὰ τοῦ τρίβωνος τὴν κενοδοξίαν.
  [k] Horat. Epistol. i. 17; Diog. L. vi.
46-56-66.

"Si pranderet olus patienter, regibus uti
Nollet Aristippus. Si sciret regibus uti,
Fastidiret olus, qui me notat. Utrius horum
Verba probes et facta, doce: vel junior audi,
Cur sit Aristippi potior sententia. Namque
Mordacem Cynicum sic eludebat, ut aiunt:
Scurror ego ipse mihi, populo tu: rectius hoc et
Splendidius multo est. Equus ut me portet,
    alat rex,

eminent measure that accomplishment, the want of which Plato proclaims to be so misleading and mischievous—artistic skill in handling human affairs, throughout his dealings with mankind.[1]

Attachment of Aristippus to ethics and philosophy— contempt for other studies. That the scheme of life projected by Aristippus was very difficult, requiring great dexterity, prudence, and resolution, to execute it—we may see plainly by the Xenophontic dialogue; wherein Sokrates pronounces it to be all but impracticable. As far as we can judge, he surmounted the difficulties of it: yet we do not know enough of his real life to determine with accuracy what varieties of difficulties he experienced. He followed the profession of a Sophist, receiving fees for his teaching: and his attachment to philosophy (both as contrasted with ignorance and as contrasted with other studies not philosophy), was proclaimed in the most emphatic language. It was better (he said) to be a beggar, than an uneducated man:[m] the former was destitute of money, but the latter was destitute of humanity. He disapproved varied and indiscriminate instruction, maintaining that persons ought to learn in youth what they were to practise in manhood: and he compared those who, neglecting philosophy, employed themselves in literature or physical science, to the suitors in the Odyssey who obtained the favours of Melantho and the other female servants, but were rejected by the queen Penelopê herself.[n] He treated with contempt the study of geometry, because it took no account, and made no mention, of what was good and

---

Officium facio : tu poscis vilia rerum,
Dante minor, quamvis fers te nullius egentem.
Omnis Aristippum decuit color, et status, et res,
Tentantem majora, ferè præsentibus æquum."

(Compare Diog. L. ii. 102, vi. 58, where this anecdote is reported as of Plato instead of Aristippus.)

Horace's view and scheme of life are exceedingly analogous to those of Aristippus. Plutarch, Fragm. De Homero, p. 1190; De Fortunâ Alex. p. 330 D. Diog. Laert. ii. 67. διό ποτε Στράτωνα, οἱ δὲ Πλάτωνα, πρὸς αὐτὸν εἰπεῖν, Σοὶ μόνῳ δέδοται καὶ χλανίδα φέρειν καὶ ῥάκος. The remark cannot have been made by Straton, who was not contemporary with Aristippus. Even Sokrates lived by the bounty of his rich friends, and indeed could have had no other

means of supporting his wife and children; though he accepted only a small portion of what they tendered to him, declining the remainder. See the remark of Aristippus, Dio. L. ii. 74.

[1] Plato, Phædon, p. 89 E. ὅτι ἄνευ τέχνης τῆς περὶ τἀνθρώπεια ὁ τοιοῦτος χρῆσθαι ἐπιχειρεῖ τοῖς ἀνθρώποις.

[m] Diog. L. ii. 70 : Plutarch, Fragm. 'Υπομνήματ· εἰς 'Ησίοδον, s. 9. 'Αρίστιππος δὲ ἀπ' ἐναντίας ὁ Σωκρατικὸς ἔλεγε, συμβούλου δεῖσθαι χεῖρον εἶναι ἢ προσαιτεῖν.

[n] Diog. L. ii. 79-80. τοὺς τῶν ἐγκυκλίων παιδευμάτων μετασχόντας, φιλοσοφίας δὲ ἀπολειφθέντας, &c. Plutarch, Fragm. Στρωματέων, sect. 9.

evil, beautiful and ugly. In other arts (he said), even in the vulgar proceeding of the carpenter and the currier, perpetual reference was made to good, as the purpose intended to be served—and to evil as that which was to be avoided: but in geometry no such purpose was ever noticed.[o]

This last opinion of Aristippus deserves particular attention, because it is attested by Aristotle. And it confirms what we hear upon less certain testimony, that Aristippus discountenanced the department of physical study generally (astronomy and physics) as well as geometry; confining his attention to facts and reasonings which bore upon the regulation of life.[p] *Aristippus taught as a Sophist. His reputation thus acquired procured for him the attentions of Dionysius and others.* In this restrictive view he followed the example and precepts of Sokrates—of Isokrates—seemingly also of Protagoras and Prodikus—though not of the Eleian Hippias, whose course of study was larger and more varied.[q] Aristippus taught as a Sophist, and appears to have acquired great reputation in that capacity both at Athens and elsewhere.[r] Indeed, if he had not acquired such intellectual and literary reputation at Athens, he would have had little chance of being invited elsewhere, and still less chance of receiving favours and presents from Dionysius and other princes:[s] whose attentions

[o] Aristot. Metaph. B. 996, a, 32, M. 1078, a. 35. ὥστε διὰ ταῦτα καὶ τῶν σοφιστῶν τινὲς οἷον ᾿Αρίστιππος προεπηλάκιζον αὐτὰς, &c.

[p] Diog. L. ii. 92. Sext. Emp. adv. Math. vii. 11. Plutarch, apud Eusebium Præp. Ev. i. 8, 9.

[q] Plato, Protagor. p. 318 E, where the different methods followed by Protagoras and Hippias are indicated.

[r] Diog. Laert. ii. 62. Alexis Comicus ap. Athenæ. xii. 544.

Aristokles (ap. Euseb. Præp. Ev. xiv. 18) treats the first Aristippus as a mere voluptuary, who said nothing generally. περὶ τοῦ τέλους. All the doctrine (he says) came from the younger Aristippus. I think this very improbable. To what did the dialogues composed by the first Aristippus refer? How did he get his reputation?

[s] Several anecdotes are recounted about sayings and doings of Aristippus in his intercourse with *Dionysius.* *Which* Dionysius is meant?—the elder or the younger? Nothing is said to indicate which of the two.

It is to be remembered that Dionysius the Elder lived and reigned until the year 367 B.C., in which year his son Dionysius the Younger succeeded him. The death of Sokrates took place in 399 B.C.: between which, and the accession of Dionysius the Younger, an interval of 32 years occurred. Plato was old, being sixty years of age, when he first visited the younger Dionysius, shortly after the accession of the latter. Aristippus cannot well have been younger than Plato, and he is said to have been older than Æschines Sokraticus (D. L. ii. 83). Compare ii. p. 41.

If, with these dates present to our minds, we read the anecdotes recounted by Diog. L. respecting the sayings and doings of Aristippus with *Dionysius,* we shall find it difficult to understand them. Several of them relate to the contrast between the behaviour of Aristippus and that of Plato at Syracuse. Now Plato once went to Syracuse, when he was forty years of age (Epist. vii. init.), in 387 B.C., while the

did not confer celebrity, but waited upon it when obtained, and doubtless augmented it. If Aristippus lived a life of indulgence at Athens, we may fairly presume that his main resources for sustaining it, like those of Isokrates, were derived from his own teaching: and that the presents which he received from Dionysius of Syracuse, like those which Isokrates received from Nikokles of Cyprus, were welcome additions, but not his main income. Those who (like most of the historians of philosophy) adopt the opinion of Sokrates and Plato, that it is disgraceful for an instructor to receive payment from the persons taught—will doubtless despise Aristippus for such a proceeding: for my part, I dissent from this opinion, and I therefore do not concur in the disparaging epithets bestowed upon him. And as for the costly indulgences, and subservience to foreign princes, of which Aristippus stands accused, we must recollect that the very same reproaches were advanced against Plato and Aristotle by their contemporaries: and as far as we know, with quite as much foundation.[t]

Aristippus composed several dialogues, of which the titles alone are preserved.[u] They must however have been compositions of considerable merit, since Theopompus accused Plato of borrowing largely from them.

As all the works of Aristippus are lost, we cannot pretend to understand fully his theory from the meagre abstract given in Sextus Empiricus and Diogenes. Yet the theory is of importance in the history of ancient speculation, since it passed with some modifications to Epikurus, and was adopted by a large proportion of instructed men. The Kyrenaic doctrine was transmitted

Ethical theory of Aristippus and the Kyrenaic philosophers.

elder Dionysius was in the plenitude of power : but he made an unfavourable impression, and was speedily sent away in displeasure. · The anecdotes recounted about Aristippus cannot well have occurred *then:* nor again (for other reasons) at the later period, when Plato visited the younger Dionysius, and when Aristippus, as well as Plato, was sixty years of age. I do not know what to make of these anecdotes, except as illustrative fiction: but I think it very probable that Aristippus may have visited the elder Dionysius, and may have found greater favour with him than Plato found, since Dionysius was an accomplished man and a composer of tragedies. Moreover Aristippus was a Kyrenæan, and wrote about Libya (D. L. ii. 83).

[t] See the epigram of the contemporary poet, Theokritus of Chios, in Diog. L. v. 11 ; compare Athenæus, viii. 354, xiii. 566. Aristokles, ap. Eusebium Præp. Ev. xv. 2.

[u] Diog. L. ii. 84-85.

by Aristippus to his disciples Æthiops and Antipater: but his chief disciple appears to have been his daughter Arête: whom he instructed so well, that she was able to instruct her own son, the second Aristippus, called for that reason Metrodidactus.   The basis of his ethical theory was, pleasure and pain: pleasure being *smooth motion*, pain, *rough motion*:[x] pleasure being the object which all animals, by nature and without deliberation, loved, pursued, and felt satisfaction in obtaining—pain being the object which they all by nature hated, and tried to avoid.   Aristippus considered that no one pleasure was different from another, nor more pleasurable than another:[y] that the attainment of these special pleasurable moments, or as many of them as practicable, was The End to be pursued in life.   By *Happiness*, they understood the sum total of these special pleasures, past, present, and future: yet Happiness was desirable not on its own account, but on account of its constituent items, especially such ·of those items as were present and certainly future.[z]   Pleasures and pains of memory and expectation were considered to be of little importance.   Absence of pain or relief from pain, on the one hand—they did not consider as equivalent to positive pleasure—nor absence of pleasure or withdrawal of pleasure, on the other hand—as equivalent to positive pain.   Neither the one situation nor the other was a *motion* (κίνησις) *i.e.* a positive situation, appreciable by the consciousness: each was a middle state—a mere negation of consciousness, like the phenomena of sleep.[a]   They recognised some mental pleasures and pains

---

[x] Diog. L. ii. 86.   δύο πάθη ὑφίσταντο, πόνον καὶ ἡδονήν· τὴν μὲν λείαν κίνησιν, τὸν δὲ πόνον, τραχεῖαν κίνησιν· μὴ διαφέρειν τε ἡδονὴν ἡδονῆς, μηδὲ ἥδιόν τι εἶναι· καὶ τὴν μὲν, εὐδόκητην πᾶσι ζώοις, τὸν δὲ ἀποκρουστικόν.

[y] Diog. L. ii. p. 87.   μὴ διαφέρειν τε ἡδονὴν ἡδονῆς, μηδὲ ἥδιόν τι εἶναι.   They did not mean by these words to deny that one pleasure was more vehement and attractive than another pleasure, or that one pain is more vehement and deterrent than another pain: for it is expressly said afterwards (s. 90) that they admitted this.   They meant to affirm that one pleasure did not differ from another *so far forth as pleasure:* that all pleasures must be ranked as a class, and compared with

each other in respect of intensity, durability, and other properties possessed in greater or less degree.

[z] Diog. L. ii. pp. 88-89.   Athenæus, xii. p. 544.

[a] Diog. L. ii. 89-90.   μὴ οὔσης τῆς ἀπονίας ἢ τῆς ἀηδονίας κινήσεως, ἐπεὶ ἡ ἀπονία οἱονεὶ καθεύδοντός ἔστι κατάστασις—μέσας καταστάσεις ὠνόμαζον ἀηδονίαν καὶ ἀπονίαν.

A doctrine very different from this is ascribed to Aristippus in Galen—Placit. Philos. (xix. p. 230, Kühn).   It is there affirmed that by *pleasure* Aristippus understood, not the pleasure of sense, but that disposition of mind whereby a person becomes insensible to pain, and hard to be imposed upon (ἀνάλγητος καὶ δυσγοήτευτος).

as derivative from bodily sensation and as exclusively individual—others as not so: for example, there were pleasures and pains of sympathy; and a man often felt joy at the prosperity of his friends and countrymen, quite as genuine as that which he felt for his own good fortune.   But they maintained that the bodily pleasures and pains were much more vehement than the mental which were not bodily: for which reason, the pains employed by the laws in punishing offenders were chiefly bodily.   The fear of pain was in their judgments more operative than the love of pleasure: and though pleasure was desirable for its own sake, yet the accompanying conditions of many pleasures were so painful as to deter the prudent man from aiming at them.   These obstructions rendered it impossible for any one to realise the sum total of pleasures constituting Happiness.   Even the wise man sometimes failed, and the foolish man sometimes did well, though in general the reverse was the truth: but under the difficult conditions of life, a man must be satisfied if he realised some particular pleasurable conjunctures, without aspiring to a continuance or totality of the like.[b]

Prudence— good, by reason of the pleasure which it ensured, and of the pains which it was necessary to avoid. Just and honourable, by law or custom—not by nature.

Aristippus regarded prudence or wisdom as good, yet not as good *per se*, but by reason of the pleasures which it enabled us to procure and the pains which it enabled us to avoid—and wealth as a good, for the same reason.   A friend also was valuable, for the use and necessities of life: just as each part of one's own body was precious, so long as it was present and could serve a useful purpose.[c]   Some branches of virtue might be possessed by persons who were not wise: and bodily training was a valuable auxiliary to virtue.

[b] Diog. L. ii. 91.

It does not appear that the Kyrenaic sect followed out into detail the derivative pleasures and pains; nor the way in which, by force of association, these come to take precedence of the primary, exercising influence on the mind both more forcible and more constant. We find this important fact remarkably stated in the doctrine of Kalliphon.

Clemens Alexandr. Stromat. ii. p. 415, ed. 1629.   Κατὰ δὲ τοὺς περὶ Καλλιφῶντα, ἕνεκα μὲν τῆς ἡδονῆς παρεισῆλθεν ἡ ἀρετή· χρόνῳ δὲ ὕστερον, τὸ περὶ αὐτὴν κάλλος κατιδοῦσα, ἰσότιμον ἑαυτὴν τῇ ἀρχῇ, τούτεστι τῇ ἡδονῇ, πάρεσχεν.

[c] Diog. L. ii. 91.   τὴν φρόνησιν ἀγαθὸν μὲν εἶναι λέγουσιν, οὐ δι' ἑαυτὴν δὲ αἱρετήν, ἀλλὰ διὰ τὰ ἐξ αὐτῆς περιγινόμενα· τὸν φίλον τῆς χρείας ἕνεκα· καὶ γὰρ μέρος σώματος, μέχρις ἂν παρῇ, ἀσπάζεσθαι.

The like comparison is employed by the Xenophontic Sokrates in the Memorabilia (i. 2, 52-55), that men cast away portions of their own body, so soon as these portions cease to be useful.

Even the wise man could never escape pain and
of these were natural: but he would keep c
passionate love, and superstition, which were not natura.,
consequences of vain opinion.   A thorough acquaintance with
the real nature of Good and Evil would relieve him from
superstition as well as from the fear of death.[d]

The Kyrenaics did not admit that there was anything just,
or honourable, or base, by nature: but only by law and
custom: nevertheless the wise man would be sufficiently
restrained, by the fear of punishment and of discredit from
doing what was repugnant to the society in which he lived.
They maintained that wisdom was attainable; that the senses
did not at first judge truly, but might be improved by study;
that progress was realised in philosophy as in other arts, and
that there were different gradations of it, as well as different
gradations of pain and suffering, discernible in different men.
The wise man, as they conceived him, was a reality; not
(like the wise man of the Stoics) a sublime but unattainable
idéal.[e]

Such were (as far as our imperfect evidence goes) the
ethical and emotional views of the Kyrenaic school: Their logical theory—nothing knowable except the phenomenal, our own sensations and feelings—no knowledge of the absolute.
their theory and precepts respecting the plan and
prospects of life.   In regard to truth and knowledge,
they maintained that we could have no knowledge
of anything but human sensations, affections, feel-
ings, &c. ($\pi\acute{a}\theta\eta$): that respecting the extrinsic, extra-
sensational, absolute, objects or causes from whence
these feelings proceeded, we could know nothing at all.
Partly for this reason, they abstained from all attention to
the study of nature—to astronomy and physics: partly also
because they did not see any bearing of these subjects upon
good and evil, or upon the conduct of life.   They turned
their attention mainly to ethics, partly also to logic as subsi-
diary to ethical reasoning.[f]

Such low estimation of mathematics and physics—and attention given almost exclusively to the feelings and conduct
of human life—is a point common to the opposite schools of

[d] Diog. L. ii. p. 92.
[e] Diog. L. ii. p. 93.
[f] Diog. L. ii. p. 92. Sextus Empiric.
adv. Mathemat. vi. 53.

Aristippus and Antisthenes, derived by both of them from Sokrates. Herein Plato stands apart from all the three.

The theory of Aristippus, as given above, is only derived from a meagre abstract and from a few detached hints. We do not know how he himself stated it: still less how he enforced and vindicated it. He, as well as Antisthenes, composed dialogues: which naturally implies diversity of handling. Their main thesis, therefore—the text, as it were, upon which they debated or expatiated (which is all that the abstract gives)—afford very inadequate means, even if we could rely upon the accuracy of the statement, for appreciating their philosophical competence. We should form but a poor idea of the acute, abundant, elastic, and diversified dialectic of Plato, if all his dialogues had been lost—and if we had nothing to rely upon except the summary of Platonism prepared by Diogenes Laertius: which summary, nevertheless, is more copious and elaborate than the same author has furnished either of Aristippus or Antisthenes.

In the history of the Greek mind these two last-mentioned philosophers (though included by Cicero among the *plebeii philosophi*) are not less important than Plato and Aristotle. The speculations and precepts of Antisthenes passed, with various enlargements and modifications, into the Stoic philosophy: those of Aristippus into the Epikurean: the two most widely extended ethical sects in the subsequent Pagan world. The Cynic sect, as it stood before it embraced the enlarged physical, kosmical, and social theories of Zeno and his contemporaries, reducing to a minimum all the desires and appetites—cultivating insensibility to the pains of life, and even disdainful insensibility to its pleasures—required extraordinary force of will and obstinate resolution, but little beyond. Where there was no selection or discrimination, the most ordinary prudence sufficed. It was otherwise with the scheme of Aristippus and the Kyrenaics: which, if it tasked less severely the powers of endurance, demanded a far higher measure of intelligent prudence. Selection of that which might safely be enjoyed, and determination of the limit within which enjoyment must be confined, were constantly indispensable. Prudence, knowledge, the art

Doctrines of Antisthenes and Aristippus passed to the Stoics and Epikureans.

of mensuration or calculation, were essential to Aristippus, and ought to be put in the foreground when his theory is stated.

That theory is, in point of fact, identical with the theory expounded by the Platonic Sokrates in Plato's Protagoras. The general features of both are the same. Sokrates there lays it down explicitly, that pleasure *per se* is always good, and pain *per se* always evil : that there is no other good (*per se*) except pleasure and diminution of pain—no other evil (*per se*) except pain and diminution of pleasure : that there is no other object in life except to live through it as much as possible with pleasures and without pains ;[g] but that many pleasures become evil, because they cannot be had without depriving us of greater pleasures or imposing upon us greater pains—while many pains become good, because they prevent greater pains or ensure greater pleasures : that the safety of life thus lies in a correct comparison of the more or less in pleasures and pains, and in a selection founded thereupon. In other words, the safety of life depends upon calculating knowledge or prudence, the art or science of measuring.

Ethical theory of Aristippus is identical with that of the Platonic Sokrates in the Protagoras.

The theory here laid down by the Platonic Sokrates is the same as that of Aristippus. The purpose of life is stated almost in the same words by both : by the Platonic Sokrates, and by Aristippus in the Xenophontic dialogue—" to live through with enjoyment and without suffering." The Platonic Sokrates denies, quite as emphatically as Aristippus, any good or evil, honourable or base, except as representing the result of an intelligent comparison of pleasures and pains. Judicious calculation is postulated by both : pleasures and pains being assumed by both as the only ends of pursuit and avoidance, to which calculation is to be applied. The main difference is, that the prudence, art, or science, required for making this calculation

Difference in the manner of stating the theory by the two.

<hr/>

[g] Plato, Protag. p. 355 A. ἦ ἀρκεῖ ὑμῖν τὸ ἡδέως καταβιῶναι τὸν βίον ἄνευ λυπῶν ; εἰ δὲ ἀρκεῖ, καὶ μὴ ἔχετε μηδὲν ἄλλο φάναι εἶναι ἀγαθὸν καὶ κακὸν, ὃ μὴ εἰς ταῦτα τελευτᾷ, τὸ μετὰ τοῦτο ἀκούετε.

The exposition of this theory, by the Platonic Sokrates, occupies the latter portion of the Protagoras, from p. 351 to near the conclusion. See above, ch. xxi. of the present work, pp. 60-89, vol. ii.

The language held by Aristippus to Sokrates, in the Xenophontic dialogue (Memor. ii. i. 9), is exactly similar to that of the Platonic Sokrates, as above cited—ἐμαυτὸν τάττω εἰς τοὺς βουλομένους ᾗ ῥᾷστά τε καὶ ἥδιστα βιοτεύειν.

rightly, are put forward by the Platonic Sokrates as the prominent item in his provision for passing through life : whereas, in the scheme of Aristippus, as far as we know it, such accomplished intelligence, though equally recognised and implied, is not equally thrust into the foreground. So it appears at least in the abstract which we possess of his theory: if we had his own exposition of it, perhaps we might find the case otherwise. In that abstract, indeed, we find the writer replying to those who affirmed prudence or knowledge to be good *per se*— and maintaining that it is only good by reason of its consequences:[h] that is, that it is not good as End, in the same sense in which pleasure or mitigation of pain are good. This point of the theory, however, coincides again with the doctrine of the Platonic Sokrates in the Protagoras: where the art of calculation is extolled simply as an indispensable condition to the most precious results of human happiness.

What I say here applies especially to the Protagoras: for I am well aware that in other dialogues the Platonic Sokrates is made to hold different language.[i] But in the Protagoras he defends a theory the same as that of Aristippus, and defends it by an elaborate argument which silences the objections of the Sophist Protagoras; who at first will not admit the unqualified identity of the pleasurable, judiciously estimated and selected, with the good. The general and comprehensive manner in which Plato conceives and expounds the theory, is probably one evidence of his superior philosophical aptitude as compared with Aristippus and his other contemporaries. He enunciates, side by side, and with equal distinctness, the two conditions requisite for his theory of life. 1. The calculating or measuring art. 2. A description of the items to which alone such measurement must be applied—pleasures and pains.—These two together make the full theory. In

---

[h] Diog. L. ii. p. 91.
[i] See chapters xxi.-xxii.-xxx. of the present work, in which I enter more fully into the differences between the Protagoras, Gorgias, and Philêbus, in respect to this point.
Aristippus agrees with the Platonic Sokrates *in the Protagoras*, as to the general theory of life respecting pleasure and pain.

He agrees with the Platonic Sokrates *in the Gorgias* (see pp. 500-515), in keeping aloof from active political life. τὰ αὑτοῦ πράττειν, καὶ οὐ πολυπραγμονεῖν ἐν τῷ βίῳ—which Sokrates, in the Gorgias (p. 526 C), proclaims as the conduct of the true philosopher, is proclaimed with equal emphasis by Aristippus.   Compare the Platonic Apology, p. 31 D-E.

other dialogues Plato insists equally upon the necessity of knowledge or calculating prudence : but then he is not equally distinct in specifying the items to which such prudence or calculation is to be applied.   On the other hand, it is quite possible that Aristippus, in laying out the same theory, may have dwelt with peculiar emphasis upon the other element in the theory : *i. e.* that while expressly insisting upon pleasures and pains, as the only data to be compared, he may have tacitly assumed the comparing or calculating intelligence, as if it were understood by itself, and did not require to be formally proclaimed.

A distinction must here be made between the general theory of life laid down by Aristippus—and the particular application which he made of that theory to his own course of proceeding.   What we may observe is, that the Platonic Sokrates (in the Protagoras) agrees in the first, or general theory: whether he would have agreed in the second, (or application to the particular case) we are not informed, but we may probably assume the negative.   And we find Sokrates (in the Xenophontic dialogue) taking the same negative ground against Aristippus—upon the second point, not upon the first.   He seeks to prove that the course of conduct adopted by Aristippus, instead of carrying with it a preponderance of pleasure, will entail a preponderance of pain.   He does not dispute the general theory.

Distinction to be made between a general theory—and the particular application of it made by the theorist to his own tastes and circumstances.

Though Aristippus and the Kyrenaic sect are recognised as the first persons who laid down this general theory, yet various others apart from them adopted it likewise.   We may see this not merely from the Protagoras of Plato, but also from the fact that Aristotle, when commenting upon the theory in his Ethics,[k] cites Eudoxus (eminent both as mathematician and astronomer, besides being among the hearers of Plato) as its principal champion.   Still the school of Kyrênê are recorded as a continuous body, partly defending, partly modifying, the theory of Aristippus.[l]

Kyrenaic theorists after Aristippus.

---

[k] Aristot. Ethic. Nikom. x. 2.

[l] Sydenham, in his notes on Philêbus (note 39, p. 76), accuses Aristippus and the Kyrenaics of prevarication and sophistry in the statement of their doctrine respecting Pleasure.   He says

Hegesias, Annikeris, and Theodôrus are the principal Kyrenaics named: the last of them contemporary with Ptolemy Soter, Lysimachus, Epikurus, Theophrastus, and Stilpon.

Diogenes Laertius had read a powerfully written book of Theodôrus, controverting openly the received opinions respecting the Gods:—which few of the philosophers ventured to do. Cicero also mentions a composition of Hegesias.[m] Of Annikeris we know none; but he too, probably, must have been an author. The doctrines which we find ascribed to these Kyrenaics evince how much affinity there was, at bottom, between them and the Cynics, in spite of the great apparent opposition. Hegesias received the surname of the Death-Persuader: he considered happiness to be quite unattainable, and death to be an object not of fear, but of welcome acceptance, in the eyes of a wise man. He started from the same basis as Aristippus: pleasure as the *expetendum*, pain as the *fugiendum*, to which all our personal friendships and aversions were ultimately referable. But he considered that the pains of life preponderated over the pleasures, even under the most favourable circumstances. For conferring pleasure, or for securing continuance of pleasure—wealth, high birth, freedom, glory, were of no greater avail than their contraries poverty, low birth, slavery, ignominy. There was nothing which was, by nature or universally, either pleasurable or painful. Novelty, rarity, satiety, rendered one thing pleasurable, another painful, to different persons and at different times. The wise man would show his wisdom, not in the fruitless struggle for pleasures, but in the avoidance or mitigation of pains: which he would accomplish more successfully by rendering himself indifferent to the causes of pleasure. He would act always for his own account, and would value himself higher than other persons: but he would

Theodôrus—Annikeris—Hegesias.

---

that they called it indiscriminately ἀγαθὸν and τἀγαθόν—(a good—The Good)—" they used the fallacy of changing a particular term for a term which is universal, or vice versâ, by the sly omission or insertion of the definite article *The* before the word Good" (p. 73). He contrasts with this prevarication the ingenuousness of Eudoxus, as the advocate of Pleasure (Aristot. Eth. N. x. 2). I know no evidence for either of these allegations: either for the prevarication of Aristippus or the ingenuousness of Eudoxus.

[m] Diog. L. ii. 97. Θεόδωρος—παντάπασιν ἀναιρῶν τὰς περὶ θεῶν δόξας. Diog. L. ii. 86, 97. Cicero, Tusc. Dis. i. 34, Ἡγησίας ὁ πεισιθάνατος.

at the same time reflect that the mistakes of these others were involuntary, and he would give them indulgent counsel, instead of hating them. He would not trust his senses as affording any real knowledge: but he would be satisfied to act upon the probable appearances of sense, or upon phenomenal knowledge.[n]

Such is the summary which we read of the doctrines of Hegesias: who is said to have enforced his views,[o] —of the real character of life, as containing a great preponderance of misfortune and suffering—in a manner so persuasive, that several persons were induced to commit suicide. Hence he was prohibited by the first Ptolemy from lecturing in such a strain. His opinions respecting life coincide in the main with those set forth by Sokrates in the Phædon of Plato: which dialogue also is alleged to have operated so powerfully on the Platonic disciple Kleombrotus, that he was induced to terminate his own existence. Hegesias, agreeing with Aristippus that pleasure would be the Good, if you could get it—maintains that the circumstances of life are such as to render pleasure unattainable: and therefore advises to renounce pleasure at once and systematically, in order that we may turn our attention to the only practicable end—that of lessening pain. Such deliberate renunciation of pleasure brings him into harmony with the doctrine of the Cynics.

Hegesias—Low estimation of life—renunciation of pleasure—coincidence with the Cynics.

On another point, however, Hegesias repeats just the same doctrine as Aristippus. Both deny any thing like absolute knowledge: they maintain that all our knowledge is phenomenal, or relative to our own impressions or affections: that we neither do know, nor can know, any thing about any real or supposed ultraphenomenal object, *i. e.* things in themselves, as distinguished from our own impressions and apart from our senses and other capacities. Having no writings of Aristippus left, we know this doctrine only as it is presented by others, and those too opponents. We cannot tell whether Aristippus or his sup-

Doctrine of Relativity affirmed by the Kyrenaics, as well as by Protagoras.

[n] Diog. L. ii. 93, 94.
[o] Compare the Pseudo-Platonic dialogue entitled Axiochus, pp. 366, 367, and the doctrine of Kleanthes in Sext. Empiric. adv. Mathemat. ix. 88-92. Lucretius, v. 196-234.

porters stated their own doctrine in such a way as to be open
to the objèctions which we read as urged by opponents. But
the doctrine itself is not, in my judgment, refuted by any of
those objections. "Our affections (πάθη) alone are known
to us, but not the supposed objects or causes from which they
proceed." The word rendered by *affections* must here be
taken in its most general and comprehensive sense—as
including not merely sensations, but also, remembrances,
emotions, judgments, beliefs, doubts, volitions, conscious energies, &c. Whatever we know, we can know only as it appears
to or implicates itself somehow with our own minds. All the
knowledge which I possess, is an aggregate of propositions
affirming facts, and the order or conjunction of facts, as they
are, or have been, or may be, relative to myself. This doctrine
of Aristippus is in substance the same as that which Protagoras announced in other words as—"Man is the measure of
all things." I have already explained and illustrated it, at
considerable length, in my chapter on the Platonic Theætêtus,
where it is announced by Theætêtus and controverted by
Sokrates.[p]

---

[p] See above, vol. ii. ch. xxvi. p. 325
seq. Compare Aristokles ap. Eusebium,
Præp. Ev. xiv. 18, 19, and Sextus Emp.
adv. Mathemat. vii. 190-197, vi. 53.

Sextus gives a summary of this doctrine of the Kyrenaics, more fair and
complete than that given by Aristokles
—at least so far as the extract from the
latter in Eusebius enables us to judge.
Aristokles impugns it vehemently, and
tries to fasten upon it many absurd
consequences—in my judgment without foundation. It is probable that by
the term πάθος the Kyrenaics meant
simply sensations internal and external:
and that the question, as they handled
it, was about the reality of the supposed
Substratum or Object of sense, independent of any sentient Subject. It is
also probable that, in explaining their
views, they did not take account of the
memory of past sensations—and the
expectation of future sensations, in
successions or conjunctions more or less
similar—associating in the mind with
the sensation present and actual, to
form what is called a permanent object
of sense. I think it likely that they
set forth their own doctrine in a narrow
and inadequate manner.

But this defect is noway corrected
by Aristokles their opponent. On the
contrary, he attacks them on their
strong side : he vindicates against them
the hypothesis of the ultra-phenomenal,
absolute, transcendental Object, independent of and apart from any sensation, present, past, or future—and from
any sentient Subject. Besides that, he
assumes them to deny, or ignore, many
points which their theory noway requires them to deny. He urges one
argument which, when properly understood, goes not against them, but
strongly in their favour. " If these
philosophers," says Aristokles (Eus.
xiv. 19, 1), "know that they experience
sensation and perceive, they must know
something beyond the sensation itself.
If I say ἐγὼ καίομαι, 'I am being
burned,' this is a proposition, not a
sensation. These three things are of
necessity co-essential—the sensation itself, the Object which causes it, the
Subject which feels it (ἀνάγκη τὰ τρία
ταῦτα συνυφίστασθαι—τό τε πάθος αὐτὸ
καὶ τὸ ποιοῦν καὶ τὸ πάσχον)." In
trying to make good his conclusion—
That you cannot know the sensation
without the Object of sense—Aristokles

at the same time asserts that the Object cannot be known apart from the sensation, nor apart from the knowing Subject. He asserts that the three are by necessity *co-essential*—*i. e.* implicated and indivisible in substance and existence: if distinguishable therefore, distinguishable only logically (λόγῳ χωριστὰ), admitting of being looked at in different points of view. But this is exactly the case of his opponents, when properly stated. They do not deny Object: they do not deny Subject: but they deny the independent and separate existence of the one as well as of the other: they admit the two only as relative to each other, or as reciprocally implicated in the indivisible fact of cognition. The reasoning of Aristokles thus goes to prove the opinion which he is trying to refute.

Most of the arguments, which Sextus adduces in favour of the Kyrenaic doctrine, show forcibly that the Objective Something, apart from its Subjective correlate, is unknowable and a non-entity; but he does not include in the Subjective as much as ought to be included; he takes note only of the present sensation, and does not include sensations remembered or anticipated. Another very forcible part of Sextus's reasoning may be found, vii. sect. 269-272, where he shews that a logical Subject *per se* is undefinable and inconceivable—that those who attempt to define Man (*e. g.*) do so by specifying more or fewer of the predicates of Man—and that if you suppose all the predicates to vanish, the Subject vanishes along with them.

CHAPTER XXXIX.

XENOPHON.

THERE remains one other companion of Sokrates, for whom
a dignified place must be reserved in this volume—
Xenophon, the son of Gryllus. It is to him that we
owe, in great part, such knowledge as we possess of
the real Sokrates. For the Sokratic conversations related by Xenophon, though doubtless dressed up and
expanded by him, appear to me reports in the main
of what Sokrates actually said. Xenophon was sparing in the
introduction of his master as titular spokesman for opinions,
theories, or controversial difficulties, generated in his own
mind: a practice in which Plato indulged without any reserve,
as we have seen by the numerous dialogues already passed in
review.

Xenophon—his character—essentially a man of action and not a theorist— the Sokratic element is in him an accessory.

I shall not however give any complete analysis of Xenophon's works: because both the greater part of them, and the
leading features of his personal character, belong rather to
active than to speculative Hellenic life. As such, I have dealt
with them largely in my History of Greece. What I have
here to illustrate is the Sokratic element in his character,
which is important indeed as accessory and modifying—yet
not fundamental. Though he exemplifies and attests, as a
witness, the theorising negative vein, the cross-examining
Elenchus of Sokrates—it is the preceptorial vein which he
appropriates to himself and expands in its bearing on practical
conduct. He is the semi-philosophising general; undervalued
indeed as a hybrid by Plato—but by high-minded Romans
like Cato, Agricola, Helvidius Priscus, &c., likely to be
esteemed higher than Plato himself.[a] He is the military

---

[a] See above, my remarks on the Platonic Euthydêmus, vol. i. ch. xix.
pp. 556-564.

brother of the Sokratic family, distinguished for ability and energy in the responsible functions of command: a man of robust frame, courage, and presence of mind, who affronts cheerfully the danger and fatigues of soldiership, and who extracts philosophy from experience of the variable temper of armies, together with the multiplied difficulties and precarious authority of a Grecian general.[b] For our knowledge, imperfect as it is, of real Grecian life, we are greatly indebted to his works. All historians of Greece must draw largely from his Hellenica and Anabasis: and we learn much even from his other productions, not properly historical; for he never soars high in the region of ideality, nor grasps at etherial visions— " nubes et inania "—like Plato.

Respecting the personal history of Xenophon himself, we possess but little information: nor do we know the year either of his birth or death. His Hellenica concludes with the battle of Mantineia in 362 B.C. But he makes incidental mention in that work of an event five years later—the assassination of Alexander, despot of Pheræ, which took place in 357 B.C.[c]—and his language seems to imply that the event was described shortly after it took place. His pamphlet De Vectigalibus appears to have been composed still later—not before 355 B.C. In the year 400 B.C., when Xenophon joined the Grecian military force assembled at Sardis to accompany Cyrus the younger in his march to Babylon, he must have been still a young man: yet he had even then established an intimacy with Sokrates at Athens: and he was old enough to call himself the " ancient guest " of the Bœotian Proxenus, who engaged him to come and take service with Cyrus.[d] We may suppose him to have

Date of Xenophon—probable year of his birth.

---

[b] We may apply to Plato and Xenophon the following comparison by Euripides, Supplices, 905. (Tydeus and Meleager.)

γνώμη δ' ἀδελφοῦ Μελεάγρου λελειμ-
μένος,

ἴσον πάρεσχεν ὄνομα διὰ τέχνην δορὸς,
εὑρὼν ἀκριβῆ μουσικὴν ἐν ἀσπίδι·
φιλότιμον ἦθος, πλούσιον φρόνημά τε
ἐν τοῖσιν ἔργοις, οὐχὶ τοῖς λόγοις ἴσον.

[c] Xenoph. Hellen. vi. 4-37. τῶν δὲ ταῦτα πραξάντων (i. e. of the brothers of Thêbê, which brothers had assassinated

Alexander) ἄχρις οὗ ὅδε ὁ λόγος ἐγρά-
φετο, Τισίφονος, πρεσβύτατος ὢν τῶν
ἀδελφῶν, τὴν ἀρχὴν εἶχε.

[d] That he was still a young man appears from his language, Anabas. iii. 1, 25. His intimacy with Sokrates, whose advice he asked about the propriety of accepting the invitation of Proxenus to go to Asia, is shown iii. 1, 5. Proxenus was his ξένος ἀρχαῖος, iii. 1, 4.

The story mentioned by Strabo (ix. 403) that Xenophon served in the Athenian cavalry at the battle of

been then about thirty years of age; and thus to have been born about 430 B.C.—two or three years earlier than Plato. Respecting his early life, we have no facts before us: but we may confidently affirm (as I have already observed about[e] Plato), that as he became liable to military service in 412 B.C., the severe pressure of the war upon Athens must have occasioned him to be largely employed, among other citizens, for the defence of his native city, until its capture in 405 B.C. He seems to have belonged to an equestrian family in the census, and therefore to have served on horseback. More than one of his compositions evinces both intelligent interest in horsemanship, and great familiarity with horses.

Our knowledge of his personal history begins with what he himself recounts in the Anabasis. His friend Proxenus, then at Sardis commanding a regiment of Hellenic mercenaries under Cyrus the younger, wrote recommending him earnestly to come over and take service, in the army prepared ostensibly against the Pisidians. Upon this Xenophon asked the advice of Sokrates: who exhorted him to go and consult the Delphian oracle—being apprehensive that as Cyrus had proved himself the strenuous ally of Sparta, and had furnished to her the principal means for crushing Athens, an Athenian taking service under him would incur unpopularity at home. Xenophon accordingly went to Delphi: but instead of asking the question broadly—"Shall I go, or shall I decline to go?"—he put to Apollo the narrower question—"Having in contemplation a journey, to which of the Gods must I sacrifice and pray, in order to accomplish it best, and to come back with safety and success?" Apollo indicated to him the Gods to whom he ought to address himself: but Sokrates was displeased with him for not having first asked, whether he ought to go at all. Nevertheless (continued Sokrates), since you have chosen to put the question in your own way, you must act as the God has prescribed.[f]

His personal history—He consults Sokrates—takes the opinion of the Delphian oracle.

Delium (424 B.C.), and that his life was saved by Sokrates, I consider to be not less inconsistent with any reasonable chronology, than the analogous anecdote — that Plato distinguished himself at the battle of Delium. See above, vol. i. ch. iii. p. 117.

[e] See vol. i. ch. 3, pp. 116-118.

[f] Xenop. Anab. iii. 1, 4-6.

The anecdote here recounted by Xenophon is interesting, as it illustrates his sincere faith as well as that of Sokrates, in the Delphian oracle: though we might have expected that on this occasion, Sokrates would have been favoured with some manifestation of that divine sign, which he represents to have warned him so frequently and on such trifling matters.   Apollo however was perhaps displeased (as Sokrates was) with Xenophon, for not having submitted the question to him with full frankness: since the answer given was proved by subsequent experience to be incomplete.[g]   After fifteen months passed, first, in the hard upward march—next, in the still harder retreat—of the Ten Thousand, to the preservation of whom he largely contributed by his energy, presence of mind, resolute initiative, and ready Athenian eloquence, as one of their leaders—Xenophon returned to Athens.   It appears that he must have come back not long after the death of Sokrates.   But Athens was not at that time a pleasant residence for him.   The Sokratic companions shared in the unpopularity of their deceased master, and many of them were absent: moreover Xenophon himself was unpopular as the active partisan of Cyrus.   After a certain stay, we know not how long, at Athens, Xenophon appears to have gone back to Asia; and to have resumed his command of the remaining Cyreian soldiers, then serving under the Lacedæmonian generals against the Persian satraps Tissaphernes and Pharnabazus.   He served first under Derkyllidas, next under Agesilaus.   For the latter he conceived the warmest admiration, and contracted with him an intimate friendship.   At the time when Xenophon rejoined the Cyreians in Asia, Athens was not at war with the Lacedæmonians: but after some time, the hostile confederacy of Athens, Thebes, and Corinth, against them was organised: and Agesilaus was

His service and command with the Ten Thousand Greeks, afterwards under Agesilaus and the Spartans.—He is banished from Athens.

[g] Compare Anabas. vi. 1, 22, and vii. 8, 1-6.

See also Plato, Apol. Sokr. p. 33 C, and Plato, Theagês, p. 129; also above, vol. i. ch. xiii. pp. 434-439.

Sokrates and Xenophon are among the most imposing witnesses cited by Quintus Cicero, in his long pleading to show the reality of divination (Cicero, De Divinatione, i. 25-52, i. 54, 122). Antipater the Stoic collected a large number of examples, illustrating the miraculous divining power of Sokrates. Several of these examples appear much more trifling than this incident of Xenophon.

summoned home by them from Asia, to fight their battles in
Greece. Xenophon and his Cyreians were still a portion of
the army of Agesilaus, and accompanied him in his march
into Bœotia; where they took part in his desperate battle
and bloody victory at Koroneia.[h] But he was now lending
active aid to the enemies of Athens, and holding conspicuous
command in their armies. A sentence of banishment, on the
ground of Laconism, was passed against him by the Athenians,
on the proposition of Eubulus.[i]

How long he served with Agesilaus, we are not told. At
His residence the end of his service, the Lacedæmonians provided
at Skillus him with a house and land at the Triphylian town of
near Olym-
pia. Skillûs near Olympia, which they had seemingly
taken from the Eleians and re-colonised. Near this residence
he also purchased, under the authority of the God (perhaps
Olympian Zeus) a landed estate to be consecrated to the
Goddess Artemis: employing therein a portion of the tithe of
plunder devoted to Artemis by the Cyreian army, and deposited by him for the time in the care of Megabyzus, priest
of Artemis at Ephesus. The estate of the Goddess contained
some cultivated ground, but consisted chiefly of pasture;
with wild ground, wood and mountain, abounding in game
and favourable for hunting. Xenophon became Conservator
of this property for Artemis: to whom he dedicated a shrine
and a statue, in miniature copy of the great temple at
Ephesus. Every year he held a formal hunting-match, to
which he invited all the neighbours, with abundant hospitality,
at the expense of the Goddess. The Conservator and his
successors were bound by formal vow, on pain of her displeasure, to employ one tenth of the whole annual produce in
sacrifices to her: and to keep the shrine and statue in good
order, out of the remainder.[k]

Xenophon seems to have passed many years of his life
either at Skillus or in other parts of Peloponnesus, and is

[h] Xenoph. Anab. v. 3, 6; Plutarch, Agesilaus, c. 18.
[i] Diog. L. ii. 51-59. ἐπὶ Λακωνισμῷ φυγὴν ὑπ' Ἀθηναίων κατεγνώσθη.
[k] Xenop. Anab. v. 3, 8-12; Diog. L. ii. 52; Pausanias, v. 6, 3.
φησὶ δ' ὁ Δείναρχος ὅτι καὶ οἰκίαν καὶ

ἄγρον αὐτῷ ἔδοσαν Λακεδαιμόνιοι.
Deinarchus appears to have composed for a client at Athens a judicial speech against Xenophon, the grandson of Xenophon Sokraticus. He introduced into the speech some facts relating to the grandfather.

said to have died very old at Corinth. The sentence of
banishment passed against him by the Athenians was Family of
Xenophon—
revoked after the battle of Leuktra, when Athens his son Gryl-
lus killed at
came into alliance with the Lacedæmonians against Mantineia.
Thebes. Some of Xenophon's later works indicate that he
must have availed himself of this revocation to visit Athens:
but whether he permanently resided there is uncertain. He
had brought over with him from Asia a wife named Philesia,
by whom he had two sons, Gryllus and Diodorus.[1] He sent
these two youths to be trained at Sparta, under the countenance of Agesilaus:[m] afterwards the eldest of them, Gryllus,
served with honour in the Athenian cavalry which assisted
the Lacedæmonians and Mantineians against Epameinondas,
B.C. 362. In the important combat[n] of the Athenian and
Theban cavalry, close to the gates of Mantineia—shortly preceding the general battle of Mantineia, in which Epameinondas was slain—Gryllus fell, fighting with great bravery.
The death of this gallant youth—himself seemingly of great
promise, and the son of so eminent a father—was celebrated
by Isokrates and several other rhetors, as well as by the
painter Euphranor at Athens, and by sculptors at Mantineia
itself.[o]

Skillus, the place in which the Lacedæmonians had established Xenophon, was retaken by the Eleians Death of
Xenophon
during the humiliation of Lacedæmonian power, not at Corinth—
long before the battle of Mantineia. Xenophon Story of the
Eleian Exe-
himself was absent at the time; but his family were getæ.
constrained to retire to Lepreum. It was after this, we are

[1] Æschines Sokraticus, in one of his dialogues, introduced Aspasia conversing with Xenophon and his (Xenophon's) wife. Cicero, De Invent. i. 31, 51-54 ; Quintil. Inst. Orat. v. p. 312.

[m] Plutarch, Agesilaus, c. 20.

[n] Xenoph. Hellen. vii. 5, 15-16-17. This combat of cavalry near the gates of Mantineia was very close and sharply contested; but at the great battle fought a few days afterwards the Athenian cavalry were hardly at all engaged, vii. 5, 25.

[o] Pausanias, i. 3, 3, viii. 11, 4, ix. 15, 3 ; Diogenes L. ii. 54. Harpokra-

tion v. Κηφισόδωρος.

It appears that Euphranor, in his picture, represented Gryllus as engaged in personal conflict with Epameinondas and wounding him—a compliment not justified by the facts. The Mantineians believed Antikrates, one of their own citizens, to have mortally wounded the great Theban general with his spear, and they awarded to him as recompense immunity from public burthens (ἀτελείαν), both for himself and his descendants. One of his descendants, Kallikrates, continued even in Plutarch's time to enjoy this immunity, Plutarch, Agesilaus, c. 35.

told, that he removed to Corinth, where he died in 355 B.C.
or in some year later. The Eleian Exegetæ told the traveller
Pausanias, when he visited the spot five centuries afterwards,
that Xenophon had been condemned in the judicial Council
of Olympia as wrongful occupant of the property at Skillus,
through Lacedæmonian violence; but that the Eleians had
granted him indulgence, and had allowed him to remain.[p]
As it seems clearly asserted that he died at Corinth, he can
hardly have availed himself of the indulgence; and I incline
to suspect that the statement is an invention of subsequent
Eleian Exegetæ, after they had learnt to appreciate his
literary eminence.

From the brief outline thus presented of Xenophon's life,
it will plainly appear that he was quite different in
character and habits from Plato and the other Sokratic brethren. He was not only a man of the
world (as indeed Aristippus was also), but he was
actively engaged in the most responsible and difficult functions of military command: he was moreover a landed proprietor and cultivator, fond of strong exercise with dogs and
horses, and an intelligent equestrian. His circumstances were
sufficiently easy to dispense with the necessity of either composing discourses or taking pupils for money. Being thus
enabled to prosecute letters and philosophy in an independent
way, he did not, like Plato and Aristotle, open a school.[q]
His relations, as active coadjutor and subordinate, with Agesilaus, form a striking contrast to those of Plato with Dionysius,
as tutor and pedagogue. In his mind, the Sokratic conversations, suggestive and stimulating to every one, fell upon the
dispositions and aptitudes of a citizen-soldier, and fructified in
a peculiar manner. My present work deals with Xenophon,

Marginal note: Xenophon different from Plato and the other Sokratic brethren.

[p] Pausan. v. 6, 3; Diog. L. ii. 53-56.

[q] See, in the account of Theopompus
by Photius (Cod. 176, p. 120; compare
also Photius, Cod. 159, p. 102, a. 41),
the distinction taken by Theopompus:
who said that the four most celebrated
literary persons of his day were, his
master Isokrates, Theodektês of Pha-
sêlis, Naukrates of Erythræ, and himself (Theopompus). He himself and
Naukrates were in good circumstances,
so that he passed his life in independent prosecution of philosophy and
philomathy. But Isokrates and Theodektês were compelled δι' ἀπορίαν βίου,
μισθοῦ λόγους γράφειν καὶ σοφιστεύειν,
ἐκπαιδεύοντες τοὺς νέους, κἀκεῖθεν καρ-
πουμένους τὰς ὠφελείας.

Theopompus does not here present
the profession of a Sophist (as most
Platonic commentators teach us to
regard it) as a mean, unprincipled,
and corrupting employment.

not as an historian of Grecian affairs or of the Cyreian expedition, but only on the intellectual and theorising side:—as author of the Memorabilia, the Cyropædia, Œkonomikus, Symposion, Hieron, De Vectigalibus, &c.

The Memorabilia were composed as records of the conversations of Sokrates, expressly intended to vindicate Sokrates against charges of impiety and of corrupting youthful minds, and to show that he inculcated, before every thing, self-denial, moderation of desires, reverence for parents, and worship of the Gods. The Œkonomikus and the Symposion are expansions of the Memorabilia: the first [r] exhibiting Sokrates not only as an attentive observer of the facts of active life (in which character the Memorabilia present him also), but even as a learner of husbandry [s] and family management from Ischomachus—the last describing Sokrates and his behaviour amidst the fun and joviality of a convivial company. Sokrates declares [t] that as to himself, though poor, he is quite as rich as he desires to be; that he desires no increase, and regards poverty as no disadvantage. Yet since Kritobulus, though rich, is beset with temptations to expense quite sufficient to embarrass him, good proprietary management is to him a necessity. Accordingly, Sokrates, announcing that he has always been careful to inform himself who were the best economists in the city,[u] now cites as authority Ischomachus, a citizen of wealth and high position, recognised by all as one of the "super-excellent."[x] Ischomachus loves wealth, and is anxious to maintain and even

His various works—Memorabilia, Œkonomikus, &c.

[r] Galen calls the Œkonomicus the last book of the Memorabilia (ad Hippokrat. De Articulis, t. xviii. p. 301, Kühn). It professes to be repeated by Xenophon from what he himself *heard* Sokrates say—ἤκουσα δέ ποτε αὐτοῦ καὶ περὶ οἰκονομίας τοιάδε διαλεγομένου, &c. Sokrates first instructs Kritobulus that economy, or management of property, is an art, governed by rules, and dependant upon principles; next, he recounts to him the lessons which he professes to have himself received from Ischomachus.

I have already adverted to the Xenophontic Symposion as containing jocular remarks which some erroneously cite as serious.

[s] To *learn* in this way the actualities of life, and the way of extracting the greatest amount of wheat and barley from a given piece of land, is the sense which Xenophon puts on the word φιλόσοφος (Xen. Œk. xvi. 9; compare Cyropædia, vi. 1, 41).

[t] Xenop. Œkonom. ii. 3; xi. 3, 4.

I have made some observations on the Xenophontic Symposion, comparing it with the Platonic Symposion, in a prior chapter of this work, vol. ii. ch. xxiv. p. 229.

[u] Xen. Œkon. ii. 16.

[x] Xen. Œkon. vi. 17, xi. 3. πρὸς πάντων καὶ ἀνδρῶν καὶ γυναικῶν, καὶ ξένων καὶ ἀστῶν, καλόν τε κἀγαθὸν ἐπονομαζόμενον.

enlarge his property : desiring to spend magnificently for the
honour of the Gods, the assistance of friends, and the support
of the city.[y] His whole life is arranged, with intelligence
and forethought, so as to attain this object, and at the same
time to keep up the maximum of bodily health and vigour,
especially among the horsemen of the city as an accomplished
rider[z] and cavalry soldier. He speaks with respect, and
almost with enthusiasm, of husbandry, as an occupation not
merely profitable, but improving to the character : though he
treats with disrespect other branches of industry and craft.[a]
In regard to husbandry, too, as in regard to war or steersmanship, he affirms that the difference between one practitioner
and another consists, not so much in unequal knowledge, as
in unequal care to practise what both of them know.[b]

Ischomachus describes to Sokrates, in reply to a string of
successive questions, both his scheme of life and his
scheme of husbandry. He had married his wife
before she was fifteen years of age : having first
ascertained that she had been brought up carefully,
so as to have seen and heard as little as possible,
and to know nothing but spinning and weaving.[c] He describes how he took this very young wife into training, so as
to form her to the habits which he himself approved. He
declares that the duties and functions of women are confined
to in-door work and superintendence, while the out-door
proceedings, acquisition as well as defence, belong to men :[d]
he insists upon such separation of functions emphatically, as
an ordinance of nature—holding an opinion the direct reverse
of that which we have seen expressed by Plato.[e] He makes
many remarks on the arrangements of the house, and of the

Marginal note: Ischomachus, hero of the Œkonomikus —ideal of an active citizen, cultivator, husband, housemaster, &c.

[y] Xen. Œkon. xi. 9.
[z] Xen. Œkon. xi. 17-21. ἐν τοῖς
ἱππικωτάτοις τε καὶ πλουσιωτάτοις.
[a] Xen. Œkon. iv. 2-3, vi. 5-7. Ischomachus asserts that his father had
been more devoted to agriculture
(φιλογεωργότατος) than any man at
Athens; that he had bought several
pieces of land (χώρους) when out of
order, improved them, and then resold
them with very large profit, xx. 26.
[b] Xen. Œkon. xx. 2-10.
[c] Xen. Œkon. vii. 3-7. τὸν δ' ἔμπροσθεν χρόνον ἔζη ὑπὸ πολλῆς ἐπι-

μελείας, ὅπως ὡς ἐλάχιστα μὲν ὄψοιτο,
ἐλάχιστα δὲ ἀκούσοιτο, ἐλάχιστα δὲ
ἔροιτο.
The διδασκαλία addressed to Sokrates
by Ischomachus is in the form of ἐρώ-
τησις, xix. 15. The Sokratic interrogation is here brought to bear upon
Sokrates, instead of by Sokrates; like the
Elenchus in the Parmenidês of Plato.
[d] Xen. Œkon. vii. 22-32.
[e] See above, ch. xxxv. pp. 216-225.
Compare also Aristotel. Politic. iii.
4, 1277, b. 25, where Aristotle lays
down the same principle as Xenophon.

stores within it: and he dwells particularly on the management of servants, male and female.

It is upon this last point that he lays more stress than upon any other. To know how to command men—is the first of all accomplishments in the mind of Xenophon. Ischomachus proclaims it as essential that the superior shall not merely give orders to his subordinates, but also see them executed, and set the example of personal active watchfulness in every way. Xenophon aims at securing not simply obedience, but cheerful and willing obedience—even attachment from those who obey. " To exercise command over willing subjects " [f] (he says), " is a good more than human, granted only to men truly consummated in virtue of character essentially divine. To exercise command over unwilling subjects, is a torment like that of Tantalus." *(margin: Text upon which Xenophon insists —capital difference between command over subordinates willing, and subordinates unwilling.)*

The sentence just transcribed (the last sentence in the Œkonomikus) brings to our notice a central focus in Xenophon's mind, from whence many of his most valuable speculations emanate. " What are the conditions under which subordinates will cheerfully obey their commanders ? "—was a problem forced upon his thoughts by his own personal experience, as well as by contemporary phenomena in Hellas. He had been elected one of the generals of the Ten Thousand : a large body of brave warriors from different cities, most of them unknown to him personally, and inviting his authority only because they were in extreme peril, and because no one else took the initiative.[g] He discharged his duties admirably : and his ready eloquence was an invaluable accomplishment, distinguishing him from all his colleagues. Nevertheless when the army arrived at the Euxine, out of the reach of urgent peril, he was made to feel sensibly the vexations of authority resting upon such pre- *(margin: Probable circumstances generating these reflections in Xenophon's mind.)*

---

[f] Xen. Œkon. xxi. 10-12. ἥθους βασιλικοῦ — θεῖον γενέσθαι. Οὐ γὰρ πάνυ μοι δοκεῖ ὅλον τουτὶ τὸ ἀγαθὸν ἀνθρώπινον εἶναι, ἀλλὰ θεῖον, τὸ ἐθελόντων ἄρχειν· σαφῶς δὲ δίδοται τοῖς ἀληθινῶς σωφροσύνη τετελεσμένοις. Τὸ δὲ ἀκόντων τυραννεῖν διδόασιν, ὡς ἐμοὶ δοκεῖ, οὓς ἂν ἡγῶνται ἀξίους εἶναι βιοτεύειν, ὥσπερ ὁ Τάνταλος ἐν Ἅδου λέγεται. Compare also iv. 19, xiii. 3-7.

[g] The reader will find in my 'History of Greece,' ch. 70, p. 103 seq., a narrative of the circumstances under which Xenophon was first chosen to command, as well as his conduct afterwards.

carious basis, and perpetually traversed by jealous rivals. Moreover, Xenophon, besides his own personal experience, had witnessed violent political changes running extensively through the cities of the Grecian world: first, at the close of the Peloponnesian war—next, after the battle of Knidus— again, under Lacedæmonian supremacy, after the peace of Antalkidas, and the subsequent seizure of the citadel of Thebes—lastly, after the Thebans had regained their freedom and humbled the Lacedæmonians by the battle of Leuktra. To Xenophon—partly actor, partly spectator—these political revolutions were matters of anxious interest; especially as he ardently sympathised with Agesilaus, a political partisan interested in most of them, either as conservative or revolutionary.

We thus see, from the personal history of Xenophon, how his attention came to be peculiarly turned to the difficulty of ensuring steady obedience from subordinates, and to the conditions by which such difficulty might be overcome. The sentence, above transcribed from the Œkonomikus, embodies two texts, upon which he has discoursed in two of his most interesting compositions—Cyropædia and Hieron. In Cyropædia he explains and exemplifies the divine gift of ruling over cheerful subordinates: in Hieron, the torment of governing the disaffected and refractory. For neither of these purposes would the name and person of Sokrates have been suitable, exclusively connected as they were with Athens. Accordingly Xenophon, having carried that respected name through the Œkonomikus and Symposion, now dismisses it, yet retaining still the familiar and colloquial manner which belonged to Sokrates. The Epilogue, or concluding chapter, of the Cyropædia, must unquestionably have been composed after 364 B.C.—in the last ten years of Xenophon's life: the main body of it may perhaps have been composed earlier.

This text affords subjects for the Hieron and Cyropædia— Name of Sokrates not suitable.

The Hieron gives no indication of date: but as a picture purely Hellenic, it deserves precedence over the Cyropædia, and conveys to my mind the impression of having been written earlier. It describes a supposed conversation (probably suggested by current traditional

Hieron— Persons of the dialogue —Simonides and Hieron.

conversations, like that between Solon and Crœsus) between
the poet Simonides and Hieron the despot of Syracuse; who,
shortly after the Persian invasion of Greece by Xerxes, had
succeeded his brother Gelon the former despot.[h] Both of
them had been once private citizens, of no remarkable consequence : but Gelon, an energetic and ambitious military
man, having raised himself to power in the service of Hippokrates despot of Gela, had seized the sceptre on the death of
his master : after which he conquered Syracuse, and acquired
a formidable dominion, enjoyed after his death by his brother
Hieron.   This last was a great patron of eminent poets—
Pindar, Simonides, Æschylus, Bacchylides : but he laboured
under a painful internal complaint, and appears to have been
of an irritable and oppressive temper.[i]

Simonides asks of Hieron, who had personally tried both
the life of a private citizen and that of a despot,   Questions put
which of the two he considered preferable, in regard   to Hieron.
to pleasures and pains.   Upon this subject, a con-   by Simonides.
versation of some length ensues, in which Hieron   Hieron.
declares that the life of a despot has much more pain, and
much less pleasure, than that of a private citizen under middling circumstances :[j] while Simonides takes the contrary side,
and insists in detail upon the superior means of enjoyment,
apparent at least, possessed by the despot.   As each of these
means is successively brought forward, Hieron shews that
however the matter may appear to the spectator, the despot
feels no greater real happiness in his own bosom : while he
suffers many pains and privations, of which the spectator
takes no account.   As to the pleasures of sight, the despot
forfeits altogether the first and greatest, because it is unsafe
for him to visit the public festivals and matches.   In regard
to hearing—many praises, and no reproach, reach his ears :

---

[h] Plato, Epistol. ii. p. 311 A. Aristot. Rhetor. ii. 16, 1391, a. 9 ; Cicero,
Nat. Deo. i. 22, 60.
    [i] See the first and second Pythian
Odes of Pindar, addressed to Hieron,
especially Pyth. i. 55-61-90, with the
Scholia and Boeckh's Commentary.
Pindar compliments Hieron upon having founded his new city of Ætna—
θεοδμάτῳ σὺν ἐλευθερίᾳ. This does

not coincide with the view of Hieron's
character taken by Xenophon ; but
Pindar agrees with Xenophon in exhorting Hieron to make himself popular
by a liberal expenditure.
    [j] Xenop. Hier. i. 8. εὖ ἴσθι, ὦ
Σιμωνίδη, ὅτι πολὺ μείω εὐφραίνονται οἱ
τύραννοι τῶν μετρίως διαγόντων ἰδιωτῶν,
πολὺ δὲ πλείω καὶ μείζω λυποῦνται.

but then he knows that the praises are insincere—and that reproach is unheard, only because speakers dare not express what they really feel. The despot has finer cookery and richer unguents; but others enjoy a modest banquet as much or more—while the scent of the unguents pleases those who are near him more than himself.[k] Then as to the pleasures of love, these do not exist, except where the beloved person manifests spontaneous sympathy and return of attachment. Now the despot can never extort such return by his power; while even if it be granted freely, he cannot trust its sincerity, and is compelled even to be more on his guard, since successful conspiracies against his life generally proceed from those who profess attachment to him.[l] The private citizen on the contrary knows that those, who profess to love him, may be trusted, as having no motive for falsehood.

Still (contends Simonides) there are other pleasures greater *Misery of governing unwilling subjects declared by Hieron.* than those of sense. You despots possess the greatest abundance and variety of possessions— the finest chariots and horses, the most splendid arms, the finest palaces, ornaments and furniture— the most brilliant ornaments for your wives—the most intelligent and valuable servants. You execute the greatest enterprises: you can do most to benefit your friends, and hurt your enemies: you have all the proud consciousness of superior might.[m]—Such is the opinion of the multitude (replies Hieron), who are misled by appearances: but a wise man like you, Simonides, ought to see the reality in the background, and to recollect that happiness or unhappiness reside only in a man's internal feelings. You cannot but know, that a despot lives in perpetual insecurity, both at home and abroad: that he must always go armed himself, and have armed guards around him: that whether at war or at peace, he is always alike in danger: that, while suspecting every one as an enemy, he nevertheless knows that when he has put to

---

[k] Xen. Hieron, i. 12-15-24.

[l] Xen. Hier. i. 26-38. Τῷ τυράννῳ οὔ ποτ' ἐστὶ πιστεῦσαι, ὡς φιλεῖται. Αἱ ἐπιβουλαὶ ἐξ οὐδένων πλέονες τοῖς τυράννοις εἰσὶν, ἢ ἀπὸ τῶν φιλεῖν αὐτοὺς προσποιησαμένων.

This chapter affords remarkable illustration of Grecian manners, especially in the distinction drawn between τὰ παιδικὰ ἀφροδίσια and τὰ τεκνοποιὰ ἀφροδίσια.

[m] Xen. Hier. ii. 2.

death the persons suspected, he has only weakened the power
of the city :[n] that he has no sincere friendship with any one :
that he cannot count even upon good faith, and must cause
all his food to be tasted by others, before he eats it : that
whoever has slain a private citizen, is shunned in Grecian
cities as an abomination—while the tyrannicide is everywhere honoured and recompensed : that there is no safety for
the despot even in his own family, many having been killed
by their nearest relatives :[o] that he is compelled to rely upon
mercenary foreign soldiers and liberated slaves, against the
free citizens who hate him : and that the hire of such inauspicious protectors compels him to raise money, by despoiling
individuals and plundering temples :[p] that the best and most
estimable citizens are incurably hostile to him, while none
but the worst will serve him for pay : that he looks back with
bitter sorrow, to the pleasures and confidential friendships
which he enjoyed as a private man, but from which he is
altogether debarred as a despot.[q]

Nothing brings a man so near to the Gods (rejoins
Simonides) as the feeling of being honoured. Power and a
brilliant position must be of inestimable value, if they are
worth purchasing at the price which you describe.[r] Otherwise, why do you not throw up your sceptre ? How happens
it that no despot has ever yet done this ?—To be honoured
(answers Hieron), is the greatest of earthly blessings, when a
man obtains honour from the spontaneous voice of freemen.
But a despot enjoys no such satisfaction. He lives like a
criminal under sentence of death by every one : and it is impossible for him to lay down his power, because of the number
of persons whom he has been obliged to make his enemies.
He can neither endure his present condition, nor yet escape
from it. The best thing he can do is to hang himself.[s]

[n] Xen. Hieron, ii. 5-17.
[o] Xenoph. Hieron, ii. 8, iii. 1, 5. Compare Xenoph. Hellenic. iii. 1, 14.
[p] Xen. Hieron, iv. 7-11.
[q] Xen. Hieron, vi. 1-12.
[r] Xen. Hieron, vii. 1-5.
[s] Xen. Hier. vii. 5-13. Ὁ δὲ τύραν- νος, ὡς ὑπὸ πάντων ἀνθρώπων κατα- κεκριμένος δι' ἀδικίαν ἀποθνήσκειν—καὶ νύκτα καὶ ἡμέραν διάγει. Ἀλλ' εἴπερ τῷ ἄλλῳ λυσιτελεῖ ἀπάγξασθαι, ἴσθι ὅτι

τυράννῳ ἔγωγε εὑρίσκω μάλιστα τοῦτο λυσιτελοῦν ποιῆσαι. Μόνῳ γὰρ αὐτῷ οὔτε ἔχειν, οὔτε καταθέσθαι τὰ κακὰ λυσιτελεῖ.

Solon in his poems makes the remark, that for the man who once usurps the sceptre no retreat is pos- sible. See my 'History of Greece,' chap. xi. p. 132 seq.

The impressive contrast here drawn by Hieron (c. vi.) between his condition

Simonides in reply, after sympathising with Hieron's despondency, undertakes to console him by showing

that such consequences do not necessarily attend
despotic rule. The despot's power is an instrument
available for good as well as for evil. By a proper
employment of it, he may not only avoid being
hated, but may even make himself beloved, beyond
the measure attainable by any private citizen. Even kind
words, and petty courtesies, are welcomed far more eagerly
when they come from a powerful man than from an equal:
moreover a showy and brilliant exterior seldom fails to fasci-
nate the spectator.[t] But besides this, the despot may render
to his city the most substantial and important services. He
may punish criminals and reward meritorious men : the
punishments he ought to inflict by the hands of others, while
he will administer the rewards in person—giving prizes for
superior excellence in every department, and thus endearing
himself to all.[u] Such prizes would provoke a salutary competition in the performance of military duties, in choric exhibitions, in husbandry, commerce, and public usefulness of
every kind. Even the foreign mercenaries, though usually
odious, might be so handled and disciplined as to afford
defence against foreign danger,—to ensure for the citizens
undisturbed leisure in their own private affairs—to protect
and befriend the honest man, and to use force only against
criminals.[x] If thus employed, such mercenaries, instead of
being hated, would be welcome companions : and the despot
himself may count, not only upon security against attack,
but upon the warmest gratitude and attachment. The citizens
will readily furnish contributions to him when asked, and will
regard him as their greatest benefactor. "You will obtain
in this way " (Simonides thus concludes his address to Hieron),
" the finest and most enviable of all acquisitions. You will
have your subjects obeying you willingly, and caring for
you of their own accord. You may travel safely wherever
you please, and will be a welcome visitor at all the crowded

as a despot and the past enjoyments of
private life and citizenship which he
has lost, reminds one of the still more
sorrowful contrast in the Atys of

Catullus, v. 58-70.
[t] Xen. Hieron, viii. 2-7.
[u] Xen. Hieron, ix. 1-4.
[x] Xen. Hieron, x. 6-8.

Marginal note: Advice to Hieron by Simonides—that he should govern well, and thus make himself beloved by his subjects.

festivals.   You will be happy, without jealousy from any one." [y]

The dialogue of which I have given this short abstract, illustrates what Xenophon calls the torment of Tantalus—the misery of a despot who has to extort obedience from unwilling subjects :—especially if the despot be one who has once known the comfort and security of private life, under tolerably favourable circumstances. If we compare this dialogue with the Platonic *Gorgias*, where we have seen a thesis very analogous handled in respect to Archelaus,—we shall find Plato soaring into a sublime ethical region of his own, measuring the despot's happiness and misery by a standard peculiar to himself, and making good what he admits to be a paradox by abundant eloquence covering faulty dialectic : while Xenophon, herein following his master, applies to human life the measure of a rational common sense, talks about pleasures and pains which every one can feel to be such, and points out how many of these pleasures the despot forfeits, how many of these pains and privations he undergoes,—in spite of that great power of doing hurt, and less power, though still considerable, of doing good, which raises the envy of spectators. The Hieron gives utterance to an interesting vein of sentiment, more common at Athens than elsewhere in Greece ; enforced by the conversation of Sokrates, and serving as corrective protest against that unqualified worship of power which prevailed in the ancient world no less than in the modern. That the Syrakusan Hieron should be selected as an exemplifying name, may be explained by the circumstance, that during thirty-eight years of Xenophon's mature life (405-367 B.C.), Dionysius the elder was despot of Syrakuse : a man of energy and ability, who had extinguished the liberties of his native city, and acquired power and dominion greater than that of any living Greek. Xenophon, resident at Skillus within a short distance from Olympia, had probably [z] seen the splendid Thêory (or sacred legation of representative envoys) installed in rich

Margin note: Probable experience had by Xenophon of the feelings at Olympia against Dionysius.

---

[y] Xen. Hieron, xi. 10-12-15. κἂν ταῦτα πάντα ποιῇς, εὖ ἴσθι πάντων τῶν ἐν ἀνθρώποις κάλλιστον καὶ μακαριώ- | τατον κτῆμα κεκτημένος· εὐδαιμονῶν γὰρ οὐ φθονηθήσῃ.

[z] Xenop. Anab. v. 3, 11.

and ornamented tents, and the fine running horses sent by
Dionysius, at the ninety-ninth Olympic festival (384 B.C.):
but he probably also heard the execration with which the
name of Dionysius himself had been received by the spectators,
and he would feel that the despot could hardly shew himself
there in person.   There were narratives in circulation about
the interior life of Dionysius,[a] analogous to those statements
which Xenophon puts into the mouth of Hieron.   A predecessor of Dionysius as despot of Syracuse[b] and also as patron
of poets, was therefore a suitable person to choose for illustrating the first part of Xenophon's thesis—the countervailing
pains and penalties which spoilt all the value of power, if
exercised over unwilling and repugnant subjects.[c]

But when Xenophon came to illustrate the second part of
his thesis—the possibility of exercising power in
such manner as to render the holder of it popular
and beloved—it would have been scarcely possible
for him to lay the scene in any Grecian city.   The
repugnance of the citizens of a Grecian city towards a
despot who usurped power over them, was incurable—
however much the more ambitious individuals among them
might have wished to obtain such power for themselves: a repugnance as great among oligarchs as among democrats—perhaps
even greater.   When we read the recommendations addressed
by Simonides, teaching Hieron how he might render himself
popular, we perceive at once that they are alike well inten-
tioned and ineffectual.   Xenophon could neither find any real
Grecian despot corresponding to this portion of his illustrative
purpose—nor could he invent one with any show of plausibility.   He was forced to resort to other countries and other
habits different from those of Greece.

To this necessity probably we owe the Cyropædia: a
romance in which Persian and Grecian experience
are singularly blended, and both of them so trans-

Marginal notes: Xenophon could not have chosen a Grecian despot to illustrate his theory of the happiness of governing willing subjects.

Marginal note: Cyropædia—blending of Spartan and Persian cus-

---

[a] See chap. 83, vol. xi. pp. 40-50, of
my 'History of Greece,' where this
memorable scene at Olympia is described.

[b] Cicero, Tusc. Disp. v. 20, 57-63;
De Officiis, ii. 7, 24-25.
"Multos timebit ille, quem multi timent."

[c] An anecdote is told about a visit
of Xenophon to Dionysius at Syracuse
—whether the elder or the younger is
not specified — but the tenor of the
anecdote points to the younger; if so,
the visit must have been later than
367 B.C. (Athenæus x. 427).

formed as to suit the philosophical purpose of the narrator.   Xenophon had personally served and communicated with Cyrus the younger: respecting whom also he had large means of information, from his intimate friend Proxenus, as well as from the other Grecian generals of the expedition.   In the first book of the Anabasis, we find this young prince depicted as an energetic and magnanimous character, faithful to his word and generous in his friendships—inspiring strong attachment in those around him, yet vigorous in administration and in punishing criminals—not only courting the Greeks as useful for his ambitious projects, but appreciating sincerely the superiority of Hellenic character and freedom over Oriental servitude.[d]   And in the Œkonomikus, Cyrus is quoted as illustrating in his character the true virtue of a commander; the test of which Xenophon declares to be—That his subordinates follow him willingly, and stand by him to the death.

(margin: toms—Xenophon's experience of Cyrus the Younger.)

It is this character—Hellenised, Sokratised, idealised—that Xenophon paints into his glowing picture of Cyrus the founder of the Persian monarchy, or the Cyropædia.   He thus escapes the insuperable difficulty arising from the position of a Grecian despot; who never could acquire willing or loving obedience, because his possession of power was felt by a majority of his subjects to be wrongful, violent, tainted.   The Cyrus of the Cyropædia begins as son of Kambyses, king or chief of Persia, and grandson of Astyages, king of Media; recognised according to established custom by all, as the person to whom they look for orders.   Xenophon furnishes him with a splendid outfit of heroic qualities, suitable to this ascendant position; and represents the foundation of the vast Persian empire, with the unshaken fidelity of all the heterogeneous people composing it, as the reward of a laborious life spent in the active display

(margin: Portrait of Cyrus the Great—his education—Preface to the Cyropædia.)

---

[d] Xenoph. Anab. i. 9, also i. 7, 3, the address of Cyrus to the Greek soldiers — "Ὅπως οὖν ἔσεσθε ἄνδρες ἄξιοι τῆς ἐλευθερίας ἧς κέκτησθε, καὶ ὑπὲρ ἧς ὑμᾶς εὐδαιμονίζω. Εὖ γὰρ ἴστε, ὅτι τὴν ἐλευθερίαν ἑλοίμην ἂν, ἀντὶ ὧν ἔχω πάντων καὶ ἄλλων πολλαπλασίων, compared with i. 5, 16, where Cyrus gives his appreciation of the Oriental portion of his army, and the remarkable description of the trial of Orontes, i. 6.

[e] Xenoph. Œconom. iv. 18-19.   Κῦρος, εἰ ἐβίωσεν, ἄριστος ἂν δοκεῖ ἄρχων γενέσθαι—ἡγοῦμαι μέγα τεκμήριον ἄρχοντος ἀρετῆς εἶναι, ᾧ ἂν ἑκόντες ἔπωνται, καὶ ἐν τοῖς δεινοῖς παραμένειν ἐθέλωσιν.   Compare Anab. i. 9, 29-30.

of such qualities. In his interesting Preface to the Cyropædia, he presents this as the solution of a problem which had greatly perplexed him. He had witnessed many revolutions in the Grecian cities—subversions of democracies, oligarchies, and despotisms: he had seen also private establishments, some with numerous servants, some with few, yet scarcely any house-master able to obtain hearty or continued obedience. But as to herds of cattle or flocks of sheep, on the contrary, he had seen them uniformly obedient; suffering the herdsman or shepherd to do what he pleased with them, and never once conspiring against him. The first inference of Xenophon from these facts was, that man was by nature the most difficult of all animals to govern.[f] But he became satisfied that he was mistaken, when he reflected on the history of Cyrus; who had acquired and maintained dominion over more men than had ever been united under one empire, always obeying him cheerfully and affectionately. This history proved to Xenophon that it was not impossible, nor even difficult,[g] to rule mankind, provided a man undertook it with scientific or artistic competence. Accordingly, he proceeded to examine what Cyrus was in birth, disposition, and education—and how he came to be so admirably accomplished in the government of men.[h] The result is the Cyropædia. We must observe however that his solution of the problem is one which does not meet the full difficulties. These difficulties, as he states them, had been suggested to him by his Hellenic experience: by the instability of government in Grecian cities. But the solution which he provides departs from Hellenic experience, and implies what Aristotle and Hippokrates called the more yielding and servile disposition of Asiatics:[i] for it postulates an hereditary chief of heroic or divine lineage, such as was nowhere acknowledged in Greece, except at Sparta—and there, only under restrictions which would have rendered the case unfit for Xenophon's purpose. The heroic and regal

---

[f] Xen. Cyrop. i. 1, 2.

[g] Xen. Cyrop. i. 1, 3. ἐκ τούτου δὴ ἠναγκαζόμεθα μετανοεῖν, μὴ οὔτε τῶν ἀδυνάτων οὔτε τῶν χαλεπῶν ἔργων ᾖ τὸ ἀνθρώπων ἄρχειν, ἢν τις ἐπισταμένως τοῦτο πράττῃ.

[h] Xen. Cyrop. i. 1, 3-8.

[i] Aristot. Politic. vii. 7, 1327, b. 25. τὰ δὲ περὶ τὴν Ἀσίαν, διανοητικὰ μὲν καὶ τεχνικὰ τὴν ψυχὴν, ἄθυμα δέ· διόπερ ἀρχόμενα μὲν καὶ δουλεύοντα διατελεῖ.

Hippokrates, De Aere, Locis, et Aquis, c. 19-23.

lineage of Cyrus was a condition not less essential to success, than his disposition and education:[k] and not merely his lineage, but also the farther fact, that besides being constant in the duties of prayer and sacrifice to the Gods, he was peculiarly favoured by them with premonitory signs and warnings in all difficult emergencies.[1]

The fundamental principle of Xenophon is, that to obtain hearty and unshaken obedience is not difficult for a ruler, provided he possesses the science or art of ruling. This is a principle expressly laid down by Sokrates in the Xenophontic Memorabilia.[m] We have seen Plato affirming in the Politikus[n] that this is the only true government, though very few individuals are competent to it: Plato gives to it a peculiar application in the Republic, and points out a philosophical or dialectic tuition whereby he supposes that his Elders will acquire the science or art of command. The Cyropædia presents to us an illustrative example. Cyrus is a young prince who, from twenty-six years of age to his dying day is always ready with his initiative, provident in calculation of consequences, and personally active in enforcement: giving the right order at the right moment, with good assignable reasons. As a military man, he is not only personally forward, but peculiarly dexterous in the marshalling and management of soldiers; like the Homeric Agamemnon[o]—

Ἀμφότερον, βασιλεύς τ᾽ ἀγαθὸς, κρατερός τ᾽ αἰχμητής.

> Xenophon does not solve his own problem—The governing aptitude and popularity of Cyrus come from nature, not from education.

[k] So it is stated by Xenophon himself, in the speech addressed by Crœsus after his defeat and captivity to Cyrus, vii. 2, 24—ἀγνοῶν ἐμαυτὸν ὅτι σοι ἀντιπολεμεῖν ἱκανὸς ᾤμην εἶναι, πρῶτον μὲν ἐκ θεῶν γεγονότι, ἔπειτα δὲ διὰ βασιλέων πεφυκότι, ἔπειτα δὲ ἐκ παιδὸς ἀρετὴν ἀσκοῦντι· τῶν δ᾽ ἐμῶν προγόνων ἀκούω τὸν πρῶτον βασιλεύσαντα ἅμα βασιλέα καὶ ἐλεύθερον γενέσθαι. *Cyrus.* τοῦ Περσειδῶν γένους, i. 2, 1.

[1] See the remarkable words addressed by Cyrus, shortly before his death, in sacrificing on the hill-top to Ζεὺς Πατρῷος and Ἥλιος, *Cyrop.* viii. 7, 3. The special communications of the Gods to Cyrus are insisted on by Xenophon, like those made to Sokrates, and like the constant aid of Athênê to Odysseus in Homer, *Odyss.* iii. 221:—

Οὐ γάρ πω ἴδον ὧδε θεοὺς ἀναφανδὰ φιλεῦντας
Ὡς κείνῳ ἀναφανδὰ παρίστατο Παλλὰς Ἀθήνη.

[m] Xenoph. Mem. iii. 9, 10-12.
[n] See what has been said above about the Platonic Politikus, vol. ii. ch. xxviii. pp. 489-496.
[o] Cicero, when called upon in his province of Cilicia to conduct warlike operations against the Parthians, as well as against some refractory mountaineers, improved his military knowledge by studying and commenting on the Cyropædia. Epist. ad Famil. ix. 25. Compare the remarkable observation made by Cicero (Academic. Prior. ii. init.) about the way in which Lucullus made up his deficiency of military experience by reading military books.

But we must consider this aptitude for command as a spontaneous growth in Cyrus—a portion of his divine constitution
or of the golden element in his nature (to speak in the phrase
of the Platonic Republic); for no means are pointed out
whereby he acquired it, and the Platonic Sokrates would
have asked in vain, where teachers of it were to be found.
It is true that he is made to go through a rigorous and long-
continued training: but this training is common to him with
all the other Persian youths of good family, and is calculated
to teach obedience, not to communicate aptitude for command: while the master of tactics, whose lessons he receives
apart, is expressly declared to have known little about the
duties of a commander.[p] Kambyses indeed (father of Cyrus)
gives to his son valuable general exhortations respecting the
multiplicity of exigencies which press upon a commander,
and the constant watchfulness, precautions, fertility of invention, required on his part to meet them. We read the
like in the conversations of Sokrates in the Memorabilia:[q]
but neither Kambyses nor Sokrates are teachers of the art of
commanding. For this art, Cyrus is assumed to possess a
natural aptitude; like the other elements of his dispositions—
his warm sympathies, his frank and engaging manners, his
ardent emulation combined with perfect freedom from jealousy, his courage, his love of learning, his willingness to
endure any amount of labour for the purpose of obtaining
praise, &c., all which Xenophon represents as belonging to him
by nature, together with a very handsome person.[r]

The Cyropædia is a title not fairly representing the con-

Views of
Xenophon
about public
and official
training of
all citizens.

tents of the work, which contains a more copious
biography of the hero than any which we read in
Plutarch or Suetonius. But the education of Cyrus[s]
is the most remarkable part of it, in which the
ethico-political theory of Xenophon, generated by Sokratic
refining criticism brought to bear on the Spartan drill and
discipline, is put forth. Professing to describe the Persian

---

[p] Xen. Cyrop. i. 6, 12-15.

[q] Compare Cyropæd. i. 6 with Memorab. iii. 1.

[r] Cyropæd. i. 2, 1. φῦναι δὲ ὁ
Κῦρος λέγεται, &c. i. 3, 1-2, πάντων
τῶν ἡλίκων διαφέρων ἐφαίνετο, φιλό-

στοργος ὢν φύσει, &c.

[s] I have already observed that the
phrase of Plato in Legg. iii. p. 694 C
may be considered as conveying his
denial of the assertion, that Cyrus had
received a good education.

polity, he in reality describes only the Persian education; which is public, and prescribed by law, intended to form the character of individuals so that they shall stand in no need of coercive laws or penalties. Most cities leave the education of youth to be conducted at the discretion of their parents, and think it sufficient to enact and enforce laws forbidding, under penal sanction, theft, murder, and various other acts enumerated as criminal. But Xenophon (like Plato and Aristotle) disapproves of this system.[t] His Persian polity places the citizen even from infancy under official tuition, and aims at forming his first habits and character, as well as at upholding them when formed, so that instead of having any disposition of his own to commit such acts, he shall contract a repugnance to them. He is kept under perpetual training, drill, and active official employment throughout life, but the supervision is most unremitting during boyhood and youth.

There are four categories of age:—boys, up to sixteen— young men or ephêbi, from sixteen to twenty-six— mature men, as far as fifty-one—above that age, elders. To each of these four classes there is assigned a certain portion of the "free agora:" i. e. the great square of the city, where no buying or selling or vulgar occupation is allowed—where the regal residence is situated, and none but dignified functions, civil or military, are carried on. Here the boys and the mature men assemble every day at sunrise, continue under drill, and take their meals; while the young men even pass the night on guard near the government house. Each of the four sections is commanded by superintendents or officers: those superintending the boys are Elders, who are employed in administering justice to the boys, and in teaching them what justice is. They hold judicial trials of the boys for various sorts of misconduct: for violence, theft, abusive words, lying, and even for ingratitude. In cases of proved guilt, beating or flogging is inflicted. The boys go there to learn justice (says Xenophon), as boys in Hellas go to school to learn letters. Under this discipline, and in learning the use of the bow and javelin besides, they

Marginal note: Details of (so called) Persian education—Severe discipline—Distribution of four ages.

---

[t] Xenophon says the same about the scheme of Lykurgus at Sparta, De Lac. Repub. c. 2.

spend the time until sixteen years of age. They bring their food with them from home (wheaten bread, with a condiment of kardamon, or bruised seed of the nasturtium), together with a wooden cup to draw water from the river: and they dine at public tables under the eye of the teacher. The young men perform all the military and police duty under the commands of the King and the Elders: moreover, they accompany the King when he goes on a hunting expedition—which accustoms them to fatigue and long abstinence, as well as to the encounter of dangerous wild animals. The Elders do not take part in these hunts, nor in any foreign military march, nor are they bound, like the others, to daily attendance in the agora. They appoint all officers, and try judicially the cases shown up by the superintendents, or other accusers, of all youths or mature men who have failed in the requirements of the public discipline. The gravest derelictions they punish with death: where this is not called for, they put the offender out of his class, so that he remains degraded all his life.[u]

This severe discipline is by law open to all Persians who choose to attend, and the honours of the state are attainable by all equally. But in practice it is confined to a few: for neither boys nor men can attend it continuously, except such as possess an independent maintenance; nor is any one allowed to enter the regiment of youths or mature men, unless he has previously gone through the discipline of boyhood. The elders, by whom the higher functions are exercised, must be persons who have passed without reproach through all the three preceding stages: so that these offices, though legally open to all, are in practice confined to a few—the small class of Homotimoi.[x]

Evidence of the good effect of this discipline— Hard and dry condition of the body.

Such is Xenophon's conception of a perfect Polity. It consists in an effective public discipline and drill, begun in early boyhood and continued until old age. The evidence on which he specially insists to prove its good results relates first

---

[u] Xen. Cyrop. i. 2, 6-16. καὶ ἤν τις ἢ ἐν ἐφήβοις ἢ ἐν τελείοις ἀνδράσιν ἐλλίπῃ τι τῶν νομίμων, φαίνουσι μὲν οἱ φύλαρχοι ἕκαστον, καὶ τῶν ἄλλων ὁ βουλόμενος· οἱ δὲ γεραίτεροι ἀκούσαντες ἐκκρίνουσιν· ὁ δὲ ἐκκριθεὶς ἄτιμος τὸν λοιπὸν βίον διατελεῖ.

[x] Cyropæd. i. 2, 14-15.

to the body.   The bodies of the Persians become so dry and
hard, that they neither spit, nor have occasion to wipe their
noses, nor are full of wind, nor are ever seen to retire for the
satisfaction of natural wants.[y]   Besides this, the discipline
enforces complete habits of obedience, sobriety, justice, endurance of pain and privation.

We may note here both the agreement, and the difference,
between Xenophon and Plato, as to the tests applied for measuring the goodness of their respective disciplinarian schemes.
In regard to the ethical effects desirable (obedience, sobriety,
&c.) both were agreed.   But while Plato (in Republic) dwells
much besides upon the musical training necessary, Xenophon
omits this, and substitutes in its place the working off of all
the superfluous moisture of the body.[z]

Through the two youthful stages of this discipline Cyrus is
represented as having passed; undergoing all the
fatigues as well as the punishment (he is beaten or
flogged by the superintendent[a]) with as much rigour
as the rest, and even surpassing all his comrades in
endurance and exemplary obedience, not less than
in the bow and the javelin.   In the lessons about
justice he manifests such pre-eminence, that he is
appointed by the superintendent to administer justice
to other boys: and it is in this capacity that he is chastised
for his well-known decision, awarding the large coat to the
great boy and the little coat to the little boy, as being more
convenient to both,[b] though the proprietorship was opposite:
the master impressing upon him, as a general explanation,
that the lawful or customary was the Just.[c]   Cyrus has been
brought as a boy by his mother Mandanê to visit her father,
the Median king Astyages.   The boy wins the affection of
Astyages and all around by his child-like frankness and
affectionate sympathy (admirably depicted in Xenophon):
while he at the same time resists the corruptions of a
luxurious court, and adheres to the simplicity of his Persian

[Marginal note:] Exemplary obedience of Cyrus to the public discipline—He had learnt justice well —His award about the two coats— Lesson inculcated upon him by the Justice-Master.

y Cyrop. i. 2, 16.
z See above, chap. xxxv. pp. 174-175.
a Cyrop. i. 3, 17, i. 5, 4.
b Cyrop. i. 3, 17. This is an ingenious and apposite illustration of the
law of property.
c Cyrop. i. 3, 17. ἔπειτα δὲ ἔφη τὸ
μὲν νόμιμον δίκαιον εἶναι· τὸ δὲ ἄνομον,
βίαιον.

training. When Mandanê is about to depart and to rejoin her husband Kambyses in Persis, she is entreated by Astyages to allow Cyrus to remain with him. Cyrus himself also desires to remain : but Mandanê hesitates to allow it : putting to Cyrus, among other difficulties, the question—How will you learn justice here, when the teachers of it are in Persis ? To which Cyrus replies—I am already well taught in justice : as you may see by the fact, that my teacher made me a judge over other boys, and compelled me to render account to him of all my proceedings.[d] Besides which, if I am found wanting, my grandfather Astyages will make up the deficient teaching. But (says Mandanê) justice is not the same here under Astyages, as it is in Persis. Astyages has made himself master of all the Medes : while among the Persians equality is accounted justice. Your father Kambyses both performs all that the city directs, and receives nothing more than what the city allows : the measure for him is, not his own inclination, but the law. You must therefore be cautious of staying here, lest you should bring back with you to Persis habits of despotism, and of grasping at more than any one else, contracted from your grandfather : for if you come back in this spirit, you will assuredly be flogged to death. Never fear, mother (answered Cyrus) : my grandfather teaches every one round him to claim less than his due—not more than his due : and he will teach me the same.[e]

The portion of the Cyropædia just cited deserves especial attention, in reference to Xenophon as a companion and pupil of Sokrates. The reader has been already familiarised throughout this work with the questions habitually propounded and canvassed by Sokrates— What is Justice, Temperance, Courage, &c. ? Are these virtues teachable ? If they are so, where are the teachers of them to be found ?—for he professed to have looked in vain for any teachers.[f] I have farther remarked that Sokrates required these questions to be debated in the order here stated. That is—you must first know what Justice

Xenophon's conception of the Sokratic problems—He does not recognise the Sokratic order of solution of those problems.

[d] Cyropæd. i. 4, 2.
[e] Cyrop. i. 3, 17-18. "Οπως οὖν μὴ ἀπολῇ μαστιγούμενος, ἐπειδὰν οἴκοι ἦς, ἂν παρὰ τούτου μαθὼν ἥκῃς ἀντὶ τοῦ

βασιλικοῦ τὸ τυραννικὸν, ἐν ᾧ ἔστι τὸ πλέον οἴεσθαι χρῆναι ἀπάντων ἔχειν.
[f] Xenop. Memor. i. 16, iv. 4, 5.

is, before you can determine whether it be teachable or not—nay before you are in a position to affirm any thing at all about it, or to declare any particular acts to be either just or unjust.[g]

Now Xenophon, in his description of the Persian official discipline, provides a sufficient answer to the second question—Whether justice is teachable—and where are the teachers thereof? It *is* teachable: there are official teachers appointed: and every boy passes through a course of teaching prolonged for several years.—But Xenophon does not at all recognise the Sokratic requirement, that the first question shall be fully canvassed and satisfactorily answered, before the second is approached. The first question is indeed answered in a certain way—though the answer appears here only as an *obiter dictum*, and is never submitted to any Elenchus at all. The master explains—What is Justice?—by telling Cyrus, "That the lawful is just, and that the lawless is violent." Now if we consider this as preceptorial—as an admonition to the youthful Cyrus how he ought to decide judicial cases—it is perfectly reasonable:—"Let your decisions be conformable to the law or custom of the country." But if we consider it as a portion of philosophy or reasoned truth—as a definition or rational explanation of Justice, advanced by a respondent who is bound to defend it against the Sokratic cross-examination—we shall find it altogether insufficient. Xenophon himself tells us here, that Law or Custom is one thing among the Medes, and the reverse among the Persians: accordingly an action which is just in the one place will be unjust in the other. It is by objections of this kind that Sokrates, both in Plato and Xenophon, refutes explanations propounded by his respondents.[h]

[g] See above, vol. i. ch. xi. p. 385; vol. ii. ch. xx. pp. 8-11, ch. xxi. p. 72.

[h] Plato, Republ. v. p. 479 A. τούτων τῶν πολλῶν καλῶν μῶν τι ἔστιν, ὃ οὐκ αἰσχρὸν φανήσεται; καὶ τῶν δικαίων, ὃ οὐκ ἄδικον; καὶ τῶν ὁσίων ὃ οὐκ ἀνόσιον; Compare Republ. i. p. 331 C, and the conversation of Sokrates with Euthydêmus in the Xenophontic Memorab. iv. 2, 13-19, and Cyropædia, i. 6, 27-34, about what is just and good morality towards enemies.

We read in Pascal, Pensées, iv. 4:—
"On ne voit presque rien de juste ou d'injuste, qui ne change de qualité en changeant de climat. Trois degrés d'élévation du pôle renversent toute la jurisprudence. Un méridien décide de la vérité: en peu d'années de possession, les loix fondamentales changent: le droit a ses époques. Plaisante justice, qu'une rivière borne! Vérité au deçà des Pyrénées—erreur au delà!

"Ils confessent que la justice n'est

Though the explanation of Justice here given is altogether

untenable, yet we shall find it advanced by Sokrates himself as complete and conclusive, in the Xenophontic Memorabilia, where he is conversing with the Sophist Hippias. That Sophist is represented as at first urging difficulties against it, but afterwards as concurring with Sokrates: who enlarges upon the definition, and extols it as perfectly satisfactory. If Sokrates really delivered this answer to Hippias, as a general definition of Justice—we may learn from it how much greater was his negative acuteness in overthrowing the definitions of others, than his affirmative perspicacity in discovering unexceptionable definitions of his own. This is the deficiency admitted by himself in the Platonic Apology—lamented by friends like Kleitophon—arraigned by opponents like Hippias and Thrasymachus. Xenophon, whose intellect was practical rather than speculative, appears not to be aware of it. He does not feel the depth and difficulty of the Sokratic problems, even while he himself enunciates them. He does not appreciate all the conditions of a good definition, capable of being maintained against that formidable cross-examination (recounted by himself) whereby Sokrates humbled the youth Euthydêmus: still less does he enter into the spirit of that Sokratic order of precedence (declared in the negative Platonic dialogues), in the study of philosophical questions:— First define Justice, and find a definition of it such as you can maintain against a cross-examining adversary—before you proceed either to affirm or deny any predicates concerning it. The practical advice and reflexions of Xenophon are, for the

pas dans les coutumes, mais qu'elle reside dans les loix naturelles, connues en tout pays. Certainement ils la soutiendraient opiniâtrement, si la témérité du hasard qui a semé les loix humaines en avait rencontré au moins une qui fut universelle: mais la plaisanterie est telle, que le caprice des hommes s'est si bien diversifié, qu'il n'y en a point.

"Le larcin, l'inceste, le meurtre des enfans et des pères, tout a eu sa place entre les actions vertueuses. Se peutil rien de plus plaisant, qu'un homme ait droit de me tuer parcequ'il demeure au-delà de l'eau, et que son prince a querelle avec lè mien, quoique je n'en aie aucune avec lui?

"L'un dit que l'essence de la justice est l'autorité du législateur: l'autre, la commodité du souverain: l'autre, la coutume présente—et c'est le plus sûr. Rien, suivant la seule raison, n'est juste de soi: tout branle avec le temps. La coutume fait toute l'équité, par cette seule cause qu'elle est reçue: c'est le fondement mystique de son autorité. Qui la ramène à son principe, l'anéantit."

most part, judicious and penetrating. But he falls very short
when he comes to deal with philosophical theory:—with reasoned truth, and with the Sokratic Elenchus as a test for discriminating such truth from the false, the doubtful, or the
not-proven.

Cyrus is allowed by his mother to remain amidst the
luxuries of the Median court. It is a part of his
admirable disposition that he resists all its temptations,[1] and goes back to the hard fare and discipline
of the Persians with the same exemplary obedience
as before. He is appointed by the Elders to command the Persian contingent which is sent to assist

Biography of Cyrus—constant military success earned by suitable qualities—Variety of characters and situations.

Kyaxares (son of Astyages) king of Media; and he thus enters
upon that active military career which is described as occupying his whole life, until his conquest of Babylon, and his
subsequent organization of the great Persian empire. His
father Kambyses sends him forth with excellent exhortations,
many of which are almost in the same words as those which
we read ascribed to Sokrates in the Memorabilia. In the
details of Cyrus's biography which follow, the stamp of Sokratic influence is less marked, yet seldom altogether wanting.
The conversation of Sokrates had taught Xenophon how to
make the most of his own large experience and observation.
His biography of Cyrus represents a string of successive situations, calling forth and displaying the aptitude of the hero
for command. The epical invention with which these situations are imagined—the variety of characters introduced,
Araspes, Abradates, Pantheia, Chrysantas, Hystaspes, Gadatas,
Gobryas, Tigranes, &c.—the dramatic propriety with which
each of these persons is animated as speaker, and made to
teach a lesson bearing on the predetermined conclusion—all
these are highly honourable to the Xenophontic genius, but
all of them likewise bespeak the Companion of Sokrates.
Xenophon dwells, with evident pleasure, on the details connected with the *rationale* of military proceedings: the wants
and liabilities of soldiers, the advantages or disadvantages of
different weapons or different modes of marshalling, the duties
of the general as compared with those of the soldier, &c.

[1] Cyropæd. i. 5, 1.

Cyrus is not merely always ready with his orders, but also competent as a speaker to explain the propriety of what he orders.[k] We have the truly Athenian idea, that persuasive speech is the precursor of intelligent and energetic action: and that it is an attribute essentially necessary for a general, for the purpose of informing, appeasing, re-assuring, the minds of the soldiers.[l] This, as well as other duties and functions of a military commander, we find laid down generally in the conversations of Sokrates,[m] who conceives these functions, in their most general aspect, as a branch of the comprehensive art of guiding or governing men. What Sokrates thus enunciates generally, is exemplified in detail throughout the life of Cyrus.

Throughout all the Cyropædia, the heroic qualities and personal agency of Cyrus are always in the foreground, working with unerring success and determining every thing. He is moreover recommended to our sympathies, not merely by the energy and judgment of a leader, but also by the amiable qualities of a generous man—by the remarkable combination of self-command with indulgence towards others—by considerate lenity towards subdued enemies like Krœsus and the Armenian prince—even by solicitude shown that the miseries of war should fall altogether on the fighting men, and that the cultivators of the land should be left unmolested by both parties.[n] Respecting several other persons in the narrative, too—the Armenian Tigranes, Gadatas, Gobryas, &c.—the adventures and scenes described are touching: but the tale of Abradates and Pantheia transcends them all, and is perhaps the most pathetic recital embodied in the works of Hellenic antiquity.[o] In all these narratives the vein of sentiment is

Generous and amiable qualities of Cyrus. Abradates and Pantheia.

---

[k] Cyropæd. v. 5, 46. λεκτικώτατος καὶ πρακτικώτατος. Compare the Memorabilia, iv. 6, 1-15.

[l] Memorab. iii. 3, 11; Hipparch. viii. 22; Cyropæd. vi. 2, 13. Compare the impressive portion of the funeral oration delivered by Perikles in Thucydides, ii. 40.

[m] See the four first chapters of the third book of the Xenophontic Memorabilia. The treatise of Xenophon called Ἱππαρχικὸς enumerates also the

general duties required from a commander of cavalry: among these, ψευδαυτόμολοι are mentioned (iv. 7). Now the employment, with effect, of a ψευδαυτόμολος, is described with much detail in the Cyropædia. See the case of Araspes (vi. 1, 37, vi. 3, 16).

[n] Cyrop. iii. 1, 10-38, vii. 2, 9-29, v. 4, 26, vi. 1, 37. Ἀλλὰ σὺ μὲν, ὦ Κῦρε, καὶ ταῦτα ὅμοιος εἶ, πρᾷός τε καὶ συγγνώμων τῶν ἀνθρωπίνων ἁμαρτημάτων.

[o] Cyrop. vii. 3.

neither Sokratic nor Platonic, but belongs to Xenophon himself.

This last remark may also be made respecting the concluding proceedings of Cyrus, after he has thoroughly completed his conquests, and when he establishes arrangements for governing them permanently. The scheme of government which Xenophon imagines, and introduces him as organizing, is neither Sokratic nor Platonic, nor even Hellenic: *Scheme of government devised by Cyrus when his conquests are completed—Oriental despotism, wisely arranged.*
it would probably have been as little acceptable to his friend Agesilaus, the marked "hater of Persia,"[p] as to any Athenian politician. It is altogether an Oriental despotism, skilfully organized both for the security of the despot and for enabling him to keep a vigorous hold on subjects distant as well as near: such as the younger Cyrus might possibly have attempted, if his brother Artaxerxes had been slain at Kunaxa, instead of himself. "Eam conditionem esse imperandi, ut non aliter ratio constet, quam si uni reddatur"[q]—is a maxim repugnant to Hellenic ideas, and not likely to be rendered welcome even by the regulations of detail with which Xenophon surrounds it : judicious as these regulations are for their contemplated purpose. The amiable and popular character which Cyrus has maintained from youth upwards, and by means of which he has gained an uninterrupted series of victories, is difficult to be reconciled with the insecurity, however imposing, in which he dwells as Great King. When we find that he accounts it a necessary precaution to surround himself with eunuchs, on the express ground that they are despised by every one else and therefore likely to be more faithful to their master—when we read also that in consequence of the number of disaffected subjects, he is forced to keep a guard composed of twenty thousand soldiers taken from poor Persian mountaineers[r]—we find realised, in the case of the triumphant Cyrus, much of that peril and insecurity which the despot Hieron had so bitterly deplored in his conversation with Simonides. However unsatisfactory the ideal

---

[p] Xenop. Agesilaus, vii. 7. εἰ δ᾽ αὖ καλὸν καὶ μισοπέρσην εἶναι— ἐξέπλευσεν, ὅ, τι δύναιτο κακὸν ποιήσων

τὸν βάρβαρον.
[q] Tacit. Annal. i. 6.
[r] Xen. Cyrop. vii. 5, 58-70.

of government may be, which Plato lays out either in the Republic or the Leges—that which Xenophon sets before us is not at all more acceptable, in spite of the splendid individual portrait whereby he dazzles our imagination. Few Athenians would have exchanged Athens either for Babylon under Cyrus, or for Plato's Magnêtic colony in Krete.

The Xenophontic government is thus noway admirable, even as an ideal. But he himself presents it only as an ideal—or (which is the same thing in the eyes of a companion of Sokrates) as a quasi-historical fact, belonging to the unknown and undetermined past. When Xenophon talks of what the Persians *are now*, he presents us with nothing but a shocking contrast to this ideal; nothing but vice, corruption, degeneracy of every kind, exorbitant sensuality, faithlessness and cowardice.[s] His picture of Persia is like that of the Platonic Kosmos, which we have read in the Timæus:[t] a splendid Kosmos in its original plan and construction, but full of defects and evil as it actually exists. The strength and excellence of the Xenophontic orderly despotism dies with its heroic beginner. His two sons (as Plato remarked) do not receive the same elaborate training and discipline as himself: nor can they be restrained, even by the impressive appeal which he makes to them on his death-bed, from violent dissension among themselves, and misgovernment of every kind.[u]

Persian present reality—is described by Xenophon as thoroughly depraved, in striking contrast to the establishment of Cyrus.

Whatever we may think of the political ideal of Xenophon, his Cyropædia is among the glories of the Sokratic family; as an excellent specimen of the philosophical imagination, in carrying a general doctrine into illustrative details—and of the epical imagination in respect to varied characters and touching incident. In stringing together instructive conversations, moreover, it displays the same art which we trace in the Memorabilia, Œkonomikus, Hieron, &c., and which is worthy of the attentive companion of Sokrates. Whenever Xenophon talks about military affairs, horsemanship, agriculture, house-management, &c., he is within the range of his

Xenophon has good experience of military and equestrian proceedings—No experience of finance and commerce.

---

[s] Cyropæd. viii. 8.
[t] See above, ch. xxxvi. p. 291 seq.
[u] Cyropæd. viii. 7, 9-19; Plato, Legg. iii. p. 694 D.

personal experience, and his recommendations, controlled as they thus are by known realities, are for the most part instructive and valuable. Such is the case not merely with the Cyropædia and Œkonomikus, but also in his two short treatises, De Re Equestri and De Officio Magistri Equitum. But we cannot say as much when he discusses plans of finance.

We read among his works a discourse—composed after his sentence of exile had been repealed, and when he was very old, seemingly not earlier than 355 B.C.[x] criticising the actual condition of Athens, and proposing various measures for the improvement of the finances, as well as for relief of the citizens from poverty. He begins this discourse by a sentiment thoroughly Sokratic and Platonic, which would serve almost as a continuation of the Cyropædia. The government of a city will be measured by the character and ability of its leaders.[y] He closes it by another sentiment equally Sokratic and Platonic; advising that before his measures are adopted, special messengers shall be sent to Delphi and Dodona; to ascertain whether the Gods approve them—and if they approve, to which Gods they enjoin that the initiatory sacrifices shall be offered.[z] But almost everything in the discourse, between the first and last sentences, is in a vein not at all Sokratic—in a vein, indeed, positively anti-Platonic and anti-Spartan. We have already seen that wealth, gold and silver, commerce, influx of strangers, &c., are discouraged as much as possible by Plato, and by the theory (though evaded partially in practice) of Sparta. Now it is precisely these objects which Xenophon, in the treatise before us, does his utmost to foster and extend at Athens. Nothing is here said about the vulgarising influence of trade as compared with farming, which we read in the Œkonomikus: nor about the ethical and pædagogic dictation which pervades so much of the Cyropædia, and

Marginal note: Discourse of Xenophon on Athenian finance and the condition of Athens. His admiration of active commerce and variety of pursuits.

---

[x] Xenophon, Πόροι—ἢ περὶ Προσόδων. De Vectigalibus. See Schneider's Proleg. to this treatise, pp. 138-140.

[y] De Vectig. 1. ἐγὼ μὲν τοῦτο ἀεί ποτε νομίζω, ὁποῖοί τινες ἂν οἱ προστάται ὦσι, τοιαύτας καὶ τὰς πολιτείας γίγνεσθαι.

[z] De Vect. vi. 2. Compare this with Anabas. iii. 1, 5, where Sokrates reproves Xenophon for his evasive manner of putting a question to the Delphian God. Xenophon here adopts the plenary manner enjoined by Sokrates.

reigns paramount throughout the Platonic Republic and Leges.
Xenophon takes Athens as she stands, with the great variety
of taste, active occupation, and condition among the inhabitants: her mild climate and productive territory, especially
her veins of silver and her fine marble: her importing and
exporting merchants, her central situation, as convenient
entrepôt for commodities produced in the most distant lands:[a]
her skilful artisans and craftsmen: her monied capitalists:
and not these alone, but also the congregation and affluence
of fine artists, intellectual men, philosophers, Sophists, poets,
rhapsodes, actors, &c.: last, though not least, the temples
adorning her akropolis, and the dramatic representations
exhibited at her Dionysiac festivals, which afforded the highest
captivation to eye as well as ear, and attracted strangers from
all quarters as visitors.[b] Xenophon extols these charms of
Athens with a warmth which reminds us of the Periklean
funeral oration in Thucydides.[c] He no longer speaks like one
whose heart and affections are with the Spartan drill: still
less does he speak like Plato—to whom (as we see both by the
Republic and the Leges) such artistic and poetical exhibitions were abominations calling for censorial repression—and
in whose eyes gold, silver, commerce, abundant influx of
strangers, &c., were dangerous enemies of all civic virtue.

Yet while recognising all these charms and advantages,
Recognised poverty among the citizens. Plan for improvement.
Xenophon finds himself compelled to lament great
poverty among the citizens; which poverty (he says)
is often urged by the leading men as an excuse for
unjust proceedings. Accordingly he comes forward
with various financial suggestions, by means of which he
confidently anticipates that every Athenian citizen may obtain
a comfortable maintenance from the public.[d]

First, he dwells upon the great advantage of encouraging
metics, or foreigners resident at Athens, each of whom paid

[a] De Vectig. c. i. 2-3.

[b] De Vect. v. 4. Τί δὲ οἱ πολυέλαιοι;
τί δὲ οἱ πολυπρόβατοι; τί δὲ οἱ γνώμῃ
καὶ ἀργυρίῳ δυνάμενοι χρηματίζεσθαι;
Καὶ μὴν χειροτέχναι γε καὶ σοφισταὶ
καὶ φιλόσοφοι· οἱ δὲ ποιηταί, οἱ δὲ τὰ
τούτων μεταχειριζόμενοι, οἱ δ' ἀξιοθεά-
των ἢ ἀξιακούστων ἱερῶν ἢ ὁσίων ἐπι-
θυμοῦντες, &c.

[c] Thucydid. ii. 34-42 ; Plutarch,
Perikles, c. 12. Compare Xenophon,
Republ. Athen. ii. 7, iii. 8..

[d] De Vectig. iv. 33. καὶ ἐμοὶ μὲν δὴ
εἴρηται, ὡς ἂν ἡγοῦμαι κατασκευασθείσης
τῆς πόλεως ἱκανὴν ἂν πᾶσιν Ἀθηναίοις
τροφὴν ἀπὸ κοινοῦ γενέσθαι.

an annual capitation tax to the treasury. There were already many such, not merely Greeks, but Orientals also, Lydians, Phrygians, Syrians, &c.:[e] and by judicious encouragement all expatriated men everywhere might be made to prefer the agreeable residence at Athens, thus largely increasing the annual amount of the tax. The metics ought (he says) to be exempted from military service (which the citizens ought to perform and might perform alone) but to be admitted to the honours of the equestrian duty, whenever they were rich enough to afford it : and farther, to be allowed the liberty of purchasing land and building houses in the city. Moreover not merely resident metics, but also foreign merchants who came as visitors, conducting an extensive commerce—ought to be flattered by complimentary votes and occasional hospitalities : while the curators of the harbour, whose function it was to settle disputes among them, should receive prizes if they adjudicated equitably and speedily.[f]

Advantage of a large number of Metics. How these may be encouraged.

All this (Xenophon observes) will require only friendly and considerate demonstrations. His farther schemes are more ambitious, not to be effected without a large outlay. He proposes to raise an ample fund for the purposes of the city, by voluntary contributions; which he expects to obtain not merely from private Athenians and metics, rich and in easy circumstances—but also from other cities, and even from foreign despots, kings, satraps, &c. The tempting inducement will be, that the names of all contributors with their respective contributions will be inscribed on public tablets, and permanently commemorated as benefactors of the city.[g] Contributors (he says) are found, for the outfit of a fleet, where they expect no return : much more will they come forward here, where a good return will accrue. The fund so raised will be employed under public authority with the most profitable result, in many different ways. The city will build docks and warehouses for bonding goods—houses near the harbour to be let to merchants—merchant-vessels to

Proposal to raise by voluntary contributions a large sum to be employed as capital by the city. Distribution of three oboli per head per day to all the citizens.

---

[e] De Vect. ii. 3-7.   [f] De Vect. iii. 2-6.

[g] De Vect. iii. 11.

be let out on freight. But the largest profit will be obtained
by working the silver mines at Laureion in Attica. The city
will purchase a number of foreign slaves, and will employ
them under the superintendence of old free citizens who
are past the age of labour, partly in working these mines for
public account, each of the ten tribes employing one tenth
part of the number—partly by letting them out to private
mining undertakers, at so much per diem for each slave: the
slaves being distinguished by a conspicuous public stamp, and
the undertaker binding himself under penalty always to restore the same number of them as he received.[h] Such competition between the city and the private mining undertakers
will augment the total produce, and will be no loss to either,
but wholesome for both. The mines will absorb as many
workmen as are put into them: for in the production of silver
(Xenophon argues) there can never be any glut, as there is
sometimes in corn, wine, or oil. Silver is always in demand,
and is not lessened in value by increase of quantity. Every
one is anxious to get it, and has as much pleasure in hoarding
it under ground as in actively employing it.[i] The scheme,
thus described, may (if found necessary) be brought into
operation by degrees, a certain number of slaves being purchased annually until the full total is made up. From these
various financial projects, and especially from the fund thus
employed as capital under the management of the Senate, the
largest returns are expected. Amidst the general abundance
which will ensue, the religious festivals will be celebrated
with increased splendour—the temples will be repaired, the
docks and walls will be put in complete order—the priests,
the Senate, the magistrates, the horsemen, will receive the
full stipends which the old custom of Athens destined for
them.[k] But besides all these, the object which Xenophon has
most at heart will be accomplished: the poor citizens will be
rescued from poverty. There will be a regular distribution

[h] De Vect. iv. 13-19.
[i] De Vect. iv. 4-7.
[k] De Vectig. vi. 1-2. Καὶ ὁ μὲν δῆμος τροφῆς εὐπορήσει, οἱ δὲ πλούσιοι τῆς εἰς τὸν πόλεμον δαπάνης ἀπαλλαγήσονται, περιουσίας δὲ πολλῆς γενομένης, μεγαλοπρεπέστερον μὲν ἔτι ἢ νῦν τὰς ἑορτὰς ἄξομεν, ἱερὰ δ' ἐπισκευάσομεν, τείχη δὲ καὶ νεώρια ἀνορθώσομεν, ἱερεῦσι δὲ καὶ βουλῇ καὶ ἀρχαῖς καὶ ἱππεῦσι τὰ πάτρια ἀποδώσομεν—πῶς οὐκ ἄξιον ὡς τάχιστα τούτοις ἐγχειρεῖν, ἵνα ἔτι ἐφ' ἡμῶν ἐπίδωμεν τὴν πόλιν μετ' ἀσφαλείας εὐδαιμονοῦσαν;

among all citizens, per head and equally. Three oboli, or half a drachma, will be allotted daily to each, to poor and rich alike. For the poor citizens, this will provide a comfortable subsistence, without any contribution on their part: the poverty now prevailing will thus be alleviated. The rich, like the poor, receive the daily triobolon as a free gift: but if they even compute it as interest for their investments, they will find that the rate of interest is full and satisfactory, like the rate on bottomry. Three oboli per day amount in the year of 360 days to 180 drachmæ: now, if a rich man has contributed ten minæ (= 1000 drachmæ), he will thus receive interest at the rate of 18 per cent. per annum: if another less rich citizen has contributed one mina (= 100 drachmæ) he will receive interest at the rate of 180 per cent. per annum: more than he could realise in any other investment.[1]

Half a drachma, or three oboli, per day, was the highest rate of pay ever received (the rate varied at different times) by the citizens as Dikasts and Ekklesiasts for attending in judicature or in assembly. It is this amount of pay which Xenophon here proposes to ensure to every citizen, without exception, out of the public treasury; which (he calculates) would be enriched by his project so as easily to bear such a disbursement. He relieves the poor citizens from poverty by making them all pensioners on the public treasury, with or without service rendered, or the pretence of service. He strains yet farther the dangerous principle of the Theôrikon, without the same excuse as can be shown for the Theôrikon itself on religious grounds.[m] If such a proposition had been made by Kleon, Hyperbolus, Kleophon, Agyrrhius, &c., it would have been dwelt upon by most historians of Greece as an illustration of the cacoethes of democracy—to extract money, somehow or other, from the rich, for the purpose of keeping the poor in comfort. Not one of the democratical leaders, so far as we know, ever ventured to propose so sweeping a measure: we have it here from the pen of the oligarchical Xenophon.

But we must of course discuss Xenophon's scheme as a

Purpose and principle of this distribution.

[1] De Vectig. iii. 9-12.
[m] Respecting the Theôrikon at Athens, see my 'History of Greece,' ch. 88, pp. 492-498.

whole: the aggregate enlargement of revenue, from his

Visionary anticipations of Xenophon, financial and commercial. various new ways and means, on one side—against the new mode and increased amount of expenditure, on the other side. He would not have proposed such an expenditure, if he had not thoroughly believed in the correctness of his own anticipations, both as to the profits of the mining scheme, and as to the increase of receipts from other sources; such as the multiplication of tax-paying Metics, the rent paid by them for the new houses to be built by the city, the increase of the harbour-dues from expanded foreign trade. But of these anticipations, even the least unpromising are vague and uncertain: while the prospects of the mining scheme appear thoroughly chimerical. Nothing is clear or certain except the disbursement. We scarcely understand how Xenophon could seriously have imagined, either that voluntary contributors could have been found to subscribe the aggregate fund as he proposes—or that if subscribed, it could have yielded the prodigious return upon which he reckons. We must however recollect, that he had no familiarity with finance, or with the conditions and liabilities of commerce, or with the raising of money from voluntary contributors for any collective purpose. He would not have indulged in similar fancies if the question had been about getting together supplies for an army. Practical Athenian financiers would probably say, in criticising his financial project—what Heraldus[n] observes upon some views of his opponent Salmasius,

[n] This passage of Heraldus is cited by M. Boeckh in his Public Economy of Athens, B. iv. ch. 21, p. 606, Eng. Trans. In that chapter of M. Boeckh's work (pp. 600-610) some very instructive pages will be found about the Xenophontic scheme here noticed.

I will however mention one or two points on which my understanding of the scheme differs from his. He says (p. 605):—"The author supposes that the profit upon this speculation would amount to three oboli per day, so that the subscribers would obtain a very high per centage on their shares. Xenophon supposes unequal contributions, according to the different amounts of property, agreeable to the principles of a property-tax, but an equal distribution of the receipts for the purpose of favouring and aiding the poor. What Xenophon is speaking of is an income annually arising upon each share, either equal to or exceeding the interest of the loans on bottomry. Where, however, is the security that the undertaking would produce three oboli a day to each subscriber?"

I concur in most of what is here said; but M. Boeckh states the matter too much, as if the three oboli per diem were a real return arising from the scheme, and payable to each shareholder upon each *share* as he calls it. This is an accident of the case, not the essential feature. The poorest citizens

about the relations of capital and interest in Attica—"Somnium est hominis harum rerum, etiam cum vigilat, nihil scientis."[o] The financial management of Athens was doubtless defective in many ways : but it would not have been improved in the hands of Xenophon—any more than the administrative and judiciary department of Athens would have become better under the severe regimen of Plato.[p] The merits

—for whose benefit, more than for any other object, the scheme is contrived— would not be shareholders at all: they would be too poor to contribute anything, yet each of them would receive his triobolon like the rest. Moreover, many citizens, even though able to pay, might hold back, and decline to pay : yet still each would receive as much. And again, the foreigners, kings, satraps, &c., would be contributors, but would receive nothing at all. The distribution of the triobolon would be made to citizens only. Xenophon does indeed state the proportion of receipt to payments in the cases of some rich contributors, as an auxiliary motive to conciliate them. But we ought not to treat this receipt as if it were a real return yielded by the public mining speculation, or as profit actually brought in.

As I conceive the scheme, the daily triobolon, and the respective contributions furnished, have no premeditated ratio, no essential connection with each other. The daily payment of the triobolon to every citizen indiscriminately, is a new and heavy burden which Xenophon imposes upon the city. But this is only one among many other burdens, as we may see by cap. 6. In order to augment the wealth of the city, so as to defray these large expences, he proposes several new financial measures. Of these the most considerable was the public mining speculation ; but it did not stand alone. The financial scheme of Xenophon, both as to receipts and as to expenditure, is more general than M. Boeckh allows for.

[o] It is truly surprising to read in one of Hume's Essays the following sentence. Essay XII. on Civil Liberty, p. 107, ed. of Hume's Philosophical Works, 1825.

" The Athenians, though governed by a Republic, paid near two hundred per cent for those sums of money which any emergence made it necessary for them to borrow, as we learn from Xenophon."

In the note Hume quotes the following passage from this discourse, De Vectigalibus :—Κτῆσιν δὲ ἀπ' οὐδενὸς ἂν οὕτω καλὴν κτήσαιντο, ὥσπερ ἀφ' οὗ ἂν προτελέσωσιν εἰς τὴν ἀφορμήν. Οἱ δέ γε πλεῖστοι Ἀθηναίων πλείονα λήψονται κατ' ἐνιαυτὸν ἢ ὅσα ἂν εἰσενέγκωσιν. Οἱ γὰρ μνᾶν προτελέσαντες, ἐγγὺς δυοῖν μναῖν πρόσοδον ἕξουσι. Ὁ δοκεῖ τῶν ἀνθρωπίνων ἀσφαλέστατόν τε καὶ πολυχρονιώτατον εἶναι.

Hume has been misled by dwelling upon one or two separate sentences. If he had taken into consideration the whole discourse and its declared scope, he would have seen that it affords no warrant for any inference as to the rate of interest paid by the Athenian public when they wanted to borrow. In Xenophon's scheme there is no fixed proportion between what a contributor to the fund would pay and what he would receive. The triobolon received is a fixed sum to each citizen, whereas the contributions of *each* would be different. Moreover the foreigners and metics would contribute without receiving anything, while the poor citizens would receive their triobolon per head, without having contributed anything.

[p] Aristeides the Rhetor has some forcible remarks in defending Rhetoric and the Athenian statesmen against the bitter criticisms of Plato in the Gorgias: pointing out that Plato himself had never made trial of the difficulty of governing any real community of men, or of the necessities under which a statesman in actual political life was placed (Orat. xlv. Περὶ Ῥητορικῆς, pp. 109-110, Dindorf).

of the Sokratic companions—and great merits they were—lay in the region of instructive theory.

Xenophon accompanies his financial scheme with a strong recommendation to his countrymen, that they should abstain from warlike enterprises and maintain peace with every one. He expatiates on the manifest advantages, nay, even on the necessity, of continued peace, under the actual poverty of the city; for the purpose of recruiting the exhausted means of the citizens, as well as of favouring his own new projects for the improvement of finance and commerce. While he especially deprecates any attempt on the part of Athens to regain by force her lost headship over the Greeks, he at the same time holds out hopes that this dignity would be spontaneously tendered to her, if, besides abstaining from all violence, she conducted herself with a liberal and conciliatory spirit towards all: if she did her best to adjust differences among other cities, and to uphold the autonomy of the Delphian temple.[q] As far as we can judge, such pacific exhortations were at that time wise and politic. Athens had just then concluded peace (355 B.C.) after the three years of ruinous and unsuccessful war, called the Social War, carried on against her revolted allies Chios, Kos, Rhodes, and Byzantium. To attempt the recovery of empire by force was most mischievous. There was indeed one purpose, for which she was called upon by a wise forecast to put forth her strength—to check the aggrandisement of Philip in Macedonia. But this was a distant purpose: and the necessity, though it became every year more urgent, was not so prominently manifest[r] in 355 B.C. as to affect the judgment of Xenophon. At that early day, Demosthenes himself did not see the danger from Macedonia: his first Philippic was delivered in 351 B.C., and even then his remonstrances, highly creditable to his own forecast, made little impression on others. But when we read the financial oration De Symmoriis delivered by Demosthenes in 354, then young, we shall duly

Xenophon exhorts his
countrymen
to maintain
peace.

<hr/>

q Xenoph. De Vectig. v. 3-8.

r See my 'History of Greece,' ch. 86, p. 325 seq.

I agree with Boeckh, Public Econ. of Athens, ut suprà, p. 601, that this pamphlet of Xenophon is probably to be referred to the close of the Social War, about 355 B.C.

appreciate his sound administrative and practical judgment; compared with the benevolent dreams and ample public largess in which Xenophon here indulges.[s]

We have seen that Plato died in 347 B.C., having reached the full age of eighty: Xenophon must have attained the same age nearly, and may perhaps have attained it completely—though we do not know the exact year of his death. With both these two illustrious companions of Sokrates, the point of view is considerably modified in their last compositions as compared to their earlier. Xenophon shows the alteration not less clearly than Plato, though in an opposite direction. His discourse on the Athenian revenues differs quite as much from the Anabasis, Cyropædia, and Œkonomikus—as the Leges and Epinomis differ from any of Plato's earlier works. Whatever we may think of the financial and commercial anticipations of Xenophon, his pamphlet on the Athenian revenues betokens a warm sympathy for his native city—a genuine appreciation of her individual freedom and her many-sided intellectual activity—an earnest interest in her actual career, and even in the extension of her commercial and manufacturing wealth. In these respects it recommends itself to our feelings more than the last Platonic production—Leges and Epinomis—composed nearly at the same time, between 356-347 B.C. While Xenophon in old age, becoming reconciled to his country, forgets his early passion for the Spartan drill and discipline, perpetual, monotonous, unlettered—we find in the senility of Plato a more cramping limitation of the varieties of human agency—a stricter compression, even of individual thought and speech, under the infallible official orthodoxy—a more extensive use of the pædagogic rod and the censorial muzzle—than he had ever proposed before.

In thus taking an unwilling leave of the Sokratic family, represented by these two venerable survivors—to both of whom the students of Athenian letters and philosophy are so deeply indebted—I feel some satisfaction in the belief, that

Difference of the latest compositions of Xenophon and Plato, from their point of view in the earlier.

---

[s] Respecting the first Philippic, and the Oratio De Symmoriis of Demo- | sthenes, see my 'History of Greece,' ch. 87, pp. 401-431.

both of them died, as they were born, citizens of free Athens and of unconquered Hellas: and that neither of them was preserved to an excessive old age, like their contemporary Isokrates, to witness the extinction of Hellenic autonomy by the battle of Chæroneia.[t]

[t] Compare the touching passage in Tacitus's description of the death of Agricola, c. 44-45.

"Festinatæ mortis grande solatium tulit, evasisse postremum illud tempus," &c.

THE END.

LONDON: PRINTED BY WILLIAM CLOWES AND SONS, STAMFORD STREET, AND CHARING CROSS.

ALBEMARLE STREET, LONDON,
January, 1865.

MR. MURRAY'S

GENERAL LIST OF WORKS.

ALBERT (PRINCE). THE SPEECHES AND ADDRESSES on Public Occasions of H.R.H. THE PRINCE CONSORT; with an Introduction giving some Outlines of his Character. Portrait. 8vo. 10s. 6d.; or Popular Edition, fcap. 8vo, 1s.

ABBOTT'S (REV. J.) Philip Musgrave; or, Memoirs of a Church of England Missionary in the North American Colonies. Post 8vo. 2s.

ABERCROMBIE'S (JOHN) Enquiries concerning the Intellectual Powers and the Investigation of Truth. 16th Edition. Fcap. 8vo. 6s. 6d.

———————— Philosophy of the Moral Feelings. 12th Edition. Fcap. 8vo. 4s.

ACLAND'S (REV. CHARLES) Popular Account of the Manners and Customs of India. Post 8vo. 2s.

ÆSOP'S FABLES. A New Translation. With Historical Preface. By Rev. THOMAS JAMES. With 100 Woodcuts, by TENNIEL and WOLF. 50th Thousand. Post 8vo. 2s. 6d.

AGRICULTURAL (THE) JOURNAL. Of the Royal Agricultural Society of England. 8vo. Published half-yearly.

AIDS TO FAITH: a Series of Essays. By various Writers. Edited by WILLIAM THOMSON, D.D., Lord Archbishop of York. 8vo. 9s.

CONTENTS.

Rev. H. L. MANSEL—*Miracles.*
BISHOP OF KILLALOE—*Christian Evidences.*
Rev. DR. McCAUL—*Prophecy and the Mosaic Record of Creation.*
Rev. CANON COOK — *Ideology and Subscription.*

Rev. GEORGE RAWLINSON—*The Pentateuch.*
ARCHBISHOP OF YORK—*Doctrine of the Atonement.*
BISHOP OF ELY.—*Inspiration.*
BISHOP OF GLOUCESTER AND BRISTOL.—*Scripture and its Interpretation.*

AMBER-WITCH (THE). The most interesting Trial for Witchcraft ever known. Translated from the German by LADY DUFF GORDON. Post 8vo. 2s.

ARMY LIST (THE). *Published Monthly by Authority.* 18mo. 1s. 6d.

ARTHUR'S (LITTLE) History of England. By LADY CALLCOTT. 130th Thousand. Woodcuts. Fcap. 8vo. 2s. 6d.

ATKINSON'S (MRS.) Recollections of Tartar Steppes and their Inhabitants. Illustrations. Post 8vo. 12s.

AUNT IDA'S Walks and Talks; a Story Book for Children. By a LADY. Woodcuts. 16mo. 5s.

AUSTIN'S (JOHN) LECTURES ON JURISPRUDENCE; or, the Philosophy of Positive Law. 3 Vols. 8vo. 39s.

——————— (SARAH) Fragments from German Prose Writers. With Biographical Notes. Post 8vo. 10s.

B

ADMIRALTY PUBLICATIONS ; Issued by direction of the Lords Commissioners of the Admiralty:—

A MANUAL OF SCIENTIFIC ENQUIRY, for the Use of Travellers. Edited by Sir JOHN F. HERSCHEL, and Rev. ROBERT MAIN. *Third Edition.* Woodcuts. Post 8vo. 9s.

AIRY'S ASTRONOMICAL OBSERVATIONS MADE AT GREENWICH. 836 to 1847. Royal 4to. 50s. each.

—— ASTRONOMICAL RESULTS. 1848 to 1858. 4to. 8s. each.

—— APPENDICES TO THE ASTRONOMICAL OBSERVA-TIONS.

1836.—I. Bessel's Refraction Tables.
II. Tables for converting Errors of R.A. and N.P.D. }8s.
    into Errors of Longitude and Ecliptic P.D. }
1837.—I. Logarithms of Sines and Cosines to every Ten }
    Seconds of Time. }8s.
II. Table for converting Sidereal into Mean Solar Time. }
1842.—Catalogue of 1439 Stars. 8s.
1845.—Longitude of Valentia. 8s.
1847.—Twelve Years' Catalogue of Stars. 14s.
1851.—Maskelyne's Ledger of Stars. 6s.
1852.—I. Description of the Transit Circle. 5s.
II. Regulations of the Royal Observatory. 2s.
1853.—Bessel's Refraction Tables. 3s.
1854.—I. Description of the Zenith Tube. 3s.
II. Six Years' Catalogue of Stars. 10s.
1856.—Description of the Galvanic Apparatus at Greenwich Ob-servatory. 8s.

—— MAGNETICAL AND METEOROLOGICAL OBSERVA-TIONS. 1840 to 1847. Royal 4to. 50s. each.

—— ASTRONOMICAL, MAGNETICAL, AND METEOROLO-GICAL OBSERVATIONS, 1848 to 1862. Royal 4to. 50s. each.

—— ASTRONOMICAL RESULTS. 1848 to 1862. 4to.

—— MAGNETICAL AND METEOROLOGICAL RESULTS. 1848 to 1862. 4to. 8s. each.

—— REDUCTION OF THE OBSERVATIONS OF PLANETS. 1750 to 1830. Royal 4to. 50s.

———————————— LUNAR OBSERVATIONS. 1750 to 1830. 2 Vols. Royal 4to. 50s. each.

———————————— 1831 to 1851. 4to. 20s.

BERNOULLI'S SEXCENTENARY TABLE. *London,* 1779. 4to.

BESSEL'S AUXILIARY TABLES FOR HIS METHOD OF CLEAR-ING LUNAR DISTANCES. 8vo.

——FUNDAMENTA ASTRONOMIÆ: *Regiomontii,* 1818. Folio. 60s.

BIRD'S METHOD OF CONSTRUCTING MURAL QUADRANTS. *London,* 1768. 4to. 2s. 6d.

—— METHOD OF DIVIDING ASTRONOMICAL INSTRU-MENTS. *London,* 1767. 4to. 2s. 6d.

COOK, KING, AND BAYLY'S ASTRONOMICAL OBSERVATIONS. *London,* 1782. 4to. 21s.

ENCKE'S BERLINER JAHRBUCH, for 1830. *Berlin,* 1828. 8vo. 9s.

GROOMBRIDGE'S CATALOGUE OF CIRCUMPOLAR STARS. 4to. 10s.

HANSEN'S TABLES DE LA LUNE. 4to. 20s.

HARRISON'S PRINCIPLES OF HIS TIME-KEEPER. PLATES 1797. 4to. 5s.

ADMIRALTY PUBLICATIONS—*continued.*

HUTTON'S TABLES OF THE PRODUCTS AND POWERS OF NUMBERS. 1781. Folio. 7s. 6d.

LAX'S TABLES FOR FINDING THE LATITUDE AND LONGITUDE. 1821. 8vo. 10s.

LUNAR OBSERVATIONS at GREENWICH. 1783 to 1819. Compared with the Tables, 1821. 4to. 7s. 6d.

MASKELYNE'S ACCOUNT OF THE GOING OF HARRISON'S WATCH. 1767. 4to. 2s. 6d.

MAYER'S DISTANCES of the MOON'S CENTRE from the PLANETS. 1822, 3s.; 1823, 4s. 6d. 1824 to 1835, 8vo. 4s. each.

——— THEORIA LUNÆ JUXTA SYSTEMA NEWTONIANUM. 4to. 2s. 6d.

——— TABULÆ MOTUUM SOLIS ET LUNÆ. 1770. 4to. 5s.

——— ASTRONOMICAL OBSERVATIONS MADE AT GOTTINGEN, from 1756 to 1761. 1826. Folio. 7s. 6d.

NAUTICAL ALMANACS, from 1767 to 1868. 8vo. 2s. 6d. each.

——— SELECTIONS FROM THE ADDITIONS up to 1812. 8vo. 5s. 1834-54. 8vo. 5s.

——— SUPPLEMENTS, 1828 to 1833, 1837 and 1838. 8vo. 2s. each.

——— TABLE requisite to be used with the N.A. 1781. 8vo. 5s.

POND'S ASTRONOMICAL OBSERVATIONS. 1811 to 1835. 4to. 21s. each.

RAMSDEN'S ENGINE for DIVIDING MATHEMATICAL INSTRUMENTS. 4to. 5s.

——— ENGINE for DIVIDING STRAIGHT LINES. 4to. 5s.

SABINE'S PENDULUM EXPERIMENTS to DETERMINE THE FIGURE OF THE EARTH. 1825. 4to. 40s.

SHEPHERD'S TABLES for CORRECTING LUNAR DISTANCES. 1772. Royal 4to. 21s.

——— TABLES, GENERAL, of the MOON'S DISTANCE from the SUN, and 10 STARS. 1787. Folio. 5s. 6d.

TAYLOR'S SEXAGESIMAL TABLE. 1780. 4to. 15s.

——— TABLES OF LOGARITHMS. 4to. 3l.

TIARK'S ASTRONOMICAL OBSERVATIONS for the LONGITUDE of MADEIRA. 1822. 4to. 5s.

——— CHRONOMETRICAL OBSERVATIONS for DIFFERENCES of LONGITUDE between DOVER, PORTSMOUTH, and FALMOUTH. 1823. 4to. 5s.

VENUS and JUPITER: OBSERVATIONS of, compared with the TABLES. London, 1822. 4to. 2s.

WALES' AND BAYLY'S ASTRONOMICAL OBSERVATIONS. 1777. 4to. 21s.

WALES' REDUCTION OF ASTRONOMICAL OBSERVATIONS MADE IN THE SOUTHERN HEMISPHERE. 1764—1771. 1788. 4to. 10s. 6d.

BABBAGE'S (CHARLES) Economy of Machinery and Manufactures. *Fourth Edition.* Fcap. 8vo. 6s.

——— Reflections on the Decline of Science in England, and on some of its Causes. 4to. 7s. 6d.

B 2

BAIKIE'S (W. B.) Narrative of an Exploring Voyage up the Rivers Quorra and Tshadda in 1854. Map. 8vo. 16s.

BANKES' (GEORGE) STORY OF CORFE CASTLE, with documents relating to the Time of the Civil Wars, &c. Woodcuts. Post 8vo. 10s. 6d.

BARBAULD'S (MRS.) Hymns in Prose for Children. With 112 Original Designs. Small 4to. 5s.

BARROW'S (SIR JOHN) Autobiographical Memoir, including Reflections, Observations, and Reminiscences at Home and Abroad. From Early Life to Advanced Age. Portrait. 8vo. 16s.

———— Voyages of Discovery and Research within the Arctic Regions, from 1818 to the present time. 8vo. 15s.

———— Life and Voyages of Sir Francis Drake. With numerous Original Letters. Post 8vo. 2s.

BATES' (H. W.) Records of a Naturalist on the River Amazons during eleven years of Adventure and Travel. Second Edition. Illustrations. Post 8vo. 12s.

BEES AND FLOWERS. Two Essays. By Rev. Thomas James. Reprinted from the "Quarterly Review." Fcap. 8vo. 1s. each.

BELL'S (SIR CHARLES) Mechanism and Vital Endowments of the Hand as evincing Design. Sixth Edition. Woodcuts. Post 8vo. 6s.

BERTHA'S Journal during a Visit to her Uncle in England. Containing a Variety of Interesting and Instructive Information. Seventh Edition. Woodcuts. 12mo.

BIRCH'S (SAMUEL) History of Ancient Pottery and Porcelain : Egyptian, Assyrian, Greek, Roman, and Etruscan. With 200 Illustrations. 2 Vols. Medium 8vo. 42s.

BLUNT'S (REV. J. J.) Undesigned Coincidences in the Writings of the Old and New Testament, an Argument of their Veracity : containing the Books of Moses, Historical and Prophetical Scriptures, and the Gospels and Acts. 8th Edition. Post 8vo. 6s.

———— History of the Church in the First Three Centuries. Third Edition. Post 8vo. 7s. 6d.

———— Parish Priest; His Duties, Acquirements and Obligations. Fourth Edition. Post 8vo. 7s. 6d.

———— Lectures on the Right Use of the Early Fathers. Second Edition. 8vo. 15s.

———— Plain Sermons Preached to a Country Congregation. Second Edition. 3 Vols. Post 8vo. 7s. 6d. each.

———— Essays on various subjects. 8vo. 12s.

BISSET'S (ANDREW) History of England during the Interregnum, from the Death of Charles I. to the Battle of Dunbar, 1648—50. Chiefly from the MSS. in the State Paper Office. 8vo. 15s.

BLAKISTON'S (Capt.) Narrative of the Expedition sent to explore the Upper Waters of the Yang-Tsze. Illustrations. 8vo. 18s.

BLOMFIELD'S (Bishop) Memoir, with Selections from his Correspondence. By his Son. 2nd Edition. Portrait, post 8vo. 12s.

BOOK OF COMMON PRAYER. Illustrated with Coloured Borders, Initial Letters, and Woodcuts. A new edition. 8vo. 18s. cloth; 31s. 6d. calf; 36s. morocco.

BORROW'S (George) Bible in Spain; or the Journeys, Adventures, and Imprisonments of an Englishman in an Attempt to circulate the Scriptures in the Peninsula. 3 Vols. Post 8vo. 27s.; or Popular Edition, 16mo, 3s. 6d.

———— Zincali, or the Gipsies of Spain; their Manners, Customs, Religion, and Language. 2 Vols. Post 8vo. 18s.; or Popular Edition, 16mo, 3s. 6d.

———— Lavengro; The Scholar—The Gipsy—and the Priest. Portrait. 3 Vols. Post 8vo. 30s.

———— Romany Rye; a Sequel to Lavengro. Second Edition. 2 Vols. Post 8vo. 21s.

BOSWELL'S (James) Life of Samuel Johnson, LL.D. Including the Tour to the Hebrides. Edited by Mr. Croker. Portraits. Royal 8vo. 10s.

BRACE'S (C. L.) History of the Races of the Old World. Designed as a Manual of Ethnology. Post 8vo. 9s.

BRAY'S (Mrs.) Life of Thomas Stothard, R.A. With Personal Reminiscences. Illustrated with Portrait and 60 Woodcuts of his chief works. 4to.

BREWSTER'S (Sir David) Martyrs of Science, or the Lives of Galileo, Tycho Brahe, and Kepler. Fourth Edition. Fcap. 8vo. 4s. 6d.

———— More Worlds than One. The Creed of the Philosopher and the Hope of the Christian. Eighth Edition. Post 8vo. 6s.

———— Stereoscope: its History, Theory, Construction, and Application to the Arts and to Education. Woodcuts. 12mo. 5s. 6d.

———— Kaleidoscope: its History, Theory, and Construction, with its application to the Fine and Useful Arts. Second Edition. Woodcuts. Post 8vo. 5s. 6d.

BRINE'S (Capt.) Narrative of the Rise and Progress of the Taeping Rebellion in China. Plans. Post 8vo. 10s. 6d.

BRITISH ASSOCIATION REPORTS. 8vo. York and Oxford, 1831-32, 13s. 6d. Cambridge, 1833, 12s. Edinburgh, 1834, 15s. Dublin, 1835, 13s. 6d. Bristol, 1836, 12s. Liverpool, 1837, 16s. 6d. Newcastle, 1838, 15s. Birmingham, 1839, 13s. 6d. Glasgow, 1840, 15s. Plymouth, 1841, 13s. 6d. Manchester, 1842, 10s. 6d. Cork, 1843, 12s. York, 1844, 20s. Cambridge, 1845, 12s. Southampton, 1846, 15s. Oxford, 1847, 18s. Swansea, 1848, 9s. Birmingham, 1849, 10s. Edinburgh, 1850, 15s. Ipswich, 1851, 16s. 6d. Belfast, 1852, 15s. Hull, 1853, 10s. 6d. Liverpool, 1854, 18s. Glasgow, 1855, 15s.; Cheltenham, 1856, 18s.; Dublin, 1857, 15s.; Leeds, 1858, 20s. Aberdeen, 1859, 15s. Oxford, 1860, 25s. Manchester, 1861, 15s. Cambridge, 1862, 20s. Newcastle, 1863.

BRITISH CLASSICS. A New Series of Standard English Authors, printed from the most correct text, and edited with notes. 8vo.

Already Published.

I. GOLDSMITH'S WORKS. Edited by Peter Cunningham, F.S.A. Vignettes. 4 Vols. 30s.

II. GIBBON'S DECLINE AND FALL OF THE ROMAN EMPIRE. Edited by William Smith, LL.D Portrait and Maps. 8 Vols. 60s.

III. JOHNSON'S LIVES OF THE ENGLISH POETS. Edited by Peter Cunningham, F.S.A. 3 Vols. 22s. 6d.

IV. BYRON'S POETICAL WORKS. Edited, with Notes. 6 vols. 45s.

In Preparation.

WORKS OF POPE. With Life, Introductions, and Notes, by Rev. Whitwell Elwin. Portrait.

HUME'S HISTORY OF ENGLAND. Edited, with Notes.

LIFE AND WORKS OF SWIFT. Edited by John Forster.

BROUGHTON'S (Lord) Journey through Albania and other Provinces of Turkey in Europe and Asia, to Constantinople, 1809—10. *Third Edition.* Illustrations. 2 Vols. 8vo. 30s.

———— Visits to Italy. *3rd Edition.* 2 vols. Post 8vo. 18s.

BUBBLES FROM THE BRUNNEN OF NASSAU. By an Old Man. *Sixth Edition.* 16mo. 5s.

BUNYAN (John) and Oliver Cromwell. Select Biographies. By Robert Southey. Post 8vo. 2s.

BUONAPARTE'S (Napoleon) Confidential Correspondence with his Brother Joseph, sometime King of Spain. *Second Edition.* 2 vols. 8vo. 26s.

BURGON'S (Rev. J. W.) Memoir of Patrick Fraser Tytler. *Second Edition.* Post 8vo. 9s.

———— Letters from Rome, written to Friends at Home. Illustrations. Post 8vo. 12s.

BURN'S (Lieut.-Col.) French and English Dictionary of Naval and Military Technical Terms. *Fourth Edition.* Crown 8vo. 15s.

BURNS' (Robert) Life. By John Gibson Lockhart. Fifth Edition. Fcap. 8vo. 3s.

BURR'S (G. D.) Instructions in Practical Surveying, Topographical Plan Drawing, and on sketching ground without Instruments. *Fourth Edition.* Woodcuts. Post 8vo. 6s.

BUTTMAN'S LEXILOGUS; a Critical Examination of the Meaning of numerous Greek Words, chiefly in Homer and Hesiod. Translated by Rev. J. R. Fishlake. *Fifth Edition.* 8vo. 12s.

BUXTON'S (Sir Fowell) Memoirs. With Selections from his Correspondence. By his Son. Portrait. *Fifth Edition.* 8vo. 16s. *Abridged Edition,* Portrait. Fcap. 8vo. 2s. 6d.

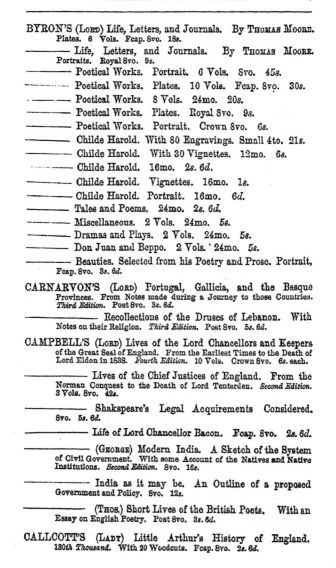

BYRON'S (Lord) Life, Letters, and Journals. By Thomas Moore. Plates. 6 Vols. Fcap. 8vo. 18s.

———— Life, Letters, and Journals. By Thomas Moore. Portraits. Royal 8vo. 9s.

———— Poetical Works. Portrait. 6 Vols. 8vo. 45s.

———— Poetical Works. Plates. 10 Vols. Fcap. 8vo. 30s.

———— Poetical Works. 8 Vols. 24mo. 20s.

———— Poetical Works. Plates. Royal 8vo. 9s.

———— Poetical Works. Portrait. Crown 8vo. 6s.

———— Childe Harold. With 80 Engravings. Small 4to. 21s.

———— Childe Harold. With 30 Vignettes. 12mo. 6s.

———— Childe Harold. 16mo. 2s. 6d.

———— Childe Harold. Vignettes. 16mo. 1s.

———— Childe Harold. Portrait. 16mo. 6d.

———— Tales and Poems. 24mo. 2s. 6d.

———— Miscellaneous. 2 Vols. 24mo. 5s.

———— Dramas and Plays. 2 Vols. 24mo. 5s.

———— Don Juan and Beppo. 2 Vols. 24mo. 5s.

———— Beauties. Selected from his Poetry and Prose. Portrait. Fcap. 8vo. 3s. 6d.

CARNARVON'S (Lord) Portugal, Gallicia, and the Basque Provinces. From Notes made during a Journey to those Countries. *Third Edition.* Post 8vo. 3s. 6d.

———————— Recollections of the Druses of Lebanon. With Notes on their Religion. *Third Edition.* Post 8vo. 5s. 6d.

CAMPBELL'S (Lord) Lives of the Lord Chancellors and Keepers of the Great Seal of England. From the Earliest Times to the Death of Lord Eldon in 1838. *Fourth Edition.* 10 Vols. Crown 8vo. 6s. each.

———————— Lives of the Chief Justices of England. From the Norman Conquest to the Death of Lord Tenterden. *Second Edition.* 3 Vols. 8vo. 42s.

———————— Shakspeare's Legal Acquirements Considered. 8vo. 5s. 6d.

———————— Life of Lord Chancellor Bacon. Fcap. 8vo. 2s. 6d.

———————— (George) Modern India. A Sketch of the System of Civil Government. With some Account of the Natives and Native Institutions. *Second Edition.* 8vo. 16s.

———————— India as it may be. An Outline of a proposed Government and Policy. 8vo. 12s.

———————— (Thos.) Short Lives of the British Poets. With an Essay on English Poetry. Post 8vo. 3s. 6d.

CALLCOTT'S (Lady) Little Arthur's History of England. 130th *Thousand.* With 20 Woodcuts. Fcap. 8vo. 2s. 6d.

CASTLEREAGH (The) DESPATCHES, from the commencement of the official career of the late Viscount Castlereagh to the close of his life. Edited by the MARQUIS OF LONDONDERRY. 12 Vols. 8vo. 14s. each.

CATHCART'S (Sir George) Commentaries on the War in Russia and Germany, 1812-13. Plans. 8vo. 14s.

CAVALCASELLE AND CROWE'S New History of Painting in Italy, from the Second to the Sixteenth Century, from recent researches in the Archives, as well as from personal inspection of the Works of Art in that Country. With 70 Illustrations. Vols. I. and II. 8vo. 42s.

———————————— Notices of the Lives and Works of the Early Flemish Painters. Woodcuts. Post 8vo. 12s.

CHAMBERS' (G. F.) Handbook of Descriptive and Practical Astronomy. Illustrations. Post 8vo. 12s.

CHARMED ROE (The); or, The Story of the Little Brother and Sister. By OTTO SPECKTER. Plates. 16mo. 5s.

CHURTON'S (Archdeacon) Gongora. An Historical Essay on the Age of Philip III. and IV. of Spain. With Translations. Portrait. 2 Vols. Small 8vo. 15s.

CLAUSEWITZ'S (Carl Von) Campaign of 1812, in Russia. Translated from the German by LORD ELLESMERE. Map. 8vo. 10s. 6d.

CLIVE'S (Lord) Life. By Rev. G. R. GLEIG, M.A. Post 8vo. 3s. 6d.

COLCHESTER (The) PAPERS. The Diary and Correspondence of Charles Abbott, Lord Colchester, Speaker of the House of Commons, 1802-1817. Edited by His Son. Portrait. 3 Vols. 8vo. 42s.

COLERIDGE'S (Samuel Taylor) Table-Talk. *Fourth Edition.* Portrait. Fcap. 8vo. 6s.

COLONIAL LIBRARY. [See Home and Colonial Library.]

COOK'S (Rev. Canon) Sermons Preached at Lincoln's Inn Chapel, and on Special Occasions. 8vo. 9s.

COOKERY (Modern Domestic). Founded on Principles of Economy and Practical Knowledge, and adapted for Private Families. By a Lady. *New Edition.* Woodcuts. Fcap. 8vo. 5s.

CORNWALLIS (The) Papers and Correspondence during the American War,—Administrations in India,—Union with Ireland, and Peace of Amiens. Edited by CHARLES ROSS. *Second Edition.* 3 Vols. 8vo. 63s.

COWPER'S (Mary Countess) Diary while Lady of the Bedchamber to Caroline Princess of Wales, 1714—20. *Second Edition.* Portrait. 8vo. 10s. 6d.

CRABBE'S (Rev. George) Life, Letters, and Journals. By his Son. Portrait. Fcap. 8vo. 3s.

——————— Life and Poetical Works. Plates. 8 Vols. Fcap. 8vo. 24s.

——————— Life and Poetical Works. Plates. Royal 8vo. 7s.

CROKER'S (J. W.) Progressive Geography for Children. *Fifth Edition.* 18mo. 1s. 6d.

———— Stories for Children, Selected from the History of England. *Fifteenth Edition.* Woodcuts. 16mo. 2s. 6d.

———— Boswell's Life of Johnson. Including the Tour to the Hebrides. Portraits. Royal 8vo. 10s.

———— Essays on the Early Period of the French Revolution. 8vo. 15s.

———— Historical Essay on the Guillotine. Fcap. 8vo. 1s.

CROMWELL (OLIVER) and John Bunyan. By ROBERT SOUTHEY. Post 8vo. 2s.

CROWE'S AND CAVALCASELLE'S Notices of the Early Flemish Painters; their Lives and Works. Woodcuts. Post 8vo. 12s.

———— History of Painting in Italy, from 2nd to 16th Century. Derived from Historical Researches as well as inspection of the Works of Art in that Country. With 70 Illustrations. Vols. I. and II. 8vo. 42s.

CUNNINGHAM'S (ALLAN) Poems and Songs. Now first collected and arranged, with Biographical Notice. 24mo. 2s. 6d.

CURETON (REV. W.) Remains of a very Ancient Recension of the Four Gospels in Syriac, hitherto unknown in Europe. Discovered, Edited, and Translated. 4to. 24s.

CURTIUS' (PROFESSOR) Student's Greek Grammar, for the use of Colleges and the Upper Forms. Translated under the Author's revision. Edited by DR. WM. SMITH. Post 8vo. 7s. 6d.

———— Smaller Greek Grammar for the use of the Middle and Lower Forms, abridged from the above. 12mo. 3s. 6d.

———— First Greek Course; containing Delectus, Exercise Book, and Vocabularies. 12mo. 3s. 6d.

CURZON'S (HON. ROBERT) ARMENIA AND ERZEROUM. A Year on the Frontiers of Russia, Turkey, and Persia. *Third Edition.* Woodcuts. Post 8vo. 7s. 6d.

CUST'S (GENERAL) Annals of the Wars of the 18th & 19th Centuries. 9 Vols. Fcap. 8vo. 5s. each.

———— Lives and Characters of the Warriors of All Nations who have Commanded Fleets and Armies before the Enemy. 8vo.

DARWIN'S (CHARLES) Journal of Researches into the Natural History of the Countries visited during a Voyage round the World. Post 8vo. 9s.

———— Origin of Species by Means of Natural Selection; or, the Preservation of Favoured Races in the Struggle for Life. Post 8vo. 14s.

———— Fertilization of Orchids through Insect Agency, and as to the good of Intercrossing. Woodcuts. Post 8vo. 9s.

DAVIS'S (NATHAN) Visit to the Ruined Cities of Numidia and Carthaginia. Illustrations. 8vo. 16s.

DAVY'S (SIR HUMPHRY) Consolations in Travel; or, Last Days of a Philosopher. *Fifth Edition.* Woodcuts. Fcap. 8vo. 6s.

———— Salmonia; or, Days of Fly Fishing. *Fourth Edition.* Woodcuts. Fcap. 8vo. 6s.

DELEPIERRE'S (Octave) History of Flemish Literature. From the Twelfth Century. 8vo. 9s.

DENNIS' (George) Cities and Cemeteries of Etruria. Plates. 2 Vols. 8vo. 42s.

DERBY'S (Edward Earl of) Translation of the Iliad of Homer into English Blank Verse. 2 Vols. 8vo. 24s.

DIXON'S (Hepworth) Story of the Life of Lord Bacon. Portrait. Fcap. 8vo. 7s. 6d.

DOG-BREAKING; the Most Expeditious, Certain, and Easy Method, whether great excellence or only mediocrity be required. By Lieut.-Gen. Hutchinson. *Fourth and Revised Edition.* With additional Woodcuts. Crown 8vo.

DOMESTIC MODERN COOKERY. Founded on Principles of Economy and Practical Knowledge, and adapted for Private Families. *New Edition.* Woodcuts. Fcap. 8vo. 5s.

DOUGLAS'S (General Sir Howard) Life and Adventures; From Notes, Conversations, and Correspondence. By S. W. Fullom. Portrait. 8vo. 15s.

————— On the Theory and Practice of Gunnery. *5th Edition.* Plates. 8vo. 21s.

————— Military Bridges, and the Passages of Rivers in Military Operations. *Third Edition.* Plates. 8vo. 21s.

————— Naval Warfare with Steam. *Second Edition.* 8vo. 8s. 6d.

————— Modern Systems of Fortification, with special reference to the Naval, Littoral, and Internal Defence of England. Plans. 8vo. 12s.

DRAKE'S (Sir Francis) Life, Voyages, and Exploits, by Sea and Land. By John Barrow. *Third Edition.* Post 8vo. 2s.

DRINKWATER'S (John) History of the Siege of Gibraltar, 1779-1783. With a Description and Account of that Garrison from the Earliest Periods. Post 8vo. 2s.

DU CHAILLU'S (Paul B.) EQUATORIAL AFRICA, with Accounts of the Gorilla, the Nest-building Ape, Chimpanzee, Crocodile, &c. Illustrations. 8vo. 21s.

DUFFERIN'S (Lord) Letters from High Latitudes, being some Account of a Yacht Voyage to Iceland, &c., in 1856. *Fourth Edition.* Woodcuts. Post 8vo. 9s.

DYER'S (Thomas H.) History of Modern Europe, from the taking of Constantinople by the Turks to the close of the War in the Crimea. 4 Vols. 8vo. 60s.

EASTLAKE'S (Sir Charles) Italian Schools of Painting. From the German of Kugler. Edited, with Notes. *Third Edition.* Illustrated from the Old Masters. 2 Vols. Post 8vo. 30s.

EASTWICK'S (E. B.) Handbook for Bombay and Madras, with Directions for Travellers, Officers, &c. Map. 2 Vols. Post 8vo. 24s.

EDWARDS' (W. H.) Voyage up the River Amazon, including a Visit to Para. Post 8vo. 2s.

ELDON'S (LORD) Public and Private Life, with Selections from his Correspondence and Diaries. By HORACE TWISS. *Third Edition.* Portrait. 2 Vols. Post 8vo. 21s.

ELLIS (REV. W.) Visits to Madagascar, including a Journey to the Capital, with notices of Natural History, and Present Civilisation of the People. *Fifth Thousand.* Map and Woodcuts. 8vo. 16s.

———— (MRS.) Education of Character, with Hints on Moral Training. Post 8vo. 7s. 6d.

ELLESMERE'S (LORD) Two Sieges of Vienna by the Turks. Translated from the German. Post 8vo. 2s.

———————— Campaign of 1812 in Russia, from the German of General Carl Von Clausewitz. Map. 8vo. 10s. 6d.

———————— Poems. Crown 4to. 24s.

———————— Essays on History, Biography, Geography, and Engineering. 8vo. 12s.

ELPHINSTONE'S (HON. MOUNTSTUART) History of India—the Hindoo and Mahomedan Periods. *Fourth Edition.* Map. 8vo. 18s.

ENGEL'S (CARL) Music of the Most Ancient Nations; particularly of the Assyrians, Egyptians, and Hebrews; with Special Reference to the Discoveries in Western Asia and in Egypt. With 100 Illustrations. 8vo. 16s.

ENGLAND (HISTORY OF) from the Peace of Utrecht to the Peace of Versailles, 1713—83. By LORD MAHON (Earl Stanhope). *Library Edition,* 7 Vols. 8vo. 93s.; or *Popular Edition,* 7 Vols. Post 8vo. 35s.

———————— From the First Invasion by the Romans, down to the 14th year of Queen Victoria's Reign. By MRS. MARKHAM. *118th Edition.* Woodcuts. 12mo. 6s.

———————— (THE STUDENT'S HUME). A History of England from the Earliest Times. Based on the History by DAVID HUME. Corrected and continued to 1858. Edited by WM. SMITH, LL.D. Woodcuts. Post 8vo. 7s. 6d.

ENGLISHWOMAN IN AMERICA. Post 8vo. 10s. 6d.

ESKIMAUX and English Vocabulary, for Travellers in the Arctic Regions. 16mo. 3s. 6d.

ESSAYS FROM "THE TIMES." Being a Selection from the LITERARY PAPERS which have appeared in' that Journal. *Seventh Thousand.* 2 vols. Fcap. 8vo. 8s.

EXETER'S (BISHOP OF) Letters to the late Charles Butler, on the Theological parts of his Book of the Roman Catholic Church; with Remarks on certain Works of Dr. Milner and Dr. Lingard, and on some parts of the Evidence of Dr. Doyle. *Second Edition.* 8vo. 16s.

FAMILY RECEIPT-BOOK. A Collection of a Thousand Valuable and Useful Receipts. Fcap. 8vo. 5s. 6d.

FARRAR'S (REV. A. S.) Critical History of Free Thought in reference to the Christian Religion. Being the Bampton Lectures, 1862. 8vo. 16s.

———————— (F. W.) Origin of Language, based on Modern Researches. Fcap. 8vo. 5s.

FEATHERSTONHAUGH'S (G. W.) Tour through the Slave States of North America, from the River Potomac to Texas and the Frontiers of Mexico. Plates. 2 Vols. 8vo. 26s.

FERGUSSON'S (JAMES) Palaces of Nineveh and Persepolis Restored. Woodcuts. 8vo. 16s.

———— History of the Modern Styles of Architecture, completing the above work. With 312 Illustrations. 8vo. 31s. 6d.

FISHER'S (REV. GEORGE) Elements of Geometry, for the Use of Schools. *Fifth Edition.* 18mo. 1s. 6d.

———— First Principles of Algebra, for the Use of Schools. *Fifth Edition.* 18mo. 1s. 6d.

FLOWER GARDEN (THE). By REV. THOS. JAMES. Fcap. 8vo. 1s.

FONNEREAU'S (T. G.) Diary of a Dutiful Son. Fcap. 8vo. 4s. 6d.

FORBES' (C. S.) Iceland; its Volcanoes, Geysers, and Glaciers. Illustrations. Post 8vo. 14s.

FORD'S (RICHARD) Handbook for Spain, Andalusia, Ronda, Valencia, Catalonia, Granada, Gallicia, Arragon, Navarre, &c. *Third Edition.* 2 Vols. Post 8vo. 30s.

———— Gatherings from Spain. Post 8vo. 3s. 6d.

FORSTER'S (JOHN) Arrest of the Five Members by Charles the First. A Chapter of English History re-written. Post 8vo. 12s.

———— Grand Remonstrance, 1641. With an Essay on English freedom under the Plantagenet and Tudor Sovereigns. *Second Edition.* Post 8vo. 12s.

———— Oliver Cromwell, Daniel De Foe, Sir Richard Steele, Charles Churchill, Samuel Foote. *Third Edition.* Post 8vo. 12s.

FORSYTH'S (WILLIAM) Life and Times of Cicero. With Selections from his Correspondence and his Orations. Illustrations. 2 Vols. Post 8vo. 18s.

FORTUNE'S (ROBERT) Narrative of Two Visits to the Tea Countries of China, 1843-52. *Third Edition.* Woodcuts. 2 Vols. Post 8vo. 18s.

———— Third Visit to China. 1853-6. Woodcuts. 8vo. 16s.

———— Yedo and Peking. With Notices of the Agriculture and Trade of Japan and China. Illustrations. 8vo. 16s.

FOSS' (Edward) Judges of England. With Sketches of their Lives, and Notices of the Courts at Westminster, from the Conquest to the Present Time. 9 Vols. 8vo. 114s.

FRANCE (HISTORY OF). From the Conquest by the Gauls to the Death of Louis Philippe. By Mrs. MARKHAM. 56th Thousand. Woodcuts. 12mo. 6s.

———— (THE STUDENT'S HISTORY OF). From the Earliest Times to the Establishment of the Second Empire, 1852. By W. H. PEARSON. Edited by WM. SMITH, LL.D. Woodcuts. Post 8vo. 7s. 6d.

FRENCH (THE) in Algiers; The Soldier of the Foreign Legion— and the Prisoners of Abd-el-Kadir. Translated by Lady DUFF GORDON. Post 8vo. 2s.

GALTON'S (FRANCIS) Art of Travel ; or, Hints on the Shifts and Contrivances available in Wild Countries. *Third Edition.* Woodcuts. Post 8vo. 7s. 6d.

GEOGRAPHY (THE STUDENT'S MANUAL OF ANCIENT). By Rev. W. L. BEVAN. Edited by WM. SMITH, LL.D. Woodcuts. Post 8vo. 7s. 6d.

——————— Journal of the Royal Geographical Society of London. 8vo.

GERMANY (HISTORY OF). From the Invasion by Marius, to the present time. By Mrs. MARKHAM. *Fifteenth Thousand.* Woodcuts. 12mo. 6s.

GIBBON'S (EDWARD) History of the Decline and Fall of the Roman Empire. *A New Edition.* Preceded by his Autobiography. Edited, with Notes, by Dr. WM. SMITH. Maps. 8 Vols. 8vo. 60s.

——————— (The Student's Gibbon); Being an Epitome of the above work, incorporating the Researches of Recent Commentators. By Dr. WM. SMITH. *Ninth Thousand.* Woodcuts. Post 8vo. 7s. 6d.

GIFFARD'S (EDWARD) Deeds of Naval Daring ; or, Anecdotes of the British Navy. New Edition. Fcap. 8vo. 3s. 6d.

GOLDSMITH'S (OLIVER) Works. A New Edition. Printed from the last editions revised by the Author. Edited by PETER CUNNINGHAM. Vignettes. 4 Vols. 8vo. 30s. (Murray's British Classics.)

GLADSTONE'S (RIGHT HON. W. E.) Financial Statements of 1853, 60, 63, and 64 ; also his Speeches on Tax-Bills, 1861, and on Charities, 1863. *Second Edition.* 8vo. 12s.

——————— Wedgwood : an Address delivered at Burslem. Woodcuts. Post 8vo. 2s.

GLEIG'S (REV. G. R.) Campaigns of the British Army at Washington and New Orleans. Post 8vo. 2s.

——————— Story of the Battle of Waterloo. Post 8vo. 3s. 6d.

——————— Narrative of Sale's Brigade in Affghanistan. Post 8vo. 2s.

——————— Life of Robert Lord Clive. Post 8vo. 3s. 6d.

——————— Life and Letters of Sir Thomas Munro. Post 8vo 3s. 6d.

GORDON'S (SIR ALEX. DUFF) Sketches of German Life, and Scenes from the War of Liberation. From the German. Post 8vo. 3s. 6d.

——————— (LADY DUFF) Amber-Witch : A Trial for Witchcraft. From the German. Post 8vo. 2s.

——————— French in Algiers. 1. The Soldier of the Foreign Legion. 2. The Prisoners of Abd-el-Kadir. From the French. Post 8vo. 2s.

GOUGER'S (HENRY) Personal Narrative of Two Years' Imprisonment in Burmah. *Second Edition.* Woodcuts. Post 8vo. 12s.

GRAMMAR (THE STUDENT'S GREEK.) For Colleges, and the Upper Forms. By PROFESSOR CURTIUS. Translated under the Revision of the Author. Edited by WM. SMITH, LL.D. Post 8vo. 7s. 6d.

——————— (THE STUDENT'S LATIN). For Colleges and the Upper Forms. By WM. SMITH, LL.D, Post 8vo. 7s. 6d.

GREECE (THE STUDENT'S HISTORY OF). From the Earliest Times to the Roman Conquest. By WM. SMITH, LL.D. Woodcuts. Post 8vo. 7s. 6d.

GRENVILLE (THE) PAPERS. Being the Public and Private Correspondence of George Grenville, including his PRIVATE DIARY. Edited by W. J. SMITH. 4 Vols. 8vo. 16s. each.

GREY (EARL) on Parliamentary Government and Reform. A New Edition, containing Suggestions for the Improvement of our Representative System, and an Examination of the Reform Bills of 1859—61. 8vo. 9s.

GREY'S (SIR GEORGE) Polynesian Mythology, and Ancient Traditional History of the New Zealand Race. Woodcuts. Post 8vo. 10s. 6d.

GROTE'S (GEORGE) History of Greece. From the Earliest Times to the close of the generation contemporary with the death of Alexander the Great. *Fourth Edition.* Maps. 8 vols. 8vo. 112s.

———— PLATO, and the other Companions of Socrates. 3 Vols. 8vo.

———— (MRS.) Memoir of Ary Scheffer. Post 8vo. 8s. 6d.

———— Collected Papers. 8vo. 10s. 6d.

GUIZOT'S (M.) Meditations on Christianity. Containing 1. NATURAL PROBLEMS. 2. CHRISTIAN DOGMAS. 3. THE SUPERNATURAL. 4. LIMITS OF SCIENCE. 5. REVELATION. 6. INSPIRATION OF HOLY SCRIPTURE. 7. GOD ACCORDING TO THE BIBLE. 8. JESUS CHRIST ACCORDING TO THE GOSPELS. Post 8vo. 9s. 6d.

HALLAM'S (HENRY) Constitutional History of England, from the Accession of Henry the Seventh to the Death of George the Second. *Seventh Edition.* 3 Vols. 8vo. 30s.

———— History of Europe during the Middle Ages. *Tenth Edition.* 3 Vols. 8vo. 30s.

———— Literary History of Europe, during the 15th, 16th and 17th Centuries. *Fourth Edition.* 3 Vols. 8vo. 36s.

———— Literary Essays and Characters. Fcap. 8vo. 2s.

———— Historical Works. Containing History of England,—Middle Ages of Europe,—Literary History of Europe. 10 Vols. Post 8vo. 6s each.

———— (ARTHUR) Remains; in Verse and Prose. With Preface, Memoir, and Portrait. Fcap. 8vo. 7s. 6d.

HAMILTON'S (JAMES) Wanderings in North Africa. Post 8vo. 12s.

HART'S ARMY LIST. (*Quarterly and Annually.*) 8vo. 10s. 6d. and 21s each.

HANNAH'S (Rev. Dr.) Bampton Lectures for 1863; the Divine and Human Elements in Holy Scripture. 8vo. 10s. 6d.

HAY'S (J. H. DRUMMOND) Western Barbary, its wild Tribes and savage Animals. Post 8vo. 2s.

HEAD'S (SIR FRANCIS) Horse and his Rider. Woodcuts. Post 8vo. 5s.

———— Rapid Journeys across the Pampas. Post 8vo. 2s.

———— Bubbles from the Brunnen of Nassau. 16mo. 5s.

———— Emigrant. Fcap. 8vo. 2s. 6d.

———— Stokers and Pokers; or, N.-Western Railway. Post 8vo. 2s.

———— Fortnight in Ireland. Map. 8vo. 12s.

———— (SIR EDMUND) Shall and Will; or, Future Auxiliary Verbs. Fcap. 8vo. 4s.

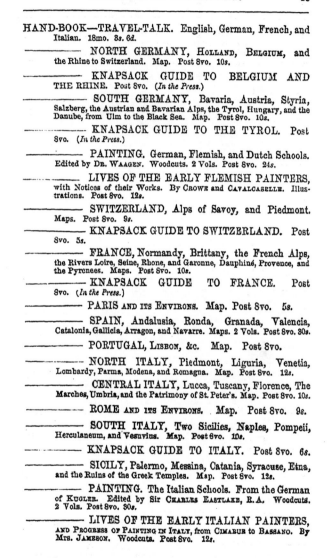

HAND-BOOK—TRAVEL-TALK. English, German, French, and Italian. 18mo. 3s. 6d.

——————— NORTH GERMANY, HOLLAND, BELGIUM, and the Rhine to Switzerland. Map. Post 8vo. 10s.

——————— KNAPSACK GUIDE TO BELGIUM AND THE RHINE. Post 8vo. (In the Press.)

——————— SOUTH GERMANY, Bavaria, Austria, Styria, Salzberg, the Austrian and Bavarian Alps, the Tyrol, Hungary, and the Danube, from Ulm to the Black Sea. Map. Post 8vo. 10s.

——————— KNAPSACK GUIDE TO THE TYROL. Post 8vo. (In the Press.)

——————— PAINTING. German, Flemish, and Dutch Schools. Edited by DR. WAAGEN. Woodcuts. 2 Vols. Post 8vo. 24s.

——————— LIVES OF THE EARLY FLEMISH PAINTERS, with Notices of their Works. By CROWE and CAVALCASELLE. Illustrations. Post 8vo. 12s.

——————— SWITZERLAND, Alps of Savoy, and Piedmont. Maps. Post 8vo. 9s.

——————— KNAPSACK GUIDE TO SWITZERLAND. Post 8vo. 5s.

——————— FRANCE, Normandy, Brittany, the French Alps, the Rivers Loire, Seine, Rhone, and Garonne, Dauphiné, Provence, and the Pyrenees. Maps. Post 8vo. 10s.

——————— KNAPSACK GUIDE TO FRANCE. Post 8vo. (In the Press.)

——————— PARIS AND ITS ENVIRONS. Map. Post 8vo. 5s.

——————— SPAIN, Andalusia, Ronda, Granada, Valencia, Catalonia, Gallicia, Arragon, and Navarre. Maps. 2 Vols. Post 8vo. 30s.

——————— PORTUGAL, LISBON, &c. Map. Post 8vo.

——————— NORTH ITALY, Piedmont, Liguria, Venetia, Lombardy, Parma, Modena, and Romagna. Map. Post 8vo. 12s.

——————— CENTRAL ITALY, Lucca, Tuscany, Florence, The Marches, Umbria, and the Patrimony of St. Peter's. Map. Post 8vo. 10s.

——————— ROME AND ITS ENVIRONS. Map. Post 8vo. 9s.

——————— SOUTH ITALY, Two Sicilies, Naples, Pompeii, Herculaneum, and Vesuvius. Map. Post 8vo. 10s.

——————— KNAPSACK GUIDE TO ITALY. Post 8vo. 6s.

——————— SICILY, Palermo, Messina, Catania, Syracuse, Etna, and the Ruins of the Greek Temples. Map. Post 8vo. 12s.

——————— PAINTING. The Italian Schools. From the German of KUGLER. Edited by Sir CHARLES EASTLAKE, R.A. Woodcuts. 2 Vols. Post 8vo. 30s.

——————— LIVES OF THE EARLY ITALIAN PAINTERS, AND PROGRESS OF PAINTING IN ITALY, from CIMABUE to BASSANO. By MRS. JAMESON. Woodcuts. Post 8vo. 12s.

HAND-BOOK—DICTIONARY OF ITALIAN PAINTERS. By
A LADY. Edited by RALPH WORNUM. With a Chart. Post 8vo. 6s. 6d.

——————— GREECE, the Ionian Islands, Albania, Thessaly,
and Macedonia. Maps. Post 8vo. 15s.

——————— TURKEY, Malta, Asia Minor, Constantinople,
Armenia, Mesopotamia, &c. Maps. Post 8vo. (In the Press.)

——————— EGYPT, Thebes, the Nile, Alexandria, Cairo,
the Pyramids, Mount Sinai, &c. Map. Post 8vo. 15s.

——————— SYRIA & PALESTINE, Peninsula of Sinai, Edom,
and Syrian Desert. Maps. 2 Vols. Post 8vo. 24s.

——————— BOMBAY AND MADRAS. Map. 2 Vols. Post
8vo. 24s.

——————— NORWAY, Map. Post 8vo. 5s.

——————— DENMARK, SWEDEN and NORWAY. Maps. Post
8vo. 15s.

——————— RUSSIA, THE BALTIC AND FINLAND. Maps. Post
8vo. 12s.

——————— MODERN LONDON. A Complete Guide to all
the Sights and Objects of Interest in the Metropolis. Map. 16mo.
3s. 6d.

——————— WESTMINSTER ABBEY. Woodcuts. 16mo. 1s.

——————— KENT AND SUSSEX, Canterbury, Dover, Rams-
gate, Sheerness, Rochester, Chatham, Woolwich, Brighton, Chichester,
Worthing, Hastings, Lewes, Arundel, &c. Map. Post 8vo. 10s.

——————— SURREY, HANTS, Kingston, Croydon, Reigate,
Guildford, Winchester, Southampton, Portsmouth, and Isle of Wight.
Maps. Post 8vo. 7s. 6d.

——————— BERKS, BUCKS, AND OXON, Windsor, Eton,
Reading, Aylesbury, Uxbridge, Wycombe, Henley, the City and Uni-
versity of Oxford, and the Descent of the Thames to Maidenhead and
Windsor. Map. Post 8vo. 7s. 6d.

——————— WILTS, DORSET, AND SOMERSET, Salisbury,
Chippenham, Weymouth, Sherborne, Wells, Bath, Bristol, Taunton,
&c. Map. Post 8vo. 7s. 6d.

——————— DEVON AND CORNWALL, Exeter, Ilfracombe,
Linton, Sidmouth, Dawlish, Teignmouth, Plymouth, Devonport, Tor-
quay, Launceston, Truro, Penzance, Falmouth, &c. Maps. Post 8vo.
7s. 6d.

——————— NORTH AND SOUTH WALES, Bangor, Car-
narvon, Beaumaris, Snowdon, Conway, Menai Straits, Carmarthen,
Pembroke, Tenby, Swansea, The Wye, &c. Maps. 2 Vols. Post 8vo.
12s.

——————— CATHEDRALS OF ENGLAND—Southern Divi-
sion, Winchester, Salisbury, Exeter, Wells, Chichester, Rochester,
Canterbury. With 110 Illustrations. 2 Vols. Crown 8vo. 24s.

——————— CATHEDRALS OF ENGLAND—Eastern Divi-
sion, Oxford, Peterborough, Norwich, Ely, and Lincoln. With 90
Illustrations. Crown 8vo. 18s.

——————— CATHEDRALS OF ENGLAND—Western Divi-
sion, Bristol, Gloucester, Hereford, Worcester, and Lichfield. With 50
Illustrations. Crown 8vo. 16s.

——————— FAMILIAR QUOTATIONS. From English Authors.
Third Edition. Fcap. 8vo. 5s.

HEBER'S (BISHOP) Journey through India. *Twelfth Edition.* 2 Vols. Post 8vo. 7s.

———— Poetical Works. *Sixth Edition.* Portrait. Fcap. 8vo. 6s.

HERODOTUS. A New English Version. Edited, with Notes and Essays, historical, ethnographical, and geographical. By Rev. G. RAWLINSON, assisted by SIR HENRY RAWLINSON and SIR J. G. WILKINSON. *Second Edition.* Maps and Woodcuts. 4 Vols. 8vo. 48s.

HESSEY (REV. DR.). Sunday—Its Origin, History, and Present Obligations. Being the Bampton Lectures for 1860. *Second Edition.* 8vo. 16s.

HICKMAN'S (WM.) Treatise on the Law and Practice of Naval Courts-Martial. 8vo. 10s. 6d.

HILLARD'S (G. S.) Six Months in Italy. 2 Vols. Post 8vo. 16s.

HOLLWAY'S (J. G.) Month in Norway. Fcap. 8vo. 2s.

HONEY BEE (THE). An Essay. By REV. THOMAS JAMES. Reprinted from the "Quarterly Review." Fcap. 8vo. 1s.

HOOK'S (DEAN) Church Dictionary. *Ninth Edition.* 8vo. 16s.

———— (THEODORE)Life. By J. G. LOCKHART. Reprinted from the "Quarterly Review." Fcap. 8vo. 1s.

HOOKER'S (Dr. J. D.) Himalayan Journals; or, Notes of an Oriental Naturalist in Bengal, the Sikkim and Nepal Himalayas, the Khasia Mountains, &c. *Second Edition.* Woodcuts. 2 Vols. Post 8vo. 18s.

HOPE'S (A. J. BERESFORD) English Cathedral of the Nineteenth Century. With Illustrations. 8vo. 12s.

HORACE (Works of). Edited by DEAN MILMAN. With 300 Woodcuts. Crown 8vo. 21s.

———— (Life of). By DEAN MILMAN. Woodcuts, and coloured Borders. 8vo. 9s.

HUME'S (THE STUDENT'S) History of England, from the Invasion of Julius Cæsar to the Revolution of 1688. Corrected and continued to 1858. Edited by Dr. Wm. Smith. Woodcuts. Post 8vo. 7s. 6d.

HUTCHINSON (GEN.) on the most expeditious, certain, and easy Method of Dog-Breaking. *Fourth Edition.* Enlarged and revised, with additional Illustrations. Crown 8vo.

HUTTON'S (H. E.) Principia Græca; an Introduction to the Study of Greek. Comprehending Grammar, Delectus, and Exercise-book, with Vocabularies. *Third Edition.* 12mo. 3s. 6d.

c

HOME AND COLONIAL LIBRARY. A Series of Works adapted for all circles and classes of Readers, having been selected for their acknowledged interest and ability of the Authors. Post 8vo. Published at 2s. and 3s. 6d. each, and arranged under two distinctive heads as follows :—

CLASS A.
HISTORY, BIOGRAPHY, AND HISTORIC TALES.

1. SIEGE OF GIBRALTAR. By JOHN DRINKWATER. 2s.
2. THE AMBER-WITCH. By LADY DUFF GORDON. 2s.
3. CROMWELL AND BUNYAN. By ROBERT SOUTHEY. 2s.
4. LIFE OF SIR FRANCIS DRAKE. By JOHN BARROW. 2s.
5. CAMPAIGNS AT WASHINGTON. By REV. G. R. GLEIG. 2s.
6. THE FRENCH IN ALGIERS. By LADY DUFF-GORDON. 2s.
7. THE FALL OF THE JESUITS. 2s.
8. LIVONIAN TALES. 2s.
9. LIFE OF CONDE. By LORD MAHON. 3s. 6d.
10. SALE'S BRIGADE. By REV. G. R. GLEIG. 2s.
11. THE SIEGES OF VIENNA. By LORD ELLESMERE. 2s.
12. THE WAYSIDE CROSS. By CAPT. MILMAN. 2s.
13. SKETCHES OF GERMAN LIFE. By SIR A. GORDON. 3s. 6d.
14. THE BATTLE OF WATERLOO. By REV. G. R. GLEIG. 3s. 6d.
15. AUTOBIOGRAPHY OF STEFFENS. 2s.
16. THE BRITISH POETS. By THOMAS CAMPBELL. 3s. 6d.
17. HISTORICAL ESSAYS. By LORD MAHON. 3s. 6d.
18. LIFE OF LORD CLIVE. By REV. G. R. GLEIG. 3s. 6d.
19. NORTH - WESTERN RAILWAY. By SIR F. B. HEAD. 2s.
20. LIFE OF MUNRO. By REV. G. R. GLEIG. 3s. 6d.

CLASS B.
VOYAGES, TRAVELS, AND ADVENTURES.

1. BIBLE IN SPAIN. By GEORGE BORROW. 3s. 6d.
2. GIPSIES OF SPAIN. By GEORGE BORROW. 3s. 6d.
3 & 4. JOURNALS IN INDIA. By BISHOP HEBER. 2 Vols. 7s.
5. TRAVELS IN THE HOLY LAND. By IRBY and MANGLES. 2s.
6. MOROCCO AND THE MOORS. By J. DRUMMOND HAY. 2s.
7. LETTERS FROM THE BALTIC. By a LADY. 2s.
8. NEW SOUTH WALES. By MRS. MEREDITH. 2s.
9. THE WEST INDIES. By M. G. LEWIS. 2s.
10. SKETCHES OF PERSIA. By SIR JOHN MALCOLM. 3s. 6d.
11. MEMOIRS OF FATHER RIPA. 2s.
12. 13. TYPEE AND OMOO. By HERMANN MELVILLE. 2 Vols. 7s.
14. MISSIONARY LIFE IN CANADA. By REV. J. ABBOTT. 2s.
15. LETTERS FROM MADRAS. By a LADY. 2s.
16. HIGHLAND SPORTS. By CHARLES ST. JOHN. 3s. 6d.
17. PAMPAS JOURNEYS. By SIR F. B. HEAD. 2s.
18. GATHERINGS FROM SPAIN. By RICHARD FORD. 3s. 6d.
19. THE RIVER AMAZON. By W. H. EDWARDS. 2s.
20. MANNERS & CUSTOMS OF INDIA. By REV. C. ACLAND. 2s.
21. ADVENTURES IN MEXICO. By G. F. RUXTON. 3s. 6d.
22. PORTUGAL AND GALLICIA. By LORD CARNARVON. 3s. 6d.
23. BUSH LIFE IN AUSTRALIA. By REV. H. W. HAYGARTH. 2s.
24. THE LIBYAN DESERT. By BAYLE ST. JOHN. 2s.
25. SIERRA LEONE. By a LADY. 3s. 6d.

₊ Each work may be had separately.

IRBY AND MANGLES' Travels in Egypt, Nubia, Syria, and the Holy Land. Post 8vo. 2s.

JAMES' (Rev. Thomas) Fables of Æsop. A New Translation, with Historical Preface. With 100 Woodcuts by Tenniel and Wolf. *Thirty-eighth Thousand.* Post 8vo. 2s. 6d.

JAMESON'S (Mrs.) Lives of the Early Italian Painters, from Cimabue to Bassano, and the Progress of Painting in Italy. *New Edition.* With Woodcuts. Post 8vo. 12s.

JESSE'S (Edward) Gleanings in Natural History. *Eighth Edition.* Fcp. 8vo. 6s.

JOHNSON'S (Dr. Samuel) Life. By James Boswell. Including the Tour to the Hebrides. Edited by the late Mr. Croker. Portraits. Royal 8vo. 10s.

——————— Lives of the most eminent English Poets. Edited by Peter Cunningham. 3 vols. 8vo. 22s. 6d. (Murray's British Classics.)

JOURNAL OF A NATURALIST. Woodcuts. Post 8vo. 9s. 6d.

KEN'S (Bishop) Life. By A Layman. *Second Edition.* Portrait. 2 Vols. 8vo. 18s.

——————— Exposition of the Apostles' Creed. Extracted from his "Practice of Divine Love." Fcap. 1s. 6d.

——————— Approach to the Holy Altar. Extracted from his " Manual of Prayer" and "Practice of Divine Love." Fcap. 8vo. 1s. 6d.

KING'S (Rev. S. W.) Italian Valleys of the Alps; a Tour through all the Romantic and less-frequented "Vals" of Northern Piedmont. Illustrations. Crown 8vo. 18s.

——————— (Rev. C. W.) Antique Gems; their Origin, Use, and Value, as Interpreters of Ancient History, and as illustrative of Ancient Art. Illustrations. 8vo. 42s.

KING EDWARD VIth's Latin Grammar; or, an Introduction to the Latin Tongue, for the Use of Schools. *Sixteenth Edition.* 12mo. 3s. 6d.

——————————————— First Latin Book; or, the Accidence, Syntax, and Prosody, with an English Translation for the Use of Junior Classes. *Fourth Edition.* 12mo. 2s. 6d.

KIRK'S (J. Foster) History of Charles the Bold, Duke of Burgundy. Portrait. 2 Vols. 8vo. 30s.

KERR'S (Robert) GENTLEMAN'S HOUSE; or, How to Plan English Residences, from the Parsonage to the Palace. With Tables of Accommodation and Cost, and a Series of Selected Views and Plans. 8vo. 21s.

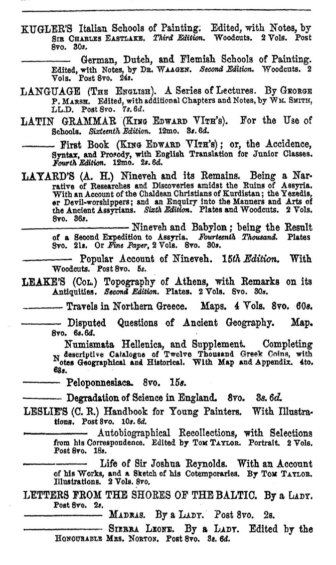

KUGLER'S Italian Schools of Painting; Edited, with Notes, by
SIR CHARLES EASTLAKE. *Third Edition.* Woodcuts. 2 Vols. Post
8vo. 30s.

—————— German, Dutch, and Flemish Schools of Painting.
Edited, with Notes, by DR. WAAGEN. *Second Edition.* Woodcuts. 2
Vols. Post 8vo. 24s.

LANGUAGE (THE ENGLISH). A Series of Lectures. By GEORGE
P. MARSH. Edited, with additional Chapters and Notes, by WM. SMITH,
LL.D. Post 8vo. 7s. 6d.

LATIN GRAMMAR (KING EDWARD VITH'S). For the Use of
Schools. *Sixteenth Edition.* 12mo. 3s. 6d.

—————— First Book (KING EDWARD VITH'S); or, the Accidence,
Syntax, and Prosody, with English Translation for Junior Classes.
Fourth Edition. 12mo. 2s. 6d.

LAYARD'S (A. H.) Nineveh and its Remains. Being a Narrative of Researches and Discoveries amidst the Ruins of Assyria.
With an Account of the Chaldean Christians of Kurdistan; the Yezedis,
or Devil-worshippers; and an Enquiry into the Manners and Arts of
the Ancient Assyrians. *Sixth Edition.* Plates and Woodcuts. 2 Vols.
8vo. 36s.

—————————————— Nineveh and Babylon; being the Result
of a Second Expedition to Assyria. *Fourteenth Thousand.* Plates
8vo. 21s. Or *Fine Paper,* 2 Vols. 8vo. 30s.

—————— Popular Account of Nineveh. *15th Edition.* With
Woodcuts. Post 8vo. 5s.

LEAKE'S (COL.) Topography of Athens, with Remarks on its
Antiquities. *Second Edition.* Plates. 2 Vols. 8vo. 30s.

—————— Travels in Northern Greece. Maps. 4 Vols. 8vo. 60s.

—————— Disputed Questions of Ancient Geography. Map.
8vo. 6s. 6d.

—————— Numismata Hellenica, and Supplement. Completing
a descriptive Catalogue of Twelve Thousand Greek Coins, with
Notes Geographical and Historical. With Map and Appendix. 4to.
63s.

—————— Peloponnesiaca. 8vo. 15s.

—————— Degradation of Science in England. 8vo. 3s. 6d.

LESLIE'S (C. R.) Handbook for Young Painters. With Illustrations. Post 8vo. 10s. 6d.

————————— Autobiographical Recollections, with Selections
from his Correspondence. Edited by TOM TAYLOR. Portrait. 2 Vols.
Post 8vo. 18s.

————————— Life of Sir Joshua Reynolds. With an Account
of his Works, and a Sketch of his Cotemporaries. By TOM TAYLOR.
Illustrations. 2 Vols. 8vo.

LETTERS FROM THE SHORES OF THE BALTIC. By a LADY.
Post 8vo. 2s.

————————————— MADRAS. By a LADY. Post 8vo. 2s.

————————————— SIERRA LEONE. By a LADY. Edited by the
HONOURABLE MRS. NORTON. Post 8vo. 3s. 6d.

LEWIS' (Sir G. C.) Essay on the Government of Dependencies. 8vo. 12s.

——— **Glossary of Provincial Words used in Herefordshire and** some of the adjoining Counties. 12mo. 4s. 6d.

——— **(M. G.) Journal of a Residence among the Negroes in the** West Indies. Post 8vo. 2s.

LIDDELL'S (Dean) History of Rome. From the Earliest Times to the Establishment of the Empire. With the History of Literature and Art. 2 Vols. 8vo. 28s.

——— **Student's History of Rome. Abridged from the** above Work. 25th Thousand. With Woodcuts. Post 8vo. 7s. 6d.

LINDSAY'S (Lord) Lives of the Lindsays; or, a Memoir of the Houses of Crawfurd and Balcarres. With Extracts from Official Papers and Personal Narratives. Second Edition. 3 Vols. 8vo. 24s.

——— **Report of the Claim of James, Earl of Crawford and** Balcarres, to the Original Dukedom of Montrose, created in 1488 Folio. 15s.

——— **Scepticism; a Retrogressive Movement in Theology** and Philosophy. 8vo. 9s.

LISPINGS from LOW LATITUDES; or, the Journal of the Hon. Impulsia Gushington. Edited by Lord Dufferin. With 24 Plates, 4to. 21s.

LITERATURE (English). A Manual for Students. By T. B. Shaw. Edited, with Notes and Illustrations, by Wm. Smith, LL.D. Post 8vo. 7s. 6d.

——— **(Choice Specimens of). Selected from the Chief** English Writers. By Thos. B. Shaw, M.A. Edited by Wm. Smith, LL.D. Post 8vo. 7s. 6d.

LITTLE ARTHUR'S HISTORY OF ENGLAND. By Lady Callcott. 120th Thousand. With 20 Woodcuts. Fcap. 8vo. 2s. 6d.

LIVINGSTONE'S (Rev. Dr.) Popular Account of his Missionary Travels in South Africa. Illustrations. Post 8vo. 6s.

——— **Narrative of an Expedition to the Zambezi and** its Tributaries; and of the Discovery of Lakes Shirwa and Nyassa. 1858-64. By David and Charles Livingstone. Map and Illustrations. 8vo.

LIVONIAN TALES. By the Author of "Letters from the Baltic." Post 8vo. 2s.

LOCKHART'S (J. G.) Ancient Spanish Ballads. Historical and Romantic. Translated, with Notes. Illustrated Edition. 4to. 21s. Or, Popular Edition, Post 8vo. 2s. 6d.

——— **Life of Robert Burns. Fifth Edition. Fcap. 8vo. 3s.**

LONDON'S (Bishop of) Dangers and Safeguards of Modern Theology. Containing Suggestions to the Theological Student under present difficulties. Second Edition. 8vo. 9s.

LOUDON'S (Mrs.) Instructions in Gardening for Ladies. With Directions and Calendar of Operations for Every Month. Eighth Edition. Woodcuts. Fcap. 8vo. 5s.

LUCAS' (SAMUEL) Secularia; or, Surveys on the Main Stream of History. 8vo. 12s.

LUCKNOW: a Lady's Diary of the Siege. *Fourth Thousand.* Fcap. 8vo. 4s. 6d.

LYELL'S (SIR CHARLES) Elements of Geology; or, the Ancient Changes of the Earth and its Inhabitants considered as illustrative of Geology. *Sixth Edition.* Woodcuts. 8vo. 18s.

———— Geological Evidences of the Antiquity of Man. *Third Edition.* Illustrations. 8vo. 14s.

LYTTELTON'S (LORD) Ephemera. Post 8vo. 10s. 6d.

LYTTON'S (SIR EDWARD BULWER) Poems. *New Edition.* Revised. Post 8vo. 10s. 6d.

MAHON'S (LORD) History of England, from the Peace of Utrecht to the Peace of Versailles, 1713—83. *Library Edition.* 7 Vols. 8vo. 93s. *Popular Edition,* 7 Vols. Post 8vo. 35s.

———— "Forty-Five;" a Narrative of the Rebellion in Scotland. Post 8vo. 3s.

———— History of British India from its Origin till the Peace of 1783. Post 8vo. 3s. 6d.

———— Spain under Charles the Second; 1690 to 1700. *Second Edition.* Post 8vo. 6s. 6d.

———— Life of William Pitt, with Extracts from his MS. Papers. *Second Edition.* Portraits. 4 Vols. Post 8vo. 42s.

———— Condé, surnamed the Great. Post 8vo. 3s. 6d.

———— Belisarius. *Second Edition.* Post 8vo. 10s. 6d.

———— Historical and Critical Essays. Post 8vo. 3s. 6d.

———— Miscellanies. *Second Edition.* Post 8vo. 5s. 6d.

———— Story of Joan of Arc. Fcap. 8vo. 1s.

———— Addresses. Fcap. 8vo. 1s.

McCLINTOCK'S (CAPT. SIR F. L.) Narrative of the Discovery of the Fate of Sir John Franklin and his Companions in the Arctic Seas. *Twelfth Thousand.* Illustrations. 8vo. 16s.

McCULLOCH'S (J. R.) Collected Edition of RICARDO's Political Works. With Notes and Memoir. *Second Edition.* 8vo. 16s.

MacDOUGALL (COL.) On Modern Warfare as Influenced by Modern Artillery. With Plans. Post 8vo. 12s.

MAINE (H. SUMNER) On Ancient Law: its Connection with the Early History of Society, and its Relation to Modern Ideas. *Second Edition.* 8vo. 12s.

MALCOLM'S (SIR JOHN) Sketches of Persia. *Third Edition.* Post 8vo. 3s. 6d.

MANSEL (REV. H. L.) Limits of Religious Thought Examined. Being the Bampton Lectures for 1858. *Fourth Edition.* Post 8vo. 7s. 6d.

MANSFIELD (SIR WILLIAM) On the Introduction of a Gold Currency into India: a Contribution to the Literature of Political Economy. 8vo. 3s. 6d.

MANTELL'S (GIDEON A.) Thoughts on Animalcules; or, the Invisible World, as revealed by the Microscope. *Second Edition.* Plates. 16mo. 6s.

MANUAL OF SCIENTIFIC ENQUIRY, Prepared for the Use of Officers and Travellers. By various Writers. Edited by Sir J. F. HERSCHEL and Rev. R. MAIN. *Third Edition.* Maps. Post 8vo. 9s. (*Published by order of the Lords of the Admiralty.*)

MARKHAM'S (MRS.) History of England. From the First Invasion by the Romans, down to the fourteenth year of Queen Victoria's Reign. 156th *Edition.* Woodcuts. 12mo. 6s.

———————— History of France. From the Conquest by the Gauls, to the Death of Louis Philippe. *Sixtieth Edition.* Woodcuts. 12mo. 6s.

———————— History of Germany. From the Invasion by Marius, to the present time. *Fifteenth Edition.* Woodcuts. 12mo. 6s.

———————— History of Greece. From the Earliest Times to the Roman Conquest. By Dr. WM. SMITH. Woodcuts. 16mo. 3s. 6d.

———————— History of Rome. From the Earliest Times to the Establishment of the Empire. By DR. WM. SMITH. Woodcuts. 16mo. 3s. 6d.

———————— (CLEMENTS, R.) Travels in Peru and India, for the purpose of collecting Cinchona Plants, and introducing Bark into India. Maps and Illustrations. 8vo. 16s.

MARKLAND'S (J. H.) Reverence due to Holy Places. *Third Edition.* Fcap. 8vo. 2s.

MARRYAT'S (JOSEPH) History of Modern and Mediæval Pottery and Porcelain. With a Description of the Manufacture. *Second Edition.* Plates and Woodcuts. 8vo. 31s. 6d.

———————— (HORACE) Jutland, the Danish Isles, and Copenhagen. Illustrations. 2 Vols. Post 8vo. 24s.

———————— Sweden and Isle of Gothland. Illustrations. 2 Vols. Post 8vo. 28s.

MATTHIÆ'S (AUGUSTUS) Greek Grammar for Schools. Abridged from the Larger Grammar. By Blomfield. *Ninth Edition.* Revised by EDWARDS. 12mo. 3s.

MAUREL'S (JULES) Essay on the Character, Actions, and Writings of the Duke of Wellington. *Second Edition.* Fcap. 8vo. 1s. 6d.

MAXIMS AND HINTS on Angling and Chess. By RICHARD PENN. Woodcuts. 12mo. 1s.

MAYNE'S (R. C.) Four Years in British Columbia and Vancouver Island. Its Forests, Rivers, Coasts, and Gold Fields, and Resources for Colonisation. Illustrations. 8vo. 16s.

MELVILLE'S (HERMANN) Typee and Omoo; or, Adventures amongst the Marquesas and South Sea Islands. 2 Vols. Post 8vo. 7s.

MEREDITH'S (MRS. CHARLES) Notes and Sketches of New South Wales. Post 8vo. 2s.

MESSIAH (THE): A Narrative of the Life, Travels, Death, Resurrection, and Ascension of our Blessed Lord. By A LAYMAN. Author of the "Life of Bishop Ken." Map. 8vo. 18s.

MICHIE'S (ALEXANDER) Siberian Overland Route from Peking to Petersburg, through the Deserts and Steppes of Mongolia, Tartary, &c. Maps and Illustrations. 8vo. 16s.

MILLS' (ARTHUR) India in 1858; A Summary of the Existing Administration. *Second Edition.* Map. 8vo. 10s. 6d.

———— **(REV. JOHN)** Three Months' Residence at Nablus, with an Account of the Modern Samaritans. Illustrations. Post 8vo. 10s. 6d.

MILMAN'S (DEAN) History of the Jews, from the Earliest Period, brought down to Modern Times. *New Edition.* 3 Vols. 8vo. 36s.

———— Christianity, from the Birth of Christ to the Abolition of Paganism in the Roman Empire. *New Edition.* 3 Vols. 8vo. 36s.

———— Latin Christianity; including that of the Popes to the Pontificate of Nicholas V. *New Edition.* 9 Vols. 8vo 84s.

———— Character and Conduct of the Apostles considered as an Evidence of Christianity. 8vo. 10s. 6d.

———— Life and Works of Horace. With 300 Woodcuts. Vols. Crown 8vo. 30s.

———— Poetical Works. Plates. 3 Vols. Fcap. 8vo. 18s.

———— Fall of Jerusalem. Fcap. 8vo. 1s.

———— **(CAPT. E. A.)** Wayside Cross. A Tale of the Carlist War. Post 8vo. 2s.

MILNES' (R. MONCKTON, LORD HOUGHTON) Poetical Works. Fcap. 8vo. 6s.

MODERN DOMESTIC COOKERY. Founded on Principles of Economy and Practical Knowledge and adapted for Private Families. *New Edition.* Woodcuts. Fcap. 8vo. 5s.

MOORE'S (THOMAS) Life and Letters of Lord Byron. Plates. 6 Vols. Fcap. 8vo. 18s.

———— Life and Letters of Lord Byron. Portraits. Royal 8vo. 9s.

MOTLEY'S (J. L.) History of the United Netherlands: from the Death of William the Silent to the Synod of Dort. Embracing the English-Dutch struggle against Spain; and a detailed Account of the Spanish Armada. Portraits. 2 Vols. 8vo. 30s.

MOUHOT'S (HENRI) Siam, Cambojia, and Lao; a Narrative of Travels and Discoveries. Illustrations. 2 vols. 8vo. 32s.

MOZLEY'S (REV. J. B.) Treatise on Predestination. 8vo. 14s.

———— Primitive Doctrine of Baptismal Regeneration. 8vo. 7s. 6d.

MUNDY'S (General) Pen and Pencil Sketches in India. *Third Edition.* Plates. Post 8vo. 7s. 6d.

———— (Admiral) Account of the Italian Revolution, with Notices of Garibaldi, Francis II., and Victor Emmanuel. Post 8vo. 12s.

MUNRO'S (General Sir Thomas) Life and Letters. By the Rev. G. R. Gleig. Post 8vo. 3s. 6d.

MURCHISON'S (Sir Roderick) Russia in Europe and the Ural Mountains. With Coloured Maps, Plates, Sections, &c. 2 Vols. Royal 4to.

———— Siluria ; or, a History of the Oldest Rocks containing Organic Remains. *Third Edition.* Map and Plates. 8vo. 42s.

MURRAY'S RAILWAY READING. Containing :—

Wellington. By Lord Ellesmere. 6d.	Balaam's Literary Essays. 2s.
Nimrod on the Chase. 1s.	Mahon's Joan of Arc. 1s.
Essays from "The Times." 2 Vols. 8s.	Head's Emigrant. 2s. 6d.
Music and Dress. 1s.	Nimrod on the Road. 1s.
Layard's Account of Nineveh. 5s.	Croker on the Guillotine. 1s.
Milman's Fall of Jerusalem. 1s.	Hollway's Norway. 2s.
Mahon's "Forty-Five." 3s.	Maurel's Wellington. 1s. 6d.
Life of Theodore Hook. 1s.	Campbell's Life of Bacon. 2s. 6d.
Deeds of Naval Daring. 3s. 6d.	The Flower Garden. 1s.
The Honey Bee. 1s.	Lockhart's Spanish Ballads. 2s. 6d.
James' Æsop's Fables. 2s. 6d.	Taylor's Notes from Life. 2s.
Nimrod on the Turf. 1s. 6d.	Rejected Addresses. 1s.
Art of Dining. 1s. 6d.	Penn's Hints on Angling. 1s.

MUSIC AND DRESS. By a Lady. Reprinted from the "Quarterly Review." Fcap. 8vo. 1s.

NAPIER'S (Sir Wm.) English Battles and Sieges of the Peninsular War. *Third Edition.* Portrait. Post 8vo. 10s. 6d.

———— Life and Letters. Edited by H. A. Bruce, M.P. Portraits. 2 Vols. Crown 8vo. 28s.

———— Life of General Sir Charles Napier; chiefly derived from his Journals and Letters. *Second Edition.* Portraits. 4 Vols. Post 8vo. 48s.

NAUTICAL ALMANACK. Royal 8vo. 2s. 6d. (*By Authority.*)

NAVY LIST. (*Published Quarterly, by Authority.*) 16mo. 2s. 6d.

NEW TESTAMENT (The) Illustrated by a Plain Explanatory Commentary, and authentic Views of Sacred Places, from Sketches and Photographs. Edited by Archdeacon Churton and Rev. Basil Jones. With 110 Illustrations. 2 Vols. Crown 8vo.

NEWDEGATE'S (C. N.) Customs' Tariffs of all Nations; collected and arranged up to the year 1855. 4to. 30s.

NICHOLLS' (Sir George) History of the English, Irish and Scotch Poor Laws. 4 Vols. 8vo.

———— (Rev. H. G.) Historical Account of the Forest of Dean. Woodcuts, &c. Post 8vo. 10s. 6d.

———— Personalities of the Forest of Dean, its successive Officials, Gentry, and Commonalty. Post 8vo. 3s. 6d.

NICOLAS' (Sir Harris) Historic Peerage of England. Exhibiting the Origin, Descent, and Present State of every Title of Peerage which has existed in this Country since the Conquest. By William Courthope. 8vo. 30s.

NIMROD On the Chace—The Turf—and The Road. Reprinted from the "Quarterly Review." Woodcuts. Fcap. 8vo. 3s. 6d.

O'CONNOR'S (R.) Field Sports of France; or, Hunting, Shooting, and Fishing on the Continent. Woodcuts. 12mo. 7s. 6d.

OXENHAM'S (Rev. W.) English Notes for Latin Elegiacs; designed for early Proficients in the Art of Latin Versification, with Prefatory Rules of Composition in Elegiae Metre. *Fourth Edition.* 12mo. 3s. 6d.

PARIS' (Dr.) Philosophy in Sport made Science in Earnest; or, the First Principles of Natural Philosophy inculcated by aid of the Toys and Sports of Youth. *Ninth Edition.* Woodcuts. Post 8vo. 7s. 6d.

PEEL'S (Sir Robert) Memoirs. Edited by Earl Stanhope and Mr. Cardwell. 2 Vols. Post 8vo. 7s. 6d. each.

PENN'S (Richard) Maxims and Hints for an Angler and Chessplayer. *New Edition.* Woodcuts. Fcap. 8vo. 1s.

PENROSE'S (F. C.) Principles of Athenian Architecture, and the Optical Refinements exhibited in the Construction of the Ancient Buildings at Athens, from a Survey. With 40 Plates. Folio. 5l. 5s.

PERCY'S (John, M.D.) Metallurgy of Iron and Steel; or, the Art of Extracting Metals from their Ores and adapting them to various purposes of Manufacture. Illustrations. 8vo. 42s.

PHILLIPP (Charles Spencer March) On Jurisprudence. 8vo. 12s.

PHILLIPS' (John) Memoirs of William Smith, the Geologist. Portrait. 8vo. 7s. 6d.

——— Geology of Yorkshire, The Coast, and Limestone District. Plates. 4to. Part I., 20s.—Part II., 30s.

——— Rivers, Mountains, and Sea Coast of Yorkshire. With Essays on the Climate, Scenery, and Ancient Inhabitants. *Second Edition*, Plates. 8vo. 15s.

PHILPOTT'S (Bishop) Letters to the late Charles Butler, on the Theological parts of his "Book of the Roman Catholic Church;" with Remarks on certain Works of Dr. Milner and Dr. Lingard, and on some parts of the Evidence of Dr. Doyle. *Second Edition.* 8vo. 16s.

POPE'S (Alexander) Life and Works. *A New Edition.* Containing nearly 500 unpublished Letters. Edited with a New Life, Introductions and Notes. By Rev. Whitwell Elwin. Portraits. 8vo. (*In the Press.*)

PORTER'S (Rev. J. L.) Five Years in Damascus. With Travels to Palmyra, Lebanon and other Scripture Sites. Map and Woodcuts. 2 Vols. Post 8vo. 21s.

——— Handbook for Syria and Palestine: including an Account of the Geography, History, Antiquities, and Inhabitants of these Countries, the Peninsula of Sinai, Edom, and the Syrian Desert. Maps. 2 Vols. Post 8vo. 24s.

PRAYER-BOOK (The Illustrated), with 1000 Illustrations of Borders, Initials, Vignettes, &c. Medium 8vo. 18s. cloth; 31s. 6d. calf; 36s. morrocco.

PRECEPTS FOR THE CONDUCT OF LIFE. Extracted from the Scriptures. *Second Edition.* Fcap. 8vo. 1s.

PUSS IN BOOTS. With 12 Illustrations. By OTTO SPECKTER. Coloured, 16mo. 2s. 6d.

QUARTERLY REVIEW (THE). 8vo. 6s.

RAMBLES in Syria among the Turkomans and Bedaweens. Post 8vo. 10s. 6d.

RAWLINSON'S (REV. GEORGE) Herodotus. A New English Version. Edited with Notes and Essays. Assisted by SIR HENRY RAWLINSON and SIR J. G. WILKINSON. *Second Edition.* Maps and Woodcut. 4 Vols. 8vo. 48s.

————————— Historical Evidences of the truth of the Scripture Records stated anew. *Second Edition.* 8vo. 14s.

————————— Five Great Monarchies of the Ancient World. Illustrations. 4 Vols. 8vo. 16s. each.
Vols. I.—II., Chaldæa and Assyria. Vols. III.—IV., Babylon, Media, and Persia.

REJECTED ADDRESSES (THE). By JAMES AND HORACE SMITH. Fcap. 8vo. 1s., or *Fine Paper*, Portrait, fcap. 8vo. 5s.

RENNIE'S (D. F.) British Arms in Peking, 1860; Kagosima, 1862. Post 8vo. 12s.

————————— Pekin and the Pekinese : Narrative of a Residence at the British Embassy. Illustrations. 2 Vols. Post 8vo.

REYNOLDS' (SIR JOSHUA) His Life and Times. Commenced by C. R. LESLIE, R.A., and continued by TOM TAYLOR. Portraits and Illustrations. 2 Vols. 8vo.

RICARDO'S (DAVID) Political Works. With a Notice of his Life and Writings. By J. R. M'CULLOCH. *New Edition.* 8vo. 16s.

RIPA'S (FATHER) Memoirs during Thirteen Years' Residence at the Court of Peking. From the Italian. Post 8vo. 2s.

ROBERTSON'S (CANON) History of the Christian Church, from the Apostolic Age to the Concordat of Worms, A.D. 1123. *Second Edition.* 3 Vols. 8vo. 38s.

ROBINSON'S (REV. DR.) Biblical Researches in the Holy Land. Being a Journal of Travels in 1838 and 1852. Maps. 3 Vols. 8vo. 45s.

————————— Physical Geography of the Holy Land. Post 8vo. 10s. 6d.

ROME (THE STUDENT'S HISTORY OF). FROM THE EARLIEST TIMES TO THE ESTABLISHMENT OF THE EMPIRE. By DEAN LIDDELL. Woodcuts. Post 8vo. 7s. 6d.

ROWLAND'S (DAVID) Manual of the English Constitution; Its Rise, Growth, and Present State. Post 8vo. 10s. 6d.

————————— Laws of Nature the Foundation of Morals. Post 8vo

RUNDELL'S (MRS.) Domestic Cookery, adapted for Private Families. *New Edition.* Woodcuts. Fcap. 8vo. 5s.

RUSSELL'S (J. RUTHERFURD, M.D.) Art of Medicine—Its History and its Heroes. Portraits. 8vo. 14s.

RUXTON'S (GEORGE F.) Travels in Mexico; with Adventures among the Wild Tribes and Animals of the Prairies and Rocky Mountains. Post 8vo. 3s. 6d.

SALE'S (SIR ROBERT) Brigade in Affghanistan. With an Account of the Defence of Jellalabad. By REV. G. R. GLEIG. Post 8vo. 2s.

SANDWITH'S (HUMPHRY) Siege of Kars. Post 8vo. 3s. 6d.

SCOTT'S (G. GILBERT) Secular and Domestic Architecture, Present and Future. Second Edition. 8vo. 9s.

———— (Master of Baliol) University Sermons Post 8vo. 8s. 6d.

SCROPE'S (G. P.) Geology and Extinct Volcanoes of Central France. Second Edition. Illustrations. Medium 8vo. 30s.

SELF-HELP. With Illustrations of Character and Conduct. By SAMUEL SMILES. 50th Thousand. Post 8vo. 6s.

SENIOR'S (N. W.) Suggestions on Popular Education. 8vo. 9s.

SHAFTESBURY (LORD CHANCELLOR); Memoirs of his Early Life. With his Letters, &c. By W. D. CHRISTIE. Portrait. 8vo. 10s. 6d.

SHAW'S (T. B.) Student's Manual of English Literature. Edited, with Notes and Illustrations, by DR. WM. SMITH. Post 8vo. 7s. 6d.

———— Choice Specimens of English Literature. Selected from the Chief English Writers. Edited by WM. SMITH, LL.D. Post 8vo. 7s. 6d.

SIERRA LEONE; Described in Letters to Friends at Home. By A LADY. Post 8vo. 3s. 6d.

SIMMONS on Courts-Martial. 5th Edition. 8vo. 14s.

SMILES' (SAMUEL) Lives of British Engineers; from the Earliest Period to the Death of Robert Stephenson; with an account of their Principal Works, and a History of Inland Communication in Britain. Portraits and Illustrations. 3 Vols. 8vo. 63s.

———— George and Robert Stephenson; the Story of their Lives. With Portraits and 70 Woodcuts. Post 8vo. 6s.

———— James Brindley and the Early Engineers. With Portrait and 50 Woodcuts. Post 8vo. 6s.

———— Self-Help. With Illustrations of Character and Conduct. Post 8vo. 6s.

———— Industrial Biography: Iron-Workers and Tool Makers. A companion volume to "Self-Help." Post 8vo. 6s.

———— Workmen's Earnings—Savings—and Strikes. Fcap. 8vo. 1s. 6d.

SOMERVILLE'S (MARY) Physical Geography. Fifth Edition. Portrait. Post 8vo. 9s.

———— Connexion of the Physical Sciences. Ninth Edition. Woodcuts. Post 8vo. 9s.

SOUTH'S (JOHN F.) Household Surgery; or, Hints on Emergencies. Seventeenth Thousand. Woodcuts. Fcp. 8vo. 4s. 6d.

SMITH'S (Dr. Wm.) Dictionary of the Bible; its Antiquities, Biography, Geography, and Natural History. Illustrations. 3 Vols. 8vo. 105s.

———— Greek and Roman Antiquities. *2nd Edition.* Woodcuts. 8vo. 42s.

———————— Biography and Mythology. Woodcuts. 3 Vols. 8vo. 5l. 15s. 6d.

———————— Geography. Woodcuts. 2 Vols. 8vo. 80s.

———— Classical Dictionary of Mythology, Biography, and Geography, compiled from the above. With 750 Woodcuts. 8vo. 18s.

———— Latin-English Dictionary. 3rd Edition. Revised. 8vo. 21s.

———— Smaller Classical Dictionary. Woodcuts. Crown 8vo. 7s. 6d.

———————— Dictionary of Antiquities. Woodcuts. Crown 8vo. 7s. 6d.

———— Latin-English Dictionary. 12mo. 7s. 6d.

———— Latin-English Vocabulary; for Phædrus, Cornelius Nepos, and Cæsar. *2nd Edition.* 12mo. 3s. 6d.

———— Principia Latina—Part I. A Grammar, Delectus, and Exercise Book, with Vocabularies. *6th Edition.* 12mo. 3s. 6d.

———————— Part II. A Reading-book of Mythology, Geography, Roman Antiquities, and History. With Notes and Dictionary. *3rd Edition.* 12mo. 3s. 6d.

———————— Part III. A Latin Poetry Book. Hexameters and Pentameters; Eclogæ Ovidianæ; Latin Prosody, &c. *2nd Edition.* 12mo. 3s. 6d.

———————— Part IV. Latin Prose Composition. Rules of Syntax, with Examples, Explanations of Synonyms, and Exercises on the Syntax. *Second Edition.* 12mo. 3s. 6d.

———— Student's Greek Grammar. By Professor Curtius. Post 8vo. 7s. 6d.

———————— Latin Grammar. Post 8vo. 7s. 6d.

———————— Latin Grammar. Abridged from the above. 12mo. 3s. 6d.

———— Smaller Greek Grammar. Abridged from Curtius. 12mo. 3s. 6d.

STANLEY'S (Dean) Sinai and Palestine, in Connexion with their History. Map. 8vo. 16s.

———————— Bible in the Holy Land. Woodcuts. Fcap. 8vo. 2s. 6d.

———————— St. Paul's Epistles to the Corinthians. 8vo. 18s.

———————— Eastern Church. Plans. 8vo. 12s.

———————— Jewish Church. Vol. 1. Abraham to Samuel. Plans. 8vo. 16s.

———————— Vol. 2. Samuel to the Captivity. 8vo. 16s.

———— Historical Memorials of Canterbury. Woodcuts. Post 8vo. 7s. 6d.

———————— Sermons in the East, with Notices of the Places Visited. 8vo. 9s.

———————— Sermons on Evangelical and Apostolical Teaching. Post 8vo. 7s. 6d.

———————— Addresses and Charges of Bishop Stanley. With Memoir. 8vo. 10s. 6d.

SOUTHEY'S (ROBERT) Book of the Church. *Seventh Edition.* Post 8vo. 7s. 6d.

——————— Lives of Bunyan and Cromwell. Post 8vo. 2s.

SPECKTER'S (OTTO) Puss in Boots. With 12 Woodcuts. Square 12mo. 1s. 6d. plain, or 2s. 6d. coloured.

——————— Charmed Roe; or, the Story of the Little Brother and Sister. Illustrated. 16mo.

ST. JOHN'S (CHARLES) Wild Sports and Natural History of the Highlands. Post 8vo. 3s. 6d.

——————— (BAYLE) Adventures in the Libyan Desert and the Oasis of Jupiter Ammon. Woodcuts. Post 8vo. 2s.

STANHOPE'S (EARL) Life of William Pitt. With Extracts from his M.S. Papers. *Second Edition.* Portraits. 4 Vols. Post 8vo. 42s.

——————— Miscellanies. *Second Edition.* Post 8vo. 5s. 6d.

STEPHENSON (GEORGE and ROBERT). The Story of their Lives. By SAMUEL SMILES. With Portraits and 70 Illustrations. Post 8vo. 6s.

STUDENT'S HUME. A History of England from the Invasion of Julius Cæsar to the Revolution of 1688. By DAVID HUME, and continued to 1858. Woodcuts. Post 8vo. 7s. 6d.
*** A Smaller History of England. 12mo. 3s. 6d.

——————— HISTORY OF FRANCE; from the Earliest Times to the Establishment of the Second Empire, 1852. By W. H. PEARSON, M.A. Woodcuts. Post 8vo. 7s. 6d.

——————— HISTORY OF GREECE; from the Earliest Times to the Roman Conquest. With the History of Literature and Art. By WM. SMITH, LL.D. Woodcuts. Crown 8vo. 7s. 6d. (Questions. 2s.)
*** A SMALLER HISTORY OF GREECE. 12mo. 3s. 6d.

——————— HISTORY OF ROME; from the Earliest Times to the Establishment of the Empire. With the History of Literature and Art. By Dean LIDDELL. Woodcuts. Crown 8vo. 7s. 6d.
*** A SMALLER HISTORY OF ROME. 12mo. 3s. 6d.

——————— GIBBON; an Epitome of the History of the Decline and Fall of the Roman Empire. By EDWARD GIBBON. Incorporating the Researches of Recent Commentators. Woodcuts. Post 8vo. 7s. 6d.

——————— MANUAL OF ANCIENT GEOGRAPHY. By Rev. W. L. BEVAN, M.A. Woodcuts. Post 8vo. 7s. 6d.

——————— ENGLISH LANGUAGE. By GEORGE P. MARSH. Post 8vo. 7s. 6d.

——————— ENGLISH LITERATURE. By T. B. SHAW, M.A. Post 8vo. 7s. 6d.

——————— SPECIMENS OF ENGLISH LITERATURE. Selected from the Chief Writers. By THOMAS B. SHAW, M.A. Post 8vo. 7s. 6d.

STOTHARD'S (Thos.) Life. With Personal Reminiscences. By Mrs. Bray. With Portrait and 60 Woodcuts. 4to. 21s.

STREET'S (G. E.) Gothic Architecture in Spain. From Personal Observations during several journeys through that country. Illustrations. Medium 8vo.

———————— Brick and Marble Architecture of Italy in the Middle Ages. Plates. 8vo. 21s.

SWIFT'S (Jonathan) Life, Letters, Journals, and Works. By John Forster. 8vo. (In Preparation.)

SYME'S (Professor) Principles of Surgery. 5th Edition. 8vo. 12s.

TAIT'S (Bishop) Dangers and Safeguards of Modern Theology. 8vo. 9s.

TAYLOR'S (Henry) Notes from Life. Fcap. 8vo. 2s.

THOMSON'S (Archbishop) Lincoln's Inn Sermons. 8vo. 10s. 6d.

THREE-LEAVED MANUAL OF FAMILY PRAYER; arranged so as to save the trouble of turning the Pages backwards and forwards. Royal 8vo. 2s.

TRANSACTIONS OF THE ETHNOLOGICAL SOCIETY OF LONDON. New Series. Vols. I. and II. 8vo.

TREMENHEERE'S (H. S.) Political Experience of the Ancients, in its bearing on Modern Times. Fcap. 8vo. 2s. 6d.

TRISTRAM (H. B.). The Great Sahara. Wanderings South of the Atlas Mountains. Map and Illustrations. Post 8vo. 15s.

TWISS' (Horace) Public and Private Life of Lord Chancellor Eldon, with Selections from his Correspondence. Portrait. Third Edition. 2 Vols. Post 8vo. 21s.

TYLOR'S (E. B.) Researches into the Early History of Mankind, and the Development of Civilization. Illustrations. 8vo.

TYNDALL'S (John) Glaciers of the Alps. With an account of Three Years' Observations and Experiments on their General Phenomena. Woodcuts. Post 8vo. 14s.

TYTLER'S (Patrick Fraser) Memoirs. By Rev. J. W. Burgon, M.A. 8vo. 9s.

VAUGHAN'S (Rev. Dr.) Sermons preached in Harrow School. 8vo. 10s. 6d.

VENABLES' (Rev. R. L.) Domestic Scenes in Russia. Post 8vo. 5s.

WAAGEN'S (Dr.) Treasures of Art in Great Britain. Being an Account of the Chief Collections of Paintings, Sculpture, Manuscripts, Miniatures, &c. &c., in this Country. Obtained from Personal Inspection during Visits to England. 4 Vols. 8vo.

WALSH'S (Sir John) Practical Results of the Reform Bill of 1832. 8vo. 5s. 6d.

VAMBERY'S (Arminius) Travels in Central Asia, from Teheran across the Turkoman Desert, on the Eastern Shore of the Caspian to Khiva, Bokhara, and Samarcand in 1863. Map and Illustrations. 8vo. 21s.

WELLINGTON'S (The Duke of) Despatches during his various Campaigns. Compiled from Official and other Authentic Documents. By Col. Gurwood, C.B. 8 Vols. 8vo. 21s. each.

———————— Supplementary Despatches, and other Papers. Edited by his Son. Vols. I. to XII. 8vo. 20s. each.

———————— Selections from his Despatches and General Orders. By Colonel Gurwood. 8vo. 18s.

———————— Speeches in Parliament. 2 Vols. 8vo. 42s.

WILKINSON'S (Sir J. G.) Popular Account of the Private Life, Manners, and Customs of the Ancient Egyptians. *New Edition.* Revised and Condensed. With 500 Woodcuts. 2 Vols. Post 8vo. 12s.

———————— Handbook for Egypt.—Thebes, the Nile, Alexandria, Cairo, the Pyramids, Mount Sinai, &c. Map. Post 8vo. 15s.

———————— (G. B.) Working Man's Handbook to South Australia; with Advice to the Farmer, and Detailed Information for the several Classes of Labourers and Artisans. Map. 18mo. 1s. 6d.

WILSON'S (Bishop Daniel) Life, with Extracts from his Letters and Journals. By Rev. Josiah Bateman. *Second Edition.* Illustrations. Post 8vo. 9s.

———————— (Genl. Sir Robert) Secret History of the French Invasion of Russia, and Retreat of the French Army, 1812. *Second Edition.* 8vo. 15s.

———————— Private Diary of Travels, Personal Services, and Public Events, during Missions and Employments in Spain, Sicily, Turkey, Russia, Poland, Germany, &c. 1812-14. 2 Vols. 8vo. 26s.

———————— Autobiographical Memoirs. Containing an Account of his Early Life down to the Peace of Tilsit. Portrait. 2 Vols. 8vo. 26s.

WORDSWORTH'S (Canon) Journal of a Tour in Athens and Attica. *Third Edition.* Plates. Post 8vo. 8s. 6d.

———————— Pictorial, Descriptive, and Historical Account of Greece, with a History of Greek Art, by G. Scharf, F.S.A. *New Edition.* With 600 Woodcuts. Royal 8vo. 28s.

WORNUM (Ralph). A Biographical Dictionary of Italian Painters: with a Table of the Contemporary Schools of Italy. By a Lady. Post 8vo. 6s. 6d.

BRADBURY AND EVANS, PRINTERS, WHITEFRIARS.

169075

Made in the USA